DATE DUE

MAY 0 3		
MAY 3 0 2017		
JUN 0 3 2017		
JUN 1 5 2017		
AUG 0 8 2017		

The House of the Dead

THE HOUSE OF THE DEAD

Siberian Exile Under the Tsars

Daniel Beer

ALFRED A. KNOPF   NEW YORK   2017

THIS IS A BORZOI BOOK
PUBLISHED BY ALFRED A. KNOPF

Copyright © 2016 by Daniel Beer

Published in the United States by Alfred A. Knopf,
a division of Penguin Random House LLC, New York,
and in Canada by Random House of Canada,
a division of Penguin Random House Canada Limited, Toronto.
Originally published in hardcover in Great Britain by Allen Lane,
a division of Penguin Random House Ltd., London, in 2016.

www.aaknopf.com

Knopf, Borzoi Books, and the colophon are registered trademarks of
Penguin Random House LLC.

Library of Congress Cataloging-in-Publication Data
Names: Beer, Daniel, author.
Title: The house of the dead : Siberian exile under the tsars / Daniel Beer.
Description: First United States edition. | New York : Alfred A. Knopf, 2017. |
"This is a Borzoi book"
Identifiers: LCCN 2016009610 (print) | LCCN 2016019798 (ebook) |
ISBN 9780307958907 (hardcover) | ISBN 9780307958914 (ebook)
Subjects: LCSH: Exile (Punishment)—Russia—History. | Exile
(Punishment)—Russia (Federation)—Siberia—History. | Exiles—Russia
(Federation)—Siberia—History. | Political prisoners—Russia
(Federation)—Siberia—History. | Penal colonies—Russia
(Federation)—Siberia—History. | Convict labor—Russia
(Federation)—Siberia—History. | Revolutionaries—Russia
(Federation)—Siberia—History. | Siberia (Russia)—History—19th century.
| Siberia (Russia)—History—20th century. | Russia—Social
conditions—1801–1917.
Classification: LCC HV9712 .B44 2016 (print) | LCC HV9712 (ebook) |
DDC 364.6—dc23

Jacket image: Ruins of a Stalinist prison camp in the marble canyon
in the Kodar mountains in Siberia. akg-images.
Jacket design by Oliver Munday

Manufactured in the United States of America
First American Edition

For Gusztáv

Contents

Illustrations

12. Portrait of Maria Volkonskaya (Copyright © Central Pushkin Museum/Bridgeman Images)

13. Portrait of Mikhail Lunin (Private collection of art critic Ilya Zilbershtein/Bridgeman Images)

14. Portrait of Fyodor Dostoevsky by Konstantin Trutovsky (Copyright AKG Images/Sputnik)

15. *Life Is Everywhere*, 1888, by Nikolai Aleksandrovich Yaroshenko (Copyright © Tretyakov Gallery, Moscow/Sputnik/Bridgeman Images)

16. *A Break for Liberty*, from George Kennan, *Siberia and the Exile System* (1891), Vol. 1 (Reproduced by kind permission of the Syndics of Cambridge University Library)

17. Convict in Siberia (Copyright © The Stapleton Collection/Bridgeman Images)

18. *The Irtysh Prison-Barge*, from Harry de Windt, *Siberia As It Is* (1891) (Reproduced by kind permission of the Syndics of Cambridge University Library)

19. "Group of Convicts on the *Yaroslavl*," from Harry de Windt, *The New Siberia* (1896) (Reproduced by kind permission of the Syndics of Cambridge University Library)

20. "Elderly Prisoners in Kara," an illustration for *The Graphic*, 13 August 1898 (Copyright © Look and Learn Illustrated Papers Collection/Bridgeman Images)

21–23. "Aged Ordinary Prisoners at Kara," from Lev Deutsch, *16 Years in Siberia* (1905) (Reproduced by kind permission of the Syndics of Cambridge University Library)

24. *The Convict Prison, Tobolsk*, from George Kennan, *Siberia and the Exile System* (1891), Vol. 2 (Reproduced by kind permission of the Syndics of Cambridge University Library)

25. "Prisoners Marching Through the Streets of Odessa," from Lev Deutsch, *16 Years in Siberia* (1905) (Reproduced by kind permission of the Syndics of Cambridge University Library)

26. Jarosław Dąbrowski (Copyright © akg-images/Interfoto)

27. A political exile in Siberia (Copyright © The Stapleton Collection/Bridgeman Images)

28. Yelizaveta Kovalskaya, from George Kennan, *Siberia and the Exile System* (1891), Vol. 2 (Reproduced by kind permission of the Syndics of Cambridge University Library)

Maps

ARCTIC

Varde

Christiania

Stockholm

Helsingfors

Kara Sea

Warsaw
Kovno
Wilno
St Petersburg

Dniepr

Uglich

Kiev
Moscow
Yaroslavl
Ryazan
Vladimir

Odessa

Kharkiv
Nizhny Novgorod

Ob

EUROPEAN
RUSSIA
Kazan

Perm

Black Sea

Volga

Uralsk
Ural
Orenburg
Tobolsk
S
I
Yenisei

Ural Mountains

Ob

Caspian Sea

Omsk
Tomsk

Irtysh

Aral Sea

L. Balkhash

PERSIA

0   200 400 600 800 km

AFGHANISTAN

Russian Empire circa 1875

O C E A N

Bering Sea

N

Kolyma

•Verkhoyansk

Lena

A

Aldan

Okhotsk

Sea of
Okhotsk

Yakutsk•

B E R I A

Sakhalin

Lena

Angara

rasnoyarsk

L. Baikal

Amur

Chita   Shilka

Khabarovsk

Amur

Irkutsk•

Vladivostok•

CHINESE EMPIRE

JAPAN

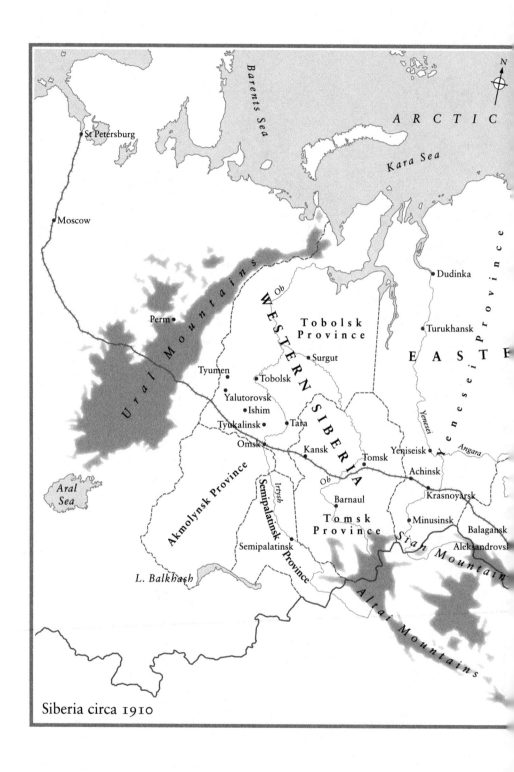

Siberia circa 1910

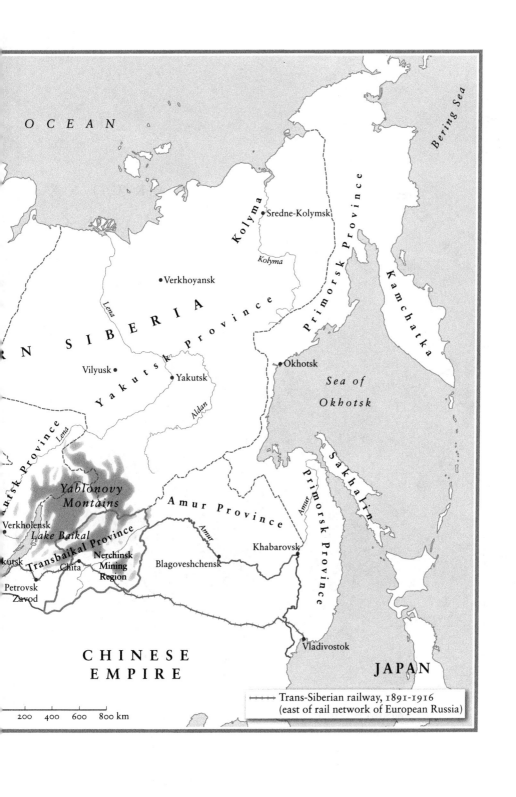

OCEAN

Bering Sea

Sredne-Kolymsk

Kolyma

Kolyma

Verkhoyansk

Primorsk Province

N SIBERIA

Yakutsk Province

Kamchatka

Lena

Vilyusk

Yakutsk

Okhotsk

Sea of Okhotsk

Aldan

utsk Province

Lena

Yablonovy Montains

Verkholensk

Amur Province

Sakhalin

Lake Baikal

Amur

Primorsk Province

Transbaikal Province

Amur

Khabarovsk

...utsk

Chita

Nerchinsk Mining Region

Blagoveshchensk

Petrovsk Zavod

CHINESE EMPIRE

Vladivostok

JAPAN

Trans-Siberian railway, 1891-1916 (east of rail network of European Russia)

200 400 600 800 km

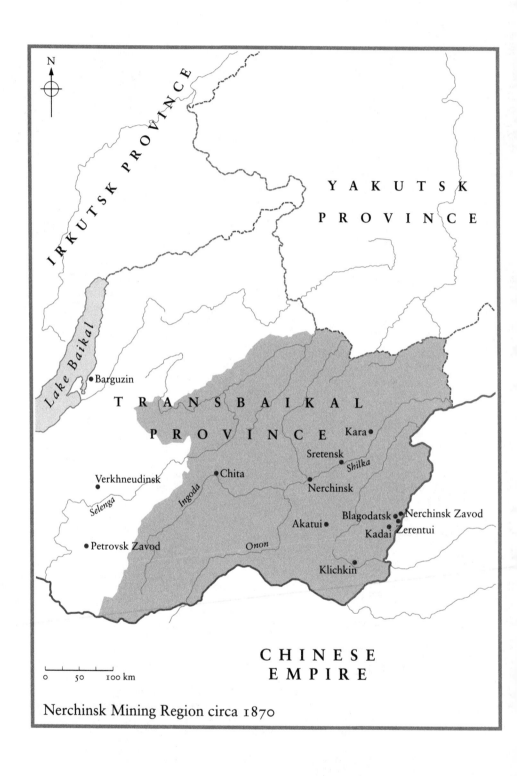

N

IRKUTSK PROVINCE

YAKUTSK
PROVINCE

Lake Baikal

• Barguzin

TRANSBAIKAL
PROVINCE

Kara •

Sretensk
• *Shilka*

• Chita

Nerchinsk

Verkhneudinsk •

Ingoda

Selenga

Blagodatsk • • Nerchinsk Zavod
Akatui • Kadai • Zerentui

• Petrovsk Zavod

Onon

Klichkin •

CHINESE
EMPIRE

0   50   100 km

Nerchinsk Mining Region circa 1870

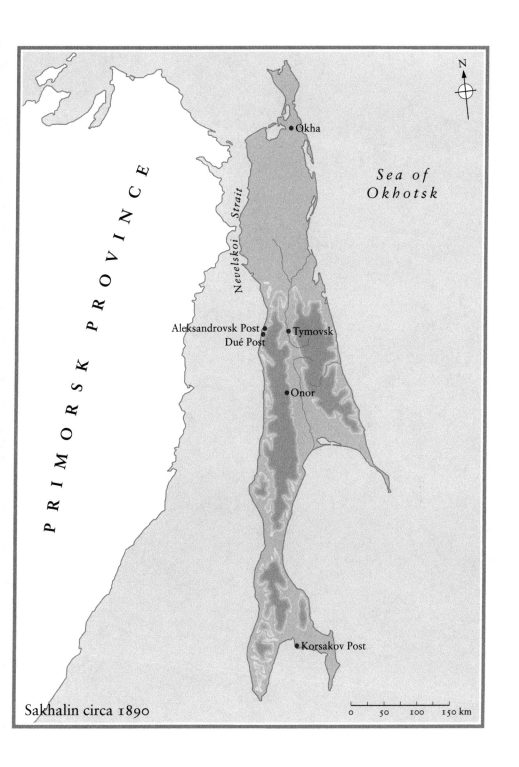

N

Sea of
Okhotsk

• Okha

Nevelskoi Strait

P R I M O R S K   P R O V I N C E

Aleksandrovsk Post
Dué Post
• Tymovsk

• Onor

• Korsakov Post

Sakhalin circa 1890

0   50   100   150 km

Author's Note

Transliteration from the Russian in the notes conforms to the standard system adopted by the Library of Congress. The main text amends this system for the Anglophone reader: "soft signs" are omitted; surnames ending in "ii" and "yi" are standardized to "y"; "e" is rendered as "ye" when appropriate, and so on. The names of Russian emperors, empresses and famous writers are given in their commonly Anglicized form.

Whenever possible, non-Russian (usually Polish) names have been restored to their original Latinate form. As it was not always possible to infer the original name from the Russian-language sources, such names sometimes appear in their Russified form. For any errors in this process, I apologize.

In the interest of allowing readers to consult the original sources, the book cites widely available translations of major Russian texts whenever possible. All other translations from the Russian are the author's own.

Throughout the text all weights and measurements have been converted from the Russian imperial system to the metric system both in the original Russian sources and in the English translations cited. Modifications to existing English translations are noted.

From 1700 to February 1918, Russia used the Julian calendar, which was between eleven and thirteen days behind the Gregorian calendar. Dates are given according to the Julian calendar.

THE ADMINISTRATION OF SIBERIA

Between 1803 and 1822, all Siberia was under the authority of a single governor-general based in Irkutsk. In 1822, Siberia was divided into two principal administrative territories: a governorate-general of Western Siberia based in Omsk, and a governorate-general of Eastern Siberia based in Irkutsk. Each of these governorates-general was run by a governor-general who answered to St. Petersburg and oversaw the governors of individual provinces. The Western Siberian governorate-general comprised Tobolsk, Tomsk and Omsk provinces (the latter was subsequently dissolved, partly merged into Tobolsk province and partly subdivided into the two new provinces of Semipalatinsk and Akmolynsk); the Eastern Siberian governorate-general comprised Irkutsk, Yenisei, Yakutsk and Transbaikal provinces. Each province (*guberniia* or *oblast'*) had an administrative capital and comprised a number of districts (*uezd*), and each district comprised a number of cantons (*volost'*). Some regions (*okrug*), such as the Nerchinsk Mining Region, stood outside of this hierarchy and were ruled by a senior official responsible directly to the tsar. In 1882, the Western Siberian governorate-general was abolished, Tomsk and Tobolsk provinces were placed under the direct control of the central government and Semipalatinsk and Akmolynsk provinces formed the new governorate-general of the Steppe. The Eastern Siberian governorate-general was subsequently subdivided into two new governorates-general: Priamursk, in 1884, and Irkutsk, in 1887. Priamursk administered the provinces of Transbaikal, Primorsk, the Amur and the island of Sakhalin; Irkutsk administered Yenisei, Irkutsk and Yakutsk provinces. Despite some further minor changes, these basic administrative units remained in place until 1917.

Here was a world all its own, unlike anything else; here were laws unto themselves, ways of dressing unto themselves, manners and customs unto themselves, a house of the living dead, a life unlike anywhere else, with distinct people unlike anyone else. It is this distinct corner that I am setting out to describe.

—Fyodor Dostoevsky, *Notes from the
House of the Dead* (1862)[1]

The House of the Dead

The Bell of Uglich

In 1891, a group of Russian merchants successfully petitioned Tsar Alexander III to allow them to transport a 300-kilogramme copper bell from the Siberian town of Tobolsk to its native town of Uglich, 2,200 kilometres to the west. The bell travelled up the Volga River in the late spring of 1892 and arrived by steamship at a jetty erected in front of the Uglich cathedral. There, it received a ceremonial homecoming exactly three centuries after having first been exiled to Siberia.[1]

The bell's fate had been sealed in the spring of 1591, when the nine-year-old son and designated heir of Ivan the Terrible, Tsarevich Dmitry, was found in Uglich with his throat slit. Dmitry's mother and her family believed that the tsarevich had been murdered on the orders of a potential rival to the throne, the tsar regent, Boris Godunov. They rang Uglich's bell to summon the townspeople in revolt. The Uglichans formed a mob and went on the rampage, murdering both the presumed assassins and an official from Moscow. The unrest attracted the Kremlin's wrath. Godunov ordered forces to Uglich to quash the rebellion, and the following spring, he dispensed justice. He had some 200 townspeople executed and others imprisoned; about 100 were flogged and had their nostrils torn out; the more eloquent lost their tongues as well. Scourged and mutilated, the rebels were banished to Siberia.

In addition to inflicting retribution on the insurgents, Godunov punished the symbol of their political unity. He had the bell lowered, subjected to twelve lashes, relieved of its "tongue" and then exiled to Siberia. The Uglichans were made to drag the mutinous bell across the Urals before finally bringing it to rest in Tobolsk, where the town's military governor registered it as "the first inanimate exile." Silenced and banished, the bell became a testament to the power of Russia's rulers both to drive their turbulent subjects beyond the Urals and to strike them dumb.[2]

Yet in the centuries that followed it also became a rallying point for opponents of the autocracy who viewed Godunov's punishment of the Uglichans as the cruel act of a usurper. In 1862, one nobleman exiled to Tobolsk, Ippolit Zavalishin, discerned in the Uglich Bell an "unquelled accuser who bears eloquent testimony to . . . the punishment of an entire blameless town!"³ By the middle of the nineteenth century, then, the bell had come to symbolize not only the supreme authority of the sovereign but also the vengeful power on which it relied.

Tobolsk played a central role in the development of Siberian exile in the centuries after the banishment of the Uglich Bell. This legacy is still visible today in the jumble of decaying wooden houses and neo-classical buildings that make up the old town. Tobolsk's central square sits atop a plateau that rears 50 metres above the muddy waters of the great River Irtysh and the lower town that sprawls to the south. It commands distant views of the surrounding countryside and the barges inching their way upstream. Two large buildings bestride the square. One is the stone kremlin, a fortified complex that projected the power and splendour of the imperial state. Its massive white walls, above which soar the blue and gold cupolas of the Sofia Cathedral, were built by exiles: Swedish soldiers taken prisoner by Peter the Great in 1709 at one of the decisive battles of the Great Northern War (1700–1721). The second building, whose imposing neoclassical façade spans the length of the square's western edge, is the Tobolsk Central Penal Labour Prison. Built in the early 1850s, the prison was the second of its kind in the town, adding much needed capacity to the existing ramshackle jail. Convoys numbering hundreds of exiles would be marched up into the town, across the square and through its gates, to be held in the prison while the Tobolsk Exile Office, the administrative centre of the entire exile system, determined their final destinations. Distributed into new convoys, the exiles would then set off on the roads and waterways of Siberia, bound for distant villages and penal settlements. Tobolsk was the gateway to a continental prison.⁴

The exile system played a central role in the colonization of Sibe-ria. Towns grew up around Siberian penal forts and colonies to house their officials and military personnel. Rare was the Siberian village left untouched by the exiles who either officially settled almost every dis-trict in every Siberian province or unofficially roamed through them as itinerant labourers, thieves and beggars. Siberia's roads were dotted with the squat ochre waystations in which the marching convoys of deportees would overnight on their long and gruelling journey. The forwarding prisons, city jails, mines, industrial enterprises and exile settlements resembled sinews of state power that stretched eastwards from St. Petersburg. When, in 1879, a devastating fire consumed three-quarters of the centre of Irkutsk—then a thriving city of 30,000 inhabitants—one of the few stone buildings to survive the flames was the central prison. Its significance as a major transit point for exiles was laid bare as it suddenly loomed above the smouldering ruins of the city.[5]

The Tobolsk Central Penal Labour Prison continued to serve as a penal institution until 1989, when the authorities finally shut it down. Like many of the tsarist-era prisons, it had been refurbished after 1917 and eventually become part of what Alexander Solzhenitsyn would call the "archipelago" of penal facilities that formed the Stalinist Gulag. Both in Russia and abroad, the Gulag has overlaid memories of the tsars' use of Siberia as a place of punishment. Long before the Soviet state erected its camps, however, Siberia was already a vast open prison with a history spanning more than three centuries.[6]

Siberia—the Russian name *Сибирь* is pronounced *Seebeer*—dwarfs European Russia. At 15,500,000 square kilometres, it is one and a half times larger than the continent of Europe. Siberia has never had an independent political existence; it has no clear borders and no binding ethnic identity. Its modern history is inseparable from Russia's. The easily surmountable Ural Mountains have acted less as a physical boundary than as the imaginative and political frontier of a European Russia beyond which lay a giant Asiatic colony and a sprawling penal realm. Siberia was both Russia's heart of darkness and a world of opportunity and prosperity. The continent's bleak and unforgiving present was to give way to a brighter future, and Siberia's exiles were intended to play a key role in this vaunted transition.[7]

For the imperial state sought to do more than cage social and political disorder within its continental prison. By purging the old world of its undesirables, it would also populate the new. The exile system promised to harness a growing army of exiles in the service of a wider project to colonize Siberia. In theory, Russia's criminals would toil to harvest Siberia's natural riches and settle its remote territories and, in so doing, they would discover the virtues of self-reliance, abstinence and hard work. In practice, however, the exile system dispatched into the Siberian hinterland an army not of enterprising settlers but of destitute and desperate vagabonds. They survived not by their own industry but by stealing and begging from the real colonists, the Siberian peasantry. The tensions embedded in this dual status of "prison colony" were never reconciled over the more than three centuries separating the banishment of the Uglichan insurgents and the implosion of the tsarist empire in 1917. Contrary to the ambitions of Russia's rulers, penal colonization never became a driving force behind Siberia's development. Rather, as the numbers of exiles grew, it became an ever greater obstacle to it.

Over the nineteenth century, the scale and intensity of Siberian exile increased so significantly that it easily surpassed the exile systems of the British and French empires. The British transported around 160,000 convicts to Australia in the eight decades between 1787 and 1868; the French state meanwhile had a penal population of about 5,500 in its overseas colonies between 1860 and 1900. By contrast, between 1801 and 1917, more than 1 million tsarist subjects were banished to Siberia.[8]

Among those exiles were generations of revolutionaries from towns and cities in European Russia and Poland. Some fought for a liberal constitution, some for national independence and still others for a socialist utopia. Siberia became a desolate staging post in the overlapping histories of European republicanism and the Russian revolutionary movement. By the end of the nineteenth century, the tsarist government was deporting thousands of dedicated revolutionaries to prisons, mines and far-flung settlements in Siberia. Amid the isolation and claustrophobia, they bickered, plotted and published political tracts to inspire and to coordinate the revolutionary underground in Russia's major cities. Their dreams of impending revolution, undiluted by the compromises of practical politics, filled the yawning Siberian skies. Siberia had become a gigantic laboratory of revolution and exile, a rite of passage for the men and women who would one day rule Russia. When revolution finally erupted in 1905, these exiled radicals transformed Siberia's towns and villages into crucibles of violent struggle against the autocracy. Scaffolds were erected in the courtyards of prisons while, beyond their walls, warders were assassinated in the streets. No longer a quarantine against the contagions of revolution, Siberia had become a source of the infection.

The biographies and writings of a few luminaries dominate historical memory of Siberian exile before the Russian Revolution. Some, such as Fyodor Dostoevsky and Vladimir Lenin, were themselves exiles; others, like Anton Chekhov and Leo Tolstoy, penned vivid portraits of convict life in Siberia in their reportage and fiction. In 1861–2, amid the "thaw" of Alexander II's Great Reforms, Dostoevsky published his acclaimed semi-autobiographical novel, the title of which is usually rendered in English as *Notes from the House of the Dead*, though the original Russian title translates more accurately as *Notes from the Dead House*, underlining Dostoevsky's belief that, whatever their crimes, the exiles ultimately fell victim to a brutal and dehumanizing prison system: a house of the dead.

Thereafter, the annual trickle of articles, memoirs and works of fiction on the exile system became a torrent that surged unabated through the final decades of the tsarist era. The Russian press carried anguished discussions of the horrors of the exile system and its disastrous consequences for Siberia itself. Other celebrated writers and artists followed in Dostoevsky's footsteps. In Chekhov's story *In Exile* (1892), the long years of banishment in Siberia have stripped an ageing ferryman of all compassion, hope and desire. The former exile is, his young companion exclaims, "no longer alive, a stone, clay."[9] By the time Ilya Repin painted his *Unexpected Return* in 1884, the hollowed-out stare of the gaunt young man entering his family's dining room and the confused and shocked reaction of his relatives needed no explanation. Each and every one of Repin's contemporaries understood that the scene depicted the homecoming of a political exile. Repin's painting belonged to a shared *imaginative* canvas of the banishment, cruelty and suffering that were indelibly associated with Siberia. When, in 1892, Alexander III finally granted permission for the exiled bell of Uglich to be returned to its original home, the Russian press hailed the gesture as an expression of the monarch's magnanimity. But in the glare of mounting public revulsion at the disastrous penal colonization of a continent, the return of the bell looked more like an acknowledgement of failure, even defeat.[10]

Abroad, too, exile was blackening the name of the autocracy. In 1880, the British satirical magazine *Judy* published a cartoon that neatly summarized the views of many Western observers. It depicts the Russian bear dressed as a gendarme, bearing a "torch of civilization" and leading a seemingly endless column of prisoners in chains to Siberia. The plight of Russian and Polish political prisoners in exile evoked outraged sympathy from audiences in Europe and the United States who denounced the tyranny of the autocracy. The most eloquent and well-informed foreign spokesman for the empire's political prisoners abroad was the American journalist and explorer George Kennan. Originally sympathetic to the Russian government's struggle with what he believed to be dangerous fanatics, in the late 1880s Kennan received permission from the Ministry of the Interior to travel unimpeded throughout Siberia and to report on what he found. What he discovered were thousands of men and women who were not, he argued, deranged and dangerous radicals, but rather martyrs to the cause of freedom. Across the world, Siberia was fast becoming a byword for the despotism of the tsars.[11]

Yet if the individual fates of famous writers and revolutionaries in Siberia became widely known and discussed both in Russia and abroad, the same could not be said of the vast majority of Siberia's exiles. For every banished radical, thousands of unknown common criminals and their families were marched off to Siberia and into oblivion. Most were illiterate and lacked the resources required to record their experiences for posterity. Their fates survive only in the police reports, petitions, court records and official correspondence that were compiled and retained by the apparatus of an increasingly developed and sophisticated police state. These documents, stitched into bundles and filed away in rough cardboard folders in the dusty and decaying collections of tsarist ministries, are today held in archives in Moscow, St. Petersburg and towns and cities across Siberia.[12]

It is from this body of archival evidence and from the welter of published memoirs and diaries that this book recovers the experiences of revolutionaries and common criminals in Siberia from Alexander I's coronation in 1801 to Nicholas II's abdication in 1917. Their voices tell the story of Russia's struggle to govern its prison empire as the tsarist regime collided violently with the political forces of the modern world.

Origins of Exile

At the end of the sixteenth century, the Kingdom of Muscovy embarked on a programme of conquest that became known as the "gathering of the lands." This territorial expansion surged into the power vacuum left by the decline of the Mongol Golden Horde, a confederation of nomadic and semi-nomadic tribes that had ruled the territory stretching from Western Siberia to Moscow since the thirteenth century, but had more recently fragmented into separate khanates. In 1582, a Cossack adventurer named Yermak Timofeyevich crossed the Urals with an army of several hundred men in an audacious raid on the waning power of the Siberian Mongol leader Kuchum Khan. After a victorious battle in Western Siberia, Yermak briefly established a toe-hold east of the Urals and claimed the lands in the name of Ivan the Terrible. Although his own victory proved short-lived (the Cossack leader drowned only three years later while escaping a Tatar ambush), the gateway to Siberia that Yermak ripped open would never close. The Russians continued their raids across the Urals, Kuchum Khan died in battle by the River Ob in 1598, and the Siberian khanate collapsed.[1]

Thereafter, the Russian advance into Siberia was inexorable. A motley collection of Muscovite emissaries, regular soldiers, foreign mercenaries, traders and émigré Cossacks from the Don and Dnieper regions of south-west Russia pushed further and further east along the Irtysh and Ob rivers and their tributaries. They established forts that served as nodal points for the projection of military power and for the collection of tribute from Siberia's native tribes. The town of Tyumen was established in 1586 and Tobolsk was founded the following year. By 1600, Muscovy's forces had claimed all of the territory between the Urals and the River Ob and were driving further eastwards towards the next great Siberian waterway, the Yenisei River, 1,600 kilometres away. Further conquest followed: Mangazeya was founded in 1601;

Tomsk in 1604. By 1630, there were some fifty fortified villages in Western Siberia and the Russians had built outposts in Yeniseisk and Krasnoyarsk on the banks of the Yenisei. Just twelve years later, they had crossed the last of Siberia's great south–north trunk rivers, the Lena, and had established a presence in Yakutsk that would eventually provide access to the desolate exile settlements in the Arctic Circle. By 1649, they had reached the shores of the Northern Pacific and founded the port of Okhotsk. Nine years later, they had advanced a further 2,000 kilometres and were on the shores of the Bering Strait, less than 160 kilometres from Alaska's Cape Prince of Wales.[2]

It is in Russia's conquest and colonization of the continent to its east that the origins of the exile system are to be found. Russia's rapid expansion was driven by Moscow's growing military strength, logistical capacities and administrative sophistication, but it also created a persistent shortage of labourers, farmers and traders in Siberia's remote and sprawling territories. From its earliest recorded instances, exile enabled the tsars not only to banish their unruly subjects from European Russia but also to press them into service as settlers and penal labourers at various strategic locations across Siberia. Exile emerged under the auspices of this wider expansionist project; punishment and colonization became intertwined.

The continent the Russians conquered stretches 8,000 kilometres from the Urals to the Pacific and 3,200 kilometres from the Arctic Circle to the Mongolian border. The Yenisei River forms a natural border between Western and Eastern Siberia, which differ significantly in topography. With the exception of the Altai Mountains, Western Siberia has a low elevation and flat, open landscapes. An abundance of rivers flows into its spongy soil, creating marshlands that flood each spring. Eastern Siberia and the Russian Far East are far more diverse: a combination of rugged mountain ranges, deep gorges, thick forests and marshy lowlands. At the heart of Eastern Siberia, the ground plunges into Lake Baikal, the world's largest and deepest fresh-water lake. Baikal's surface, which freezes over each winter, spans some 32,000 square kilometres.

Contrary to popular perception, Siberia is not enveloped in ice and snow year-round. The permafrost landscape of the tundra exists only above the 60th parallel, a latitude which runs through Sweden and Alaska. In fact, most of Siberia is covered by the taiga, a dense belt of coniferous and deciduous forests between 1,000 and 2,000 kilometres wide. South of the taiga lies the steppe, a flat, treeless territory of grasslands and deserts. The majority of Siberians live below the 60th parallel in climates similar to those in which Europeans live. Summer temperatures in most Siberian towns and cities (which actually lie further south than Moscow) can easily climb high into the 30°sC. But the winters in this most continental of climates are ferocious. Temperatures frequently plunge below zero in September and reach –20°C by December, though a bone-chilling –30 to –40°C is not uncommon. They begin to climb above zero again only in late spring.[3]

In the late sixteenth century Siberia was covered by the thinnest of human membranes. There were in total about 230,000 indigenes, who between them spoke no fewer than 120 distinct languages. They included reindeer herders in the tundra of the north, hunters in the thick forests of the taiga and nomads in the steppe to the south. Among the first tribes to encounter the Russians were the Ostyaks of Western Siberia, who herded reindeer, hunted and trapped, and fished the waters of the Ob and Irtysh rivers. The south-central regions of Siberia were dominated by the semi-nomadic Turkic peoples, the Tatars and the Kirghiz, who herded their own flocks, sowed wheat, mined iron and traded silk. The Tungus roamed the taiga of both Western and Eastern Siberia, hunting and herding reindeer. The Yakuts had built a way of life centred on raising cattle and horses in the Lena River valley. Although they gradually adopted many Russian customs, they continued to live in yurts made of hides or birch bark in the summer and of clay, bark and cattle dung in the winter. The warlike Buryats tended their flocks in the rough lands of the Transbaikal (the region beyond Lake Baikal in Eastern Siberia) and, by the seventeenth century, had begun to trade in furs and leather with the Chinese to the south. Further south-east, in the Amur River Basin, lived the Gilyaks—farmers and fishermen who dressed in fish skins and dog fur. To the far north-east, in the most inhospitable climate in the whole of Eurasia, were the Chukchi and the Koryaks, fierce fishermen and hunters who lived off reindeer, whale and seal meat. Most of Siberia's natives used shamans to communicate with their gods and venerated the animals they hunted and herded. Some, such as the Yakuts, converted to Christianity in the seventeenth century; others, like the Buryats, began to replace their tribal shamans with Buddhist priests.[4]

In a land yet to discover significant deposits of precious metals, the magnet that pulled the Russians eastwards was fur. Widespread demand for Siberia's pelts in both Europe and Asia transformed the wilderness into a seemingly inexhaustible treasure trove. Cossacks, soldiers, state officials, and private fur traders known as *promyshlenniki* crossed the Urals and, following the continent's network of rivers and, using portage to navigate stretches of land, pushed ever deeper into the Siberian interior. Working in groups as small as two or three or as large as sixty and more, often financed by Siberian governors based in Muscovy's fortified towns and settlements, they embarked on expeditions to gather fur. It usually took a winter and two summers to make a round trip between Russia and the towns and forts of Western Siberia; journeys as far afield as Yakutsk and Transbaikal could take up to three times as long. Travel was beset with all manner of perils. Distances of several hundred kilometres might separate one settlement from another; relatively minor injuries or bouts of sickness could easily prove fatal in the unforgiving forests, swamps and mountains. But in an otherwise impoverished rural economy, the rewards were astonishing. The pelts of squirrels, foxes, ermines, martens and, most prized of all, sable that the *promyshlenniki* brought back fetched astronomical prices in Russia and beyond. A single black Arctic fox fur was enough to purchase a good-sized farm, complete with horses, cattle, sheep and fowl.[5]

As they advanced eastwards, the Russians used a mixture of incentives and violence to extract tribute from Siberia's indigenous peoples. Those who cooperated with the *promyshlenniki* could expect payment and protection; those who did not, and who were suspected of concealing their wealth, paid a terrible price. Torture, hostage-taking and murder were commonplace; entire villages were wiped out. Some tribes, such as the Ostyaks, were accustomed to paying tribute to their former Mongol rulers and tried to come to terms with the advancing Russians only to be shocked by the greed of their new masters. Others, like the Buryats, resisted invasion from the outset. But even when they did sometimes show themselves capable of uniting in a coordinated defence of their lands, Siberia's tribes could offer only scattered resistance. None could match the firepower of the Russian forces, and tens of thousands succumbed to the diseases that the invaders brought with them. Only the snowbound outer reaches of Chukotka in the far

north-east offered sufficiently daunting natural obstacles and sufficiently meagre fur yields to stall the Russian advance.[6]

Over time, the Russians' use of both coercion and incentives
achieved the desired results: Siberia's native peoples embraced or submitted to the new trading empire, sought peace with their new masters,
and paid tribute. The *promyshlenniki* gathered enormous numbers of
furs in what proved to be an extraordinarily successful state-managed
conquest of territory. In the summer of 1630, they transported 34,000
sable pelts through Mangazeya; in the summer of 1641, no fewer than
75,000 sable pelts passed through the tsar's customs house in Yakutsk.
So ruthlessly efficient was the expanding Russian state in overseeing
this harvest of Siberian fur that by 1700, the supply of "soft gold" was
running dry.[7]

Over time, Russian governance imposed itself in this new frontier world by building on a complex set of relations—often mutually
beneficial but sometimes antagonistic—between traders, trappers and
Cossacks, on the one hand, and the early governors whom the tsar
placed in charge of Siberia's settlements, on the other. Cash-strapped
Muscovy's eastward expansion had to be self-financing, so governors
were allowed to support themselves and their subordinates by trading
in furs, alcohol and women in a practice known as "feeding," provided
they turned over a fixed share to the state. Some amassed extraordinary
sums. In order to ensure that they did not exceed what were considered reasonable levels of extortion and embezzlement, the government
established checks on the main roads leading back to European Russia
to search returning governors and confiscate surplus loot. While tolerated, the practice of "feeding" established a pattern of unaccountabil-
ity, not to say impunity, among Siberia's officials that would plague St.
Petersburg well into the nineteenth century. Thievery, graft and bribery
flourished at every level of the administration, from Siberia's provincial governors down to lowly scribes. Yet for all its rough edges and
its improvised and informal power structures, the Russian imperial
enterprise proved remarkably efficient not only in gathering Siberia's
fur harvests but also in conquering, holding and, ultimately, administering great swathes of territory. The conquest of Siberia transformed
Muscovy from a second-rank kingdom on the edge of Europe into the
world's largest continental empire.[8]

They first came to Siberia as warriors, trappers and traders, but over the course of the seventeenth century, Russians turned from furs to farming and from tribute collection to settlement. In 1622, there were about 23,000 Russians and assorted foreigners living east of the Urals; by 1709, it was 227,000 and rising. The frontier forts of the early fur-rush days evolved into more settled towns and centres of trade. The second half of the seventeenth century saw Tobolsk emerge as the seat of Russian government, religion and commerce in Western Siberia. By 1700, Tomsk had come to play a similar role in south-central Siberia while Yeniseisk, the transit point for all trade passing to and from Yakutsk and the Far East, occupied the same position further north. Founded in 1652, Irkutsk also grew rapidly, first as a collection centre for fur tribute from the Buryat natives of Transbaikal and, later, as a commercial hub for goods traded between China and the Russian Empire.[9]

In the last decades of the seventeenth century, waves of new migrants were forging a settled population of Europeans in Siberia. Peasants migrated from impoverished regions of European Russia. Some were government-sponsored settlers; others were fugitive serfs who knew their masters had little prospect of tracking them down if they escaped beyond the Urals. As early as 1670, there were about 34,000 peasants in the region of Tobolsk alone. State officials, Cossacks, other soldiers and prisoners of war made up a significant proportion of those living in Siberia's small towns and settlements and lent them a distinctively military character. Thousands of religious dissenters fled persecution in European Russia to establish colonies further east where they could practise their beliefs unmolested by the authorities.[10] By the turn of the eighteenth century, Siberia had a native population of about 200,000 and a Russian and European population of about 150,000 men and 76,000 women. These various groups intermarried and interbred. Many Russian settlers took (sometimes literally) native women as wives and fathered children with them. A century after Yermak first crossed the Urals, a Siberian way of life was beginning to take shape. Russian soldiers, craftsmen and peasants mingled with Siberian indigenes and emerged over time as a settled population of colonists known as the *sibiryaki* or *starozhily* (Old Siberians).[11]

Yet living alongside the Old Siberians were men and women who had not chosen to come to Siberia; rather they had been forcibly uprooted from their native regions and cast into what became known as the "vast prison without a roof." Siberia was both a land of opportunity and a penal realm, a land of free migrants and of unfree exiles. Under the tsars, it became apparent that there was a fundamental contradiction between these two roles—a contradiction that would dominate Siberia and the exile system in the centuries that followed.[12]

Exile was an act of expulsion. The bishop of Tobolsk and Siberia, Ioann Maksimovich, declared in 1708: "In the same way that we have to remove harmful agents from the body so that the body does not expire, so it is in the community of citizens: all healthy and harmless objects can abide within it, but that which is harmful must be cut out."[13] Imperial ideologues repeatedly returned to the image of Siberia as a world beyond the imaginative frontiers of the state into which the sovereign could purge impurities to protect the health of the bodies politic and social. The metaphors changed over time but the basic conviction remained that Siberia was a receptacle for the empire's own disorder.

The expulsion of malefactors from Russian society was publicly performed in a brutal ceremony that both underlined the gravity of the offence and asserted the power of the sovereign. Those guilty of serious crimes were flogged in public places; male felons also had their faces branded and their nostrils ripped out. On his travels through the Russian Empire in the 1770s, the English historian William Coxe came across one such flogging of a convicted murderer in the central market in St. Petersburg. Pushing his way through the crowd, Coxe clambered onto the roof of a cottage on the edge of the square and, from his vantage point, witnessed the proceedings. The executioner wielded the most terrible of all instruments of corporal punishment, the knout. Consisting of a stiff thong of rawhide, about four centimetres in diameter, it was fastened by a bronze ring to a braided leather whip, about a metre in length, which was in turn attached to a long wooden stick held by the executioner:

> The executioner, before every stroke, receded a few paces, and at the same time drew back the hand which held the knout; then, bounding forwards, he applied the flat end of the thong with considerable force to the naked back of the criminal in a

perpendicular line, reaching six or seven inches from the collar
to the waist. He began hitting the right shoulder, and continued
his strokes parallel to each other quite to the left shoulder; nor
ceased till he had inflicted 333 lashes, the number prescribed
by the sentence. At the conclusion of this terrible operation, the
nostrils of the criminal were torn with pincers; his face marked
with a hot iron; and he was re-conducted to prison, in order to
be transported to the mines of Nerchinsk in Siberia.[14]

Such brutal retribution was actually evidence of imperial clemency.
From the reign of Peter the Great (1696–1725), rituals of "civil execution" or "political death" stripped away the convict's juridical rights
and titles and confiscated all lands and wealth in an awesome demonstration of the might of the Russian state. Then, in 1753, Empress
Elizabeth (1741–62) formally replaced the gallows with penal labour
in Siberia. A ruling from the State Senate clarified that those guilty of
capital crimes would henceforth submit to a "political death" and exile
"to eternal penal labour." From that time on, capital offenders were
pronounced "civilly dead"; all were publicly knouted at market by an
executioner. A typical judgment of a felon from the eighteenth century
ran as follows:

> Sentence him to death, bring him to the scaffold, order him to
> lie down upon the executioner's block and then remove him
> from it and say We, the Great Sovereign, show him mercy and
> grant him life instead of death. We did not order him executed
> but ordered . . . that for his theft, his nostrils be torn out piti-
> lessly, so that others watching have no wish to steal or to say
> harmful things about us, the Great Sovereign.[15]

Civil executions were thus intended to be humiliating and traumatic
experiences. After 1785, the Russian nobility was exempt from corporal punishment since shame and dishonour were themselves believed
to wield a terrible punitive power for the upper orders. But for the
lower orders, considered insensible to such elevated emotions, there
was nothing ceremonial about the rituals that marked their expulsion
from imperial society.[16]

Coxe wryly observed that, whatever the monarchical mercy

shown in these rituals: "Upon a general calculation, perhaps it will be found, that notwithstanding the apparent mildness of the penal code, not fewer malefactors suffer death in Russia, than in those countries wherein that mode of punishment is appointed by the laws."[17] The lethal realities that awaited notwithstanding, the abolition of capital punishment meant that Siberia's penal labourers owed the tsar not just their punishments but also their very lives. The sovereign's power, not simply to take life but also to grant it, remained a cornerstone of the exile system in the centuries that followed.

Beyond the performance of autocratic might, exile to Siberia also came in the seventeenth and eighteenth centuries to embrace economic goals. As the Russian state expanded and its appetite for territory and resources grew, banishment *from* (*vysylka iz* in Russian) became replaced by exile *to* (*ssylka v*). In the wake of the banishment of the Uglich insurgents in 1592, the state continued to send criminals, deserters, prostitutes and mutinous populations to Siberia, often to regions that failed to attract sufficient numbers of voluntary migrants. By one estimate, a total of 19,900 men and 8,800 women were exiled to Siberia in the decades between 1662 and 1709.[18] The deployment of penal labourers under Peter the Great on large-scale construction projects in St. Petersburg, along the Baltic Coast and around the Sea of Azov expanded to include sites in Siberia. Some 20,000 of Peter's Swedish prisoners of war (including those who built the Tobolsk kremlin) were marched in chains to towns and villages across Siberia, where they were later joined by Peter's defeated political adversaries and small numbers of runaway serfs. The Petrine use of prisoners to harvest raw materials at labour sites across Siberia expanded as the state sought not simply to tap Siberia's natural resources but also to settle and colonize the land.[19]

The construction of a rudimentary infrastructure over the course of the eighteenth century was a step change in this colonization effort. Primitive roads were built to supplement Siberia's river network as the primary means of transportation, making travel easier and faster. The sparseness of Siberia's population and the huge distances between settlements led the government to rely on the local population for both transportation and communication. The unpaved roads were maintained by teams of peasants and natives who, during the reign of Catherine the Great (1762–96), were rewarded for their labours with exemption from the Siberian tribute. By 1725, there were already around 7,000 coachmen employed along Siberia's highways. In the 1740s, efforts were made to link the various Siberian forts by means of post houses, each manned by coachmen and stocked with fresh horses. The going was so arduous that the post houses were built relatively short distances from each other (there were as many as twenty between Tara and Tobolsk in 1745, a distance of only 380 kilometres). Construction of the Great Siberian Post Road linking Moscow with Yakutsk began in the 1760s. The Post Road was built at a great cost, both in roubles and in the lives of convicts and serfs, but it did eventually allow for the improved flow of wheeled traffic.[20]

Nonetheless, travel across Siberia remained an ordeal. Negotiating the roads on foot or by cart varied with the seasons between the merely gruelling and the utterly impossible. Each spring and autumn, the mud flowed axle-deep under the carts. The Russian term for this period is *rasputitsa;* literally, the "time without roads." The horse-drawn carts frequently became stuck in bogs; wheels and axles broke as they clattered over rocks and logs. In summer, clouds of dust choked travellers, and ponds and streams alongside the road turned brown and brackish in the heat, unleashing ferocious swarms of mosquitoes and horseflies. "I . . . took some rest," the American traveller John Ledyard confided to his diary upon finally reaching Irkutsk in 1787,

> after a very fatiguing route—rendered so by several very disagreeable circumstances—going with the Courier, and driving with wild tartar horses at the most rapid rate over a wild and ragged Country—breaking and upsetting several [covered wagons]—beswarmed by Musquetoes—all the way hard rains and when I arrived at Irkutsk I was, and had been the last 48 hours, wet thro' and thro'—and one complete mass of mud.

It was only in winter, when snow blanketed the dust and the plummeting temperatures froze the mud solid, that the Great Siberian Post Road was more easily travelled; but journeys could still take many months, even years. Even into the 1830s, the road to Okhotsk on the shores of the Pacific was littered with the carcasses and skeletons of horses that had not survived the journey.[21]

As the roads slowly extended and improved, the practical distances between Siberia and Russia shrank. By the end of the eighteenth century, a government courier could travel on horseback the 10,500 kilometres from St. Petersburg to Okhotsk in less than eighteen weeks; Nerchinsk in Transbaikal could be reached in seventy-five days. Yakutsk in north-eastern Siberia lay 100 days' journey from the capital and the towns of western and central Siberia were considerably closer than that. It had become possible for the Russian emperor to issue a directive in the Winter Palace and to be reasonably confident that it would arrive in the hands of the intended Siberian official in a matter of months.[22]

For the migrants crossing the Urals, however, the distances between European Russia and Siberia's towns and villages remained enormous. Many of the Russian peasants making the journey either as settlers or exiles had never ventured more than a few dozen kilometres from the villages where they had been born. Parts of Siberia remained as physically inaccessible and as psychologically remote from St. Petersburg and Moscow as Botany Bay was from London in the 1790s.[23]

The migrants still came, though, and in ever greater numbers as the eighteenth century wore on. By 1762, more than 350,000 male peasants had settled in Siberia; by 1811, the number had leapt to over 600,000. The growth in trade and agriculture gradually transformed Siberia's frontier settlements into bustling towns. Surrounded by fertile arable lands, Tobolsk flourished as a centre of trade. In 1782, 348 merchants and 2,761 artisans composed more than half the town's inhabitants in addition to 725 exiles, 487 coachmen, 151 indigenous converts to Christianity and 300 retired military servicemen. By 1790, Tobolsk boasted a dozen icon painters, 18 silversmiths, 35 gunsmiths, 45 blacksmiths, a clockmaker and a host of other artisans including tailors, dressmakers and cobblers.[24] When the Scottish explorer Captain John Dundas Cochrane visited the town in the early 1820s, he found that:

> it has many handsome churches . . . the streets are paved with wood, and in general the buildings are of the same material. The markets and bazzars are well regulated, and the town in general is very clean . . . Numerous flocks of cattle are seen in the neighbourhood of Tobolsk: provisions are cheap and abundant . . . But what is perhaps more remarkable, very good society is to be enjoyed here, and the strongest features of content[edness] are displayed in this hitherto supposed metropolis of barbarism and cruelty.[25]

Following Catherine the Great's administrative division of Siberia into East and West in 1775, Irkutsk became, like Tobolsk, a regional capital. By the 1790s, as many as 7 million roubles of goods were passing through Irkutsk each year, and as many as 10,000 sledges gathered there each winter to ferry freight westwards from China. Administrative power and burgeoning trade brought wealth and an expanding class of Siberian merchants who intermarried with Russian officials to form the beginnings of a provincial polite society. Irkutsk's first public library opened in 1782; by the end of the eighteenth century the town also boasted an amateur theatre and a forty-piece orchestra. Cochrane wrote of Irkutsk that "the streets are wide and run at right angles . . . The houses are for the greater part of wood, although many are of brick and constructed on a superior style of architecture."[26]

Still, by the beginning of the nineteenth century, only three Siberian towns—Tobolsk, Tomsk and Irkutsk—had a population of more than 10,000; none had more than 15,000 and most had fewer than 5,000. Siberia's total population, now a combination of native peoples, Russian peasant settlers and exiles, amounted to only about 1 million, concentrated in the towns and villages of Western Siberia and in a few centres east of the Yenisei River. Most Siberian towns were in fact little more than large villages, separated from each other by great swathes of tundra, taiga and steppe, dotted with tiny settlements whose inhabitants engaged in agriculture, trade and crafts. Despite the differences in the formal legal categories ascribed to them by the state, Cossacks, retired soldiers, peasants and settled exiles lived side by side and shared the unrelenting challenges of Siberia's harsh climate and often inhospitable terrain. Most villages were scattered along Siberia's waterways, post roads and trade routes; some were situated near mines, salt works and distilleries. A variety of involuntary migrants toiled in these industrial enterprises, which belonged either to the crown or to private landowners. Some were convicts sentenced to penal labour (*katorga*), some were army deserters and fugitive serfs; others were state peasants or private serfs who had been forcibly transferred by their masters to Siberia from European Russia.[27]

As it centralized its power in the eighteenth century, the state pushed for greater social regimentation. A host of previously innocent activities—

felling oak trees, gathering salt, vagrancy, trespassing, begging and so forth—became criminalized and punishable by exile to Siberia. Under empresses Anna (1730–40) and Elizabeth, penal colonization developed in an ad hoc fashion amid a jumble of legislation that added debtors, religious dissenters and convicts to the ranks of Siberia's involuntary recruits. The empire also witnessed, or at least was now able to record, an apparent increase in both petty crime and serious organized banditry. The struggle with both yielded further recruits for Siberia's penal enterprises. Prostitutes, thieves, drunks and beggars were periodically rounded up in Russian cities and marched off to Siberia.[28]

As the institution of serfdom tightened its grip on the Russian peasantry, it brought about violent clashes between the state and a population reluctant to surrender its freedom. In the eighteenth century, the empire was rocked by violent insurgencies: the Bulavin Revolt of 1707–8 and, most spectacularly, the Cossacks' and peasants' rebellion of 1773–5, led by Yemelyan Pugachev. The defeated insurgents, if they escaped massacre and the gallows, found themselves chained in marching convoys bound for Siberia.[29] Tens of thousands more did not revolt but simply fled the burdens of serfdom and twenty-five-year terms of military service, and disappeared into the Russian countryside. Itinerant labourers and beggars unable to provide internal documents were (often rightly) taken for runaway serfs or deserters, and were flogged and exiled. These attempts to fix and discipline the population culminated in the criminalization of vagrancy in 1823, which caused a surge in the numbers being annually exiled to Siberia. In the period 1819–22, over 4,000 people were exiled to Siberia each year; in 1823, that number increased to almost 7,000 and it nearly doubled the following year. In the two decades between 1826 and 1846, 48,500 of the 160,000 men and women exiled to Siberia had been sentenced as vagabonds.[30]

The late eighteenth century also saw the first stirrings of ideological opposition to the state. Almost two centuries after the Uglich insurgents were banished to Tobolsk, the autocracy still regarded Siberia as a convenient dumping ground for dissidents and subversives. Successive tsars saw religion as an ideological bulwark of political legitimacy. Catherine the Great exiled thousands of Old Believers (Orthodox Christians who rejected the reforms to the liturgy that were enacted in the 1660s) and the members of utopian sects such as the Flagellants and the Milk Drinkers. These deportations set a pattern for the persecution and exile of religious dissenters that would continue until the beginning of the twentieth century.[31]

In the wake of the French Revolution, even Catherine, that most enlightened of despots who admired Montesquieu and corresponded with Voltaire and Diderot, was inclined to view all and any criticism of her domain as revolutionary both in meaning and purpose. The writer Aleksandr Radishchev was banished to Siberia for the sweeping critique he offered of the Russian Empire's political, social and moral turpitude in his *A Journey from St. Petersburg to Moscow* (1790). Despite the author's decidedly counter-revolutionary (and prophetic) warnings of the violent consequences that would ensue if the state failed to tackle the evils of serfdom and rural poverty, Catherine was outraged. She denounced Radishchev as "a man worse than Pugachev," and tried him on charges of sedition and *lèse majesté*. Radishchev was found guilty and condemned to death, a sentence Catherine commuted to ten years of exile in the remote fortress settlement of Ilimsk in Eastern Siberia. Radishchev served only five years of his sentence, however, before being recalled to St. Petersburg by Paul I (1796–1801), who delighted in reversing his mother's decisions. He was a lone political exile in Siberia at the end of the eighteenth century but, viewed from the end of the nineteenth, Radishchev would seem an outrider for further generations of ideological rebels who would take up the pen, and later the gun, against the autocracy.[32]

The tsarist regime went on to use both judicial and extra-judicial mechanisms to banish subjects whose behaviour, religious and political beliefs were considered harmful to the public good. The system of "administrative exile" enabled the regime to bypass legal niceties and public rituals. People were arrested quietly and, with no right of appeal, were removed from Russian society. One scribe from Kazan province, who in 1821 made allegations of corruption against the governor, found himself denounced as "suspicious" and banished to the West Siberian city of Tomsk. Bureaucratic incompetence, venality and indifference created a labyrinth of absurd regulations, shadowy accusations and secret arrests.[33]

Despite the rise in the numbers of exiles in the eighteenth century, the state's expanding penal enterprises in Siberia continued to face chronic labour shortages. The government sought to address this recruitment shortfall in part by bestowing powers of administrative exile on a range of social and institutional authorities throughout the empire. In 1736, the private owners of factories, mines and smelteries and the managers of state-owned factories received the right to exile workers "who show themselves to be intemperate." Noting that "in Siberia, in Irkutsk province and in the Nerchinsk region, there are many areas suitable for settlement and agriculture," in 1760 the Imperial Senate promulgated a decree allowing landowners and monasteries to turn over their serfs to the state. Landowners could now draw on lists typically prepared by village elders to select for removal to Siberia men and women labelled "indecent," "obscene" or guilty of "immoral conduct." In an added incentive, such males who were over the age of fifteen could be accepted as substitutes for the military recruits whom serf owners had to levy for the state. The legislation sought to rid European Russia of troublesome peasants while providing the expanding industrial sites of Eastern Siberia with a pool of cheap labour.

Administrative exile also allowed serf owners to divest themselves of serfs who were disobedient or feckless or to whom they simply took a dislike. In his autobiographical novella of 1874, *Punin and Baburin,* Ivan Turgenev portrayed his own family's despotic treatment of the serfs on their estate. The narrator's grandmother (a character inspired by Turgenev's own mother) singles out a young serf whom she accuses of failing to show her sufficient deference. She has him exiled to Siberia, dismissing him with a wave "of her handkerchief towards the window as if driving away an importunate fly."[34]

Russian peasants were not, however, passive victims of despotic masters; they too wielded exile as a tool of social control and cleansing. Peasant communities regularly colluded with serf owners in the administrative exile of the disabled and the mentally ill. Both serfs and their lords had a vested interest in ridding themselves of those who represented an economic burden on the village, even if their only offence was their incapacity or ineptitude.[35] Of the 97,000 criminal exiles in Siberia at the beginning of 1835, 28,500 were designated "incapable." Moreover, according to legislation dating back to 1669, peasant and merchant communities—themselves legally constituted bodies—could, like serf owners, refuse to accept the return of men and women who had already served out their sentences. A criminal might be found guilty, flogged and sentenced to a term of imprisonment, only to discover, upon his eventual release, that his former community would not take him back. In such cases, the offender was liable to find himself or herself administratively exiled to Siberia even if the original offence did not merit this punishment. One case among tens of thousands was that of Aleksei Lebedev, the son of a Moscow merchant who was convicted in 1846 of petty theft. Following a flogging and a brief custodial sentence, his merchant community refused to re-admit him and Lebedev was exiled to Siberia.[36]

Peasant and merchant communities were granted more than simply the right to reject returning convicts. A decree from 1763 empowered them to administratively exile their own members to Siberia, even if their guilt had not been proven but they simply fell under suspicion. In the absence of an effective rural police force, the tsarist state relied on these devolved punitive practices to maintain law and order in European Russia. In 1857 in the central Russian province of Yaroslavl, a territory that stretched across 36,000 square kilometres with a population of 950,000, the Ministry of the Interior could rely on just 244 policemen to keep the peace. Across the whole empire by 1900, the government employed a total of only 1,600 constables and 6,900 sergeants to police a widely dispersed rural population approaching 90 million. Unable to entrust its own agencies with upholding the law, the tsarist state effectively farmed out legal responsibility for investigating crimes, apprehending malefactors and determining guilt to a host of communes, guilds and institutions. Hapless individuals would find themselves summarily pronounced guilty and turned over to the authorities for deportation to Siberia. Exile was never simply a tool of repressive government but also a punishment wielded by peasant and merchant communities against their own members.[37]

For serf owners, factory owners, village assemblies and merchant guilds, administrative exile thus provided a useful tool for both policing and removing troublemakers and the unproductive. The scope for abuse was almost limitless. Everyone from thieves, murderers and rapists to the victims of slander, superstition and the noxious cauldron of village politics could find themselves fettered in convoys marching eastwards. The use and abuse of administrative exile fed a surge in exile numbers in the first half of the nineteenth century. From the 1830s onwards, more than half the exiles who set off for Siberia had never seen the inside of a courtroom or heard the rulings of a judge. Many of those sentenced by Georgian England to deportation to the colonies might have been guilty of shockingly petty crimes, but they had at least been convicted by a magistrate or a jury of their peers. The exclusion of the overwhelming majority of the empire's population of peasants and merchants from any meaningful legal protections supplied a steady stream of recruits for Siberia's exile settlements and penal colonies.[38]

By the late eighteenth century, Catherine the Great's absolutist regime had expanded exile into a full-blown state-led project to colonize the Siberian landmass.[39] The first two decades of Catherine's reign alone saw the deportation to Siberia of around 60,000 insurrectionists, religious dissenters and political prisoners, together with the usual colourful collection of criminals, prostitutes, administrative exiles and their families. The empress's concern with the productivity of her involuntary colonists led her to attempt to reform the exile system. The corporal punishments often meted out to Siberia's exiles were thus prohibited from being so brutal as to incapacitate them because they had to remain capable of work. For the same reason, Catherine attempted to block the deportation of the elderly and the infirm but, in a reflection of the limited power the autocrat wielded in territories thousands of kilometres distant from St. Petersburg, her instructions had little apparent effect. The powers of exile granted to serf owners, peasants and merchants still ensured the selection of Siberian recruits not for their potential productivity, but precisely for their lack of it.[40]

Though colonization gave imperial policies in Siberia a wider purpose, exile remained chaotic, driven by the ad hoc accumulation of edicts, laws and temporary legislation. It was rationalized for the first time under the reforming energies of the great nineteenth-century statesman Mikhail Speransky (1772–1839). Appointed governor-general of Siberia by Alexander I in 1819, Speransky set about streamlining the exile system. In 1822, he implemented a raft of reforms that marked the beginning of the imperial state's coordinated and sustained pursuit of the penal colonization of Siberia. Henceforth, exiles convicted of major crimes were sentenced to varying terms of penal labour followed by exile to settlement (ssylka na poselenie) to a particular district in Siberia; less serious offenders were sentenced directly to various terms—ranging from a few years to their entire lives—of exile to settlement (again within a particular district). Upon completion of their sentences, exiles were permitted to leave their officially designated district and reside anywhere in Siberia. Both punishments therefore envisaged the eventual integration of the exiles into the ranks of the Siberian peasantry. Exiles were allowed to return to European Russia only if the authorities granted them express permission (and an internal passport) to do so. They were obliged to secure the consent of their own peasant and merchant communities, which often was not forthcoming, and they had to pay for the return journey themselves. While these laws were not infrequently flouted by local authorities acting on their own initiative, they nevertheless constituted the foundations of the exile system. The legal barriers to the exiles' return to their native regions after they had served out their sentences were deliberately calculated to ensure that most remained in Siberia. Speransky's administrative, penal and logistical reforms shaped the exile system for the remainder of the century.[41]

The wider ambition of colonization now demanded that criminals be disciplined and even rehabilitated. Ideally, penal labourers and exiles would be transferred to the sparsely populated expanses of Irkutsk and Yenisei provinces and deployed to specific industrial sites and mines such as Aleksandrovsk, Nerchinsk and Kara. Just as the exile system purged Russia of its villains, so the rigours of exile in Siberia would purge these villains of their vices. The gender imbalance among Siberia's exiles meant that, by the middle of the eighteenth century, the authorities were already concerned that a shortage of women in Siberia was preventing the emergence of a stable population of penal colonists. Accordingly, the state encouraged women to follow their husbands beyond the Urals, believing that their presence would exert a pacifying and rehabilitative influence over the men. The government even passed new legislation obliging the wives of administrative exiles and, with the consent of the serf owner, their children to follow their husbands and fathers to Siberia, and then compensated the serf owner for the loss of their human possessions. Through the establishment of stable and productive family units, the goal of individual regeneration neatly dovetailed with the state's colonial agenda.[42]

There was, however, a persistent gulf between the state's designs and its ability to implement them in the remote, sparsely populated and thinly administered regions of Siberia. On the ground, colonization and punishment were wildly at odds with each other. Chronically underfunded, hopelessly mismanaged and brutalized by the conditions of their captivity, exiles lacked the incentives, the skills and the financial and organizational wherewithal necessary to establish themselves as independent farmers and traders in Siberia's unforgiving climate and terrain. Yet even though the contradictions between punishment and colonization were already obvious in the reign of Alexander I, the state persisted doggedly with exile as its primary tool of punishment until the beginning of the twentieth century.

In the absence of precise statistics, the best estimates of numbers of exiles living in Siberia at the end of the eighteenth century suggest a few tens of thousands, a total of some 35,000 males having been exiled between 1761 and 1781. By the time Alexander acceded to the throne in 1801, these exiles were dispersed among about 360,000 natives and around 575,000 Russian and European migrants, and therefore made up less than 5 per cent of the total inhabitants of Siberia. Over the course of the nineteenth century, exiles rarely exceeded 10 per cent of the continent's overall population. The uneven concentrations of exiles and penal labourers meant, however, that they could constitute a significant percentage of inhabitants in a given town or region. In 1840, they made up only 4 per cent of the inhabitants of Yalutorovsk district in Western Siberia but they constituted 31 per cent of the population of Kainsk district in central Siberia and no fewer than 38 per cent of those living in Marinsk district, further east.[43]

As reported crime, social unrest, religious dissent and sedition increased throughout the nineteenth century, the numbers of exiles surged. Over the course of the 1830s, 78,000 exiles crossed the Ural Mountains; by the 1870s, their number had climbed to almost 167,000. The cumulative effect of this penal migration meant that by the time of the empire-wide census of 1897, there were 300,000 exiles living among an overall Siberian population of 5,760,000. Though twenty years were still to pass before the Russian Revolution, this expanding outcast population and the tensions it provoked already testified to deepening social and political conflict. Imperial Russia struggled to cage social and political disorder beyond the Urals, but by the end of the nineteenth century it had begun to resemble a society devouring itself.[44]

2

The Boundary Post

Over the course of the nineteenth century, convoys of prisoners marching across the Ural Mountains into exile would pass a simple 3.5-metre column made of plastered bricks. Standing in a forest clearing some 2,500 kilometres east of St. Petersburg, it bore on one side the coat of arms of the province of Perm and the word "Europe"; on the other, that of the province of Tobolsk and the word "Asia." The simplicity of the boundary post between Russia and Siberia belied its significance as a marker of the wrenching separation of exiles from their homeland. The exiled anarchist Prince Peter Kropotkin noted drily that "the inscription of Dante's Inferno would be more appropriate to the boundary-pillar of Siberia than these two words which pretend to delineate two continents."[1] The American George Kennan witnessed the scenes at the boundary post when he travelled throughout Siberia in 1888:

> No other spot between St. Petersburg and the Pacific is more full of painful suggestions, and none has for the traveller a more melancholy interest than the little opening in the forest where stands this grief-consecrated pillar. Here hundreds of thousands of exiled human beings—men, women, and children; princes, nobles, and peasants—have bidden good-by forever to friends, country, and home . . . The Russian peasant, even when a criminal, is deeply attached to his native land; and heart-rending scenes have been witnessed around the boundary pillar . . . Some gave way to unrestrained grief; some comforted the weeping; some knelt and pressed their faces to the loved soil of their native country, and collected a little earth to take with them into exile . . .[2]

Exiles passing the post would sometimes scrawl final valedictory messages on it: "Farewell Masha!" read one inscription; "Farewell life!" another. Others, in a bid to stave off the oblivion they sensed awaited them, would etch their own names into the plaster. The boundary post has not survived to the present day (although a likeness of it has been reconstructed) but for as long as it stood, this modest marker of an administrative boundary loomed large in the popular imagination as a monument to the torments of Siberia's exiles.[3]

The scenes of sorrow and grief that played themselves out time and again beneath the post were a measure of the tsars' power to drive their subjects around the vast territories of the empire, as the 1649 Penal Code had stipulated, "to wherever the sovereign shall direct."[4] The journey into exile was thus a measure of autocratic authority, each footstep eastwards a homage to the ruler. By the end of the eighteenth century, the forced movement of criminals and their families had also come to fill a central role in St. Petersburg's colonial ambitions beyond the Urals.

The European empires all struggled with the formidable logistical problems of penal migration. Britain's transports to its Australian penal colonies in the late eighteenth century were dreadful ordeals for the convict passengers. Prisoners languished in the ships' holds, "chilled to the bone on soaked bedding, unexercised, crusted with salt, shit and vomit, festering with scurvy and boils." Of the 1,006 convicts who sailed on the Second Fleet in 1790, 267 died at sea and at least another 150 after landing.[5] The British government took swift and decisive action to curb the lethal excesses in transportation because the organized and efficient transfer of healthy convicts was understood to be necessary to the wider project of penal colonization. It bombarded the private contractors responsible for transportation with demands for improvements in conditions, and deferred payment for each convict until he or she disembarked in decent health. A naval surgeon was placed on board each vessel and was answerable to the government, not to the contractors. Negligence and abuse still continued on some ships but, by 1815, the death rate in the transports had fallen to one in eighty-five. By the end of transportation in 1868, it was only one in 180.[6]

The deportation of convicts to Siberia presented logistical difficulties not less (and possibly even more) daunting than those of the roiling

waters of the Atlantic and Indian oceans. The annual deportation of
thousands of unruly and sometimes violent convicts several thousands
of kilometres across the most inhospitable territory would have taxed
the resources of any contemporary European state. The Siberian continent boasted only the sketchiest network of roads, and rivers that
flowed unhelpfully south to north and north to south, rather than west
to east, and turned each winter into a hazardous ocean of snow.

When compared with its European rivals, the tsarist empire's state
machinery was primitive and already creaking under the weight of its
administrative burdens. St. Petersburg's remit did not run as deep as
that of London or Paris. Even within European Russia, the state had little direct contact with its own population. It devolved governance onto
the landed nobility, the Church, merchant guilds and village assemblies. The Imperial Army was the only direct and sustained confrontation with state power that most Russian subjects—the peasantry—ever
experienced. The enormous distances separating Siberia's administrators from their masters in the capital amplified the effects of this
bureaucratic weakness. Under-resourced and virtually unaccountable,
officials manoeuvred within the deportation system for private gain,
neglecting, exploiting and robbing the convicts in their charge.

After several months, sometimes years on the road, convicts who
had departed hale and hearty from European Russia finally reached
their destinations in Eastern Siberia as ragged, sickly, half-starving
mockeries of the robust penal colonists envisioned by officials in St.
Petersburg. The deportation process itself thus frustrated the state's
wider strategic ambitions for the penal colonization of Siberia. The
downcast and desperate figures trudging eastwards in marching convoys were indictments of the imperial state's weakness and incompetence. The boundary post was not so much a symbol of the sovereign's
power as a marker of its limitations.

At the beginning of the nineteenth century, exiles almost all made the
journey to Siberia on foot. They would set out from one of five cities in the empire: St. Petersburg, Białystok in the Kingdom of Poland,
Kamenets-Podolsk and Kherson in Ukraine, and Tiflis in Georgia. Most
were funnelled through the Central Forwarding Prison in Moscow,
from where they and their families would march eastwards through

the town of Vladimir that gave its name to the road that wound its way eastwards. Synonymous with Siberian exile, the *Vladimirka* gained such notoriety over the nineteenth century that Isaak Levitan's eponymous landscape painting from 1892, which today hangs in Moscow's Tretyakov Gallery, seemed to echo to the clumping steps of exiles marching eastwards.

Leading out of Russia through Kazan and Perm, the *Vladimirka* crossed the Urals and joined the Great Siberian Post Road. Siberia's artery snaked across the open plains of Western Siberia, through the cities of Tyumen, Tobolsk and Tomsk before plunging into the thick swampy forests of Eastern Siberia and passing through the towns of Achinsk and Krasnoyarsk, eventually to reach the regional capital of Irkutsk. Anton Chekhov described the road as "the longest and, I should think, the ugliest . . . on earth." Indeed, the Great Siberian Post Road was in reality nothing more than a narrow dirt track. Deportation convoys were a familiar sight on the road. The English traveller William Spottiswoode woke beside it one morning in 1856: "The chill grey morning draws on; and beneath the double row of birch trees, which seem drooping to shelter them as they pass, is a long line of drab-clad figures marching in the same direction as ourselves. We instinctively know what it is, but can still hardly believe that a story so sad, so strange, so distant, is being realised before our eyes."[7]

Exiles in the marching convoys were issued with regulation clothing: coarse grey smocks, each boasting a bright scrap of cloth, in the shape of the ace of diamonds, sewn onto the back to facilitate identification (male convicts entering Siberia also had one side of their head shaved). As winter approached and temperatures plummeted, convict parties strung out along the road were also provided with sheepskin coats. The standard-issue coats and boots were often, as one contemporary noted, "of such poor quality and so carelessly stitched together that, when given out in Tobolsk, they did not even last until the convict had reached the next . . . district town." The exiles were then obliged to purchase replacement items at their own expense from local inhabitants who enthusiastically exploited their captive market. Those without the funds to replace their worn-out garments and footwear walked barefoot and in rags. The further the marching convoys proceeded eastwards, the more they came to resemble columns not so much of regimented prisoners as of bedraggled refugees.[8]

The convicts walked all year round. During the intense heat of the summer, those at the rear of the marching column choked on the great dust clouds raised by hundreds of tramping feet. On the open steppe, the treeless horizon and cloudless skies offered no respite from the burning sun. Dehydration and sunstroke saw many convicts collapse as they marched. The autumn rains brought only temporary respite from the heat before they transformed the roads into a churning quagmire through which the convicts squelched knee-deep. Late September would already bring the first searing winter frosts. At 20°C below, the breath froze onto the men's beards, forming chunks of ice; at 30°C below, the cold burned the lungs. In January 1828, one young woman making her way by carriage across Siberia to join her exiled fiancé encountered a marching convoy in temperatures of –46°C:

> I heard a noise, still strange to me at that time, but which afterwards became all too familiar. It was the noise of the fetters . . . an entire party of people was in chains—some were even chained to a metal pole. These unfortunates were a terrible sight. To protect their faces from the cold, they had covered them with some dirty rags into which they had cut holes for their eyes.[9]

The freezing temperatures, impenetrable blizzards and deep snowdrifts frequently turned the marching convoys into a lethal ordeal.

Government inspectors reported that many of the exiles were not equipped with sufficient money or adequate clothing before they set out from their provinces in European Russia; others had their funds stolen by officials en route. Still others, although properly provided for by their local officials, "had, from carelessness and fecklessness, frittered away their allowance before completing half their journey." A large number of the exiles in marching convoys were eventually obliged to sell their coats; they suffered shortages in both food and clothing and became exhausted, reliant for food on the alms of the Siberian villagers in whose cabins they were put up for the night.

Record-keeping was in a desperate state with different convict parties mingling and documents being lost and altered. In 1806, Alexander I acknowledged in a decree that the Siberian authorities "did not accurately know the sex or the number of the people sent to them for settlement." To address these shortcomings, the government proposed the establishment of officials at the first settlement inside the border of each province through which the exiles passed. It would be their job to draw up accurate lists of the numbers of exiles arriving, their condition and their destination. But such measures amounted to very little and record-keeping within the system remained haphazard and incomplete. A combination of escapes, deaths and exiles waylaid in the provinces through which they marched defied the compilation of accurate statistics on exile numbers and their location.[10]

In practices that ran completely counter to the state's own attempts to populate its industrial enterprises with labourers, local authorities along the route also routinely filtered out fit and healthy exiles for work in their own regions, allowing only the sick and frail to proceed. As early as 1786, the head of the Nerchinsk Mining Region in Transbaikal wrote to St. Petersburg complaining that he was being sent underage and sick exiles, incapable of working in the mines. Nearly a fifth of the 970 exiles assigned to the mines and factories were too young, too sick or too frail to be capable of manual labour. More than half of those currently working were over the age of fifty and were, therefore, "without prospects in the near future." St. Petersburg acknowledged that healthier exiles were indeed being detained in the provinces through which they passed, and ordered that the practice be stopped.[11]

In the decades that followed, however, it showed no signs of abating. In 1813, Minister of the Interior Osip Kozodavlev fired off an angry letter to the Siberian governor-general, Ivan Pestel, complaining that of the 1,100 male souls destined for Irkutsk province between 1809 and 1811 only 625 had actually arrived; 490 had remained in Tomsk province, 180 to settle, 220 because they were apparently too sick to travel, and the rest because they had been put to work in local factories. While acknowledging that the sick should indeed be allowed to remain in Tomsk province to be cared for by local communities, the minister noted that "under this pretext, perfectly capable people are being detained." Five years later, less than half the allocated number of exiles was reaching Eastern Siberia. Investigations revealed that the "best people in terms of age and abilities" were remaining in many Russian and Siberian provinces to be used as labourers. They were being sent on to Irkutsk only when periods of up to ten years of penal labour had already destroyed their health.[12]

The majority of prisoners travelled from distant Russian provinces, and to reach their assigned locations took two years. However, if they had fallen ill and had been hospitalized, it could take as many as three years. There were examples of some convicts taking four or five. The authorities were concerned that prisoners condemned to penal labour would, if their penal servitude were to begin from the moment of their conviction, drag their heels in the marching convoys, and seek to while away their sentences in hospitals along the route in order to delay their arrival in the mines or factories. They therefore stipulated that a penal labourer's sentence would begin only when he or she arrived at their final destination in Siberia. One convict reached Irkutsk after eight years and only when he finally entered the prison factory did the first minute of his eight-year sentence begin.[13]

Conditions in the marching convoys unsurprisingly eroded the health of the convicts and their families. One inspector reported in 1802 that the sick and any pregnant women were being treated "negligently" as they followed the convict parties on the *telegi*—springless wooden carts—"in the most pitiful and dangerous conditions . . . Some died on the route and the women gave birth in the wagons." A battery of ailments afflicted the exiles tramping along the Great Siberian Post Road: fevers, catarrhal and rheumatic attacks, pneumonia and consumption, ulcers from the fetters, rashes from the dirt and typhus from the overcrowding in the buildings. By some estimates, one third of all the exiles marching the 5,000 kilometres to Eastern Siberia required treatment and convalescence in the field hospitals and medical stations along the route. "They arrived," one report noted, "exhausted, prematurely enfeebled, having contracted incurable diseases, having forgotten their trades, and having grown quite unaccustomed to labour . . ."[14]

In a custom that had developed over the seventeenth and eighteenth centuries, marching convoys would overnight in the villages strung out along the route. Smaller groups could be accommodated in peasant huts and barns but larger parties were sometimes forced to sleep in the open air. Local peasant communities were charged both with supplying guards for the marching convoys and with maintaining the roads and bridges along which they travelled. In 1804, the governor-general of Siberia, Ivan Selifontov, highlighted in a report to the capital how onerous was the Siberian population's responsibility for transferring exiles "across Siberia's vast and sparsely settled provinces." This unwanted distraction from the peasants' work in the fields was a source of considerable rancour.[15] Even though the villagers were themselves liable for any prisoners who absconded on their watch, many were themselves former exiles, and had no particular enthusiasm for risking their lives to ensure the security of the convoys. Escapes were commonplace and the fugitives then formed themselves into marauding bands of vagrants that attacked entire merchant caravans journeying along Siberia's isolated highways. Selifontov called for the establishment of military units with mounted Cossacks along the main Siberian roads "in order not only to put an end to such acts of banditry and brigandage, but also to remove the danger for inhabitants and travellers." Selifontov calculated that 2,880 soldiers, based in post offices along the main routes, would be required to undertake the transportation of prisoners successfully. He understood, however, that it would be difficult to raise the required numbers without severely impinging upon the army's duties elsewhere, so he settled for 1,825. Alexander approved his request and the Internal Watch was eventually established in 1816. The Cossacks who manned it proved, however, no more reliable than the peasants they replaced. Officials lamented that they often released the convicts they were accompanying in return for payment. The endemic nature of escapes and the waves of crime unleashed by fugitives in the Siberian provinces of Tobolsk and Tomsk were an unending concern for the authorities.[16]

Overlaying these administrative problems in the years prior to the sweeping reforms to the exile system in 1822 were the expanding numbers of exiles being marched off to Siberia. An annual average of 1,600 were exiled between 1807 and 1813, but the annual average for the period from 1814 to 1818 jumped to 2,500 and from 1819 to 1823 it rose again to 4,600. The increasing use of administrative exile by both landowners and peasant communities, compounded by mounting conflict between the peasants and their masters under the impact of the Napoleonic Wars, fuelled this growth in numbers. By the end of the second decade of the nineteenth century, the system was teetering on the verge of collapse. Responsibility for stabilizing and overhauling it was entrusted to the new governor-general of Siberia, Mikhail Speransky.[17]

Speransky nurtured a vision of Siberia's eventual integration into the Russian Empire and believed that moral energy and administrative reform could tackle the problems of the exile system. He approached the task of deporting convicts to Siberia as a purely logistical project. His "Statutes on Exile Transfer Within Siberian Provinces" was part of the wider "Statutes on Exiles" published in 1822 and comprised thirteen articles and 199 clauses. The construction of purpose-built waystations or *étapes* along the Great Siberian Post Road had already begun in 1819. Speransky's "Statutes on Exile Transfer" accelerated and expanded the process, mapping out a new route along a series of stages, punctuated by a succession of *étapes*. Each was separated by a day's march from a semi-station (*poluetap*) and then another day's trek to the next *étape*. Semi-stations were designed to accommodate marching convoys for a single night; *étapes* for two nights and a rest day. Speransky ordered the construction of forty such stages in Western Siberia and another twenty-one in Eastern Siberia. Each had its own command, drawn from the Internal Watch and answerable to the Ministry of War, responsible for relaying marching convoys under armed guard along the route. The marching convoys were usually led by an officer, a non-commissioned officer and a drummer, flanked by armed soldiers on both sides and with Cossacks on horseback at the front and the rear.[18]

The convoys were processions of misfortune. At the front marched the penal labourers. Those sentenced not simply to exile but to penal labour were considered (for the most part, with good cause) to be more dangerous and more likely to attempt an escape. Their hands were manacled and they wore heavy leg fetters connected by a chain that ran through a ring attached to a belt. They were then shackled in pairs to a pole, later replaced by a chain, to prevent escapes. When one collapsed, all had to stop; when one had to defecate, all had to attend. One contemporary observed that "the heavy fetters, even though surrounded by leather, chafed legs exhausted from walking; but most unbearable of all for these unfortunates was being shackled in pairs: every convict suffered from each jerking movement of his partner through the manacles, especially if they were of different heights and builds." If there were not enough fetters to go around, convicts would be shackled together in a single set. Following them trudged those exiled to settlement, wearing only leg fetters. Next came administrative exiles, who were not shackled. The final group comprised the family members voluntarily following their relatives into exile. Behind the column rumbled four carts, each drawn by a single horse. These bore the exiles' belongings (their lives were condensed into a maximum weight of 12 kilogrammes). If space allowed, the old, the young and the sick were permitted to ride with the baggage; if not, they could hire extra horse-drawn carts from local villages at their own expense. If they did not have the funds, they had to walk.[19]

In Speransky's technocratic vision, the design of the *étape* system would allow the orderly movement of exiles to their assigned destinations and enforce accountability for their transfer. The great reformer was meticulous in his detailing of the route and scheduling of the marching convoys: exiles beginning their journey at the First *Étape* Command in the village of Tyguloye, on Tobolsk province's western border, would march two days via a semi-station to the next full station at Perevalovo, where they would be turned over to the Second *Étape* Command. At this station, they received a day's rest and were permitted to use the bathhouse. The convoy command would then march the prisoners on to Tyumen, where it transferred them to the Tyumen Invalid Command, responsible for delivering them to Tobolsk, 280 kilometres away.[20]

It was in Tobolsk that Speransky's reforms established the headquarters of the Exile Office, transforming the town into the nerve centre of the exile administration. Setting out from Tobolsk, exiles would first march a staggering 1,560 kilometres to the city of Tomsk over a twelve-week period with never more than a single day of rest at any stop. Another 590 kilometres stood between Tomsk and Krasnoyarsk on the Yenisei River, the boundary between Western and Eastern Siberia, where the prisoners would be allowed to rest for a week. After another 1,050 kilometres of marching, again with never more than a single day's rest at a time, the convoy would finally reach Irkutsk and another few days of precious respite. The final leg was no less arduous: penal labourers destined for the silver mines of Nerchinsk had another 1,600 kilometres to march. According to Speransky's calculations, an exile would, on reaching Irkutsk, have walked 3,570 kilometres (the approximate distance overland from Madrid to St. Petersburg or from Washington, DC, to Salt Lake City, Utah) in twenty-nine and a half weeks, at an average distance of 27 kilometres per day.[21]

Speransky's "Statutes on Exile Transfer" was a document of imperial hubris. From the lofty heights of St. Petersburg's ministries, it crafted a virtual world of orderly, timetabled departures and arrivals, efficient convoy commands working in synchronized harmony to deliver their charges to Siberian destinations along a meticulously planned route. From this altitude, plotting the forced migration of people was a matter of slotting numbers together in a coherent sequence: roubles per convict, convicts per marching convoy, *étapes* per hundreds of kilometres and so on. Yet the remote and recalcitrant realities of Siberia subverted Speransky's imperial ambitions, confounding the reformer's attempts to micromanage this traffic in human beings.

In particular, Speransky's plans for the orderly transfer of exiles foundered on an explosion in the numbers banished each year beyond the Urals. Speransky appeared convinced that annual totals would remain fairly static but they in fact more than doubled across the 1820s (to a large degree because of the 1823 criminalization of vagrancy), from an annual average of 4,600 between 1819 and 1823 to an annual average of 11,100 over the next three years. One official noted ruefully in 1825 that, whereas in the years before 1822, the state was exiling between sixty and seventy individuals each week, it was now deporting in excess of 200. In the period between 1823 and 1831, 11,000 penal labourers and 68,600 exiles (79,600 individuals overall, of whom 9,200 were women) passed through the Tobolsk Exile Office.[22]

Seeking to reduce the number of escapes as exiles marched eastwards in the summer months, the "Statutes on Exile Transfer" set a limit of sixty exiles in each deportation convoy during the summer and a maximum of 100 in winter when the ferocious cold dissuaded almost all from attempting to flee. Penal labourers, considered more dangerous than exiles, were to number no more than ten in each party. Speransky additionally stipulated that no more than one party should set out each week from the collection point in Tyguloye. As the number of exiles in the 1820s increased, however, officials were obliged to ignore these limits and thus to compromise the security of the convoys. In the early 1820s, marching convoys swelled to in excess of 400 exiles. Subsequent attempts to limit their size were defeated by the sheer weight of numbers flooding into the exile system. In 1835, senior government inspectors noted that the huge and unforeseen increase in exile numbers made it "extremely difficult, not to say impossible, for local officials to carry out their duties in accordance with the rules laid out in the 'Statutes on Exile Transfer.'" They noted that marching convoys regularly consisted of more than 250 souls. Alternatively, the authorities were obliged to detain exiles exceeding the requisite number in the towns along the route, delaying their arrival at their official destination.[23]

The *étapes* beyond the Siberian frontier were constructed according to a set of prescriptions spelled out in Speransky's statutes, and usually took the form of low stockades enclosing a yard. They contained three one-storey log buildings painted in regulation ochre, one housing the convoy commander and the other two the soldiers and exiles. Inside the exiles' barracks were three or four large cells, each of which contained a Russian stove and rows of upper and lower planking, which ran along their walls and on which the convicts could sit, sleep and store their belongings. Semi-stations were even more primitive: a wooden stockade containing two huts, one for the officer and convoy soldiers and another for the exiles. The responsibility for their maintenance was given to a local population with nothing to gain from investing in the state's prison buildings. A mere decade or so after most were constructed, one government inspector reported to St. Petersburg that almost all the prison buildings in Tobolsk province "were in an absolutely terrible state, both cramped and badly designed." Instructions to improve the construction of the *étapes* by building with stone were flouted by local authorities. As late as 1848, even the Central Forwarding Prison in Tobolsk was still built of wood.[24]

In many waystations and semi-stations, the cells were poorly heated and ventilated; exiles struggled for space on the benches; hardened and aggressive criminals occupied premium positions near the stove in winter and by the windows in summer. The weak and the sick were forced to sleep under the benches on the filth-encrusted floors. As one anonymous contemporary recorded, "the hut for the convicts is divided into a number of cells, which combined could accommodate 30–40, but, as parties of 100, sometimes 200 and more spend half a day and night in them, the convicts sleep on the benches, under the benches, on the floor by the doorway, in the corridors and sometimes even outside in the courtyard whatever the weather." The *étapes* were infested with a galaxy of ravenous insects. A strip of the wall running above the benches in the cells was usually stained red with the blood of crushed mosquitoes, as exile after exile had attempted to put an end to his tormentors.[25]

The congestion and squalor in the waystations almost reduced the convicts to the state of livestock. "It was so crowded on the benches," one exiled nobleman remembered,

> that it was scarcely possible to turn over; some made room for themselves at the feet of others, at the very edge of the benches; the rest on the floor and under the benches. One can imagine how fetid it is, especially in foul weather, when all arrive soaked through in their dirty rags. And then there are the so-called *parashas*, wooden tubs that met the nocturnal needs of prisoners. The stench from these *parashas* was unbearable . . .

These leaking vats of excrement and the terrible ventilation ensured that the *étapes* were incubators of typhus, dysentery, cholera and tuberculosis.[26]

For all the government's professed concern for the delivery of healthy and productive exiles to its penal labour sites, the Great Siberian Post Road was no place to fall ill. Each waystation boasted only a single medical room containing six beds, hopelessly inadequate for the numbers of exiles taken ill in the marching convoys. In 1845, the government decreed that the sick be immediately transported on the *telegi* to the medical facilities in each of the district towns along the route. In Western Siberia, however, there were only six such towns across a distance of nearly 2,000 kilometres. Those in need of medical care had to endure up to 200 kilometres and more of jolting along Siberia's notoriously potholed roads—a journey lasting sometimes more than two weeks. As late as 1880, there were only three such medical facilities in the 590 kilometres separating Tomsk from Krasnoyarsk. Kennan witnessed the sufferings of stricken exiles in the open carts: "When a prisoner is suffering from one of the diseases of the respiratory organs that are so common in *étape* life, it is simply torture to sit in a cramped position for six or eight hours in an open *telega*, breathing the dust raised by the feet of 350 men marching in close column." Those fortunate or hardy enough to survive the journey often discovered that the medical facilities in Siberia's towns offered little respite. Some would admit the sick only if they could pay; others had no qualified medical staff. Overcrowding was, as ever, a constant peril: in 1868, as a result of "acute overcrowding," typhus tore through the Krasnoyarsk prison into which more than 1,500 convicts were crammed. Built for eighty beds, the prison hospital was struggling to cope with 250 patients.[27]

The marching convoys reserved special torments for women. Despite the fact that most female convicts had no history of vice, the assumption of officials was that all female convicts were prostitutes even before they entered the marching convoys. In 1839, one Polish exile, Justynian Ruciński, observed at first hand how every female exile was obliged to take a lover in the marching convoy. The choice of partner was not her own, though, but that of the convicts, who auctioned the women off to the highest bidder among her "suitors." If a woman rejected the proposed union, she "was subjected to terrible reprisals." On several occasions, Ruciński "witnessed horrible rapes in broad daylight." The failure to separate small numbers of women from large groups of men created a combustible swirl of passions, lusts and jealousies that could erupt into violence. Another exile in a marching convoy that numbered some 300 men and only a few female convicts recalled how "all kind of romantic affairs developed, and one beautiful young woman ended up with her stomach sliced open in one of the waystations." Amid more relaxed censorship in the reign of Alexander II, Russian authors began to depict the fate of women en route to Siberian exile. Nikolai Leskov's *Lady Macbeth of Mtsensk* (1865) offered a grim portrait of women in the marching convoys competing in the exchange of sexual favours for protection and for material assistance from the men.[28]

The authorities had long been troubled by this traffic in women's bodies, but they tended to view the women who sold themselves as depraved rather than desperate. They were concerned not so much with protecting the women as with addressing the threat venereal disease posed to the physical health of the exiles in the deportation convoys. In 1826, the authorities instructed that women and children should follow the men at an interval of two days in separate convoys, but convicts of both sexes continued to be transported together as officials on the ground had neither the resources nor the incentive to separate them. Besides, convoy soldiers themselves frequently outdid the convicts as sexual predators and made no effort to spare the female exiles' honour and dignity. Many regarded the sexual favours of their charges as one of the perks of the job and took advantage of them to buy and sell women's bodies.[29]

When challenged by St. Petersburg over the parlous state of affairs within the exile administration, officials routinely pointed to "the shortages in secretarial resources needed to cope with the growth in the number of cases following the 1823 edicts on vagabonds." In this, they had a genuine case to make. In 1856, the staff of the Tobolsk Exile Office, charged with equipping, processing and distributing almost every exile entering Siberia, had a total of just seven members of staff: a director, two assessors, two bookkeepers and two secretaries. By 1873, the number had leapt to nine.[30]

If chronic underfunding and the huge increase in the numbers of exiles both frustrated Speransky's plans for the deportation of exiles, the malfeasance of the Siberian authorities also played a decisive part. Postings to Siberia's small towns, waystations and remote penal settlements were scarcely among the most desirable in the empire and officials at all levels of the administration were keen to offset the monotony and hardship of everyday life with graft. Speransky had envisaged the Tobolsk Exile Office as the efficient administrative headquarters of the exile system. In fact, it was a pit of corruption. Report after report highlighted cases of embezzlement, the theft of exiles' possessions and a brisk illicit trade in places of banishment. One extensive investigation in the 1830s discovered that officials in the Exile Office had sold to more than 2,000 exiles bound for Eastern Siberia permission to remain in Tobolsk province and even some permits to return to the provinces from which they had originally been exiled. They also arbitrarily reduced the sentences of those able to pay for clemency.[31]

Corruption remained so difficult to root out in part because even the most senior officials were themselves heavily involved in embezzlement and bribery schemes. Between 1822 and 1852 five of the eleven governors of Tobolsk were dismissed for corruption. In 1847, the governor-general of Eastern Siberia, Vilgelm Rupert, was forced to resign after an inquiry found him guilty of a whole spectrum of abuses, including the commandeering of penal labourers to work on his own private residence. Such expansive venality dwarfed the misdemeanours of minor officials in exchange for a few roubles here and there, but even petty bribes and pilfering undermined the efficiency of the exile deportations.[32]

The Tobolsk Exile Office's embezzlement of funds intended for the provision of warm clothing left the exiles desperately vulnerable to the ferocity of the Siberian winter. One official reported in 1864 that exiles were setting out from Tobolsk with clothes of such poor quality that "if they had not had their own clothing, they would have been quite unable to make the journey." Some were arriving in Tomsk with severe cases of frostbite, having lost fingers and toes to the cold.[33]

Under-equipped at the outset of their journey, exiles were thrown on the tender mercies of the convoy commands. The captains of the British convict transport ships that set sail from England for New South Wales were the same captains who delivered their charges to the colonial authorities six months later. Accompanied by surgeons who were answerable to the crown, they could be held accountable for the state of the convicts on board. The flagrant abuse of convicts might be detected and punished, if not by the law, then at least by the refusal of payment. The transport ships were sealed units, surrounded by great expanses of ocean that made the shirking of official accountability no less difficult than escape. By contrast, over the 7,000 kilometres that separated St. Petersburg from Nerchinsk, convicts would pass through up to 100 different convoy commands. Each was staffed by soldiers and officers who could, if they chose, neglect, rob and mistreat their charges almost with impunity and then pass them on to the next convoy command before turning their eager attentions to the next hapless party of convicts delivered into their custody. Not all were corrupt and rapacious, but many were. Prisoners were sometimes forced to sell their clothes in order to supplement the meagre rations provided by the state. Convoy officers would make available a daily allowance, or would sometimes simply hand over a certain sum when the convoy set out on a given stage along the route. These funds were almost always insufficient to purchase food from the local villages through which the convoy passed. The convoy soldiers and their families then charged extortionate prices for bread and supplies at the waystations and semi-stations in which they operated monopolies.[34]

Some convoy officers laced their corruption with outright sadism.

One nameless convict recorded in his diary in 1857 his party's treatment at the hands of one particular convoy command:

> When you arrive at the waystations, even if the temperatures are well below freezing, they search everyone down to his shirt. In [one village], it was so cold that it was impossible to stand three minutes without gloves and, arriving at the waystation, the convoy commander subjected us to a search like that. He is more savage than a terrifying wild beast, released from its cage, and much nicer to his horse and his dogs than to people . . . Feeding the people with rotten food was profitable for him and so, following this rule, the food he gave us was so bad that many in our party fell ill.[35]

The venality of the convoy soldiers often proved fatal. The nameless exile recorded in his diary on 10 February 1858 after leaving Perm that "two of our party died today, an old man and a little baby. Both froze to death on the carts." In October 1852, four convicts froze to death in a snowstorm in a marching convoy in the Nerchinsk Mining Region. They had not merely lacked the necessary warm clothing but had also been effectively starving when the snowstorm struck, having been unable to purchase more supplies of bread from the Cossacks at the waystations because the price charged for the food exceeded their daily allowance.[36]

The minister of the interior, Aleksandr Timashev, wrote to the governor-general of Eastern Siberia, Nikolai Muravyov (later, Muravyov-Amursky), in the wake of the affair pointing out that "if what has been described can happen under the noses of the Yenisei provincial authorities, one can only imagine what occurs in localities far removed from such supervision." Not for the first time, Timashev drew the attention of provincial governors to the risks attendant upon allowing convoy soldiers and their families to run monopolies over the sale of provisions to the marching convoys. He demanded "the severest prosecution of those guilty of these abuses." Here too, however, the government was unable to force its will on the convoy commanders in *étapes* thousands of kilometres away from St. Petersburg. Throughout the nineteenth century, exiles perished in the marching convoys from cold, hunger and disease in numbers so high they elicited protests from the local peasantry who were charged with disposing of the corpses. In 1844, St. Petersburg was obliged to clarify that the local authorities should make available funds for the burials.[37]

Convicts responded to this brutal environment by organizing themselves into *arteli*, or prisoners' associations, for the duration of the journey into exile. In ethnographer Sergei Maksimov's lyrical description, "the prisoners love their own *artel*; without it the journey through *étapes* and life in the prisons are impossible. The *artel* is the source of life and joy to the prisoner family—its solace and its peace." Actual joy and peace might have proved beyond the remit of the *artel* but it did offer convicts a basic form of collective organization and protection. Composed of representatives from groups of approximately ten prisoners in each convoy, this unofficial but powerful community was effectively a duplication of the communal traditions of the peasant village. It held sway over all aspects of the convicts' lives in the marching convoy. Its primary function was the collective defence of its members against the authorities. Headed by an elected official—the elder—the operations of the *artel* were governed by traditions embracing commercial activity, a central exchequer and draconian codes of discipline and punishment.[38]

Setting out from European Russian cities, the marching convoy would elect an elder for the duration of the journey to Tobolsk. The convicts usually selected an individual familiar with Siberia from previous periods in exile, often a vagabond who had escaped only to be recaptured and who possessed useful skills and trades. Once the authorities had confirmed his election, he could not be dismissed by any of the convoy officers or *étape* guards without the consent of the entire *artel*. On reaching Tobolsk, the *arteli* dissolved and were re-formed within the new marching convoys organized by the Tobolsk Exile Office.[39]

While the *artel* was not an official institution, the exile administration did recognize its existence and to some extent its necessity. The authorities not only turned a blind eye to many of its illegal practices but also even relied upon its goodwill in order to manage the operation of the convoys. The convicts, in turn, valued the trust of the convoy commanders and would seek to simplify their duties by obeying instructions and sticking to commitments undertaken. On one occasion, the exiles even helped the convoy soldiers to extinguish a blaze that had taken hold in one of the waystations. None tried to escape.[40]

At the outset of the journey, the *artel* established a communal fund under the control of the elder into which each convict had to pay a levy. The kitty was used principally as a source of bribes in order to purchase various concessions from the convoy soldiers and *étape* commanders. This form of collective bargaining could be used to secure permission to beg for alms in the villages through which the convoy passed. Appealing to the famed generosity of the Siberian peasants and merchants, the convicts would sing of their misery:

> Take pity on us, our fathers!
> Take pity on us, our mothers!
> Take pity on us poor convicts for the love of Christ!
> We are captives!
> Captives in stone prisons,
> Behind iron bars,
> Behind oak doors,
> Behind heavy padlocks.
> We have bidden farewell to our fathers and our mothers,
> To all of our kinfolk—to our people![41]

The *artel* would also strike bargains with the convoy officers. In violation of Speransky's "Statutes on Exile Transfer," they would secure the removal of the hated leg fetters outside of towns and villages in exchange for a promise that no escapes would be attempted. The *artel* would collectively vouch for the conduct of its members. Should any of the convicts break the terms of this bargain, he would be hunted down not only by the convoy soldiers, but also by other exiles in the marching convoy. Three exiles fled a 300-strong marching convoy near the town of Tyumen, whose *artel* had just negotiated an extra day's rest from the convoy commander. Outraged by this violation of their collective agreement and fearful lest it jeopardize the concessions they had secured, the *artel* dispatched a group of exiles in pursuit of the fugitives. By morning they had caught up with their quarry, and dragged them back to the convoy commander, who ordered that each man receive 100 strokes of the birch rod. Finding such leniency unsatisfactory, the *artel* went on to administer a further 500 strokes of their own with such vigour that their cruelty shocked even the convoy officer.[42]

Another of the *artel*'s primary responsibilities was the enforcement of contracts, from the strictly financial to the very personal, among its members. Backed by the threat of violence, the *artel* oversaw, and indeed made possible, the constant bartering of goods and services among convicts. From the repairing of boots to the purchasing of vodka, the *artel* ensured that undertakings to defer payment would be honoured. Some had only their names—and fates—to barter. Each convict sentenced to exile or penal labour was issued with a card that bore his name, his rank, his origins, his crime, his punishment and a very brief description of his appearance. This paperwork often contained clerical errors—names misspelt or exile destinations mixed up—resulting in individuals marching thousands of kilometres to the wrong places. It could take several months to rectify mistakes. The name of one reluctant exile, Yusef Novitsky, disappeared from the list of those in a convoy marching from Tobolsk to Irkutsk in 1848. Listed under a different name, he subsequently appeared in another deportation convoy destined for the Western Siberian town of Ishim, a less onerous destination than remote Irkutsk. Once the mistake had been discovered, Novitsky was eventually apprehended and confessed that he had, together with a number of other exiles, bribed a scribe at one of the *étapes* to enter their names in the list of deportees to Ishim.[43]

The exiles themselves were acutely aware that the pieces of paper recording their identities, crimes and sentences determined their fate. Guards in the marching convoys were keen to ensure that they arrived with the full complement of the exiles in their charge but they were preoccupied with names rather than faces. It was quite impossible for convoy commanders to remember each individual and, at the changeover from one stage command to another, only the overall number of convicts was counted; there was no roll call. Such laxity in record-keeping presented an opportunity to determined and unscrupulous exiles. For the months, sometimes years, spent in the marching convoys provided scope for the formation not only of new friendships but also of more sinister and exploitative bonds. Fyodor Dostoevsky explained the practice of exchanging names in *Notes from the House of the Dead*:

> A gang of convicts under escort is on the march to Siberia, for example. There are all kinds of criminals: some are going to prison, some to penal factories, others are going to the settle-

ments; they are all marching together. At some point along the road, in Perm province, let us say, one of the convicts decides he wants to exchange his name with that of another. For example some Mikhailov or other, a man who has committed murder or some other capital offence, considers that it will hardly be to his advantage to go to prison for many years . . . At last he comes across Sushilov. Sushilov is a manor serf and is merely being sent away to settlement. He has already marched some 1,600 kilometres without a kopeck in his pocket, needless to say, for Sushilov is incapable of possessing a kopeck—marched in weariness and exhaustion, fed on nothing but government rations, without the merest passing morsel or anything tastier, dressed in prison clothes, waiting on everyone in return for a few wretched brass bits. Mikhailov starts talking to Sushilov, gets on close, even friendly terms with him, and finally plies him with vodka at one of the stops along the way. Now he asks Sushilov if he wouldn't like to swap names with him . . . Sushilov, somewhat intoxicated, a simple soul, full of gratitude towards his new friend Mikhailov, does not dare to refuse . . . They arrive at an agreement. The unscrupulous Mikhailov, taking advantage of Sushilov's extraordinary simple-mindedness, buys his name in exchange for a red shirt and a silver rouble, which he gives Sushilov there and then in front of witnesses. The next day Sushilov is no longer drunk, but he is given more vodka to drink, and he feels he cannot go back on his word: the silver rouble has already been spent on vodka, and so, a little later, has the woven red shirt. If you don't want to do it, give the money back. But where is Sushilov to get a whole silver rouble from? And if he doesn't give it back, the *artel* will force him to . . . Otherwise it will get its teeth into him. The men will beat him up, or perhaps simply kill him . . . Finally, Sushilov sees that he cannot cry off, and decides to comply with the agreement in full . . . So the end result of it all is that Sushilov arrives in . . . [the prison] in exchange for a silver rouble and a red shirt.[44]

Anyone attempting to renege on such agreements would incur the wrath of the *artel* and might be, in Kennan's words, "condemned to death by this merciless Siberian Vehmgericht."* Over the head of such traitors, "hung an invisible sword of Damocles, and sooner or later, in one place or another, it was sure to fall."[45]

At the beginning of the nineteenth century, exiles were already changing names in large numbers on the road to Siberia. The practice only spread as the size of the marching convoys swelled in the 1820s. In 1828, the government passed a new law that punished with five years of penal labour each exile to settlement who exchanged names with a penal labourer. Penal labourers caught trafficking in identities were to be punished with 100 blows of the birch rod and a minimum of twenty-five years of penal labour in the place of their original exile. More draconian laws followed, but the traffic in identities remained impossible to root out. Cases of individuals who had switched names, and so had been delivered to the wrong destinations to serve out the wrong sentences, were clogging up local courts.[46] In subsequent decades, officials continued to complain that the practice of name changing was so widespread that it was subverting the very foundation of the exile system.

Many convicts would look back on their journey to Siberia as the most torturous part of their exile. Torn from their towns and villages, their friends and their family, they found themselves hurled into an unfamiliar and frightening world of exhausting forced marches, overcrowded *étapes*, disease, penury and the ever present threat of violence. These privations and torments were, however, as much a consequence of the state's failure to implement its own directives as they were the measure of a deliberately sadistic policy emanating from St. Petersburg. The autocracy proved unable to finance properly and to administer efficiently the complex logistical operation that involved moving hundreds of thousands of captives under armed guard across a continent.

Officials dispatched to investigate the state of the Siberian exile system were well aware that the state's colonial ambitions were turning to ashes in the deportation convoys. Convicts were finally reaching their destinations, ailing and exhausted, their appetite for hard work all but lost and replaced by a readiness to beg, steal and murder. The 1835 report of one Siberian inspector captured the self-defeating nature of

---

* A medieval German fraternal tribunal

the state's mismanagement of the deportation of exiles to Siberia in a criticism that lost none of its acuity over the decades that followed:

> The exile's long journey, unavoidably in the company of hard-ened criminals . . . and spent in prisons in which they can barely be squeezed inside the walls, has a harmful influence on whatever is left of their morality. Having passed through this school of corruption, a person who has only just set out on the path of vice arrives in Siberia ready to commit every kind of crime.[47]

For convicts, to march past the boundary post and cross the Siberian frontier was to enter a dark world in which the weak and vulnerable were delivered into the hands of the cynical, the ruthless and the corrupt. The post bore mute witness to both the frailties of state power and the torments of the men, women and children trudging into exile.

3

Broken Swords

At three o'clock in the morning of 13 July 1826, guards unlocked the narrow prison cells buried deep within the musty casements of the Peter and Paul Fortress in the heart of St. Petersburg. The heavy oak doors swung open and more than thirty young officers stepped out of their cells. Darkness makes only the most fleeting of visits to the skies of Russia's northern capital in July and dawn was already breaking as the prisoners were led out to the courtyard. Assembled before them were ranks of soldiers drawn from the city's regiments and dozens of officials and dignitaries. In the distance, beyond the northern entrance to the fortress, the prisoners could discern the gallows that had been erected for the execution of their leaders. The Supreme Court of the Russian Empire had convicted the men, known to posterity as the "Decembrists," of an attempt to overthrow Tsar Nicholas I. They had led a brief but violent revolt that began on 14 December 1825 on Senate Square in the capital and ended two weeks later with the doomed rebellion of the Chernigov Regiment outside Kiev. A symbol of the Russian autocracy looming above the waters of the Neva, across from the imperial seat of power in the Winter Palace, the Peter and Paul Fortress was to be the site of the state's retribution.

The Decembrists were drawn up into lines and led one after the other to a crackling brazier. Their sentences were read out in turn: civil execution followed by exile to penal labour in the mines of Eastern Siberia. Their epaulettes were torn from their shoulders and thrown, together with their military greatcoats, into the flames. Each officer was made to kneel, and an executioner took a sword, specially filed down at the middle of its blade, and broke it over his head. The prisoners were then dressed in the rough grey smocks issued to convicts and pronounced "civilly dead." The ceremony enacted their expulsion from Russian society and reaffirmed the sanctity of the laws they had violated. Civil death also brought the annihilation of the men as legal subjects of the tsar and entailed the "loss of all rights and privileges of rank." The Decembrists' spouses were free to remarry, their children to inherit their estates. Exile to penal labour in Siberia was a suspended death sentence. After the ceremony one of the Decembrists, the book-ish Aleksandr Muravyov, even wrote to Nicholas thanking him cra-venly for "granting me life!"[1]

The Decembrists themselves understood their sentences as a pro-nouncement of absolute annihilation. After the ceremony, twenty-six-year-old Nikolai Basargin returned to his cell in the fortress "with the conviction that all my relations and accounts with the world were now finished and that I would spend the rest of my life in a far flung and gloomy region . . . in constant suffering and with every kind of pri-vation. I no longer considered myself an inhabitant of this world."[2] The condemned men would exchange their wealth, privilege and influ-ence for poverty and oblivion; their glittering careers in the army and government service for hard labour among the common criminals of Siberia's silver mines. Exile defended the autocrat's impregnable power and ensured the obliteration of his enemies. Such was the design behind the sentences read out in the courtyard of the Peter and Paul Fortress on that July morning, but it backfired. For in Siberia the Decembrists would find not political oblivion but political renewal. Exiled as the defeated leaders of a crushed rebellion, they would win a new moral authority as martyrs to the cause of freedom and reform. Theirs is the first part of the story of how Siberia was transformed from a political wasteland into a central stage in the development of European republi-canism and the Russian revolutionary movement.

The uprising on Senate Square had intellectual roots that stretched back into the European Enlightenment and Romanticism, but the Decembrist movement had taken shape a decade earlier in the Impe-rial Army. The future Decembrists had discovered the Russian nation while fighting Napoleon and the invading French in 1812. The con-flict had forged new bonds of fraternity and loyalty between the offi-cers and their men. Russian peasants, many of whom were serfs, had shown themselves capable of loyalty, dependability and devotion to the motherland. Upon their return to Russia at the end of the conflict, the young noblemen struggled to reconcile their inspiring experiences of fighting alongside men who remained their legal property as serfs. The institution of serfdom became for them a shameful reminder of the empire's backwardness and of the yawning gulf between the educated and wealthy elite and the desperately impoverished peasantry. Forged in the crucible of 1812, the officers' patriotic loyalties to the Russian people began to eclipse their dynastic loyalty to the tsar.[3]

Many Russian officers also returned from the Napoleonic Wars with their heads full of new political ideas. One officer observed that "if we took France by force of arms, she conquered us with her customs." Many leaders of the Decembrist movement, such as Sergei Volkonsky, Ivan Yakushkin and Mikhail Fonvizin, had returned triumphantly in 1815 only to chafe at the strict hierarchies and stifling parade-ground discipline of military life. Having fought against "Napoleonic despotism" in Europe, they struggled to reconcile themselves to a Russia that was essentially the personal fiefdom of the tsar.[4] Nikolai Bestuzhev attempted to explain his participation in the rebellion in a letter to Nicholas after his arrest:

> We delivered our homeland from tyranny but we are tyrannised once again by our own sovereign . . . Why did we free Europe, only to be placed in chains ourselves? Did we grant a constitution to France only to not dare to speak of one for ourselves? Did we pay with our blood for primacy among nations only to be oppressed at home?[5]

Others, such as Mikhail Bestuzhev-Ryumin and Dmitry Zavalishin, too young to have fought Napoleon, were nevertheless driven by the ideas of Voltaire, Adam Smith, Concordet and Rousseau. In the wake of Russia's victory over Napoleon, they found inspiration in the rebellions led by liberal officers in other countries demanding constitutionalism and independence.[6]

From 1816 onwards, these young patriotic idealists began to gather in informal groups and "secret societies" to discuss reform. Over the following decade, their meetings took on an increasingly conspiratorial bent and gradually evolved into two clusters: a "Northern Society" based in St. Petersburg under the leadership of Colonel Sergei Trubetskoi, Captain of the Guards Nikolai Muravyov and the poet Kondraty Ryleyev, and a "Southern Society" based in Ukraine, directed by Colonel Pavel Pestel and Colonel Sergei Muravyov-Apostol. There were extensive contacts between the Decembrists' secret societies and the Polish Patriotic Society, which would itself eventually contribute a substantial Polish contingent to Siberia's exiles. Alexander I's sudden death in 1825 had, however, precipitated the Decembrist Revolt before a firm alliance with the Poles could be secured. The Poles in the early 1820s, more conservative in outlook, were overwhelmingly concerned with securing their own independence and the return of their lost provinces. They shied away from the Decembrists' more radical republican agenda.[7]

The authorities were aware of the existence of these secret societies and the various pamphlets the conspirators wrote and discussed. Initially, however, they treated them with a measure of indulgence and took no decisive action to break up the meetings, let alone arrest the participants. When inspecting Major-General Sergei Volkonsky's regiment in 1823, Alexander put his officer on notice: "You would do better to continue your work [with your troops] and not to concern yourself with the government of my empire, which, I'm afraid, is none of your business."[8] Volkonsky ignored the warning.

In the autumn of 1825, the Decembrists had been drawing up plans to stage a rebellion the following summer. When, however, the childless Alexander died unexpectedly while travelling in southern Russia on 19 November 1825 and his younger brother Konstantin refused to ascend the throne, the conspirators believed that the moment to strike had arrived. In the temporary authority vacuum, while preparations were underway for Alexander's youngest brother Nicholas to be crowned tsar, the Decembrists hastily cobbled together plans for an armed rebellion. On 14 December, when garrisons were due to assemble in the capital to swear the oath of allegiance to the new tsar, they planned to march their loyal troops out onto Senate Square. There, they would refuse to take the oath, demand the overthrow of the autocracy and proclaim a constitution. Relying on troops ignorant of the goals of the rebellion, however, the Decembrists lacked a unified leadership and clear strategic vision. The troops they commanded might have supported them personally but had next to no idea of their political ambitions. The result was less a serious rebellion than a badly executed piece of political theatre in which many forgot their lines.

On the morning of 14 December, the rebel officers led some 3,000 troops onto a snow-covered Senate Square. The soldiers thronged around Falconet's glowering statue of Peter the Great, which depicts the emperor astride his rearing charger as it crushes a Swedish serpent beneath its hooves. This monument to a ruthless imperial sovereign scattering his enemies seemed to command the drama playing out before it. Ill-prepared and chaotic, the revolt was doomed before it began. Trubetskoi, the Decembrists' appointed leader and interim "dictator" of the new Russian Republic, failed to appear on the square; he had abandoned his comrades and sworn the oath of loyalty to the new tsar before taking refuge in the Austrian embassy. The rebels banged their drums, unfurled their regimental banners and called for a constitution, but they succeeded only in demonstrating their own isolation and impotence.

Forces loyal to the tsar quickly surrounded them and, as the day wore on, and Nicholas's patience wore out, the rebels found themselves outnumbered and rudderless. After attempts to negotiate the overthrow of the autocracy unsurprisingly failed, skirmishes ensued. Government troops dispersed the insurgents with cannon fire and grapeshot. The rebel officers fled. In the days that followed, they were rounded up and arrested. Even those who, like Trubetskoi, had not participated directly in the rebellion, were also incarcerated in the Peter and Paul Fortress.[9] News of the failed rebellion in St. Petersburg reached the rebels in the south only on 23 December and the brief but bloody revolt of the Chernigov Regiment outside Kiev on 31 December came to naught. Its leader, Muravyov-Apostol, was unable to rally sufficient troops to his cause, and the mutinous forces in his command were easily defeated.[10] The revolutionaries had failed to seize power, even for a day.[11]

The Decembrists' undeniably amateurish, nervous and ill-timed attempts to stage a coup have sometimes obscured the radicalism that animated their rebellion. The great Russian poet Alexander Pushkin, who numbered several Decembrists among his close friends, made light of their plotting in a long-suppressed verse from his narrative poem of 1833, *Eugene Onegin*:

> At first, these plots, initiated
> 'Twixt a Lafite and a Cliquot
> Were in friendly tone debated

And the rebellious science was slow
To kindle a defiant passion,
All this was mere ennui and fashion,
The idleness of youthful minds,
Games that a grown-up scamp designs.[12]

Pushkin's condescending dismissal of the Decembrists' ideas does not do justice, however, to the scale and significance of the rebels' ambitions. The Decembrists drew inspiration from the republican models of antiquity and from Russia's own historical republican traditions. They planned a total overhaul of the Russian state structure based on republican patriotism and civic nationalism, both familiar from the American and French revolutions. They envisaged the "tyrannicide" of Nicholas himself and the murder of the imperial family. The autocracy would be overthrown, replaced by either a constitutional monarchy or a republic; in either case, a radical transfer of sovereignty from the ruler to the people. They intended to do away with serfdom, the aristocracy and the complicated patchwork of corporations and guilds within society. In their place, they would introduce the institutions of a modern state. Whether as a centralized government or a federal system modelled on the United States, these institutions would foster a unitary nation by drawing together the various nationalities and religions of the empire on the basis of equality and universal rights. No longer would different sets of rights and responsibilities be parcelled out to different social estates and sub-groups; instead, there would only be the common entitlements and duties of citizens who would be equal before the law. The Decembrists stood very much within the European republican tradition; in the Russian Empire of the 1820s, such ideas were explosive in their radicalism.[13]

Educated Russian society's reaction to the rebellion and its aftermath was ambivalent. On the one hand, many were shocked by the violence of the revolt (some 3,000 people died on both sides) and by the planned murder of the imperial family; on the other hand, there was, in many quarters, broad sympathy with the Decembrists' desire for reform, especially their intention to introduce a constitution and to abolish serfdom. Moreover, the suppression of the revolt struck at the very heart of the Russian imperial elite. Many of the Decembrists were drawn from the most eminent St. Petersburg and Moscow families, and were themselves *habitués* of the intimate world of the imperial court. In some families, two or three brothers were involved. The Bestuzhevs and Bestuzhev-Ryumins were protagonists in both the Northern and Southern societies; so too the Muravyov clan, which also included the Muravyov-Apostols, three of whom marched onto Senate Square on 14 December. Thirteen Decembrists were the sons of senators, seven of provincial governors, two of state ministers and one was the son of a member of the Imperial Russian State Council. But none was closer to the palace than the family of Prince Sergei Volkonsky, the scion of one of the oldest and wealthiest noble families in Russia and a childhood playmate of Nicholas himself. The tsar took his role in the rebellion as a personal betrayal.[14]

Even within the suffocating formality of the court, some of the Decembrists' families struggled to save their sons and brothers from the tsar's wrath. They bombarded Nicholas with petitions for mercy, arguing that the officers had been young and foolish and that to punish them would be to punish entire families who were faithful subjects of the tsar. In responding to these, Nicholas encountered an obstacle thrown up by the very nature of his own autocratic power. In a case as important as the trial of the Decembrists, the Investigative Commission and the Supreme Court deferred in all matters of judgment and sentencing to the young tsar. No one was under any illusions that what would determine the fate of the Decembrists was not the letter of the law but Nicholas's personal vengefulness or magnanimity. The great Russian historian and conservative statesman Nikolai Karamzin observed at the beginning of the nineteenth century that "in Russia the sovereign is the living law: he pardons the good, executes the bad and the love of the former constitutes the terror of the latter . . . The Russian monarch embodies the union of all powers; our rule is paternal, patriarchal."[15]

In the official ideology of the state, Nicholas was, indeed, a father to his subjects. He stood at the pinnacle of power and authority that in turn legitimated all the patriarchal institutions of the empire: the landlord and his serfs; officers and their soldiers; fathers and their households. As in many contemporary European monarchies, this paternalist exercise of power in the Russian Empire embodied a compact between the ruler and the ruled: service, obedience and deference were to be rendered by the tsar's subjects in return for his protection and care. This very paternalism at the heart of the autocrat's power posed, however, a dilemma when dealing with the appeals of the rebels' families.[16]

Ivan Odoyevsky, the father of the Decembrist poet Aleksandr Odoyevsky, wrote to Nicholas in January 1826. A distinguished commander in the Napoleonic Wars, Odoyevsky acknowledged that his son had "covered me and himself in shame." Conscious of the righteousness of the tsar's anger, he could not bring himself to ask for a pardon, as his son's guilt "exceeds the limits of my imagination," but he did appeal to the tsar's compassion for his son's youth and the "tears of his 57-year-old father." He begged the emperor to punish his son "by returning him to me for correction, so that I can make him worthy to bear the name, as I do, of a loyal servant." Pyotr Obolensky, the father of Yevgeny Obolensky, who had taken command of the troops on Senate Square after Trubetskoi failed to appear, also petitioned Nicholas. Obolensky was the head of one of the most ancient aristocratic families in Russia and a former governor of Tula province. His son's crime was not, he claimed, "true to his character. The Lord accepts the repentant and the contrite: You are like God on earth . . . I beseech you, affectionate father to your subjects, do not take my son away from me and my family!"[17] Such appeals to the tsar's paternalism from leading figures in the imperial elite could not be completely ignored.

Not all the Decembrists' family members lobbied the sovereign in this way. Some merely counselled prostration before Nicholas. Volkonsky's elder brother Nikolai Repnin-Volkonsky, himself an adjutant general and a powerful state official, wrote to Sergei in prison emphasizing the suffering he had inflicted on his own family: "Your imprisonment, my dearest Sergei, is almost more unbearable for me than it is for you." In what amounted to a manifesto for the patriarchal authority of the crown, Nikolai urged Sergei to break with his fellow conspirators and to confess all to the investigators: "After these events, no bonds of friendship can exist. They all dissolve before the sacred obligations which none of us should betray; and it is not only your honour at stake here but also mine, and that of our ancestors . . ." Nikolai argued that obedience and loyalty to the tsar trumped the bonds of comradeship among the rebels. Fraternity and patriarchy were incompatible; one had to choose between the two. Each brother made a different choice.

Sergei chose his comrades and incurred the tsar's fury by refusing to incriminate them at his trial. The tsar fulminated: "Volkonsky is a liar and a scoundrel . . . not answering anything, standing there as if in a stupor. He is the very picture of a disgusting, ignoble criminal and an idiotic human being!" Nikolai chose his sovereign and went on to disown his brother utterly. He never once wrote to Sergei in the three decades his brother went on to spend in Siberia.[18]

After long months of exhaustive interrogations, closely directed by Nicholas himself, the Supreme Court delivered its guilty verdict on 1 June 1826. It sentenced the five alleged ringleaders to death by quartering, a further thirty-one to decapitation and most of the others (making a total of 121 officers) to civil execution followed by lifelong penal labour (*katorga*) in Eastern Siberia. The death penalty had been de facto abolished for almost seventy years in Russia and the prospect of its sudden reintroduction for the ringleaders was unsettling to many. In Moscow, the Polish poet Adam Mickiewicz observed the shudder of horror that ran through Russian society at the draconian severity of the sentences.[19]

Nicholas was aware of this popular disquiet but he promised to be unmoved. He confided to the French envoy, Count de la Ferronays: "The leaders and instigators of the conspiracy will be shown no pity, no mercy. The law dictates punishment, and I will not use my right of clemency for them. I will be implacable. I am obliged to give this lesson to Russia and to Europe."[20] But he was exaggerating. The young tsar might have been vindictive but he was also cautious, and with good reason. He was, after all, the grandson of the cruel and hapless Paul I, who had been murdered in 1801 by his own praetorian guard in a palace coup. Nicholas knew that there were limits to the Russian aristocracy's tolerance for bloody retribution when so many of the Decembrist rebels were drawn from the bosom of its own families.

Clemency was a prerogative of the sovereign and a demonstration of his power. The tsars traditionally exercised clemency in order to commemorate the birth of heirs, significant anniversaries in the history of the state and, of course, coronations. It was in light of this established tradition that, as the great radical thinker Alexander Herzen recalled, "everyone expected, on the eve of the coronation, that the condemned would have their sentences commuted. Even my father, his caution and scepticism notwithstanding, would say that the death sentences would not be carried out, that it was all simply intended to make an impression on people." After a fashion Nicholas did show mercy: he commuted the thirty-one sentences of decapitation to extensive terms of penal labour followed by lifelong exile, "lessening the sentences as far as his duty to justice and the security of the state permitted." Siberia offered, therefore, an expedient punishment. It enabled the monarch to cleanse Russian society of the stain of sedition while keeping to a minimum the amount of noble blood shed in the process. By extending mercy to the rebels, the young Nicholas was also burnishing his own credentials as the supreme ruler of the empire.[21]

Once the civil execution of their comrades in the fortress courtyard had ended, the five alleged ringleaders of the rebellion underwent something altogether less ceremonial. The movement's chief ideologue, Pavel Pestel, the leader of the rebellion in the south, Sergei Muravyov-Apostol, the poet Kondraty Ryleyev, the eighteen-year-old Mikhail Bestuzhev-Ryumin and the staunchly republican Pyotr Kakhovsky were led out of their cells and beyond the fortress ramparts to where the gallows stood. Nicholas had extended a clemency of sorts to the five by "delivering them from bloodshed": he had commuted their death sentences from quartering to hanging.[22]

If hanging was intended to appear as an act of merciful retribution, it failed. As the nooses were tightened and the stools kicked from under their feet, some of the ropes, swollen with moisture from that night's rain, snapped. Three of the condemned tumbled from the scaffold into the ditch below. Half choked, they were helped back onto the gallows to be hanged for a second time. Muravyov-Apostol noted drily that he was glad of the opportunity to die for his country not once but twice. Ryleyev exclaimed, "Cursed land! Where we do not know how to organize a conspiracy, how to judge people or even how to hang them!" At the second attempt, however, he and his comrades were indeed hanged and left to swing for an hour from the gallows. The signs bearing the inscription "criminal—regicide" hung from their necks. As news of the botched execution spread, though, the corpses swinging from the gibbet came to symbolize for many not so much the compassionate justice of the sovereign as his vengeful wrath. Indeed, in the century that followed, Russians repeatedly returned to the hanging of the five Decembrist leaders as a symbol of violent tyranny.[23]

Nicholas might have spared the lives of the remaining Decembrists, but his decision to subject them to a civil execution followed by banishment to Siberia was an injunction to the Russian elite to forget them. The tsar's proclamation on the day of the executions was intended to frame their meaning for public consumption. It offered an endorsement of his own patriarchal authority, an emphatic rejection of the "dreamy excesses" of the rebels and a stern warning to families to take greater care of the "moral education" of their children. There was also a note of triumph in its emphasis on the repudiation of many of the rebels by their own families: "we have seen new examples of devotion: we have seen how fathers have not spared their criminal children, relatives have renounced the suspects and delivered them to the court; we have seen all the ranks united in a single thought: the trial and punishment of the criminals."[24]

Indeed, for many families, the punishment forced them to choose between brothers and sons on the one hand, and the tsar on the other. Some chose Nicholas. Pavel Bestuzhev-Ryumin, the father of the youngest Decembrist to hang, instructed the rest of his family to "destroy" the memory of their brother. "To a dog—a dog's death!" he proclaimed as he tore a portrait of his son to pieces. Herzen was indignant at this "shameless repudiation of loved ones." In their loyalty to the emperor, many relatives and friends "proved themselves to be fanatical slaves— some out of baseness and others, which was even worse, out of conviction." Deeply distressed by the shame of Volkonsky's arrest, his mother, Princess Aleksandra, also placed her loyalty to the emperor before her feelings for her son. A lady-in-waiting to the empress dowager, she continued to attend the court in the Winter Palace. The imposing battlements of the Peter and Paul Fortress where her son was incarcerated were clearly visible across the waters of the River Neva. The Decembrist Aleksandr Muravyov called the fortress "a hideous monument of absolutism [that] faces the Monarch's palace like a fateful warning that the one can only exist because of the other."[25] Fearful of demonstrating any sympathy for her son, Princess Aleksandra even attended a ball to celebrate Nicholas's coronation on the very day Volkonsky began his journey into exile. Her unfailing sense of propriety and loyalty was rewarded with the Order of St. Catherine. Her behaviour, so soon after the executions of the Decembrist leaders, made a lasting impression on the Frenchman Count Jacques-François Ancelot, who attended the coronation as part of an official delegation:

We all believed that this bloody catastrophe, which had preceded the coronation ceremony by so few days, would sadden
the forthcoming festivities. For there were almost no families
in Russia that did not have victims to weep for. Such was my
astonishment . . . when I saw the parents, the brothers, the
sisters, the mothers of the condemned taking an active part
in the brilliant balls, the marvellous feasts and the sumptu-
ous reunions! Some of the noblemen . . . ceaselessly on their
knees before the throne were doubtless afraid lest their sadness
be taken for sedition . . . In a despotic state one can explain
this neglect of the most natural sentiments by the weakness of
humanity that imposes itself on a man who is terribly ambi-
tious for honours and for wealth. But what does one say of a
woman, a mother in the twilight of her life who, bent by her
years towards the grave, comes every day, covered in diamonds
to take part in boisterous performances of public elation, while
her son is setting off for a painful exile where perhaps death
awaits him?[26]

For loyal supporters of the throne, the civil execution was a literal
one. Privately, they mourned as if for a deceased member of the family.
In the years following his exile, members of Sergei's family could be
heard declaring, "Il n'y a plus de Serge." It was against such instances
of slavish obeisance to the patriarchal authority of the tsar that the
decision of some of the Decembrists' wives to follow their husbands to
Siberia would sear itself into the consciousness of contemporaries, and
later, of posterity.[27]

The Decembrists' young wives had been quite ignorant of their husbands' conspiracy, and news of the arrests shattered their cossetted and
privileged lives. In their prison cells in the fortress, the men expressed
remorse and guilt at the suffering they had inflicted on their blameless
spouses. Nikolai Muravyov wrote to his wife, Aleksandra, at the end
of December 1825, confessing his involvement in the uprising and begging her to forgive him: "There were so many times that I wanted to
reveal to you my fateful secret. My vow of silence and a false sense of
shame shielded my eyes from all the cruelty and recklessness of what I

had done, binding your fate to the fate of a criminal. I am the cause of your misfortune and of the misfortune of your family." "I can barely write," Aleksandra confided to her sister, "I am so crushed by grief."[28]

Distraught at the news of their husbands' role in the rebellion, several of the Decembrists' wives, including the daughters of influential and fabulously wealthy families, Maria Volkonskaya, Aleksandra Muravyova and Yekaterina Trubetskaya, declared their intention to follow their husbands into exile. Much ink has been spilled in the last two centuries over the momentous decision of the *Dekabristki* to share their husbands' fate in Siberia. Many have seen in it an inspirational example of romantic love and self-sacrifice, a repudiation of the formal codes of duty and honour that governed the lives of the aristocracy in Nicolaevan Russia. Nikolai Nekrasov's epic poem "Russian Women," first published in 1873, commemorated the lives of the Decembrist wives and was crucial in fashioning this romantic archetype for posterity. In Nekrasov's poem, passionate love drove the women to follow their husbands to Siberia. Volkonskaya declares to her father in the poem:

> Terrible torture awaits me here.
> Yes, if I obey you and stay,
> Separation will torment me.
> Knowing no peace and night and day,
> Weeping over my poor orphan,
> I will keep thinking of my husband
> And hear his meek reproach.

In truth, a number of factors impelled Trubetskaya, Volkonskaya and Muravyova to follow their husbands, by no means all of them romantic.[29]

Languishing in the cells of the Peter and Paul Fortress, the Decembrists judged correctly that if they escaped the gallows, Siberia beckoned. They came to cling to the hope that their young brides would follow them into exile. In voluminous correspondence from his cell in the fortress—he was writing several letters each week—Sergei Trubetskoi appealed to Yekaterina's love for him. But he appealed even more to her religious sense of duty as a wife. In January 1826, he confessed, "I do not have the strength not to ask for the happiness of being together with you." Trubetskoi presented his punishment and the possibility of exile as a test of his wife's Christian virtues: "I know, my sweet friend, that you will regret nothing, if the Lord allows us to be together; you will not complain about your fate, whatever it might be." By May, Trubetskoi was writing of his conviction "that everything that the Lord has sent us is entirely just" and that "God will send us the strength to endure our fate, no matter how testing it might be." Acknowledging the worldly riches that Yekaterina would be forced to forgo, Trubetskoi emphasized that such "advantages and enjoyments were quite unnecessary for salvation and can, perhaps, only deflect us from the righteous path." Neither was he above emotional blackmail. He wrote on the eve of his civil execution: "without you my life is a heavy burden that I would be happy to cast off."[30]

Even more difficult was the choice for the twenty-year-old Maria Volkonskaya, the daughter of General Nikolai Rayevsky, one of the heroes of 1812. Born in 1806, Maria was a beautiful young woman with dark pensive eyes and delicate features framed by thick black curly hair. She had married the rugged and imposing Sergei Volkonsky, whom she barely knew and who was already thirty-four years old, when she was only seventeen. They had been married for just over a year, during which Sergei had been overwhelmingly absent, caught up in preparations for the conspiracy in the south, before he had sealed his fate on Senate Square. Maria gave birth to the couple's first child, Nikita, in January 1826 and spent the next several weeks fighting a fever that threatened to take her life. Fearful for her health, her family initially kept her in the dark about the uprising in St. Petersburg and her husband's central role in it.[31]

When she finally did learn of Sergei's imprisonment at the beginning of March, she immediately wrote to him: "My beloved Sergei, two days ago I found out about your arrest. I will not allow my soul to be shattered by it. I put my hope in the mercy of our magnanimous Emperor. I can assure you of one thing: whatever your fate, I will share it." There ensued an undignified struggle between the Rayevsky and Volkonsky families over Maria's future. The former were determined that she should spare herself the torments of Siberian exile and that her place was with her child in the bosom of her family; the latter did their best to persuade her to follow her husband into exile to offer him succour and support. Confronting a dreadful choice, Maria wrote to her husband in mid-June: "Unhappily for me, I see very clearly that I will always be separated from one of you; I cannot risk the life of my child, by taking him everywhere with me." Maria's was not, however, a straightforward choice between familial honour and romantic love.[32]

Romanticism in Russia, as elsewhere in Europe, was more than simply a celebration of the emotions; it offered a series of public codes for virtuous behaviour. Byronic literary works, so fashionable among the Russian elite, presented models for educated contemporaries to emulate. The Decembrist wives were inspired by the true story of a young princess who had voluntarily followed her husband, Prince Ivan Dolgoruky, into Siberian exile when he was banished by the Empress Anna in 1730.[33] On the eve of the uprising in 1825, Decembrist leader Ryleyev had immortalized her sacrifice in his poem "Natalya Dolgorukaya":

> I have forgotten my native city,
> Wealth, honours and family name
> To share with him Siberia's cold
> And endure the inconstancy of fate.[34]

Such ideals were commonly accepted within Russian society, and many believed that the sanctity of the marriage vows meant that the Decembrists' wives should share their husbands' fate. In the months leading up to the rebellion, as Nikolai Basargin was reading to his wife from another of Ryleyev's poems, he wondered aloud whether he might not himself end up in Siberia. Unsuspecting, she answered without hesitation: "Well what of it? I'd go with you so as to take care of you and to share your fate. That could never separate us, so what's the point in thinking about it?" Aware of these cultural expectations of spousal devotion and duty, the Rayevskys struggled to keep Maria on the family estate of Boltyshka in Kiev province, insulated from a public opinion that would only encourage her to follow her husband. Maria insisted, though, on travelling to the capital, where she was granted a brief and awkward meeting with her husband in the presence of prison officials during which Sergei managed to slip her a note containing scrawled lines of reassurance and endearment. The sight of her husband in chains sealed Maria's determination to follow him.[35]

Appalled by the risks to her health of a hazardous journey of several thousand kilometres to Eastern Siberia, Maria's parents tried to persuade Volkonsky to release his wife from her marriage vows by instructing her to remain with her child. "Be a man and a Christian," wrote Maria's mother, "demand of your wife that she quickly leave to be with her child, who needs the presence of his mother. Part with her as calmly as possible." Maria's father meanwhile was more forthright. Fearing that Maria might not be dissuaded from following Volkonsky, he wrote to the imprisoned Decembrist in January while Maria was gravely ill following childbirth: "You used to call me father, so obey your father! You know your wife's mind, her feelings and her attachment to you: she will share the fate of a disgraced convict—she will die. Don't be her assassin!"[36] That summer, in the face of Maria's continuing determination to leave, her father again pleaded with Volkonsky:

> Think, my friend, whether she will be able to survive several months of travelling; whether those months might not be enough to condemn your little boy to death; about what help she will be able to offer you or him! Think about the fact that she will relinquish her status and that any children you might have will enjoy none. Your heart must tell you, my friend, that you should write to her yourself, and tell her not to follow you.[37]

But Sergei refused to tell his wife to remain with their child and Maria remained unflinching in her resolve. Her decision eventually caused a breach in her relations with her father: "My father and I separated in silence; he gave me his blessing and then turned away unable to say a word. I looked at him and said to myself, 'It's over. I will never see him again, I have died for my family.'"[38]

Amid the public ambivalence and private lobbying over the fate of the Decembrists, the government was keen to avoid creating martyrs to the causes of reform and revolution. Just as the timing of the execution was chosen in order to limit the potential number of sympathetic onlookers, so the deportation of the Decembrists to Siberia was to be clandestine. The tsar instructed that "the departure of the criminals to their places of banishment should take place at night and in secret, that none of them should be sent through Moscow, that those travelling to Siberia should be sent along the Yaroslavl road and, finally, that no one should be informed of the routes." This secrecy was an expression of state weakness, not strength. Dmitry Zavalishin recalled, "the government was at a loss as to what to do with us. Not only did it not dare to send us on the usual route with a party of convicts marching to Siberia, but it was even afraid of dispatching us all together in a separate group."[39]

So, unlike the thousands who trudged into exile each year along the "road of fetters" from St. Petersburg to Irkutsk, the majority of the Decembrists were sent in groups of no more than four, and not on foot but in wagons. Fearful of escapes, the government decided that each prisoner be accompanied by two gendarmes and a special courier, and that they be clapped in heavy leg irons. The humiliation of the fetters made quite an impression on the Decembrists: "It was quite unexpected," one of the rebels from the Chernigov Regiment, Ivan Gorbachevsky, remembered, "when they brought the chains and began to shackle us. When we finally stood up and the chains began to clank on my legs . . . It was a terrible sound." The Baltic German Andrei Rozen wondered why the state was inflicting on the Decembrists a punishment usually reserved for recidivists and those guilty of having attempted escape. He noted with thinly veiled irony that some put this down to the state's compassion: "It was said that the solicitous government was fearful of the common people's fury and vengeance, that they might have torn us limb from limb on the road."[40]

Even here Nicholas's decision to punish and humiliate the prisoners contained elements of black comedy that underlined the amateurish and improvised nature of state power. Zavalishin recalled how instructions arrived just before departure that the leg irons should not be sealed shut with iron pins but should rather be padlocked so that they could, if required, be more easily opened during the journey. There were no padlocks to be found and soldiers were sent off to purchase some in the town. They returned with locks designed to seal gift boxes, which commonly bore an inscription. Zavalishin's legs were thus shackled by a lock that boasted "I give this to the one I love"; Bestuzhev's legs by another declaring "I value not your gift, but your love."[41]

The failure of the revolt, the humiliations and shame of their interrogations and the punishing conditions of their long captivity in the Peter and Paul Fortress had broken the spirits and the health of many of the Decembrists. Even after thirteen years of exile, Nikolai Basargin still vividly recalled "the dark feeling of helplessness, the sense of moral defeat" that overwhelmed him in the casements, where he faced quite alone "the unlimited power of the autocracy." Nikolai Muravyov was consumed by regret as he confided to his wife: "Every day, I pray to God to forgive me for having participated in this madness and law-lessness and for having laboured to build this new Tower of Babel." Trubetskoi meanwhile had abased himself before Nicholas during his interrogations and begged for mercy. In his first month in prison, he exclaimed in a letter to his wife, Yekaterina: "If only you knew how difficult it is to be a criminal before [Nicholas] . . . I pray to God that he gives me the chance to show our benefactor that I feel my crime and his blessing and that at least my heart is not ungrateful." On the eve of his departure, after half a year behind the cold dank walls of the fortress, and apparently suffering from tuberculosis, he was "spit-ting platefuls of blood." Others, such as Obolensky, had denounced their comrades in a bid to mitigate their punishment. Even Volkon-sky, who had maintained a defiant dignity throughout his interroga-tions, had fallen ill during his incarceration and was fearful that he would not survive the journey.[42] The Decembrists left St. Petersburg as broken men.

The first groups of prisoners were dispatched in late July 1826 and, over the course of the next twelve months, a total of ninety-three men, almost all "stripped of all rights and privileges of rank," set out for Eastern Siberia. Since the government wished to minimize con-tact between the prisoners and the inhabitants of the towns and vil-lages through which they passed, the deportations were undertaken at breakneck speed. The wagons were to travel day and night and to rest only every third day.[43] The convoy guards were under instructions to convey the prisoners as quickly as possible and often rode the horses literally to death. Mikhail Bestuzhev and his companions demanded that their convoy captain show them his written instructions. If he had not been explicitly ordered "to kill them," they would report him at the first opportunity. Bestuzhev was, indeed, almost killed when thrown from his cart as it careered down a hill. His chains were caught in the wheels and he was "dragged like Hector behind the chariot of Achilles." Convoy captains struggled to maintain their place in the time-table amidst the frenetic pace of the deportation parties. The Bestuzhev brothers and their companions were denied their allocated day's rest in Tobolsk because the convoy captain feared they might be overtaken. "O bureaucratic Russia!" Nikolai Bestuzhev mused. "Administrators are ready to drive us to exhaustion, even to death, as long as they do not violate the numerical order: 1, 2, 3, 4 and so on." The state of the roads and the forced pace of the journey were not the only torment for the exiles. They struggled to grow accustomed to the chains that would accompany their every movement until they were eventually permitted to remove them some four years later. The fetters chafed against their ankles, causing bleeding wounds to appear. When Volkonsky tripped over his chains while descending some steps, a peasant remarked mock-ingly, "Learn to live with them, master!"[44]

To the Decembrists, their physical privations were undoubtedly overshadowed by psychological anguish. For noblemen, many drawn from the most illustrious and wealthy St. Petersburg and Moscow families and steeped in the Romantic patriotism of the age, it was a wrenching journey. They confronted not only the forfeiture of their wealth, power and status but also banishment from their native coun-try. "The very name 'Siberia,'" one Russian explorer commented in 1830, "is enough to terrorize a Russian, who sees in it only inexorable separation from his homeland, a vast dungeon, inescapable and eter-nal." Many Decembrists, like Sergei Krivtsov, were filled with dread at the prospect of spending the rest of their days "at the frontier of an unpeopled realm, where ice and frost, like Herculean pillars, draw the line for man, declaring *non plus ultra*." Artamon Muravyov repeatedly reviled the Cossack adventurer Yermak for having ever "conquered" Siberia, a "source of anguish and of graves for exiles." Depression and despair hung heavily over most of the exiles as they jolted their way eastwards on their wagons. Convoy gendarmes reported that "all the convicts, especially while they were still travelling through Rus-sian provinces, were very miserable, for the most part silent, and often wept, Vasily Davydov, who was grieving for the five children he had left behind, more than most."[45]

To cross the Ural Mountains was for almost all the Decembrists to plunge over a frontier and into a foreign land. Nikolai Lorer recalled the moment:

In the morning we silently ascended 21 kilometres to the way-station, which stood alone, dejectedly on the very peak of the mountain. From the summit, a boundless sea of forests, blue and violet and a road twisting through them, stretched out before us. The coach driver pointed ahead with his whip and said, "That's Siberia!"

And so, we were no longer in Europe! Separated from all the civilised world![46]

The Decembrists' spirits began, however, to lift after they left the Urals behind. They discovered not the frozen wasteland of the Russian imagination but a beautiful and varied landscape, one in which the peasants were not oppressed by the slavery of serfdom. Basargin noted that "the further we travelled into Siberia, the more fetching it seemed in my eyes. The common people seemed freer, more lively and more educated than our Russian peasants, especially the serfs."[47] Such observations would feed into a growing Romantic perception among reform-minded Russians of Siberia as a democratic alternative to the rigid and suffocating hierarchies of European Russia.

Nevertheless, for all their moral torments and physical discomfort, the manner in which most Decembrists were deported to Siberia marked them out as men of exceptional status. First, they rode in wagons, rather than walked, something quite unimaginable for the thousands of exiles who made the arduous journey over the Urals every year in the 1820s. Officials and convoy soldiers were also unsure of how to treat their eminent charges. Even if they had been "deprived of all rights and privileges," the Decembrists were still identical in language, bearing and manners to their superiors. As Zavalishin observed, "everywhere we went, we were called princes and generals . . . many, wishing to satisfy both the rules of our current status and their desire to show us respect, addressed themselves to us as 'Your former Highness, Your former Excellency.'" The guards' hesitant enforcement of the strict rules meticulously laid out by government ministers was rendered all the more confused by favours the Decembrists themselves purchased through bribes. Alexander Benckendorff, the head of Nicholas I's Third Section, which had been established to combat sedition in the wake of the Decembrist Revolt, learned that the initial two groups of exiles "were wining and dining" en route and plying their convoy soldiers and gendarmes with food and drink. Obolensky was permitted to write to his wife and Davydov was allowed to shave. The Decembrists were expressly forbidden from riding in their own carriages but, armed with 1,000 roubles from his wife, Fonvizin did just that and managed to obtain warm blankets for himself and his travelling companions into the bargain. During the course of their journey, he and his comrades were "waited on" by their gendarmes.[48]

As they rode into exile, the Decembrists encountered not the baying mob of which Rozen, the Baltic German, had been warned, but curiosity, sympathy and generosity from both officials and the wider Siberian population. Fonvizin wrote to his wife from the route that the governor of Tobolsk, Dmitry Bantysh-Kamensky, and his family "received me warmly and generously—I am obliged to them that our convoy officer treated us very well and even agreed to forward you this letter." Basargin recalled how the elderly governor of the small town of Kainsk, a certain Stepanov, approached them "accompanied by two men dragging an enormous basket with wine and foods of every kind. He made us eat as much as we could and then take the leftovers with us. He also offered us money with words that surprised us: 'I acquired this money'—he said pulling out a large packet of notes—'not entirely cleanly, in bribes. Take it with you; my conscience will rest easier.'" In Krasnoyarsk, the inhabitants argued over who should have the honour of accommodating the exiles as they took a day's rest in the town. Merchants entertained the Decembrists in the best rooms of their houses, sparing no expense on the food and drink they lavished upon their guests.[49]

Such experiences did not simply reflect the Decembrists' exceptional status. One of Siberia's established traditions was the giving of alms to the "unfortunates" who passed through settlements in the deportation convoys. Official attempts to keep the journey secret notwithstanding, Basargin recalled how, at the waystations, people would crowd around to catch a glimpse of the prisoners. The more courageous would approach the wagons and throw coppers into them for the prisoners. "I still keep," he wrote in his memoirs, "a copper coin given to me by an old beggar woman. She entered our hut and, showing us some pennies, said: 'This is all that I have: take it sirs, our dear fathers. You need it more than me.'"[50]

Although the government had still to decide upon a specific local-

ity, the Decembrists were bound for the sprawling penal zone of the
Nerchinsk Mining Region, 1,700 kilometres to the east of Lake Baikal.
Exhausted from a journey of 6,000 kilometres in a mere thirty-seven
days, the first two parties of Decembrists arrived in the regional capital,
Irkutsk, in late August 1826 and finally at the Blagodatsk silver mine in
Nerchinsk two months later.[51]

The extent to which the Decembrist leaders benefited from the
crown's nervous indulgence and wider public sympathy is starkly
apparent when their experiences are compared with those of less distinguished officers involved in the rebellion. When one exiled official
observed "it is possible to learn to live anywhere," he might have added
that the learning curve was steeper for some than for others. Educated
Russians from the upper classes sentenced to penal labour struggled to
find their bearings amid the insecurity, violence and destitution of the
marching convoys. Civilly dead and stripped of their rights and rank,
they suddenly found themselves thrust into the company of the common people. The hierarchies and discipline of the Imperial Army, the
aristocratic household and serfdom no longer structured their dealings
with peasants, tradespeople and soldiers.[52]

A small number of Decembrist officers exiled to Siberia experienced this cultural collision with the lower orders. Sentenced after the
immediate official panic about the rebellion had subsided, they were
deported not from the capital but from provincial towns. These men
did not benefit from the combination of state anxiety, personal wealth
and public generosity during their journey into exile. The authorities
in St. Petersburg were content to forgo the secrecy and speed that had
accompanied the initial waves of Decembrist deportations. Rather than
being hurried eastwards on wagons and on sledges, they walked to
Eastern Siberia in the company of common criminals. For tsarist officials in charge of the marching convoys in the localities, they became
simply more names in the lists of exiles. Treated as common criminals
guilty of a capital offence, they were to join standard exile convoys
between 100 and 200 strong. Their experiences served to underline the
relative indulgence of the authorities that their comrades to the north
had enjoyed.[53]

One such young officer, Vasily Kolesnikov, recorded his experiences
for posterity. Like most noblemen who plunged into the raucous, violent and seedy world of the marching convoys, Kolesnikov was more

appalled by the apparent immorality of the exiles themselves than by the dehumanizing conditions in which they were forced to exist:

> In general, the philanthropist finds here a complete absence of the idea of love for his fellow man . . . These unfortunates almost compete with each other in cruelty, attempting to reveal as much as they possibly can of the baser sides of their humanity. They are steeped in immorality, inured to every kind of vice. Amongst them the constant noises, shouts, cards, bones, disputes or songs, dancing . . . My God! What dancing! . . . In a word, it was an authentic hell!

In December 1827, after three months on the road, Kolesnikov finally reached Tobolsk. He was locked up in a narrow, freezing, dank cell, where he fell sick "from exhaustion and cold" but received no medical attention. When the marching convoy set off five days later, he was, however, allowed to travel on one of the wagons. In September 1828, after repeated bouts of illness that delayed him in various infirmaries along the route, Kolesnikov arrived in the settlement of Chita, 320 kilometres to the east of Lake Baikal, after a full year on the road.[54]

In his punishment of the Decembrists, Nicholas encountered difficulties in striking a diplomatic balance between righteous wrath and paternal mercy, but the decision of the wives to join their husbands placed him in a particular quandary. By the 1820s, the Romanov dynasty was already setting great store by the public demonstration of familial virtue, something it continued to emphasize right up until 1917. To deny Volkonskaya, Muravyova, Trubetskaya and the other women the right to fulfil their duty as wives would be to publicly disavow the sanctity of marriage. The enforced separation of devoted wives from their husbands could not but reflect badly on the moral authority of the autocracy.[55]

But allowing the Decembrist wives to proceed risked undermining the status of the convicts and drawing attention to their fate just as the state sought to cast them into obscurity. In an attempt to dissuade them from making the journey, the tsar refused the wives the right to take their children with them. This raising of the stakes was politically ill-judged, for it forced the women into the public agony of choosing between husbands and children. In October of 1826, Nicholas went further and clarified that the normal statutes governing the spouses of penal labourers would, in this case, also be enforced. If they joined their husbands in Nerchinsk, failing an amnesty or the dissolution of their marriages, they would only be permitted to return to Russia after the death of their spouses.[56]

Granted a meeting with his wife, Anastasia, and their children in Yaroslavl as he journeyed eastwards, Ivan Yakushkin was informed of Nicholas's refusal to allow the children to follow their fathers. Although Anastasia wished to take her place by his side in Siberia, Yakushkin was insistent that she should not abandon her children as "the care of their mother was essential." It was the last time he would ever see his family. "When the moment of our definitive and eternal separation came," he recalled, "I bade farewell to my wife and children and wept like a little boy whose sole remaining and favourite toy had been taken away." Almost six years later, as the children were now older, Yakushkin would write to give consent for Anastasia to join him without them. By then, however, permission for the Decembrist wives to join their husbands in Siberia had been withdrawn and Nicholas refused the request.[57]

In late October, as Yakushkin was forbidding his wife to abandon their young children in Yaroslavl, Sergei Volkonsky had already entered the Nerchinsk Mining Region. Volkonsky was no longer under any illusions as to what awaited Maria if she followed him. He was clearly torn between his reluctance that she should share this fate and his desire to have her by his side. He wrote to his sister: "The more I think about my situation, the more I start to think that it is my duty to forbid my darling Mashenka to come to live with me. Her duty to our son and my miserable position both raise obstacles that I believe are insuperable." A mere month in Nerchinsk divested Volkonsky of these scruples. He wrote to his wife on 12 November 1826:

> With your arrival here, you will have to make many sacri-
> fices . . . you will be stripped of your rank and you will have to
> separate from our son . . . I am duty bound to describe to you
> all the horrors of my situation, I am nonetheless . . . too sure of
> your strength of character to think that you . . . might change

your decision, which you have repeated to me in your letters. I know that you can only be at peace, by being together with me or by having the possibility of seeing me. I would be deceiving you if I began to reassure you that seeing you is not the only possible solace for me in my bitter fate . . .[58]

A week later, on 18 November, Volkonsky wrote another letter, the romanticism of which was designed to prise his wife apart from her child. Maria faced, he claimed, "a permanent separation from me or a temporary separation from our son." Temporary because Volkonsky knew in his heart that, "in the face of my spiritual torments, my life will be a very short one . . . Mashenka, come to me before I am lowered into a grave! Let me look upon you once more; let me fill your heart with all the feelings in my soul!" On 15 December, Maria wrote to Nicholas formally requesting permission to follow her husband.[59]

It has been claimed that Nicholas sprang a trap on the Decembrist wives, cynically keeping them in ignorance of his intention to prevent them from ever making the return journey to European Russia until they had already reached Irkutsk. In fact, the tsar had made such constraints clear to all concerned in his reply to Volkonskaya's petition on 21 December: "I feel obliged once again to repeat here my warning, which I have already given you, about what awaits you, should you travel beyond Irkutsk. You should of course pursue whatever course of action seems to you the most appropriate in your current situation." When Maria later claimed to her parents that she did not understand the meaning of these words, she was most probably seeking to assuage their anger and distress. At the very least, she had wilfully chosen to misunderstand the warning. Nicholas did not want the women to leave for Siberia and had no reason to conceal from them that they would not be allowed to return. But erecting such obstacles in the path of the young wives did not dissuade them. Far from backing down, Volkonskaya wrote to her father: "My son is happy but my husband is unhappy—my place is with my husband. [Such is] my sense of duty."[60]

Maria's decision also needs to be understood within the wider culture of the aristocratic family in early nineteenth-century Russia. The sentimental literary cult of motherhood and domesticity, already well established in eighteenth-century Britain and France, influenced many but by no means all mothers in Russia. Some aristocratic women remained preoccupied with the running of their households and estates, and with the advancement of their children's prospects at court. Some were physically and emotionally remote from their young children, whom they entrusted to wet nurses and nannies.[61] When, on the eve of her departure in December 1826, Maria wrote to Sergei that she was reconciled to her decision to leave her child for her husband, she expressed sentiments familiar to her class:

> My sweet, now I can say to you that I have endured a great deal in order to achieve my goal but now I am leaving and I will forget everything, everything. Without you I am as if without life: only my obligations to our son could lead me to separate from you but I part from him without sadness. He is surrounded by care and will not feel the absence of his mother: my soul is calm on our angel's account. Hope, and the knowledge that I will soon see you, inspire me. It seems to me that I have never before been happy.[62]

She never saw her son again; a year later, he was dead.

Maria's anguished father was convinced that his daughter was determined to follow her husband under the Volkonskys' influence: "They had praised her heroism and persuaded her she was a heroine—and, like an idiot, she went." He might well have been right, but the voluntary exile of the *Dekabristki* was a powerful myth in the making. A few days after the departure of Aleksandra Muravyova and Maria Volkonskaya from Moscow on New Year's Eve 1826, the poet Pyotr Vyazemsky wrote to a friend: "Over the last few days, I've seen Muravyova and Volkonskaya setting off. What a moving and noble fate! We must thank these women! They have added a few beautiful lines of verse to our history." Vyazemsky was an astute observer. Even though they were impelled by their own private motives, the decision of the *Dekabristki* to follow their husbands to Siberia became publicly understood as an act of political defiance.[63]

The casting of the Decembrists as martyrs began before the majority had even reached Siberia. On the eve of Maria Volkonskaya's departure from Moscow to join her husband, Pushkin read out his "Message to Siberia" to a gathering of her friends and supporters in one of the most celebrated literary salons of the day:

> In deep Siberian mines retain
> A proud and patient resignation;
> Your grievous toil is not in vain
> Nor yet your thoughts' high aspiration.
>
> Grief's constant sister, hope, is nigh,
> Shines out in dungeons black and dreary
> To cheer the weak, revive the weary;
> The hour will come for which you sigh,
>
> When love and friendship reaching through
> Will penetrate the bars of anguish,
> The convict warrens where you languish,
> As my free voice now reaches you.
>
> Each hateful manacle and chain
> Will fall; your dungeons break asunder;
> Outside waits freedom's joyous wonder
> As comrades give you swords again.[64]

Volkonskaya carried with her a copy of the poem when she set out from Moscow. Although unpublished for another four decades, Pushkin's poem circulated through the salons and drawing rooms of the empire's two capitals and echoed like cannon fire across the nineteenth century. It established a grip on the public imagination, shaping perceptions of the Decembrists in exile and helping to immortalize their memory as victims of a vindictive and arbitrary state.

Nicholas and his ministers had sought, if not the physical, then the political annihilation of the Decembrists as representatives of constitutional reform within the Russian elite. But in these terms they failed, for the story of the Decembrists' exile to Siberia is the story of a victory snatched from defeat. Lionized by their supporters, their moral authority only grew over the course of Nicholas I's reign and would inspire a subsequent generation of radicals after his death. In exile in

London, Herzen became the leading draughtsman of the inspiring legend of the Decembrists and their wives. His journal, *The Polar Star*, took its name from an almanac published by the executed Decembrist poet Ryleyev, and boasted a masthead adorned with the faces of the five hanged ringleaders of the rebellion. Herzen established himself as the most influential radical intellectual of the first half of the nineteenth century and was one of the leading architects of the Russian revolutionary movement in the 1860s and 1870s. The tale he crafted of the revolutionary martyrs of 1825 went on to inspire a later generation of the autocracy's enemies.[65]

The Decembrists' uprising and their exile also resonated far beyond Russia itself. In the Italian peninsula, Giuseppe Mazzini and his republican movement, Young Italy, saluted the memory of the men "who gave their lives for the liberation of the Slavic peoples, thus becoming citizens and brothers of all who struggle for the cause of Justice and Truth on earth." The Decembrists had also blazed a trail for Polish patriots. By the end of the 1820s, republicanism in Poland, buoyed by developments elsewhere in Europe, was very much in the ascendancy. Polish rebels would look to the Decembrists' attempt to restore "ancient Russian freedom" as a source of inspiration. The next armed challenge to Nicholas I would come not in the streets of the imperial capital, but on the westernmost periphery of his empire, in Warsaw. Siberia would beckon for the Polish rebels as it had for the Decembrists.[66]

The Decembrists were exiled as traitors broken in spirit, many of them having betrayed both their comrades and their cause. Those who survived Nicholas, however, would return to European Russia hailed as heroes and patriots. The men could not have envisaged this possibility as they knelt before the brazier in the courtyard of the Peter and Paul Fortress while the swords were being broken over their bowed heads. Yet decades later, Basargin would look back on his exile to Siberia with a note of defiance:

> I am now sure that if, instead of condemning us so cruelly, the government had punished us more moderately, it would have better achieved its goals . . . Having deprived us of everything and having suddenly placed us as outcasts on the very lowest step of the social ladder, it gave us the right to see ourselves as

the purifying agents of a future transformation of Russia. In a word, the government turned us from the simplest and most ordinary of people into political martyrs for our ideas. In so doing, it elicited general sympathy for us and assumed for itself the role of an embittered and merciless persecutor.[67]

4

The Mines of Nerchinsk

Sprawling across 1,300 kilometres of hilly, wooded territory, from the eastern shores of Lake Baikal to the Chinese border, the Nerchinsk Mining Region was the most feared place of exile in the empire of Nicholas I. Mining had first begun in the region in the late sixteenth century and the first silver smeltery had been established in 1704 in the town of Nerchinsk Zavod, 1,600 kilometres east of the Eastern Siberian capital, Irkutsk. This remote and inhospitable territory had never attracted much voluntary labour, so the authorities had recruited miners from a mixture of penal labourers and conscripted peasants. Nerchinsk was the empire's only silver mining region until the 1740s, and production remained on a small scale until the 1760s, when Russia's involvement in the Seven Years' War (1756–63) fuelled demand for metals and led to an expansion in mining. If, in the decades between 1704 and 1750, Nerchinsk had mined and smelted only 9,000 kilogrammes of silver, in the 1780s alone production leapt to 76,000 kilogrammes. By the beginning of the nineteenth century, Nerchinsk had expanded into a major site of silver, lead, copper and gold mining and into the principal site of penal labour in Siberia.[1]

By the 1820s, seven smelteries and twenty silver mines radiated out from an administrative centre in the town of Nerchinsk. Clustered around each of the labour sites were settlements inhabited by 17,000 factory workers, mine employees and soldiers, and about 6,000 exiles, one third of them penal labourers. Shale and rocks, coated in a thin layer of vegetation in the summer and a dusting of snow in the winter, covered the hills that rose above the mines. Thick woods encircled the settlements; wild animals could be heard prowling through them at night. The engineer and ethnographer Grigory Spassky recorded his dismal impression of Nerchinsk Zavod in 1820: "Walking towards the town, one descends 6 kilometres, as if into a deep pit in which ramshackle structures are scattered about the slopes in a disorderly manner. It is only on reaching the main street that it is possible to see the buildings of the smeltery." Inside, furnaces belched out thick black smoke that choked the air; the cries and curses of the miners rang out through the dirt roads and dilapidated buildings. The mines had won such notoriety by the 1820s that Alexander Pushkin could allude to "the road to Nerchinsk" in his poem "Tsar Nikita and His Forty Daughters" as to the dreadful fate that awaited those who fell foul of the tsar. Siberia's mines had a terrible reputation and, in Nerchinsk, they lived up to it.[2]

In October 1826, three months after they set out from St. Petersburg, the first group of Decembrists—Sergei Volkonsky, Sergei Trubetskoi and their six companions—arrived at the Blagodatsk mine. The mine was, as Maria Volkonskaya later recalled, "a village consisting of a single road, surrounded by hills scarred with pits in which lead, containing silver, was dug up . . . It would have been a beautiful place if the woods for 50 kilometres around had not been chopped down for fear that fugitive penal labourers might hide in them; even the bushes had been chopped down. In winter, it was desolate."[3]

The Decembrists were quartered in pairs in small narrow storerooms in a barracks heated by a large Russian stove. The men arrived bearing several thousand roubles with which they were permitted to purchase necessities before the head of the Nerchinsk Mining Region, Timofei Burnashev, confiscated the money and subsequently released it to them in instalments. With these funds, the Decembrists were able to secure the services of their four guards, who, as Yevgeny Obolensky recalled, "prepared our food, set the samovar, served us and shortly came to like us, becoming the most useful of assistants." Burnashev was "a little rough, but in his orders could be sensed his wish to improve our situation." Although the Decembrists had been sentenced to work in the mines as common penal labourers, no less than the governor-general of Eastern Siberia, Aleksandr Lavinsky, wrote to Burnashev that they "were not to be worked to the point of exhaustion."[4]

These relative benefits notwithstanding, Volkonsky wrote to his wife in November 1826 with a characteristic lack of stoicism: "From the moment of my arrival in this place, I have been put to work in the mines. I spend my days in hard physical labour and spend my hours of rest in a dark cell always under the strictest supervision, even stricter than during my incarceration in the fortress. So you can imagine how unbearable is my lot and in what a dreadful position I find myself."[5] Obolensky was rather less melodramatic in his assessment of conditions in Blagodatsk: "The work itself was not so onerous, but conditions underground were very awkward: we had to work in a hole, leading to a vertical wall, in which we had to kneel and, adopting various positions depending on the height of the ceiling, to wield a hammer weighing 6 or 8 kilogrammes." And yet, as Obolensky recalled, "in our work underground we had no set tasks—we worked and rested as much as we chose; on top of this, the work would end at eleven o'clock and the rest of the time we enjoyed complete freedom." Conditions above ground were, paradoxically, much worse: "The holidays were days of punishment: in a stuffy cell, in which it was barely possible to turn around, millions of bugs and various loathsome creatures covered us from head to toe and gave us no peace. Added to that was the offensive attitude of the officials, who were used to dealing with penal labourers and considered it their duty to hurl abuse and all manner of expletives at us."[6]

Nicholas ordered the "state criminals" placed under close supervision by the authorities in Nerchinsk and demanded that monthly reports on their health and spirits be dispatched to St. Petersburg. Officials reported that the men were obedient but sometimes fell into despondency.[7] The Decembrists were roused from their meekness on only a single occasion, in a confrontation with a zealous mine official who suddenly decreed that their cells were to be locked at all times when their occupants were not working. Seeking to defend their right to socialize in their free time and protesting that incarceration in the poorly ventilated storerooms for eighteen hours at a stretch would destroy their health, the Decembrists embarked on a hunger strike. Within a couple of days, Burnashev intervened. Keen to diffuse the situation and to avoid any casualties among his eminent charges, he ordered the doors to the storerooms unlocked, the mine official replaced, and the earlier routine re-established.[8]

On 10 February 1827, six weeks after her departure from Moscow, Maria Volkonskaya reached the Blagodatsk mine and met up with

Yekaterina (Katya) Trubetskaya, who had arrived a few days before. Before receiving permission to see their husbands, the two women had been obliged to sign an undertaking that they would only meet the men every three days in the presence of an officer. All correspondence was to pass through the hands of the Nerchinsk Mining Region military commander, Major-General Stanislav Leparsky. Volkonskaya and Trubetskaya were not to supply their husbands with any writing materials or other goods, or to transmit any correspondence from them. They were allowed to retain the services of only a single male and a single female servant. They were permitted to talk to their husbands only in Russian (as opposed to French), a language they were accustomed to using only when addressing servants and serfs and one they did not speak very well.[9] The next day, Maria was taken to see her husband in the mine barracks for their first encounter since Sergei had been marched out of the Peter and Paul Fortress in St. Petersburg in July of the previous year:

> At first I couldn't make anything out, it was so dark. They opened a small door on the left and I entered my husband's cell. Sergei rushed towards me; I was taken aback by the clanking of his chains: I had not known that he was in fetters . . . The sight of his chains overwhelmed and moved me so much that I dropped to my knees and began to kiss first his chains, and then Sergei.[10]

Together, Volkonskaya and Trubetskaya rented a small cabin in the mining settlement. "It was so cramped," Maria recalled, "that when I lay down on my mattress on the floor, my head touched the wall and my feet the door. The stove produced a great deal of smoke and it was impossible to use it when it was windy in the courtyard; the windows had no glass, only mica." The first few months in Blagodatsk were a testing time. Arriving in Blagodatsk with relatively small sums of money, swiftly abandoned by their servant girls, who took off with local Cossacks, and quite unprepared for the most basic of chores, the two women were forced to adapt to a harsh new life. Like Volkonskaya, the vivacious Katya Trubetskaya was the daughter of a fabulously wealthy aristocratic family in St. Petersburg and had grown up surrounded by servants tending to her every need. Raised in a palace that boasted marble tiles that had belonged, it was claimed, to the emperor Nero, she found herself scrubbing her own floor clean.[11] Maria for the most part maintained a stoical, even cheerful disposition but clearly found her existence in Blagodatsk extremely challenging, as she hinted to her mother in a letter in October 1827: "Sweet mother, what courage is needed to live in this country! How fortunate for you that we are forbidden to write openly of life here."[12]

Their own hardships notwithstanding, Volkonskaya and Trubetskaya were able to offer the Decembrists both moral and material support. As soon as the women appeared in the mine, their husbands began to recover their spirits.[13] The women grew concerned, however, that the men's poor diet was destroying their health. Trubetskoi was again spitting blood; Volkonsky was suffering from chest pains and Artamon Muravyov from colic.[14] Trubetskaya dug out a cookbook she had brought with her and began to prepare the men meals on the wooden stove in the hut she shared with Volkonskaya, sending them to the prisoners through soldiers bribed as messengers. The women began to write letters in their own name, but on the men's behalf, to friends and family in Moscow and St. Petersburg, rupturing the silence that had surrounded the Decembrists since their arrival in Blagodatsk. Once the families were alerted to the whereabouts of the exiles, letters, parcels and money started to arrive. Assisted by the women, the prisoners began to win various concessions from the authorities. Volkonsky and Trubetskoi were allowed to visit their wives in their cabin, and the Decembrists were permitted to take walks in the countryside around Blagodatsk on the days they were not working. Writing to his brother a few years later, Obolensky described Maria and Katya as "guardian angels." With the appearance of "these two gentlewomen," he confided, "Russian in their hearts and noble in their character . . . we established a family."[15]

Without the benefit of the Decembrists' exceptional status, private funds and solicitous wives, the common penal labourers in the Nerchinsk mines endured a far worse fate. The barracks housing them were, one inspector noted, "falling down, poorly designed . . . terribly cramped, badly maintained and filthy." In some of the mining settlements, between eighty and 120 men were crammed into such buildings, measuring nine square metres, in which "there was neither order nor fresh air." Destitution and squalor reigned everywhere. The Scottish naval officer and explorer John Dundas Cochrane visited the Nerchinsk Mining Region in the early 1820s and found it "impossible to conceive the haggard, worndown, wretched, and half-starved appearance" of the penal labourers.[16]

The mine shafts in which the convicts toiled were primitive narrow tunnels dug into the side of the hills. The Zerentui mine was, for example, a hole approximately 4 metres in diameter that plunged 50 metres into the limestone at the foot of a hill. Through its entrance, inside a small shed, miners would enter the shaft with lamps suspended from their necks. Using hammers and crowbars, they would hack away at the walls to break off lumps of rock that would then be ground down and sifted outside. They sometimes used dynamite to open up smaller tunnels that fanned out from the main shaft. The heat in the mine was stifling; the walls dripped with moisture that trickled out through a gutter cut into the uneven floor. Part of the shaft was already flooded. In the words of one visitor to the mines, "the humidity, reminiscent of a bathhouse, was itself one of the forms of punishment."[17]

The miners worked in daytime and night-time shifts, each lasting twelve hours. Many lived in permanent darkness: for months of the year, they would enter the mines in the early morning, hours before sunrise, and leave only long after night had fallen. In the superstitious culture of the Russian peasantry, the earth was a dark underworld populated by a host of evil demons. Infested with squealing rats scurrying about in the impenetrable gloom, the mines seemed to play host to these "unclean spirits" in terrifying numbers. At the Zerentui mine, the convicts referred to the two principal shafts as two monsters, "growler" and "ringer," that sought daily to devour them. And devour them the shafts did. Miners perished in the frequent cave-ins occasioned by the use of dynamite in the boreholes, falling rocks and collapsing supports. At another of Nerchinsk's mines, three miners suffocated, as each refused to abandon a comrade to sulphurous fumes and died trying to retrieve him. The miners spoke of being "crushed by the mountain" or "beaten by the hole."

The work was not only dangerous; it was also grindingly monotonous. Badly designed and hastily dug, the shafts burrowed into the hillside in such a chaotic manner, and were so scarred with pits and mounds, that it was impossible to use even conventional wheelbar-rows, let alone mining carts, to transport the ore to the surface. It was all carried out of the mine by men in pairs on roughly made stretch-ers; there was little use of mechanization anywhere in the region. New arrivals at the Kara gold fields in the east of the Nerchinsk Mining Region would be set to work "clearing away the tail," that is, load-ing the earth disgorged from the mouth of the mine shafts into carts and then dragging it away. Even peasant convicts were aware that this Sisyphean labour was really work for draught animals and this knowl-edge, the ethnographer Sergei Maksimov observed, "tormented them without limit."[18]

So arduous and soul-destroying was the labour that many convicts resorted to drastic measures to avoid it. They would claim they had committed dreadful crimes that required the attention of the district court. In so doing, they hoped to prompt an investigation and thereby delay the moment of their return to the mines. They would claim to have murdered men and dumped their corpses in some remote loca-tion, simply in order to extend the time it took to clear up the case. If no evidence of their supposed crimes was uncovered, they would invent new atrocities to buy themselves time in the hope of staging an escape or changing identities with a fellow exile. Some simply preferred incarceration in the Nerchinsk prison to the dangerous work under-ground.[19]

Self-harm was another favoured means of avoiding the back-breaking labour. Some would stick pins into the inside of their cheeks and then stand outside in winter temperatures of −30°C and below, causing the cheeks to swell up. Others would intentionally inflict frost-bite on their hands, even to the point of having fingers amputated. One tactic was to simulate the symptoms of syphilis by inserting finely chopped horse hair into tiny incisions on the penis. The suppurations were enough to persuade all but the most experienced of camp doctors that the convict was no longer fit for work.[20]

The only activity in the mines that the penal labourers did approach assiduously, with energy and ingenuity, was the theft of gold and sil-ver. Specialists in this particular art form would circumvent all the spot checks and searches performed by their guards by squirrelling away the valuable fragments to fences beyond the penal settlements. On one occasion, convicts succeeded in burrowing their way under a mine's storage facilities to steal a year's worth of accumulated gold. Nerchinsk's courts were teeming with prosecutions for the theft of precious metals.[21]

Organized not in the spirit of enterprise but in accordance with bureaucratic dictates from St. Petersburg, and manned by a deeply reluctant workforce, the mines were, unsurprisingly, inefficient. On an average day in 1851, each man still produced only about 200 kilogrammes of earth that could be sifted for gold; in the private mining enterprises across Irkutsk province that employed free labour, the average was up to 1,370 kilogrammes per man per day. One inspector of Siberian penal labour lamented that, before the recent discovery of gold deposits in Kara in the 1830s, "the Nerchinsk mines did not turn any kind of profit." It was no surprise that across Siberia mine officials preferred free labourers to the ragged convicts whose only incentive to work was the avoidance of punishment.[22]

Conditions in Nerchinsk exposed a fundamental flaw in the state's attempt to combine punishment and colonization in Siberia. Mikhail Speransky's 1822 reforms of the exile system had envisioned penal labour as an instrument of reform. The mines and smelteries were supposed to yield not only iron, silver and gold but also a host of rehabilitated, energetic and hardy convicts. In reality, they forged destitute and dangerous criminals who had nothing to lose and were fleeing in droves. Governor-General of Eastern Siberia Aleksandr Lavinsky reported to the capital in January 1829 on the "intolerable, even calamitous" condition of the penal labourers:

> They receive a wage insufficient even for subsistence and are used in the most exhausting forms of labour. Housed in awful, cramped, filthy barracks, they are subject to dangers that exceed human powers. Owning no property that might divert them from the vices in which they are so steeped, these criminals flee the mines at the first opportunity and, gathering in groups of up to 10 men and more, embark on new crimes, including violent robbery and brigandage. There are examples of some getting as far as Yenisei and even Tomsk provinces [in Western Siberia] before they are finally captured.[23]

The exiles and penal labourers living in barracks scattered about the various mining settlements were never under lock and key and wore no fetters. One official explained to St. Petersburg in 1831 that "keeping all the penal labourers in fetters and in prison is quite impossible given their large number . . . and the lack of suitable buildings." During the summer months, escape, although usually punished with a severe beating, was a matter of heading off into the surrounding woods.[24]

With little to confine them in this remote and scarcely populated land, exiles absconded in their thousands during Nicholas's reign. Though the murderous cold had only just begun to recede in Nerchinsk in the spring of 1830, by 1 May, 163 penal labourers had already escaped. Most were eventually captured or simply turned themselves in, but not before they had disrupted the work of the mines and frequently committed serious crimes. Poorly equipped and isolated from reinforcements sometimes by hundreds of kilometres of taiga, prison authorities were outnumbered, and not infrequently outgunned, by the convicts in their charge. In 1828, there were just ten officers, forty junior officers and 524 soldiers in charge of an exile population of approximately 6,000 dispersed across a gigantic territory. Over the course of 1830, the military commander of the Nerchinsk Mining Region, Major-General Stanislav Leparsky, repeatedly wrote to Governor-General Lavinsky begging for reinforcements to pursue the fugitive exiles. Although he recognized that the endless escapes and the resulting crime spree across the Nerchinsk Mining Region were damaging the state's economic interests in the mines, Lavinsky was only able to scrape together 121 regular soldiers to bolster the numbers. In 1833, the authorities decreed that any soldier apprehending a fugitive exile would receive a reward of three silver roubles. Even so, such measures proved quite inadequate to stem the flow of destitute and dangerous fugitives.[25]

Murders in Nerchinsk were commonplace, committed both by exiles in the penal settlements and by the vagabonds who roamed the surrounding countryside. In 1828, reports from the head of the Nerchinsk Mining Region, Mine Captain Fyodor fon Frish, abounded with incidents of families butchered for the smallest of sums, rapes and kidnappings. As the only part of the Nerchinsk population with disposable incomes, and usually the object of the exiles' enmity, the region's officials were especially vulnerable to attack. The deputy head of one of the smelteries in Nerchinsk, Ivan Baldauf, an official "of good character who had diligently carried out his duties around the mine," ordered the flogging of two penal labourers who had tried to escape. When he approached the two men to read out the sentence, one of them, Ivan Ivanov, bowed before him and suddenly produced a knife he had concealed inside his shirtsleeve. Before any of the guards present were able to react, Ivanov stabbed Baldauf in the stomach. Despite the ministrations of the local physician, Baldauf died two days later, leaving behind a wife and five children. In February 1828, exile Anton Zakharov stabbed to death the wife and son of one of the Nerchinsk soldiers for the princely sum of seventeen roubles. In July, another exile slit the throat of an official's wife at the Kadai mine.[26] The convicts even celebrated the murder of officials in their songs:

> The mine foreman finally got his retirement
> But he couldn't hide from the vengeance of justice
> His skull was smashed to pieces with a hammer
> Once an exile got hold of him.[27]

As they mingled with the local population of officials, settled exiles and factory peasants, the penal labourers had easy access to the alcohol—vodka and wine—sold in the various drinking dens that littered the penal settlements. Alcohol added a combustible element to the various tensions, resentments and hatreds that festered in the mines. In March 1828, what began as a vodka-fuelled attempt to murder Mine Captain Aleksandr Taskin and his wife in the Klichkin mine, 180 kilometres from the town of Nerchinsk, ended in a riot. During a night of heavy drinking in the mine tavern, a group of exiles led by Timofei Ivanov forced the tavern-keeper to hand over wine at knifepoint. The following day, still drunk, Ivanov assaulted a mine official, an offence for which he knew he would be flogged. Determined to exact vengeance on Taskin for ordering him to "desist from drinking and rowdiness," Ivanov broke into the official's lodgings intent on murder. Ivanov discovered no one at home, but the noise he had made breaking the locks alerted Taskin's neighbours, who seized him. Yet when his drinking companions, all still drunk, witnessed his arrest, they attacked the neighbours and freed Ivanov. Together, they then proceeded to the tavern with their knives, boasting of their intention to murder Taskin, "burn the settlement at one end, and cut the throats of everyone at the other." Other convicts began to join them and only towards evening, when a unit of military and mining personnel was assembled in sufficient numbers, was it possible to seize them. The men were knouted and sentenced to lifelong penal labour.[28]

The authorities in Nerchinsk were becoming increasingly concerned that the penal labourers—many of them former soldiers—were showing a capacity for coordinated, military resistance. Leparsky complained in June 1828 that "the conspiracies of the exiled penal labourers are growing more intricate every year." The previous August, fifty-seven convicts entering the mining region in a marching convoy had staged a rebellion against their guards, and twenty-five of them had managed to flee on postal horses. One Cossack, Sobolev, organized a party to give chase and, finally cornering the fugitives on the shores of a lake, demanded that they surrender. When the exiles refused, the Cossacks attacked and a four-hour firefight ensued during which Sobolev himself was badly wounded, two exiles were killed and several more injured. The remaining fugitives were eventually seized; only one managed to flee. The following month, another convoy of prisoners marching into Nerchinsk attacked their Cossack and peasant guards and locked them in a waystation before also seizing postal horses and fleeing into the surrounding forests, robbing peasant homes and wounding three people. Although they numbered no more than twenty-eight men and, Leparsky reported, "were eventually defeated by frontier Cossacks right on the border with China, while defending themselves, they had attacked and withdrawn in formation." Their intention had been "to attack different mines and force the other penal labourers, either by persuasion or by violent threats . . . to join them. So reinforcing themselves, they planned to make for the Chinese border." Such instances of organized and disciplined resistance, Leparsky noted bleakly, "did not occur in earlier times," and he appealed for the military forces at his disposal to be strengthened.[29]

Denunciation and slander were almost a form of currency in this shadowy world of violent convicts and frightened officials. Exiles would report knowledge of plots, real and imagined, to the authorities in the hope of acquiring benefits and concessions for themselves. Timofei

Filippov, condemned in 1823 to the knout followed by lifelong penal labour, sought to delay his arrival in Nerchinsk by writing repeated denunciations of plots to assassinate Alexander I. His claims were investigated, but officials believed them to be false, dreamed up with the sole purpose of delaying the passing of his sentence, or in order to have himself called to St. Petersburg. "Filippov was seeking," they concluded, "to save his own life, not the tsar's." Undeterred, Filippov escaped from a marching convoy on its way to Nerchinsk in 1827 by switching names with a fellow convict in Tomsk. Once exposed, he was taken to Irkutsk. There, desperate to delay punishment, he launched a volley of new denunciations of plots against the lives of the imperial family hatched by Masonic conspirators. On this occasion, Filippov appeared to have overplayed his hand: his claims reached Count Alexander von Benckendorff, the head of the imperial secret police, the Third Department, who flatly rejected them. In 1830, he was publicly punished with forty-five blows of the knout, branded and sent to his original destination in the Nerchinsk mines.[30]

The Decembrists were an obvious target for denunciations levelled by exiles seeking to curry favour with the authorities. The exiled officers Andrei Rozen and Dmitry Zavalishin both observed the nervousness of the authorities at the arrival of the Decembrists in Siberia.[31] The rebels' crime had been an organized and collective assault on the very autocracy they were sworn to protect. If the original revolt had stumbled in part because the troops on Senate Square had little understanding of the cause for which they were being ordered to fight, perhaps in Nerchinsk, with a solidarity born of common desperation, things would be different. The Decembrists' arrival in the region over the course of 1827 and 1828 threatened to bring political leadership to the destitute and desperate convicts.

One of those who sought to capitalize on the government's anxieties was Roman Medoks, a man who appeared to have stepped straight out of the pages of one of Nikolai Gogol's satires. The most extraordinary Russian adventurer, embezzler, womanizer and fraudster of the nineteenth century, Medoks proved extremely adept at manipulating the authorities with his denunciations of seditious conspiracies. Medoks was the son of an English acrobat, Michael Maddox, who had travelled to Moscow in 1766 and eventually founded the Petrovsk Theatre, which later rose from the ashes of a devastating fire in 1805 as the Bolshoi.[32] Born some time between 1789 and 1795, Medoks joined the cavalry, but in 1812 he embezzled 2,000 roubles and fled from his regiment to the Caucasus. Using forged papers, he passed himself off as an envoy from the Ministry of Finance and received further substantial funds from the local authorities in southern Russia. Finally unmasked, he was sent to St. Petersburg and, in 1813, Alexander I ordered him imprisoned in the Peter and Paul Fortress. He languished there for fourteen years, sharing months of confinement with the Decembrist rebels in 1826.

In March 1827, his pleas to the tsar for mercy were finally answered and Medoks was exiled to the town of Vyatka, 960 kilometres to the east of Moscow. He once again absconded in 1828 only to be arrested and then escape again. He finally appeared in Irkutsk in March 1831 in the home of the exiled Decembrist Aleksandr Muravyov. Eager to win the favour of the tsar, Medoks promptly offered his services to Benckendorff as a spy, and soon uncovered an enormous anti-government plot. The imprisoned Decembrists were conducting an extensive correspondence with their supporters in various Russian cities, hatching a new conspiracy, the "Society of the Great Cause," against the state. Medoks reported to Benckendorff that, "for all my feelings of revulsion at writing denunciations, I have a sacred duty to write to Your Excellency both to reveal a secret that might have the most extreme consequences, and to divest myself of any suspicion of involvement in the affair." Medoks went so far as to elaborate a complex system of codes that, he claimed, enabled the Decembrists to conduct their correspondence in secret. The conspirators used the sign of a dagger, for example, to represent the Decembrists Ivan Yakushkin and Aleksandr Yakubovich because "they were sharpened like daggers" in their readiness for renewed rebellion.[33] He also claimed that the criminals had won over a number of the state's leading representatives in Siberia, including the governor of Irkutsk, Ivan Tseidler, and even the military commander of Nerchinsk, Leparsky himself. Medoks claimed that his information would "save the fatherland" but insisted on being brought home from Siberia, since he could not reveal anything in detail in Irkutsk for fear of reprisals from his enemies. Leading figures in the government responded with some scepticism to Medoks's claims but Nicholas appeared to believe this vision of another empire-wide conspiracy against the throne. In October 1833, Medoks was recalled to Moscow, where he was put up in one of the best hotels and generously provided for by Nicholas's secret police while he prevaricated about the evidence for his claims. It was only when pressure began to mount on him to prove his case that he finally fled once again. This time, however, his luck deserted him and, once more apprehended, he was clapped in chains and returned to the Peter and Paul Fortress. He was left there to rot for another two decades until Alexander II finally amnestied him in 1856.[34]

In September 1827, after eleven months at the Blagodatsk mine, the Decembrists and their wives were transferred to Chita. The authorities in St. Petersburg, alarmed by reports of violence in Nerchinsk and fearful of conspiracies among the "state criminals," had decided on a policy of concentrating all the Decembrists in a single location, where they could be more effectively confined and monitored.[35] Nicholas had charged Leparsky with finding a suitable temporary site in which to hold the Decembrists while a permanent prison was built in Petrovsk Zavod. Leparsky chose Chita. Founded in the seventeenth century as the fur trade in Siberia was booming, Chita was a collection of ramshackle huts with 300 residents and a small church. On the site of an abandoned Cossack fort, the St. Petersburg authorities ordered the construction of a wooden stockade prison, which was completed in August 1827. A month later, the Blagodatsk eight, cheered at the prospect of joining their friends and comrades, set out for Chita under an armed guard of twelve Cossacks and a junior officer.[36] The fate of one of the Decembrists' comrades in Nerchinsk, Ivan Sukhinov, would give them cause to count their blessings that they had been removed from the violent and unstable world of the mines.

On the morning of 13 June 1828, a year after the transfer of the Blagodatsk eight to Chita, a dog in the Zerentui mine entered the settlement and presented its master with a human arm. The limb soon led to the discovery of a head, a torso and items of clothing scattered in the vicinity of a disused mine shaft in the surrounding woods. Wild animals had torn the body to pieces, but the remains were recognized as those of a penal labourer, Aleksei Kazakov, who had disappeared from the camp a few weeks earlier.

Kazakov had last been seen on 24 May, when the overseer of the Zerentui mine, Chernigovtsev, had returned to his lodgings after a three-day inspection of a neighbouring mine. Exhausted from his journey, Chernigovtsev had taken to his bed to rest but was soon roused by an unaccustomed knocking at the door of his cabin. He hurried to the window and opened it to discover Kazakov standing on the porch "quite drunk and in a state of excitement." Kazakov informed Chernigovtsev of a conspiracy hatched by a group of fellow prisoners who were drinking and plotting in the mine's tavern. Under the leadership of the exiled Decembrist Ivan Sukhinov, the convicts were preparing an armed rebellion in Zerentui that very night: "They planned first of all to seize the soldiers' weapons and ammunition from the armoury and, once armed, to enter the barracks where the penal labourers lived and force them to escape, to destroy the prison and to liberate all the convicts under guard. They then planned to burn the entire settlement around the Zerentui mine, to go on to Nerchinsk and beyond, destroying everything that stood in their path." Chernigovtsev instructed Kazakov to go to the mine office and wait for him there. The intoxicated convict lumbered off and vanished. He only reappeared, dismembered, on 13 June, by which time he was at the centre of an unfolding drama of plots, rebellion and betrayal.[37]

Kazakov's drunken denunciation to Chernigovtsev set in motion a chain of events—later known as the "Zerentui Conspiracy"—that would reach its bloody climax some six months later.[38] The case exposed the dark heart of the state's under-resourced, incompetent and brutal management of its exile population under Nicholas. Fearful and uncertain, the men who administered the penal labourers were quick to see threats in the shadowy corners of the barracks and in the gloom of the mines. They resorted to fearsome displays of punishment and retribution in an attempt to terrify the penal labourers into submission.

Upon hearing Kazakov's denunciation of exiles plotting murder and rebellion in the settlement, Chernigovtsev was seized by fear for his own and his family's safety. He immediately ordered the arrest of the men Kazakov had named. One was Ivan Golikov, a former sergeant major in the Imperial Army. While Chernigovtsev had been away from the mine, Golikov had spent three days on a drinking binge with his fellow convicts. Chernigovtsev had Golikov beaten for his drinking and, at the same time, he put to him Kazakov's allegations. The beating and the questioning were, Chernigovtsev subsequently affirmed, "a coincidence of two different circumstances at the same time."[39] It is improbable that they appeared very coincidental to Golikov.

Given the methods of persuasion employed during questioning, Golikov's confession offered a warped version of the preoccupations of his interrogators. The exile admitted that, from the end of April, he had frequently visited the apartment Ivan Sukhinov shared with two other Decembrist officers, Venyamin Solovyov and Aleksandr Mozalevsky. Sukhinov had recruited both Golikov and Vasily Bocharov, the exiled son of an Astrakhan merchant, promising to reward them if they could find up to twenty "good exiles" to stage a rebellion in Zerentui. Under the birch rod, the allegations of an armed revolt to launch an escape bid morphed into nothing less than a political rebellion with the goal of liberating the Decembrists 290 kilometres away in Chita. Golikov now admitted that Sukhinov had told him:

> We can gather in numbers and first of all seize the soldiers' weapons from the stores and, once armed, enter the barracks and force all the convicts living there to escape together . . . Then we will go to Nerchinsk Zavod and do the same there: first seize the battlefield weapons, freeing all the convicts from the prison, . . . and then force all the inhabitants of the mining complex to join our party of brigands . . . With the increase in our party and its armaments, nothing will be able to stop us. After that we will go through the mines and factories, adding people to our party, before travelling right up to the Chita fort and freeing all the Decembrists.[40]

The confession was the sum of all the authorities' fears: a violent insurgency, directed by a seasoned officer, capable of renewing and unleashing the dormant revolutionary forces of the Decembrists in Nerchinsk. Subjected to similar methods of interrogation, two other convicts, Fyodor Morshakov and Timofei Nepomnyashchy, corroborated this story and confessed to having been recruited to the conspiracy by Golikov on 24 May. Later that day, the alleged leader of the conspiracy, Sukhinov, was also arrested and questioned.[41]

Ivan Sukhinov had played a leading role in the brief and bloody rebellion of the Chernigov Regiment in the environs of Kiev at the end of December 1825. Born in 1794 in Kherson province into the family of a nobleman of modest means, at fifteen he had joined the Hussars and fought in the Napoleonic Wars, picking up seven wounds and a medal for gallantry. In 1816, he had returned from the conflict to Russia, where, in 1819, following a brief demobilization due to his injuries, he had been promoted as an officer into the Chernigov Regiment. Like many of his fellow officers returning from the conflict, Sukhinov had found the regimentation and strict hierarchies of life in Alexandrine Russia stifling. In September 1825, his commanding officer, Sergei Muravyov-Apostol, had recruited him into the Decembrists' Southern Society.[42]

Sukhinov scarcely had the makings of a revolutionary hero. After the failure of the Chernigov Regiment's rebellion, he fled and then wrote to Nicholas I from hiding: "Forgive me magnanimously, my sovereign, my crime. I am neither a murderer nor a barbarian. If I am guilty, then it is only of following the orders of Muravyov-Apostol." Sukhinov managed to evade capture until 15 February 1826, when, after the authorities intercepted a letter he sent to his brother begging for money, he was apprehended in Debaser in Bessarabia. He appeared before a military tribunal on 26 February and was found guilty of "illegally attempting to overthrow the existing state order." Nicholas I confirmed the sentence of lifelong penal labour in Eastern Siberia on 12 July 1826 and, on 1 August, Sukhinov and his comrades from the Chernigov Regiment, Solovyov and Mozalevsky, were all subject to a civil execution in the small town of Ostrog before a gathering of the purged and newly re-formed regiment. They set out for Siberia on 5 September.[43]

Sukhinov and his companions did not reach Moscow until the end of 1826 and Tobolsk until May of the following year. Exhausted from the journey and disconsolate at his fate, Sukhinov expressed despair and remorse to a state official charged with reporting on the mood of the exiled insurgents. Delayed by bouts of illness along the route, the officers finally arrived at the Zerentui mine in Nerchinsk on 9 March, after a year and a half on the road.[44] A mere two months later, Sukhinov found himself accused of masterminding a conspiracy to stage a violent rebellion against the state.

Taken in for questioning, Sukhinov testified that he knew his alleged accomplices: Golikov from the moment he had begun to employ him to undertake his penal labour duties, and Bocharov only by sight. Golikov had begun pestering him, Mozalevsky and Solovyov for money, and had been refused entry to their cabin the day before the arrests. Sukhinov flatly denied that he had ever asked Golikov to recruit men for a rebellion, protesting that he would never have dreamed of "such criminal actions, being always convinced that sooner or later the sovereign's mercy would be extended, and he had always sustained himself in that comforting hope." Sukhinov concluded that Golikov's slander was motivated by "revenge and ingratitude towards Sukhinov for the times when Sukhinov had refused his requests [for money] . . . and had barred him from his cabin."[45]

A week later, Golikov and his accomplices were once again interrogated at the mine office and, now sober and aware of the gravity of their situation, they sought to distance themselves from their original confessions. Golikov explained that, "although Sukhinov had talked about escaping with him, it had only been out of pity for the penal labourers who were in such an impoverished state that [Sukhinov] had said that he would, in their position, either immediately escape or kill himself." It was for this reason that, when drunk, Golikov had invited everyone to flee, but he had never, in fact, heard of any actual plans from Sukhinov. His previous testimony had been false, "given because, after three days of drinking, he was drunk and hungover and lied in order to try to clear himself." Nepomnyashchy and Morshakov claimed their initial testimony had been beaten out of them. Bocharov denied any knowledge of a plot, claiming he had been too drunk to remember the discussions in the tavern.[46]

Once summoned into being by both a denunciation and a confession, however, the existence of a conspiracy proved difficult to deny and the retraction of the convicts' earlier testimony failed to head off a full investigation. When Chernigovtsev's superior, fon Frish, learned of the allegations, he was alarmed not only by the ongoing threat of social disorder in the mines under his command, but also by the apparent involvement of a Decembrist. He wrote to Leparsky, the military commander of Nerchinsk, stating that there were "strong grounds to believe in a conspiracy" led by Sukhinov. Leparsky responded by instructing fon Frish to strengthen the guard in Zerentui and to get to the bottom of the affair.[47] Fon Frish set up an investigative commission that arrived in Zerentui one day after Golikov had retracted his initial confession, charged with "bringing clarity to the whole [affair] by the most scrupulous means." An official already rumoured to have tortured two exiles to death in Nerchinsk was selected to head the investigation. In keeping with the judicial procedures of Nicolaevan Russia, he and his colleagues confined their activities to the repeated interrogation of the suspects.[48]

Then, just as the investigation was beginning its work, Rudakov's dog presented its grisly find. Kazakov's dismembered corpse seemed to offer incontrovertible proof of the allegations the exile had made on 24 May. The suspects were transferred from Zerentui to the town of Nerchinsk, where the interrogations became still more brutal. Beatings combined with moral exhortations of the clergy were widely used as a means of extracting confessions in the penal settlements of Siberia.[49] So, when fon Frish later reported to his superiors in St. Petersburg that the new interrogations were accompanied by "direct methods of persuasion from the legal officials," it left little to the imagination. Nepomnyashchy was the first to break and, by 22 June, he had returned to his original confession. The others quickly followed suit. Golikov himself finally admitted that, having learned of Kazakov's denunciation from a fellow convict, he had told Bocharov to lure Kazakov into a copse not more than 30 metres from the barracks with the promise of more alcohol. He had then followed the pair and attacked Kazakov, beating him to death with a rock. Golikov and Bocharov had dumped the body in a disused mine shaft before returning to the settlement tavern to continue drinking. Due perhaps to his traditional exemption from the persuasive power of the birch rod as a (former) member of the nobility, the only accused not to change his story in his subsequent interrogations was Sukhinov.[50]

News of the alleged conspiracy in Zerentui reached Nicholas in August 1828 while he was summering in Odessa. The tsar's shock at the conditions in the mines to which he had exiled the Decembrists spoke volumes about his ignorance of his own penal settlements. Nicholas expressed indignation at the "weak supervision of the penal labourers in the mines" and at the fact that the authorities in Nerchinsk punished drunken exiles only lightly with the birch rod. Particularly alarming was the discovery that "the criminal Sukhinov moved around freely . . . and that he even had another exile working for him as a servant." The tsar immediately ordered the establishment of a military tribunal to try the accused, with the clear implication that those found guilty would be executed. By late September, the tribunal of four officers was ready to hear the case in the town of Nerchinsk.[51]

The working assumption of military tribunals under Nicholas I was that an order to try was an order to convict. Proceedings were based on "the inquisitorial principle": the confession of the accused was considered compelling evidence. Even better was the congruent testimony of two different witnesses, and the tribunal now had the evidence of a number of witnesses who had, over the course of the summer, aligned their various statements. Ordinarily, of course, the testimony of an officer and a gentleman would have outweighed that of men from the lower orders. As the court observed, however, Sukhinov's involvement in the Decembrist Revolt "was already sufficient proof of his guilt."[52]

When the tribunal duly delivered its verdict to Leparsky on 4 November, it convicted Sukhinov of conspiring to stage an uprising in Zerentui with the ultimate goal of liberating his fellow Decembrists in Chita. Golikov and Bocharov were convicted of recruiting men to the cause and of the murder of Kazakov once the latter had denounced them. The alleged ringleaders were sentenced to be knouted between 280 and 400 times, branded on their faces and imprisoned "in order to prevent them from committing similar crimes in the future." The other members of the conspiracy were sentenced to up to 200 blows of the knout (or whip if their crime was considered more minor), branded and condemned to lifelong penal labour.[53]

According to military law, Leparsky had the right to alter the sentences, and on 29 November he duly exercised his discretion. Sukhinov and his close associates were to be spared the knout (which would anyway have almost certainly proven fatal) and to face the relative honour and humanity of a firing squad. Leparsky decided to travel from Chita to Nerchinsk to oversee the passing of the sentences on 3 December himself. He was meticulous in his preparations for the execution, stipulating how many soldiers and how many bullets were required, and the dimensions of the pit into which the bodies of the condemned were to be cast.[54]

Leparsky was to discover, though, that even the best-laid plans go awry. The conspiracy's mastermind never reached the execution site. A fellow captive stumbled over Sukhinov in the night of 1 December lying on the floor, his head in a noose made from his belt not more than 30 centimetres from the ground. He had tied his belt to his leg fetters and fixed it to the wooden frame of the stove. The weight of Sukhinov's legs had then pulled the noose tight around his neck and he had slowly, in an almost horizontal position, asphyxiated.[55]

In hindsight, the execution cast Sukhinov's suicide as a dignified choice. On 4 December, a clearly indignant Leparsky reported on the proceedings. Comprising 170 privates, the Fifth Mining Battalion stationed in Nerchinsk had been "unable to muster more than 40 rifles for the 70 men who were to attend the execution by shooting of the condemned criminals." Of the weapons, only fifteen had been deemed fit for use and half the selected soldiers "could not shoot properly"; it was only by reducing the quantity of gunpowder that it became possible to use weapons which had been in the possession of the battalion since 1775. Leparsky complained bitterly that "the battalion was armed worse than if it had wielded only spears."[56] He omitted from his report grisly details about the deaths of the condemned men, but rumours of a botched and barbaric execution began to circle throughout the Nerchinsk Mining Region.

His business concluded, Leparsky ordered that Sukhinov's fellow Decembrists in Zerentui, Solovyov and Mozalevsky, be transferred to join the other Decembrists in Chita. There, Solovyov offered his comrades and their supporters the story, finally published in the reign of Alexander II, of both a heroic, if ill-fated, attempt to free the Decembrists and the state's gruesome retribution. The condemned men had survived the initial volley of gunfire, he reported, and the firing squad had been obliged to run them through with bayonets. Bocharov had been thrown into the execution pit "still half alive."[57] A rash of Decembrist memoirs published in the second half of the nineteenth century would return to the story of Sukhinov's desperate and tragic bid to free his comrades in Chita. The hapless Decembrist became enshrined in an emerging pantheon of heroic opponents of tsarist tyranny.[58]

As it turned out, official fears of the dangers posed by Decembrists in exile were exaggerated. The exiled officers never manifested any enthusiasm for staging a renewed rebellion, but what did pose an insidious threat to the tsarist regime was their gradual reinvention as martyrs in the public eye. Sukhinov could not have envisaged this wider shift in perception as he made a noose from his belt in his cell on 1 December 1828, but Siberia was becoming a central stage in the political history of the Russian Empire. Sukhinov's comrades in Chita would take up the story.

5

The Decembrist Republic

A decade after the Decembrists were exiled, merchants and officials in Irkutsk began to dispatch their servants to the bleak settlement of Petrovsk Zavod with orders for jewellery. The popularity of these adornments in the polite society of Eastern Siberia in the 1830s reveals much about the fate of Decembrists in the culture of Nicolaevan Russia. For after the prisoners' arrival in Petrovsk Zavod in the autumn of 1830, Nikolai Bestuzhev—the Decembrist with "the golden fingers"— had set about forging rings and bracelets from the prisoners' discarded fetters. These he then sent back to his relatives in St. Petersburg. Bestuzhev recalled how the accessories subsequently became an unexpected hit in educated circles: "Irkutsk ladies, our wives' acquaintances, wanted to have them; their husbands and brothers also wanted to wear them—some out of vanity and others out of primitive liberalism." He noted with some indignation how local locksmiths in Petrovsk Zavod opened up stalls offering "Decembrist jewellery," like "forged antiques in Rome." The Decembrists' fetters, "a sacred deposit, an emblem of our suffering for truth, became a crude decoration . . . of every Irkutsk dandy!"[1] In his distaste at this trade in trinkets, however, Bestuzhev overlooked the fact that it was ultimately a testament to the Decembrists' moral victory over the autocracy. A decade after the men's civil execution in the courtyard of the Peter and Paul Fortress, their fetters had become symbols of the state's tyranny, and icons of their own martyrdom.

Nicholas I's entire reign was a protracted epilogue to the Decembrist Revolt. In the decades that followed the revolt's suppression, the Russian state recoiled from the evils of revolution abroad and sedition at home. In so doing, it dragged official culture into outright reaction. Government mouthpieces in education and the arts spawned the ideol-

ogy of "Official Nationality," a cultural trinity of autocracy, Orthodoxy and "national spirit." Part of the European-wide restoration and
reaction that followed the Napoleonic Wars, "Official Nationality"
sought to refurbish the symbolic foundations of the autocracy. Government censorship ruthlessly suppressed tsarism's ideological rivals: liberalism, nationalism and constitutionalism.[2] European Russian culture
was stifled by censorship, hierarchies, traditions and a stubborn refusal
on the part of the government to allow educated society any say in the
development and governance of the state. Nicholas I's reign witnessed
"a parting of the ways" in which educated Russians' support for the
tsarist regime began to erode. Many, frustrated at the lack of civic and
intellectual freedoms and wary of the attentions of the imperial secret
police, the Third Department, sought refuge in the private world of
their estates and in the abstractions of philosophical idealism.[3] In a
small corner of Siberia, the exiled Decembrist rebels were, however,
paradoxically free, even in their fetters, to experiment with new forms
of political authority and social organization. They offered a model of
democracy, patriotism and social activism both for their contemporaries and for posterity. It is in this sense that the roots of 1917 stretch
back to 1825.

Two weeks after they had set off from the Blagodatsk mine, Sergei Volkonsky, Sergei Trubetskoi, their wives and their six comrades reached
the Chita fort in the west of the Nerchinsk Mining Region, where the
state was now concentrating the exiled Decembrists. A skilled artist as
well as a gifted jewellery maker, Nikolai Bestuzhev left a series of excellent aquarelles and sketches of Chita in the late 1820s. Situated in a
wide valley ringed by hills that were covered in scrub, the 3-metre-high
stockade of sharpened logs, which reminded Maria Volkonskaya of
ships' masts, surrounded a series of barracks into which, by the end
of 1827, were crammed some eighty-two prisoners and several wives.
A few kilometres to the north of Chita lies Lake Onon, where, Andrei
Rozen observed, "Genghis Khan held his court of justice. (He used to
drown criminals in the seething waters on his march into Rus.) The
descendants of his Mongols, the Buryats, still wander with their felt
tents through this country abounding in rivers and lakes." The winters were long and cold, but without the penetrating damp of much of

Nerchinsk; the summers filled Chita with a blazing heat and a profusion of vegetation. The vale of Chita was, Rozen recalled, "renowned for its flora, for which reason the region is called 'the Garden of Siberia.'" These were far healthier climes. On setting out from Blagodatsk, Volkonsky had looked, in the opinion of Leparsky, "thin and rather weak." Once in Chita, his health swiftly recovered.[4] The Decembrists would spend three years in the Chita fort and these would prove to be a halcyon episode in their Siberian exile.

The men were housed in groups of between ten and twenty in one of four large barracks within the prison. Nikolai Bestuzhev's brother, Mikhail, wrote that they were "packed like herrings in a barrel" in poorly ventilated rooms that at night grew, as Rozen remembered, "intolerably oppressive." Nikolai Basargin recounted how "each man had half a metre on which to sleep on the planks, so that in turning over onto one's side during the night one had necessarily to knock a neighbour—especially as we wore chains that were not taken off at night and which made a quite extraordinary noise and caused a perceptible pain with every careless movement. But is there anything to which youth cannot grow accustomed? What can it not endure? We all slept as well as in luxurious beds or on feather mattresses."[5]

In Chita, the Decembrists' wives found replacements for the servants they had lost in Blagodatsk. They were initially permitted to see their husbands, in accordance with the tsar's instructions, only twice a week, for three hours. Maria complained bitterly that their lot was worse than that of the wives of common penal labourers: "After I left my parents, my child, my homeland, after I travelled 6,400 kilometres and signed an undertaking to renounce any protection from the law, I am informed that I cannot even rely on the protection of my husband. So state criminals should be subject to the severity of the law, just like common penal labourers, but they are not to enjoy a family life, which is granted to the most terrible criminals and monsters!"[6] Maria highlighted one of the principal dilemmas for the authorities: the enforcement of these rules was clearly also to the detriment of the women, who were regarded with sympathy in Chita by the residents and prison officials alike. "We see our husbands twice a week for three hours and we are allowed to send them dinner," Maria wrote in December 1827. "Often the clanking of their chains summons us to the window, from which we watch with a bitter-sweet joy as they go to work."[7] Volkonskaya, Trubetskaya and the other wives would walk up to the prison garden and snatch moments of conversation with their husbands through the cracks in the palisade of thick timbers. Fearful that Leparsky might catch them, the women bribed the guards to warn them if he approached.[8]

Nicholas had ordered that the Decembrists be "put to work and treated as regular penal labourers."[9] But the penal labour to which the men were subject was perfunctory and only expressed, in Zavalishin's opinion, "the abnormality of conditions in Russia and the impotence of the government." In the summer months, the men were sent out to work filling in a roadside hollow known as "the Devil's grave." Their day began, Zavalishin recalled, as follows:

> Before going out to work, there was hustle and bustle among the guards in the barracks and the servants in the wives' cabins. Books, newspapers, chessboards, breakfast, a samovar, tea and coffee were all taken out to our place of work. State workers carried out the hods, the wheelbarrows and the shovels if we were going to work on the "Devil's grave." Finally, an officer would arrive and say, "Gentlemen, to work? Who's going today (because each day many would say they were sick and didn't feel like working)?" If too few were willing, the officer would say "someone else is needed, gentlemen, otherwise the commandant will notice that there are too few." Then someone would say, "Well alright, perhaps I'll go too" . . . Then we'd go out, some of us would pick up a shovel for his own amusement, and some not. The soldiers would carry the spare shovels. One of us would begin to sing, accompanied by the noise of the clanking of chains . . . More often than not we would strike up a revolutionary song, "Our Fatherland Is Suffering Beneath Your Yoke" and so on. The officer and the soldiers would calmly listen to the song and march along to it, as if everything were as it should be . . . The work site turned into a club; some would read newspapers, some would play chess and still others would, for their amusement, start to load earth into the wheelbarrows and laugh uproariously as they tipped the

contents of the barrow—both soil and hods into the gully . . . the officer or overseer would help himself to what was left of our breakfast or tea and, only if he saw the commandant somewhere in the distance, would, for the sake of appearances, cry out, "What is this, gentlemen, you are not working?"[10]

In the winter months, when it was impossible to work outside, the men took turns working in a mill that Leparsky had constructed next to the prison. Here the work, comprising two daily shifts of three hours each, was no more onerous. "We were obliged to grind 60 kilogrammes of rye in all," Ivan Yakushkin recalled, "but since no more than two men could work at a given time at each of the four hand-mills, we changed places several times during the work session. Needless to say, this labour was not taxing, but a few who lacked the strength to do their share themselves hired a guard to grind it for them. Those who were not working smoked or played chess, or read and chatted in another room." Yevgeny Obolensky wrote to his brother of the Decembrists' debates "about philosophy, science, about anything to kill three or four hours in the day."[11] Not everyone appreciated the perfunctory nature of the work. Pyotr Svistunov complained to his brother Aleksei that, "essentially, we are not forced to do anything here, and it might all seem to be like going for a stroll, if it were not for the fact that we are obliged to go to work . . . the obligation to undertake utterly useless work is also a kind of torture. The authorities have never lacked inventiveness when it comes to inflicting punishment while preserving the appearance of mercy."[12]

Nicholas sent Leparsky detailed instructions governing the treatment of the prisoners and their wives. The commandant was to submit fortnightly reports on the Decembrists' "behaviour, their mood, whether they undertook any labour, and everything that concerns them." The Decembrists were forbidden to write to friends and family; their wives were permitted to correspond, but only if they first passed their open letters to Leparsky in order that they might be censored. The prisoners were allowed to receive correspondence and parcels sent to Leparsky for verification. Both prisoners and their wives could receive only such financial support "as was necessary for their maintenance" and they could only "keep the most essential possessions." The men were instructed to avoid interacting with the other exiles in the area. As ever, these instructions from the capital wielded but limited authority in Eastern Siberia, where Leparsky proved unwilling to enforce them.[13]

An elderly Russified Pole, Stanislav Leparsky knew Latin, wrote in French and German and was, in Rozen's opinion, "a completely honourable man with a kind heart." He submitted reports on the Decembrists' conduct only for a brief time, and quietly ignored many of St. Petersburg's more stringent directives governing the treatment of the prisoners. Contrary to his instructions, he allowed the Decembrists not only to maintain contact with other exiles but even to employ them as personal servants and to pay them to perform their own labour duties. He also turned a blind eye to the Decembrists' use of their wives as secretaries. By 1828, there were eight women in Chita. "Each woman took responsibility for a number of men in the prison," Yakushkin recalled, "for whom she would constantly write and re-write the letters she was given as if they were from herself, adding only 'so and so asks me to pass on to you this and this.'" Rozen marvelled at how the women "formed a link between the living and the politically dead."[14] Despite these efforts, however, the threat of censorship was a source of terrible frustration, as Nikolai Bestuzhev discovered:

> Even our correspondence with our close relatives was terse and cautious; we thought through every phrase ten times over before committing it to paper in order that it would pass Leparsky's censorship and not compel our women to rewrite the letters once again . . . This correspondence was so colourless and lifeless! It bore such a vulgar stamp of officialdom that every time I wrote letters, I was seized by madness.[15]

Once the women arrived in Chita, their very presence placed officials in an invidious position. Officials could not restrict the men's access to their wives without at the same time publicly punishing selfless and devoted women who had already suffered a great deal. Rozen grasped the state's dilemma: "The presence of the women was most beneficial to us even where our life in prison, upkeep, and treatment by officials were concerned . . . They became witnesses, one might say participants, in our lives and they enjoyed all their rights; consequently, they could complain not only privately to their relations, but even to the government—which was obliged to spare them if only so as not to arouse public opinion against itself, to earn the charge of cruelty and to submit to the just condemnation of posterity and history."[16] In fact, the women had signed away their rights, but Rozen's neglect of this fact spoke volumes. The Decembrists' wives were assertive, articulate and wielded a moral authority that Leparsky found difficult to resist. Basargin recalled how, on the occasions when the general did deny some petition for an improvement in the men's conditions, he found himself assailed by their wives:

> More than once, in their ignorance of criminal and civil law and refusing to acknowledge the unlimited power that the government wielded over the condemned, and standing on their own sense of justice and humanity, the women would, provoked by some measure that restricted our freedom, enter into a struggle with the commandant. They would say to his face the harshest and most acerbic words, calling him a jailer and adding that no decent man would have assumed his position unless it was, whatever the consequences and the tsar's fury, to alleviate our lot. If he did act in this way then he would earn not only their respect and ours but the respect of every man and of posterity as well; if, however, he did not, they would look upon him as a common jailer who had sold himself for money, and he would leave behind the most undesirable memory. Such words could not fail to influence the old man, not least because in his heart he knew them to be just. "In God's name, do not become so heated," he would reply to such outbursts. "Be reasonable! I will do everything in my power, but you are demanding of me something that will compromise me in the eyes of the government. I am sure that you do not want me to be demoted to the ranks for not having followed my instructions." "Well, better to be a private, General," they replied, "but be an honourable man!" What was he to do after that?[17]

The Decembrists and their wives were well aware that exile was not oblivion. Their appeals to the court of posterity were clear evidence of their awareness of the public stage upon which they lived their lives in Siberia. And their words were well chosen. Honour was perhaps the highest of all the currencies that circulated among the Russian aristocracy. For Leparsky, a nobleman from Kiev province, to be castigated for his lack of honour by women from eminent aristocratic families from the capital was a humiliation indeed. Leparsky once remarked that he would rather deal with 100 political exiles than with half a dozen of their wives.[18]

In order to alleviate their conditions, the Decembrists in Chita could draw not just on the arsenal of their wives' indignant protests, but also on their own families' often fabulous wealth. The government had restricted the sums of financial aid the Decembrists might receive: 2,000 roubles for "settlement purposes" and not more than 1,000 roubles annually. Trubetskoi and Nikolai Muravyov both received, however, between 2,000 and 3,000 roubles a year from their families, Volkonsky received 2,000, and Mikhail Fonvizin up to 1,000. The wives were exempt from any restrictions and acted as conduits not just for correspondence flowing out of Chita but also for funds flowing in. By one estimate, in the ten years the Decembrists spent as state convicts, the men received almost 355,000 roubles and their wives another 778,000. And these were only the monies officially declared and recorded. In Eastern Siberia, they were immense sums.[19]

In addition, the Decembrists enjoyed a steady stream of supplies from St. Petersburg and Moscow that could not be purchased locally. Furniture, clothing, foodstuffs, scientific equipment and painting materials were all delivered to Chita. Maria wrote to her mother requesting ivory-handled forks and spoons and asked her mother-in-law for English port, as Sergei's health was in need of a "strengthening remedy." Sergei later also required the *Fly-Fisher's Entomology* and guides to the preparation of tobacco.[20]

The rituals of marriage, birth and death bound the Decembrists together. In March 1828, a young French woman, Pauline Guèble, arrived in Chita. The representative of a French couture house, she had travelled in 1823 to Moscow, where she found life captivating and fell in love with the brother of one of her customers, Ivan Annenkov. Propriety had precluded the possibility of marriage between the wealthy aristocrat Annenkov and a French dressmaker, but the Guards officer's civil execution and exile to Siberia suddenly made the union a feasible prospect. Guèble sought and obtained permission to travel to Siberia to marry Annenkov, first from the Decembrist's mother and then from Nicholas himself.[21] Leaving Moscow in December 1827,

Guèble arrived in Chita at the end of March the following year. Within three days, she and Annenkov were married in the little village church in the presence of all the Decembrists. Leparsky gave away the bride. "It was a curious wedding, perhaps even unique," Basargin recalled. "Annenkov had his chains removed during the service, only to be clapped in them again and returned to prison when it finished. He was then treated as the other married men and allowed to visit Madame Annenkova twice a week in her lodgings."[22]

Joyful moments like the Annenkovs' wedding could quickly give way to tragedy, though. "In Chita I received news of the death of my poor Nikolai, my first child, whom I had left behind in St. Petersburg," Maria Volkonskaya noted grimly in her memoirs. The two-year-old died on 17 January 1828, but Maria, exiled across time as well as distance, learned the terrible news only in March. Nikolai was buried in the Alexander Nevsky monastery in St. Petersburg. His grave bore an epitaph penned by Pushkin:

> In radiance, in joyful repose,
> At the throne of the Eternal Creator,
> With a smile he looks upon earthly exile
> Blesses his mother and prays for his father.[23]

Maria wrote to her father of how she had "withdrawn from everyone and could not, as before, see my friends. I have such moments of despair when I do not know what will become of me." By the first anniversary of her son's death, Maria had yet to recover her spirits: "With each day, I feel the loss of my son more and more strongly," she confided in a letter to her sister. She later wrote from Chita that, "in all the world that surrounds me, there is only one place close to my heart—the patch of grass covering my child's grave."[24]

The regime in Chita gradually relaxed further. In August 1828, two years into their sentence, the men finally had their chains, long a source of discomfort and of shame, removed. Yakushkin remembered how the chains continually intruded into the thoughts of the prisoners: "No sooner would I become absorbed in reading something, sometimes a letter from one of my relatives, my thoughts carrying me far away from Chita, and suddenly the door would be flung open and some young men would burst into the room laughing . . . and clanking their chains.

When this happened, one involuntarily felt oneself to be back again in Chita." By the summer of 1828, the rules governing contact between the husbands and their wives were being altogether ignored, as Yakushkin recorded: "The husbands went to visit their wives every day and if one of them was sick, the husband would stay the night. After a while, the husbands did not live in the prison at all but continued to go out to work when it was their turn." Maria wrote to her father in May 1829: "It has now been three days since I received permission to join Sergei. The calmness that I feel since being able to take care of Sergei and to share with him the days outside of his work . . . has returned to me an emotional tranquillity and happiness that I had long ago lost."[25]

Leparsky did much to alleviate conditions for the Decembrists but remained fearful of being denounced for failing to implement the letter of the law. On one occasion, a message from Pauline Annenkova was forwarded to St. Petersburg without having first passed through Leparsky's censorship. The general anxiously summoned Annenkova to his office to enquire after the contents of the letter. "I only wrote that the General is an honest man," Annenkova replied. Putting his head in his hands, Leparsky began to pace the room, muttering, "I am lost." When some of the women became pregnant and began to write to their relatives requesting various supplies from the capitals, Leparsky became alarmed at the news and the impression it might make on the government. He summoned the expectant mothers and explained to them in great confusion, "Permit me to say, *mesdames,* that you have no right to become pregnant. Once the babies are born, that is a different matter."[26]

The Decembrists finally received the order to leave behind the wooden fort at Chita in August 1830 to trek about 670 kilometres under armed guard to the purpose-built prison in Petrovsk Zavod. The exiled officers and their wives spent a month and a half on the open road. Nothing captured the spirit of fraternity and liberation from the hierarchies and conventions of Nicolaevan Russia like the progress of their convoy in glorious summer weather and a carnivalesque atmosphere, as Basargin remembered:

> We almost died of laughter, looking at our costumes and our comical procession, usually led by Zavalishin in a round hat with an enormous brim and in some sort of black frock coat of his own invention, similar to a Quaker's caftan. Rather a small

man, he held a large stick much taller than himself in one hand
and a book he was reading in the other. Next came Yakushkin
in a little jacket *à l'enfant*, then Volkonsky in a woman's fur-
trimmed jacket. Some wore full-length sacristans' frock coats;
others Spanish coats; still others were in blouses. In a word, it
was such a funny and motley collection of clothes that, if we
had encountered some European or other who had just left
the capital, he would certainly have taken us for a group of
lunatics who had been taken out of an institution for a walk.[27]

En route, the Decembrists celebrated news of the July Revolution in
Paris with a glass of champagne and a noisy rendering of the "Mar-
seillaise." The journey "was very pleasant and good for our health.
It replenished our energies for many years to come," wrote Mikhail
Bestuzhev. Their destination was, however, a far less agreeable place
than the Chita fort. Upon arrival, Bestuzhev "entered the walls of our
Bastille" to discover his cell was "dark, damp and stuffy. A perfect
grave!" During the 1830s, Petrovsk Zavod held seventy-one Decembrists. There was enough space for each prisoner to have his own cell,
but no accommodation was provided for the Decembrists' wives, who
were supposed to live beyond the walls of the prison in privately rented
rooms.[28]

When they had first learned in early June 1830 of the impending
move to Petrovsk Zavod, Katya Trubetskaya, Aleksandra Muravyova
and Aleksandra Davydova were all nursing infants born in Chita and
Maria Volkonskaya was already expecting a second child. The women
had been dismayed to discover that in Petrovsk they would be forced
to choose between living inside the prison with their husbands or living
beyond its walls and seeing them only twice a week, as the regulations
stipulated. In desperation, Trubetskaya had written to the head of the
Third Department, Count Alexander von Benckendorff, asking him to
intercede with Nicholas:

7 June 1830, Chita Fort

General,

For almost five years now my only desire has been to share
my husband's imprisonment, which as long as it only affected
me, has been possible. But now I have a child and I am fear-

ful for him. I am not sure he will be able to survive the damp and unhealthy air of the prison. If I am forced to take him into the jail, I will, perhaps, be putting his life in danger. There, I will be deprived of all assistance, of all means of caring for him should he fall sick. Since I have no one with whom I can leave my child, I will be obliged to live outside the prison. But I am scared that my strength will give out if I am only able to see my husband every three days—I will not be able to bear it. Besides, any sudden illness that seizes either my child or me will strip me of even these brief meetings with my husband because, according to the regulations we have been shown, in Petrovsk [Zavod] the meetings are only to take place in the prison. General, I have given up everything so as to only not be parted from my husband. I live only for him. For God's sake, do not take away the possibility of being with him . . .

> In complete devotion,
> Yekaterina Trubetskaya

Davydova had written on the same day, appealing to Benckendorff "as a father and husband. I am sure that you will not remain indifferent to a poor innocent infant and his mother." When the letters reached Nicholas in August 1830, however, the emperor denied their requests.[29]

The women had with good reason become concerned. After arriving at Petrovsk Zavod, they were obliged to tramp back and forth between their rented cabins and the prison itself in temperatures that within a month were plunging to below −20°C. "I spend the whole day running from the prison to home and from home to the prison," Muravyova wrote to her father. "My heart bleeds for my child, who is left alone at home. On the other hand, I'm terribly worried about Nikita . . . It has already been two days since I have seen him, because I am seriously ill and cannot leave home." The authorities confiscated this letter, and Benckendorff himself commented:

> This letter should not be passed on, and the wives should be told that they aggrieve their relatives in vain. Their husbands have been exiled as a punishment, and everything has been done that compassion and leniency could contrive to allevi-

ate their richly deserved sentence . . . The women are already allowed to live with their husbands, but it is impossible to build premises for the children inside the prison because we do not know how many of these unfortunate victims of reckless love there will be.[30]

Yakushkin recalled that Muravyova would run back and forth several times a day between her daughter Nonushka at home and her husband in the prison. With each year, her health deteriorated. One time, in September 1832, Muravyova visited the prison during the day dressed very lightly, but in the evening when she returned home, she felt she had caught a cold, and that night she suffered terribly from chest pains. A doctor was called and confirmed that she had developed pneumonia. Yakushkin later wrote: "Over the next two months, the sick woman was fading. No treatments were able to restore her diminishing strength. Two days before she died, she expressed a wish to see me. I sat with her for half an hour at her bedside. She was barely able to speak, but from her words it was clear that she had readied herself to part for ever from those close to her heart." Concerned by public disquiet at the twenty-eight-year-old Muravyova's untimely death, two months later the authorities in St. Petersburg issued a new directive allowing the husbands to visit their wives outside of the prison.[31]

The Decembrists' wives did not merely share their husbands' fate; they transformed it. The desire of the Decembrists and their wives to raise families necessarily involved a struggle with the authorities. Volkonskaya, Trubetskaya, Muravyova and the others might have signed away their legal rights when they crossed the frontier of the Nerchinsk Mining Region, but the state could not strip them of their moral rights. Nicholas had sought to banish the Decembrists into obscurity, where they could be punished at will, far from the gaze of the Russian aristocracy. Through their correspondence with friends and family, however, the women ensured that news of the Decembrists would continue to circulate in Russian towns and cities. The wives' correspondence from Nerchinsk meant that the tsar found himself very publicly playing the part of a petty and vindictive tyrant, gratuitously separating children from their parents and inflicting suffering on women who were not only innocent but also embodied the very highest virtues of spousal devotion and self-sacrifice.[32]

Educated Russians viewed the private sacrifices of the Decembrists' wives as public acts of courage and patriotism, repeatedly returning to the image of these virtuous and selfless women. In so doing, they effectively enshrined them as secular saints and apostles of the reformist movements in the empire. The socialist thinker Alexander Herzen wrote from exile in London in 1866, "The wives of those exiled to penal labour were stripped of all their civil rights, they left behind their wealth, their rank and they set off for a life of captivity in the terrible climate of Eastern Siberia under the terrible oppression of the police there."[33] In 1873, Nikolai Nekrasov, a poet with radical sympathies and a keen commercial nose for the literary tastes of the Russian reading public, immortalized the lives of Maria Volkonskaya and Katya Trubetskaya in a narrative poem called "Russian Women." The last scene of the poem embellished Maria's first encounter with her husband in Blagodatsk:

> I rushed towards him, my soul as I went
> Was stirred by the most sacred feeling.
> And now, only now in this underground Hell
> Where deafening clamour persisted,
> And seeing his chains did I visage full well
> The torments in which he existed,
> His strength and his patience, enduring these pains
> In which his destroyers had placed him,
> I fell on my knees to him. Lifting his chains
> I kissed them, before I embraced him.[34]

Nekrasov's Trubetskaya is radicalized by her journey through the "kingdom of paupers and slaves" to join her husband in Nerchinsk. She expresses "contempt for the hangmen, the knowledge of our rightness will sustain us."[35] In the decades that followed the death of Nicholas, poets, journalists and historians fashioned an image of the women as democratic and patriotic heroines who believed that, by joining their husbands in Siberia, they would keep their revolutionary ideals alive in exile. Languishing in the cells of the Shlisselburg prison in St. Petersburg at the dawn of the twentieth century, the radical Vera Figner found inspiration in the example of the Decembrist wives: "Do we not find in these women something exceptional that also struck and inspired their

contemporaries? Do we not in all sincerity find in them . . . torchbear-
ers who illuminated the future of our revolutionary movement?"[36]

While the Decembrists' families embodied in exile a new ideal of self-
sacrifice, friendship and deep emotion, the men found their relations
with kin in Russia increasingly strained. Many felt their family members
were distancing themselves, writing only very infrequently and betray-
ing a lack of enthusiasm for lobbying the government on their behalf.
Obolensky wrote from Petrovsk Zavod in 1830, "I have often thought
how odd it is that people confuse a man's political behaviour with
his civic and family relations . . . Let actions within a family be judged
by the family and political actions by the political authorities; why
add familial punishments to political ones?" It is strange, he regretted,
"that penal labour . . . could destroy those feelings that should have
lasted until the end of our lives."[37] Maria's family never forgave Sergei Volkonsky for his involvement in the doomed Decembrist Revolt
and so for dragging their daughter off to Siberia to live as the wife of
a disgraced "state criminal." Maria's mother, Sofia Rayevskaya, was
uncompromising in her accusation that Maria's "adored husband"
was to blame for everything: "Only a little virtue would have been
needed in order not to marry when the man was party to that damned
conspiracy!" Maria also sensed her father's disapproval, pleading with
him, "How can I be happy, even for a moment, when the blessings you
give me in all your letters are not extended to Sergei?" Rancour erupted
over family finances as well. With some justification, the Rayevskys
complained that the Volkonskys were mean-spirited in their financial
support for Sergei and Maria, leaving the burden to fall on them. It was
true that the Volkonskys almost never sent money. Sergei's own sister,
Sofia, had seized his part of the family estate for herself. "If I had the
misfortune to have my son in Siberia and my unfortunate and blameless daughter-in-law had followed him there," Maria's mother wrote,
"I would have sold my last dress in order to send her money." Sergei
himself became embittered that his family had cheated him out of his
inheritance and that it had made no effort to have his children officially acknowledged as heirs to the Volkonsky estates. Only once did
they petition the emperor to have Sergei transferred to the ranks of the
Imperial Army in the Caucasus. Sergei's relations with his sister broke

down entirely. She was, he wrote at the end of his exile, like "a bone stuck in my gullet." In 1848, he wrote to fellow Decembrist Ivan Push-chin: "I don't much care for aristocratic family relations; our prison family is more honest and trustworthy." Volkonsky was not alone in his reference to the prison family. Obolensky and Nikolai Basargin also spoke of the Decembrists as a family characterized by bonds of mutual assistance, affection and solidarity.[38]

First in Chita and later in Petrovsk Zavod, the Decembrists remained faithful to their values of egalitarianism, solidarity and serving the interests of the common people. And the state paradoxically made such endeavours possible. Its failure to restrict effectively the wealth to which the Decembrists had access and its reluctance to force them to engage seriously in potentially exhausting labour left highly educated and energetic young men to their own devices. Most important of all, fearful of the Decembrists' seditious influence over the wider exile population, the regime had concentrated them together. For Mikhail Bestuzhev, "the prison gave us a political existence beyond the frontiers of political death."[39] Basargin agreed:

> If the government had dispersed us around different smelter-ies, and stripped us of the company of our comrades and of the opportunity of supporting each other; if it had mixed us together with common penal-labourers, and had subordinated us to the local officials and the general labour regulations, the majority of us might easily have been morally destroyed by their circumstances . . . We might easily have lost our sense of dignity and have perished irretrievably, dragging out the most pitiful, undignified existence . . . Acting as it did, the government gave us the means not only to maintain our moral dignity but also even to raise it still higher.[40]

The social distinctions among the Decembrists quickly evaporated in captivity, replaced by egalitarian bonds of comradeship derived from their common experiences. Zavalishin remembered how virtues of generosity and mutual support shaped the Decembrists' relations with each other "in a revival of the Christian commune." Not all Decembrists enjoyed great personal wealth. Those who received no monies from their families were entitled to a derisory annual state subsidy of

114 roubles, the annual salary of a private in the army. But, in order to ensure that none fell into real hardship, the Decembrists established a prisoners' *artel,* or association, into which each paid sums commensurate with his income. Basargin was elected treasurer and kept accounts, ensuring that each man, irrespective of his means, received no less than 500 roubles annually.[41] Goods sent from St. Petersburg were placed on a common table (there was, after all, only a common table, as Zavalishin himself wryly observed) and were shared. The institution of the *artel,* described in ironic terms by Pyotr Svistunov in a letter from Petrovsk Zavod in September 1831, embodied this general enthusiasm for solidarity and equality:

> It really is our small Lilliputian "state." Each year by means of
> a majority in a secret ballot, we elect a ruler and a chancellor,
> who will enact the will of the *artel* and whose privileges consist
> in the fact that the work that should fall on them is carried
> out by the other members. The public opinion of the *artel* is
> its highest court and decides all and any conflicts. We have a
> codex of rules, our own budget, our own special commissions,
> electors and deputies. In a word, we are playing at a repub-
> lic in the most innocent way, as if consoling ourselves in our
> misfortune. It is a parody of our dreams, which could provide
> material for research into the deficiencies of the human mind.[42]

Despondent and lonely, Svistunov could not possibly have discerned in 1831 the influence the Decembrist "republic" would come to wield over the popular imagination in the decades that followed. If their republicanism had failed as a political project in St. Petersburg, enacted in their small community in Nerchinsk it became a clarion call to a later generation of opponents of the autocracy.

Across virtually the whole of the nineteenth century, the Decembrists were among the least isolated of Siberia's exiles. Books, journals and newspapers flooded from Russia, first into Chita and then into Petrovsk Zavod, keeping the Decembrists abreast of events in the empire and Europe, albeit with a delay of two or three months. "It was quite impossible," Rozen wrote in his memoirs, "for any one of us to read all the journals and newspapers we received from one postal delivery to the next. For that reason, they were distributed among many readers who then reported orally on the most important events and discoveries." They followed the suppression of the November Insurrection in the Polish kingdom in 1830–31 with keen interest and sympathized with the plight of the Polish insurgents who would in fact soon be joining them in Eastern Siberia. The authorities attempted to operate a primitive kind of censorship over the stream of publications—Russian, French, German and English—being sent to Nerchinsk, but with little success. Confounded by the literary appetites of the polyglot Zavalishin, Leparsky struggled to assess the seditious content of books written in Arabic and Hebrew.[43]

Even prohibited books and newspapers often reached the Decembrists, passing through the tsar's own private chancellery, to which the Nerchinsk region was subordinate. "We used the following trick," Zavalishin explained. "The contents page would be cut out of the book and in its place would be glued the contents of another common book, usually a scholarly 'treatise on archaeology, on botany' and so on." As a result, the exiled revolutionaries immersed themselves in Gibbon, Montesquieu, Franklin and Rousseau, to name but a few. Nikolai Muravyov, Trubetskoi and Volkonsky had their libraries sent from St. Petersburg. Mikhail Lunin had a "huge library of religious volumes, including priceless original editions of all the Greek and Latin fathers of the Church," while Zavalishin "had a library in fifteen different languages." Within a few years, the Decembrists' collection numbered more than 100,000 volumes (Zavalishin was probably guilty of exaggeration when he estimated that it contained almost half a million).[44]

Drawn from the very highest echelons of the Russian elite, many of the Decembrists had received a classical education. Several began to give lectures to their comrades. Nikolai Muravyov had an excellent collection of maps that he used to illustrate lessons on military strategy; Nikolai Bestuzhev gave talks on military history and seamanship. A qualified physician, Ferdinand Volf taught anatomy and physics, while Obolensky lectured on literature and Pavel Bobrishchev-Pushkin on mathematics. Between them, the men were fluent in dozens of languages that they set about teaching each other. Obolensky and Lunin learned Greek; Svistunov took up Latin, English and German and the dazzling linguistic talent Zavalishin mastered Latin, German, Italian, modern Greek and Polish. Reading and writing were one thing; accurate pronunciation quite another. Lunin, who was proficient in English, would entreat his pupils, "Gentlemen, read and write English

as much as you like, only please do not attempt to speak it!" Another
exiled officer, Nikolai Belyayev, remembered how this period of the
Decembrists' exile "was a wonderful moral, intellectual, religious and
philosophical school."[45] First Chita and, later, Petrovsk Zavod became
the most vibrant cultural centres anywhere in the tsarist empire east of
the Urals. Surveying the community of Decembrists in 1834, the writer
and diplomat Semyon Cherepanov recorded in his journal, "Petrovsk
Zavod comprises a sort of academy or university with 120 academics
or professors."[46]

The men also turned their attentions to practical matters. Nikolai
Lorer recorded how "craftsmen of all kinds appeared among us: locksmiths, cabinet-makers whose work really could rival that of craftsmen in St. Petersburg." The outstanding polymath of the academy was
Nikolai Bestuzhev. He made clocks, shoes, toys, cradles and coffins. As
a favour to Maria Volkonskaya, he learned to repair and tune the piano
she had shipped from St. Petersburg. He executed a series of impressive
portraits of the Decembrists and their wives in addition to landscapes
of Chita, Petrovsk Zavod and their environs. Volkonsky and Aleksandr
Poggio, meanwhile, proved themselves ingenious and skilled horticul-
turalists and directed their energies towards the cultivation of a garden
in the grounds of the Chita fort. "Growing produce for 100 people
throughout the winter is no mean task," Obolensky wrote with pride.
"In the autumn we harvest vegetables from the rows, pickle cabbages,
beetroot, store the potatoes, turnips, carrots." Volkonsky ordered
seeds delivered from St. Petersburg and turned Maria's room into an
improvised botanical garden. By constructing greenhouses, Poggio succeeded in growing asparagus, melons and cauliflowers.[47]

The frenetic activity in which Nikolai Bestuzhev and the other
Decembrists immersed themselves never, however, quelled a deep sense
of despair at the failure of the revolt and at their banishment to Siberia: "I long for life, but I am lying in a grave. I got my calculations
all wrong. I did everything to deserve to be shot and never expected
to emerge with my life, and now I do not know what to do with it,"
Bestuzhev wrote from Petrovsk Zavod to a comrade in 1838. "If I must
live, then I have to act! Inactivity is worse than purgatory and so I saw,
plane, dig, and paint, but time still trickles in cold little drops onto my
hot and feverish head, and I immediately feel pangs in my poor, broken
heart."[48]

The Decembrists' ability to forge a meaningful community along democratic principles and their pursuit of agricultural and educational activities among the native population of Siberia offered inspiring examples for others to follow. Looking back on the Decembrists' decades of exile, Zavalishin saw something genuinely new in their relations with the local population in Siberia: "We were the first people to appear in Siberia from the higher orders who were accessible to all. We behaved in accordance with an ethos that was completely at odds with what the inhabitants had grown accustomed to see in their social superiors and their officials. They encountered sympathy and common endeavour rather than coercion and extortion."[49] In the tsarist empire of Nicholas, such values—an implicit rejection of the hierarchies that governed all relations between the various social classes—carried a radical charge.

Contrary to the mythologies developing around them, the Decembrists were no saints. In their memoirs, they were generally loath to speak ill of their comrades, but Zavalishin did not flinch from describing the less savoury aspects of their life in Petrovsk Zavod. He recounted how the sense of community started to weaken as, after a few years, the wealthier Decembrists began to construct their own private homes around the prison: "They assured us that it was to alleviate the overcrowding, but in fact that was not the reason . . . It destroyed the equality and liberated some individuals from the control of social supervision, and it promoted not only privileges for the rich but also servility among the emerging proletariat." The Volkonsky and Trubetskoi households, for example, each came to number around twenty-five servants, including a midwife and a bookkeeper. The Muravyovs even had their own governor. In the prison there were another forty servants: bodyguards, cooks, bakers, gardeners, swine-herders. As a consequence, some began to "take the sides of more privileged individuals, in order to gain private advantage from them, and so patrons, partisans and private factions emerged." Cards and alcohol, "previously unthinkable, began to appear in the prison and began to undermine our moral standing." Many turned to prostitutes and the purchase of sexual favours from the daughters of peasant families in the surrounding area. Ivan Sukhinov's erstwhile companion from Zerentui, Aleksandr Mozalevsky, was discovered by Leparsky to have "embarked upon sordid relations and the most indecent acts." Svistunov turned to pimping and prostitution. He received large sums of money from his brother Aleksei but turned over only very little to the *artel*, "spending what remained on orgies and on the seduction and purchase of innocent young girls from dishonest parents in the villages." Aleksandr Kuchevsky so mistreated his young bride that he had to pay for her to be tracked down after she fled.[50]

After Nicholas commuted their sentences to shorter terms of penal labour—an instance of autocratic mercy that did little to challenge the image of a punitive martinet—the Decembrists began in 1835 to be released from penal labour to settlement. Some, like Nikolai Bestuzhev's younger brother Aleksandr, obtained permission to travel to the Southern Caucasus to join the Imperial Army in its colonial wars in the region. Most, though, were assigned to small towns and villages across Siberia. Unlike the senior administrators and governors of Siberia, who served terms in what they saw as a kind of temporary colonial posting, the Decembrists, by now aware that Nicholas had no intention of ever granting them an amnesty, made Siberia their home. They continued their agricultural, ethnographic and educational efforts among the native population. Basargin and Rozen taught the Buryats how to cultivate buckwheat, rye, barley and hemp. Bestuzhev began to import scythes from China to improve the harvesting and storage of fodder for their cattle. In Chita, Poggio showed the Buryats how to use hotbeds to begin planting early, and demonstrated that it was possible to grow tobacco, asparagus, cucumbers and watermelons.[51]

Zavalishin founded a school for the children of the local peasants and Buryats in Chita; Nikolai and Aleksandr Bestuzhev and Obolensky, another in Nerchinsk; Yakushkin, a third in Yalutorovsk in Western Siberia. Progressive British educational theories underpinned the instruction in all three. Yakushkin even went on to found a school for girls, which, within four years, had no fewer than fifty pupils. The Decembrists also numbered some trained doctors, and they helped to organize and promote basic medical services among the native Tungus and Buryats. The most famous among them was Ferdinand Volf, who, in 1836, was granted permission to practise medicine, and became a physician at the newly opened Tobolsk Central Penal Labour Prison in 1852.[52]

In receipt of generous financial assistance from their families, the

Volkonskys were exiled to settlement in the village of Urik just outside Irkutsk. There they established a successful farm and raised a family before enjoying reintegration into the polite society of officials and wealthy merchants in the town. In Irkutsk, Maria Volkonskaya established a foundling hospital and several schools. She also hosted soirées and concerts in the Volkonskys' large and handsomely furnished house in the centre of the city (today a museum dedicated to the Decembrists). The Volkonsky home became a cultural institution in the life of Irkutsk, transmitting the tastes and manners of elite metropolitan Russia to provincial Siberian society. Even today, the impressive municipal architecture of Irkutsk, with its opera house, museums and art galleries, owes something to the cultural influence of the Decembrists.[53]

Basargin undertook a general survey of Siberia's economic, social and administrative problems, Matvei Muravyov-Apostol conducted a statistical analysis of the Yalutorovsk region. The brothers Pyotr and Andrei Borisov compiled and catalogued an extensive collection of insects, and Nikolai Bestuzhev produced detailed ethnographic studies, including the compilation of a Buryat–Russian dictionary. Some Decembrists also entered state service in Siberia, finding employment as statisticians and agronomists in an administration that was desperately short of competent officials. While himself still a "state criminal," Aleksandr Briggen rose to the position of chairman of the district court in the district of Kurgan, in Western Siberia. Zavalishin, an acknowledged expert on Russia's Far East even before his arrest, became one of the most important advisers to the Eastern Siberian authorities and made an influential study of the Amur region.[54]

With these various projects to benefit the local population, the Decembrists effectively set down the roots of a European intelligentsia in Siberia. Decembrists such as Basargin themselves took great pride in the "moral and educational benefits" and "several new and useful ideas" they had introduced to the inhabitants of the regions in which they settled.[55] It was in this narrow sense that the government's use of exile did benefit the overall development of the continent. Over the course of the nineteenth century, educated exiles, drawn from the ranks of the nobility and the intelligentsia, made a powerful and lasting contribution to the development of civil society in Siberia. They did so not because they were criminals who found redemption and reform beyond the Urals but because in exile they continued to pursue the very same republican ideals of patriotic service to their country that had brought them into conflict with the autocracy in the first place. A later generation of political exiles in the 1860s and 70s would follow in the footsteps of the Decembrists. Denied the opportunity of pursuing their democratic goals at home, some political exiles would find an outlet for their reforming energies and civic activism in Siberia.

The government remained, however, deeply suspicious of the Decembrists' political influence in Siberia. After their release to settlement, the exiles were officially not permitted to reside in the same town in groups of more than three (although the ruling was widely flouted by the local authorities); they remained under police supervision, and were prohibited from travelling beyond their assigned districts without express permission. As a result, the men now endured a far more isolated existence than they had in Chita and Petrovsk Zavod, as Nikolai Bestuzhev remarked in a letter to Obolensky in 1840: "I have more freedom now—much more than in prison—so now at least a physical existence is possible. But as far as the life of the mind is concerned—adieu!" Bestuzhev found his desire for social engagement and practical work frustrated by the constraints under which he was forced to live in the tiny village of Selenginsk in Transbaikal: "Having been released to settlement and possessing reserves of energy, I wanted to be a useful member of society, at least to be active and not a layabout; but the restrictions imposed on us from every side mean that, even with the best will in the world, we are left with nothing to do."[56]

The official restrictions on their movements and activities also deprived most Decembrists of the opportunity to support themselves. Zavalishin wrote to Benckendorff from Chita in 1842 explaining that his lack of freedom of movement prevented him from earning a living either from agriculture or from any other kind of trade, and he begged to be allowed to publish his books. With the exception of the Baltic German Andrei Rozen, who did prove to be a competent and successful farmer, most of the Decembrists at settlement either were subsidized by their families in European Russia or struggled to earn a living. "So many of our friends are enduring real poverty," Volkonsky wrote to his comrade Aleksandr Pushchin in 1841: "The Muravyovs and Trubetskois are well off and we have no debts, but there are others who haven't got a kopeck . . . We help as much as we can."[57]

Poverty and isolation eventually took their toll on many Decembrists. When Mikhail Bestuzhev commented in Chita that "if we had been dispersed around the various mines, . . . we would probably have perished like Sukhinov, or would have succumbed morally under the yoke of need and privation," he unwittingly anticipated the fate of several of his comrades after their release to settlement. The 33-year-old officer Konstantin Igelstrom wrote in despair on the eve of his release to settlement in 1832, "Now I am told to till the soil. I have spent ten years in the military academy, ten years in the army and now seven in various prisons. So the question is where was I supposed to have learned agriculture?" Aleksandr Baryatinsky died of syphilis in a filthy shack in Tobolsk in 1844; the Borisov brothers eked out a living selling sketches of the insects they studied in Eastern Siberia. Pyotr died on 30 September 1854 and Andrei, who had long struggled with mental illness, hanged himself a few days later.[58]

Mikhail Lunin had always predicted that only three courses were open to the Decembrists: "Some will marry, some will enter a monastery, and the rest will drink themselves to death." He himself, however, defied his own predictions. One of the most remarkable Decembrists, Lunin understood perhaps better than any that, in retrospect, the power of the Decembrist Revolt lay not in its armed challenge to the autocracy in St. Petersburg but in its crafting of an inspiring example of patriotism and republican virtue. Unlike his comrades, who conducted themselves "quietly and submissively" in their dealings with the authorities, Lunin remained defiant and fearless.[59]

A devout Catholic, Lunin had always remained somewhat aloof from the other Decembrists in Chita and Petrovsk Zavod. After his release to settlement at the end of 1835, he joined the Volkonskys and Muravyovs in the village of Urik. There he began to write letters to his sister, Yekaterina Uvarova, filling them with acerbic commentaries on his exile in Siberia and on the corruption and injustices of the tsarist system. Before long, this reckless correspondence, which Lunin knew would pass through the Third Department, began to draw the ire of the government.[60]

From his isolated little village in Eastern Siberia, Lunin understood that the state's punishment of the Decembrists had only elevated them in the eyes of the Russian educated public. "No one has the power," he wrote to his sister in 1837, "to disgrace people who have not deserved it. I have stood before the gallows and have worn fetters. But do you really think me disgraced? My political opponents do not think so. They had to use brute force because they had no other means to refute the progressive ideas I expressed." A year later, Lunin wrote: "In prison and in exile my name has been changed several times and has, with each change, grown longer. In official documents I am now called 'state criminal, exiled to settlement' so there is now an entire phrase attached to my name. In England they would say: 'Lunin, member of the opposition.'" He was convinced that "the ideas for which I have been sentenced to political death will in a few years be a necessary condition for civic life." Benckendorff's assistant wrote to his master that these letters were "evidence of the inveterate nature of Lunin's false ideas."[61]

Benckendorff forbade Lunin from corresponding for a year, but when the Decembrist was finally allowed to take up his quill once again in 1839, he showed no signs of having been intimidated. On the contrary, Lunin threw caution to the wind. In letters that he knew must incur the wrath of St. Petersburg, he scorned the "slavery that expresses itself in our norms, customs and institutions," writing that "we do not fear death on the battlefield, but do not dare to speak up in the State Council for justice and humanity." He criticized serfdom and took aim at the stifling censorship that reigned in Russia: "In our time it is virtually impossible to say 'hello' without the word containing some kind of political meaning." He wrote that the last wish of the Athenian general Themistocles, exiled to Argos, "was that his earthly remains be brought to his fatherland and buried in his native soil; my last wish is that my thoughts . . . are taken from the desert of Siberia to be spread and developed in the minds of my fellow countrymen." He asked his sister to "circulate copies of my letters. Their goal is to shake people out of their apathy."[62]

Lunin's fate was sealed by the discovery of some political essays that excoriated Russia's political and social order. In one of many rhetorically powerful passages, Lunin offered a searing indictment of autocracy since the suppression of the Decembrist Revolt:

> If from the depths of Siberia's wastelands our exiles could raise their voices, they would first say to the leaders of the ruling party: "What have you done for the people over the last fifteen years? . . . You committed yourself to listening to and developing all the legally expressed opinions about improving the state

of the country but have made that impossible by imposing new restraints on the freedom of the press, by impeding relations with Europe and by paralysing the operation of civilised principles with the help of a reactionary system. We advocated the cult of the law; you advocated the cult of personality, storing the clothes of sovereigns in churches as if they were a new kind of relic. You have taken it upon yourself to cleanse Russia of the contagion of liberal ideas and have plunged her into an abyss of dissolution, into the vices of spying and the darkness of ignorance. With the hand of the executioner, you have extinguished the minds that illuminated the social movement and directed its development. What have you put in their place? We in turn will summon you before the court of our contemporaries and of posterity: answer for yourselves![63]

Benckendorff gave the order in February 1841 to arrest Lunin "and to send him immediately to the Akatui mine but not to put him to work there, rather to subject him to the strictest prison regime, separate from all the other criminals, in order that he have no contact, either personal or written, with anyone." A month later, Lunin was taken into custody on his farm in Urik and sent to what his sister later called "an exile within exile." His destination concealed from friends and family, he reached Akatui in April.[64]

Even by the bleak standards of Nerchinsk, the Akatui mine was a desolate place. Leparsky had considered it as a possible location for a prison for the Decembrists but had found the great "pit" in which it stood too "terrible and unhealthy." The air was said to be so heavy with fumes from the smelteries that no bird could live within a radius of 300 kilometres of the mine. Exiles believed Akatui to be a place where prisoners were buried alive; no one ever returned from there.[65]

It became all but impossible for Lunin to smuggle letters out from the prison (through Polish prisoners whom he encountered there), but he did manage to send word to Volkonsky in January 1842:

> The architect of the Akatui prison inherited, without a doubt, Dante's imagination. My former cells were boudoirs compared to my current lodgings. They do not let me out of their sight; the guards are at the doors and the windows—everywhere. My

comrades in captivity are a group of 50 murderers, assassins, brigands and forgers. We get on, by the way, extremely well. These good people have taken to me. They give me their little treasures for safekeeping and confide in me their little secrets, which belong, of course, in the pages of blood-soaked adventure stories.[66]

Put on a starvation diet by the authorities, Lunin realized that he was "condemned to a slow death in the prison rather than to a swift one on the scaffold." In 1843, Lunin wrote to Maria Volkonskaya: "I am encased in darkness, deprived of air, space and food." Moisture trickled down the walls of his cell and the air was so damp that his books quickly became covered in mould. His final letter to the Volkonskys was written sometime after October 1844. What became of him over the following year is unknown, but he drew his final breath in his dark cell on 3 December 1845. His body was discovered the following day, surrounded by his priceless but decaying Greek and Latin editions of Plato, Homer, Herodotus, Tacitus, Cicero and Augustine.[67]

Stories matter in politics and, amid the stifling cultural orthodoxies of Nicholas's reign, they mattered more than ever. The Decembrists had been banished to Siberia as traitors, broken in spirit, their rebellion against the autocracy distinguished only by its dilettantish incompetence. In Siberia they found, however, not political oblivion but political rebirth. Of course, the rebels were never the morally pristine and implacable revolutionary martyrs painted by their supporters. But their lives in exile did furnish contemporaries with the ingredients of an inspiring story of republican ideals and patriotic virtues. In Chita and in Petrovsk Zavod, the Decembrists' ongoing commitment to liberty, equality and fraternity was an implicit repudiation of tsarism's oppressive social hierarchies. Their civic activism in Siberia—their horticulture, their teaching, their ethnography—expressed a passionate commitment to the common good that flew in the face of the social quietism demanded by the crown. In short, they carved out an existence for themselves that remained faithful to the ideals of 14 December 1825.

The march of time, politics and technology during their exile eventually brought the Decembrists' lives in Siberia much closer to the world of the Russian capitals. Following the death in 1842 of his comrade Nikolai Muravyov, Volkonsky mused: "It is not sad to die in Siberia, but it is a pity that there is not one single grave for the bones of all of us disgraced individuals. This does not occur to me out of pride or personal vanity. Separated, we are, like all people, specks of dust. But clustered together, our bones would, with a bit of good fortune, be a monument to the great cause of our motherland and a worthy funeral feast for future generations." But Volkonsky was a practical man and, from his farmstead in Urik, he could have no inkling of the torrent of publications that would pour out of Siberia and into the public realm in the reigns of Nicholas's successors. These memoirs, letters and published records did indeed fashion a towering literary monument to the Decembrists' exile in Siberia and the ideals that had taken them there. Far from being lost to posterity, the Decembrists became icons for both reformers and revolutionaries in the second half of the nineteenth century. One of the most enduring and talismanic poems for a later generation of the autocracy's enemies was written by the Decembrist poet Aleksandr Odoyevsky, a man who, Mikhail Bestuzhev wrote, "poured his entire life in captivity into poetic sounds."[68] In the Chita fort at the end of 1827, Odoyevsky penned a poetical reply to Pushkin's "Message to Siberia," the poem Maria Volkonskaya had taken with her when she left Moscow in December 1826:

> The sound of your prophetic harp,
> Impassioned, came to us at last.
> Swiftly our hands reached for the sword,
> But found that shackles held them fast.

> Yet, singer, fret not: we are proud
> Of these chains as of our fate.
> Locked in our prison cells, we scoff
> At the rulers of the State.

> Our grievous toil will not be lost,
> The spark will quicken into flame;
> Our people, blindfolded no more,
> A new allegiance will proclaim.

> Beating our shackles into swords,
> Liberty's torch we will relight,
> And she will overwhelm the Tsars,
> While nations waken in the night.[69]

Three years later, on 29 November 1830, in part inspired by the example of the Decembrists, it was to be the Polish, not the Russian nation, that would "waken in the night." The rebellion was to prove the single most serious internal challenge to Russian imperial might in the long reign of Nicholas.

Of the 121 Decembrist officers sent into exile, only a few dozen outlived their nemesis. After Nicholas's death on 18 February 1855, his successor, Alexander II, moved swiftly to break with much of his father's legacy of stagnation and repression. Alexander's coronation manifesto, issued on 26 August 1856, made provisions for the amnesty of the surviving Decembrists. A total of twenty-one, including Sergei Trubetskoi, Yevgeny Obolensky and Sergei Volkonsky, together with Maria, made the return journey to European Russia. At the dawn of a new reign, amid mounting optimism among the progressive members of the Russian nobility and intelligentsia, the sudden appearance of these men and women seemed to promise that, at long last, the ideals that had led them to Siberia might now be on the verge of being implemented by the state. In Moscow's salons, the figures of these elderly exiles, now bent with age, were an inspiration to a younger generation of Russian students and intellectuals who revered Volkonsky as a "sort of Christ who had emerged from the Russian wilderness." Travelling in Europe in 1861, the Volkonskys met the young Leo Tolstoy in Florence. Tolstoy was enchanted by the "remarkable old man," Volkonsky, and began planning a novel about the Decembrists that would eventually evolve into his masterpiece *War and Peace* (1869).[70]

After he met Volkonsky in Paris in the summer of 1861, the long-time dissident writer Herzen hailed the Decembrists as the progenitors of a long line of revolutionaries who would continue the struggle against the autocracy: "The ghosts of these venerable old custodians will rise from the earth and, summoning their grandsons over the graves of their sons, they will show them the way."[71] In the 1860s, the returning exiles became a living connection between the democratic and patriotic ideals of the Decembrists and a new generation of radicals who emerged to challenge the autocracy: the Populists.

Maria Volkonskaya died in 1863 and Sergei two years later. In the final months of his life, Sergei sat down to write his memoirs. He was unapologetic about his part in the rebellion and everything that had flowed from it: "The path I chose took me to the Supreme Court, to Siberia, to penal labour and into a thirty-year-long exile from my homeland, and yet, I do not renounce a single one of my words."[72]

6

Sybiracy

Long after night fell on the sleepy garrison town of Uralsk in southern Russia on 21 November 1839, a young man stepped from one of the wooden cabins with a knapsack on his back. He made his way purposefully through the searing frost and along barren streets to the edge of town. Plunging into open fields, he tramped through knee-deep snow to the banks of the Ural River, some 3 kilometres away. The meandering waters were sealed by a layer of ice thick enough to support the weight of a man. With a cautious tread, the figure searched the river for a point where the ice was thinner and weaker. He finally discovered an ice hole used by some nearby Cossack cabins to draw water from the river. By stamping on the thin film of ice that had formed that evening, he was able to reopen the hole. Casting furtive glances into the inscrutable darkness, he snatched a bundle of clothes from his knapsack and scattered them on the ice around the hole. His task complete, he regained the riverbank and fled. He ran for the first 500 metres, panting heavily in the frosty air as he hurried towards the town. He stole along the deserted streets, avoiding the occasional pool of light falling from the cottage windows he passed. Taking every care not to be seen or heard, he reached his cabin. He climbed the steps and opened the door, and was greeted on the threshold by a dark-haired young woman, her eyes flashing with alarm. She flung her arms around his neck, they exchanged some flustered words of reassurance and endearment, and he hurried inside. Moments later, the young man stepped into a large wardrobe in the bedroom, pulled aside a false wall and clambered through. Drawing the partition back into place, he settled down to wait. A mere half an hour passed before the first knock at the door ruptured the silence. The young man was an exiled Polish revolutionary named Wincenty Migurski; the woman was his wife, Albina. Together, they had just staged his death.[1]

Wincenty Migurski was born in 1805 into a modest landowning family of the Polish nobility, or *szlachta,* in Sandomierz, in today's south-eastern Poland. The region's turbulent fortunes in the late eighteenth and early nineteenth centuries were part of Poland's bitter history. In 1772, the Polish-Lithuanian Commonwealth, comprising the Kingdom of Poland and the Grand Duchy of Lithuania, was partitioned by the neighbouring powers of Russia, Austria and Prussia. Sandomierz passed to Austria. Further partitions in 1792 and 1795 saw what remained of Poland annexed by the three empires. Desperate to regain their independence, the Poles turned to Napoleon in 1806, only to see their territory further dismembered in the wake of his defeat. At the Treaty of Vienna in 1815, the European powers established Congress Poland and placed it under the protection of Tsar Alexander I on condition that he safeguard Poland's constitutional liberties. Migurski grew up amid the Romanticism and the ardent republicanism of young Polish noblemen who were inspired by the ideals of the French Revolution and by their fathers' experience of fighting alongside the *Grande armée.* Thousands of Poles captured during Napoleon's chaotic retreat from Moscow in 1812 had been exiled to penal battalions in Siberia and the Caucasus, where they were held until Napoleon's defeat in the west.[2]

In the 1820s, the Polish nobility grew increasingly restive under rule from St. Petersburg. Alexander had never really accepted Polish autonomy, and Nicholas I's repressive regime alienated many. Throughout the 1820s, St. Petersburg steadily undermined many of the terms of the Treaty of Vienna—freedoms of the press were withdrawn, taxes were imposed without the consent of the Polish parliament and liberal opponents of tsarist rule found themselves persecuted. Such policies only laid bare the tensions between Polish constitutionalism and nationalism, on the one hand, and Russian autocracy and imperialism, on the other.

In 1823, the authorities uncovered a secret society of Polish students, the Philomaths, at the University of Wilno (Vilnius). The leaders of the group, which included the great Polish Romantic poet Adam Mickiewicz, were steeped in a European Romanticism and political nationalism. They moved from the study of patriotic Polish and Lithuanian literary works to a more active role in promoting Poland's independence from the Russian Empire. Betrayed by one of their number, the group was exposed. After a trial lasting several months in 1824,

104 students were convicted of subversive activities and twenty of them were imprisoned or exiled to Siberia. In the same year, the director of the Wilno high school investigated a small number of students who had scrawled patriotic slogans on the classroom blackboard. Their history teacher had made no efforts to remove them and had delivered his lecture standing before them. Other unknown persons daubed anti-Russian graffiti on the walls of the Dominican monastery in Wilno. Such instances of anti-Russian feeling and pro-Polish sentiment even drew the attention of the heir to the Russian throne and governor of Congress Poland, Grand Duke Konstantin.[3]

Konstantin was unpopular in many quarters because of his often arbitrary rule and casual brutality in the barracks and on the parade ground. Strained relations between the Polish nobility and the Russian autocracy finally snapped when St. Petersburg insisted that the Polish army assist in the suppression of the July Revolution in Paris in 1830. Inspired by events in France and by the almost simultaneous rebellion in Brussels that would see Belgium win independence from a United Netherlands and establish a constitutional order, a young republican named Piotr Wysocki instigated a revolt of young Polish officers in Warsaw. On the night of 29 November 1830, the rebels seized arms from their garrison and attacked the Belweder Palace, the seat of the grand duke, in a bid to kill Konstantin. The governor managed to escape, but Wysocki's forces succeeded in capturing the city's arsenal and forced the withdrawal of Russian forces from the Polish capital.[4]

The Polish rebels shared the republican ideas of the Decembrists; theirs was a political and cultural nationalism that saw itself working in concert with the progressive nations of Europe, especially France and Italy. They sought to replace the autocratic "Holy Alliance of Monarchs" born of the Congress of Vienna in 1815 with a "Holy Alliance of Peoples." Wysocki and his comrades rebelled under the slogan "For our freedom, and yours!"—making clear that their enemy was the Russian Empire, not its people. In Warsaw, the ceremonial dethronement of the Romanovs was preceded by a ceremony in honour of the Decembrists, organized by the Polish Patriotic Society. Five empty coffins, symbolizing the five executed ringleaders of 14 December 1825, were paraded through the streets of the Polish capital, and a religious service was held in the Orthodox Church, after which Wysocki addressed the crowd in front of the Royal Castle.[5]

If the Poles had looked abroad for inspiration, their own insurrection catapulted them to the forefront of the European republican movement. There was an outpouring of support in the European press for the "French of the North" and calls (resisted by Louis Philippe I) for France to intervene in support of the rebels. French republicans, such as Godefroi Cavaignac and his fellow members of the Society of the Rights of Man, acknowledged their own debt to the Poles for having deflected Nicholas's armies from intervention in France itself. The French general and hero of both the American War of Independence and the July Revolution, the Marquis de Lafayette, pushed unsuccessfully for France to recognize Poland. In Britain, there was a surge of indignation, followed by meetings and rallies in support of Poland, denouncing Russia and pushing for British intervention in the conflict. In July 1831, *The Times* fulminated: "How long will Russia be permitted, with impunity, to make war upon the ancient and noble nation of the Poles, the allies of France, the friends of England, the natural, and, centuries ago, the tried and victorious protectors of civilized Europe against the Turkish and Muscovite barbarians?" Across the Atlantic, there was also a tide of American public sympathy for the Polish rebels.[6]

The November Insurrection, as it became known, quickly erupted into a full-scale military confrontation between the Poles and the Russians, with both sides fielding the largest armies Europe had witnessed since the Napoleonic Wars. The insurgents had, however, overplayed their hand. They faced the might of the Imperial Russian Army while they were internally divided and commanded by hesitant men who could not decide whether to fight the Russians or negotiate with them. On 25 February 1831, a Polish force of 40,000 repelled 60,000 Russians on the Vistula to save Warsaw but managed to secure not a decisive victory but only a postponement of defeat. As Russian reinforcements poured into Poland, the rebels found themselves outnumbered and overwhelmed. After months of stubborn Polish resistance, tsarist troops ground their way back towards Warsaw and finally retook the city in October 1831.[7]

Russian retribution fell heavily on the prostrate Polish provinces. A government edict of 15 March 1833 reassigned 11,700 Polish officers and soldiers to penal battalions and fortress labour at a variety of remote and unattractive locations throughout the Russian Empire. Several thousand more were sentenced to penal labour and settlement in Siberia. The tsar was especially vengeful in the Western Borderlands of Russia, in today's Lithuania, Belarus and Ukraine, which were better integrated into the empire than the Kingdom of Poland. The insurgents there, many of them Polish noblemen, were tried by field courts martial and summarily shot. Russian allies of the Poles were singled out for especially brutal treatment. One of many, Nikita Gumbarsky from Vyborg province, north of St. Petersburg, was sentenced for "participation in the rebellion of 1831, for murder, arson and other criminal acts" to 120 blows of the birch rod and lifelong penal labour.[8]

Wysocki himself was sentenced to death. When the court suggested that he appeal to the tsar for mercy, Wysocki replied, "I did not take up arms only to then ask the tsar for mercy but rather so that my people would never again have to ask for it." Perhaps reluctant to avoid a repeat of the martyrdom of the Decembrists' leaders, Nicholas commuted his sentence to twenty years of penal labour in Siberia.[9] Throughout the 1830s, thousands of Poles were marched eastwards in convoys that took up to two years to reach their destination. Between 1832 and 1835 alone, some 900 Polish political prisoners passed through the Tobolsk Exile Office.[10] This was the first of two major deportations of Poles in the nineteenth century; the second was to follow in the 1860s. These Poles came to be known as the *Sybiracy*, Polish for "Siberians."

Polish exiles struggled in the inhospitable terrain of Siberian penal settlements to preserve their political ideals and their cultural identity. If Siberia had liberated the Decembrists from the stifling hierarchies of Russian society and enabled them to put their republican ideals into practice, it brought the exiled Poles only oblivion. Yet in their lonely, tormented struggles to maintain their roots and ideals, the *Sybiracy* yielded a searing tale of martyrdom that did much to cement Polish Romantic nationalism. None exemplified that struggle better than Wincenty Migurski.

In the wake of the suppression of the November Insurrection, between 7,000 and 8,000 insurgents fled the threat of Siberian deportation, crossing over the Kingdom of Poland's western and southern borders into emigration. Many became active in various republican organizations that made up Young Europe (Young Poland was itself modelled

on Giuseppe Mazzini's Young Italy). Entering this continent-wide revolutionary underground, frequently centred in Masonic lodges in eastern French towns and cities, the Poles saw themselves as the vanguard
of a revolutionary movement that would liberate their own homeland
from autocratic rule and thereby inspire revolution in Russia proper.
One of the first actions of the Polish National Committee in Paris was
to issue a friendly proclamation to the Russians (partly authored by
Mickiewicz). It paid homage to the Decembrists, promoted the idea
of a free federation of Slavic nations, and summoned the Russians to
overthrow the autocracy, abandon their conquests and unite with the
Poles in a common fight for freedom.[11]

Migurski was one of those plotting against St. Petersburg. In
1831, he had fled to France, spending two years in Besançon, where he
actively participated in the Polish organizations of republican émigrés
from across Europe. Migurski's group lobbied for British and French
support in the liberation of Poland and believed that an active partisan
war on Polish soil would secure the support of powerful geopolitical
allies.[12]

Following the "Great Polish Emigration of 1831," many of the
defeated rebels stole back into the Kingdom of Poland, organizing conspiratorial networks that were to prepare the ground for a renewed
uprising. Migurski himself was dispatched to the Austrian-held territory of Galicia. Laying low in a provincial town in March 1834, he met
and fell in love with Albina Wiśniowska, the seventeen-year-old daughter of a provincial nobleman. Their romance was cut short a month
later when Migurski received orders to make his way to Warsaw to
liaise with his comrades.[13]

En route, however, Migurski was arrested on suspicion of having
false papers, and when he finally arrived in Warsaw, it was under armed
guard. During sustained interrogation in the city's notorious citadel,
Migurski was overcome with despair: he "had done nothing to serve
his country and had ruined Albina, robbing her of happiness forever."
He took poison in a bid to end his life, but the retching convulsions
that resulted saved him. Undeterred, Migurski seized a knife that he
had successfully smuggled past his captors and, grasping a heavy book,
hammered the blade five times into his stomach and once into the area
of his heart. He folded his hands on his chest and, "with a prayer on
my lips, waited for death." But death never came. His guards discov-

ered Migurski's prone figure in the cell and sounded the alarm. The ministrations of a doctor saved him, and two months of convalescence saw his strength eventually return. The investigative commission established by St. Petersburg to uncover Polish conspiracies had by then finished its work. In January 1836, in a sentence apparently softened by compassion at his sufferings, a military tribunal exiled Migurski to the town of Uralsk, 500 kilometres north of the Caspian Sea, to serve as a private in the Imperial Army.[14]

Some of Migurski's most committed fellow emissaries were followers of Szymon Konarski, a disciple of Mazzini, a radical republican and one of the founders of Young Poland. Konarski had also taken refuge in France before returning to the Kingdom of Poland intent on instigating a partisan war against the Russians. In February 1835, he set up the "Commonwealth of Polish People," an umbrella organization based in Cracow that aimed to unite the various underground groups in the Western Borderlands to the east of the Kingdom of Poland. It sought the creation of a sovereign and independent Poland, but one which saw the aspirations of the Polish nation as indivisible from those of humanity as a whole. For "people of all countries are brothers . . . members of a great and united brotherhood. They are obliged to offer each other help in securing and defending their common freedom. Men, families, castes, peoples who ultimately seek to oppress other peoples, become the enemies of all mankind." Konarski's conspiratorial efforts took him deep inside the territory of the Russian Empire to today's Lithuania.[15]

The tsarist secret police, the Third Department, eventually infiltrated the Commonwealth of Polish People. Konarski was arrested near Wilno in May 1838 and executed by firing squad the following February. The Third Department succeeded in forcing some of Konarski's followers to confess their plans and reveal the identities of their co-conspirators. Many were arrested and exiled to Siberia. A military tribunal convicted one, Josef Antoni Beaupré, a thirty-eight-year-old physician from Krements in Volhynia province, of having been active in the Commonwealth of Polish People. Working as chief secretary in the provincial administration under the *nom de guerre* "Tojad," or "Wolf's Bane," after the bright but lethally poisonous flower, Beaupré had allegedly used his position to gather statistical data "in order to carry out a partisan war . . . with the aim of galvanising minds for the revival of Poland." He was found to have supplied other conspirators with money, letters and books. Beaupré was sentenced to death on 21 February 1839, a sentence subsequently commuted to twenty years of penal labour and the confiscation of his estates.[16] One of Beaupré's close associates in Krements and another of Konarski's followers was Ewa Felińska. Also caught up in the Third Department's dragnet, Felińska was the first female political exile banished to Siberia. On the personal intervention of Nicholas, who had declared: "I have no reason to like Polish men, but I cannot abide Polish women," she was sentenced to the confiscation of her estates and "permanent settlement" in Tobolsk province, but not to the loss of her noble rights. Felińska spent five years in exile and, upon her return to Poland, published her Siberian memoirs, *Revelations of Siberia. By a Banished Lady*, in London in 1852. Full of astute and amusing anthropological observations of life in Siberia, it fascinated a sympathetic British audience. Within two years the book was already in its third edition.[17]

Deportations of Polish revolutionaries persisted throughout the 1830s and 40s as Nicholas endeavoured to cleanse the Kingdom of Poland, Bessarabia and the Western Borderlands of subversive elements. New legislation stripped many Polish noblemen of their rank and sentenced them as if they were peasants. In 1833, Viktor Burghardt from Białystok was deprived of his noble titles and exiled to settlement in Siberia for "writing a pamphlet full of revolutionary ideas in the name of the inhabitants of Warsaw, calling for insurrection, disturbing the peace and security of the state and foul and derogatory statements directed at the sovereign." Around 54,000 rebels were deported between 1832 and 1849 from Lithuania, Podolia and Volhynia to the Caucasus or beyond the Volga. Of these (the records are incomplete), somewhere between 10,000 and 20,000 were exiled to Siberia.[18]

Deprived of the speed, secrecy and relative comfort of the Decembrists' deportation, these men made the 4,000-kilometre journey to Siberia on foot. Tramping eastwards in one convoy was Justynian Ruciński. A follower of Konarski and active in the revolutionary underground, Ruciński had been arrested in Zhitomir to the west of Kiev in 1838 and had been sentenced to twenty years of penal labour in Eastern Siberia. In February 1839, after six months in a Kiev prison, he was clapped in irons and deported to Tobolsk, where he encountered "dozens of exiles, exhausted and tortured to the point of being unrecognisable." Arranged into a marching convoy with a mixture of his countrymen and common criminals, Ruciński then set out for the Nerchinsk Mining Region on a journey that would take thirteen months:

> A life began for us that is difficult to name, let alone adequately to describe. It seemed there can be no harsher existence on earth. It comprised daily marches of 20 to 25 kilometres in chains, overnighting in prisons on filthy wooden benches, . . . lacking undergarments, clothes and boots, a starvation diet, extreme hunger, icy slush, heat, frosts and all the time we had to keep marching onwards and onwards. There was the unceasing surveillance of the convicts, whose lives were full of the most cynical kinds of depravity, usually encouraged by corrupt convoy commanders. We found ourselves torn away from our pasts, in the midst of an unimaginable Siberian wasteland, lacking any news whatsoever of the wives and families we had left behind, unable to send them word or any sign of life. Our bodies were terribly exhausted through physical exertion and our minds through anxiety and homesickness. That is but a pale rendering of our bitter fate.[19]

When they finally reached Nerchinsk, Konarski's followers—the *konarshiki*—considered the most dangerous and inveterate of Poland's revolutionaries, were subject to especially close surveillance by the authorities.[20]

Migurski had, meanwhile, travelled to Uralsk from Warsaw by carriage relatively swiftly, on what would ultimately prove to be his own circuitous and tortuous route to Nerchinsk. Upon his arrival, he immediately wrote to Albina, "the sole and unchanging object of my feelings," telling her of his imprisonment, attempted suicide and banishment. For a young patriotic nobleman in the age of Romanticism, Migurski's love for Albina was an expression of his basic humanity. Republicans of the nineteenth century believed that romantic love, solidarity and patriotism all sprang from the same source: the natural dignity of human beings. "Our rights," he wrote to Albina, "are sacred, and even the distance of 3,000 kilometres separating us should not influence them."

To love in defiance of distance was, for Migurski, to love in defiance of St. Petersburg. He would not permit himself, however, to ask Albina to join him, as he considered this too great a sacrifice to demand of anyone. But Albina responded to his letter with a volley of impassioned declarations that she would follow him to Russia: "No difficulties, distances, public opinion would deter me from this step." Moved by her selfless devotion, Migurski declared: "On my knees, I ask you. Believe me that only your joining me will be able to bring me happiness . . . In the name of the Lord and our sacred love, I beg you, come!" Albina finally arrived in Uralsk in the spring of 1837 and was reunited with Migurski. They were married within a month in a ceremony that, for the young Polish revolutionary, was laced with ambivalence. Onlookers at the wedding "could perceive bitterness, hatred and indignation in me, because on my face was etched not only joy at the ceremony but also the thought that this was not the fate that should have befallen my darling Albina."[21]

The couple settled down together in Uralsk, where they struggled with the suffocating tedium of life in a small provincial Russian town so deftly rendered by Alexander Pushkin in *The Captain's Daughter* (1836) and by Anton Chekhov in his short stories half a century later. Migurski had been demoted to the ranks but not sentenced to penal labour and, as a consequence, Albina had not been forced, when she joined him, to relinquish her own rights and privileges as a noblewoman. Both were well-educated members of the nobility, and buoyed by the income that Albina was able to draw from her family, they began to excite first the jealousy, and later the animosity, of many of the provincial denizens of Uralsk: "My wife was for them a complete enigma," Migurski recalled. "They could not understand how this person had, in leaving her homeland, forsaken all the elevated pleasures and privileges she enjoyed there in order that her entire world should be concentrated in a life united with mine." The couple endured gossip and even outright insults in the street.[22]

Albina became pregnant in the summer of 1837 and gave birth to a daughter, Michalina, the following spring. But the hot, humid climate in Uralsk was, Migurski recalled, "unbearable, the cause of mass mortality among new-borns," and "the Lord delivered the most terrible blow to our tormented hearts": Michalina survived only a few short weeks. The local authorities denied the couple's request to have the child buried in the local church because, at that time, they did not consider the Catholic Poles Christians. Outraged by this insult to his feelings as a parent and as a devout Christian, Migurski resolved to ensure that his child would one day be buried not in Russia but in Poland. He carefully embalmed the tiny body and interred it outside the grounds of the cemetery.[23]

After Michalina's death, Albina petitioned the empress, Aleksandra Fyodorovna, for permission to return to Galicia or at least for Migurski to be released from military service so that the couple could move to another part of Russia with a less lethal climate. The petition was declined, and the attempts of Migurski's parents to secure a pardon from the throne proved similarly fruitless. It was then that Migurski began to hatch a plan "to win freedom." Albina shared her husband's sense that languishing in Uralsk "was an insult to the natural dignity of Man, a base existence and a sin. Anyone who had the opportunity and did not attempt to change his lot was committing a crime. In a word, having talked it through, we decided to escape from Russia."[24] Action and the rights of man were both central to republican thinking in the 1830s. These virtues invested the Migurskis' decision with a political significance beyond the grief-stricken desire to return home. Escape was a defiant act of Polish patriotism.

And escape the Poles did, in large numbers, throughout the 1830s and 40s. They usually absconded within a couple of months of arriving in the penal settlements, once the conditions of their captivity and forced labour had become clear. Alan Rokicki arrived at the Aleksandrovsk penal distillery, some 70 kilometres northwest of Irkutsk, on 27 January 1835 and, on 9 March, he fled; Leon Romanowski arrived at the Irkutsk salt works at the end of March and, by 4 May, the hunt for him was on, as well.[25] When, in the night of 22 June 1835, the leader of the November Insurrection, Piotr Wysocki, fled with six comrades from the Aleksandrovsk penal distillery, the state's response was brutal. Wysocki and his fellow fugitives managed to elude their pursuers in the forests for only two days before being recaptured. When questioned, some of Wysocki's accomplices confessed that their leader had planned to seize weapons and join forces with exiled Poles from the Irkutsk salt works before returning to Poland via India. Such Promethean ambitions seemed confirmed by the discovery that the fugitives were carrying maps of Asia and European Russia. A field court martial sentenced

Wysocki and his accomplices to a relatively lenient sentence of between sixteen and twenty-four blows of the lash. The head of the Nerchinsk Mining Region, Major-General Stanislav Leparsky, felt that such punishments were insufficient to act as a deterrent and increased the sentence to one of the most terrible forms of corporal punishment in the empire. Wysocki and his comrades were each to "run a gauntlet" of 500 soldiers.[26]

Graphically described in Leo Tolstoy's 1903 short story "After the Ball," the gauntlet was used in the Russian military and in armies throughout Europe in the nineteenth century. The offender was stripped to the waist and forced to run between two lines of soldiers, each armed with a birch rod and charged with delivering a stinging blow to the criminal as he passed. There could be up to 1,000 soldiers deployed in the lines, and criminals were sometimes made to stagger past them as many as six times, generating a pulverizing total of 6,000 blows. In 1834, Nicholas had halved this number for soldiers, but Siberia's governors argued that this dispensation did not apply to exiles. In 1851, the gauntlet replaced the knout as Siberia's most feared instrument of punishment.[27]

Wysocki and his comrades survived the gauntlet and were put to work as penal labourers in irons in separate factories "under close guard." Each was to spend four months chained to wheelbarrows, a punishment reserved for the most dangerous recidivists. Wysocki was then sent to the feared mining settlement at Akatui, where he was to be confined "until his morality is corrected." Yet even though he "behaved very well indeed," he remained in chains. While in the desolate prison, he befriended Mikhail Lunin and assisted the Decembrist in smuggling out correspondence to his comrades across Siberia.[28]

Escapes by Poles, with the attendant threat of disorder, became so common that, in 1835, the commander of the Siberian Corps and Omsk province, Major-General Semyon Bronevsky, wrote to Minister of War Aleksandr Chernyshev: "In order to deprive them of the opportunity of escaping, all Poles currently sentenced to penal labour in the factories of Irkutsk and Yenisei provinces, and some who are sentenced to settlement, should be sent separately, under close guard, by minor roads beyond Baikal to the mines of Nerchinsk." Once there, the authorities were to submit monthly reports on the behaviour of their prisoners and forward detailed digests to St. Petersburg every three months.[29] The Nerchinsk authorities were warned that, "if, because of carelessness and weak surveillance, one of these individuals escapes, then the officials are to be tried and punished with the fullest force of the law, for these criminals can inflict great harm on the state." As ever, though, the authorities put their faith not so much in the vigilance of their guards as in "Baikal and the barren mountainous wastes that offer, without a firm grasp of the locality, no means of subsistence with which to traverse them." The indigenous Buryat and Tungus nomads also proved effective in "pursuing the fugitives into the most impenetrable of places." The numbers of Poles escaping did indeed decline after their transfer to Nerchinsk.[30]

Almost 6,000 kilometres away in Uralsk, Migurski was planning his own escape. With Albina's support, he hatched a plot to fake his own suicide and thus free Albina to make the journey home, ostensibly as a widow. For months, he waited for a man of his approximate age, height and appearance to die in the environs of Uralsk so that he could make use of his corpse to stage a violent death. Albina, once again, became pregnant, however, and fearful that they would be unable to make their escape before she gave birth, they decided to bring forward their plans. On 21 November 1839, Migurski wrote a letter to his commanding officer: "The extremity of my suffering and despair does not permit me to remain the guardian of my wife, who has devoted her entire life to me." Underlining Albina's misery in Uralsk, Migurski claimed that only his death would release her from her marriage vows and "from her sufferings." It would grant her the possibility of returning to her family in Galicia. That night, Migurski scattered his clothes next to the hole in the ice on the Ural River and then concealed himself behind the false wall in the bedroom wardrobe. When the local commander opened the letter the following morning and hurried to Migurski's cabin, he discovered a pale and frightened Albina. The young woman played her part to perfection, turning her genuine fear that the plot would be exposed into a convincing performance of grief.[31]

The authorities remained suspicious, though. They ordered extensive searches for Migurski in the vicinity, believing that he might simply have absconded. They also placed Albina under "the strictest secret surveillance," in case her husband should contact her. After a month, Albina began to appeal for permission to return to Galicia: "After the death of my husband, I have nothing left but to return to the bosom of my family." The authorities insisted, however, upon waiting for the ice on the river to melt so that Migurski's corpse could be recovered and his suicide confirmed.[32]

As the months passed, the tension and fear that haunted Albina in this period could not but tell upon her health. Her second child, born in April 1840, survived for only three weeks. Migurski also embalmed its little corpse and concealed it together with its dead sibling in anticipation of the time when it might be returned to Galicia for burial. Migurski remained all the while inside the cabin, concealing himself whenever visitors called. Albina again wrote to the authorities imploring them to allow her to return home. She complained that no proper search for her husband's body had been carried out. "Would anyone in their right mind," she enquired, "having decided to escape, warn the authorities of his impending disappearance . . . when it would have been possible to conceal the fact of his flight for several days?" Her appeals eventually reached the capital. A noblewoman, Albina was also a Habsburg and not a Russian subject, a fact which made her continued detention in southern Russia a diplomatically sensitive issue. In May, the minister of war himself, under some pressure from the Austrian ambassador in St. Petersburg, acceded to Albina's requests and granted her permission to leave Uralsk for home. On 13 June 1840, in a closed carriage and under the armed escort of a single young Cossack, she set out for Galicia.[33]

Unbeknown to the coachman and her escort, Albina Migurska travelled not alone, but in the company of her two dead children, whose bodies were concealed in her luggage. Migurski had hidden himself in the carriage beneath his wife's seat, hoping to remain undetected across the 2,000 kilometres that stood between them and the Polish border. Such ambitions were desperately naive. The group had journeyed a mere four days before the Cossack overheard a male voice inside the carriage and opened the door to discover Migurski beneath his wife's seat. After a brief struggle, the soldier succeeded, with the help of some passing peasants, in overwhelming the fugitive and delivered him, bound, to the town of Petrovsk. There, Migurski was formally arrested before being transferred to Saratov, where the governor duly reported on events to St. Petersburg.[34]

The attempted flight of this grieving couple with the embalmed bodies of their two dead children was a gesture of defiance to the throne.

Nicholas was furious that the Migurskis had "declined" to leave the
bodies of their children in Russian soil, and demanded punishment, in
order to deter anyone else from attempting something similar in the
future. Returned to Orenburg under armed guard to stand trial before
a military tribunal in February 1841, Migurski did his utmost to excul-
pate his wife. He declared that the plot was all his idea and that he had
indeed originally planned to take his own life, before recoiling from
the deed at the last minute and returning to his wife to persuade her to
help him to escape. After many months of interrogations and investigations of an escape that had embarrassed the local military authorities
in Uralsk and infuriated the tsar, the military tribunal found Migurski
guilty of attempting to flee his place of banishment and of illegally
attempting to smuggle the corpses of his dead children out of Russia.
The tribunal stripped Migurski of all rights of rank and, following the
personal intervention of the tsar, sentenced him in November 1841 to
serve in the 13th Eastern Siberian Battalion in Nerchinsk.[35]

While Migurski languished in a military prison, Albina had in the
meantime been returned to Uralsk while the authorities investigated
her own complicity in the escape. She was again pregnant and, separated from her husband, gave birth to another infant who survived
but a few days in the disease-infested town that had already claimed
the lives of her two earlier children. Denied permission to see his wife
before he left for Siberia and concerned that, if she attempted once
again to follow him, she would not survive the journey, Migurski sent
Albina a desperate plea:

> Save your soul, if you can no longer save your body, my dearest
> Albina! Return home and pray there for our enemies, for they,
> as Christ said, really know not what they do . . . Do not worry
> about me, my darling. I have accepted my fate and the will of
> God, and will leave peacefully and devote my last breath to
> Him, dying in the conviction that the Lord will not abandon us
> and will unite us in the next life.[36]

But Albina remained determined to join her husband. After a court,
reluctant to convict a foreign noblewoman who had already suffered so
much, had cleared her of any wrongdoing, she declared her intention to
follow Migurski to Nerchinsk.[37]

In March 1842, in the town of Omsk, Migurska caught up with her husband en route to Nerchinsk. They had not seen each other since their foiled escape. Migurski remembered their meeting with a mixture of tenderness and horror:

> After eighteen months of separation and overcome with emotion, I took her in my arms, kissed her, hugged her and wept! Poor, unhappy Albina had changed terribly! She had become so pale, thin and exhausted, that if I had encountered her in the street I might not have recognised her. "Oh Lord!" I thought, looking at her. "Am I really not supposed to smoulder with hatred and the desire to take revenge on all of humanity! What have they done with her? Why have they done this? You hear, why have they done this?" . . . I began again to kiss her for she was, even in her pitiful state, as dear to me as ever, and even dearer as the loss of my love drew nearer.[38]

The couple journeyed together to Nerchinsk, stopping for a week in Urik at the home of Sergei and Maria Volkonsky, who welcomed them as fellow republicans and patriots. They crossed the frozen waters of Baikal and arrived in Nerchinsk in October 1842. Enjoying a kind of tragic celebrity among the educated exiles and officials of Siberia, Migurski was not required to work as a soldier but used the money he had received from his relatives to buy a small cabin and some livestock. Albina was again pregnant but her strength was ebbing. She had contracted tuberculosis on the journey to Siberia and passed the disease on to the child now born to her, Konrad. As consumption ravaged her body, Albina knew she did not have long to live. She begged Migurski: "You are still young, my darling and adored husband, so do not shackle yourself and, if you meet someone worthy of you, marry! Even though I love you more than life, I would be rightly condemned if I allowed my jealousy from the grave to bind your desire and your will!" At the age of twenty-five, Albina Migurska died on 3 June 1843. Her son survived her by a little over a year. Migurski buried them both with his own hands.[39]

Posterity rescued the Migurskis from the Siberian oblivion into which Nicholas had endeavoured to cast the Polish rebels. Amid the stifling censorship of Nicolaevan Russia, only the great lexicographer

Vladimir Dal recorded their story, albeit in vague terms, in 1846. Four years after Nicholas's death, however, Migurski—now himself an old man with only a few years left to live—finally took up his pen to write his memoirs in his modest cabin in Irkutsk. He began with the words: "When my dear wife died in my arms in Nerchinsk, I resolved to tell the world the story of her life. I now do this with the ardent hope that her love and loyalty . . . will serve as a model for Polish women." His tragic tale of romance, patriotism and defiance was published in 1863, beyond the reach of the Russian censor, in the Habsburg Polish city of Lviv, and it seized the imagination of Polish contemporaries. In Russia, too, amid the more relaxed censorship of the Great Reforms, the Siberian ethnographer Sergei Maksimov was able in 1870 to describe briefly the fate of Wincenty, Albina and their children. He dwelt on Albina's gravestone, "the resting place of one of the true heroines of all the history of Polish bondage."[40] Albina's terrible fate beyond Lake Baikal confirmed a new image of Siberia as the graveyard of Polish nationhood.

The Migurskis' tale found a monumental epitaph in Russian literary culture only with the publication of Leo Tolstoy's account of their lives half a century later, in 1906. By then, liberated from the constraints of censorship by the 1905 Revolution, Tolstoy's searing indictment of the cruelty of the autocracy even took as its title Migurski's distraught exclamation when he met his dying wife in Omsk: "Why have they done this?" Tolstoy made the story of Wincenty, Albina and their children known across the Russian Empire and Europe. At the very moment when the autocracy was fighting a renewed insurgency in Poland and the Western Borderlands, it would be haunted by the corpses of a Polish noblewoman and her dead child buried in the stony ground of Nerchinsk.[41]

Wincenty Migurski himself finally reached his beloved Poland in September 1859, a quarter of a century after he had been exiled to Uralsk. When he died four years later in Wilno, the Kingdom of Poland was once more in flames. Seizing the torch of rebellion raised by Migurski and his compatriots in 1830, Poles had again launched themselves on a desperate and ill-fated bid to wrest independence from St. Petersburg.[42]

·   ·   ·

Not all Migurski's comrades in Siberia suffered such a bitter fate. A number of wealthy and educated Polish exiles were able to draw upon material and diplomatic support from their families to improve their circumstances in exile. For many Polish noblemen, as for the Decembrists who had preceded them, the work in the mines was of a perfunctory nature and labour duties could be circumvented by bribes. Polish memoirists recalled handsome family homes in Nerchinsk and a library boasting some 3,000 volumes in the Polish language. Like the Decembrists, the Poles established a commune, or *ogół*, that subscribed to newspapers, arranged correspondence (the Poles were subject to the same restrictions as the Decembrists) and distributed material goods to the poorer members of the exile community.[43]

But there were important differences between the Decembrists and the Polish exiles. If the Decembrists in Siberian exile experienced a liberation of sorts from the oppressive hierarchies of Nicolaevan Russia, the Poles underwent only a wrenching sense of cultural dislocation. The relative freedom offered to the Poles exiled in settlements in Eastern Siberia brought with it an insidious threat. With official permission, they could reside almost anywhere they pleased, but their dispersal increased the chances, especially for deracinated young bachelors, of losing themselves in the alien culture of the Siberian peasantry. Maksimov observed the Poles' struggle with their own "Russification." In Akatui, Wysocki tried to dissuade his comrades from "mixing Polish and Russian blood." In order to marry local women, the Poles were obliged to convert from Catholicism, the religious mainstay of their national identity, to Orthodoxy, the religion of their conquerors. Marriages with Siberian women were therefore considered a "betrayal of the fatherland." Maksimov noted that the Polish exiles were deeply concerned with "the preservation of national sentiments and patriotic belief, with all of its extreme and strange manifestations, right down to the most minor details."[44]

This resistance to cultural assimilation enjoyed only qualified success. When the rebel Justynian Ruciński arrived in Nerchinsk in 1840, he encountered many of his compatriots exiled following the November Insurrection. Young, educated and mostly with no direct experience whatsoever of agriculture, they struggled to adapt to farming in Siberia's harsh climate: "These poor men, from different educations, family traditions and pasts, and cut off from their homeland, faced a bitter fate and lost their way. Some married local girls and became forever Siberians; others were driven by necessity to work as labourers for the peasants. Only a few were able to stand up in the adversity and preserve their original, uncorrupted character."[45]

Across Siberia, the Poles bombarded the authorities with petitions, protesting their innocence and demanding improvements to their conditions. From his vantage point in the little village of Urik, outside Irkutsk, Lunin observed that the guilt of many had never been proven: "Do not seek among them only men guilty of revolution, even agitators . . . Among our exiles there are many who were tricked into revolt, subjected to great danger and then abandoned." Others were simply reckless youths. One Polish nobleman had been convicted of "spitting on a portrait of the Emperor while drunk, stealing a Cossack's pistol, singing mutinous songs, insulting his Imperial Majesty and posting slogans and poems of a rebellious nature." He was sentenced to fifteen years of penal labour in Eastern Siberia. As the authorities themselves tersely conceded, further investigation of some individuals' alleged crimes revealed that "the extent of their guilt was less than originally believed." Many Poles succeeded in having their cases reinvestigated and their sentences overturned.[46]

Repeatedly, Nicholas ordered clemency extended to political exiles, either by commuting their sentences of penal labour to sentences of "exile to settlement" or by granting them permission to return home. The extension of imperial clemency was a tsarist tradition, one of the Romanovs' "scenarios of power." Just as Nicholas had spared the lives of the Decembrist rebels, he would also, in order to commemorate events in the life of the imperial dynasty, offer pardons to political prisoners who had shown good behaviour and suitable levels of remorse. This clemency was an expression of autocratic paternalism; it allowed the tsar to express both power and benevolence and also to offer correctives to government policies while not calling into question the entire edifice of the state. To celebrate the wedding of his son Alexander in 1841, Nicholas commuted the sentences of dozens of exiles, many of them politicals, in Eastern Siberia. His demonstrations of autocratic omnipotence and mercy were somewhat undermined, however, by the failure of the Siberian authorities to locate many of the beneficiaries of his clemency.[47] Again in February 1851, on the twenty-fifth anniversary of his accession to the throne, Nicholas graciously ordered the further release of penal labourers to settlement. More releases followed in the remainder of his reign.[48] Yet even these gestures of imperial magnanimity revealed a system steeped in bureaucratic formalism. In 1855, a decree from the emperor extended permission to return home to all Poles with families who had been exiled to settlement in Siberia for more than ten years. One Polish rebel, Mieczysław Wyżykowski, who had been exiled to Tomsk province, was initially denied the right of return to Warsaw because his wife and child who had accompanied him into exile had both died, leaving Wyżykowski a widower. It was only following the personal intervention of the governor-general of Western Siberia, Gustav Gasford, that, after a year's delay, Wyżykowski was finally permitted to leave for Poland. Despite the decades in exile and the creeping effects of cultural assimilation, when Alexander II issued a general amnesty to political prisoners on his accession to the throne in 1856, only twenty-seven Poles elected to remain in Siberia. The readiness of most to leave may well have had as much to do with their underwhelming material conditions as it did with their undimmed patriotic fervour.[49]

The new sovereign's magnanimity did not, however, embrace them all. In 1833, fifteen-year-old Polish nobleman Hilariusz Weber had been convicted of participating in an insurgent party that had murdered four Russian soldiers, including an officer. He was stripped of his rank and title and sentenced to lifelong penal labour. Weber spent twenty-five years in the Nerchinsk mines but found himself excluded from the dispensations of the 1856 amnesty that saw the Decembrists return home. For, in 1841, Weber had been caught forging an official document—a serious crime that threatened to subvert the state's control over its own exile population—and had been sentenced to sixteen lashes. This stain on his record meant that he had displayed insufficient "moral improvement and questionable repentance" in Siberia. He was, therefore, not eligible for clemency.[50]

Released from penal labour to settlement in 1858, Weber sought permission the following year to appeal to the emperor for a pardon. The head of the Third Department, Adjutant General Vasily Dolgorukov, was sympathetic. Since 1841, Weber had, he argued, "behaved irreproachably." The offence he committed in that year was but an "impulsive response to his poverty and circumstances." Weber had committed his original crime in the Kingdom of Poland at the tender age of fifteen out of "inexperience." For more than twenty years, he had led an honest and industrious life, useful for the economy of the region. Bearing his long years of privation and suffering with stoicism, obedience and repentance, he had atoned for his crime, and he and his family deserved relief from their fate. But only the viceroy of the Kingdom of Poland, General Mikhail Gorchakov, had the right to submit Weber's petition to the emperor, and he remained unpersuaded. Weber's "guilt was too great" and his behaviour in Siberia "was not enough to merit the clemency granted in the manifesto of 1856."[51]

A year later, Weber renewed his petition for a pardon and this time enjoyed the backing of none other than the powerful and liberal-minded governor-general of Eastern Siberia, Count Nikolai Muravyov (later Muravyov-Amursky).[52] Despite being himself a veteran of the campaign to suppress the rebellious Poles in 1830–31, Muravyov-Amursky had clearly taken a shine to Weber. He argued that there were many criminals who had benefited from the amnesties of the previous few years who were "just as guilty as Weber, and some who had, like him, been charged with more serious crimes during their exile and been sentenced by the courts." Many of them had, however, been sentenced only to settlement and had not suffered Weber's "exhausting and interminable" years of penal labour. The governor-general believed that Weber had "atoned for his crime and deserved the sovereign's mercy." Weber's position and that of his family "were extremely difficult despite the fact that his broad-ranging and specialist knowledge, his honest, energetic and inventive work, had been of considerable benefit to state enterprises . . . and to the local population." Since his release from penal settlement two years earlier, Weber had been active in promoting navigation along the Amur. He had even been involved in talks with Americans about the possibility of running a private steamboat along the river. Even so, if he was to make a success of this venture, he needed to regain his rights of rank, since he could not conduct contractual business as an exiled settler. Muravyov-Amursky argued that Weber should be given the opportunity to "deploy his knowledge, skills and honest industry for his own and for the public's good." Gorchakov quickly reversed his decision "out of respect" for a figure with Muravyov-Amursky's standing, and submitted a petition to the capital. The authorities in St. Petersburg restored Weber's rights of rank and gave him permission to reside anywhere in Siberia so that "he might benefit the region." Pushed to choose between punishment and colonial interests, the government opted for the latter. It refused, nevertheless, to grant Weber permission to return to Poland.[53]

For those who did make the return journey to the Kingdom of Poland, the homecomings were bittersweet affairs. Across the nineteenth century, returning exiles experienced a painful dislocation from the societies they had been forced to leave behind. Having made the long-awaited journey of several thousand kilometres back across the length of the empire, they often found themselves stranded and penniless in a land that had moved on and left them behind. Piotr Wysocki, the leader of the November Insurrection, was allowed to return to Poland in 1857, and he spent the next twenty years eking out an existence on a small farm near Warsaw before dying in poverty.[54] Life in Siberia had been distant from the quickening pace of change in European Russia and in the Kingdom of Poland. Reaching home prematurely aged not only in body but also in mind, former exiles would shuffle about their former towns and villages as representatives of a bygone era. When Justynian Ruciński received the emperor's permission to return to European Russia in 1848, he discovered that:

> a fifteen-year exile never really ends. Its traces cannot but remain. Even those who sentenced me to exile cannot erase them . . . Life in my homeland had continued to take its natural course. After more than a decade of banishment, the exile returns. Everywhere he meets old, familiar faces; everywhere he is welcomed joyously and warmly. But there it ends: everyone returns to his own affairs, to his daily life. The exile remains an exile because the golden thread that had tied him to the practical and business affairs of his country has been severed . . . An indeterminate sadness pursues him everywhere. His soul remains forever scarred.[55]

Thousands of Polish returnees experienced the same quiet tragedy of estrangement in the land for which they had sacrificed themselves. If as individuals many fell into obscurity, however, as a group the rebels of 1830 bestrode the European consciousness, galvanizing Romantic views of Polish nationalism and blackening the name of the Russian autocracy.

Polish exiles living in Western Europe exchanged their swords for quills and forged the inspiring image of Poland as a martyred nation. Adam Mickiewicz inveighed against Russian despotism from the vaunted lecture halls of the Collège de France in Paris. His drama *Dziady* (1823–32) and his epic verse *The Books of the Polish Nation and of the Polish Pilgrimage* (1832) were immediately translated into English and French and forged an image of Poland as the "Christ of nations," crucified by her neighbours in the partitions of Poland in the 1770s and 90s and crushed in her noble desire for freedom in 1830. The torments of Polish exiles in Siberia stood centre stage in his searing vision of national suffering. Freedom had been banished from Poland, but it would return:

> And finally Poland said: "Whosoever will come to me shall be free and equal for I am FREEDOM."
>
> But the Kings, when they heard of this, were terrified in their hearts and said: "We banished freedom from the earth; but lo, it returneth in the person of a just nation, that doth not bow down to our idols! Come, let us slay this nation . . ."
>
> And they martyred the Polish Nation and laid it in the grave, and the Kings cried out: "We have slain and have buried Freedom."
>
> But . . . the Polish nation did not die: its body lieth in the grave, but its spirit hath descended from the earth, that is from public life, to the abyss, that is to the private life of people who suffer slavery in their country and outside of their country . . .
>
> But on the third day the soul shall return to the body, and the Nation shall arise and free all the peoples of Europe from slavery.[56]

Mickiewicz's compatriot in Paris, Frédéric Chopin, put some of the poet's verse to music in his haunting ballades, ensuring that indictments of Russian tyranny could be heard from pianos across Europe.[57]

In this emerging Romantic narrative of national martyrdom, the thousands of Polish exiles to Siberia became a monastic, fraternal, religious community. Inspired by Mickiewicz's verse, Polish patriots believed their countrymen exiled to Siberia were assuming the burden of the sins of the entire nation and thereby securing its redemption.

The Siberian wilderness—almost unimaginably remote for Poles in the 1830s—assumed the sanctity of Golgotha: a place of both execution and spiritual rebirth.[58]

The impact of Nicholas's ruthless suppression of the November Insurrection and of the ensuing fate of Polish exiles in Siberia was amplified abroad because it coincided, elsewhere in Europe, with the renewed advance of liberal nationalism. As the fears inspired by the French Revolution receded, liberals were once again assailing the *anciens régimes* that had been reinstated by the Congress of Vienna in 1815 in the wake of Napoleon's defeat. These renewed progressive energies culminated in the July Revolution in Paris in 1830 (news of which the Decembrists had greeted with champagne and toasts as they trekked from Chita to Petrovsk Zavod), in the 1830 revolution in Belgium and in the extension of the franchise in Britain ushered in by the Reform Bill of 1832. The idea of popular sovereignty and representative governance underpinned by constitutions—whether through a plebiscitary Bonaparte in France or a parliament as in Britain and Belgium—would henceforth dominate westernmost Europe.[59]

Amid this revival of liberal nationalism in the wake of 1830, the image of a chivalric nation that had sacrificed her finest sons to the cause of freedom came to exercise an almost irresistible appeal upon the Romantic sensibilities of the day. In 1831 the French poet Casimir François Delavigne composed the iconic verse "La Varsovienne," put to music by Karol Kurpiński, which contained the lines:

> Either we win—or we are ready
> To build a barrier of our corpses,
> To slow down the giant,
> Who wishes to bring chains to the world.

If the partitions of Poland in the 1770s and 90s had already elicited sympathy in England and France, the spectacle of Polish patriots being shackled and cast into the wastelands of Siberia provoked outrage among both liberals and republicans. In Paris, the French republican Jules Michelet wrote *Democratic Legends of the North,* which portrayed freedom-loving Poland's struggle against Russian despotism (Michelet had the text republished in 1863 in the midst of the next Polish rebellion under the title "Martyred Poland"). In Hungary, the

Romantic nationalist poets Mihály Vörösmarty and Sándor Petőfi penned odes to Polish martyrdom. Lajos Kossuth, the youthful lawyer and future leader of the Hungarian Revolution against Vienna, declared: "The cause of the Poles is the cause of Europe, and I can boldly affirm that whoever does not honour the Poles . . . does not love his own motherland."[60]

If Poland was a virtuous martyr among nations, the Russian Empire was an ignoble executioner. This new image was a striking reversal of Europeans' indulgent view of the Russian autocracy as an outpost of enlightened absolutism under Catherine the Great and as a magnanimous liberator of peoples from Napoleonic tyranny under Alexander I. Nicholas's exile of the Decembrists had revealed him to be a vengeful dynastic legitimist at home; his exile of the Polish rebels projected that image across Europe. The autocracy appeared now not as a bulwark of conservative tranquillity but as a granite bastion of militant reaction.[61]

No one propounded this view more influentially, or indeed more acerbically, than the Marquis de Custine, a Frenchman who visited Russia in 1839 and who wrote a travelogue which became an international bestseller. Custine's sensational indictment of the Russia of Nicholas I appeared convincing because he was himself an opponent of the liberalism that was on the march in Europe. Custine had travelled to Russia in order to observe and extol the virtues of a state uncontaminated by the revolutionary pathogens attacking the *anciens régimes* of Europe. His nostalgic conservatism did not, however, incline Custine to side with Russia in its conflict with Poland. Custine was a devout Catholic, and his sympathies lay with his defeated co-religionists. He had many friends among Polish exiles in Paris in the 1830s and had been influenced by Mickiewicz's anti-Russian verse even before he set out for St. Petersburg.[62]

Custine portrayed the autocracy as an oriental despotism reaching out to crush an indubitably European nation. Russia, he wrote, had banished the patriotic sons of Poland into the darkest snowbound recesses of an Asiatic landmass:

Does the world know that, at the present hour, the roads of Asia are once again covered with exiles torn from their hearths and proceeding on foot to their tomb, as the herds leave their pastures for the slaughterhouse? This revival is attributable to a pretended Polish conspiracy, a conspiracy of *youthful mad-men*, who would have been heroes had they succeeded; and who, their attempt being desperate, only appear to me the more generously devoted. My heart bleeds for the exiles, their families, and their country. What will be the result when the oppressors of this corner of the earth, where chivalry once flourished, shall have peopled Tartary with all that was most noble and courageous amongst the sons of ancient Europe?[63]

The impact of Custine's travelogue is difficult to overstate. From its initial publication in Paris in 1843, it ran to four editions within three years with even more editions appearing in Brussels. English, Danish and German translations followed, and abridged pamphlets appeared in other European countries (needless to say, the book was officially banned in Russia). Overall, it must have sold several hundred thousand copies. For all its inaccuracies and exaggerations, it became by far the most influential description of the Russian Empire penned by a foreigner during the reign of Nicholas. It also played a significant role in blackening the name of the autocracy in the years leading up to the outbreak of the Crimean War.[64]

When Custine met Nicholas, he fancied he could discern a dark reality amid the pomp and ceremony of the imperial court:

> When I closely consider this personage, distinguished from all others upon earth, I fancy that his head has two faces, like that of Janus, and the words violence, exile, oppression, or their full equivalent, SIBERIA, is engraved on the face which is not presented towards me. This idea haunts me unceasingly, even as I speak to him.[65]

In the decades that followed, this was the face the autocracy increasingly turned to Europe. In 1848, Nicholas would send forth his armies to quash the Hungarian Revolution. In 1863, with a brutality that shocked the continent, his successor, Alexander II, would crush the second rebellion in the Kingdom of Poland and exile thousands more Poles across the Urals. Beyond the dazzling culture of Russia's European cities, Siberia had become the Stygian recess of autocratic power.

7

The Penal Fort

Europe's "springtime of peoples" in the historic year of 1848 became swiftly enveloped in a freezing fog of political reaction. Armies loyal to princes, kings and emperors retreated, rallied and then returned to crush the revolutions that a year earlier had promised to sweep the old order away. In a testament to the brutal efficiency with which Nicholas I dealt with dissent at home, the Russian Empire remained largely unperturbed by the convulsions that rocked much of the continent. There was no reprise of the Decembrists' rebellion in St. Petersburg, and even the Kingdom of Poland remained quiet. Wary, nevertheless, of the contagions of liberalism and nationalism and keen to uphold dynastic authority in the neighbouring Habsburg Empire, in June 1849 Nicholas dispatched 300,000 soldiers to suppress the Hungarian Revolution. With Russia's western frontier secured, on 22 December 1849, the tsar publicly turned his attention to a smattering of opponents at home.[1]

Languishing in the Peter and Paul Fortress in St. Petersburg, in the very cells that had held the Decembrists a quarter of a century earlier, were several dozen students, officials and writers. They had been convicted of membership in a subversive discussion group that convened once a week in the home of a radical young nobleman named Mikhail Petrashevsky. Most of the *Petrashevtsy*, as they came to be known, were critical of the institution of serfdom, inspired by the ideals of 1848 and hopeful of reform at home. They were no revolutionaries, but the upheavals in Europe had provoked the Russian state into a further clampdown on all forms of dissent. The Petrashevsky Circle had caught the attention of the imperial secret police, the Third Department. Arrested in April 1849, the men had been held in isolation in the fortress over a long summer while they were subjected to intensive interrogations about their ideas, their activities and their links abroad. In September, a commission of inquiry had found twenty-eight of them guilty of seditious crimes. Sentencing, however, had not yet taken place. Thus, when their cell doors opened on the morning of 22 December and the prisoners were led out into the icy darkness, they were still ignorant of their fate.[2]

In Russia's northern capital day breaks only shortly before noon in December. Transported under armed guard in sealed carriages through streets still cloaked in gloom, the men caught mere glimpses of passing buildings through frosted windows. After what seemed like an endless journey, the carriages finally came to a halt on Semyonovsky Square, a brisk walk from the central thoroughfare of Nevsky Prospect. The carriage doors were opened and the prisoners stepped out into knee-deep snow. They found themselves surrounded by regiments from the city, drawn up to form a square. In the centre of this formation, a rough wooden staircase led up to a platform hung with black cloth. The men's joy at being at last reunited after so many months of isolation in separate prison cells was cut short by the appearance of an official who informed them that their sentences were about to be carried out. He led the prisoners, many of whom had themselves been officers in the Petersburg regiments, past the ranks of soldiers and up onto the scaffold. The ensuing spectacle was intended to underline to the watching soldiers the price of disloyalty to the crown.[3]

Another official ordered the men to stand in line and remove their hats. He moved along the line, pausing before each man to read out the list of his imputed crimes and his punishment. Over the full half an hour it took him to perform his duties, "one sentence echoed and re-echoed like the tolling of a funeral bell: 'The Field Criminal Court has sentenced you to death by shooting.'" The emperor had personally approved each sentence with the word "Confirmed." The horror dawned on the men that they were about to die. Each was handed a long white peasant blouse and nightcap to put on. The first three prisoners, including Petrashevsky himself, were seized by the arm and led off the platform and each one was tied to a post that stood in the ground below. The firing squad walked to within 4 metres of the condemned men and raised their rifles. Surveying the drama from the scaffold in the next group of three prisoners, consumed by "mystic terror," stood the twenty-eight-year-old writer and author of *Poor Folk* (1846),

Fyodor Dostoevsky.[4] What passed through his mind in those moments as the firing squad took aim, knowing that he was next in line to die, can perhaps be surmised from a scene in his 1868 novel *The Idiot*. It was one of the most famous passages Dostoevsky ever wrote:

> Those five minutes seemed to him an infinite length of time, an immense richness; . . . nothing was so hard for him at the time as the incessant thought: "What if I didn't have to die? What if I could get my life back—what an infinity it would be! And it would all be mine! Then I would make each minute into a whole lifetime, I would lose nothing, would account for each minute, waste nothing in vain!" . . . this idea finally turned into such fury that he wanted them to shoot him as quickly as possible.[5]

On Semyonovsky Square, however, the shots never rang out. At the very last moment, an aide-de-camp galloped onto the square to deliver a pardon from Nicholas. Overcome with terror and confusion, the *Petrashevtsy* learned that the tsar had graciously spared their lives; their fate was not to die at the hands of a firing squad but to join the ranks of common criminals in penal forts across Siberia. One of them, Nikolai Grigoryev, was left unable to appreciate the tsar's magnanimity. He had already been manifesting signs of mental illness in prison; the ordeal drove him out of his mind altogether and he never recovered his senses. Dostoevsky himself learned that he was sentenced to four years' penal labour in Omsk, followed by a lifetime of military service. Petrashevsky was sentenced to penal labour for an indeterminate period. The "unconsummated" execution was then enacted in ritual form. The men were divested of their execution blouses; two executioners stepped forward to break swords ceremoniously over the prisoners' heads as they knelt. They were issued with convict clothing, dirty sheepskin coats and felt boots. A peasant cart pulled up, Petrashevsky was put in fetters and driven off on the first leg of his journey to Siberia. The others were to follow in the coming days.[6]

The theatrical director of the entire grisly pageant was none other than Nicholas himself. The mock execution served to underscore in the most brutal terms that the convicts owed their lives to the mercy of the emperor. Unlike the Decembrists, the *Petrashevtsy* would enjoy no special dispensations. Nicholas's order of clemency was very specific: "When the Tobolsk Exile Office determines their location, they should be treated as convicts in the full sense of the word. Any softening of their sentences in the future should depend upon their behaviour and upon the Emperor's mercy, but under no circumstances upon the initiatives of local authorities."[7]

Returned that day to his cell in the Peter and Paul Fortress, Dostoevsky penned a feverish letter to his brother Mikhail. He declared his burning ambition to savour every moment of his life: "Life is a gift, life is happiness, every minute could be an age of fortune! . . . Now, changing my life, I will be reborn in a new form. Brother! I swear to you that I will not lose hope, I will maintain my spirits and I will keep my heart pure. I am being reborn as something better. That is my great hope and my great consolation!" But Dostoevsky was daunted by the prospect of being silenced in Siberian exile: "Will I really never again take a pen in my hand? . . . I will send you everything that I write if I ever do write anything ever again, dear God! . . . Yes, if it is impossible to write, I will die! Better fifteen years' imprisonment with a pen in my hand!"[8]

As the clocks struck midnight on 24 December, Dostoevsky was put in leg irons. In the company of two other *Petrashevtsy,* he took his seat in a convoy of sledges guarded by gendarmes, and set out from St. Petersburg. "It was a sad moment as we crossed the Urals," Dostoevsky later recalled. "The horses and sledges had foundered in the drifts. We were in the middle of a snowstorm. We got out of the sledges—it was night—and stood waiting while they were dragged out. All around us was snow and the blizzard; it was the frontier of Europe; ahead was Siberia and our unknown fate, while the whole of our past lay behind us. It was so depressing that I wept." Dostoevsky reached Tobolsk by carriage on 9 January 1850. The party took the steep road up from the lower town to the central square perched on the edge of the plateau above the River Irtysh. As they climbed up towards the Tobolsk Forwarding Prison, they passed the Bell of Uglich, that mute reminder of the sovereign's power and of the exile's oblivion beyond the Urals.[9]

While being held in the Tobolsk Forwarding Prison, Dostoevsky received an unexpected visit. Pulling strings with the local exile officials, three of the Decembrists' wives secured a meeting with the young writer. Dostoevsky wrote of the encounter:

We saw these great martyresses who had voluntarily followed their husbands to Siberia. They gave up everything: their social position, wealth, connections, relatives, and sacrificed it all for the supreme moral duty, the freest duty that can ever exist. Guilty of nothing, they endured for twenty-five long years everything that their convicted husbands endured . . . They blessed us on our new journey; they made the sign of the cross over us and gave each of us a copy of the Gospels, the only book permitted in the prison. This book lay under my pillow during the four years of my penal servitude.[10]

Each copy of the New Testament, passed on almost as a talisman from one generation of Siberia's political exiles to the next, contained ten roubles in banknotes hidden in the binding. Dostoevsky and his fellow convicts departed Tobolsk on 20 January 1850 and reached the Omsk prison fort eleven days later.[11]

Captivity in Omsk would leave Dostoevsky a changed man. Life among the common criminals in the timber barracks forced him to fundamentally rethink his own moral and political convictions. Over the next four years, he scrawled notes that would form the basis for the most influential book to be published on Siberian exile across the whole of the nineteenth century. *Notes from the House of the Dead* (1861–2) caused a sensation both as a work of literature and as a glimpse into a horrifying world of which most educated Russians were wholly ignorant. Written from the perspective of a fictional narrator named Goryanchikov—a literary device to ease the book past the censor—the work was semi-autobiographical. Contemporaries understood it to be a memoir, rather than a work of fiction. It produced, one reviewer wrote at the time, "a striking impression. The author was seen as a new Dante who had made the descent into hell, one more terrible in that it existed not in the poet's imagination but in reality." Leo Tolstoy declared of *Notes from the House of the Dead*, "I know of no better book in all modern literature, and that includes Pushkin."[12]

Notes from the House of the Dead was one of the first of a stream of publications in the reigns of Alexander II and his successors to document for public scrutiny the unsavoury realities of Siberian exile. In the decades that followed, almost every single published report, every single piece of independent journalism, every single prison memoir offered the same damning critique of the failure of Siberia's prisons and penal forts to reform penal labourers and prepare them for settlement.[13]

Dostoevsky entered the Siberian penal system in 1850, at a time when its infrastructure and administration were suffering from decades of underfunding and neglect. The penal fort in Omsk was typical of penal settlements across Siberia in the nineteenth century. Dostoevsky's narrator, Goryanchikov, describes "a large courtyard, two hundred yards long and a hundred and fifty yards wide, completely enclosed all round by a high stockade in the form of an irregular hexagon, that is a fence of high posts, driven deep into the earth, wedged closely against one another in ribs, strengthened by cross-planks and sharpened on top: this was the outer enclosure of the prison." Inside the stockade, arranged around a central courtyard, stretched "two long, single-storeyed buildings with wooden frames."[14] These were the barracks where the convicts lived. In a letter to his brother Mikhail, written in February 1854 just a week after his release, Dostoevsky remembered how their cramped conditions forced convicts into a squalid intimacy that was as punishing as the prison regime itself:

We lived on top of each other, all together in one barrack. Imagine an old, dilapidated, wooden construction, which should have been torn down long ago, and which was no longer fit for purpose. In summer, it was unbearably stuffy; in winter, unendurably cold. All the floors were rotting through and were covered in an inch-thick layer of filth such that one could slip and fall. The little tallow windows were so coated with frost that it was almost impossible to read at any time of the day. There was an inch of ice on the panes. The ceilings were dripping; everywhere there were draughts. We were packed in like herrings in a barrel. The stove took six logs at once but produced no heat (the ice in the room barely thawed), only intolerable fumes—and this, all winter long. The convicts used to wash their clothes right there in the barracks, splashing everything with water. There was not even room to turn around. We were not allowed to leave the barracks to relieve ourselves from dusk till dawn because they were locked. Tubs

were placed inside the door to meet our nocturnal needs and so
the stench was unbearable. All the convicts stank like pigs . . .
We slept on bare planks and were allowed only a pillow. We
spread out sheepskin coats over us, and our feet were always
uncovered. We shivered all night. There were fleas, lice, and
cockroaches by the bushel.[15]

Almost all visitors to Siberian penal camps were struck by the
appalling lack of ventilation in the prisons and the stench from the tubs
lingered in the cells. And little changed in the decades that followed.
The American George Kennan offered the following description of the
air in one of the prisons he visited in the mid-1880s:

I can ask you to imagine cellar air, every atom of which has
been half a dozen times through human lungs and is heavy
with carbonic acid; to imagine that air still further vitiated
by foul pungent, slightly ammoniacal exhalations from long
unwashed human bodies; to imagine that it has a suggestion of
damp, decaying wood and more than a suggestion of human
excrement—and still you will have no adequate idea of it.[16]

The squalid and lice-infested barracks and cells were home to a
varied collection of prisoners. Men who had slit the throats of entire
families in order to steal the smallest of sums rubbed shoulders with
hapless victims of miscarriages of justice. The prisons also teemed with
petty criminals who had fled their original place of exile only to be
recaptured and punished with terms of penal labour. By the middle of
the nineteenth century, Siberia's penal forts and prisons also boasted
increasing numbers of educated Russians and Poles who had been sentenced to penal labour for their political activities.[17]

Crammed with prisoners, the barracks were a hive of activity that
generated an unrelenting cacophony of noise. A former prisoner at the
Omsk prison fort, the ethnographer and journalist Nikolai Yadrintsev,
remembered how each prisoner attended to his own affairs, offering up
contrasts that were, by turns, darkly comical and repulsive:

A mixture of sounds, chatter, commotion and guffawing, the
din in the fort cells is unimaginable. On one side you hear a

hammer beating . . . Someone is filing down some animal bones; here a piece of metal is being sharpened; there, someone has started playing some frenzied prison tunes. Somewhere there is the clanking of chains as an exile makes his way down the corridor; some unknown person is beating on a closed door with a stick. The sounds sometimes merge together and sometimes fragment, crashing into each other in striking contrasts. In one cell someone is reading the Bible aloud while alongside him another convict is dancing in the most disgusting manner. The chaste prayers of a sectarian can be heard together with the foulest swearing; an honest Muslim sings out verses from the Koran; a Jew weeps over his Psalms; and at the same time the vagabond's carefree song can be heard; for a moment the howl of a woman brought into the fort cuts through the air, followed by the curses of the overseers and shouts of endearment. Suddenly there erupts the hymn of some exile or other, full of longing and triumph, full of hopeful prayers. All of this is subsumed within the cackling chorus of the tempestuous fort, which flows into one wild and chaotic concert.[18]

Not all were able, like Yadrintsev, to appreciate the melodies of the barracks. The suffocating and forced intimacy of prison life was unbearable for those with more developed notions of privacy than the peasants or soldiers habituated to communal living. In *Notes from the House of the Dead*, Goryanchikov recalls: "I could never have conceived how terrible and agonising it would be not once, not even for one minute of all the . . . years of my imprisonment, to be alone. At work to be constantly under guard, in the barracks to be with two hundred other convicts and not once, never once to be alone!" Dostoevsky later confided to his brother that his captivity in the Omsk fort had been "a ceaseless, merciless assault on my soul . . . eternal hostility and bickering all around, cursing, cries, din, uproar . . . All that for four years!"[19]

One of Dostoevsky's fellow prisoners in Omsk, the Pole Szymon Tokarzewski, once mocked what he took to be the author's excessive preoccupation with his status as a nobleman: "It seems to me that there is no aristocracy and no nobility in the fort; there are only people here who have been stripped of all rights; only penal labourers." There was bitter irony in this observation. In the formal sense, the civil death that accompanied sentences to penal labour obliterated rank. For practical purposes, however, members of the educated classes remained conspicuously different from the common people. Like foreigners in their own land, they spoke, walked and ate differently from the mass of peasants, artisans, merchants, workers and soldiers. As Goryanchikov observes, "in spite of the fact that they have already been deprived of all their rights and are completely on a par with the other convicts, the men never accept [the noblemen] as their companions. This is not out of any conscious prejudice, but . . . a sincere and unconscious predisposition."[20]

Expelled from a society in which the vertiginous hierarchies of rank and status were encoded in manners, speech and education, most educated Russians did not benefit from the special dispensations afforded the Decembrists. Unaccustomed to the harshness of life in captivity, educated Russians also lacked the necessary social and manual skills to adapt to life in the penal forts, as Goryanchikov explains in *Notes from the House of the Dead*:

> When the common man goes to prison he arrives among his own kind of society, perhaps even among a society that is more developed than the one he has left. He has, of course, lost a great deal: his country, his family, everything—but his environment remains the same. An educated man, subject by law to the same punishment as the commoner, often loses incomparably more. He must suppress in himself all his normal wants and habits; he must make the transition to an environment that is inadequate for him . . . And often the punishment the law considers equal and apportions equally becomes ten times more painful for him.[21]

Common convicts often viewed educated prisoners with suspicion and even downright hostility, but even so, they remained psychologically and culturally conditioned to respect them. Memoirs of Siberia's penal settlements also recorded examples of kindness and generosity shown to the educated classes by common convicts. One peasant exile took

pity on a disoriented and fumbling nobleman travelling in a marching convoy and inexplicably and selflessly took care of him on the
long journey into exile, refusing any kind of payment for his labours.
And yet the gulf between the common people and educated society
remained, for the most part, unbridgeable. It was a painful separation
for educated Russians to ponder as many had been exiled precisely for
their attempts to bring freedom to the masses.[22]

Siberia's prisons and penal barracks proved an inhospitable terrain for
the forging of friendships. The exiled revolutionary Pyotr Yakubovich
found that "everyone looks at everyone else not as a comrade in misery
but as a wolf looks at another wolf, an enemy at an enemy. The very
word 'comrade,' for which in fact the convicts have a great affection, is
not used in our cultured sense: Men are called 'comrades' if they drink
and eat together from the same bowls . . . [which is] usually a matter
of chance." In place of friendship and solidarity, one-upmanship and
verbal sparring dominated relations between the convicts, and the barracks echoed to the sounds of relentless bickering. The penal labourers
held wit and the ability to turn a cutting phrase in high regard. "They
swore with finesse, with artistic skill," Goryanchikov recalls in *Notes
from the House of the Dead*. Yakubovich perceived a "form of artistic
competition" in the convicts' foul language and insults.[23]

Some prisoners would also try to outdo each other in conspicuous
cynicism. One convict in the Irkutsk prison recounted to a political
prisoner how, together with a "comrade," he had slaughtered a family:

> What on earth for?—I couldn't restrain myself.
> For money, obviously—my interlocutor grinned calmly.
> Yes, but why kill them all, even the children?
> We did the whole lot. Another time we butchered two fam-
> ilies . . .
> And God?—I asked—are you really not scared?
> What God? . . . Wherever we've been . . . In the furthest
> flung places, where crows don't even carry bones and where
> animals don't go, we've seen neither God nor the Devil.[24]

Educated observers, from Alexander Herzen to Anton Chekhov, repeatedly noted (and lamented) that the Russian village was a legal world

unto itself. Popular understandings of crime, justice and punishment were often in sharp conflict with official legal culture. Peasants would either brutally punish or turn a blind eye to the same crime, depending on whether the victim was a member of their village or an outsider. The peasantry often had an indulgent attitude to violence against women, against members of other faiths and against strangers. Rape, arson and murder were all forms of retribution sanctioned by peasant communities. Ignorant of the empire's legal statutes, convicts found themselves exiled to Siberia for acts that they struggled to understand as crimes.[25] Ivan Yefimov, the commandant of the Aleksandrovsk penal distillery in Irkutsk province, tried and failed to convince one otherwise amenable convict that "slitting the throats of 'yids'" was, in fact, a crime. The man "remained convinced that it was a mere trifle." Dostoevsky's narrator, Goryanchikov, discerns in these expressions of indifference to the crimes they had committed many convicts' complete isolation from the laws of the Russian Empire: "The majority of them did not feel that they had done any wrong whatsoever . . . the criminal knows for a certainty that he will be acquitted by the judgment of his own people, who will never finally condemn him and who will for the most part fully acquit him, as long as the crime is not against one of his own kind, his brothers, his common kith and kin." Many convicts were sustained in prison by their desire for revenge against those they believed to have wronged them.[26]

Violence threaded its way through the very fabric of prison life. Brawling among prisoners was frowned upon as it elicited the unwanted attentions of the warders.[27] When the convicts had been drinking, however, fights were wont to erupt. Shortly after his arrival in Omsk, Goryanchikov encounters the fearsome Gazin: "he was horribly strong, stronger than anyone else in the prison; he was taller than average, of Herculean build, with an ugly disproportionately large head . . . the convicts would have it, I do not know with what justification, that he was an escaped convict from Nerchinsk; that he had already been exiled to Siberia and escaped several times, that he had changed his name and finally ended up in our prison." When Gazin drank, he would "start by picking on men with taunts of the most vicious kind, calculated and seemingly prepared long in advance; finally, when he was completely intoxicated, he would pass into a fearful rage, grab a knife and go for men with it." Unable to defend themselves individually, the convicts would respond by attacking Gazin as a group:

> A dozen or so men from the barrack he belonged to would rush him together and begin beating him. It is impossible to conceive of anything more cruel than this beating: they beat him in the chest, in the heart, in the solar plexus, in the stomach, they beat him long and hard, and only stopped when he was completely unconscious and looked as if he were dead. They could not have brought themselves to beat anyone else like this: to beat a man in this fashion meant to kill him—Gazin, however, they could not kill. After they had beaten him up they would wrap him, quite unconscious, in a sheepskin coat and carry him to the plank bed. "They say he gets over it once he's had a rest." And so it was: the next morning he would get up almost well again, and would go out to work morosely and in silence. And every time Gazin got drunk, all the men in the prison knew that the day would end in a beating for him. He knew it too, but he went on getting drunk just the same.[28]

Once given, or at least taken, offence could easily end in killing.[29] The Okhotsk salt works was one of the most punishing penal sites in Siberia, a bleak settlement in the far north-east, on the coast of the Sea of Okhotsk. Penal labourers there would toil over large salt-pans distilling salt from seawater. The salt works was reserved for recidivist criminals who had already committed murders in Siberia's prisons and forts. An official there in the 1820s remembered the almost casual brutality and the spontaneity with which prisoners would turn on each other. One convict, Ivan Medyantsev, was a merchant from Yaroslavl, forty-four years of age, lean, well-built and "remarkably strong." Convicted of murder, he had been knouted and sentenced to penal labour in the Nerchinsk mines, where he had gone on to kill again. As a recidivist, he had then been sent to Okhotsk, where he again took the life of a fellow prisoner. When the official entered the cell in the aftermath of the killing, he saw Medyantsev reading the Bible, for "he always liked to read the Bible" after committing a murder:

> Talking to Medyantsev, I urged him not to commit any more murders. Apart from pointing out the punishments that

awaited him in the next life, I tried to appeal to his reason, emphasising that crimes could be atoned for, that they could be committed foolishly, out of man's weaknesses, but that once a life is taken, it cannot be returned and no atonement can be made. Man is God's creation and belongs to Him; such a crime cannot be forgiven neither in the here and now nor in the afterlife. Medyantsev responded with a sigh: "I'm not happy about it myself—do you think it's fun to kill a man?" "But you have been killing for a long time!" "There are times when a man is so miserable that he can do evil things and not even look upon the light. Whatever you see turns red before your eyes, soaked by the blood of the living. You are so tormented that you would gladly hide away, but then along comes some snivelling idiot to bother you. You don't remember yourself how you smashed his skull in with your fetters, but then you see that you've killed him. Suddenly the shell falls away, the torment subsides and the red mist clears from your eyes. You feel sorry for the man, but there's nothing to be done."[30]

In the Aleksandrovsk penal distillery, Yefimov remembered being roused from his bed before dawn one winter morning in 1849 to attend a crime scene. One elderly labourer had stabbed another to death in a dispute over their breakfast. The two had known each other for a long time and always ate together in the prison barracks. On this occasion, when one of them began to cut the bread and onion, the other waited patiently for his turn with the knife and then plunged it into his companion's breast: "The murder was pointless and without purpose . . . In response to all questions, the murderer simply replied 'I don't remember what for; I don't know why I did it . . .'" One morning shortly afterwards, the warders entered one of the locked and guarded distilleries only to discover a "corpse in a pool of blood surrounded by a few copper coins and discarded greasy playing cards." The victim proved to be a Jewish coppersmith named Kornyushka, who had spent the night gambling with two other penal labourers tasked with guarding the alcohol in the distillery. They had played cards for many hours until an argument broke out, whereupon one of the men had seized an axe and delivered such a blow to Kornyushka's neck that he "almost completely severed his head." The assailants had been planning to dispose of the body that evening but were found out before they could cover their tracks.[31]

The barracks were not simply dens of iniquity and violence. Once they were locked shut for the night, they transformed into hives of commercial activity as the men sat in their accustomed places and took up their various crafts. Some stitched boots or tailored new clothes from material they had acquired; others repaired watches and carved ornaments. Many demonstrated extraordinary artistry and were capable of fashioning, "from splinters and slats . . . wooden model birds which any merchant of moderate means would have had no hesitation in hanging from the ceiling of his living room or hallway." Others would create intricate and beautifully finished children's toys from dried bread and animal bones. Whenever the opportunity presented itself, convict watch-makers, carpenters, tailors and musicians would ply their trades in the surrounding towns and villages. One convict named Tsezik, who had lived in a variety of different Siberian prisons, was a masterful creator of model creatures. His works adorned the refined studies of directors of gold mines and of senior government officials; they only increased in value after Tsezik passed away.[32]

In this way, money could be earned; alternatively, it could be made. Counterfeiters were the artisanal elite of Siberia's penal forts and prisons. Usually drawn from the ranks of vagabonds, they specialized in forging contracts, documents and, most importantly, money. The most gifted and successful had been trained as engravers, draughtsmen and scribes, and their skills secured for them a celebrity status. One such individual, Kozhevnikov, was famed for both his skill and his spontaneous acts of "generosity" towards the local peasantry, upon whom he would on occasion bestow expertly forged *assignaty*, or banknotes, to a value that would dwarf the peasants' own income. The penal forts were famous throughout Siberia for their production of counterfeit money. The illiterate Siberian peasantry proved gullible victims of the wily forgers. The arts of forgery, of smuggling and of theft were all taught in Siberia's penal settlements and passed on from hardened convicts to fresh-faced newcomers. One exile described them as "academies of crime."[33]

Earned, forged or stolen, money had, Goryanchikov discovers in

Notes from the House of the Dead, a "terrible significance and power in the prison." It was necessary to obtain goods, bribe guards, secure deals with fellow inmates and fund escapes. But beyond these practical applications, Goryanchikov understands that the funds convicts earned, forged and stole purchased something far more valuable:

> It is safe to say that the convict who had any money at all in the prison suffered ten times less than the one who had none at all, even though the latter was provided with all the regulation prison issue and had, it was thought, according to the administration's reasoning, little use for money . . . if the convicts had been deprived of the chance of earning their own money they would either have gone insane or would have died like flies . . . or would have ended by stooping to unheard of acts of villainy—some out of boredom, others in order to be executed and put out of their misery as soon as possible . . . If after earning his kopeck by practically sweating blood or devising extraordinarily complicated ruses, often involving theft and fraud, in order somehow to obtain it, the convict goes on to spend it carelessly like a child . . . he is throwing it away on something he considers to be a degree higher in value than money. What is it that has a higher value than money? It is freedom, or at least the dream of freedom.[34]

"Freedom" could be purchased from the *maidan*—from the Turkish *meydan* meaning "public square" or "ring"—which the convict communes operated in each penal settlement. The *maidan* provided a range of goods and services both permitted and illicit. Thread for mending clothes, leather or felt for making new boots, tools for budding craftsmen, ink for forgers: these could all be ordered and acquired through the storekeeper or *maidanshchik*. The *maidan* also stood at the centre of a roaring clandestine trade in alcohol. Both commodity and currency, vodka was trafficked into the prisons and camps by convicts who procured it from exiles who lived around the penal settlements. The bootlegging was an art form involving ingenious methods of concealment. Mules working for the *maidanshchik* would collect the vodka from an agreed drop beyond the walls of the fort or prison. They would fill the rinsed-out lungs and intestines of slaughtered cattle with the alcohol, would wrap them around their bodies beneath their ragged clothing and then, displaying "skill and thievish cunning," would smuggle the contraband past the guards and sentries. Dostoevsky's fellow captive in the Omsk fort, Tokarzewski, recalled that the "smuggler who succeeded in delivering vodka from the tavern to the fort was, in the minds of the penal labourers, a real 'hero.'"[35]

Like all the other goods and services purveyed by the *maidan*, vodka was freely available to those with money, albeit at grotesquely inflated prices. Convicts would drink away what little money they had and then sell their food; finally they would draw on credit from the *maidanshchik*, who, as a consequence, came to wield great economic power over his fellow prisoners. The *maidanshchik* and the suppliers were the prison's "only capitalists." The mark-up on alcohol was as much as 150 per cent and the extortionate prices, propped up by the *maidan*'s monopoly, devoured the convicts' meagre funds.[36]

For vodka and wine offered an illusion of freedom. Convicts went on drinking binges that lasted days, fuelling spells of personal oblivion that offered a temporary respite from the regimented claustrophobia governing daily life. Tokarzewski encountered "unbridled revelry and drunkenness" when convicts managed to get their hands on vodka. Work details beyond the prison walls provided an opportunity to drink. In one instance, an inebriated convict was left sleeping under a bush when the guards returned to the Krasnoyarsk prison with their penal labourers. It was only after he had spent a day working off his hangover that he reappeared at the prison gates. Yadrintsev reported how in one penal fort, the *maidanshchik* was an exiled nobleman who turned a ward in the infirmary into a veritable tavern with shelves stocked with wine, vodka and leather flasks hanging to dry from the bars on the window. He could be found "amidst a battery of bottles and jars, pouring out measures with the artistry of an old tapster." One prankster had scrawled "drinking establishment and liquor store" in chalk on the wall above.[37]

The forced idleness and squalor of the prisons and penal forts drove the prisoners not only to drink, but also to gamble. The games involved cards and bones (though Kennan recorded convicts in the marching convoys, presumably deprived of the luxury of either, using live insects). Card games were a reigning obsession in the prisons and penal forts. More than just a general store, the *maidan* was also a gambling den where the *maidanshchik* was master of ceremonies. He would unfurl a greasy length of carpet, provide dice, bones and cards upon request and administer the pot. Players would pay a fee to join the game—thirty kopecks for the first game, twenty for the second and one for the third, after which they could play for free. The playing cards were either purchased and smuggled into the prison or meticulously fashioned by the convicts themselves in a decorative homage to the power that chance wielded over their lives. The red suits of hearts and diamonds were sometimes coloured using the blood of the card-makers themselves, "such were the lengths to which the men were prepared to go to be able to gamble!" The *maidanshchik* would receive a cut—between 5 and 10 per cent—of the winnings. These monies then flowed (at least in theory) back into the general kitty, so the prisoners' commune had a direct financial stake in the card games. The unofficial rules further stipulated that one third of the winnings be returned to the loser at the end of the game. This constraint upon the brutal economics of the gambling den was intended to prevent prisoners from falling into complete destitution. It also ensured that they lived to gamble another day. Yet such efforts to temper the passions were unable to address the reckless abandon with which convicts would gamble everything and anything they either possessed or even promised to acquire.[38]

"They were all games of chance," Goryanchikov remembers. "Each player placed a heap of copper coins in front of him—all that he had in his pockets—and got up only when he had lost everything or had taken all his companions' money." Lookouts were a necessary precaution, as the warders would confiscate both the cards and the pot if they caught men gambling. An assiduous prison warder in Tobolsk received a tip-off one night that a game was underway in one of the prison barracks. His attempts to steal into the building unnoticed were undone, however, for the floor of the barracks was strewn with the bodies of sleeping men. As the warder and the sentries crept into the barracks in darkness, they trampled on the sleeping convicts, whose shouts of indignation alerted the players to the danger. The cards vanished from view, and the intruders were forced to beat a retreat from the incensed prisoners.[39]

Interior Ministry official Vasily Vlasov reported in 1870 that the convicts' "passion for gambling leads them to such extremes that having lost their money, the convicts go on to lose their clothing and food."

He observed with grim fascination how, "left without food and cloth-ing, the loser would hide himself beneath the plank beds or behind the stove until he acquired new clothing and, until such time as his debt was paid off, he would live off the alms of his comrades." Such alms were proffered, he surmised, because the loser's fellow prisoners "saw in him an unfortunate victim of chance, a fate that might just as easily befall them."[40] The principled desperation of the gambling convicts, when they were called upon to repay their debts, impressed the English anthropologist Charles Henry Hawes on his travels through Siberia at the end of the nineteenth century:

> If they have no money or secret store of food, and there are extraordinary underground ways of possessing these, the Crown tools lent them to repair their boots will be staked, then their clothes, and finally their rations even to a month ahead. Should the gamester lose all these, he regards the last as a debt of honour, and he succeeds in paying it in a novel manner. In fact, it reflects a standard of honour that even Monte Carlo could not exceed. The loser is put into a cell, and with his own consent starved for every two days, and fed on the third, thus accumulating rations to his credit which are taken in payment of his debt.[41]

Men who had gambled or drunk away all their money were known as the *zhigany*, a caste of unfortunates in the prison whose destitu-tion made them especially vulnerable and exploited. They were forced to undertake the most menial and revolting jobs, emptying the tubs full of human waste, cleaning the filthy barracks and working as man-servants for the more successful gamblers. During the card games, a *zhigan* would be paid a pittance to be on lookout while the game was in progress. He would freeze and shiver in the darkness of a passage in a temperature of −30°C for some six or seven hours at a stretch, listening for every warning sound that came from outside. In 1897, journalist Vlas Doroshevich encountered one such prisoner "with gal-loping consumption" in a prison infirmary on the island of Sakhalin. "He had lost everything, including his bread ration. For months, he had been consuming nothing but the gruel that Sakhalin's swine ate only with reluctance. In the infirmary, he had begun betting medicine.

The exhausted, dying man's listless and extinct eyes only glittered and blazed with life when he spoke of gambling."[42]

The vicissitudes of the cards meshed with a devil-may-care fatalism among the prisoners. In a world in which violence and insecurity were inescapable, the cards offered convicts (at least the illusion of) agency and the possibility of escape from the destitution that daily gnawed at them. To play cards was to challenge fate—to attempt, even against the odds, as the convicts would cry, "To beat the devil!" For Yakubovich, gambling and alcohol supplied a little colour to lives coarsened beyond measure: "Without cards or vodka, or even perhaps without the birch rod, without something spicy, stimulating, life would not be life to these men."[43]

Dostoevsky's narrator, Goryanchikov, sees in the convict's irrational and self-destructive behaviour, through drinking or gambling or fighting, a brief assertion of personality, a minor act of defiance against the baseness of captivity:

> One convict or another can have lived quietly for several years . . . when suddenly for no apparent reason whatever—as if the devil had got into him—he starts to behave waywardly, to go on binges, get mixed up in brawls, and sometimes even to take the risk of committing a criminal offence: he is openly disrespectful to a senior official, or he commits murder or rape etc. . . . The cause of this sudden outburst in the man . . . is nothing more than an anguished, convulsive manifestation of the man's personality, his instinctive anguish and anguished longing for himself, his desire to declare himself and his humiliated personality, a desire which appears suddenly and which sometimes ends in anger, in frenzied rage, in insanity, fits, convulsions . . . If he is to go on a binge, then he goes on a binge with a vengeance, if he takes a risk, he risks everything, even murder. It is enough for him only to get started: when the man grows intoxicated, there is no holding him back.[44]

This human compulsion to express individual autonomy, even if through acts of irrational self-destruction, would echo through many of Dostoevsky's later works, from *Notes from Underground* (1864) to *Demons* (1871).

. . .

Brutal and chaotic though they undoubtedly were, the prisons and penal forts were far from lawless. Prisoners governed themselves through an intricate web of traditions and practices overseen by the commune (*obshchina*). George Kennan described the convict's commune as the "body politic of the criminal world; and it fills, in the life of the exile, the same place that the commune fills in the life of the peasant."[45] A stable and extended version of the *artel,* that self-governing organization of convicts in the marching convoys en route to Siberia, the prisoners' commune operated in all penal settlements along similar lines. Its primary functions were to afford its members protection from the authorities and to collectivize some of their resources in order to secure various benefits. Each commune usually had up to some 100 members, drawn from a particular barracks or prison wing; there might be several of them in the larger penal forts and settlements. Each one would elect an elder, or *starosta,* responsible for administering funds paid into a central kitty and for negotiating with the prison authorities. The prison warders would confirm the appointment of the *starosta* and would then deal with him directly. Dependent on a basic level of cooperation in their dealings with the convicts, the warders could only remove the *starosta* from his position with the consent of the rest of the commune. The commune similarly distributed tasks among the various prisoners; exemptions from such labours could be purchased by funds paid directly into the kitty. The commune was obliged to offer credit to its poorer members, who then had to work to pay off the debt. Prisoners who arrived in the forts and prisons without a kopeck to their name were assigned the most onerous and unpleasant tasks. The rules of the commune were the aggregation of decades of customs, forged within the prisons. For ethnographer Sergei Maksimov, they had become "fixed within the air itself, passed on by the very prison walls to each new generation of convicts."[46]

The commune was not without power in its struggles with the authorities. At the Irkutsk salt works, the commune conspired to bring about the dismissal of a particularly unpopular disciplinarian and (most importantly) incorruptible junior officer. A vagabond was paid to stagger about the prison feigning drunkenness. As expected, the man was seized and subjected to a beating for his drinking, while the head of the prison demanded to know who had supplied him with vodka. The wily vagabond, who had agreed a rate of two kopecks for every blow of the birch rod, then denounced the junior officer as the chief purveyor of alcohol in the prison. His claims were initially met with incredulity and with blow after blow of the rod—more than 200 in total—but still the vagabond stuck to his story. Eventually, the overseer asked to see inside the junior officer's bag and discovered a bottle of vodka that another prisoner had planted there moments before. The vagabond received four silver roubles and the commune freed itself from the tiresome vigilance of the overzealous junior officer, who was removed from his post.[47]

The only real crime the commune recognized was betrayal. As Kennan observed, "the exile may lie, he may rob, he may murder if he will, provided his action does not affect injuriously the interests of the *artel* to which he belongs; but if he disobeys that organization, or betrays its secrets to the prison authorities, even under the compulsion of the lash—he may count himself dead already." Informers and spies were especially loathed as their betrayals threatened the very fabric of communal life. Their whispered reports might expose a route used by smugglers to bring goods into the prison or they might foil a planned escape. Two hardened vagabonds in the Omsk fort had been planning an escape when, only days before their intended departure, their fetters were tightened and the guard strengthened. The two men spent months investigating who had tipped off the prison authorities. They came to suspect their cellmate and, over a couple of nights, they removed the planks that covered one of the walls in their cell and dug a shallow grave inside the wall. On the third night, they seized the man while he slept, stopped up his mouth, shoved him into the grave and buried him alive. The following morning, when the cell was opened at roll call, the guards could find no trace of the convict and assumed that he must have made his escape in the night. The entire prison knew what had happened to the informer but no one reported the crime.[48]

Punishments were sometimes meted out collectively, in the best traditions of the peasant commune.[49] Gangs of prisoners would inflict a punishment they called "covering someone in darkness." They would assault malefactors by throwing a hood over their heads before subjecting them to a savage beating. Vengeance could be exacted at any moment. In the Omsk fort, one young joiner, placed in charge of a work detail in the prison, made the fatal error of reporting to the authorities a tunnel that the men had dug through to the women's quarters to facilitate visits to their lovers. The tunnel was uncovered and closed. The enraged prisoners later caught up with the joiner on the roof of the building and shoved him off the fourth floor. He was fortunate to survive the fall from what Yadrintsev called an "improvised Tarpeian Rock."* The most serious violators of the commune's codes would be brought before a "gathering" of up to 100 of its members. They would be harangued, humiliated and, if found guilty by the more senior and authoritative members of the commune, subjected to a violent and sustained beating. A crowd of convicts would sometimes furiously shake and trample an informer "until all his insides were pulverised and his bones broken." If the man was not killed straightaway, he would be dumped on his bench in the barracks and left to languish in agony and abject disgrace. The victim of the commune's justice would not dare to complain or even to visit the infirmary to seek medical attention for his wounds. Yadrintsev noted drily that the "prison forts were inventive in their punishments."[50]

Those who sought refuge from the authorities would invariably be hunted down and murdered, even after transfer to another prison. One informer in the Tara penal fort took refuge in solitary confinement under special guard for a year until those he betrayed had already left the penal fort. When he did finally emerge, however, he was still stabbed to death, by a new group of prisoners he had never before encountered. Vagabonds would carry forth the names and descriptions of informers to penal settlements across Siberia and the convicts would still exact retribution, sometimes a generation after the offence.[51]

Such brutal punishments were intended to maintain a disciplined observance of the commune's codes and, in so doing, enjoyed a certain rationality. A prisoner guilty of a crime, but not yet caught, did not fear betrayal by his fellow convicts; if indeed identified as the culprit, he in turn would never betray his accomplices. The commune's elder was on occasion obliged to submit himself to corporal punishment on behalf of the entire commune rather than divulge the identities of its members who had committed a crime within the prison. The scars on

---

* A steep cliff overlooking the Roman Forum from which murderers, traitors, perjurers and larcenous slaves were flung to their deaths.

his back assured his position and his continued standing among his fellow convicts.[52]

The *starosta*'s loyalty to the commune was not beyond reproach, though. Elders were known to gamble away the commune's kitty and brazenly steal from the common supplies. Especially egregious violations of the commune's collective morality could result in an unpopular *starosta* being deposed. By and large, however, the prisoners' commune took little interest in the sanctity of private property, the very idea of which did not fare well in the barracks and prison cells.[53]

Prisoners would initially conceal in holes in the walls the few personal belongings they had managed to carry with them into exile, or cram them into small padlocked boxes. But concealment and locks were no safeguard against determined and experienced thieves. Pilfering was both rife and shameless, regarded almost as a legitimate way of circulating goods within the prisons rather than as a violation of moral norms. Newcomers to the prison were especially vulnerable. They would find themselves warmly welcomed by a group of inmates who would engagingly explain the rules of the prison at great length while unseen hands grabbed their hats, scarves or some or other of their possessions and tossed them into the crowd. The newcomers would search for them everywhere, but in vain; their belongings would end up being sold in local markets.[54]

Convicts would go to elaborate lengths to conceal any money they possessed. They would glue it into the pages of books, sew it into their underwear, stuff it into the heels of their boots, which were specially hollowed out for the purpose; they wore it in belts strapped around their knees. The other convicts knew all these tricks and used to keep close watch on each other to see who was using which methods. If they realized that a fellow prisoner had money, they would lose no time in stealing it, together with the object in which it was concealed. The arts of theft and concealment developed in tandem. Some convicts were able to steal belongings from under the noses of their fellow prisoners, while other specialists were able to conceal them in places they would never be found. One contemporary recalled: "They would stash them under floors, in chimneys, bury them in the yard." A contractor from a neighbouring town, who had antagonized the convicts in one of Siberia's penal forts, left his horse in the yard when coming to visit the overseer. When the contractor emerged from his meeting, he discovered the horse was missing. A commotion ensued and a senior official was summoned. A search failed to uncover the horse and eventually the official asked the convicts to reveal its whereabouts, promising them that no action would be taken against them. The prisoners took the official to the bathhouse, pulled aside some planks from the floor and led the horse out into the yard.[55]

At the end of their sentences of penal labour, Siberia's convicts stepped from their prisons unprepared for a life of agricultural labour. They were, however, rigorously schooled in the arts of smuggling, pilfering and forgery, skills they would bring to bear in the hapless communities into which they would be dispersed as settled exiles.

Aged only thirty-four, Dostoevsky was finally released from the Omsk penal fort in February 1854. His sentence had been commuted to service in the ranks of the 7th Line Battalion of the Siberian Army Corps in Semipalatinsk.[56] He had survived his four years of penal labour but the experience marked him for life and was crucial for the development of his writing and philosophy. The men with whom he shared his captivity offered compelling psychological studies for the thieves and murderers who filled the pages of his great post-Siberia novels: *Crime and Punishment* (1866), *The Idiot* (1868), *Demons* (1871) and *The Brothers Karamazov* (1880). The writer's observations in Siberia of the darker impulses of the human psyche fed into a relentless obsession with crime, responsibility and morality.[57]

Russian intellectual life in the middle of the nineteenth century was dominated by debates over the nature of the peasantry and the shape of Russia's development. Romantic conservatives such as Aleksei Khomyakov and Ivan Aksakov, known as the Slavophiles, believed that the intelligentsia should reject the westward orientation of Russia's modernization since Peter the Great. Instead, it should seek to embrace the true Orthodox Christian values of the peasantry and recover the organic unity of pre-Petrine Russia. The Slavophiles claimed that the Russian peasantry, with its communal way of life, its peaceful existence and its natural humility, was the only true Christian people, uncontaminated by the selfish individualism and materialism of the West. Populists such as Alexander Herzen and Nikolai Chernyshevsky stood in the tradition of the early liberal Westernizers. They saw the peasantry as essentially rational, as champions of liberty and as the bearers of a collectivist spirit, embodied in the village commune, which heralded a bright socialist future for Russia.[58]

Both conservatives and radicals, however, superimposed their own ideological ambitions onto the values and psychology of a people they knew only superficially as serfs, household servants and soldiers. Dostoevsky later attacked the abstractions that underpinned the thinking of both ideologies:

> The question of the common people and our view of them, our present understanding of them, is our most important question, a question on which our whole future rests; one might say it is the most practical question at the moment. However, the common people are still a theory for all of us and still stand before us as a riddle. All of us who love the common people look at them as if at a theory and, it seems, not one of us loves them as they really are but only as each of us imagines them to be. And even if the Russian people eventually were to turn out to be not as we imagined them, then we all, despite our love for them, would likely renounce them at once with no regrets. I am speaking about all of us, including even the Slavophiles, who, perhaps, would be the first to renounce them.[59]

Four years in the Omsk prison fort had given Dostoevsky, by contrast, ample opportunity to observe the common people at close quarters, and he took pride in the insights he gained. "My time there has not been in vain," he wrote to his brother a week after his release, "if I did not discover Russia, then I did at least get to know its people well, so well as only a few people know them."[60] Living cheek-by-jowl with criminals in a world unstructured by the social hierarchies of tsarist Russia, Dostoevsky discovered little to love and little to admire. He found there neither the selfless, humble Christians imagined by the Slavophiles, nor the rational collectivists imagined by the Populists. He found instead "coarse, hostile and embittered" men, prone to all manner of vices, from drunken excess to violent cruelty. Most shattering of all, for a young idealist convinced of the innate goodness of all human beings, was the convicts' complete lack of remorse. Goryanchikov in *Notes from the House of the Dead* remembers:

I saw among these people not the slightest trace of repentance, not one sign that their crime weighed heavily on their conscience . . . the majority of them consider themselves to be completely in the right. Of course, vanity, bad examples, foolhardiness and false shame are the causes of much of it . . . Yet it must surely have been possible over so many years to have noticed something, to have caught at least some feature of these hearts that bore witness to an inner anguish, to suffering. But this was absent, quite definitely absent.[61]

The population of the penal fort seemed to expose the self-deluding nature of the intelligentsia's ambition to reshape the peasantry in its own image. Both Slavophiles and Populists sought, each with their own prescriptions, to bridge the "chasm" between the educated class and the "dark people," between what Herzen had decried in 1851 as the "two Russias."[62] In Omsk, Dostoevsky endured at first hand the incomprehension and enmity that filled this "chasm." Even though his fellow prisoners "had no understanding of our crimes," he wrote to his brother in 1854:

> The hatred of the common criminals for the gentry knows no bounds and that is why they greeted us, noblemen, with hostility and took perverse pleasure in our misery. They would have eaten us alive, given the chance. You cannot imagine how vulnerable we were, having to live, drink, eat and sleep alongside these people for several years and when it was quite impossible even to complain about the countless insults of all kinds. "You're noblemen, iron beaks that used to peck us to death. Before, you used to be masters, you used to torment the people, but now you're the lowest of the low. You've become one of us"—that was the theme on which they played variations for four years. One hundred and fifty enemies could never tire of terrorising us . . . we did not understand each other and so we [noblemen] had to endure all their vengeance and persecution.[63]

The picture Dostoevsky sketched out to his brother in his letter was not, however, unremittingly grim. The convicts might have been coarse, but some were still capable of flashes of humanity despite the squalor and brutality of their lives. "Over the four years of penal servitude among the brigands, I did finally discover some human beings," he wrote. "Believe it or not: There were among them some deep, strong and magnificent characters and it was so uplifting to discover these gold nuggets beneath such a rough surface."[64]

In the years following his release from exile, Dostoevsky went on to re-imagine his collision with the dark and horrifying world of the penal fort. In his post-Siberia novels, he pointed to the opportunities for moral resurrection that could be found in exile. The anti-hero of *Crime and Punishment,* Rodion Raskolnikov, finally succeeds in shedding his nihilist convictions and fanatical utilitarianism to find love, spiritual redemption and even acceptance among the penal labourers of Siberia.[65] During his trial for parricide in *The Brothers Karamazov,* the dissolute nobleman Dmitry Karamazov embraces his own moral guilt for wishing his father dead, even though he is innocent of the murder. He welcomes a probable sentence of penal labour in Siberia's mines as an opportunity for moral purification:

> During these last two months I have felt a new man in myself, a new man has been resurrected within me! He was imprisoned within me, but he would never have appeared had it not been for this lightning bolt. I am afraid! Oh, what do I care if I have to chip out ore in the mines for twenty years with a hammer—of that I am not afraid at all; no, it is something else I am afraid of now: that the resurrected man may leave me! It is possible there, too, in the mines, under the earth, beside one, in another convict and murderer like oneself to find a human heart and to consort with him, for there, too, it is possible to live, and love, and suffer! It is possible to resuscitate and resurrect in that convict the heart that has stopped beating, it is possible to nurse him for years and bring out, at last, from the den of thieves into the light a soul that is lofty now, a consciousness that is that of a martyr, resuscitate an angel, resurrect a hero![66]

The author's ordeal in the Omsk penal fort might have stripped away his idealistic preconceptions about the common people, but it ultimately ended up reaffirming—or perhaps necessitating—a belief in their spiritual sensibilities and thirst for redemption.[67] In an essay he published in his *Diary of a Writer* in 1876, Dostoevsky described the "miraculous" moment at which he had become able to discern the essential humanity of the convicts. Surrounded in the barracks by convicts who were busy administering another beating to the drunken and violent Gazin, Dostoevsky lay down on his bunk to escape the mayhem and fell into a reverie. He remembered an episode from his own childhood when, as a nine-year-old boy, he fled in terror from a forest where he thought a wolf was prowling and found himself in one of the fields on his family estate. There, one of his father's serfs, a peasant called Marey, took pity on him and did his best to comfort him:

> He quietly stretched out a thick, earth-soiled finger with a black nail and gently touched it to my trembling lips.
>
> "Now, now," he smiled at me with a broad, almost maternal smile. "Lord, what a dreadful fuss. Dear, dear, dear!"
>
> [. . .] And so when I climbed down from my bunk and looked around, I remember I suddenly felt I could regard these unfortunates in an entirely different way and that suddenly, through some sort of miracle, my former hatred and anger in my heart had vanished. This disgraced peasant, with shaven head and brands on his cheek, drunk and roaring out his hoarse, drunken song—why he might also be that very same Marey; I cannot peer into his heart, after all.[68]

This conversion, so Dostoevsky wrote, marked the beginning of the author's long journey from the utopian socialism of the *Petrashevtsy* to a new political philosophy that was now much closer to the thinking of the Slavophiles. As his own religious and nationalist convictions strengthened, Dostoevsky began to re-imagine that not just a small minority but *all* his erstwhile companions in Omsk were men imbued with an acute sense of moral responsibility and a yearning for forgiveness: "I believe that perhaps not one of them escaped the long inner suffering that cleansed and strengthened him. I saw them in church praying before confession . . . in his heart not one of them considered himself justified!" It was the convicts' resilient faith, which survived even the inhumanity of the prison fort, that would, in his view, provide the basis for healing the rift of mutual fear and enmity that divided

Russia's educated classes and the common people; all would become spiritual equals.[69]

This redemptive memory of his encounter with the common people in the Omsk penal fort became the touchstone of Dostoevsky's subsequent messianic nationalism: the author hailed his "direct contact with the People, the brotherly union with them in common misfortune, the awareness that we ourselves had become as they, equal to them, and even placed on the very lowest of their levels." He had, he remembered, been able to "return to the root of the common people, to discover the Russian soul, to recognise the common people's spirit."[70]

When he eventually returned to St. Petersburg in 1859, Dostoevsky joined a group of writers known as the "grassroots" movement (*pochvennichestvo*), which argued that a new fraternity in Orthodox Christianity would enable Russia to answer its great spiritual calling as a leader of nations. Far more than a memory, Siberia became for Dostoevsky an imaginative canvas on which to explore the possibilities of individual and collective redemption, and a vision of Russia's unique national destiny.[71]

8

"In the Name of Freedom!"

Following his quashing of the November Insurrection in the Kingdom of Poland in 1831, Nicholas I ordered the construction of a massive fortified complex in the centre of Warsaw. This forbidding edifice on the banks of the Vistula was designed to bolster the tsarist military presence and also to serve as a symbol of Russian imperial domination in the unruly city. The Citadel boasted a standing garrison of 5,000 soldiers and heavy artillery pieces that could cover most of the city with fire. Hundreds of prison cells were built inside the Citadel's casements. The most notorious among them were those of the Tenth Pavilion, which, over the course of the nineteenth century, held a succession of notable Polish rebels and revolutionaries. The whole complex was dubbed the "Warsaw Bastille."

The Citadel proved its worth for Nicholas's heir, Alexander II, when in 1863 the Poles staged their second doomed attempt to fight their way to independence. The immediate origins of what became known as the "January Uprising" lay in Alexander's Great Reforms of the early 1860s, which had sparked hopes for increased autonomy and liberalization in the Western Borderlands and the Kingdom of Poland. St. Petersburg's refusal to countenance such concessions, however, fomented political discontent. Nationalist demonstrations across Poland spilled over into rioting. The tsar's viceroy in the kingdom, General Karl Lambert, responded by imposing martial law in October 1861 and arresting leading nationalists. Combined with long-standing economic grievances, the political discontent turned to unrest, and unrest to outright rebellion. Triggered by protests at military conscription, what began as an uprising in Warsaw quickly spread north and east, into the Western Borderlands and into a prolonged insurgency that lasted from 1863 to 1865.[1]

In the complex ethnic and religious patchwork of these territories, the rebels included Germans, Jews and those describing themselves as Ukrainians or Belorussians. Most, though, were ethnic Poles. They came from a wide range of social estates, the majority from the poorer nobility, or *szlachta,* and the urban intelligentsia, but others hailed from the artisanal classes and the peasantry. Even republicans from other European nations, radicalized in the 1848 revolutions and in Giuseppe Garibaldi's Italian campaigns in the 1850s, fought alongside the Poles. Both the uprising and its aftermath were international affairs.[2]

The rebels of 1863 were militarily weaker, but politically better organized, than their compatriots had been in 1830. Dispersed in a series of localized rebellions across a vast area, they waged a lengthy and bitter guerrilla campaign against forces loyal to the autocracy. The uprising became a civil war in which various classes and ethnic groups allied themselves either with the rebels or with the Russian state. As in 1830, the rebels were no match for the might of the Imperial Army, which at the height of the conflict was fielding almost 170,000 troops. Over the course of 630 military engagements, the insurgents were eventually ground down, their ranks depleted by casualties and capture. Government forces still needed sixteen months to finally crush the uprising and root out the rebels' extensive network of underground government. The Warsaw Citadel won notoriety in the tsarist counter-insurgency campaign. It served as a launchpad for military operations and as a giant holding prison for thousands of captured insurgents. The leader of the rebellion, Romuald Traugutt, was hanged outside the Citadel in 1863.

Tsarist retribution in the Kingdom of Poland and the Western Borderlands was swift and heavy. Military tribunals sentenced hundreds to death. Not only armed insurgents, but also politicians, journalists, Catholic priests and student activists were caught up in the government's dragnet. Some 35,000 were banished to various locations throughout the empire. The repression was designed to dissuade the Poles from all and any outward manifestations of support for independence: one fifteen-year-old girl was arrested by the authorities for singing patriotic Polish songs and for wearing black mourning clothes in the rebellion's aftermath.[3]

As in the 1830s, most accused of armed involvement in the insurrection were exiled administratively or extra-judicially by field courts martial. Between 18,000 and 24,000 people were deported beyond the Urals. About 3,500 rebels, charged with the most serious "state crimes," were sentenced to lifelong penal labour in the mines or to shorter terms in the forts and factories of Nerchinsk. Those convicted of lesser crimes, and the beneficiaries of imperial clemency, were stripped of their civil rights and exiled to settlement in either Western or Eastern Siberia, depending on the alleged seriousness of the offence. The constitutional privileges and relative autonomy of the Western Borderlands were withdrawn and the Kingdom of Poland was dissolved, both replaced by direct rule from St. Petersburg. A Polish uprising against the Russian Empire had, once again, failed.[4]

Like their predecessors, this second generation of Polish rebels to be exiled endeavoured to remain faithful in Siberia to their patriotic and republican principles. Exile crushed many both in body and in spirit, but many more continued to battle the Russian state using all the means at their disposal. Some struggled to free themselves from captivity by disputing the justice of their sentences in petitions and letters; others staged daring escapes; some turned to armed revolt.

For the Polish rebels and their allies, these acts of resistance to the Siberian authorities were political acts, a continuation of their struggle against the Russian state. But they were also an extension of the nationalists' and republicans' wider battle with the monarchies and empires of Europe. The Poles pitted their patriotic, fraternal values against the patriarchal authority of the autocracy. In appeals, in suicide notes and in testimony to military tribunals in Siberia, the Poles spoke the language of rights, justice, liberty and tyranny. Carried forth by those who escaped and those who were released, their tales of defiance, heroism and suffering reverberated across the Russian Empire and beyond. For many sympathetic contemporaries in Europe, the rebels' struggles against their jailers in Siberia were the struggles of the Polish nation itself.

Today, the Tenth Pavilion inside the Warsaw Citadel is part of Poland's National Museum of Independence. In one of its galleries hangs an enormous oil painting by the Romantic artist Aleksander Sochaczewski. It depicts a marching convoy of dozens of exiled rebels, both men and women, at a rest stop, surrounded by desolate expanses of snow. Dressed in convict smocks, many of the shackled figures, their heads shaved, have collapsed to the ground from exhaustion and despair. Some offer up anguished prayers; others weep disconsolately. In the centre of the painting, the boundary post that separates the provinces of Perm and Tobolsk looms over the huddled groups of Poles. Beyond the post, Siberia beckons. Sochaczewski was one of the rebels of 1863 who were exiled to Siberia in the wake of the January Uprising. He painted *Farewell to Europe* after returning from twenty years of penal labour in Nerchinsk. It is one of the ironies of history that this stark portrait of the torments of Polish exiles hangs today in what used to be a bastion of Russian imperial might.[5]

The scale of the state's retribution in the wake of the rebellion had grave consequences for the Siberian exile system. The authorities could not cope with the sudden influx of Polish penal labourers sentenced to Siberia's towns, villages, mines, forts and factories. Even though, by the 1860s, the deportation of exiles to Siberia was becoming semi-industrialized, the journey the Poles made remained a gruelling one. The government had turned first to waterways and later to railways to ensure a faster, smoother and more orderly transfer of convicts eastwards. From 1862, trains transferred convicts from Moscow and other collection points to Nizhny Novgorod, via Vladimir. The converted trains into which the convicts were crammed comprised third-class carriages with bars on the windows, as depicted by Nikolai Yaroshenko in his 1888 canvas *Life Is Everywhere*. The overcrowding forced convicts to sit not simply on the benches but also beneath them and in the aisles. The sealed doors and the absence of ventilation took their toll. The 440-kilometre journey to Nizhny Novgorod lasted a day and a night. Elsewhere, the physical infrastructure of the deportation system was in a woeful state: waystations were so old and dilapidated, one official reported, that "no amount of repairs and alterations would render them in a state fit for the winter." In one such waystation on the road to Tyumen, even the ceilings had collapsed.[6]

Beyond the limitations of the infrastructure for deporting the prisoners eastwards, the Siberian authorities simply lacked the spare capacity to deal with the numbers of new exiles. The governor of Tomsk, German Lerkhe, wrote to his superiors in St. Petersburg in July 1864 that the prison fort was capable of accommodating only 400 prisoners but "it rarely has fewer than 600 and the average is between 700 and

750 convicts." The prison was mismanaged by a corrupt and incompetent administration that was in "need of a complete overhaul."[7]

Unable to accommodate the Poles, Siberian officials scrambled in time-honoured fashion to have them transferred to more remote regions further east. In April 1864, the governor-general of Western Siberia, Aleksandr Dyugamel, wrote to St. Petersburg to request that, "due to the lack of necessary facilities," all political prisoners sentenced to penal labour in forts under his command be sent to work in the industrial enterprises of Eastern Siberia. But further east, the authorities were themselves struggling to cope with the influx of exiles. Mikhail Korsakov, the governor-general of Eastern Siberia, ordered the transfer of a full company of riflemen "with officers who were reliable and not of Polish background" from the Amur River Basin to Nerchinsk. In October 1864, he instructed the head of the Nerchinsk Mining Region, Shilov, to disperse the new exiles across the mines. Four hundred had already arrived in Nerchinsk over the summer, with another 800 to 1,000 expected in the coming months, and the authorities there responded that it was "quite impossible" to find productive work for them. Shilov insisted that, "despite the best efforts of the administration, [prison buildings] could not be constructed at such short notice." New building work could only begin in the spring and, until that time, the exiles would need to be quartered in the towns along the route to Nerchinsk: in Krasnoyarsk, Irkutsk and Chita. Overcrowding became endemic. The retributive instincts of the Russian state had outstripped the government's punitive capacities.[8]

As early as August 1864, the exile authorities were registering serious alarm about the mutinous potential of tens of thousands of "state criminals" entering Siberia. Between 1863 and 1867, some 4,000 Poles were exiled to settlement in Tobolsk province, while 4,400 were sent to Yenisei province. It was proving extremely difficult to maintain even the most rudimentary forms of surveillance and control over such large numbers of exiles. Eager to bring the numbers of Poles down to more manageable levels, Minister of the Interior Pyotr Valuyev wrote to all Siberia's governors asking them to draw up lists of individuals who might be released early from exile and returned to complete their sentences in their native lands. In May 1866, the tsar ordered a series of measures to commute the sentences of those convicted of involvement in the January Uprising. Poles condemned to lifelong penal labour had their sentences reduced to periods of ten years; those sentenced to periods of fewer than six years in the mines, forts and factories were released to settlement, and some were freed to return home. A further amnesty followed two years later, which released to settlement all penal labourers "not charged with murders and armed robbery, and not having been convicted of any further political crimes," and made provision for the return of some to European Russia and Poland.[9] Such demonstrations of clemency had less to do with the sovereign's magnanimity and more to do with the practical problems of accommodating the huge numbers of political exiles.

The vast majority of Poles deported to Siberia in the wake of the January Uprising—around 80 per cent—were exiled to settlement. Another, much smaller category, exclusively reserved for noblemen, was "exiled to residence" and permitted to live in towns and cities.[10] Fearful of the influence of these Polish exiles in wider Siberian society, the government issued an edict in January 1866 preventing them from engaging in teaching, pharmacy, printing, photography, medicine and the sale of wine, from residing in buildings in which postal or telegraph services were stationed and from serving in all government offices. In short, they were forbidden from engaging in almost any form of productive labour to which their training and professional experience might have suited them. Many circumvented, or simply ignored, these restrictions, but all that remained for others was farming. Like their predecessors in the 1830s and 1840s, Polish rebels in the 1860s struggled to establish themselves as agriculturalists. They lacked the knowledge, stamina and ambition to make a success of farming in sub-Arctic conditions. Even if they had possessed the requisite characteristics, there was also a desperate shortage of arable land. Many tried to eke out a living by hiring themselves out as farmhands, thus putting themselves at the mercy of the Siberian peasantry. By the end of the 1860s, only around 150 of the nearly 960 Poles settled in Kansk district worked as traders and artisans; the rest were dependent on the charity of the local population and the meagre government handouts intended to keep them from starvation.[11] The ethnographer Sergei Maksimov witnessed their despair:

The political exile bears the conviction that his life has been wasted irrevocably and, for that reason, he is utterly indiffer-

ent to his surroundings, or is irritable, unsettled and tense. If
he does still cherish the hope of returning home, then this hope
itself, which so sustains him, impedes him from working, from
properly settling down: Siberia is for him like a postal station,
a brief stopover in life . . . But as the years pass, weakening
their hope and strength, these men become gloomier; their
irritability becomes reinforced by idleness. Dissatisfaction bur-
rows deeper and turns into hatred.[12]

After his original sentence of penal labour was commuted to "exile
to settlement" in the amnesty of May 1866, Maurycy Sulistrowski
wrote to his brother from Balagansk district in Irkutsk province:

There are around one and a half thousand exiled settlers in
Irkutsk province. It is difficult for numbers like that to find
work. Things are all right for those who receive funds from
their relatives, but those who receive nothing and do not know
any trade very often work for some [peasant] farmer or other,
but what sort of work is it? He is given strong tea in the morning, some cabbage soup and a piece of bread for supper. You
can satisfy your belly with the food but to clothe your body
and meet the needs of your soul, what remains? Only tears,
disappointment, misery and rags! Such is the picture of settlement! In my view, it is worse than penal labour.[13]

Desperate to avoid such a fate, Polish exiles and their families bombarded the tsarist authorities with petitions and pleas for clemency.
The mass of illiterate peasants and tradespeople languished silently
in Siberian exile without families able to lobby the government intensively on their behalf. By contrast, most of the Poles were literate and
many came from families versed in the arts of petition and patron-
age. Their pleas, bolstered by appeals from their relatives, underlined
the injustice of the sentences handed down. Exiles claimed either that
their punishments were excessive or that no crime had been committed. They further drew attention to their terrible plight in Siberia and
also to the penury and suffering of wives and children whom they had
been forced to abandon when they set out in the marching convoys.[14]
One exiled insurgent, a nobleman from Kiev named Iwan Dąbrowski,
appealed to the authorities from the village of Irbei in Irkutsk province

in July 1865. Dąbrowski claimed to have been "seized by a gang of rebels and forced under duress to remain in their party," but had fled the group at the earliest available opportunity and had made a full and frank declaration to the authorities of his involuntary participation in the revolt. He had hoped to be pardoned in 1863, "but the new law did not take my sincere regret into consideration." Dąbrowski had been exiled to settlement in Eastern Siberia "with the loss of all rights and properties." He made so bold as "to fall at your Imperial Majesty's feet to pray for mitigation of my fate, which is accompanied by the misery of my four suffering children and of my wife who has been left without the means to support herself."

Two years later, in October 1867, Dąbrowski's four children themselves petitioned Korsakov, the governor-general of Eastern Siberia, detailing their father's record of service to the Russian crown. Dąbrowski had fought in the Imperial Army in 1847 and 1848, participating in the suppression of the Hungarian Revolution, and had sustained head injuries that explained the "attacks of madness that were the cause of his misfortune." He was in poor health, they wrote, unable to engage in farming and dependent for food on the meagre financial support of his family. Destitute, he had been unable to pay the bribes demanded by the local authorities in exchange for permission to remain in Irkutsk province and had found himself transferred in February 1867 to Yakutsk province, several hundred kilometres further north-east, "to a land where any man from our climate will die a slow death. What penal labour can compare with such a cruel fate?" Their father should have benefited, they claimed, from the amnesty of May 1866, but instead had been doomed by "unfounded slander and denunciation." They ended their petition:

> Your Excellency, please graciously forgive our bold petition! But we are children, distressed by the injustices done to our poor and ailing father who has been stripped of everything, severed from his own blood, pronounced guilty because he is unable to work to support himself . . . We can only conclude that there is no justice in the courts. Your Excellency's will is the law for our father and for us; your word is a sentence of life and death . . . Be merciful! Consider his former service, his pitiful condition as a man afflicted with attacks of weak-mindedness, and consider our young years, for the oldest of

us is only seven! Heed the voice of us poor orphans, save our father from an inevitable hungry and cold death! . . . Return our father from Yakutsk province to Irkutsk to live with his cousin, the political exile Karol Drogomirecki, who would be able to look after him.

The petition was signed by the unpractised hand of each young child: Kamila, Yumen, Iwan and Honorata. Two months later, in what appears to have been a coordinated campaign of appeals from Dąbrowski's family, his sister Wincentyna also wrote to the governor-general, protesting her brother's innocence. She begged that he not be left in the "exceptionally harsh climate" of Yakutsk province, where "virtually nothing grows and where moving from one yurt to another, without any comfort at all and in poor health, he would die a slow death." Wincentyna was counting on, she declared, the governor-general's "humanity" and on the "magnanimity of our most merciful monarch."[15]

What Dąbrowski's relatives really thought of the Russian government they expressed in private letters sent to Dąbrowski that were unfortunately intercepted by the authorities in Irkutsk: "You won't believe how distressed and angry we are by the behaviour of the authorities," one stated. "They are not people but heartless beasts! Sending you without any explanation or justification to live among savages!"[16]

In part influenced by the contents of these letters, the authorities in Eastern Siberia were unmoved by Dąbrowski's pleas and those of his relatives. Dąbrowski had been removed to Yakutsk province, not because of his poverty and inability to farm, but because he was "unreliable." His alleged poor health had not been officially certified, and his correspondence with members of his family "was a precise measure of his moral sentiments" and proof of his "hostile attitude to the government." Letters from his brother in Kiev were full of "indecent and abusive expressions about the field courts in Kiev province"; they boasted that the law did not exist for the Poles and they gave advice on how to bribe the authorities. But eventually, in June 1870, the petitioning did pay off, and Dąbrowski was allowed to relocate to Penza province in central Russia seven years after his original petition.[17]

The sudden expulsion of so many insurgents brought administrative chaos to the exile system. Minister of the Interior Pyotr Valuyev com-

plained to provincial governors that many Poles were being exiled without the correct paperwork, something which was generating confusion
about their identities and their sentences. Perhaps tellingly, Valuyev's
concern lay not with the possible injustice of convicts serving out the
wrong sentences. Rather, he was agitated by the fact that many exiles
from the lower orders of Polish society were availing themselves of the
administrative confusion in record-keeping. They were claiming that
they in fact hailed from the privileged classes and so were entitled to
better rations and seats on the wagons that accompanied the marching convoys, all at greater expense to the treasury. The Tobolsk Exile
Office bombarded St. Petersburg with a string of requests for clarification of the identities and sentences of the exiles now passing through
its forwarding prisons.

At the beginning of 1865, an exile claiming to be an Italian,
Ludovico Perevosti, arrived in Tobolsk. He testified that he had been
exiled for political crimes by the authorities in Warsaw but had no
idea of his intended destination. The Exile Office contacted Warsaw
for further information, but after two months it received only a con-
firmation that Perevosti was indeed an Italian, from Palermo, and that
he had been exiled on 14 August 1864. His destination, however, was
a mystery. One nobleman from Vitebsk, Michał Blażewicz, was discovered en route to Siberia to be carrying another insurgent's papers.
Blażewicz's intended destination was not Siberia but rather a small village in Perm province. In April, the governor of Tobolsk, Aleksandr
Despot-Zenovich, wrote to the governor of Warsaw to complain about
the consequences of the chaos: exiles arriving without the necessary
documentation had to be detained in the city's prison while enquiries
were conducted, a state of affairs that "significantly increases the number of prisoners held in transit, causing serious difficulties in accommodating them and making excessive demands on the state's finances."
Some political exiles had been detained "often for more than a year,
which inflicts an undeserved punishment on them and is harmful to
their morality and health." By the spring of 1865, there were 280 Poles
in Tomsk province about whom the authorities had no information
concerning their class or their sentences.[18]

The administrative chaos offered opportunities to the quick-witted,
the courageous and the resourceful. Jarosław Dąbrowski was a twenty-
four-year-old radical republican whose biography appears to have been
drawn from the pages of nineteenth-century Romantic fiction. The son

of an impoverished nobleman from Zhitomir, he had studied at the elite Nicolaevan Academy of the General Headquarters in St. Petersburg before going on to fight with the tsarist armies in the Caucasus in the 1850s. When he returned to the capital, he became involved in the conspiratorial circles of republicans that flourished amid the apparent new-found pluralism of the reform era. In February 1862, he travelled to Warsaw and found himself at the centre of preparations for the uprising. There, he met and fell in love with a young Polish noblewoman, Pelagia Zgliczyńska, and the two were betrothed. But Dąbrowski's conspiratorial activities had not escaped the attentions of the authorities: he and several of his associates were arrested in August 1862 and imprisoned in the Warsaw Citadel. With the uprising already underway, Dąbrowski and Zgliczyńska were married in prison on 24 March 1864. Shortly afterwards, Pelagia Dąbrowska was herself convicted of involvement in the rebellion and sentenced to exile in the town of Ardatov, 400 kilometres east of Moscow in Nizhegorodsk province.[19] In October, a military tribunal condemned Dąbrowski to death by firing squad, a sentence commuted by Fyodor Berg, the tsar's last governor-general of the soon-to-be-extinct Kingdom of Poland. On 2 December 1864, with Dąbrowski already en route to Nerchinsk, the government published details of his crimes in the official newspaper, *Russian Veteran*: "For establishing a secret society in St. Petersburg with the goal of preparing a rebellion in the Western Borderlands of Russia, for criminal links with the members of an insurgent party in the Kingdom of Poland and for participation in the preparations of this party, [Dąbrowski] is stripped of his rank, his nobility, his medals commemorating the wars of 1853–1856 . . . and is sentenced to penal labour in the mines for fifteen years; all his properties . . . are confiscated by the state." Dąbrowski had held out hopes for a milder sentence and the possibility of being exiled to join his wife in Ardatov. "Fate has given us so much evidence of its favour," he wrote to Dąbrowska, "that it is unlikely to abandon us in the future. Keep your courage and belief because only he who loses hope is unhappy."[20]

Dąbrowski reached Moscow in a marching convoy of Polish exiles on 11 November 1864. There, the party was held up in a local military barracks due to a shortage of convoy officers and soldiers. As a prison official later explained to his superiors, "although he was under instructions to conduct a roll call, it proved impossible because the guard did not have a list of all the convicts, and the cramped conditions in the barracks meant that those who had had their names called out could not be separated from the others, so the roll call served no purpose." On the morning of 2 December, ninety-nine convicts (the guards reported that they had counted out the men "two or three times") were taken to the bathhouse, leaving another thirty-one, including Dąbrowski, in the barracks. By the changing of the guard that evening, Dąbrowski had, still dressed in the military uniform in which he had been transported from Warsaw, simply marched up to the front gate of the barracks and, having been taken for an officer by the guard, walked out of the barracks and to freedom. By the time readers of *Russian Veteran* were learning of Dąbrowski's heinous crimes against the state, the Polish officer was already on the run.[21]

Minister of War Dmitry Milyutin was incensed to learn of Dąbrowski's escape and demanded to know why such an important and dangerous convict had not been inserted into another marching convoy that had left Moscow for Eastern Siberia in the intervening weeks. A search for Dąbrowski succeeded only in intercepting an unsigned letter, dated 8 December, addressed to Pelagia Dąbrowska in Ardatov: "At the behest of your husband, I have the honour of informing you that he succeeded in escaping the grasp of his tormentors at the beginning of the month and has now already travelled abroad."[22] But the letter was a decoy. Dąbrowski did, indeed, plan to flee abroad, but not without his wife.

In June 1865, General Aleksei Odintsov, the embarrassed governor of Nizhegorodsk province, wrote to Minister of the Interior Valuyev to report that Dąbrowska had vanished from "under police supervision" on 19 May. Extensive searches had failed to uncover the fugitive's whereabouts but had shed some light on the means of her escape. A week before her disappearance, "a tall blond man in his mid twenties with a long aquiline nose, long hair, a Spanish beard, dressed in a dark frock coat . . . carrying nothing but a suitcase and an umbrella and smoking expensive cigars" had travelled from St. Petersburg to Ardatov, "probably to warn Dąbrowska of the impending escape." The two had arranged a rendezvous at a monastery on the outskirts of Ardatov before travelling together by train to Moscow. The mysterious individual proved to be a friend of Dąbrowski, a fellow officer and conspirator from St. Petersburg, Vladimir Ozerov. In August, General Odintsov forwarded a letter to the capital that he had personally received; it was unlikely to assuage the indignation of his superiors:

> My wife's departure from Ardatov has probably given rise to an investigation. I know very well from experience what such investigations amount to. I have discovered that investigative committees never really uncover anything, but frequently and for mercenary motives incriminate innocent people. For that reason, wishing to spare everyone suspicion and unpleasantness, I am writing to inform you of the circumstances of the escape. In fact, I misspeak, for it was not an escape but an abduction. Not only did my wife's relatives know nothing of my intentions, but neither did my wife herself right up until the last moment. I made no attempt to forewarn her, fearing that my plans might become known and be undone.

Dąbrowski concluded: "Allow me, dear Sir, to express the hope that although this adventure might be rather unpleasant to you personally as governor of the region, as a man, you can take solace in the thought that this minor unpleasantness for you will be a source of happiness for people who have already suffered a great deal." The letter was signed "Jarosław Dąbrowski, 15 June, Stockholm."[23]

Dąbrowski also had a message for the wider population of the Russian Empire. The Polish rebellion had unleashed a wave of polonophobia in a Russian society that was now intolerant of any criticisms of Russian actions in Poland. In April 1863, the authorities had closed down the magazine *Time,* which was edited by Fyodor Dostoevsky and his brother Mikhail, after it published an article by the Slavophile Nikolai Strakhov that was judged to be too sympathetic to the Polish insurgents. In such a climate, liberal opinion was intimidated into almost complete silence on the "Polish question," venturing only the most oblique criticisms of the counter-insurgency. Commentary in the conservative press was altogether more voluble. The ferociously reactionary Mikhail Katkov kept up a steady stream of anti-Polish articles in the conservative daily *Moscow News,* which became so influential that many observers believed that Katkov was spurring the Russian government to even greater repression in Poland.[24]

1. A deportation convoy of exiles, 1900.

2. *The Vladimirka*, Isaak Levitan's iconic painting of the "road of fetters"
along which convicts marched into exile, 1892.

3. *Farewell to Europe!*, 1894, former exile Aleksander Sochaczewski's painting of his fellow Polish rebels of 1863 taking leave of Europe at the Siberian Boundary Post. The painting now hangs in Poland's Museum of National Independence in Warsaw.

4. Sick and elderly prisoners journeying
into exile on open wagons, 1880s.

5. *Russian Civilisation*, a scathing view of Russian government
repression in the British satirical magazine *Judy*, 3 March 1880.

6. A cell in the Tomsk forwarding prison crammed with male convicts and with women and children following their husbands and fathers into exile, 1880s.

7. Roll call of prisoners at a waystation en route to Siberia, turn of the twentieth century.

8. Scenes of grief among common convicts at the Siberian Boundary Post, 1880s.

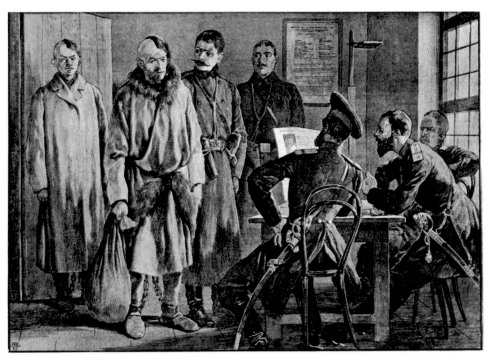

9. Prisoners arriving at the Krasnoyarsk forwarding prison, 1891.

10. *The Unexpected Return*, Ilya Repin's portrayal of
the sudden arrival from Siberia of a political exile, 1884.

11. Sergei Volkonsky

12. Maria Volkonskaya

13. Mikhail Lunin

14. Fyodor Dostoevsky

From Stockholm, Dąbrowski penned a scornful open letter to Katkov, denouncing him for fanning the flames of anti-Polish sentiment in the Russian press:

> It is true that you have, for a time, succeeded in awaking the bestial instincts and fanaticism of the Russians, but your lies and deception will not triumph for long. Hundreds of our exiles have borne an understanding of our efforts and our people into the darkest corners of Russia. Their appearance has everywhere been an eloquent protest against the lies spread by official and hired slanderers, and has awoken humane instincts in the soul of the Russians.

The letter was published in the Polish journal *Fatherland* and in Alexander Herzen's liberal London-based publication, *The Bell,* which was widely available in Russia. Herzen's magazine had maintained a staunchly pro-Polish line throughout the conflict, arguing that Poland's struggle was also the struggle of Russian democrats and socialists against the autocracy. In the grip of anti-Polish hysteria, however, Russian readers cancelled their subscriptions in droves; circulation dropped from 2,500 to 500 copies over the course of 1863.[25]

The effects of Russia's crackdown in the Kingdom of Poland and the Western Borderlands rippled across the continent as Europe's collective conscience was once again pricked by the fate of Poland. Societies devoted to the cause of Poland enjoyed a short-lived but vibrant existence in London, and the Houses of Parliament debated the government's diplomatic (though never military) response to the rebellion. The British press denounced Russia's actions and expressed solidarity with the Polish rebels; *The Times* railed against "acts of barbarism and cruelty which are a disgrace to a civilised government, and which disgrace the age in which they are committed."[26]

An ardent republican, Dąbrowski now took his revolutionary experience and military skills back to Western Europe. From Stockholm, he travelled with his wife to France, where, although hounded by the authorities at the behest of the tsarist government, he went on to play an active part in the Polish revolutionary underground. When Paris erupted in civil war in 1871, Dąbrowski, assuming the *nom de guerre* Dombrowski, took military command of the Commune. After coordinating the doomed struggle of the insurgents for two months, General Dombrowski finally fell on the barricades on 23 May 1871. His brother Teofil later explained Dąbrowski's motives: "We joined the Paris revolution because we saw in it a social revolution which, if successful, could overthrow the existing order in Europe. Could Poland lose anything in it? Nothing. Could she win something? Yes, everything."[27]

In a bitter echo of Alexander II's crushing of the Polish rebellion, some 4,500 of Dąbrowski's defeated comrades were themselves exiled from Paris to the French penal colony of New Caledonia, in the South Pacific. Dąbrowski's heroic and desperate defence of the city ensured that his name became synonymous with republicanism's defeat on the streets of Paris. When, in the 1930s, the International Brigades rallied in defence of the Spanish Republic in its struggle with fascism, one of the brigades, dominated by Poles, proudly bore the name of the "Dąbrowski Battalion."[28]

The Polish rebellion and the exile of rebels to Siberia were central moments in the history of European republicanism. The struggle of the Poles against St. Petersburg attracted support from across Europe. Italian and French republicans, energized by the experience of the 1848 revolutions, travelled to Poland to join the ranks of the rebels. The Italian General Francesco Nullo led what became known as the Garibaldi Regiment of Italian volunteers. The French officer François Rochebrune led a detachment of French volunteers, named the "Zouaves of Death" after the French light infantry units that had fought in the Crimean War. In the wake of their defeat in Poland, thirty of these men were also clapped in leg irons and marched to Siberia. They set out on their 10,000-kilometre journey in July 1863. Their rations en route were gradually cut from seven kopecks per day between Tobolsk and Tomsk, to six kopecks per day on the road to Krasnoyarsk, then to 3.5 kopecks per day between Krasnoyarsk and Irkutsk and, finally, to a starvation ration of 2.5 kopecks per day between Irkutsk and Chita; 400 grammes of black bread in Eastern Siberia cost as much as four kopecks.[29]

By the time the French, Italian and Swiss republicans finally reached Petrovsk Zavod bordering the Nerchinsk Mining Region after eight months on the road, they were physically shattered. The local doctor had all thirty of them admitted to the infirmary. Two were showing the early symptoms of pulmonary tuberculosis; another was suffering from tuberculosis and venereal disease, and a fourth, Giuseppe Clerici, had a large ulcer on his right flank, which had developed from a gunshot wound out of which a bullet and a fragment of his rib had been extracted. The ulcer was showing no signs of healing and gangrene was setting in around the rib.[30]

The Garibaldians saw themselves as part of a proud genealogy of republicanism that stretched back to the American and French revolutions. In Siberia they discovered the human detritus of earlier revolts against the autocracy, such as the sixty-five-year-old Decembrist Ivan Gorbachevsky, who had chosen to remain in Nerchinsk after Alexander II's amnesty in 1856. The old man befriended his fellow republicans and counselled stoicism in enduring their fate: "Do not become angry and embittered, face down cruel fortune with a clear head. Renunciation, spiritual harmony, concentrating on scholarly work—these are the best, the only ways of ignoring the weight of your fetters, of not being marked by them, so that when they are finally removed, you will still be young!"[31]

Once they had recovered their strength, the Garibaldians were dispersed into small groups around various mines throughout Nerchinsk. Luigi Caroli, a young officer from an influential aristocratic family in Bergamo, and a Frenchman, Émile Andreoli, were sent to the Kadai mine, which was situated only a dozen or so kilometres from the Chinese border. Andreoli described the psychological condition of his companions:

> However severe our physical sufferings and our privations, they were as nothing when compared with the inner torments that slowly but surely weigh down on the heart of a penal labourer in Siberia. Woe is he who does not more or less willingly devote himself to some or other challenging pursuit or spiritual labour, which allows him to not think of everything that he once had, his distant homeland, his relatives, about everything that he loves.[32]

The Garibaldians tried to keep their spirits up with the study of languages and local history, but it was a Herculean effort. Caroli struggled to remain occupied as his anguished longing for Italy and his

family began to consume him. Initially buoyed by rumours of an imminent amnesty that failed to materialize, Caroli eventually succumbed
to depression and his health began to deteriorate rapidly. After enduring nine months in Kadai, he died on 8 June 1865 and was buried
by his comrades. Funerals for exiled republicans offered a stage for
the affirmation of fraternal bonds and shared idealism, and so Caroli's
comrades raised a cross, inscribed with the words "To the Italian Luigi
Caroli from Polish exiles," above his grave. The Polish Romantic
painter and veteran of the rebellion, Artur Grottger, immortalized the
scene.[33]

Nerchinsk became the furthest flung graveyard of European republicanism, a desolate terminus for men whose political struggles had
often taken them across the European continent from one battlefield
and revolution to the next. One of many such Romantic rebels, and
another of Caroli's fellow prisoners in Transbaikal in 1864, was the
forty-three-year-old nobleman and lieutenant colonel in the Hussars
Andrei Krasowski. Born in 1822, Krasowski was the son of Afanasy
Krasowski, a famous general and veteran of both the Russo-Turkish
War of 1806–12 and the Napoleonic campaigns. A Russified Pole and
an Orthodox Christian, Krasowski's father had even been a commander
in the Imperial Army's suppression of the 1830 November Insurrection. Andrei Krasowski enjoyed all the benefits of an elite education at
the Page Corps in St. Petersburg, the traditional preparation for a dazzling career in the Guards. He grew up alongside the highest echelons
of the Russian aristocracy and had been a personal acquaintance of
Alexander II in his youth. He knew English, French, German, Swedish,
Italian and Polish, and had travelled widely in Europe as a young man.
While abroad, he was exposed to the republican and liberal ideas that
were seizing the imagination of the continent's educated youth and he
even met Alexander Herzen in London. Krasowski fought bravely in
the Crimean War, picking up several wounds and a medal for gallantry.
He later settled in Kiev, married and had three children. Krasowski
became interested in the life of the Ukrainian peasantry, in its folklore, songs and customs. Travelling through the Italian peninsula in
the spring of 1860, he encountered Garibaldi and joined the Italian's
volunteer army, fighting incognito first in its Sicilian campaigns and
then in its march on Naples.[34]

Following his arrival in Kiev later that year, Krasowski became

involved in the reformist student circles that flourished in the early years
of the reign of Alexander II. In the midst of the peasant disturbances
that spread throughout the Ukrainian countryside in the wake of the
emancipation of the serfs, Krasowski was denounced and arrested in
June 1862 for having circulated copies of a leaflet that he had penned
to Russian troops. He had called on the troops to disobey their orders
to attack the rioting peasants: "You are being ordered not to be friends
or saviours to the people to whom you also belong, among whom are
your fathers, brothers, sisters and mothers. Your officers are ordering you to cut them down and shoot them in the interests of the very
bureaucrats and landowners who anyway rob and ravage the unfortunate peasant."[35] Krasowski was charged with "attempting to incite
the lower ranks to revolt." He had used "inflammatory slogans and
forbidden, outrageous and libellous writings, condemning the government's steps to pacify the rebellious peasantry." A military tribunal
convicted Krasowski in October 1862. He was stripped of his rank,
of his medals for service in the Crimean War and of all his property,
and was condemned to death by firing squad. He greeted the tribunal's
verdict with the words: "I thank you with all my heart. Death is now
a blessing for me!"[36]

Alexander II commuted the sentence to a civil execution followed
by twelve years of penal labour in the mines of Nerchinsk. At seven
o'clock in the morning on 26 October 1862, Krasowski was led out
from the Kiev citadel and onto a scaffold that had been erected on an
esplanade before the city's garrison. Having fastened Krasowski to a
stock, an executioner pronounced the sentence and symbolically broke
a sword over the prisoner's head. Days later, Krasowski was marching
eastwards in a deportation convoy alongside fellow republicans. It was
only a year later, in November 1863, that he finally reached Irkutsk.
He had been hoping to be reunited in the city with his wife, who set
out to follow him into exile. Instead he learned that she had died of
typhus en route. After fifteen arduous months in the filthy and disease-
infested waystations, in February 1864 Krasowski finally reached
Petrovsk Zavod, sick with tuberculosis.[37] He arrived "in an extreme
physical and mental state, in which a man is ready to do anything," as
he recounted in a letter to the head of the prison, Cossack Lieutenant
Razgildeyev, in March 1864. The loss of his wife had been a "crushing
blow," he wrote:

I learned of the death of my beloved wife together with whom
I had lived so happily for 14 years. I had eagerly awaited her
arrival as my only solace in my bleak position. However hard
this irreversible loss was to bear, more terrible still was the
thought that my three orphaned children had lost their mother
at an age when her life could not have been more essential
for them. They now live on charity in the homes of strangers
who are perhaps indifferent to them and who cannot possibly
replace their mother . . .

After a month in the barracks of Petrovsk Zavod, "where conditions leave their mark on even the strongest and healthiest of men," Krasowski's health gave way and he was admitted to the infirmary where
the doctor treating him "would not vouch for my life, let alone my
health, if I am once again subjected to confinement in the prison . . ."
Krasowski continued with a bewildered and defiant condemnation of
his treatment at the hands of the tsarist state:

> It cannot be the goal of a rational and educated government in
> the nineteenth century to exact merciless revenge against crimi-
> nals *even after* they have been punished. It cannot therefore
> seek systematically, step by step, to finish off a sick and pow-
> erless old man and to do so *at the very moment when* he has
> been driven to the ends of the world, to a place so dreadful that
> not even Mazzini and Garibaldi would be able to cause any
> trouble here! It cannot seek to finish him off when he is now
> meekly and unconditionally in the iron grip of the authorities,
> deprived of any opportunity to do harm. No! I believe that it
> will take into account the illness of the political criminal it has
> condemned; it will take into account the more than 20 years
> that he served that state while he was young and strong; it will
> remember the reasons for his poor health, the five wounds that
> he picked up, fighting battles against the enemies of Russia and
> its emperor, for whom he did not spare his life or his blood![38]

In view of his "infirmity from wounds and weakness," Krasowski
begged to be allowed to live outside the prison while he served the
remainder of his penal labour. Krasowski's request was declined, but

he was transferred from Petrovsk Zavod to the healthier climate of the prison in Aleksandrovsk, and his sentence was reduced from twelve to eight years of penal labour. Then, in September 1867, he was permitted to reside outside the prison in a private dwelling "under strict and unwavering supervision."[39]

Such concessions came too late for the sick and despairing Krasowski. Having waited for the murderous cold to recede, he set out on horseback in a final desperate bid for freedom on 20 May 1868. Disguised as a soldier and with forged documents, he planned to head for the border with China and to travel from there into India. Krasowski never thought, however, that he stood much of a chance. Before his departure, he left a testament. It began with the republicans' trinity "in the name of freedom, equality and sacred fraternity, amen!" and ended with a bleak resolution: "I have decided in the case of any misfortune to take my life and not to give myself up alive. My death is almost a certainty."[40]

And, indeed, the ailing fugitive did not get far. Alerted to his flight, the authorities dispatched search parties to hunt him down, but it was only after two weeks that they discovered his decomposing corpse, a mere 17 kilometres from Aleksandrovsk. Krasowski had shot himself in the head. A note scrawled in blood was found on his body: "I had set out for China. My chances are extremely slim—I have lost valuable belongings that I needed to show me the way. It is better to die than to deliver myself alive into the hands of the enemy. A.K." His starving horse was tethered to a tree beside him. A search of surrounding woodland turned up Krasowski's overcoat, which contained a map and a passport sewn into the lining.[41]

Individual tragedies like Krasowski's played themselves out in penal settlements across Siberia, where the fate of the Poles was incomparably harsher than that of the Decembrists. Krasowski's sense of incredulity and outrage at the conditions of his captivity in Siberia was widely shared by his countrymen. But not all of them were so broken in mind and body that suicide remained their only recourse. Jarosław Dąbrowski's resourcefulness and ingenuity might have been exceptional, but his defiance of the government was not. Many of the Polish exiles of the 1860s were officers drawn from the nobility. Their patriotism had been battle-hardened in the doomed rebellion against St. Petersburg and their banishment to Siberia had left many embittered towards their Russian captors. Most were bound by a common tongue, Polish, a common religion, Catholicism, and a common political ideology, republicanism, that set them apart from the overwhelming majority of Siberia's exiles. Such bonds of solidarity helped to sustain their ideological conviction and rebellious energy, and made the Poles difficult to subdue.

Some officials grew concerned about the disorder that the new influx of Polish insurgents might bring to Eastern Siberia. Konstantin Shelashnikov, the governor of Irkutsk, was alarmed that the shortage of prison facilities meant that these political exiles were not being properly confined and monitored.[42] What really presented a challenge to the administrators of exile, however, was the Poles' solidarity, individual dignity and contempt for the authority of their guards and warders. Steeped in the patriotic traditions of European republicanism, the exiled revolutionaries had a keen sense of their own natural rights, rights that could not be stripped away or denied, even by the autocracy. Despot-Zenovich, the governor of Tobolsk, discerned these qualities in the new political prisoners entering Eastern Siberia:

> I know the men who make up the administration of Eastern Siberia, and I know how they deal with the exiled Poles. It will be no surprise if the soldiers' constantly rough treatment of men who have a very strong sense of their own human dignity provokes them. Therefore, I cannot guarantee that there will not be some kind of demonstration on the part of the exiles. For all their political crimes, they remain men who are in the majority extremely civilized and there are limits to any man's endurance.[43]

Despot-Zenovich proved an astute observer.

Steeled by an awareness of their own dignity, the Poles protested against their treatment and insisted that there were limits to the state's power over them. In December 1865, Poles in the region of Chita rioted in protest at the conditions in their prison and had to be subdued by soldiers wielding bayonets. In July 1866, a group of Poles sentenced to penal labour in Nerchinsk refused to leave their cells to work on a

Sunday (one declared he would have to be carried forth from his cell on bayonets). No fewer than sixty-seven prisoners signed a petition setting out their grievances. They insisted upon rights not encoded in the penal statutes of the Russian state but rather rights fundamental to all human beings. They had been abruptly informed by the authorities that they would now be required to work on feast days and Sundays, "which constituted a clear assault on our rights of conscience." The instruction was, they maintained, "a direct repudiation of all those general human rights and Christian rights that constitute the dignity of everyone and, consequently, of all those who are exiled to penal labour for their political convictions. We cannot believe that the Russian government, being a European and Christian government, could approve such an instruction." The prisoners pointed out that it was not only the Catholic but also the Orthodox Church that followed the Ten Commandments. "The sick and the frail have been left shackled without sufficient food, fresh air, or freedom to move around. Does this not constitute an inhuman perversion of those rights that all the suffering and helpless enjoy?" The Poles also invoked Alexander II's legal reforms of 1864: "At a time when a range of reforms are introducing an open judicial process safeguarding each of us against abuse, we have been subject to starvation and chains without any judicial process . . ." The head of the Nerchinsk Mining Region, G. Vorontsov, found "nothing in the prisoners' petition apart from an eloquent elucidation of their refusal to submit themselves to their deserved punishment, as appointed by the laws." He responded by having the men shackled in their cells and deprived of their rations of meat.[44]

Shortly afterwards the new head of the Nerchinsk mines, Adolf Knoblokh, took a particularly tough line when Polish exiles refused to work in one of the mines under his command due to the "lethal air." Knoblokh himself visited the mine and ordered the withdrawal of all the prisoners' samovars, books, fiddles and other objects of entertainment and amusement. He had put the prisoners in fetters and locked down in their cells on a diet of bread and water: "I promised them that they themselves would beg me to be returned to the mine shafts." Knoblokh reported triumphantly that his disciplinary measures proved "a great success": some of the prisoners "asked for forgiveness with tears in their eyes, explaining that they had been scared of losing what was left of their health in the deep, narrow shafts that were full of suffocating fumes." All ended well; the Poles were reduced to a suitably submissive state and the incident would "be a lesson to them."[45]

Revolt was, nonetheless, in the air. In February 1866, Nikolai Serno-Solovyovich, the exiled Russian revolutionary, colleague of Herzen and Chernyshevsky and co-founder of the Russian revolutionary party Land and Liberty, arrived in Kansk, in Yenisei province. He issued a call to all Poles in Eastern Siberia to rise up "in the name of truth and freedom" against a common enemy. Serno-Solovyovich blended the socialist propaganda of the Russian revolutionary movement with the republican slogans of the Polish insurgents: "Poles! You have been exiled to Siberia for your fatherland! You are martyrs to freedom! You have been stripped of everything by the same tsar who oppresses the Russian people! You have been defeated only because the Russian people did not understand and did not know what you fought for. Rise up as one with the Russian people for fatherland and for freedom!"[46]

Four months later, the Poles did rebel, and not in the mines of Nerchinsk but on the shores of Lake Baikal. Unable to accommodate the Poles within the Nerchinsk Mining Region itself, the authorities had dispersed them in work gangs throughout Transbaikal. Hundreds had been dispatched in groups of several dozen, each guarded by only a handful of soldiers, to work on the construction of a road along the southern edge of the lake. There, the men had found themselves underfed, exposed to the elements and subject to the customary indignities by their guards.[47] On the night of 25 June 1866, the Poles' dissatisfaction with their conditions erupted into open rebellion. Led by two Polish officers, Narcyz Celiński and Gustaw Szaramowicz, one group of exiles succeeded in overpowering its guards and seizing their weapons before launching a desperate bid for freedom in the direction of the Chinese border. What started as a localized revolt spread as the insurgent party moved south and other Poles swelled its ranks. In total, around 300 exiles joined the escape. The authorities in Irkutsk ordered a major deployment of two companies of Cossacks on horseback and three companies of infantry to crush the rebellion. Exhausted, malnourished and armed with only a handful of stolen weapons, the Poles were no match for the tsarist troops ranged against them. Once again, they found themselves outnumbered, outgunned and divided as to whether they should attempt to fight their way past the Russian troops or simply flee. On 28 June, a brief but decisive skirmish was fought near the village of Mishikhi, on the shores of Baikal. The rebels either surrendered or fled into the forests; seven were killed. In the weeks that followed, the authorities hunted down and arrested the remaining Poles, imprisoning them in Irkutsk.[48]

A military field court was convened to try them. Nearly 700 men were charged with involvement in the revolt and almost half were found guilty of "an armed rebellion" and of perpetrating "unrest, violence and murder." Seven of the ringleaders were sentenced to death by firing squad, 197 were condemned to lifelong penal labour and 122 had their existing sentences extended. One of the men sentenced to death, Leopold Ilyashevich, spoke at his trial not to the military tribunal arrayed before him, but to the court of history itself:

I will be judged by the whole of Russia, by the whole of Europe. In time people will give their verdict on our actions, and the blood of those you convict will be on your hands and on your children's hands. It will be remembered that we had been left here for all eternity and that we attempted to free ourselves. Will you really convict me for that attempt?[49]

It is possible to exaggerate the ideological coherence of the Polish exiles and to discern conspiracy and planning behind what were spontaneous eruptions of defiance and disorder provoked by the conditions of their captivity. But the Poles' protests and revolts cannot be reduced to an expression of practical concerns about welfare. What began as local grievances over food, accommodation and working conditions could quickly acquire a political charge when expressed in terms of powers abused and rights denied. For natural rights and human dignity *were* political issues in the exile system. Protest and escape both challenged the authority of the sovereign to exercise unlimited power over those who anyway remained alive only by his good graces. Besides, the Poles were political prisoners, not common criminals, a fact that invested their defiance of the authorities with political significance. Sympathetic contemporaries saw in the rebellion on the shores of Baikal a continuing struggle for Polish sovereignty and independence from Russian domination. Herzen's émigré journal *The Bell* thundered: "It is difficult to murder peoples, even with all the Mongol ruthlessness in the world . . . They have smashed Poland again and again . . . and yet Poland still lives . . . She rose up in Siberia! Without hope and in despair but preferring, all the same, death to slavery!"[50]

The rebels' own voices carried beyond the confines of Siberia to a community of Polish patriots and republicans scattered throughout Europe. The young Polish painter Aleksander Sochaczewski was one of the ill-fated Luigi Caroli's companions in Eastern Siberia. Sochaczewski had trained at the Warsaw Academy of Fine Arts before being sentenced to twenty years of penal labour for his part in the rebellion. Unlike many of his countrymen, Sochaczewski did not benefit from any of the imperial amnesties and served out the full term of his sentence before finally emigrating to Munich in 1883. Back in Europe, he put his talents to work, creating a series of epic, Romantic paintings, including *Farewell to Europe,* immortalizing the plight of his comrades in Siberia. One depicts fugitive exiles huddled in snowdrifts as black crows circle overhead; another, the broken body of a penal labourer slumped over his wheelbarrow.[51]

Some of Siberia's republican exiles told their story not with the palette but with the pen. The Frenchman Andreoli had been deported to Nerchinsk with the Italian Caroli but benefited from the amnesty in 1866 and was permitted to return to France. There, he denounced the amnesty as a cynical gesture intended to curry favour with European countries horrified at Russia's treatment of Poland. His "journal of captivity," the diary he had kept in Siberia, was published in the influential republican journal *Revue moderne.* Andreoli believed the tsarist state had made a mistake in ever releasing him from captivity: "If one has prisons like those in Siberia, they need to be forgotten; no man can ever be allowed to leave them. Russia . . . should have realised that once we were free, we would talk."[52]

Andreoli detailed the stinking filth of the waystations and prisons, the state's casual mixing of political and common criminals, the plight of women and children, the callous incompetence and corruption of officialdom and the brutal floggings of convicts. Siberia was, he declared, "an empire of evil," a "cesspit of vice, of corruption." Andreoli spared the common people his criticisms; they were "blinded by ignorance, and might soon themselves submit to the same treatment to which we had been condemned." He directed his ire rather at Alexander II himself. Echoing the Marquis de Custine's 1843 indictment of the "Asiatic despotism" of Nicholas I, he wrote: "You have made me traverse the immensity of your empire. I have seen there the abject state of your subjects, the corruption of your officials, the dreadful results of your despotism."[53]

Andreoli believed that the day was coming when the tsars would reap the whirlwind. He had shared his captivity in the Kadai mine with the radical socialist journalist Nikolai Chernyshevsky and described encounters in Siberia with "people who aspire to liberty in that land of imperial prison guards." He had heard "sentiments of independence, protests against tyranny, cries of hatred against the tsar." Andreoli reckoned that, although small in number and cast out into Siberia, these opponents of the regime would one day gain sufficient strength to defeat the autocracy. There were echoes of Percy Bysshe Shelley's 1818 verse "Ozymandias" in the lines he wrote:

> Pitiless tsar, what you now only discern as a black dot on the horizon, might tomorrow become a terrible hurricane that will blow away everything that today is the source of your vanity. The army of which you are so proud will be ranged against you . . . it will not stop the revolution. Together with your flatterers and your courtesans, you will disappear like straws in the wind; your palaces and your thrones will all rejoin the cinders and dust of what were once great empires.[54]

The paintings and memoirs of the exiled rebels of 1863 ensured that the martyrdom and the defiance of their comrades were seared into the European political imagination. The Poles politicized Siberia. They cast it not simply as a place of banishment and punishment but also as an arena of defiance and struggle. In the decades that followed, that battle would be joined by a new generation of radicals from across the empire.

9

General Cuckoo's Army

A bird's eye view of the Siberian taiga in the nineteenth century would have revealed a steady trickle of figures, stooped under heavy bundles, trudging westwards either alone or in small groups. The "hunchbacks," as the peasants called them, were escaped convicts who had fled the marching convoys, the mines, the prisons and the penal settlements and were making their way across the forests in the direction of European Russia. Answering the spring call of the migrant cuckoo and taking advantage of the warmer weather, thawed waterways and thickening vegetation that provided them with camouflage and with food, the fugitives set forth. These were the foot soldiers of what became known as "General Cuckoo's Army."[1]

The numbers of fugitives told a sobering tale. Abandoned and imprisoned in penury and squalor and with quite literally nothing to lose, Siberia's convicts absconded from every single prison, factory, settlement and mine in their thousands. Between 1838 and 1846, the authorities apprehended almost 14,000 male and 3,500 female fugitives in Siberia (figures that probably represented just half of those convicts who were at large).[2] In the second half of the nineteenth century, the numbers of escapes only increased as the overall exile population expanded. One government report on the state of exile in Eastern Siberia in 1877 recorded that, in three districts surveyed in Irkutsk province, half of the more than 20,000 prisoners had run away, their "whereabouts unknown."[3] By 1898, a quarter of the exiles assigned to Yenisei province, 40 per cent of those assigned to Irkutsk province and 70 per cent of those assigned to Primorsk province in Eastern Siberia were unaccounted for. Purpose-built penal labour sites witnessed a similar exodus. Such figures would suggest that, by the last quarter of the nineteenth century, anywhere up to a third of Siberia's 300,000 exiles were on the run in what ethnographer Nikolai Yadrintsev termed "an endless perpetuum mobile from Eastern Siberia to the Urals."[4]

The tsarist government was populating Siberia not with industrious colonists but with hordes of destitute and desperate exiles who roamed Siberia as beggars, at best, and petty thieves and violent brigands, at worst. Their victims were the Siberians themselves, both the indigenes and the migrant peasant settlers from Russia. Brutalized by the conditions of their captivity, fugitives visited a plague of theft, arson, kidnapping, violent robbery, rape and murder on Siberia's real colonists. Seeking strength and protection in numbers, they sometimes formed armed gangs capable of terrorizing not just isolated villages but entire towns and cities. The exile system had transformed Siberia into Russia's "Wild East."

Some exiles known as *brodiagi*, or vagabonds, made for themselves a life of escape, recapture, spells in prison and then escape again. Overwhelmingly male, the *brodiagi* embraced a semi-nomadic existence in Russia, fuelled by a combination of charity and criminality. Like most pre-industrial societies, the Russian Empire had a rich variety of migratory traditions and a large diaspora encompassing fugitive peasants, Cossacks, peddlers, gypsies, migrant hunters, pilgrims, peripatetic sectarians, travelling merchants and the nomadic tribes of the taiga, steppe and tundra. These migratory peoples had played a significant role in Russia's expansion across Siberia in the sixteenth and seventeenth centuries. In 1823, the state criminalized vagrancy in European Russia, a fact which accounted for a large part of the sudden upsurge in the numbers exiled to Siberia over subsequent decades. Between 1827 and 1846, the almost 50,000 vagrants constituted 30 per cent of all those exiled. Most of those convicted of vagabondage in Russia in this period were deserters from the army and fugitive serfs, and they presented in either case a direct challenge to Nicholas I's cherished vision of a disciplined society. The numbers arrested for vagabondage declined in European Russia after the abolition of serfdom effectively decriminalized the unauthorized movement of people. In Siberia, however, the exile system gave vagabondage a new lease on life.[5]

The authorities made little distinction between hapless runaway exiles who fled in desperation or despair and the vagabonds who made

escape and roaming Siberia their vocation. In reality, though, the vagabonds formed a separate caste within the exile population. A vagabond would boast that the penal fort was his "father" and the taiga his
"mother" and that he spent his life running between the two. "Aristocrats" among the convicts, the vagabonds cultivated a rakish noncha-
lance and a conspicuous disdain for the rules of the prison forts and
for the "herd" of common prisoners who filled them. They enjoyed a
kind of authority and status born of their repeated escapes and of their
willingness to endure the beatings that recapture brought.[6]

Those who absconded from Transbaikal had to make their way
through the Yablonovy Mountains and around the shores of Lake Baikal to Irkutsk province. They set off in groups of ten, twenty, sometimes forty; their numbers swelled with fugitives from factories and
mines along the route. Circumventing towns and villages, they clung
wherever possible to the Great Siberian Post Road as it alone offered
refuge from the thick forests, swamps and rivers of the taiga. Once
they had left Baikal behind, the increased population density offered
improved opportunities to beg but also a greater risk of capture. Even
in the summer months, food could be hard to come by, and it was not
uncommon for fugitives to die of starvation. Others drowned while
attempting to cross rivers swollen by melting snows, or sank without
trace in quagmires. Many were racked by typhus. They were a common sight tramping along Siberian roads and, their heads sometimes
still half-shaved and their bodies dressed in convict smocks, many
made no real effort to hide their origins.[7]

Traversing Irkutsk province, the "hunchbacks" would cross Yenisei province and skirt Krasnoyarsk before heading for Tomsk. After
they entered Western Siberia, where the risk of arrest increased, larger
groups of vagabonds would begin to fragment into smaller ones. Once
in Tomsk province, some would head north for Achinsk; others set out
for Tobolsk. Ultimately, almost all fugitives sought to evade capture
and starvation long enough to leave Siberia itself. Their goal was to
reach Russia or to conceal their identity and so improve their fate by
submitting to a comparatively mild punishment for vagabondage. If
they were arrested before they crossed the Urals and managed to avoid
identification, a beating and a sentence of four years' penal labour in
Western Siberia was a considerable improvement on the sentences to
which many had originally been condemned. By 1842, the existing
punishment of twelve lashes for an initial escape, sixteen for a sec-

ond and twenty-four for a third was no longer considered adequate to the challenge of deterrence. St. Petersburg ordered that, in the future, recaptured exiled penal labourers were to be knouted up to fifty times. Even so, if they succeeded in making their way as far as European Russia, and were able to remain unidentified, captured fugitives would be exiled to a mere five years' settlement in Siberia. What emerged was a vicious circle of escape and recapture with a steadily mounting incentive for captured vagabonds to flee once again. The brutal floggings administered to the recaptured foot soldiers of General Cuckoo's Army were considered a price worth paying for a chance to improve their fate.[8]

Many exiles notched up multiple escapes. Kalina Korenets had been sentenced to twenty years of penal labour and had received ninety lashes. For his first escape, he received twenty lashes and ten years added to his sentence. He fled a second time only to be captured again, lashed forty times and have his existing thirty-year sentence extended by a further fifteen. For his third unsuccessful escape, he was punished by a further sixty lashes and a sentence of lifelong penal labour. Still, a fourth time he fled, and this time he succeeded in passing himself off as a different penal labourer and so "won back" several dozen blows of the lash and a sentence of "only" twenty years of penal labour. He was just twenty-eight years old.[9]

Andrei Karelin, condemned to fifty lashes and twenty years of penal labour for brigandage and armed robbery, escaped in July 1872 from a marching convoy bound for Siberia. He was captured, carrying forged documents and a revolver, six months later in Yaroslavl. Held in the Ufa prison while his case was being investigated, he escaped once again by tunnelling his way under the prison walls but succeeded in remaining at large only a short time. He was sentenced to eighty blows of the lash and had his sentence extended by a further fifteen years. Karelin "boasted that he would once again escape," something the authorities thought "entirely possible." Anxious enquiries from Yaroslavl as to whether he had reached his destination in Transbaikal in Eastern Siberia revealed that he had tried to file through the bars on the window of his convict barge but that this attempt to flee had been foiled. The Exile Office was unable to account for Karelin's precise whereabouts and could only assure the governor of Yaroslavl that this fearsome criminal had passed through Tyumen on 28 June 1874.[10]

To flee the exile settlements and villages across Siberia usually required little more than a resolve to pack one's knapsack and set out on the road. Indeed, Siberian peasants, eager to divest themselves of the burden of supporting the often hapless and impoverished exiles assigned to their villages, would abet their escape. They would provide would-be fugitives with provisions and fail to report their absence to the authorities. In the spring of 1828, officials in Irkutsk, Yenisei and Tobolsk provinces observed a sudden and dramatic increase in the number of exiles making their way westwards along the Great Siberian Post Road. Over the course of two weeks, more than 2,000 fugitive settlers had abandoned their villages and set out in large groups. The governor of Tomsk, Major-General Pyotr Frolov, reported that the exiles were intending to return to their native regions in European Russia.[11]

When the fugitives were questioned, it transpired that the "main cause of events" was an exiled settler in Tomsk region named Yankel Shkolnik who had spread the rumour that Russia and Turkey had entered into an agreement whereby the whole of Siberia would be transferred to Turkish control. The Russian government, not wishing to lose the population of Siberia, had granted all its subjects, including its exiles, permission to move to Russia. Investigations revealed that Shkolnik had simply told a scribe and a peasant that, while visiting Tomsk, he had read of this new government decree in the newspapers. The "pernicious storyteller" was turned over to the courts for harsh sentencing, but by August, sixty-nine fugitive exiles and vagabonds had already been caught. The would-be returnees apparently made no effort to conceal themselves and refrained from the usual criminality that accompanied escape. The exodus did not cease until the autumn frosts descended. By then 536 exiles had been recaptured, ninety of them on "the very border of Tomsk province." The authorities were keen to blame Shkolnik, rather than the conditions in which the exiled settlers lived, for the sudden widespread desire to make the long and arduous journey back to Russia.[12]

Escape from penal labour colonies often posed no greater challenge than escape from the exile settlements and villages. In the 1880s, the Irkutsk salt works, despite being a permanent and established penal labour site, had no prison buildings. Its seventy-five penal labourers were housed in cabins and privately rented rooms in the vicinity of the factory. Escapes took place on such a scale that officials in Siberia's factories would factor them into their calculations of provisions required to maintain the population of penal labourers. They would announce to newly arrived parties of convicts that clothing would "only be issued to those intending to stay; whoever is going to escape won't get any!" Other prison, factory and mine officials would secretly turn a blind eye to escapes they could have prevented in order to continue to claim the prisoner's subsistence allowance for personal profit. As in Gogol's masterpiece, these prison officials would accumulate "dead souls" who provided them with a steady income but caused them little trouble.[13]

Escape from under armed guard in the waystations, prisons, penal distilleries, forts and factories sometimes required more ingenuity. Exiles dug tunnels, filed their way through prison bars, disguised themselves as visitors or soldiers, bored holes through the roofs of prison buildings and burrowed their way out of outhouses and bathhouses. Prison guards in the older of Tobolsk's two prisons discovered a tunnel beneath the walls of the laundry. Almost 20 metres in length, it was only 3 metres short of the grounds beyond the prison and already contained a lamp and items of clothing.[14]

Attempts to curb the numbers absconding from under the noses of their guards proved dangerously ineffective. In 1872, the Ministry of the Interior issued an instruction to convoy soldiers to open fire on any convict leaving prison or waystation buildings to visit the outhouse unattended: "Guards are obliged to see a criminal intent upon escape in every such unaccompanied convict." Later that year, one guard opened fire on a prisoner who, it later transpired, had been taking linen to the bathhouse to be washed. The shot missed its target but other suspected runaways were less fortunate. In July 1873, a convict was shot dead in the Vladimir forwarding prison because a guard believed he was arming himself with a stone. A few months later in Pokrovsk in Yakutsk province, another prisoner was shot dead by guards as he ran towards the prison gates to greet his wife. An officer's sabre struck still another prisoner as he, following a doctor's instructions, exercised in the prison courtyard to alleviate his symptoms of scurvy. Some soldiers were rather less zealous and would even strike deals with prisoners to allow them to escape so that they could share with the fugitives the reward for their recapture.[15]

Even without the assistance or connivance of guards, there was little to prevent the most determined and ingenious prisoners from taking flight. Ethnographer Sergei Maksimov recorded the case of one veteran vagabond named Tumanov who staged a spectacular escape from the Tobolsk penal fort. Awaiting sentence to the gauntlet by a military tribunal for crimes he had committed in exile, Tumanov declared to his fellow innates: "One way or another I have to escape." Something of a conjurer, he put on performances for the prisoners that were so successful that the guards and warders learned of them and would even attend with their families. In preparation for his next prison performance, Tumanov rehearsed how to form a human pyramid in the prison yard. The amused guards looked on, suspecting nothing. When a religious holiday was due, the prison was full of rumours that Tumanov was intending to stage an extraordinary and unprecedented performance; the entire prison was in attendance: prisoners, guards, warders, even the prison warden and some invited guests.

Sporting a comical flaxen beard, Tumanov began his performance with some familiar tricks before building to the dramatic climax featuring the human pyramid. The acrobats assumed their positions and Tumanov mounted the pyramid, a balancing pole in his hands. The human pyramid began to move about the yard, Tumanov teetering at its summit, higher even than the wooden palisade of the prison courtyard. The spectacle delighted the assembled crowd, which roared its approval. And Tumanov had one more trick up his sleeve. As the pyramid tottered towards the edge of the courtyard, he suddenly leapt from his perch and vanished over the palisade. By the time the warders and soldiers had recovered their wits, run the length of the courtyard to the gates and begun to scour the grounds around the prison, Tumanov was gone. Search parties scoured the surrounding forests, ravines and bushes, but they could find no sign of the fugitive acrobat. His pursuers found only Tumanov's flaxen beard, nailed to the wooden palisade. So outraged was the governor of Tobolsk when he learned of the incident that he threatened to make the prison commander wear the beard to "his dying day."[16]

The avoidance of punishments proved a powerful motivation for convicts to flee. One exiled soldier from Yaroslavl notched up an impressive record of escapes. Sentenced to no fewer than seventeen separate punishments, he never submitted to a single one. On each occasion, he managed to flee before the sentence was executed and then assumed a fresh identity. He escaped the penal fort in Tomsk dressed as a medical orderly; imprisoned in Kainsk, he tunnelled his way to freedom; he managed to smuggle himself out of the Omsk prison in one of the outhouse barrels carrying human waste.[17]

Others fled because they simply could not reconcile themselves to the monotony of the villages and penal settlements. Many saw the convicts' desperate and often doomed attempts to escape as expressions of a craving for freedom, or at least for a temporary release from the existential burden of living within the walls of a prison or within the confines of a particular village. Launching oneself into the taiga was for the strong and determined, but the desire to flee did not always fade with old age. Anton Chekhov encountered one elderly exile named Altukhov on Sakhalin who escaped regularly in the following manner: "He takes a hunk of bread, locks up his cabin, and walking not more than 500 metres from the post, he sits down on the hill and gazes at the taiga, the sea and the sky; after sitting like this for three days or so, he goes back home, draws his provisions and goes back to the hill again . . . In the past they used to flog him, but now they simply laugh over these 'escapes' of his."[18] George Kennan met another elderly vagabond, now settled beyond the walls of a prison in the Kara gold-mining district, who begged the prison warden to imprison him during the summer because, even though he knew that he would not survive out in the wild, he was incapable of resisting the temptation to flee. There was, Kennan found:

> something pathetic in this inability of the worn, broken old convict to hear the cry of the cuckoo without yielding to the enticement of the wild, free, adventurous life with which that cry had become associated. He knew that he was feeble and broken; he knew that he could no longer tramp through the forests, swim rapid rivers, subsist upon roots, and sleep on the ground, as he had once done; but when the cuckoo called he felt again the impulses of his youth, he lived again in the imagination the life of independence and freedom he had known only in the pathless woods, and he was dimly conscious that if not prevented by force he "must go." As Ulysses had himself bound in order that he might not yield to the voices of the sirens, so the poor old convict had himself committed to prison in order that he might not hear and obey the cry of the cuckoo.[19]

Other fugitives were simply desperate to satisfy their longing to return to their families. Over the course of several years, one convict fled three times from Nerchinsk but, on each occasion, he never got farther than Perm province, 5,000 kilometres away. Each time he was captured, he was knouted and sent back to the mines with an increase in his term of penal labour. On the fourth occasion, however, he succeeded in reaching his native village near Yaroslavl and managed to persuade his wife to follow him to Siberia. The couple presented themselves to the local authorities; the husband turned himself in as a fugitive and the wife declared her wish to follow her husband back to Nerchinsk. Eleven months later, the convict received his new sentence: sixty lashes and a very long term of penal labour. He was deported once again eastwards but this time, after eight years of struggle, in the company of his wife and children.[20]

One Nerchinsk official noted that Muslim exiles from the Caucasus would flee in order to "breathe the air of their native mountains" before returning to Siberia. The desire to see home could seize exiles like a kind of delirium, Yadrintsev observed:

> The passionate hope of one day reaching his native village becomes the goal of an exile's life and never abandons him whatever the trials and sufferings that befall him. He dreams of home while hungry in the exile settlements; it inspires him when, having escaped, he lies without food beneath some bush; if captured, he consoles himself with the idea of home while languishing on the plank beds through the long nights in prison, hatching new plans to escape . . . The loss of his homeland is the source of the exile's moral torments and the cause of his constant escapes.[21]

Even established exiles who had spent forty years at settlement might, in the twilight of their years, suddenly gamble everything on one desperate bid to see their homeland again before they died.[22]

Escape also gave fugitives a chance to "test their fortune." The roaming diaspora of pilgrims, merchants and travellers, dispersed throughout the Siberian landmass, offered a camouflage of sorts to fugitive exiles who would seek to conceal their prison past altogether.[23] In Tobolsk, one fugitive exile masqueraded as a "holy fool," a religious figure believed to be gifted with wisdom and foresight. He grew his hair down over his face in order to conceal his tell-tale brands and cultivated a lack of personal hygiene imposing enough to deter the town's residents from approaching him too closely. He enjoyed the charity of the townsfolk before some sharp-eyed locals, who noticed the faded brands on his face, eventually unmasked him. Another fugitive from justice passed himself off as a Turkish naval captain. He was able to borrow substantial sums of money in Tobolsk and then move on to enjoy the hospitality of the well-to-do residents of Tomsk before finally being exposed in Krasnoyarsk. In the 1850s, two exiles posed, in Gogolian fashion, as government inspectors, travelling with forged documents and striking fear into the hearts of local officials.[24]

If they possessed neither the papers nor the requisite dramatic skills to pass themselves off as anything other than exiles, fugitives would, when apprehended or when turning themselves in, claim the identities of exiles they knew to have been sentenced to punishments less onerous than their own. Fugitive penal labourers from the mines and factories would claim they had been exiled to settlement; those sentenced to permanent settlement would claim they were administrative exiles facing a term of five years. Fugitives from Eastern Siberia would claim that they had been banished to Western Siberia. Exploiting the chaos that reigned in the state's record-keeping, fugitives could reasonably expect many months of detention in prisons or penal settlements while their cases were investigated—long enough to escape once again.[25]

The last recourse of the captured vagabond was to refuse to divulge any identity at all. Many assumed sobriquets such as "Ivan Nepomnyashchy" or "Ivan I-Don't-Remember." One of the characters of Fyodor Dostoevsky's *Notes from the House of the Dead* is Shapkin, a convict who merrily recalls an encounter with a district policeman attempting to establish the identities of himself and a small group of his fellow fugitives. When asked to show his documents, Shapkin replied that he did not have any; he and his travelling companions were "in the pay of General Cuckoo":

> The district police officer says to me: "Who the hell are you then?" . . . I say: "Your honour, I don't remember, your honour, I've forgotten." . . . Then he says to the next fellow: "And who might you be?"
> "Scarper, your honour."

"That's your name, is it, Scarper?"

"That's my name, your honour."

"Right then, you're Scarper, and who are you?" he says to the third man.

"Scarper'n all, your honour."

"And is that your name?"

"That's my name. Scarper'n all, your honour."

"And who gave you a name like that, you villain?"

"Kind folk did, your honour. There's kind folk in the world, you know, your honour."

"And who were these kind folk?"

"I don't remember, your honour, begging your honour's pardon."[26]

Vagabonds thus assumed false names in a deliberate and brazen attempt to frustrate the authorities' attempts to identify them. "Ivan I-Don't-Remember"s proliferated, appearing in every exile settlement and penal colony across Siberia. Yadrintsev encountered no fewer than forty in a single prison fort. The prison doctor at the Kara penal settlement, Vladimir Kokosov, found the prison bursting with hundreds of vagabonds named "Ivan I-Don't-Remember," or variations thereof.[27]

The number of vagabonds being apprehended across Siberia was, by the middle of the nineteenth century, overwhelming the state's ability to punish them all in accordance with the law. Prisons and penal labour sites were overflowing with unidentified vagabonds serving out their sentences. The state's inability to cope with them was resulting in excessively lenient sentences that only increased the incentive to flee, as Minister of Justice Viktor Panin observed in exasperation:

The numbers of vagabonds in our prisons have increased to such an extent that it will soon be impossible to accommodate any more of them. The prison forts of Western Siberia are already overcrowded. As a result, the vagabonds . . . knowing that, owing to their significant numbers, there is no room for them in the penal battalions, have nothing worse to fear than a birching and exile to settlement.[28]

After decades of struggling unsuccessfully against this welter of fabricated, borrowed and stolen identities, the Siberian authorities resorted in 1895 to deporting all vagabonds refusing to divulge their identities to settlement on the island of Sakhalin, which by then already enjoyed a fearsome reputation among Siberia's exiles. The threat of Sakhalin duly provided an effective *aide-mémoire,* as one report drily noted: "From that moment their number began to fall and many began to remember their names."[29]

The government also struggled to combat the contraband in identities by ensuring that convicts remained visually distinct in order to render their escape more difficult and their detection easier. From 1824, all male and non-noble convicts in the deportation convoys sentenced to penal labour had half their heads shaved before setting out and were prohibited from wearing their own clothes (although officials frequently complained that the instructions were ignored).[30]

Branding, meanwhile, inscribed the convicts' status on their very bodies. Until 1817, when it was finally prohibited as an inhumane punishment, the state would slit the nostrils of penal labourers in public ceremonies before their deportation. In the seventeenth century, executioners would also sear the convict's flesh with hot irons, but under Peter the Great this practice was replaced by branding with ink rather than with fire. Markers of a penal labourer's shame and exclusion as well as a means of identifying him, the brands consisted of iron stamps that bristled with needles in the shape of individual letters. They pierced the flesh and then gunpowder was rubbed into the wound to leave a permanent mark. The nature of the brands changed over time, but consisted initially of the letters "B-O-P" (pronounced "V-O-R") etched into the flesh of the forehead and each cheek, spelling out the Russian for "thief." In 1845, the new penal code ordered those letters replaced with "K-A-T," which stood for "KATORZHNIK" or "penal labourer." The brands were, as one contemporary jurist observed, "not a punishment in the proper sense of the word but a preventative police measure." They were designed to prevent the exile population from melting back into the wider population and to render easier the detection, capture and punishment of fugitives. In 1840, the State Council charged Siberian governors with ensuring that all escaped exiles be properly branded and that the brands differ by province in order to help identify a fugitive's origin, or at least his most recent place of capture.[31]

At the same time, officials were becoming concerned that the brands were not proving durable enough and that, over time, they were fading away. In 1842, the Ministry of the Interior charged the Imperial Medical Council with devising a new dye "such that it would be difficult or, indeed, impossible for the criminals to remove their brands." The Medical Council considered various alternatives, testing them on convicts and dogs, but rejected most on the grounds of cost. After a two-year period of testing, during which it proposed to dispense with gunpowder in favour of soot from Holland mixed with linseed or hempseed oil, the Medical Council was unable to produce significantly improved results: "Whatever means are used for creating brands on the skin of convicts, if these brands do not penetrate deep into the body, it will always be possible to remove them by allowing the skin to fester and so, given the current state of our science, there is no such thing as a permanent branding of convicts."[32]

They were right. Fugitive exiles were understandably keen to shed the stigmata that marked them out, in convict parlance, as "branded horses." Brands might easily prove their undoing, foiling their attempts to pass themselves off as innocent pilgrims, or at least as settlers rather than penal labourers. Some resorted to drastic means: they would use poisonous plants, sulphuric acid, blister beetles, blistering plasters, silver nitrate and hot iron to burn out the brands. Alternatively, they would make incisions in the brands and then allow the wounds to fester for many months so that the putrefying flesh removed all trace of the dye. Some even injected their own flesh with syphilis. But these painful self-mutilations did not always ensure anonymity, as apprehended fugitives were sentenced for their scars just as they were for the brands. Some accumulated multiple brands in a testament to their undimmed enthusiasm for freedom. Yadrintsev encountered one old vagabond whose body was a veritable document of repeated escape and recapture: "On his back he had the marks of the knout and the gauntlet, on his buttocks the scars of birch rods and the lash. He had brands on his back, on his hands and on his face. He was as thin as a rake and walked with a crutch, yellow and with sunken cheeks."[33]

Branding, flogging, chaining and draconian increases in sentences in reality did little to stem the tide of exiles who fled. Although the 1822 "Statutes on Exiles" stipulated that supervision over the exiled settlers was the responsibility of the Tobolsk Exile Office, in practice the office's writ simply did not run into the villages scattered about Siberia's remoter provinces. Local legal officials, already short-staffed and overburdened with administrative duties, were obliged, in order to inspect their districts, to travel between 500 and 1,000 kilometres. It was, one official protested, "quite impossible for them to maintain direct supervision of the exiles." In fact, the state was not even able to protect its own offices adequately. The agricultural administration building in Ishim district was burgled in 1873; contract papers, stamps and money were stolen. The two men guarding the building—a retired soldier and an exiled settler—had been bludgeoned to death in their sleep.[34]

Many fugitives were eventually captured, but not before they had committed crimes and diverted the energies of state forces. When, prompted by a particularly high-profile or grisly murder, the authorities conducted periodic sweeps of Siberian towns, they netted astonishing numbers of vagabonds. Following a murder in Omsk in 1866, the state arrested 180 vagabonds in a week. The governor of Tomsk carried out one such round-up in his town in a single morning in 1875 and caught no fewer than 800 vagabonds.[35]

Tomsk province was a thoroughfare along which those escaping from Eastern Siberia made their way westwards. There were villages in which up to 3,000 vagabonds would spend the winter while they waited to resume their journey in the spring. Due to its central location and the ineffectiveness of its police force, the town of Tomsk itself was, for a time in the 1860s, Yadrintsev observed, "a central resting place for exiles, like an enormous coaching inn, and the backstreets in the town were like an enormous bazaar."[36] By the 1890s, semi-official refuges for vagabonds operated in Siberian towns. Set up by private benefactors with at least tacit support from the authorities, they sought to relieve the pressures that hordes of vagabonds brought to bear on the town's inhabitants. An official report described how a merchant named Shkroyev had set up one such refuge on the outskirts of Kainsk in Yenisei province, a town "teeming with vagabonds" in the 1890s. Conditions inside were a vision of utter destitution: more than 100 men crammed into two small rooms, lolling about on plank beds and on the earth floor, such that it was impossible even to count them properly. Half of them were "completely naked"; the other half "dressed in rags." The shed resounded to "groans, ceaseless coughing, sneezing and spluttering" and the "stench inside was incredible." Most had drunk their way through their alms and their clothes and "presented the combined effects of extreme poverty and moral collapse to a degree that defies the imagination."[37]

Such refuges were doubtless tolerated in part because the authorities simply did not have the prison facilities necessary to contain all this surplus itinerant population. Nikolai Kaznakov, the governor-general of Western Siberia, admitted in 1874: "There are so many vagabonds that it is impossible to keep them under guard and the authorities are obliged officially to instruct the districts to 'cease the persecution of the vagabonds.'" Count Vladimir Sologub, the chairman of the Committee on Prison Reform in the 1870s, conceded the state's impotence: "The only exiles who do not escape are those who do not wish to do so."[38]

The state's principal ally in containing the exiles was the winter. Like a giant Cerberus looming over the continent, it was the greatest obstacle in the path of the fugitives trudging westwards. For if the spring call of the cuckoo heralded the onset of the seasonal exodus of exiles, the arrival of the first autumn frosts signalled its abrupt and often lethal termination. Those who had not managed to establish themselves under assumed identities in towns and villages usually opted to return to the safety of the prison forts. Experienced vagabonds would appear at the gates, announce themselves as "Ivan I-Don't-Remember," and accept the flogging that was the price of refuge from the winter. Not all were fleet enough of foot, however, and some simply lost themselves in the taiga. Siberia's blinding winter snowstorms or *purgi*—blizzards and howling gales accompanied by plummeting temperatures—could descend in a matter of minutes, with fatal results. One group of fugitives was caught by a *purga* near Barnaul; some ran ahead and managed to gain the sanctuary of a village, but six of their companions lost their way and froze to death. Each spring, the retreat of the winter snows revealed forests strewn with the frozen corpses of vagabonds. Groups of fugitives fleeing Transbaikal would sometimes attempt to take advantage of the thick ice that sealed the waters of Lake Baikal in order to spare themselves the thousands of kilometres required to circumnavigate the shoreline. Yet the trek across Baikal's frozen expanses offered no refuge from the pitiless winter storms, and the men would sometimes freeze to death in huddled groups.[39]

Some Siberian officials betrayed a nonchalant attitude to the thou-

sands of fugitives spewing forth from exile villages and penal settlements. One official declared to the British journalist Edmund Noble:
"Siberia is a huge prison. In which of its cells a convict is confined
matters little. The great thing—and this we accomplish pretty successfully—is to prevent him from getting over its walls." Another senior
official in Western Siberia declared: "Let them flee! Whatever the case,
they won't get beyond the Urals." Such confidence was misplaced.[40]

Between 1827 and 1846, of the 155,000 men and women exiled
to Siberia, 18,500 were already fugitives from Siberia who had been
recaptured in European Russia. The annual numbers reaching Russia
were between 400 and 1,400. As the nineteenth century progressed,
roads, waterways and railways opened up some of Siberia's more
remote locations. Siberia's peasant colonists thus found themselves sus-
taining hordes of parasitical vagabonds on their journey westwards.
Meanwhile, the police were apprehending increasing numbers of Siberian vagabonds who had crossed the Urals and reached Russian towns
and cities. Regional governors in European Russia and the Caucasus
were complaining of the large numbers of exiles from their regions who
were making their way home from Siberia and "posed a threat to the
welfare and security of the province."[41] A government inquiry into the
state of the exile system in 1877 argued that the view that Siberian exile
removes criminals from European Russia is "entirely mistaken." The
report freely acknowledged that "the primary cause of vagabondage
in European Russia today is the exile system." Vagabondage placed a
tremendous burden on the treasury, which was obliged to finance the
deportation of the same exile two or three times. By 1878, for every
28,000 exiles deported to Siberia at a cost of around 300 roubles per
person, 1,000 were fugitives being returned to their original place of
banishment.[42]

The vagabonds and fugitives who fled the exile settlements and penal
labour sites rejected the role the state had assigned to them in its vision
for the penal colonization of the continent. Yet the real subversive
power of the fleeing exiles lay in the plague of begging, pilfering and
violent crime they visited upon Siberia's true colonists: the Siberian
peasantry. Every single destitute and desperate vagabond who begged
for alms, stole livestock and pilfered tools from peasant farms sapped

the resources of those upon whose shoulders the development of Siberia ultimately depended.

Some were harmless enough and, indeed, often themselves fell victim to the Siberian peasants. Dressed in rags and half-starving, they begged alms from villagers and served as a pool of itinerant labourers on farms. Beyond both the reach and the protection of the law, they were vulnerable to exploitation by unscrupulous peasants. Farmers frequently cheated them, threatening them with denunciation to the authorities if they objected. Some even murdered vagabonds to avoid paying them.[43]

Yet thousands of Siberia's vagabonds turned to crime, and often to very violent crime.[44] Indeed, by the second half of the nineteenth century, Siberia was succumbing to an epidemic of robberies, murders and rapes. Even though the exasperated peasantry reported only a small minority of the actual crimes committed, the numbers painted a picture of regions under siege. In Tobolsk and Tomsk provinces, there were some 2,850 recorded crimes in 1876, 56 per cent of them robberies and 8 per cent murders. Over the preceding five years, 8,000 vagabonds had been arrested in the two provinces. "It is a rare village on the way back to Russia that is free from theft, a rare town that is spared the most terrible atrocities, a rare road not strewn with dead bodies," the governor-general of Western Siberia, Nikolai Kaznakov, observed in 1877. Exiles butchered impoverished peasants for the smallest of sums. In June 1899, an entire family was slaughtered in the village of Sheragul in Irkutsk province; three months later, an exiled settler slit the throat of two sisters in the same village in order to rob them of the pittance they had saved. Vodka, rather than money, was sometimes the motive for the crime. In 1872, two exiles murdered a tavern-keeper in Tomsk province because he had refused them credit.[45]

Peasants occasionally succeeded in defending their homes from violent attack. One well-known brigand, a Cherkess named Dzhanteirov, had already spent four years in prison for robbing a postal coach. He went on to commit a string of armed robberies and murders before finally being arrested and sentenced to exile in Yakutsk district. He escaped, however, and on the night of 28 December 1898, he and two accomplices attempted to rob the house of a wealthy settled exile named Izbushkin. They tricked their way into the house and shot dead a labourer before stabbing Izbushkin and attacking his wife. But

Izbushkin's thirteen-year-old son rushed to his mother's defence, and opened fire on the attackers with a rifle and a shotgun, killing Dzhanteirov and one of his accomplices. The last remaining assailant fled empty-handed.[46]

The Siberian press abounded with tales of robberies and gruesome murders in which the perpetrators, if apprehended, almost invariably proved to be exiled criminals. The Irkutsk weekly *Siberia* reported that, in Yenisei province in the first six months of 1875, six churches were burgled and a sexton was murdered. In Tobolsk in June 1875, a retired local official, Burdukov, and his twenty-year-old ward were strangled in their beds. *Siberia* stated that, in the first six months of 1877, there were no fewer than twenty-eight murders and armed robberies and "countless cases of theft night and day" in the city of Tomsk. It had "become dangerous even to go out into the street in the evening: sometimes night-time hunters have appeared who ride about with hooks and lassos stripping residents of their fur coats and hats. And that is not the least of it! Robberies are carried out not only in the streets and in homes in the usual way through doors and windows but even underground by means of tunnels!" The small town of Balagansk in Irkutsk province had a total population of less than 5,000 but there were sixty-seven murders there in 1887. Understaffed, poorly trained and often corrupt, Siberia's rural police force was no match for the crime wave. Countless murders went unsolved.[47]

Yet, however inadequate the police in Siberia's towns, they offered at least a modicum of protection. In the sprawling expanses of the Siberian wilderness, there was no defence whatsoever against well-planned and ruthlessly executed assaults. In June 1845, four vagabonds hunted down and murdered an entire group of gold prospectors in the forests surrounding Yeniseisk in order to rob the merchant, Vasily Yerin, who was leading the expedition. Led by one Ivan Nepomnyashchy, the fugitive exiles had joined the party under false pretences and then waited until the expedition had dispersed into smaller search parties. They proceeded to pick off Yerin, his three stewards and their eight employees in small groups after they had penetrated into deserted areas of the forest. Betrayed by one of their number, three of the exiles attempted to flee the scene of their crime by sailing down the Yenisei River. The local magistrate and a group of armed Cossacks and peasants gave chase, following the fugitives downstream for five days and nights with occasional exchanges of gunfire that wounded Nepomnyashchy in the leg. In the end, their boat holed by gunfire, and utterly exhausted by lack of sleep, the criminals put down their weapons and surrendered. Transported to the Krasnoyarsk penal fort, the men were each sentenced to run a gauntlet of 1,000 soldiers between three and five times, branded and sent to lifelong penal labour.[48]

Merchant caravans—the lifeblood of Siberian commerce—were especially vulnerable to assault as they made their way through thick forests along Siberia's isolated roads. In August 1875, in the vicinity of Minusinsk, in Yenisei province, two peasants who had been tasked with delivering spirits for a local nobleman were discovered by the side of the road with their skulls staved in. Organized bands of brigands would waylay entire merchant families on the road and extort their money, one journalist reported, "with the most terrible forms of torture—with axe butts, needles, nails, fire and knives." In one case, they crushed the heads of the children and infants under the wheels of the carriage and slaughtered the adults. Such highwaymen were so active along the Great Siberian Post Road between Irkutsk and Tomsk that, in 1886, coachmen took to heavily arming themselves and riding in large groups to improve their chances of fighting off the bandits. Several of the worst stretches of road had to be patrolled by mounted Cossacks.[49]

An inspiration to thousands of other exiles who were preparing for flight, the audacious and brutal exploits of some vagabonds made them legends in their own time. The ethnographer Maksimov described one such convict, named Korenev, who was both an "incorrigible murderer" and a "role model beloved of the exiles who followed him." His exploits were famous across Siberia's penal forts and prisons, and were remembered, and even praised, after he was laid to rest. One former exile-turned-vagabond named Svetlov, renowned for his physical strength, became the head of a gang of brigands that terrorized Tomsk province. Svetlov was generous with his loot, it was said, and would give it away to passing vagabonds. Another, named Sokhaty, was captain of a pirate ship that attacked merchant barges on Lake Baikal and staged a spectacular robbery of the annual Chertovkinsk fair on one of the islands in the mouth of the Selenga River. The names of famous bandit chiefs still lingered in Siberian folklore at the end of the nineteenth century.[50]

15. *Life Is Everywhere,* Nikolai Yaroshenko's portrait of exiles and their families in sealed trains awaiting deportation to Siberia, 1888.

16. An attempted escape by exiles from a marching convoy, 1880s.

17. A convict chained to a wheelbarrow—one of the most terrible
punishments inflicted on recidivist criminals, 1890s.

18. Convicts on a prison barge on the River Irtysh, 1880s.

19. Convicts on a prison steamship, 1880s.

20. Elderly prisoners in Kara in the Nerchinsk Mining Region, late nineteenth century.

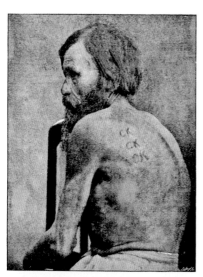

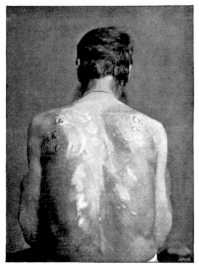

21. A convict branded with the letters "CK," an abbreviation of "Siberian Penal Labourer," late nineteenth century.

22. The executioner in Kara, late nineteenth century.

23. Scarring from corporal punishment, late nineteenth century.

24. The Tobolsk Central Penal Labour Prison, 1880s.

25. Exiles bound for Siberia marching through Odessa,
turn of the twentieth century.

26. Jarosław Dabrowski

27. A political exile in Siberia,
late nineteenth century.

28. Yelizaveta Kovalskaya, 1880s.

29. Facial brands of the kind that exiles
endeavoured to remove in order to conceal
their identity, late nineteenth century.

30. Vagabonds or *brodiagi*, fugitive exiles making their way
through the taiga, late nineteenth century.

Peasant culture across the Russian Empire was very violent; those who violated the communal laws governing village life could be shamed and brutally beaten. Even so, crimes in Siberia stood out for their savagery. The ethnographer Yadrintsev explained that most murders and armed robberies were perpetrated by penal labourers: "Penal labour of course accumulates experienced killers who go on to repeat their crimes, but our penal labour sites also bring about the brutalization, embitterment and barbarization of individuals. Physically tortured, tempered by suffering, embittered by persecution, the penal labourer naturally loses all and any gentle and human feelings." Many of Siberia's killers did, indeed, appear to revel in brutality. On 5 October 1873, the widow of an Irkutsk merchant, her daughter, their janitor and a Buryat servant were all killed and their bodies thrown into the River Angara. The killers also assaulted their young cook, raping, torturing and strangling her and finally leaving her for dead. Remarkably, she survived and was able to identify her assailants, who turned out to be three exiled settlers and three vagabonds. At their trial, they showed complete indifference to their victims and were later hanged. In the same year, a young chambermaid disappeared from the Krasnoyarsk high school for girls. Soon after her disappearance, some grisly human remains were discovered: first a mutilated head, then a severed arm being dragged by a dog, and finally the victim's torso, horribly disfigured, with the breasts sliced off and the genitals savagely mutilated. Suspicion fell on the school caretaker and a clerk from a local office, both of whom had disappeared at the same time as the girl. When the pair were finally arrested and their guilt established, the investigation revealed that both were escaped convicts living under false identities.[51]

Sexual violence against women and children was widespread. Vagabonds would abduct women from their farms at knifepoint; many were gang-raped and then killed. Yadrintsev reported on two vagabonds who could not agree on who should have one such kidnapped woman and abandoned her in the forest. She was found "naked, tied by her pigtails to a tree; her entire body had been devoured by mosquitoes and horse-flies and her flesh had swelled up; she was foaming at the mouth and was unconscious, barely alive." In 1894, Irkutsk was besieged by a gang that would ride into town at twilight on horse-drawn sledges and would capture innocent bystanders with lassos before dragging them out of town and robbing them. The perpetrators rode off with a young girl whom they raped and then dumped, naked, in the snow outside the city. Strengthened patrols in Irkutsk were unable to apprehend them, as the criminals always seemed to be one step ahead of the authorities. It was only after a gang of exiles was caught in a raid on an abandoned house not far from the governor's residence that the attacks halted.[52]

Given this epidemic of crime, it is little surprise that Siberia became synonymous with Russia's "Wild East." "Yeniseisk and its surroundings boast such an unprecedented number of murders, thefts and armed robberies," one correspondent for the popular *St. Petersburg News* reported to a shocked and fascinated audience in the capital in 1871. "After sunset, nobody dares venture out in the town. It is just like Bukhar or Chechnya in the 1840s."[53] Such comments were not mere journalistic hyperbole. A major official report published in 1900 denounced the double standards and injustice of a government that banished its criminals to Siberia and then turned a blind eye to the havoc they wreaked there:

> The crimes committed by the exile population are truly remarkable for their astonishing cunning, their bloodcurdling cruelty, and their complete fearlessness in the face of punishment . . . Almost all these crimes, if they had been committed in European Russia, would have caused a national sensation and been the talk of the reading public for a very long time, but in Siberia, they are lost among the welter of similar "events" and go completely unnoticed . . . The unavenged corpses [of the victims] do not and cannot disturb anyone's conscience: They are simply the fruits of the deeply imbibed poison of Siberian exile, and against this the local authorities are powerless.[54]

As the numbers of vagabonds spiralled in the second half of the nineteenth century, so did the demands they made of the Siberian peasantry. The begging and pilfering, to say nothing of more violent crimes, corroded established traditions of giving shelter, food and alms to passing vagabonds. Peasant charity seemed increasingly to be motivated not by pity and generosity but by fear that menacing vagabonds, if disappointed, would commit acts of theft or arson. Governor-General Kaznakov observed in 1877 that "there was a time when the local population was sympathetic to the exiles, and called them 'unfortunates.'

That time has now passed . . ." The terrified inhabitants of Western Siberia, "fearing acts of arson and retribution, leave out food at night for the embittered wanderers and seek to defend themselves in acts of lawless revenge and even in lynch-mobs."[55]

Unable to deal on its own with the marauding vagabonds in Siberia, the government had in fact long ignored the killing of exiles and had even sought to co-opt the peasants themselves in what sometimes resembled a low-intensity civil war. As early as 1813, the governor-general of Siberia, Ivan Pestel, had pressed St. Petersburg to lift the threat of any sanction against locals dealing with the problem of marauding fugitive exiles. The government had responded with a ruling that peasants, native tribes, military units and other individuals who were hunting down fugitive exiles should, "if their lives were in danger, deal with them as if with important state criminals. Those assisting the state should be reassured that they will not be blamed if they resort to drastic measures against escaped exiles."[56] This ruling amounted to a licence to kill and to a declaration of open season on Siberia's vagabonds.

Periodically, the peasants and native peoples did, indeed, declare war on the vagabonds. In a world in which the theft of livestock and farming implements could bring utter destitution to peasant families, retribution was brutal. Captured thieves were subject to violent and often fatal public beatings. A group of peasants who seized a convict for stealing horses drove seven wooden needles into his heels and then left him to crawl away into the forest. Years later, the man still bore the scars on his legs from where the needles had protruded through his calf muscles.[57] In 1879, a group of Buryats captured two vagabonds in a village outside Irkutsk and stripped them naked in a farmyard before beating them with a knout to within an inch of their lives. They then tossed the battered bodies of the men onto their own cart and whipped their horse in the direction of Irkutsk. When one of the men finally came to his senses on the approach to the town, he discovered his companion lying dead next to him. In Marinsk district, peasants caught up with an exile who had stolen their horses, and stuffed finely broken glass into his eyes, taunting him that he would never again find his way to their village. Over the course of 1884, the Ishim town surgeon conducted no fewer than 200 post-mortems on the bodies of fugitive exiles murdered by peasants in his district alone.[58]

Vagabonds retaliated with brutal acts of vengeance of their own, arson being a favoured weapon. On two separate occasions in October 1879, buildings in the same village on the outskirts of Tobolsk were set on fire amid high winds. Only the vigilance of the villagers prevented a conflagration that might have consumed the entire settlement. In 1898, another village, suspected of energetic assistance to the authorities in hunting down fugitive exiles in the vicinity, was set on fire in an act of organized reprisal. Sixty-four farmsteads were burned to the ground.[59]

The authorities not only turned a blind eye to the killing of vagabonds; rewards of three roubles were officially offered for each captured fugitive, dead or alive. Siberian peasants and natives had little compunction in tracking down such human quarry, and bounty-hunting flourished as a cottage industry. According to a popular saying, "A squirrel's pelt is worth five kopecks, but you'll get fifty for a hunchback." There were districts in Siberia that were "famed for their extermination of vagabonds." In the district of Verkholensk, in Irkutsk province, some sixty or so corpses of escaped exiles were found every year, most of them killed by peasants. Some peasants won reputations for themselves as fearless bounty-hunters. One named Bitkov plied his trade up and down the River Angara, opening fire from the shore on vagabonds drifting downstream on rafts. There were peasants who notched up sixty, sometimes ninety, kills. One peasant was said to have delivered 100 captured vagabonds to the authorities, half of them dead. The Gilyaks and Buryats of Eastern Siberia were particularly skilled and ruthless bounty-hunters and specialized in tracking down, attacking and killing organized gangs of brigands on Siberia's roads. The exiled Decembrist Dmitry Zavalishin observed that, if the peasantry had not culled so many exiles in this way, Siberia would never have been able to cope with them all.[60]

By the 1870s, however, Siberia was no longer coping. Kaznakov, the governor-general of Western Siberia, pointed out that in 1877 the crime rate in districts with exiles was five times higher than in those with none: "The exile population, bound together in the misery of its circumstances and by the solidarity of its interests, has virtually forged an alliance extending across all of Siberia, which is conducting a secret war against the civilian population."[61] Others had recourse to the same metaphor. Siberian towns were, the *Siberian Gazette* lamented:

constantly blockaded by all of the human refuse sent to our country from all over the Empire . . . Any person unfamiliar with our way of life in Siberia, walking down the road at night, might think that Omsk was a town under siege. All night there are armed sentries walking the streets, there are military units and private militias . . . On every corner you hear the challenge "Who goes there?" It is like martial law, as if the city is surrounded by an invisible enemy.[62]

Siberia looked to the ethnographer Yadrintsev like a "battlefield." The destructive contradictions of the state's penal and colonial policies in Siberia were clearly exposed in the increasingly violent and merciless struggle between the peasants and the vagabonds: "We see two clearly distinct figures, both with a historical significance: one is the representative of penal colonization who has fled from his place of exile; the other is a peasant, a representative of a civic order, standing with his rifle before his farmstead, defending his home, his property, his family and his prosperity."[63] Almost all observers, state officials and journalists alike, made the same point: the presence of exiles in Siberia was a terrible burden on the continent's free population and a brake on its economic development.

10

Sakhalin Island

My dear wife! I write to inform you that we have arrived, thank God, safely on Sakhalin! The climate here is marvellous and, for growing all manner of things, the soil is second to none! Black earth as far as the eye can see! As soon as his wife arrives, every convict is given everything he needs to set up a farmstead for free: two horses, six cows, six ducks and cockerels; a completely finished cabin, a wagon, a plough, a harrow and such like, everything that is necessary for a successful farm. So as soon as you get this letter, sell everything that you have for whatever you can get and appeal to the authorities without delay to have yourself arrested and come here![1]

So read a letter sent by one of Sakhalin's convicts to his wife at the turn of the twentieth century. It was, like countless others, written in the hold of a transport ship and posted in the port of Aden, months before its author ever reached the shores of the island. Many women fell victim in this way to the calculating deception of their own husbands. There was a caustic proverb on the island that ran: "The clever are taken there; the idiots go on their own."[2] Yet however desperate or cynical the convicts who attempted to lure their unsuspecting wives into following them to Sakhalin may have been, most had little idea of what really awaited them. Sakhalin was, in fact, the very antithesis of the fantastical pastoral idyll beguilingly crafted by the letter's author. On the island, women and children discovered not well-provisioned farmsteads, but a dark world of destitution, violence and sexual exploitation. Sakhalin did not support families; it devoured them.

Exile families wielded great symbolic and practical significance in Siberia. They both embodied the moral virtues of the tsarist political order and served as outposts of Russian imperial power. The paternalism of the Russian autocracy itself sanctified the conjugal and filial ties that bound together all families in the Russian Empire. Fathers and husbands were not simply breadwinners; they were figures of authority, charged with moral responsibility to protect, and provide for, their wives and children.[3]

Practical considerations underscored this respect for the sanctity of marriage. Unruly exile populations were unproductive and a drain on the resources of the Siberian peasantry upon whom they depended for alms, or from whom they simply stole. From the earliest recorded cases of exile to Siberia in the late sixteenth century, the state had viewed women as "frontier domesticators." They were needed to pacify their husbands, raise children and play a central role in the establishment of a stable and industrious colonial population. The domesticating influence of wives and the sober responsibilities of fatherhood would, it was believed, convert wayward criminals into hardworking homesteaders and law-abiding subjects of the tsar.[4]

Ideas of penal reform began to gain ground from the late eighteenth century, challenging older religious views of crime as an indelible sin. By the reign of Alexander II, the rehabilitation of convicts was declared to be a central, "humane" goal of the exile system. On the eve of the Great Reforms, Minister of the Interior Sergei Lanskoi explained that the state provided the criminal with all the means for his rehabilitation and reintegration into civil society. The penal labourer had the opportunity to transfer to the ranks of the exile settlers and, after a certain number of years, to the state peasantry. He "thereby becomes, once again, a member of society."[5]

The new-found emphasis on rehabilitation also served the state's wider colonial ambitions. It was one thing for penal labourers to be put to work at discrete industrial sites across Siberia, extracting natural resources. But the full-blown colonization of the continent demanded more than simply disciplined and hard-working penal labourers; it required the establishment of economically productive, settled communities that would promote commerce, industry and culture. Government officials were not blind to the obvious challenges in converting exiled criminals into resilient and law-abiding settlers. And so they turned, with a mixture of idealism and pragmatism, to the family.[6]

Throughout the reigns of Nicholas I and Alexander II, senior officials in the administration of the exile system repeatedly extolled the reforming powers of marriage and child-rearing among Siberia's exiles. Lanskoi enthused:

> Of all the material and moral means to reform penal labourers, marriage is the most important. It is true that relief from labour, permission to live outside the penal forts and the provision of resources to establish households all significantly contribute to the criminal's moral regeneration. They cannot, however, in and of themselves, bring about the kind of beneficial transformation that marriage can. A man sentenced to penal labour is stripped of all those interests that bind an individual to life and make his life appealing. With marriage, he finds a new, reinvigorated bond with the world. He finds in his wife, or at least hopes to find, a person who, with her care and her love, will alleviate life's difficulties and with whom he can share life's joys . . . Entering into family life and having a household, the criminal settles down and abstains from escapes and other crimes for fear of losing the property he has accumulated through his labours, and the comforts of his family life . . . Married life is the safest guarantor of the penal labourers' material well-being and moral reform.[7]

The exile family stood at the very heart of the state's colonial ambitions in Siberia, championed by officials as an instrument of rehabilitation, a guarantor of industry and a bulwark against disorder.

Women might have been hailed as agents of rehabilitation and material prosperity among the exile population, but there were very few of them—only approximately one fifth of the total numbers being exiled to Siberia each year. Across the two decades between 1827 and 1846, 25,500 women, as against 134,000 men, were exiled to Siberia. In some regions, the deficit of women was even more acute. In 1828, there were just 372 women exiles for 7,000 men in Yenisei province. Women also numbered but a fraction of penal labourers in many of the penal factories and distilleries across Siberia. There were only seventy-two women alongside 1,400 men toiling in the Nerchinsk mines in 1829.[8]

This gender imbalance continued throughout the second half of the nineteenth century. Women made the journey to Siberia more frequently as the spouses of convicts than as convicts themselves. Of the more than 148,000 exiles (not including penal labourers) who entered Siberia between 1882 and 1898, a mere 5 per cent were women. The numbers of families joining penal labourers increased as the opening of river routes, sea routes and railway lines simplified and accelerated the journey into exile. A total of 229,000 individuals entered Siberia through the Exile Office between 1882 and 1898: 65 per cent were men, 10 per cent were women and 25 per cent were children.[9]

The exile authorities had long been concerned about the possibility that this shortage of women among the exiles could itself become a source of violent crime in Siberia. In 1833, a Ministry of the Interior report noted that, in situations in which there were seven times more men than women, one exile frequently "seduces the wife of another or is persuaded by her to murder her husband." Exiles also murdered girls who would not consent to marry them. The report listed several violent crimes of passion: exile Yeremeyev had murdered the exiled settler Krasnoshchenkova because she refused to marry him; exiled settler Osipov had buried a hatchet in the skull of the peasant woman Khaldeyeva for the same reason.[10]

The government responded to the violence and insecurity by encouraging exiles to establish families, but found it extremely difficult to persuade the Siberian peasantry to marry off its daughters to exiles. In 1831, the Siberian authorities set up a fund of 15,000 roubles out of which incentives of 150 roubles could be paid to each Siberian peasant or merchant who betrothed his daughter or sister to an exile—funding for a total of 100 marriages. Such state largesse did little, however, to boost the numbers of Siberians giving away brides. Within a year, the governor of Yenisei province reported a mere eleven such marriages across his territory.[11]

If wives for exiles were proving difficult to recruit within Siberia itself, the state was also struggling to persuade the spouses of Russia's criminals to follow them across the Urals. Throughout the reigns of Alexander I and Nicholas I, the numbers of women who chose to follow their husbands to Siberia remained very small. At the beginning of 1835, there were just under 3,000 women and male children who had followed their husbands and fathers to Siberia out of a total exile population of nearly 100,000.[12]

In a bid to boost the numbers of women making the arduous journey eastwards, the state resorted to compulsion. The 1822 "Statutes on Exiles" stipulated that wives of peasants and tradesmen who had been administratively exiled by their communities to Siberia were obliged to follow their husbands, whether they wished to do so or not. In 1828, the government extended this ruling to include the wives of all state peasants exiled by the courts to Siberia. Four years later, the government ruled that the wives of male state serfs banished to Siberia had to follow their husbands, even if they were not themselves serfs.[13]

Amid the administrative chaos that reigned in the exile system, some women were in practice unable to join their husbands because the state could not even locate the men. The wife of Iwan Czasak, a Pole sentenced to twenty years of penal labour in Nerchinsk, wrote repeatedly to the authorities over several years asking for information about her husband's health and whereabouts. Enquiries revealed only that Czasak had last been registered leaving Tobolsk for Tomsk on 5 January 1868 before vanishing. Franciszka Czasak was still trying to establish what had become of her husband twenty-five years later.[14]

As the Decembrist wives had discovered, the state made it all but impossible for women to return to European Russia once they had joined their husbands in Siberia. The "Statutes on Exiles" had stipulated that a woman who voluntarily followed her spouse was allowed to make the journey home only in the event of her husband's death, or if the marriage was dissolved because her husband committed further crimes in exile. In other words, when women, innocent themselves of any wrongdoing, followed their husbands to Siberia, they found themselves stripped of their legal protections and rights, joining their husbands in a state of civic annihilation.[15]

These laws upheld, in principle, the sanctity of marriage, but rather more prosaic motives also played their part. In 1842, the Ministry of the Interior wrote to the Senate in St. Petersburg asking for clarification on whether the wives of exiles in Siberia might be permitted temporarily to return to European Russia to attend to family affairs, such as deaths, matters of inheritance and so forth. The proposal was to grant such women leave of absence on a case-by-case basis. The State Senate, however, rejected any changes to the law with a revealing explanation: permitting women to return for even limited periods, "quite apart from eroding family relations," could also have "harmful consequences." The returnees might "spread false accounts of life in Siberia and so deter future settlers from moving there."[16]

Many women were not made aware of the irrevocable nature of their decision to follow their husbands until they reached Siberia. In 1873, Aleksandra Uspenskaya voluntarily followed her husband, a political exile, to Nerchinsk. When she arrived together with her child, she was informed that, if she saw her husband, she would lose all her civil rights and be denied the right to return to European Russia as long as her husband lived. Uspenskaya recoiled from such a step but was permitted to remain in the town in order to be near her husband while she waited for him to be released to settlement. She took a job as a midwife to support herself and her child. Two years later, in November 1875, in failing health and depression, her husband attempted suicide. Frantic, Uspenskaya begged the authorities to be allowed to see him "under the strict supervision of the prison warders and guards." No one informed her that to do so, even under these extreme circumstances, would entail the loss of her civil rights and of any possibility of ever returning home. When she subsequently applied for permission to leave Eastern Siberia to visit her mother in St. Petersburg, the request was initially rejected. It was only following extensive lobbying that she was able to secure a dispensation from the emperor himself to return to European Russia. Clemency was forthcoming on this occasion, but the draconian legislation intended to prevent women from returning from Siberia remained in force.[17]

The tsarist authorities called all women who joined their husbands in exile "volunteers." If the term had indeed been applicable to the Decembrists' wives, however, it captured few of the brutal realities that pushed most women from the lower orders to follow their husbands. Women who chose to stay in their villages often faced grinding poverty and social ostracism from communities with no interest in supporting fatherless families. In May 1885 in Novgorod province, the wife of one peasant exiled to eight years of penal servitude in Siberia petitioned the governor of Moscow, imploring him to intervene after the authorities' refusal to allow her to follow her husband to Siberia. Since his arrest in November 1883, Maria Pavlova had been caring for their five children—the oldest was eleven and the youngest one—on her own. Unable to work, she had been forced to sell the family's small farm and was now "living in terrible poverty without support from anyone." Pavlova said that she felt sorry for her husband and, believing it to be "the only way out of my disastrous position, I decided to follow my husband wherever he was sent and so wrote to the Novgorod administration asking them to arrest me and my children and to send us together with my husband to the Moscow forwarding prison." For reasons that were obscure, however, the Novgorod authorities had rejected her request and "cast me alone with my children out on the tyranny of fate in an unknown city . . . Arrest for me would now be an act of salvation from my hopeless poverty," she wrote in desperation, and begged the governor to "save my children." The archival documents remain silent on her fate.[18]

Rumour, deceit and naivety also played their part. The blameless women who followed their husbands into exile often had little idea of what awaited them in Siberia. In 1889, a group of destitute wives of penal labourers in the Transbaikal region besieged the regional procurator, begging him for alms and claiming that they faced starvation. The official enquired why they had followed their husbands to Siberia; they had known that the state would not maintain them and that they would not be able to draw on the support of their husbands for the duration of the men's imprisonment. Invoking an image familiar from the supplications of the Russian peasantry, the women responded that they were only "dark people" and that they had been told that they would be clothed and fed by the state both en route and in exile, and that husbands were allowed to live outside the prison with their families. Their credulity was understandable. The procurator noted that many husbands, who naturally had an interest in their wives following them, offered such assurances before they left for Siberia. The women were disinclined to believe tsarist officials who pointed out that no such provisions would be made because "they always suspect ulterior motives are behind the sober words of officials."[19] The women often fell victim, then, to the duplicity of their husbands, the state authorities and their own desperate hopes.

Nowhere in Siberia more graphically illustrates the fate of exile families than the island of Sakhalin. The origins of the penal colony on the island lay in the slow collapse of the penal labour system in the rest of Siberia in the middle of the nineteenth century. The authorities' ad hoc and flailing attempts to cope with the sudden influx of exiled Polish insurgents after 1863 had exposed the creaking infrastructure of the exile system and the urgent need for reform. The Nerchinsk mines and the various penal factories and forts scattered about the continent were simply unable to accommodate the unrelenting waves of convicts being deported from European Russia. Between 1866 and 1876, the annual number of exiles reaching Siberia nearly doubled from 11,000 to 20,500.[20] For the approximately 12,000 penal labourers in Siberia in 1877, there was work for only about 5,000; 7,000 were idle and, of those, Siberia's prisons and forts could only accommodate 4,600, meaning 2,400 were being crammed inside ordinary prisons in European Russia. The overcrowding was so acute that it was killing the convicts. One hundred and sixty-eight out of a total of 744 men sentenced to penal labour in Siberia died in the Wilno (Vilnius) prison in 1875 before the authorities had managed to deport them. Even in Siberia itself, it became increasingly difficult for the authorities to find suitable forms of penal labour for the convicts in their charge. One government inquiry in 1877 was blunt:

> There is no question of hard labour. Even the operation of the usual workshops is rendered extremely difficult by the remoteness of many prisons and the inadequate facilities on site ... The penal labourers' activities are limited almost exclusively to domestic chores in the kitchens, in the yard and in the allotment where they exist. Of the huge numbers of convicts, no more than one fifth can actually be put to work.[21]

Besides, the influx of free labour to Siberia following the emancipation of the serfs in 1861 went some way towards fulfilling an ambition long nurtured by Nerchinsk's administrators: to replace inefficient penal labour with far more productive free labour. Serfdom had been a major obstacle to peasant migration, and the decades that followed its abolition saw tens of thousands flee poverty at home for a new life beyond the Urals. As the numbers flooding into the exile system continued to surge in the 1870s, the authorities became increasingly concerned by the spiralling costs of supporting idle and unproductive penal labourers.[22]

Other major causes of concern were the number of exiles escaping and the hordes of destitute and sometimes violent criminals roaming Siberia. The authorities struggled to reconcile the demands of punishment with those of colonization. On the one hand, penal labour sites should be located in isolated regions, remote from populated areas, in order to minimize the possibility of escape and of contact between the penal labourers and the free population; on the other, such locations proved unsuited to settlement once the convicts had served out their terms of penal labour. Siberia's own senior officials were only too anxious to reduce the numbers of exiles and especially of penal labourers being sent to their own territories. It was with an optimism born of desperation that the authorities looked to the island of Sakhalin as a solution to at least some of the manifest shortcomings of the exile system.[23]

Sakhalin lies in the North Pacific Ocean, off the eastern coast of Siberia, separated from the mainland by only a few kilometres of open water at the narrowest point of the Nevelskoi Strait. The island is 948 kilometres in length and between 25 and 170 kilometres in width, and it covers a total of almost 77,000 square kilometres, slightly larger than Ireland. Its northern part is covered in taiga and tundra; the southern by dense forests and mountain ranges. The climate varies significantly across the various regions of the island; temperatures are more hospitable than in inland cities on the same latitude such as Irkutsk, but range between a clammy 20°C in the summer and a perishing –20°C in the winter.[24]

The Siberian authorities had identified Sakhalin as a source of valuable coal deposits back in the 1850s, but its appeal as the site for a penal colony increased dramatically in the 1860s as the mines of Nerchinsk began to run dry. In the 1860s, the first few hundred convicts were shipped to the island. In the middle of the nineteenth century, sovereignty over Sakhalin was divided between the Russian and the Japanese empires; the Russians controlled the north of the island and the Japanese the south. After much negotiation, the two powers signed a treaty in 1875, granting Russia sovereignty over the whole of Sakhalin.[25]

Sakhalin was perfect as a place of containment: an island separated from the mainland by several kilometres of treacherous waters. In 1867, the Ministry of the Interior commissioned a major investigation into the state of the empire's penal system and tasked it with drawing up a raft of reforms. Highlighting the parlous state of the exile system in Eastern Siberia, the investigation gave a cautious welcome to the prospect of a penal colony on Sakhalin, provided that hard labour could be properly organized there. While the central government weighed its decision, a further 450 penal labourers were sent to Sakhalin in 1869.[26]

All the same, from the time the island was first proposed as a site of convict labour, there were real reservations about its suitability. First, the mines that had initially caught the attention of Siberia's administrators proved too limited to employ any more than a few hundred of the thousands of exiles who were eventually banished there. Secondly, the island's climate and soil fertility gave rise to serious doubts about the prospects for agriculture. But the Ministry of the Interior and the exile administration disregarded available meteorological data and warnings from officials on the island that there was no prospect of developing an agricultural economy. Buoyed by some wildly optimistic reports about the potential for farming on the island—reports that echoed the fantastical visions penned by convicts eager to lure their wives into following them into exile—the government finally decided in 1875 to push ahead with the establishment of a major penal colony on Sakhalin.[27]

Convicts destined for Sakhalin either marched there in convoys that wended their way through the Nerchinsk Mining Region to the port city of Vladivostok before making the crossing to the island or, more usually, made the voyage to Sakhalin in the holds of steamships that navigated around the coast of Asia from the Black Sea port of Odessa. The ships would sail out of the Black Sea, setting anchor in Constantinople before passing through the Suez Canal, Port Said, Aden, Colombo, Singapore, Nagasaki and Vladivostok on a voyage that lasted between two and three months. The two ships that the government used for this purpose, the *Petersburg* and the *Nizhny-Novgorod,* could each carry up to 600 prisoners and sailed twice a year. It was a punishing journey for the fettered prisoners confined in the stifling humidity of the ships' holds.[28]

The penal colony began to take shape as the numbers of convicts arriving on the island each year increased rapidly from an initial trickle to several hundred per annum in the mid-1880s and to more than 1,000 every year by the end of the decade. There were about 6,000 penal labourers and 4,000 settled exiles on the island in 1890 and, by the time of the empire-wide census of 1897, the total exile population had swelled to 22,000. Of the roughly 4,000 women on the island, about two thirds were female convicts and the rest were free-status women (wives who had followed their husbands or the peasant off-spring of exiles). Over the following two years, a further 5,000 men and 300 women were exiled to Sakhalin.[29]

Sakhalin offered the government something of a *tabula rasa*: an opportunity to bring to bear the fruits of a century of experience in administering large-scale penal colonies in Siberia. It was also the government's last chance to show that punishment could lead to the rehabilitation of exiles and their transformation into small-holding agricultural colonists. Key to this vaunted transition were the women of Sakhalin. They would also come, tragically, to symbolize its failures.

"Siberia is a big, cold country," Anton Chekhov wrote to his brother Aleksandr from Irkutsk in June 1890:

> There seems to be no end to the journey. There is little of novelty or interest to be seen, but I am experiencing and feeling a lot. I've battled with rivers in flood, with cold, unbelievable quagmires, hunger and lack of sleep . . . Experiences you couldn't buy in Moscow for a million roubles. You should come to Siberia! Get the courts to exile you here.[30]

At the age of thirty, and knowing that he had already contracted tuberculosis, Chekhov had set out on a gruelling eleven-week journey across Siberia to visit the penal colony on Sakhalin. He was no supporter of the exile system and had left with the determination to document conditions on the island and then to bring them to the attention of the Russian reading public. En route to Sakhalin, he fulminated to his editor, Aleksei Suvorin:

> It is quite clear from the books I have been reading and am still reading that we have let *millions* of people rot in gaol, and let them rot to no purpose, treating them with an indifference that is little short of barbaric. We have forced them to drag themselves in chains across tens of thousands of kilometres in freezing conditions, infected them with syphilis, debauched them, hugely increased the criminal population, and heaped the blame for the whole thing on red-nosed prison supervisors.

All Europe now knows that the blame lies not with the super-visors, but with all of us, but we still regard it as none of our business, we're not interested.[31]

Chekhov spent just over three months on the island working intensively. He rose early and spent each day interviewing Sakhalin's penal labourers and settled exiles. The extensive notes he made on the island formed the basis of the part-travelogue, part-sociological study serialized to great acclaim in 1893–4 in the liberal monthly *Russian Thought*. *Sakhalin Island* would prove instrumental in turning the tide of public opinion against the Siberian exile system.[32]

Chekhov discovered that only around 5 per cent of Sakhalin's women could read, let alone write. As a consequence, their stories were most commonly told, if they were told at all, by men. Official reports acknowledged that the women were the victims of sexual exploitation and sexual violence, but they rarely recorded the women's own voices in the form of petitions and appeals. The most graphic accounts of the lives of women and children on Sakhalin came from the men who observed and sometimes interviewed them. Chekhov's own account was followed by a slew of publications by journalists, government inspectors, physicians and foreign travellers, all of which dwelt in har-rowing detail on the fate of the island's women and children. Some, like journalist Vlas Doroshevich, employed the sensationalist style of the *feuilletonist,* but even he prided himself on the factual basis of his writing.[33] Most authors—the government officials, the physicians and Chekhov himself—strove for dispassionate reportage. The majority of these men were, or at least became, avowed opponents of the exile system. They understood that the corruption of women and children and the destruction of families were things that the autocracy could not possibly defend. The plight of Siberia's convicted criminals might have left many consciences back in Moscow and St. Petersburg untroubled; the brutalization of innocent women and children did not.

Of the female convicts sentenced to penal labour on Sakhalin, most had been condemned by the courts for crimes of passion: "I've come 'cos of my 'usband" or "I've come 'cos of my mother-in-law," Chek-hov heard them say. Peasant women were no strangers to misogyny. Wives who had endured years of violent beatings from their husbands would sometimes snap and reach for a knife or for poison. Some had murdered newborns they could not afford to support. Others had been exiled as thieves, forgers and arsonists. For some economically marginal women, prostitution proved a gateway to a wider criminal underworld and was a source of stigma that rendered them, like the female heroine of Leo Tolstoy's *Resurrection* (1899), Katyusha, vulnerable to all manner of accusations. By the end of the nineteenth century, however, the number of women prosecuted for "fornication" was in steep decline.[34]

Chekhov observed that, by the time a woman reached Sakhalin, her "human dignity, . . . femininity and modesty . . . are not taken into account in any circumstances; the implication seems to be that all this has been wrung out of her by her shame, or that she has lost it trudging around the prisons and waystations on the way to Siberia." Even innocent women following their husbands were not spared this fate. In a continuing violation of the regulations that stipulated that women should travel separately from the men, they often found themselves locked up overnight together with hardened criminals. Exiles' wives were also sometimes forced into sex by criminals in the marching convoys or passed around by their spouses in exchange for money, vodka or physical protection. The criminologist and Ministry of the Interior official Dmitry Dril, who visited Sakhalin in 1896, was blunt: the women, both convicts and those voluntarily following their husbands, "are often corrupted to the core in deportation parties, and arrive as prostitutes at the penal camps."[35]

Women were especially vulnerable when they were pregnant or carrying newborns. In 1837, the State Senate had ruled that women should not be sent into exile if they were pregnant or breast-feeding, but, as with many directives from the centre, the Siberian authorities routinely ignored this instruction. Indeed, given the length of the journey into exile and the pressures on the women to have sex with the men in the marching convoys, many became pregnant en route. Nikolayevna, a female convict in a group of penal labourers being transported by steamship down the Amur River in 1870, was in the final days of pregnancy and begged to be permitted to remain in Blagoveshchensk until her child was born. The authorities ignored her request, however, and she went into labour four hours after the ship had set sail. Allowed on deck, she gave birth, shielded from the eyes of onlookers and from the bad weather by only a few convict smocks. The child died within an hour.[36]

Women often followed their husbands with several young children in tow. One group of families accompanying penal labourers in 1885 was awaiting departure from Kiev for Sakhalin via Odessa. It included the wife of Lavrenty Shvoren, who had a son of nine and three daughters aged seven, five and one, and the wife of Osip Chumak, who had four daughters aged thirteen, eleven, nine and five. Their names were not even recorded.[37]

The American explorer George Kennan observed girls as young as ten being made to walk 30 kilometres a day because there was no room for them on the wagons. In 1875 alone, 1,030 children died en route to Siberia in the forwarding prisons of Moscow, Nizhny Novgorod, Kazan and Perm and in the *étapes* beyond. Two years later, a further 400 did not survive the journey. Indeed, ethnographer and journalist Nikolai Yadrintsev estimated that, as a result of woefully inadequate medical facilities, half of all children died on the way to their parents' place of exile.[38]

In addition to hunger, cold and lack of adequate medical care, the children faced the predatory appetites of the convicts with whom they shared the crowded waystations, train carriages and ships' holds. A senior Ministry of the Interior official, Vasily Vlasov, reported in 1873 that the authorities' failure to ensure that children were kept separated from the convicts in the marching convoys resulted in their exposure to "orgies and illegal acts." Exile women would complain that male convicts in the deportation convoys were "corrupting their children." Vlasov discovered that "some of the male criminals are so immoral and cynical that they have amorous relations in broad daylight in front of children," something which "not only corrupted the children's morality but also served to prematurely awaken their own sexual desires." Travelling with Chekhov on a steamer down the Amur to Sakhalin "was a convict in leg irons who had murdered his wife. His daughter, a motherless little girl aged six, was with him . . . hanging on to his fetters. At night the little girl slept hugger-mugger with the convicts and soldiers." There were reports of the rape of young girls on board the transport steamers on the Amur.[39]

Exile officials found the plight of the children in the marching convoys especially troubling. One hardened waystation officer "who had already grown indifferent to a great deal" exclaimed to the ethnographer Sergei Maksimov, "'The poor children! . . . In winter it's terrible to look at them: Numb with cold, drained, sick, coughing, many have broken out in sores and they are covered in rashes . . .'" Women who sold themselves could be condemned as depraved prostitutes, but young children forced to witness or participate in sex could not be so easily dismissed. Mirroring the ambivalence of educated society to the child prostitutes in Russia's cities, however, officials viewed the sexually exploited children of the exiles with a mixture of sympathy and disgust.[40] Vlasov had at least the decency to observe of the children that "it is impossible to reproach these victims of circumstance." But he was still shocked by their "impudent behaviour towards the soldiers and sailors, which outstripped the street walkers of large cities." In one convoy, two twelve- and fourteen-year-old daughters of penal labourers were already infected with syphilis. Ethnographer Vasily Semyovsky accompanied a party of 500 exiles and family members to the Lena gold fields in 1878; among them were eleven-year-old boys who drank, played cards and were interested in women; there was also a twelve-year-old girl "considered common property by the convict party."[41]

When women exiles finally did reach Sakhalin, they were treated as habitual prostitutes; the camp administration even organized the sale of their bodies. After a visit to Sakhalin in 1871, Vlasov reported that the authorities had turned the female section of the prison into a brothel. His report, although girded by the bureaucratic language of officialdom, nonetheless simmered with outrage. Only those guilty of an offence on the island or "not worthy of men's favour" ended up working in the kitchen; the rest "served needs" and drank themselves silly.[42]

The prostitution of the island's exile women set a pattern that would endure in the years that followed. Sakhalin's chief physician, Dr. Leonid Poddubsky, observed how, upon arrival on the island, female penal labourers were "lusted after and molested" by warders and soldiers who demanded sex from them. If the women offered any resistance to the "base instincts of the local authorities," they paid a heavy price. They were dragged to the hospital every week for medical examinations as prostitutes, or the guards accused them of having committed some "imaginary crimes." They then sent them to live with a settler in some isolated village, which amounted to "a sentence to the most unbridled prostitution, as such villages have between two and five women for some 50–60 bachelors." Poddubsky was indignant at this "mockery of the goals appointed in the laws." He even encountered cases where a husband and wife, sentenced together to penal labour on Sakhalin for the same crime, would arrive at different times of the year, only for the woman to be given to another settler.[43]

After the clerks and warders had helped themselves to the female convicts they desired, the rest were taken to the settlement at Korsakovsk Post, where Chekhov observed scenes that resembled the proceedings of a cattle market. The district governor and officials from the local administration decided which of the settled exiles and peasants "deserved to obtain a woman." Those selected were instructed to attend the prison on the appointed day, when they were given the opportunity of inspecting the new arrivals: "Each man chooses . . . perfectly seriously, treating 'with humanity' plainness, old age and their prisoner-like appearance; he gazes attentively, wishing to surmise from their faces—which of them is a good housewife?" The settlers regarded the women as "not exactly a human being, a housewife, and not exactly a creature even lower than a domestic animal, but somewhere between the two."[44]

The authorities deliberately circumvented laws designed to maintain sexual propriety and traditional morality among the exile population. Chekhov understood that convict women were parcelled out to the settled exiles across Sakhalin in the guise of agricultural labourers, "but this [is] only a screen against the law forbidding immorality and adultery," since they were in reality unlegalized wives.[45] "A woman on Sakhalin becomes," one of the physicians on the island, Dr. Nikolai Lobas, commented, "an object in the full sense of word, an object that can be handed over, dispatched, received, borrowed." Women were indeed passed around from one exile to the next in a series of squalid transactions arranged by the authorities, sometimes for personal profit. One of the few literate convict women, Natalya Linevaya, wrote a petition protesting against her treatment:

> When I arrived on the island of Sakhalin, I was sent to the Porechenskoye settlement, where I moved in with the settler Pavel Fomin, together with whom I lived for just over two months. I became pregnant by him and wanted to get married . . . but the settlement overseer arrived and for some rea-

son did not like the look of our home. He took me away from Pavel Fomin and wanted to hand me over to another settler.

Lobas witnessed dreadful scenes: a woman with two young children on her knees, begging an official not to send her to live with an exile, the two frightened children clinging to her, crying and shaking. Her prayers and tears did not help, and the woman was forced to comply. Sakhalin's women became, in effect, the prisoners of prisoners.[46]

Most relationships that emerged from these mercantile and administrative calculations were sordid caricatures of marriage. Many men and women despised their cohabitants and remained strangers to each other. Even years after they had been living under the same roof, they did not know how old the other was, where they were from in Russia, or their patronymic. Without the formal ties of marriage, women passed through the hands of several men. One woman lived with a settler for three years and bore him two children. When the man decided to move to Vladivostok, he simply handed her over to another: "I've got a woman. You can have her if you like."[47]

Some women fled forced cohabitation with settlers who abused and exploited them. The authorities took a dim view of this rejection of their own efforts to bring about the women's well-being and moral improvement. Their inevitable capture usually brought a stint in solitary confinement followed by dispatch to an even further-flung settlement. Within four to six months, the will of most women was broken by life with their designated settler. Even if they started out as reluctant prostitutes, many eventually became hardened professionals. Some settlers would quickly spend their way through any money or belongings that a female exile brought with her to Sakhalin before driving her to prostitution, often with their fists.[48]

Prostitution offered a bargaining chip of sorts to some of the women who moved in with settlers. If their partners did not permit them to receive clients at home, they would leave them, "although this did not often happen as the co-habitant shares her income." Aleksandr Salomon, the head of the Main Prison Administration, which had been established in 1879, also found women on Sakhalin who had set up their business quite independently. At Aleksandrovsk Post, the name of one such woman had already been long forgotten; she was known simply as "five kopecks," after the cost of a visit. Another woman at Rykovsk was in her seventies and charged only three kopecks.[49]

Men also turned to prostitution, although contemporary sources are very reticent on the topic. Salomon found what he described as "pederasty" to be widespread. On an expedition to study the flora of Sakhalin, the botanist Andrei Krasnov commented that the absence of women combined with the overcrowding in the prisons to form a "source of corruption" that spread out from Russian penal forts. Orientalizing homosexuality as something fundamentally "other" and un-Russian, Krasnov blamed the island's indigenous people for promoting a form of "sexual psychopathy that infects a significant part of the exile population." Sakhalin itself created the conditions for the "very perversions for which people are exiled from Russia." Poverty, gambling debts and the ever-present threat of violence drove some men to sell themselves. Doroshevich wrote of the *khamy* or "bitches" on Sakhalin: "It is impossible to sink any lower. A *kham* is convict-speak for another man's lover. '*Zakhamnichat*' means to take it, and not to give it. A *kham* is a man without even a sliver of something approaching a conscience . . . The *khamy* commit vile acts among the convicts." In the Aleksandrovsk infirmary, Lobas treated young boys who had contracted syphilis through such "acts of pederasty."[50]

Nevertheless, love did also sometimes flourish amid the squalor and brutality. Yadrintsev recalled "Don Juans," hair greased back and clutching bunches of flowers, courting female convicts in the prison corridors. Some convicts on Sakhalin grew so attached to their companions that they deliberately provoked extensions to their own terms of incarceration in order to avoid the separation that release to the mainland would bring.[51]

Exiles' wives fared little better than the convict women, and sometimes even worse. Many a "volunteer" arrived on the island already destitute or having had her belongings pilfered, only to discover that there was nowhere to earn any money, nowhere to beg alms and nothing but her husband's meagre prison rations to share. Chekhov described the bewilderment and horror that seized the women:

> During the first period after her arrival here, a free-woman wears a look of total stupefaction. The island, and the conditions encompassing the penal labour, stagger her. She will say with despair that, when travelling to her husband, she did not

deceive herself and expected only the worst, but the reality had turned out to be more frightful than all expectations . . . She weeps day and night, and chants lamentations for the deceased, and prays for her forsaken relatives as if they were dead, while her husband, acknowledging his huge guilt towards her, sits sullenly, but suddenly, coming to himself, begins to beat her and abuse her for having come here.[52]

Salomon visited Sakhalin in 1898 and painted a dismal picture of the exile settlements scattered across the island. A majority of the settlers' dwellings were "badly built," and inside they lacked "domestic utensils and any semblance of good house-keeping." They were a pitiful imitation of the state's visions of a virtuous hearth and home, resembling "not so much peasant huts but rather small prison cells."[53] Chekhov was scathing about the vegetative misery in which families languished: "In the same place there will be juveniles and two or three cradles in the corners, plus, right there, hens and dogs too, while outside in the street around the cabin, there is refuse, puddles of slops, there is nothing to occupy yourself with, nothing to eat, you are fed up with talking and quarrelling—how monotonously dismal and filthy it all is, what depression!" Beyond the poverty, there was also a gnawing rootlessness in each exile cabin:

There is no grandfather or grandmother, no old icons or furniture handed down through the family: consequently, the household lacks a past, lacks tradition . . . it's as if the family is living, not in its own home, but in quarters, or as if they have only just arrived and still have not had time to settle in; there are no cats, no crickets are heard on winter evenings . . . and the main thing, it is not their home country.[54]

An even bleaker existence confronted those forced, for want of cabins, to live in the "married barracks" at Sakhalin's Dué Post settlement, in filthy buildings already long condemned for demolition. In a single cell, Chekhov discovered six couples, including six free-status women, and a total of sixteen children. "From these barbaric lodgings and their conditions," he mused, "where girls of fifteen and sixteen are forced to sleep side by side with penal-labour convicts, the reader may judge with what disrespect and contempt are surrounded here the women and children who have voluntarily followed their husbands and fathers into penal servitude, how little they are valued here and how little thought is given to the concept of an agricultural colony."[55]

Struggling in conditions of absolute penury, not only female convicts assigned to settlers but even faithful free-status wives maintained their families through prostitution. One exile settler, whose farmstead was distinguished by obvious signs of hard work, told Salomon "that he could not really complain because, 'thanks to the Good Lord,' he hadn't yet had to sell his wife"![56]

Convict women who were considered attractive and were able to find a wealthy or influential sponsor on the island fared considerably better than both the female convicts set to work making brushes, washing linen and scrubbing the floors of the buildings, and the women who had voluntarily followed their husbands to Sakhalin. The promise of sexual favours, domestic labours and even companionship enabled some women to establish themselves as the consorts of officials and so to avoid the worst that the island had to offer. In the autumn of 1870, several women penal labourers were delivered to the Korsakov Post on Sakhalin. Lieutenant Pavlushin took for himself a woman who called herself Akulina Kozhenetskaya. When enquiries were made about the category of settlement to which she had been sentenced, it was discovered that she was in fact Yelena Kryzhanovskaya, and not Akulina Kozhenetskaya, with whom she had exchanged identities. Kryzhanovskaya had been sentenced not to settlement but to penal labour, but by the time her deception was discovered, she was already rumoured to have won over Pavlushin. When the authorities received instructions to distribute the women, including Kryzhanovskaya, to the penal works, Pavlushin ensured that she was registered as working at the infirmary at the Korsakov Post, although she in fact simply remained his consort.[57]

Vlasov believed that "honest and exemplary women" must surely "look with envy on the convict prostitutes" and that, in their hearts, they must "wonder whether crime does not give a woman the right to a comfortable existence and a privileged position." When Doroshevich asked one embittered free-status woman who had joined her husband on Sakhalin what she would do if she had no children to care for, she replied unhesitatingly, "I'd work as a prostitute . . . I'd have someone take me in. When we were in the convoy on the way here, we had to fend off the convicts! Just look at how those girls live now! . . . I don't even want to look, I'm so jealous!"[58]

Some exiles obtained women primarily with the aim of pimping them out to fellow convicts. They would send not only their cohabitants but also their free-status wives and daughters to work as prostitutes. The women sometimes needed no prompting. Chekhov described how the free-status woman's "heart becomes hardened over the course of time, and she comes to the conclusion that on Sakhalin you will never get enough to eat with delicate feelings, and goes off to earn her five- and ten-kopeck bits—as one of them put it—'with my body.'" Couples would also begin to sell their daughters from the age of twelve. "Anyone who has a good-looking wife and a daughter makes a decent living here," one exile explained to Dril, "and doesn't need to bother with livestock."[59]

Brimming with confidence in the early years of the penal colony, the commandant of Sakhalin, A. I. Ginue, had expressed his conviction that the future ultimately lay in the exiles' children:

> Care for a wife and children fosters diligence and thrift. Fear of punishment that might separate them from their family or damage their farms teaches them to weigh their actions carefully and to restrain their bad impulses . . . Once they have grown up, the children of these penal labourers form a part of the population that shares the values of the government and is more effective in ensuring public calm than any number of bayonets.[60]

Such noble ambitions for the island's children were delusional. The children grew up to be socialized not in the values of the government but in the corruption of the penal labourers.

In December 1901, an exiled settler on Sakhalin named Ipaty Vasilyev applied to the court for compensation from a young free-status woman. On the appointed day, the plaintiff and the respondent attended the courthouse to have the case heard. When summoned before the magistrate, Vasilyev stepped out of the crowd of assembled petitioners, a tall, thick-set man of forty with red hair. A thin little girl with a pale face and eyes that blazed feverishly also stepped forwards. She was the respondent, thirteen-year-old Vasilisa Ilyutina. Vasilyev had come to an arrangement with Ilyutina's parents whereby he would provide them with a cow in exchange for their daughter. Ilyutina had lived with Vasilyev for only a short time, however, before returning to her parents, taking with her the gifts Vasilyev had presented her with when she moved in. A few days later, Ilyutina moved in with another settler, Plotnikov. Ilyutina claimed that she had "earned" the gifts and explained that "my family needs to start sowing and Ipaty doesn't have any oats, so I went over to Plotnikov for 20 roubles."[61]

Many parents busied themselves trafficking their children. Vlasov observed how mothers arriving on Sakhalin had been so corrupted by their experiences on the journey to the island they were ready to sell their children "for a quart of spirit." When the English explorer Charles Henry Hawes visited Sakhalin in 1903, he was appalled at the ease with which "fathers traded with their daughters" and was probably guilty of only slight exaggeration when he claimed that "there is not a girl over nine years of age on the island who is a virgin." There were certainly cases of girls as young as eight cohabiting with adult men. Dril discovered a girl of nine in the hospital at Aleksandrovsk Post already "manifesting the symptoms of syphilis on her genitalia."[62]

The exile settlements provided a dubious education for the exile children. Chekhov spoke to one young boy whom he found alone in a settler's hut in one of the villages:

> What's your father's patronymic?
> I don't know.
> What do you mean, you don't know? You're living with your father and you don't know his name? For shame!
> He's not my real father.
> What do you mean—not your real father?
> He lives with my ma.
> Is your mother married or a widow?
> Widow. She came because of her husband.
> What do you mean, because of her husband?
> She killed him.
> Do you remember your father?

No, I don't. I'm illegitimate. Ma had me when she was . . .
[in] Kara.[63]

Hawes witnessed children surrounded by "openly vicious practices and
scenes of unblushing prostitution. The very 'game' of concubinage is
in vogue in the mixed schools." Children could be observed playing
"vagabonds" and acting out scenes of arson and lynchings: " 'I'll be
your live-in woman and we'll go to settlement together,' babbled a very
small girl. 'I'll slit your throat,' a boy threatened."[64]

Whatever the state's fond imaginings, on the island people would
call the children "a new generation of penal labourers in the making."
Of course, the problem of children being raised by destitute and desperate exiles was not confined to Sakhalin. In fact, officials charged
with writing unbiased assessments of the exile system had long recognized its corrupting effects on the convicts' children. In the 1880s,
exiled revolutionary Vladimir Korolenko's short stories of Siberian
exile confronted a broad readership with tales of children sucked into
criminality by their exile parents. On Sakhalin, however, the corruption of children was especially acute. Wise beyond their years in the
conspiratorial culture of theft, dissimulation and violence, Sakhalin's
children gave the lie to officialdom's claims about the rehabilitative
properties of the exile system and to the declared paternalism of the
autocracy.[65]

Visitors to Sakhalin were almost universally appalled at the conditions in which the settlers and their families were living. One nurse
wrote in a private letter of her disgust at the levels of sexual degradation on the island: "Oh my God! Oh my God! You won't be able to
imagine what is happening here: complete debauchery! I have on my
ward girls of fifteen, seventeen and nineteen, who started to have sexual relations when they were twelve and now cannot manage without
vodka, filth and foul language . . . If only they knew back in St. Petersburg what penal labour here is like!"[66] By the end of the nineteenth
century, however, the authorities in St. Petersburg were well aware of
the conditions for families on the island.

Official enthusiasm for Sakhalin gradually faded as the penal colony began to take shape. The head of the Main Prison Administration,
Mikhail Galkin-Vraskoi, had found reasons to be optimistic about the
prospects for the exile settlers when he visited the island in 1881. Set-

tlers' homes in Aleksandrovsk Post were "noted for their cleanliness and tidiness," the agriculture on the island seemed to be flourishing, and the schools and hospitals he inspected were all in good order. Yet Galkin-Vraskoi saw what he wanted to see and was, by no means, the only senior official to turn a blind eye to the exiles' grim existence on Sakhalin. When Chekhov visited the island nine years later, he attended a ceremonial dinner held by Andrei Korf, the governor-general of Priamursk. The most senior official in all of Eastern Siberia made a short speech to the gathering: "On Sakhalin," he declared, "I am convinced that the 'unfortunates' live better than anywhere else in Russia, or even in Europe." Chekhov struggled to reconcile Korf's delusional praise with "starvation, the prostitution endemic among the exiled women and brutal corporal punishments."[67]

Evidence of the state's failure to establish a self-sustaining penal colony was to be found in the very low birth-rates among exiles on the island, which were less than half those of European Russia. For mothers on Sakhalin, children often represented simply "an extra mouth to feed." Chekhov observed that "the birth of each new human being is not received cordially in the family; they do not sing lullabies over the baby's cradle, but only sinister lamentations are heard. The fathers and mothers say that there is nothing to feed the children with, that they will never learn anything worthwhile on Sakhalin, and 'the best thing would be if the Merciful Lord took them as soon as possible.'"[68]

The exile population was increasing only by virtue of the annual infusions of fresh convicts. Released to settlement at the conclusion of their terms of penal labour, exiles found themselves under-resourced in a harsh and inhospitable climate. The task that confronted the settlers of taming the virgin taiga and setting up sustainable farmsteads was far more difficult than penal labour. Isolated, impoverished, indebted to the state and equipped with poorly made tools, Sakhalin's "involuntary colonists" toiled for a time to no discernible effect before finally sinking into hungry destitution. With a journalist's flair for the pithy epithet, Doroshevich coined the aphorism "penal labour starts when it ends."[69]

If they survived their ordeal as exiled settlers, the convicts on Sakhalin, as elsewhere in Siberia, were permitted to join the ranks of the Siberian peasantry. The government initially decided that such reformed exiles would be allowed to return to the mainland to reside outside the cities in Eastern Siberia. The settled exiles showed no enthusiasm for remaining on the island a day longer than necessary: "God forbid we should have to stay on Sakhalin! Even if they bury me alive, I don't want to stay!" one declared. Another nurtured the ambition "at least to die on the mainland." Keen to stem the tide of departing exiles, in 1880 the government withdrew the right of return to the mainland and obliged them to engage in agriculture on the island until they had settled all the debts they had accumulated in state subsidies. From 1894, when such restrictions were lifted, the numbers returning to Russia each year soared, from 220 in 1894 to 2,000 in 1898. In 1899 alone, 760 farms were abandoned on Sakhalin in what the Main Prison Administration acknowledged to be a "mass migration" of settlers and peasants.[70]

Chekhov had left Sakhalin in October 1890 "with many unpleasant memories . . . Now I am able to contemplate it in retrospect, Sakhalin appears to me like a complete hell." The publication of his account of his visit to the island caused such a public scandal that it prompted the government to set up a secret committee to discuss the future of the penal colony and to launch a series of investigations into conditions there.[71] As the evidence of squalor, sexual exploitation and corruption of families relentlessly piled up, Siberia's administrators abandoned the pretence that Sakhalin served either to rehabilitate offenders or to establish a stable and settled population. The physician Poddubsky's detailed accounts of conditions for women and children on Sakhalin were discussed within the Main Prison Administration and the Society for the Care of the Families of Penal Labourers before being forwarded, in May 1899, to Minister of Justice Nikolai Muravyov. A lady-in-waiting even pressed a copy of Poddubsky's report into the hands of Nicholas II in St. Petersburg. The doctor's findings also entered the public sphere, when they were published and discussed in the prominent weekly legal journal *Right* and in the official *Prison Herald* at the turn of the century. Far from proving the building blocks of a flourishing and industrial community of exile settlers, Sakhalin's families became a symptom of the penal colony's poverty and moral collapse. The real villains of the sordid drama on the island were, in a sense, not even the hard-eyed convicts who sold their wives and daughters for sex; they were the tsarist authorities, who had failed to properly administer and resource the exiles in their charge. Sakhalin had become a major embarrassment to the autocracy and presented a grotesque caricature of the state's aspiration to marry penal and colonial ambitions across Siberia as a whole.[72]

Inertia still reigned, however, in St. Petersburg. Many officials clung to the belief that the problem was one of management and funding rather than of an underlying conflict between the agendas of punishment and colonization. Salomon tried to sound a positive note during his visit to the island in 1898, but found himself forced to dispel rumours about the imminent closure of the penal colony. A project on which more than 20 million roubles had already been spent since 1879 could not, he assured officials on the island, be simply abandoned. The shortcomings on the island "needed to be addressed through hard work," but Salomon conceded that the current state of affairs made "an unfavourable impression."[73]

Once back in St. Petersburg, now retired and so freer to speak his mind, Salomon was scathing about the squalid reality of family corruption and degradation on Sakhalin. The prisons were destructive "not only for morally impressionable people," but also for those whose original crimes "were of a purely formal nature" such as violations of military discipline. The only real industries on the island were gambling, vodka and prostitution. "There can be no question," he concluded, "of rehabilitation in the Sakhalin penal colony."[74]

The government's doomed experiment on Sakhalin was eventually brought to an end not by a change of heart in St. Petersburg but by the superiority of Japanese naval power. The annexation of the Amur River Basin in the second half of the nineteenth century had brought the Russian Empire face-to-face with the expanding power of industrialized Japan. Simmering tensions came to a head at the turn of the century with the construction of the Chinese Eastern Railway through Manchuria, linking Chita with Vladivostok. The Japanese feared that this new projection of Russian imperial power would threaten their own designs on Korea and parts of Manchuria. Diplomatic relations broke down between the two rival empires, and in January 1904, the Japanese launched a devastating strike against the Russian naval base at Port Arthur on the Liaodong Peninsula.[75] Following the destruction of the Russian fleet at the Battle of Tsushima during the Russo-Japanese War in May 1905, Japanese forces occupied the southern part of Sakhalin Island. They crushed feeble resistance from the soldiers stationed on the island and a ragtag band of convict settlers promised an amnesty if they fought the invaders. That summer, the Japanese military in the south, together with the Russian authorities in the north, oversaw a chaotic and brutal evacuation of the penal colony to the Russian mainland. Some 7,600 men, women and children were unceremoniously dumped on the shores of the bay of De Castri, opposite Sakhalin. From there, they had to tramp through 60 kilometres of almost impenetrable taiga to the nearest settlement of Marinsk. Held over the following year in barracks, they were eventually dispersed across Transbaikal. The Russian government finally abolished the penal colony on the island by decree on 1 July 1906.[76]

There was no more eloquent indictment of the failure of the penal colony on Sakhalin than the graves scattered about its desolate cemeteries. The cemetery at the Korsakov Post, on the southern coast, clung to one of the windswept, treeless hills overlooking the settlement. When he visited Sakhalin in 1897, Doroshevich came across the undignified burial of an exiled settler in the graveyard. The man had been a witness to the violent miseries of life on the island. In a fit of jealousy, he had murdered the woman with whom he had been living, before ending his own life with one of the poisonous plants that flourished on the island. His body had been discovered in the taiga only days after his suicide. A dozen penal labourers were manhandling a wooden cart carrying a roughly made coffin up the hill to the cemetery. A warder followed them with a revolver stuffed into his belt. At the graveside, they lowered the coffin into the ground and began to shovel in the heavy clay soil. When the coffin was buried they stuck into the small mound of earth a hurriedly cobbled together cross formed of two unpainted sticks. There was no inscription. "A few of the men crossed themselves; a few did not." They turned and left, accompanied by the barked orders of the prison warder.

In a society that was still deeply religious, most of the graves in the cemetery did not even feature that most rudimentary symbol of Christian burial. The crosses planted on the graves had been uprooted or broken off, leaving a single abject stick protruding from the earth. Doroshevich found himself standing among graves that were nothing but bare mounds of soil. One exile explained that "the settlers gather [the crosses] up for firewood . . . They're too lazy to go out into the taiga, so they drag them off from here." The wooden cross on one incongruous, well-tended grave now had a hole at its centre where a holy figure had been carved. Someone had torn the carving out of the cross, the exile observed, "for the sake of a few kopecks to blow on cards."

Elsewhere in the cemetery was the grave of a young woman, a teacher from St. Petersburg named Naumova, who had given up her life in the capital to move to Sakhalin, where she had founded the island's first orphanage. The idealistic young woman "lacked the strength to endure Sakhalin's hard-heartedness, spiritual corruption and indifference to the suffering of neighbours. She was unable to endure her struggles with Sakhalin's officials, who eyed her 'undertakings' with hostility; she could not stand the atmosphere of the penal colony and shot herself." The cross marking Naumova's grave had also been uprooted, and the exile accompanying Doroshevich was no longer able to find her exact resting place, even though she had been buried not two years earlier. The governor-general of Priamursk had sent a "marvellous iron wreath with a bronze plaque bearing a beautiful inscription" to replace the stolen cross. Local officials had decided, however, to hang it in the police station for fear that it, too, would be stolen from the graveyard.[77]

Sakhalin's cemeteries were peculiar assemblies of the dead. They were filled with corpses of men, women and children drawn from all four corners of the empire, united only by crime and punishment, poverty and misery. The hillside at the Korsakov Post had even acquired an appetite for the exiles. It was pitted with empty graves, dug in anticipation of the next bout of fever to tear through the infirmary. Once filled, these graves would, like the others, be quickly forgotten. The dead slipped from the memory of the neighbours and families who abandoned the island. The exile population never sanctified the cemeteries with the commemorative rituals of an authentic community. For many exiles, the significance of death diminished in the shadow of their bleak lives. Like the state's ambitions for the Sakhalin penal colony, the graves sank into the earth without trace.

11

The Lash

In 1890, a fugitive penal labourer named Prokhorov was captured while trying to cross the Nevelskoi Strait separating the island of Sakhalin from the mainland. It was discovered that he had, by clerical error, escaped an earlier sentence of ninety lashes for the murder of a Cossack and two of his granddaughters near Khabarovsk the previous year. Anton Chekhov described the flogging that followed to the readers of the popular monthly *Russian Thought*:

> At last Prokhorov is bound. The executioner takes up the lash with three tails and, without haste, smoothens it out.
>
> "Ready—bear up!" he says, not loudly, and without swinging his arm, as if he is simply measuring his length, he delivers the first blow.
>
> "O-one!" says the overseer in a voice like a Church sexton.
>
> For the first instant Prokhorov is silent, and even the expression on his face does not alter; but now a convulsion of pain runs through his body and a sound rings out—not a scream but a squeal.
>
> "Two!" calls the overseer.
>
> The executioner stands sideways on and strikes in such a way that the lash falls across the body. After every five blows, he slowly walks round to the other side and gives himself half a minute's rest. Prokhorov's hair is stuck to his brow, his neck is swollen; after five or ten blows his body, still covered by weals from previous lashings, has already turned crimson and dark blue; the skin splits from every blow.
>
> "Yer Excellency!" we hear through the screeching and weeping. "Yer Excellency! Be merciful, yer Excellency!"

And later, after twenty or thirty blows, Prokhorov seems to be intoning a ritual lament, as if drunk, or exactly as if he is delirious:

"What a poor unfortunate chap I am, ground down to the ground I am, that's what I am, I am . . . Just what am I being punished like this for?"

And now there is a curious stretching-out of the neck, the sounds of retching . . . Prokhorov does not utter a single word, but simply bellows and wheezes; it seems as if, since the punishment began, a whole eternity has passed, but the overseer is calling only: "Forty-*two*! Forty-*three*!" . . .

Ninety at last. They rapidly untie Prokhorov's hands and feet and help him stand up. The area where he has been beaten is dark-blue-crimson from bruises and is bleeding. His teeth are chattering, his face is yellow and wet, his eyes are wandering. When he is given medicinal drops, he bites the glass convulsively . . . They moisten his head and lead him away to the sickbay.

"That's for the murder—there'll still be something specially for the escape," they explain to me as we are returning home.[1]

Corporal punishment underpinned the architecture of power and authority in the penal settlements, dispensed by officials in order to drive prisoners into compliance and submission. Like so much else in the Siberian exile system, however, the violence proved detrimental to the state's colonial ambitions. Floggings and beatings were not effective instruments of discipline and correction but rather savage weapons of punishment. Corporal punishment served to brutalize further an already violent criminal population and even conferred status and power on a dehumanized minority. When they fled or completed their terms of penal labour, the men with scarred backs often unleashed terrible violence upon the innocents they encountered in Siberian towns and villages. By the middle of the nineteenth century, senior officials and educated observers in Siberia were expressing grave misgivings about the effects of corporal punishment.

Corporal punishment also became the subject of fierce public debate. Significantly curtailed throughout the rest of the Russian Empire in 1863, beatings remained the authorities' punishment of choice in Siberia right up to the collapse of the exile system in 1917. In the hands of questionable men with dubious motives, whips, chains and punishment cells resembled tools not of discipline but of that Russian term, redolent of despotism, *proizvol*. Denoting arbitrary power, unconstrained by laws or justice, the word *proizvol* was used increasingly from the middle of the nineteenth century by exiles and observers alike in their criticism of the lawless power of exile officials. For many onlookers, the punishments inflicted on Siberia's exiles were a shameful symptom of Russia's brutality and backwardness, underscoring the tyranny of the tsarist state.[2]

Guards and warders in the prisons and penal settlements of Siberia faced the convicts with a range of weapons in their grasp. The most feared was the knout, a thong of rawhide attached by a bronze ring to a braided leather whip, approximately one metre in length, which was fastened to a long wooden handle. Capable of removing a layer of skin with each blow when wielded energetically by an executioner who knew his business, the knout shredded the victim's back. Moreover, it often proved fatal. One of the many virtues of the knout, as perceived by the tsarist authorities, was the deep and permanent scarring it left on the convict's back. Not only an effective and necessary tool of punishment, the knout thus also facilitated identification of a fugitive as a penal labourer if he took flight and was recaptured.[3]

Next in the hierarchy of pain, the lash comprised a wooden handle attached to a tube of rawhide some 25 centimetres long that passed through a metal ring before ending in two long braided rawhide tails that grew thinner towards their tips. It was a fearsome instrument, capable in the hands of an experienced executioner of rendering a criminal senseless with two or three blows. Lastly there were the birch rods, which were made from slender switches. Each was one metre in length and, in order to ensure that the blows were strong and painful, the switches had to be neither too fresh, nor too dried out. Consequently, they were usually stored in damp places, tied together in bunches of ten or fifteen and each switch was sufficient for ten blows, after which it became unusable.[4]

Floggings and beatings were the stitches that formed the fabric of authority and control in the exile system, but as such they began increasingly to fray. As early as the 1820s, under pressure from modernizers concerned that the Russian Empire should not be left behind

by the penal reforms in other European powers, Nicholas I's government had faced a dilemma. The state was caught between mounting
concern about the savagery of beatings, on the one hand, and fear that
their abolition would deprive the authorities of their necessary tools
of punishment and deterrence, on the other. Keen to preserve the terrifying reputation of the knout but increasingly averse to the numbers
who died beneath it, in 1830 Nicholas's government secretly limited
to fifty the number of blows that could be administered. The Senate
ruled in 1832 that physicians should attend the most severe floggings
to guard against unplanned fatalities. Their task was to intervene and
call a halt to proceedings when they perceived the convict to be on the
verge of death. But such interruptions earned the convict only a suspension of the punishment, and not a reprieve. Taken to the infirmary, he
would be allowed to convalesce; the wounds on his back given time to
heal. He would then be led out for a resumption of the flogging. The
doctors, often sympathetic to the convicts and opponents of corporal
punishment, would invent medical reasons why a flogging could not be
carried out, or at least why the number of blows should be reduced.[5]

Amid mounting disquiet at its lethal brutality, the knout was abolished in European Russia by the 1845 penal code. Yet in the face of
the increasing numbers of exiles and the rising threat of disorder they
brought with them, Siberian officials argued that there could be no
softening of the punishments meted out to recidivist criminals. They
claimed that the lash was too lenient for hardened criminals while
"birching does not intimidate criminals . . . Heads of households, village elders, and fathers often use this instrument. People cry under the
rod but, after being punished, mock the birching. [The birch] can neither penalise serious and inveterate criminals nor provide an example
to others." Given the widespread use of corporal punishment throughout Russian society, the Siberian authorities believed it was one thing to
spare a first-time offender the knout; exempting him from it altogether
would "endanger state security." If the knout was to be abolished in
the 1845 penal code, the authorities needed to retain something no less
terrible: the gauntlet, in which the condemned man was made to run
between two lines of soldiers, each of whom was armed with a birch
rod and charged with delivering a blow to the prisoner as he passed.[6]

Ultimately, of course, the exile authorities wielded the death penalty. Capital punishment had still been used on an ad hoc basis by mili-

tary tribunals for the most serious crimes since its ostensible abolition by Empress Elizabeth in 1753. Even so, in the wake of the Decembrist Ivan Sukhinov's alleged rebellion in 1828, the head of the Nerchinsk Mining Region requested wider powers to apply the death penalty to violent penal labourers who threatened guards and officials.[7] In 1833, Nicholas I ruled that governors-general in Siberia could execute penal labourers who committed further serious crimes in exile, if their original sentences had been ten years or more. Officially, such criminals were alive only because a magnanimous sovereign had spared them the gallows. By ordering their execution, the tsar was therefore simply revoking his clemency.[8]

In theory, the arsenal of punishment that Siberia's guard, overseers and officials had at their disposal was both a sober instrument of justice and a necessary tool for disciplining the exile population. In practice, its use rarely proceeded from a dispassionate application of the law. As Chekhov observed on Sakhalin, the power to order that a convict be flogged was also an expression of status within the hierarchies of the camp administration:

> A person found guilty of an offence is most commonly given thirty to 100 strokes of the birch. This depends, not on guilt, but on who has ordered the punishment, the district governor or the prison governor; the former has the right to give up to 100, the latter up to thirty. One Prison Governor always scrupulously awarded thirty then when on one occasion he had temporarily to fulfil the duties of district governor he at once raised his usual quota to 100 as if these 100 strokes were an indispensable token of his new authority.[9]

Camp warders wielded the power to order floggings on their own initiative for the most minor of infractions. One of Sakhalin's physicians, Dr. Nikolai Lobas, witnessed guards beating the convicts "with whatever lay to hand" and found "nothing surprising in the fact that corporal punishment serves to corrupt badly educated and ignorant men, such as the majority of the Sakhalin prison warders."[10] Chekhov discovered that penal labourers might receive between thirty and 100 strokes of the birch rod for "failure to complete the day's convict-labour task (for instance, if a shoemaker has not finished sewing the requisite three pairs of ladies' shoes, they flog him), drunkenness, rudeness, disobedience . . . if twenty or thirty workmen have not finished a task, they flog all twenty or thirty." It was risky even to complain about prison conditions, abuses of authority and unjustified beatings. The lash and the birch rod could also be used to silence troublesome convicts, as one official on the island boasted:

> The prisoners, especially those in irons, love to hand in all kinds of absurd petitions. When I was appointed here, and went round the prison for the first time, around fifty requests were handed to me; I accepted them, but declared to the applicants that those whose petitions proved to be unworthy of attention would be flogged. Only two of them turned out to be deserving of consideration—the rest were rubbish. I ordered forty-seven men to be flogged. Following that, the next time there were twenty-five, then fewer and fewer each time, and now they don't give me any requests at all any more. I've taught them a lesson.[11]

Punishments in exile often accompanied, rather than followed, the investigation of crimes committed by exiles. The commandant of Sakhalin Island admitted that processes of investigation were commenced without sufficient cause, conducted slackly and maladroitly, and that the prisoners were detained without justification. When a settled exile was murdered on the island, a suspect was locked up in a punishment cell, clapped in irons, given hot food only every third day and told he would receive 100 strokes of the birch rod. He was "kept in this way, in the dark, half-starving and in terror, until he confessed."[12]

Camp overseers frequently showed themselves to be petty tyrants, some no less brutal than those in their charge. The head of the Omsk penal fort was the widely reviled Major Krivtsov, who wielded almost an unlimited power over 200 men.[13] A companion of Fyodor Dostoevsky in Omsk, the Pole Szymon Tokarzewski, described Krivtsov's casual use of corporal punishment:

> To be sentenced to the "sticks" [birch rod], it was enough to sleep on one's right side. Yes, this is not a joke—it is the purest truth! [Krivtsov] frequently burst into the barracks at night, and

whoever on the plank bed slept on his right side was flogged. He justified this punishment by saying that Christ always slept on his left side; consequently everybody was required to follow his example.[14]

Krivtsov was also fond of persecuting individual prisoners. One of Tokarzewski's comrades, Alojzy Mirecki, had been the first Polish political prisoner to arrive in Omsk in 1846. Sentenced for conspiratorial activity to run a gauntlet of 500 soldiers and to ten years of penal labour, Mirecki had spent an entire year in the fort before his comrades joined him. In that time, Krivtsov had robbed him of everything, and had once had him beaten 100 times with birch rods. Krivtsov then assigned Mirecki to the lowliest position in the barracks, that of the *parashnik* charged with carrying out the tubs of human waste and maintaining the pits into which they were emptied. On occasion, Mirecki was required to climb down into the cesspits on a rope. As a result of his labours, he lost his sense of smell.[15] Despite his deep contempt for the common criminals in Omsk, Tokarzewski still saw the irony of their being placed in the charge of a man like Krivtsov:

A clever, vengeful hypocrite, a man of the worst behaviour, a debauch, a gambler and a drunkard—in a word, the very personification of evil . . . His task was to exert a corrective influence over the morals and customs of men who had never thought of anything apart from the satisfaction of their animal instincts.[16]

Not only camp guards took pleasure in the lash and the birch rod. Chekhov encountered a medical assistant on Sakhalin who positively revelled in the floggings: " 'I love to see them punished,' he said, joyfully . . . 'I love it! They're such villains, such rogues . . . they should hang 'em!' " One elderly prison governor would say to the prisoner beneath the lash: " 'What are you hollering for, for Christ's sake! It's nothing, it's nothing, stand up to it! Thrash him, thrash him! Lay into him!' "[17]

In an environment in which overseers could behave with impunity, sadistic impulses could touch not just convicts but also their families, themselves innocent of any wrongdoing. An overseer at the Kara gold mines named Demidov uncovered a murder committed by one of the penal labourers. In order to force a full confession from the suspect, Demidov ordered the executioner to torture first his wife, a free woman who had voluntarily followed her husband into exile, and then his daughter. The eleven-year-old girl was suspended in the air and the executioner beat her with a birch rod from her head to her toes; when the child begged for something to drink, she was given salted fish. The torture would have continued if the executioner had himself not finally refused to beat the girl further. Memoirs abounded with similar stories of the brutality that flourished in the darker corners of the exile system.[18]

If authority and tyranny were almost indistinguishable in Siberia, there was, nevertheless, a certain logic to the infliction of spectacular punishments. Frequent escapes, murders and riots in the penal settlements were all evidence of the authorities' precarious control over the convicts in their charge. Ministry of the Interior official Vasily Vlasov believed that instances of brutality often resulted from guards' and overseers' own sense of vulnerability. Understaffed and underequipped, the authorities sometimes resorted to demonstrative displays of brutality to keep the convicts in check. The director of the Dué Post settlement on Sakhalin in the 1860s, a man named Nikolayev, was a former serf who had risen to the rank of major. Something of an innovator in the field of punishment, Nikolayev found an alternative use for the barrels that the convicts would roll along planks in order to transport coal. He would force convicts guilty of an offence into the barrels themselves and then have them rolled down to the shore: "Roll 'em vigorously for about an hour, and before you know where you are, they'll be as meek as lambs!"[19]

It was not always the prisoners who came off worst in these violent confrontations. Murderous assaults on officials could seemingly erupt from nowhere. In 1882, a warder at the Tymovsk prison on Sakhalin, Anton Derbin, had an altercation with one of the penal labourers working in the bakery, Ivan Kudryashev. When Kudryashev insulted him, Derbin stepped forward and struck the convict across the face. Kudryashev then threw himself on Derbin, seizing him by the collar and shouting, "You don't do that to me!" He threw the official to the ground and, seizing a knife, began to stab him repeatedly in the chest, the stomach and the thighs. Having heard Derbin's cries, guards arrived at the scene and came upon Kudryashev standing over Derbin's body, the knife outstretched in his hand. He declared, "I'm ready!" The other four penal labourers in the bakery had made no attempt to save Derbin, who died within minutes from his wounds. When taken into custody for questioning, Kudryashev was "calm, sober and had all his wits about him." Convicted of the murder by a military tribunal, he was hanged.[20]

Of the many factors that determined the severity of a flogging, none mattered more than the zeal of the executioner himself. An executioner, or *palach,* possessed tremendous powers of discretion when it came to flogging; he wielded in many cases the power of life and death over the exile stretched out on the block. Like so much else in the exile system, the state's appointed laws governing the punishment of convicts were subject to a web of informal calculations and practices based on bribery and corruption. Punishment and mercy were also for sale.

Executioners proved difficult to recruit. The state's preference was for free labourers to assume the work, but shortages of volunteers forced the government to draw upon the services of exiles or penal labourers who themselves faced a lashing. A deal would be struck: the exile would be spared his own punishment if he agreed to work as an executioner. Some did not have to be coerced but took real pleasure in their work. Executioners were paid a relatively generous 200–300 roubles a year, in addition to double the subsistence pay issued to penal labourers. Their real source of income derived, however, from the bribes they accepted as payment for restraining the ferocity of their blows. One of the primary functions of the prisoners' communes was to strike such deals with executioners. Humane, rather than brutal, beatings could be purchased with funds from the general kitty; the commune usually set aside 30 per cent of its income for just this purpose. More generally, the commune would ensure that all the executioner's needs were satisfied: if he needed a new coat or new boots, they were provided; if he wished to drink, he was given as much vodka as he could consume. The enduring revulsion of the other penal labourers offset, nonetheless, these perks of the job.[21]

Yet the deals struck still left the executioner needing to perform a delicate balancing act. On the one hand, he needed to satisfy the terms agreed with the individual prisoner, backed by the supervision of the commune. Failure to do so would leave the executioner himself vulnerable to retribution by his fellow convicts. On the other hand, the executioner could never really let a man off lightly; he would answer for that with his own back. Ethnographer and journalist Niko-lai Yadrintsev heard of one executioner in the town of Yeniseisk who consistently erred in his calculations and so suffered "terrible torments that he was only able to survive because of his mightily robust con-stitution." The head of police once demanded an especially vigorous punishment, but the executioner wanted to satisfy the prisoners at all costs and so softened his blows. As a consequence, after the flogging the poor man had to submit to the same punishment himself. He was thrashed and sent for a time into the prison, where the convicts got him drunk and so replenished his debt to them. The next time he was called upon to inflict a beating, he considered it his obligation to repay them with magnanimity and so once again bore the punishment him-self. The other convicts marvelled at this executioner's generosity and long remembered "their hero and benefactor."[22]

Most executioners had themselves been the recipients of brutal beatings at one time or another and therefore felt little sympathy for their victims. Many came to derive savage pleasures from their work. One such executioner, Komlev, had undergone a brutal apprenticeship on Sakhalin. Originally sentenced to twenty years of penal labour for armed robbery, he was caught in 1877 trying to flee the island and sentenced to ninety-six lashes and a twenty-year extension to his term. In prison and awaiting sentence, he had been recruited as an assistant by Sakhalin's over-burdened "celebrity" executioner, Tersky. When, however, Komlev had again tried to flee in 1889 and been captured and sentenced to an additional forty-five blows of the lash and another fifteen years on top of his existing forty-year sentence, it was Tersky who flogged him, saying, "Lie down, my pupil, I'll show you how to flog a man." Komlev later told the journalist Vlas Doroshevich: "I've been rotting ever since." Doroshevich confirmed that his body looked as if it had been scarred with a hot iron. "It was terrible to behold. In places, it was covered in white scars; in others, with fine red weals." Komlev showed Doroshevich how, when squeezed, "the weals burst and emitted a white pus."

When Tersky himself was later caught taking a bribe in exchange for a lighter flogging, and sentenced to 200 blows of the birch rod, it was Komlev's turn to show how much he had learned: "'You taught me how to use the lash; now I'll show you what can be done with the rod.' . . . What Tersky had done to Komlev was a trifle compared with what Komlev did to him." Physicians who attended Komlev's floggings described them as a "refined form of torture." When asked why he was so cruel, Komlev would reply, "Have they not beaten me? I've been beaten all my life!"[23]

Brutal floggings did not only make a lasting impression on those who wielded the lash and the rod. When the Kara prison doctor Vladimir Kokosov had to attend his first flogging, the bloody scene he witnessed left him traumatized. The prisoner, terrified and sobbing, begged for mercy on his knees and, when the first blow of the lash fell across his back, "he gave out an inhuman, wild cry." By the end of the ordeal, the convict's "pulse was intermittent, weak, barely detectable . . . his eyes were rolling around in their sockets, wild, dilated, and streaming . . . His chest was heaving with liquid and he was nauseous and began to vomit." Kokosov was left to reanimate the "pitiful, pitiful, tortured, lifeless corpse." All through the night, he sat at the bed of the flogged man and "burning tears of shame and helplessness dimmed my eyes."[24] The old medical assistant Aleksei Morozov, who worked together with Kokosov, had witnessed so many floggings that it had left him a demoralized, nervous wreck. He poured out to Kokosov his deep sense of revulsion at the spectacle of men being made to run the gauntlet:

> They brought us a man, stripped him down, tied his hands . . . he was pale, white as clay, only his mouth was wide open, sucking in air; he was shivering as if he had a fever . . . "Atteeens-hun! Beeeeegin!" And they get to work; the "green street" stirs, the rods whistle through the air, and scraps of flesh and blood fly off his back! And he cries . . . how he cries! . . . as if his back is being burnt off . . . His whole back is covered in shredded flesh; the blood flows and still they beat him! And still they beat him![25]

Most convicts regarded the birch rod, the lash and the gauntlet with undisguised terror. Some would feign madness in a desperate attempt to avoid them. For the most part, however, they were quickly unmasked or realized themselves that their performance had failed to convince the authorities. After two or three days in the infirmary, "carrying on absurdly," they would "suddenly return to their senses, calm down and gloomily begin to ask to be discharged." But in some cases, the madness was not feigned. In *Notes from the House of the Dead*, Dostoevsky describes one poor, babbling wretch in the Omsk infirmary who had just been sentenced to 2,000 blows of the birch rod. His mounting terror at the prospect of such a brutal beating had driven him out of his mind.[26] Others resorted to still more desperate means to avoid punishment. On the eve of their sentences, some would stab a fellow convict just to institute another set of proceedings and thereby postpone the hour when the lash would slice into their backs. Prisoners in the infirmaries would warily eye the men who were brought in to recover between instalments of their floggings, in case they suddenly reached for a blade.

Some, however, seemed almost insensible to the beatings.[27] Their powers of endurance and readiness to encounter floggings at the hands of guards and warders imbued these exiles with a terrible authority throughout the penal settlements. In the early 1850s, Ivan Yefimov, the head of the Aleksandrovsk penal distillery, encountered one such convict, named Ivan Karatsupenko. A hardened criminal with "red hair, an unpleasant freckled face and a strangely misshapen head," Karatsupenko had been found guilty of three separate attempted escapes and had been sentenced by a district court to fifty blows of the knout. He was led onto the square in front of the prison distillery so that the assembled penal labourers could witness the carrying out of the sentence. When the police official began to read out the sentence pronouncing the words "administer fifty blows of the knout to the penal labourer Karatsupenko for his third escape," the convict hurled himself upon him and seized the sentence in his teeth. The soldiers in attendance almost ran him through with their bayonets, but the police official, having managed to tear himself free, shouted, "Use your rifle butts!" A fight ensued in which Karatsupenko managed to tear up the sentence, punch the executioner on the nose and almost mutilate one of the soldiers, before he was finally bundled to the ground. It was only with the assistance of some of the watching convicts that he was tied down to receive his flogging. The executioner stepped forward not only to administer the punishment but also to exact revenge for his own injury. Yet from the first to the last of the fifty blows, Karatsupenko, despite all the efforts of the resentful executioner, did not let out a single cry of pain. During the punishment, he swore at everyone without exception and promised to slaughter all of them. Yefimov was worried that Karatsupenko, once untied, might kill someone, and ordered him placed in a strait-jacket and transferred to the prison hospital. The convict turned contemptuously to the executioner and mocked him for failing, despite his best efforts, to elicit a single cry of pain: "If I get hold of you one day, you'll be squealing and then you'll kick the bucket!" After enduring a flogging that would have rendered most men senseless with agony, Karatsupenko was able to walk to the hospital unaided. Later he was transferred to the Irkutsk salt works, where, for another serious offence, he was sentenced to run a gauntlet of 1,000 men three times. He endured some 1,800 blows without a sound before falling. His body was placed on a cart and carried for the remainder of the punishment between the columns of men.[28]

Vagabonds who had staged repeated escapes bore the grisly accumulation of scars from the floggings that followed recapture like badges of honour and distinction. Some convicts endured so many floggings that their shoulder blades were permanently visible, like shafts of polished ivory, through skin that had never healed over. The power to endure particularly brutal floggings had an almost sacralizing effect on some men, who were known in the Nicolaevan era as "Ivans"—"aristocrats" among the penal labourers. The "Ivans" distinguished themselves by their fearsome exploits and their ability to remain defiant and unbowed in the face of the lacerating punishments that were meted out by the state, as the journalist Vlas Doroshevich explained:

> They became "Ivans" by enduring no fewer than 2,000 lashes of the whip; the birch rod did not count at all. Such beatings conferred upon them an aura of martyrdom and elicited respect. The authorities thrashed them but also feared them. These were men who would, without a second thought, plunge a knife under your ribs or who, with their manacles, would dash in the skull of any man who offended them.[29]

Exiled revolutionary Lev Deikh remembered the power of the "Ivans" and their authority over the convicts' commune: "All members are supposed to have, *de jure,* equal rights in the organisation; but, *de facto,* the confirmed criminals, the old experienced rogues and vagabonds, are the preponderating element, and it is the 'Ivans' that govern the rest ruthlessly in their own proper interest. It is *their* will that passes for the will of the whole body." It was only after the abolition of the knout that the Ivans' mantle of inhuman resilience began to fray and their standing among the convicts diminished.[30]

For all their horror, the beatings and chains never served as an effective deterrent against a whole range of minor and major offences. Observers such as Yadrintsev were convinced the floggings only severed the final strands of humanity linking the prisoners to wider society: "A man who has suffered the lash and the rods, who has stood on the scaffold . . . no longer fears anything. What is more, he becomes cruel, cold-blooded towards the suffering of others." Yadrintsev believed that corporal punishment was "useless in preventing crimes and, even more so, in promoting rehabilitation. Rather, it inculcated savagery."[31]

For officials with an eye on the bigger picture of the exile's role in the development of Siberia, the state's primitive repertoire of punishment seemed only to undermine its colonial ambitions. Violent recidivists should simply be put to death, the officials argued; those guilty of relative misdemeanours, such as escape, should receive lenient punishments geared towards correcting, rather than terrorizing, them.[32] Some senior figures in the government betrayed a certain scepticism towards the rehabilitative benefits that the exiles might accrue. Minister of the Interior Pyotr Valuyev objected that only floggings could discipline convicts who were beyond the reach of moral persuasion.[33]

With the whip and the lash, the state was promoting a brutality that would subsequently be unleashed across Siberia when penal labourers were released to settlement. But it was also fomenting another, more subtle and indirect, threat to the state's ambitions for penal colonization: the mounting public disquiet its punishments were eliciting among an educated audience back in European Russia.

For most of the nineteenth century, officials believed that corporal punishment could serve as a deterrent that would dissuade other exiles from perpetrating crimes. The flogging of malefactors before large groups of their fellow prisoners proved, however, of questionable pedagogical merit and resulted often in expressions of sympathy with the man bleeding and whimpering on the executioner's block. In 1880, St. Petersburg ordered that these spectacles of horror be taken inside and out of sight.[34] Yet, by then, nowhere in Siberia was really out of sight. Those who worked in the exile system and those who visited it witnessed brutal floggings and were increasingly sharing their testimony with a shocked audience thousands of kilometres beyond the walls of Siberia's jails. The impact of these descriptions of punishments meted out to Siberian exiles can only be understood in terms of broader shifts in attitudes to criminals after the Great Reforms of the 1860s. At the beginning of the nineteenth century, criminals in Russia, as elsewhere in Europe, were viewed as sinful, even evil. But modern psychiatric explanations of criminal behaviour gradually supplanted such religiously defined views among educated Russians. By the 1880s, Russian criminologists were attending international conferences in Paris, Brussels and London to discuss the latest criminological theories. The serious press carried digests of their work and ensured that they reached a wide audience. A significant body of liberal and progressive opinion in Russian cities—the readers of publications such as *Russian Thought, Notes of the Fatherland, Herald of Europe* and *Russian Wealth*—were sympathetic towards the plight of Russia's criminal classes and believed that social reform was the key to tackling crime in the empire. Modern penal systems in which the behaviour of offenders could be carefully monitored, structured and disciplined were hailed as institutions of progress and enlightenment. With the rise of these modern penal sensibilities, the flogging of exiles appeared a throwback to an earlier age of barbarism that many now associated with Russia's long centuries under the "Mongol yoke."[35]

Sakhalin's Dr. Lobas was quite open about his desire to confront his readers in European Russia with the horror of punishments in Siberia: "May the reader forgive me," he wrote in an 1898 article published in both the Russian Empire's most influential medical journal, *The Physician*, and in the United States, "if I lead him against his will into a place of weeping and grinding teeth, a place with all the appearances of a torture chamber, if I force him to behold a scene he would prefer not to see."[36] Such accounts stressed that the lash and the birch rods were not instruments of justice and discipline but weapons of tyranny that exploited the rightless condition of penal labourers and exiles.

No less disturbing to contemporary sensibilities were the punishment cells in Siberia's prisons and penal forts in which exiles convicted of serious and violent crimes were locked after they had been flogged. They were gloomy, cramped dungeons with no furniture; to one visitor's eyes, they looked like "stone caves" and many had no daylight.[37]

Incarcerated for long periods in these dungeons, convicts rotted alive. Following his arrest for vagrancy, a religious sectarian named Yegor Rozhkov was exiled in 1872 to the gold mines in Kara. He steadfastly refused to undertake any of the labour tasks assigned to him there and declared that he had been punished unjustly. Over a period of two years, the guards responded to his intransigence with brutal beatings and finally put him, with manacled hands and feet, into solitary confinement on a diet of bread and water. Six months later, the newly arrived Kara prison doctor, Kokosov, was summoned to attend to Rozhkov in his punishment cell:

> The warder opened the door . . . and we were assaulted by the smell of a decomposing body. Nothing was visible in the total darkness. There was the noise of someone wheezing and snuffling. The stench was unbearable. A tallow candle was brought and I entered the cell. The room was 2 metres long and 1 metre wide . . . There was no window, only a small glass peephole in the door. On the floor, next to the plank bed, was a wooden tub full of excrement; the floor was wet and slimy. On the plank bed, wheezing and snuffling, was a half-man, half-corpse . . .

Unable to examine the prisoner in the sepulchral gloom of the cell, Kokosov ordered that Rozhkov be carried out into the light of the corridor:

> His hands and feet, swollen with scurvy, did not fit inside the iron rim of his fetters; the iron cut into his swollen body. His hands and feet had turned blue and were covered in ulcers of a dirty grey colour. Lice swarmed over the fetters and crawled over the ulcers. The blacksmith struggled to release the fetters. While forcing out the rivets, the chisel slipped and sliced into

the body; the blood began to flow. The filthy, rotting shirt and trousers were all his clothing; his feet were bare. The hat and overcoat carried out of the cell, which had served as a pillow and blanket, were smeared in excrement . . . Rozhkov had the appearance of a decomposing corpse.

Kokosov was appalled by Rozhkov's condition and penned an angry report to his superior, denouncing what he saw as "the most lawless kind of torture."[38]

Treated by Kokosov in the prison infirmary over the course of the subsequent two months, Rozhkov began to "reacquire a human form." Astonishingly, he remained unbowed. He explained to the doctor his own radical, religious view of human freedom that brooked no intervention from a coercive state: "I am free in body and mind; I live as I please, do what I like . . . You are a hireling—you don't do as you please but what you're ordered to do . . . I know you almost weep when they flog a man, but you still participate in it! I wouldn't have anything to do with it!" Following Kokosov's protests, the prison authorities were reluctant to return Rozhkov to the punishment cells and effectively gave up trying to deal with him. He was hidden during an imperial visit for fear that he would manifest some kind of insubordination. And in 1874, he was released to settlement in Chita, where he died in penury in 1885, adored by the children in the local village.[39]

Worse even than solitary confinement was to be locked in a cell and chained to a wall. Small numbers of penal labourers who had committed the most serious crimes—arson, violent robbery and murder—were punished with the knout and then chained to a wall for a period of up to ten years. In the late 1840s, the Decembrists' former prison at Petrovsk Zavod was brought back into use to hold such individuals. These unfortunates would be shackled to the walls by a chain attached to their leg fetters. The prison had enough space to accommodate up to sixty such prisoners in a group if "they showed signs of repentance" and in solitary confinement "if they remained incorrigible and violent." Prisoners thus chained to the wall would, the authorities believed, "feel the full force of their punishment and will not harm society by committing further crimes."[40]

Petrovsk Zavod confined some twenty such recidivists by chaining them to the walls of solitary but adjacent cells. The prisoners were

generously afforded a chain some 2 metres in length, long enough to
enable them to lie down on the ground and stick their heads out over
the threshold of their cells and into the corridor. As many cells adjoined
the corridor, the horizontal inmates were thus able to entertain themselves. One would tell a story while the others listened; then the next
would begin, followed by a third and so on, each in turn. It was, nevertheless, a tormented existence for the men. Many would get hold of
sharp items—knives and so forth—and try to cut their own throats.
Placed on reduced rations, over time the prisoners chained to walls
weakened in both body and mind. Their muscles atrophied through
enforced indolence; their faces grew pale; their innards swelled up and
they developed stomach pains; moving, insofar as the chains allowed,
made them nauseous. By 1851, there were fifteen prisoners whiling
away ten-year stretches chained to the walls of Petrovsk Zavod. There
were a few dozen throughout the rest of Siberia.[41]

In the penal distillery in Iglinsk, under the command of Ivan Yefimov, four men were chained to the wall for crimes they had committed as exiles. One of them was reasonably literate, so Yefimov lent
him books to read aloud to the others. When he visited the cell to
ask whether they were enjoying the reading, "they thanked me for the
books and for the reading and said that they were no longer as bored
as they had been before." Ethnographer Sergei Maksimov marvelled
at the inventiveness of some of the men detained in this way: "Many
learned to sew, turned themselves into cobblers or engravers." Locked
away in these cells, convicts contrived to communicate with each other
through pipes and crevices. Some were even provisioned with supplies
by means of a "telegraph" of ropes used to deliver items to their cell
windows.[42]

Some recidivist convicts were chained not to walls but to wheelbar-
rows that they dragged around with them for five- or ten-year stretches,
a punishment that was both a moral torment and an obstacle to escape.
Whenever the head of one prison approached a convict chained to a
wheelbarrow, the latter would "with bitter prayers and unfeigned tears
beg to be unshackled from it: 'I'm so sick of it! It turns my stomach!
I'd give anything not to have to look at it!'"[43] One of Sakhalin's most
notorious criminals, Fyodor Shirokolobov, was a man with a string of
armed robberies and murders and daring escapes to his name. He had
been deported from Eastern Siberia to the island of Sakhalin, where,

following another unsuccessful escape bid, he was finally chained to a wheelbarrow for five years. In his autobiography, he described his existence chained to his "wheelbarrow wife":

> I dragged the barrow around with me for five years and four months . . . When I went out to work with the barrow, it filled me with hatred. I suffered it . . . like a dumb beast . . . I had lost any kind of human form and the state had turned me into a kind of absurd, labouring chattel. I would look at my wheelbarrow wife with a sense of bitterness, absurdity and shame . . . a sense of human shame. It might seem unlikely that a moral abomination such as myself could feel a sense of human shame . . . but my soul was outraged by this punishment.[44]

Shirokolobov's sentiments were widely shared from the 1860s, when educated Poles arrived in Siberian prisons and penal settlements and pioneered and promoted ideas of individual sovereignty and natural rights. Following his expedition to Sakhalin in 1892, geographer and botanist Andrei Krasnov reported that all the convicts "suffered from their awareness that they enjoyed no rights . . . that they were pariahs, castoffs from society."[45] Of course, critics of the exile system made much of the prisoners' own sense of inalienable rights and dignity, and there were few who, like Shirokolobov, recorded in any detail their moral responses to the punishments they endured. Yet even if these writers projected as much as they observed, their descriptions fed into a mounting revulsion at the brutal punishment of Siberia's exiles.

The greatest scandal was still to come, though. In 1892, news of one of the very darkest episodes in the history of Siberian exile, the "Onor Affair," began to seep out to the public sphere. An illiterate overseer at the Rykovo prison on Sakhalin, Alimpy Khanov, had been tasked with supervising the construction of a new road through thick forests and swamps to connect the remote settlement of Onor, in central Sakhalin, with the south of the island. The 500 convicts in his charge were assigned exhausting labour duties: clearing undergrowth, felling and uprooting trees, building dykes and moving earth. In the winter, they froze in the searing cold that descended on Sakhalin's forests; in the summer, swarms of midges feasted on their exposed flesh. As Doroshevich later commented, a "supernatural force was required to force men to carry out work like that. The prison authorities found such a supernatural force . . . in the shape of senior overseer Khanov." A former penal labourer who had served his sentence in the Kara gold mines before being transferred to Sakhalin, Khanov was a man of questionable integrity.[46]

Between February and December 1892, 226 men fled the construction site and a further seventy died in mysterious circumstances. Assigned to the Tymovsk district infirmary in 1892, Dr. Lobas arrived on Sakhalin just as rumours of terrible brutality on the Onor tract were spreading among the exiles:

> The warders supervising the works, and especially the senior overseer Khanov, were starving the convicts to death, punishing them by withdrawing bread rations, driving them to exhaustion with crippling workloads and subjecting them to the most dreadful beatings and torture, which frequently resulted in death. It was said that the penal labourers were driven by hunger to steal bread from each other. The situation became so critical that a convict, going to sleep, would bury his chunk of bread in the ground and lie on top of it, something which was of little use as his hungry companions would succeed in stealing the concealed bread by digging tunnels under his body. Starvation drove the penal labourers to murder their comrades and eat their flesh . . . In order to escape the works on the Onor tract, the men would chop off their hands and feet, and they confessed to murders they had not committed in order to be imprisoned . . . It was also said that, in the vicinity of the tract, the stench of discarded rotting corpses filled the air.[47]

Lobas undertook an investigation of the post-mortem reports on some of the seventy penal labourers who perished on the Onor tract and discovered that many had been falsified. Physicians had certified the cause of death without ever having seen the bodies of the dead convicts and had failed to carry out post-mortems even in cases where

the death had clearly been a violent one. Lobas found that the physicians' conclusions were evidence of "a negligent attitude towards
forensic matters of great importance" and even "a malicious intent to
conceal and disguise the real state of affairs." Khanov's own reports
were a litany of misfortune: on 27 May, Olgy-Aga-Mamed-Khilil had
been murdered by his comrades; the following day, penal labourer
Obydenkov had been killed by a falling tree; two days after that, penal
labourer Sherebkov had died suddenly after dinner; on 29 June, Olgy-
Gussein-Kizakh had been beaten to death by unknown persons; on 1
July, Anton Kainatsky had died from exhaustion and epilepsy; on the
same day, Mizin Trofim had died from pneumonia; on 7 July, Averian
Bely from dysentery; on 11 July, Nikita Zhuravlyov from heart disease;
on 30 July, Ali-Meshadi-Akhmet from food poisoning, having eaten
mushrooms. And so the list went on. Lobas was outraged by what he
discovered:

> Penal labourers were dying almost every day on the Onor tract,
> many of them met untimely ends and their deaths were in most
> instances extremely suspicious. Yet the authorities showed no
> interest. Receiving the overseer's reports of the deaths of penal
> labourers, the officials simply dashed off a note to the doctor,
> asking him to certify the cause of death and, *if necessary*, con-
> duct an autopsy on this or that penal labourer who had died in
> mysterious circumstances . . . In a word, the prison authorities
> and the doctor sat in their offices hundreds of kilometres away
> from the scene of these terrible human dramas and contented
> themselves with a spot of correspondence and some formal
> replies. Medical assistants and overseers understood very well
> the attitude of the officials and acted accordingly, and mean-
> while the penal labourers were groaning under crippling work,
> starving and dying from exhaustion and beatings.[48]

Doroshevich interviewed some of the "Onor Affair" cannibals.
One, named Pavel Kolokosov, had fled the road works with another
starving penal labourer who subsequently died on the run. Kolokosov
was later apprehended carrying a sack containing pieces of partially
cooked human flesh. He admitted to having chopped up and seared the
meat in order to preserve it, but, to the complete disbelief and derision
of the other penal labourers, Kolokosov denied that he had either killed

or eaten his fellow fugitive. He claimed that he had merely simulated cannibalism in order to be imprisoned and not returned to the Onor construction site. The appalled penal labourers had to be restrained from lynching him, and they forced Kolokosov to eat the flesh in front of them. Other prisoners suspected of cannibalism were subjected to brutal beatings, some of which proved fatal. The penal labourers subsequently immortalized the horrors of the Onor tract in song:

> As we marched from Tyumen,
> We ate geese,
> But as we marched towards Onor,
> It was people we gobbled up![49]

Despite a series of official investigations, Khanov remained in his post for apparent lack of evidence. Yet stories of the atrocities on the Onor tract began to leak out. In the summer of 1893, Krasnov returned from Sakhalin to write about the "Onor Affair" in the popular magazine *Books of the Week*. Chekhov also mentioned it in his *Sakhalin Island*. The Siberian press began to pick up the story. Two articles authored by acquaintances of Lobas appeared in the newspaper *Vladivostok* in the autumn of 1893, and, by February 1894, London's *Evening Standard* and *The New York Times* also ran with the story.[50] Under the headline "Horrors from Russia: Convicts Follow Murder by Cannibalism and Are Anxious to Die," the latter stated:

> The report of the commission of inquiry into conditions at the convict station at Onor, Sakhalin, reveals numerous instances of merciless floggings and of fingers and arms lopped off with sabres. Cannibalism, prompted by famine, is a common occurrence. Murder, followed by cannibalism, is frequently committed, solely with a view to procuring execution as a termination of the misery of life . . . During 1892 almost a continuous string of convoys with mutilated corpses passed from Onor to Rykovskoye, where the officials reside. No inquiries were made, but the bodies were forthwith buried. Neither of the two doctors in Rykovskoye ever visited Onor.[51]

The "Onor Affair" exposed not just the sadistic tyranny of one individual, but an entire bureaucratic web of incompetence, indifference and corruption within the administration of the Sakhalin penal colony. It was a damning indictment of the exile system as a whole that such horrors could be allowed to take place under the noses of the island's administrators.

The whips, chains and solitary confinement that underpinned authority and power in Siberia's penal colonies and prisons were the blunt instruments of a weak state. Savagery and horror were no substitutes for discipline and justice. Unable to reform its exiles, the state relied on savage punishments to keep them in check. In a world in which corrupt and vindictive officials and executioners enjoyed tremendous powers of discretion, the boundaries between the law and despotism remained blurred, not to say invisible. To the prisoners themselves, the selective enforcement of laws appeared arbitrary and unpredictable. In onlookers, the punishments inspired revulsion.

Increasingly seen as the shameful vestige of a pre-modern past, by the end of the nineteenth century, corporal punishment was eliciting ever greater condemnation from a well-informed and assertive educated public. For many, the image of the sadistic executioner towering, whip in hand, above the prostrate body of an exile was fast becoming a symbol of the autocracy.

12

"Woe to the Vanquished!"

On a May morning in 1864, a bespectacled man, dressed in the sort of dark frockcoat beloved of Russian intellectuals, prepared for his civil execution on Mytnaya Square in St. Petersburg. Editor of the radical journal *The Contemporary*, Nikolai Chernyshevsky had been found guilty of "plotting to overthrow the existing order." As he knelt before a crowd of between 1,000 and 2,000 spectators, a sword was broken over his head and his sentence was read out. He was to be "stripped of all rights of estate and sent to 14 years of penal labour in the mines followed by settlement in Siberia forever."[1] In many respects, the authorities judged quite accurately the dangers this mild-mannered journalist posed through his steady stream of publications. His ideas were an intellectual broadside against the ideological foundations of the tsarist order and an inspiration to successive generations of radicals who would conduct an ultimately successful struggle against the state for the next half century. *What Is to Be Done?*, the novel Chernyshevsky wrote while awaiting trial in the Peter and Paul Fortress, was a clarion call to a generation of radicals. Its utopian vision of a revolutionary world seemed to many, including a youthful Vladimir Lenin, to flesh out a feasible—and tantalizingly imminent—future governed by secularism, equality, harmony and reason. Chernyshevsky's demands for reform chimed with the "repentant noblemen" of the 1860s and 70s who felt a great moral responsibility to the impoverished and downtrodden peasantry. Guilt would prove a psychological inspiration for the coming revolution.[2]

The crowd of onlookers on Mytnaya Square had gathered not in opprobrium but in sympathy. The severity of the sentence meted out to the soft-spoken intellectual generated a backlash among educated Russians. Chernyshevsky was, however, only the most celebrated of the hundreds of young radicals caught up in the government's repression of the 1860s. Many were guilty of little more than circulating and discussing the scientific and political ideas that were all the rage in the reform era. One such radical detained by the authorities was Varvara Aleksandrovskaya, the wife of a minor official. She was held in solitary confinement in St. Petersburg for two years before being convicted in 1869 of "membership in an illegal group dedicated to changing the existing order in Russia and for attempting to circulate criminal compositions." Aleksandrovskaya was sentenced to the loss of all rights of rank and to lifelong exile in Eastern Siberia. Hundreds more were banished to Siberia in the years that followed.[3]

The Russian revolutionary movement in the reign of Alexander II was a shifting cluster of parties, ideological orientations and individuals inspired by the writings of radical thinkers such as Chernyshevsky, Mikhail Bakunin, Pyotr Lavrov, Pyotr Tkachev and Nikolai Mikhailovsky. The doctrines they espoused—Materialism, Utilitarianism, Darwinism, Socialism, Anarchism and, later, Marxism—acquired an aura of infallible truth among their acolytes in the second half of the nineteenth century and inspired a generation of radicals to political action. The revolutionaries were, however, divided over how best to pursue their aims. Some believed that gradualist campaigns of agitation and propaganda among the peasantry would rouse the people from their political slumber and bring about the overthrow of the government. Others, of a more impatient political and psychological disposition, favoured violent action and propaganda by deed. They believed, naively as it turned out, that the assassination of the tsar would trigger the collapse of the autocracy. Whatever the preferred revolutionary tactics, subversive ideas in the post-Emancipation era wielded an almost material power.[4]

The radicals of the 1860s and 70s picked up the torch of reform and revolution that had first been raised by the Decembrists on Senate Square in 1825. Although many of the earlier rebels had since died in obscurity on their farms in Siberia, it was in the reform era of the 1860s, with its relaxation of censorship, that the story of their failed rebellion and their experiences in Siberia, told in a flood of published memoirs, began to enter the consciousness of a younger generation. Nikolai Nekrasov's poem "Russian Women," celebrating the self-sacrifice of the Decembrists' wives, was published a year before the "mad summer" of 1874, which proved a turning point in the history of the revolutionary movement. Thousands of students left their lecture theatres to fan out into the countryside in a "movement to the people." They sought to spread the socialist gospel among the peasantry by living alongside them, deploying their newly acquired skills as craftsmen and artisans and thereby winning their trust. They were disappointed. The activists were denounced by uncomprehending and suspicious villagers, arrested and prosecuted in a succession of major political trials. At the "Trial of the 193" in the autumn of 1877, most of the defendants were acquitted by sympathetic jurors, but the years spent in pre-trial detention had done little to mollify them. Two of those who walked free, Sofia Perovskaya and Andrei Zhelyabov, went on to lead the new revolutionary party, the People's Will, and to plan the successful assassination of Alexander II in 1881.[5]

State officials in the late nineteenth century looked on the secular ideologies of revolution as if on a plague. The arch-conservative statesman Konstantin Pobedonostsev, Procurator of the Holy Synod—a position akin to minister for religion—and tutor to both Alexander III and Nicholas II, likened the mounting influence of a revolutionary sentiment among the empire's youth to a "moral epidemic." If, in the eyes of officialdom, socialism, anarchism and nihilism were dangerous epidemics, Siberia was a realm of political quarantine.[6]

Like the Decembrists, Chernyshevsky was borne into exile posthaste by carriage, under armed guard, and not by the usual route. The authorities seemed almost in awe of the influence he wielded. Following the refusal of the Poles to work in the Akatui mine in the Nerchinsk Mining Region in 1866, the tsarist secret police, the Third Department, enquired whether Chernyshevsky had orchestrated their disobedience (he had not). When the authorities eventually released him to settlement in 1871, they were reluctant, given his celebrity within the radical movement, to allow him to settle in any of the larger Siberian towns: "The importance of his crimes and the authority he has among his acolytes demand that the government take special measures to deny Chernyshevsky the possibility of escape and the possibility of spreading his harmful influence on society." They chose, therefore, to send him to the Vilyusk prison fort in Yakutsk district, about 2,300 kilometres to the north of Nerchinsk. In so doing, the authorities succeeded simply in elevating Chernyshevsky to something akin to a secular saint.[7] The secret police even intercepted letters addressed to Chernyshevsky from admirers abroad. One, posted in New York on 1 March 1881, read as follows:

Dear and Eternal Sir,

Would you be kind enough to favour a daughter of the New World with your autograph? . . . Dear martyr, a day will soon come, I hope, when your sovereign will relent and give you liberty that you may again breathe the air, which was man's gift.[8]

By the time the letter was stamped in New York, however, the emperor to whom it made reference lay dead, his legs blown off by a revolutionary's bomb on the Yekaterinsky Canal in St. Petersburg.

Alexander II's assassination was the culmination of a determined and ruthless campaign of violence waged by the members of the People's Will. Between 1878 and 1881, revolutionaries killed two provincial governors and staged six (failed) attempts on the life of the tsar, the most spectacular of which was the bombing in February 1880 of the Winter Palace that claimed the lives of eleven soldiers and wounded a further fifty-six. Alexander's government responded to the "emperor hunt" with a series of ad hoc laws designed to radically increase the administrative powers of the police and of the governors to put under surveillance, detain, imprison and exile individuals suspected of involvement in, or even sympathy with, the revolutionary movement. These sweeping powers enabled the authorities to bypass the open courts and juries, which were proving unreliable allies in this war on terror.

And yet the government still struggled against a tide of popular sympathy with the aims of the terrorists, if not exactly with their methods. On 24 January 1878, Vera Zasulich entered the offices of the staunchly conservative governor of St. Petersburg, Fyodor Trepov, and shot and seriously wounded him. Tried in open court, Zasulich freely admitted responsibility but argued that her assassination attempt was a justified response to Trepov's order to have a young revolutionary brutally flogged for his refusal to remove his cap before the governor in the Peter and Paul Fortress. Much to the dismay of the government, the jury acquitted Zasulich on 31 March 1878. Convinced that the courts were now working to undermine them, the emperor and his advisers introduced a new law on 9 May 1878 that deprived anyone accused of attacks on government officials of the right to a trial by jury. In the future, such defendants would be tried in camera, by military courts. The use of emergency police powers to detain suspects and of military tribunals to secure convictions proved deeply unpopular. Nonetheless, the measures appeared to be having the desired effect: the activities of the People's Will were severely disrupted by the secret police and their finances fell into disarray. But then, on 1 March 1881, the terrorists got their man.[9]

After the assassination, the Okhrana, the successor organization to the Third Department, which was now equipped with telegraphs, card catalogues and extensive networks of spies and informers, hunted down and destroyed the People's Will. Paralysed by the arrests and by the infiltration of its networks, the revolutionary movement was effectively routed for a generation and would not again challenge the autocracy with bullets and bombs before the beginning of the twentieth century. As a form of propaganda by deed, the assassination was an abject failure. It did not provoke the prophesied outbreak of revolution. Instead, the peasantry rounded on its supposed revolutionary benefactors by attacking the empire's Jews, whom it blamed for the assassination. In several towns and cities, pogroms—a mixture of violent looting, murder and rape—claimed the lives of dozens of people and devastated Jewish businesses.[10]

Even in defeat, however, the People's Will clinched a vital victory in what was becoming a battle for hearts and minds. During the "emperor hunt," the lines between political conviction and political action had blurred and the state's persecution of all and any dissent, real or imagined, had reached paranoid proportions. Then, on 14 August 1881, in response to the assassination, Alexander III's government promulgated the "Statute on Measures for the Preservation of Political Order and Social Tranquillity." Intended as temporary legislation, it in fact remained in force right up until 1917 and was described by Lenin as the "de facto constitution of Russia."[11] The law effectively gave the government the right to sentence anyone it suspected of seditious activity to between three and five years of administrative exile in Siberia (extended to eight years after 1888). The American George Kennan explained the powers conferred by the new legislation:

Exile by administrative process means the banishment of an obnoxious person from one part of the empire to another without the observance of any of the legal formalities that, in most civilised countries, precede the deprivation of rights and the restriction of personal liberty. The obnoxious person may not be guilty of any crime . . . but if, in the opinion of the local authorities, his presence in a particular place is "prejudicial to public order," or "incompatible with public tranquillity," he may be arrested without a warrant, may be held from two weeks to two years in prison, and may then be removed by force to any other place within the limits of the empire and there be put under police surveillance for a period of from one to ten years . . . He has no right to demand a trial, or even a hearing. He cannot sue out a writ of habeas corpus. He cannot appeal to his fellow citizens through the press. His communications with the world are so suddenly severed that sometimes even his own relatives do not know what has happened to him. He is literally and absolutely without any means whatever of self-defence.[12]

The emergency legislation was an effective suspension of the rule of law, and it remained in place long after public revulsion at the assassination of a popular monarch had subsided. What followed were two decades in which the state failed to distinguish between dangerous radicals and moderate reformers. Astute observers, even those with little sympathy for the revolutionary movement, were almost unanimous in their denunciation of the laws. In the eyes of its critics, the emergency legislation was not simply a fundamental repudiation of the culture of openness and legality ushered in by the legal reforms of 1864 but also a recruiting sergeant for the revolutionaries. Political exiles, both those convicted of crimes by military tribunals and those exiled administratively, underwent in the public imagination a moral transformation from dangerous and misguided fanatics into sympathetic martyrs. The stage for this reinvention was Siberia.[13]

Between 1881 and 1904, the state exiled 4,100 individuals for their "political unreliability" and a further 1,900 for factory disturbances. The figures were not great when contrasted with the roughly 300,000 exiles located in Siberia by 1898. Yet the numbers mattered much less than the influence and standing of the men and women who found themselves caught up in the dragnet. Many, if not most, were educated, and some hailed from prosperous and well-connected families. A military tribunal in Kiev sentenced Maria Kovalevskaya, the daughter of a famous Russian nobleman and the sister of one of the empire's leading economists, to fourteen years of penal labour in Siberia for her revolutionary activity. Sons and daughters of the nobility, students, journalists, merchants and even state officials found themselves exiled for little more than possessing subversive literature. On 20 December 1881, nobleman Valentin Yakovenko was administratively exiled as "unreliable" following a search of his property that uncovered notes in code and the addresses of individuals believed to be engaged in revolutionary activity. A year later, another young radical was sentenced to settlement in Eastern Siberia for composing an insolent epitaph for Alexander II after his assassination. One man found himself administratively exiled to Siberia because he was "suspected of an intention to put himself into an illegal situation." The journalist Mikhail Borodin was banished in 1881 to the territory of Yakutsk on account of a manuscript of "dangerous and pernicious content" discovered in his possession. This was a spare copy of an article about the economic condition of Vyatka province that Borodin had submitted to the progressive journal *Notes of the Fatherland*. Three or four months after his arrival in one of the most desolate reaches of Eastern Siberia, he discovered that his article had been cleared by the St. Petersburg censorship committee and published in one of the most widely circulated magazines in the empire.[14]

The political exiles of the 1870s and 80s were not content, as the Decembrists had been, to accept their banishment from the political stage and to act out their ideological commitments within the narrow confines of their own exile community. Following the example of the Poles in the 1860s, this new generation was determined to take its political struggle to the authorities. Although many, if not most, of the revolutionaries had never been put on trial, they set about converting the waystations, prisons and towns of Siberia into a giant public courtroom.

One form of struggle was escape. But escape for political prisoners was never simply about the pursuit of personal freedom. For those banished to Siberia for sedition, escapes were organized acts of political resistance, collectively planned and prepared. One former prisoner at the Kara penal settlement in the Nerchinsk Mining Region remembered the convicts' cells being set up like "expeditionary camps" with various individuals assigned different tasks to equip the would-be fugitives: sewing suitable clothing, toasting bread, salting fish and meat and so on. If they managed to flee the prisons, revolutionaries could draw upon extensive networks of sympathizers among the political exiles serving out their own terms of banishment across Siberia's towns and villages. (One group of escaped exiles holed up in a house in the town of Barzugin in Irkutsk province was captured because its noisy celebrations of the assassination of the tsar attracted the attention of the authorities.) By the 1890s, there were clandestine networks of exiles across Siberia who specialized in spiriting fugitive state criminals abroad.[15]

The authorities similarly treated the escapes of "state criminals" as acts of political resistance. When, in November 1878, a group of politicals that included the influential revolutionary Ivan Debogory-Mokrievich succeeded in changing names with common criminals as their deportation convoy left Irkutsk bound for Transbaikal, the minister of the interior, Lev Makov, deemed the news important enough to warrant the emperor's attention. When another group fled from the Klyuchi waystation near Achinsk, Alexander II personally condemned the "unforgivable blunder" and demanded that "those guilty should be sharply reprimanded." When Maria Kovalevskaya was returned to Kara following three years in the Irkutsk prison, the Ministry of the Interior insisted that her transfer be entrusted not to rank-and-file soldiers but rather to specially selected junior officers. The Siberian authorities also put up much larger rewards for the capture of political prisoners. Catching a common criminal would earn a Siberian peasant three roubles, while a political prisoner brought in fifty, a sum that, as officials reported, sent "not just the peasants but also their women" out on the hunt for such fugitives.[16]

One of the tsarist regime's most implacable foes in Siberia was a diminutive, dark-haired, pale-faced young woman named Yelizaveta Kovalskaya. Born in 1850 in Kharkiv province in today's Ukraine, Kovalskaya was the illegitimate daughter of a landowner and one of his serfs. Her childhood in a world in which her father still had the right to sell her mother imbued her with a deep loathing for the tsarist state. In the 1870s, Kovalskaya became an active member of the revolutionary underground, involved in the spread of subversive literature and in agitation among the working classes of Kharkiv, St. Petersburg and Kiev, where she was finally arrested in October 1880. From the moment a Kiev military tribunal sentenced her the following June to lifelong penal labour, Kovalskaya became a thorn in the side of the Siberian authorities.[17]

En route to Kara in a deportation convoy in September 1881, she was reported to be "the main instigator of disturbances in Krasnoyarsk," where she "provoked her guards" and "swore at the convoy commander." She led her fellow politicals on a hunger strike that won them some concessions before their party was broken up into smaller groups and taken to Irkutsk under heavily armed guard. Having arrived in the Irkutsk prison, Kovalskaya turned her mind to escape and, on 16 February 1882, together with fellow revolutionary Sofia Bogomolets, she quite simply walked out of the jail. The two women had fashioned dummies lying in their beds to fool the evening watch and then Kovalskaya had disguised herself as a female warder and led Bogomolets through the prison gates. A manhunt ensued and the two women were arrested ten days later with an accomplice in a house in Irkutsk. Kovalskaya was finally delivered to the women's prison in Kara in the early spring of 1882.[18]

Kovalskaya led several hunger strikes in protest at conditions there. Unruly and a bad example to other prisoners, in 1884 she was returned to Irkutsk, where she staged another escape. Leaving bundles beneath her bedding to fool her guards into believing she was asleep, she acquired a guard's uniform with the apparent connivance of one of the warders. Early in the morning of 2 September 1884, the guards manning the entrance to the Irkutsk prison opened the gates to allow a group of five prisoners accompanied by a warder to leave on a work detail. They realized too late that the warder was none other than Kovalskaya. The fugitive "disappeared without trace after her escape despite thorough searches of the town and surrounding exile settlements," which suggested to the Irkutsk procurator that the escape "was well-prepared in advance."[19]

This time, Kovalskaya remained at large for a month and a half, sheltered by a sympathetic physician in Irkutsk. Eventually, however, her luck ran out and a retired soldier discovered her whereabouts, captured her and turned her over to the authorities. He was handsomely rewarded to the tune of 200 roubles. Returned to the Irkutsk prison, Kovalskaya was put in solitary confinement. Still, she remained unbowed. Within months, she had joined another hunger strike in protest at conditions in the prison and, believing that her death would force the authorities into making concessions, she attempted to hang herself. Only the timely intervention of a warder saved her from strangulation. The Irkutsk provincial court sentenced Kovalskaya to ninety lashes for "her accumulated crimes over a period of thirteen and a half years." But Sergei Nosovich, the governor of Irkutsk, countermanded the punishment, worried as he was about the public perception of the flogging of a diminutive woman in poor health who was guilty of little more than non-violent, if fanatical, defiance. He argued that, in general, "women are spared corporal punishment and Kovalskaya has been certified as being unable to withstand the punishment." He decided to sentence her instead to lifelong penal labour in the gold mines of Kara, and as a regular criminal, not as a political exile. Kovalskaya refused to attend her own sentencing. A solitary female prisoner in the company of six gendarmes, she crossed the ice of Lake Baikal in the direction of the Kara penal settlement in Nerchinsk on 14 April 1885.[20]

In the wake of Alexander II's assassination in 1881, all those who had already been administratively sentenced to Siberia without formal charges ever having been brought were forced to swear an oath of allegiance to the new tsar, Alexander III. Many refused. In May 1879, the novelist and revolutionary Vladimir Korolenko had been exiled administratively to the town of Vyatka in European Russia as "politically extremely unreliable and harmful for public tranquillity." When, in June 1881, he was invited to take the oath "to be a loyal subject of the sovereign emperor," he declined. The minister of the interior, Nikolai Ignatyev, decided that, "in view of the hostile attitudes Korolenko has revealed and of his earlier harmful activities, it is necessary to exile him to residence in Eastern Siberia under close police supervision." Korolenko arrived in Yakutsk, more than 8,000 kilometres east of Moscow, in November of that year. In the absence of any funds of his own, he was awarded a monthly allowance of a miserly six roubles.[21]

 Some fared far worse. George Kennan made the acquaintance in 1888 of a couple, Ivan and Aleksandra Chernyavsky, who had been administratively exiled to Siberia ten years earlier. It had been shortly after the birth of their child in Tobolsk province in 1881 that they were instructed to take the oath of allegiance. They refused and, having once again betrayed their treasonous instincts, were sent further eastwards, first to Krasnoyarsk and then, following a second refusal, to Irkutsk. By then, winter had set in and they were travelling in an open carriage across hundreds of kilometres of frozen taiga. Aleksandra struggled to keep her baby warm during the journey, but when she removed its wrappings in the last waystation before Irkutsk, she found that it had died of cold. She was beside herself with the shock of this discovery, weeping and singing nursery rhymes to the dead infant. Kennan reported their case to horrified readers in the United States and Europe: "In the courtyard of the Irkutsk forwarding prison, in a temperature of thirty degrees below zero, Chernyavsky stood for half an hour waiting for his party to be formally received, with his wife raving in a delirium beside him and his dead child in his arms."[22]

The refusal to take the coronation oath set a pattern for never asking any quarter from the authorities. Sergei De-Karrer, a senior Ministry of the Interior official dispatched to Siberia in 1888 to investigate the conditions of "state criminals," offered the latter some advice. He suggested, especially to those with families, that their complaints would be best framed in terms of an appeal "with open-hearted repentance, to monarchical mercy." The exiles' response, he reported, was unequivocal: "No, we won't hear of it: We have suffered too great a punishment for that! The government might be able to tear us away from the environment in which it believes we can be harmful, but it cannot force us to renounce our convictions." The revolutionaries understood very well that the exercise of clemency was an exercise of sovereign power. To accept the tsar's mercy was to submit to his right to grant it. When one political prisoner, Sofia Shekhter, was informed that an imperial amnesty on 15 May 1883 had freed her from penal labour, she wrote to the authorities: "Believing no one to have the right either to punish or to show me mercy, and seeing both as acts of coercion, I hereby declare that I reject this act of clemency . . . I undertake to complete the entire sentence." For this act of defiance she was sent to settlement in the frozen wasteland of Yakutsk.[23]

Politicals could find their sentences of administrative exile suddenly extended without explanation. In 1887, Yegor Sinev had been admin-

istratively exiled for a period of three years to the village of Uzhur in
Yenisei province, where he busied himself with farming. At the end of
his term of exile, however, he was not released but, "without warning or explanation," found himself transferred to another district on
the orders of the governor-general of Eastern Siberia, Aleksei Ignatyev.
He wrote to the minister of the interior, Dmitry Tolstoi, to demand
an explanation for this unexpected extension of his exile: "I know of
no crimes on my part that might have entailed such a punishment, all
the more so as I have not spread any subversive ideas among the peasants . . . and if I had anything to do with them, it was only a result of
our mutual economic interests." Sinev protested that he had invested
a great deal of energy and resources in his farm and that it would be
quite impossible to engage in agriculture in his new place of banishment. The state subsidies were, Sinev argued, wholly inadequate and
he was now "suffering terrible hardship." The governor-general's office
declined, however, to revoke the extension of Sinev's term of administrative exile or even to offer an explanation for it. Sinev's crime, and the
reason for the three-year extension to his administrative exile and his
transfer to another region of Yenisei province was clear in the authorities' own internal correspondence. In September 1889, Sinev had sent
a petition to the minister of the interior containing "sharp criticisms of
the government's treatment of political prisoners and had expressed his
sympathy with them."[24]

Even though their sentences could be extended without explanation, some exiled radicals, like the Decembrists half a century earlier,
paradoxically found greater freedom in Siberia than in their native
lands. The relative weakness of state surveillance, the chronic shortages
of professional skills and the comparative indulgence of overburdened
and understaffed local administrations all contrived to create a more
permissive atmosphere in Siberia than in Russian towns and cities.
"Out here, nobody worries about saying what he thinks," Chekhov
remarked in a letter home to his family in June 1890. "There's no one
to arrest you and nowhere to exile you to, so you can be as liberal as
you please."[25] Banished for their political and civic activism in European Russia, many discovered in Siberia new opportunities to pursue
their economic, publishing and educational interests.

Administrative exiles—some of whom had been banished for being
"politically unreliable"—found work as accountants, officials and

inspectors even within the Siberian bureaucracy. Many turned to scholarship, continuing a tradition begun by the political exiles of the 1820s and 30s of investigating the continent's geography and geology. The democratic ideals of the politicals led many to study Siberia's indigenous peoples. Others organized expeditions to explore the remote regions of Transbaikal and the far north, and their findings benefited Siberian administrations keen to better understand and govern their own territories. The ethnographic research of one group of political exiles in the 1890s assisted the governor of Yakutsk province, Vladimir Skrypitsyn, with the drafting of land reforms designed to tackle the poverty of the indigenous Yakuts.[26]

Some political exiles continued their work as writers and journalists. The regional press found itself under less scrutiny from censors than the metropolitan press and won a reputation for unvarnished commentary on Siberia's administrative, social and economic problems. Political exiles dominated the editorial boards of newspapers and journals such as *Eastern Review* and *Siberian Gazette*.[27]

Although officially barred from teaching, exiles also played a key role, often behind the scenes, in promoting the development of education in Siberia. They acted as tutors in the homes of Siberian merchants and officials and helped to establish many of the libraries, museums and reading clubs in Siberian cities. They also worked to set up primary and secondary schools throughout their regions, wrote widely on the educational needs of the local population, and even championed teaching in the native languages of Siberia's indigenous peoples.[28]

These modest opportunities for activism notwithstanding, life for Siberia's administrative exiles remained a litany of petty official intrusions, daily humiliations and senseless restrictions. In many cases, the exiles were not permitted to leave the village without official permission and had to report at regular intervals to the police station; their correspondence passed through the hands of the Siberian authorities. They were, like the Poles before them, denied the right to practise their professions. One young medical student named Nifont Dolgopolov was exiled in 1880 from Kharkiv to Tyukalinsk in Tobolsk province for protesting against the brutal dispersal of a student demonstration. In Siberia, he worked unofficially as a doctor among the local peasantry and was severely reprimanded for doing so by the local chief of police. When, one autumn, the mother of the mayor of Tyukalinsk was accidentally shot in the leg, the local doctor, arguing that he did not have the requisite expertise, declined to extract the bullet himself. He recommended that the mayor turn to Dolgopolov as to "a skilled surgeon." With some reservations about the consequences for himself, Dolgopolov successfully performed the operation to remove the bullet. He was promptly arrested and imprisoned in the Tyukalinsk district prison, where he contracted typhus. Despite expressions of sympathy from the townspeople who brought him food and flowers in jail, and despite the prisoner's dangerously sick condition, the local police chief had him deported to the town of Ishim. Surprisingly, Dolgopolov eventually recovered in hospital. The case even found its way into the pages of the London *Times* in January 1884.[29]

Outraged at what they saw as the injustice of their punishments, politicals engaged in a host of acts of minor defiance. They refused to leave their cells for roll call; they refused to travel on barges together with common criminals; they refused to remove their hats in the presence of prison officials. One political exile in Balagansk insulted a portrait of the emperor in the local administration building, a crime which earned him a stint in the town's prison.[30] The authorities frequently noted that punishment of a single prisoner elicited a wave of protest from his or her comrades. The authorities found themselves locked in cycles of retaliation and escalation, which they could win only through the imposition of brute force. But for a government attempting to shore up its moral authority in the age of a flourishing, if still censored, regional and national press, such tactics carried risks of their own.

De-Karrer noted the very high level of solidarity among the politicals. He observed how, "as soon as one of them learns of the arrival of an administrative exile, even if he or she is a complete stranger, the rest rush to greet them and arrange a visit. They often find out in advance if someone is to be punished and offer to send them money and items, to assist in sending on their correspondence and so forth." In December 1884, a group of twenty-three administrative exiles passing through Yalutorovsk in Tobolsk province defied the orders of their convoy officer when they tore themselves free of their guards to greet a group of political exiles resident in the town. When the soldiers used their rifle butts to drive the exiles back into line, one exile attempted to seize a soldier's rifle and another stepped forward and tore the convoy officer's epaulettes from his shoulder. For these acts of resistance, the two exiles were sentenced to two and three months of imprisonment, respectively.[31]

This sense of solidarity rendered the authorities' task of disciplining and controlling the politicals far more challenging. It also meant that the perceived mistreatment of individuals could quickly spiral into a collective confrontation with officials. In 1888, one group of twenty administrative exiles under police supervision in the town of Surgut in Tobolsk province wrote to the governor, Vladimir Troinitsky, requesting that, in case of sickness, they should be allowed to travel to the town of Tobolsk for treatment without having to request his express permission on each occasion. Troinitsky refused. Tensions came to a head when one of their number, Ivanov, who was gravely ill, was finally released for transfer to Tobolsk only to die en route. Outraged, twenty-one exiles denounced the "reckless, lawless, unjust and immoral attitude of the authorities," and wrote to Troinitsky: "Our patience has run out, and the faint hopes we had that you might still have some shreds of decency have vanished. Your mockery of our sick comrades' requests and your attitude in general force us to look on you not as the governor of Tobolsk but as a *monster*! Consequently, we refuse to follow any more of your orders."[32]

Both revolutionaries and officials understood that, in a culture governed by deference and the authority of rank, to abuse the direct representative of the tsar was to abuse the autocracy itself. Troinitsky had the men arrested (to shouts of "Hail freedom!" and "Down with the government!") and, after two months in the Tobolsk prison, the ringleaders were exiled to Yakutsk province in north-eastern Siberia, "to territories less favourable to escape and among populations less susceptible to revolutionary propaganda." The rest were dispersed to far-flung villages across Tobolsk province. These punishments were administrative measures that required no further trials that "would have presented the political exiles with a platform to protest and to complain about their conditions."[33]

In provoking confrontations with the authorities, the political exiles played quite deliberately to a public gallery they knew to be sympathetic to their plight, though not always to their cause. If an official insisted upon implementing a strict observance of the law governing exiles and penal labourers, the politicals would "declare war on him in the Siberian press." De-Karrer noted with indignation:

> It is enough to peruse any edition of *Eastern Review* or *Siberian Gazette* to determine whether or not a particular official is strict with the exiles. It is well known that the majority of the newspapers' correspondents . . . are administrative exiles. The newspapers have, moreover, a broad readership and so even senior local officials take account of what they write. I have heard people saying, "did you read what they did to so and so?"[34]

In some cases, officials were intimidated by the exiles, fearful of the consequences for their own careers and postings should their captives escape.[35]

Concentrated in stable groups in Siberia's prisons, revolutionaries condemned to penal labour were even more difficult to manage. In 1880, the Ministry of the Interior ruled that all political prisoners serving terms of penal labour in European prison facilities should be transferred to Siberia. For political offenders, a sentence of penal labour had become, in effect, a term of imprisonment in one of Siberia's prisons. Most were sent to Nerchinsk, the men to the Lower Kara prison, the women further down the River Kara, to the Ust-Kara prison in the river mouth. Kara's importance as a site of penal labour had been in decline since the 1860s, but in the 1880s it became the central location in Eastern Siberia for the confinement of state criminals. At the beginning of 1882, there were 430 political exiles in Eastern Siberia; all 123 of those sentenced to penal labour for serious crimes were imprisoned in Kara.[36] The local authorities struggled to cope with prisoners who actively sought out confrontation with officials, as one report acknowledged:

> With only very few exceptions, political penal labourers do not consider themselves to be criminals. Not only do they express no remorse but, on the contrary, they seek out every opportunity to demonstrate their superiority. As a result, they are rude and insolent in their dealings with the authorities; they never

request anything but always insist and insist that their demands be instantly satisfied. If they are not, they declare "protests." They repeatedly violate prison discipline for no good reason but simply to express their scorn for the authorities . . . Even the most basic instructions by officials elicit scenes of the most unbridled disobedience and disorder and, of course, the instigators always find complete support and solidarity throughout the whole prison such that any individual disturbance immediately turns into a prison-wide rebellion.[37]

Some prison officials opted for a quiet life, pursuing a policy of not antagonizing the politicals, acceding to most of their demands and allowing them considerable freedoms and privileges. The liberal-minded head of the Lower Kara prison, Vladimir Konovich, permitted a relatively lax regime whereby prisoners were not fettered, were not required to undertake any work, were permitted to wear their own clothing and were allowed to live outside the prison in private cabins. One of Kara's political prisoners, Gavriil Belotsvetov, described conditions in a letter intercepted by the authorities: "Penal labour is not nearly as bad as people in Russia imagine . . . We all live in one prison . . . There are no warders inside, which in itself spares us a great deal of unpleasantness." The prisoners received all manner of journals and magazines from Russia and even found time to launch one of their own, entitled *Kara,* and to organize the occultist communions with the spirit world that were so fashionable among educated Russians at the time.[38]

Another of the politicals explained that, through his concessions, Konovich hoped to win assurances from the politicals that they would not attempt to escape, but they gave none; their principle, they declared, was "never to enter into any forms of obligation with the authorities." And indeed, the politicals considered escape an entirely legitimate form of revolutionary struggle. Konovich's liberal regime foundered on the determination of the political exiles of Kara to behave not as privileged prisoners but as implacable enemies of the state. In April 1882, eight "state criminals" escaped from the prison through the roof of an outbuilding. One of the organizers of the breakout was Ippolit Myshkin, who had been arrested for spreading revolutionary propaganda in the Russian countryside and sentenced to ten years of penal labour in the "Trial of the 193."[39] The authorities succeeded in tracking down and

capturing all eight within a matter of weeks but found the fugitives
to be carrying revolvers, bullets and daggers made available, it was
believed, by the laxness of the prison regime. Myshkin and a comrade
had got as far as Vladivostok before they were caught.[40]

The escape prompted Konovich's removal and a crackdown in the
jail. The surveillance regime was tightened up: prisoners were once
again fettered, their cells were searched, their reading material was
confiscated and their correspondence with their relatives was severely
restricted. But it was not until May 1882 that the flashpoint came.
In response to rumours that the authorities were preparing to shave
their heads, the prisoners barricaded themselves in their cells. The state
responded with a show of force. Some 800 Cossack infantrymen moved
into the prison and removed the convicts from their cells, chained them
and marched them out of the prison. The authorities decided to temporarily disperse this rebellious group of politicals among Kara's prisons
for common criminals while they redesigned the layout of the Lower
Kara prison in order to make collective protest more difficult.[41]

Responding to this crackdown, which they dubbed the "pogrom
of 11 May," seventy-three of the 113 political prisoners in the Kara
prisons declared a hunger strike. In a letter to the authorities written on
19 July, one week into the hunger strike, Myshkin listed the prisoners'
grievances. They ranged from the forced return to European Russia of
the mother of one of the inmates caught smuggling illicit correspondence out of the prison, through the shaving of prisoners' heads, to a
"mass of petty cavils and insults" from the prison authorities. Myshkin stressed how husbands were prevented from seeing wives who had
journeyed all the way to Siberia with the permission of senior government officials. The prisoners had been taken thousands of kilometres
from their family and friends, deprived of the right of corresponding
with their fathers, mothers, brothers and sisters. This constraint was,
Myshkin argued, evidence not of the "application of the law" but of
the "despotism of the local authorities." The final straw, however, had
been the flogging of a prisoner named Tsyplov, who although convicted
as a common criminal, had been punished for smuggling the politicals' correspondence out of Kara. "None of us," Myshkin protested,
"can now feel himself safe from such a humiliating retribution, which
outrages the spirit of anyone not morally deformed." The hunger
strike would continue until such time as the authorities gave written
assurances that "there would be no hangman's retribution for politi-

cal prisoners." Otherwise, Myshkin assured the authorities, the political prisoners at Kara would "rather die from hunger." But Myshkin was bluffing. The political prisoners in Kara were not yet ready to die for their cause. Having dispersed the convicts into smaller groups, the authorities daily brought food into their cells and left it overnight to seduce them into eating. The strategy worked and, one by one, the prisoners abandoned their hunger strike.[42]

The strike failed in its immediate purpose to force a return to the earlier, more tolerant regime in the prison. But in its secondary aim to foment discontent across Eastern Siberia and to cause outrage across the whole of Russia, the "hungry mutiny" succeeded for a time; joined by the female prisoners held in the Ust-Kara prison, the disturbances even reached the "common criminal convicts who conspired to escape and stopped working."[43]

In order to crush what threatened to develop into an organized revolt, the authorities proceeded to target the ringleaders of the hunger strike. Some were transferred to the Aleksandrovsk Central Penal Labour Prison, 70 kilometres outside Irkutsk, while eight, in a testimony to the Siberian authorities' own inability to cope with committed revolutionaries, were sent back to St. Petersburg. Myshkin was one of those returned to the capital, first to the dank casements in the Peter and Paul Fortress and, later, to the Shlisselburg prison. Following a violent confrontation with one of his warders in December 1884, Myshkin was sentenced to death by a military tribunal. He died before a firing squad on 7 February 1885.[44]

When the remaining male political prisoners were returned to the Lower Kara prison six weeks later, they discovered that the authorities had divided up the large barracks into smaller cells for groups of three to five, as opposed to the previous groups of twenty to twenty-five. Although warders were unable to prevent the prisoners from communicating with each other by means of knocks and shouts through the wooden walls, they noted with satisfaction that "the distribution of people into smaller groups significantly weakened the mutinous spirit of the convicts that had developed from their concentrations in large rooms."[45]

The disturbances in Kara had shown that the prisoners were determined to defend both their dignity and a set of rights conferred not by the state but common to all human beings. Corporal punishment could deliver a devastating psychological blow to this determination, however. Many, if not most, prisoners subjected to a flogging would break down and beg convulsively for mercy. The birch rods and the lash thus threatened physiologically to destroy the defiant dignity that many political prisoners maintained, often at great personal cost, during their captivity. On this occasion, officials in Kara gave the politicals assurances that none of them would face corporal punishment. It would be another seven years before this détente would unravel.[46]

When the exiled revolutionary and Kiev University lecturer Ivan Belokonsky made the journey to Eastern Siberia in 1880, he experienced the full range of transport means then at the state's disposal: marching convoys and waystations, river barges and railways. Over the previous two decades, the transfer of exiles to Siberia had become an enormous enterprise that sucked in increasing quantities of manpower and resources. Deportation to Siberia now reflected the Russian Empire's drive towards industrialization. Pre-modern and modern forms of transport were all deployed to process the burgeoning number of deportees in the second half of the nineteenth century.[47]

In 1867, the authorities had begun transporting convicts from Nizhny Novgorod to Perm along the Volga and Kama rivers. Two barges ploughed the route. The smaller, which was called the *Fabrikant,* was designed to carry 322 convicts; the larger, called the *Sarapulets,* could carry 475 and sailed with an escort convoy of twenty-eight soldiers. Through the summer months, the two ships each made twenty-five trips, delivering a total of about 9,000 convicts to Perm each summer. Overcrowding on the barges was a problem and became unbearable as the number of exiles surged. When Belokonsky travelled on the *Fabrikant* in 1880, he was one of forty-two political exiles among a total of more than 500 criminals on board. Conditions below deck were punishing: "The stuffiness in the cells was terrible, especially as there was only any ventilation through the open windows when the barge was in motion."[48]

An average of 11,200 exiles and their families entered Siberia each year in the 1860s; in the 1870s, it was up to 16,600, an average annual increase of 48 per cent from one decade to the next. No fewer than 28,500 exiles passed through Moscow in 1876; 15,000 were dispatched by train to Nizhny Novgorod, a further 11,500 were sent on to Siberia by other routes. In 1867, the contractors operating convict barges between Tyumen and Tomsk delivered a total of 5,000 exiles and their families; by 1876, the size of the human cargo had more than doubled. The company transported a total of 10,500 people: 8,000 exiles and 2,600 women and children accompanying their husbands and fathers.[49]

The convicts' journey into exile might have speeded up, but it still proved gruelling and, not infrequently, fatal. Prisoners, including political exiles, were setting out from Moscow already malnourished and weakened, provisioned on occasion only with dry bread and rotting fish. Women and children voluntarily following their husbands and fathers into exile continued to be locked up en route, in violation of rules that St. Petersburg had repeatedly affirmed. The state of the roads rendered travel on the springless carts a torture.[50]

Their health undermined by the bruising ordeal of the roads and rivers, both the exiles and their families fell sick in large numbers in the overcrowded, draughty and inadequately heated forwarding prisons and waystations. Polish revolutionary Wacław Sieroszewski, who made the journey to Yakutsk in 1879, gave a vivid impression of one of them:

> At night, when the cells were locked, and the tubs left out for our nocturnal needs, the air became saturated with a stench as if from a disinterred grave . . . Countless insects and fearsome biting cockroaches would hurl themselves on the sleeping men and women. There was no defence and no salvation from the parasites: bedbugs, fleas, lice and ticks. They used to fall from the ceiling, crawl out of every cranny to gather in the folds of our clothing. If they were killed, they would simply gather again in the same numbers. It was a rare convict whose skin on his chest and back was not covered with disgusting blisters and bite marks. The insects spread epidemics of typhus and skin diseases from one deportation party to another by means of clothing and especially linen, which was often old and badly washed when it was handed out.[51]

Throughout the 1880s and 90s, hundreds of prisoners died on their way to Siberia from tuberculosis, pneumonia, typhus and a range of other ailments and infirmities.[52]

The physical hardship, forced communalism, squalor and indignities of the journey elicited a mixture of shock and outrage among the political exiles, many of whom hailed from the empire's privileged classes. Deportation convoys accordingly became the site of confrontations between the political exiles and their guards. One group arriving in Krasnoyarsk in 1883 demanded the following concessions from the prison authorities: they must all be allowed to remain in one group; their prison cells must not be locked at any time; they must be allowed to keep their own clothes, bed linen and belongings; they must be allowed to eat together; they must be sent on as a single party, just as they had set out from Tomsk. It was only after the governor of Yenisei province arrived to threaten them with being driven into their cells by force that they finally submitted and entered the prison.[53]

In June 1888, a party of twenty-two administrative exiles reached the Tyumen forwarding prison by rail. When they learned that they were to continue their journey to Omsk on carts and on foot in the company of common criminals, they refused to proceed and demanded that horses or steamships be made available to transport them. One of the exiles later explained that, worn out from extended solitary confinement and not being blessed with robust health, they were very scared of the prospect of such a lengthy and exhausting journey. "Besides, we had heard of the horrors to which political exiles were subjected in the deportation convoys, including cases of convoy soldiers beating political prisoners, and attempting to rape the women." The authorities did not give way, and a tense standoff ensued inside the prison as the political prisoners refused to leave their cells and threatened to defend themselves. Dragged one by one into the courtyard, they again formed a huddle, shouted abuse at the warders and attempted to push their way back into the prison buildings. But the exiles were no match for the armed soldiers who outnumbered them. They eventually resigned themselves to proceeding on foot.[54]

The authorities took a dim view of this relatively minor display of defiance. Indifferent to the exiles' insistence that theirs was an "act of disobedience, not resistance" and, following the personal intervention of Alexander III, who urged "severe punishments," the authorities handed down heavy sentences. The leader of the group was stripped of his rights of rank and condemned to eight years of penal labour, two others were sentenced to settlement in Yenisei province and the rest received prison terms of up to one year. Having been administratively exiled to Siberia without any judicial process, they now found their initial sentences altered to extended periods of exile and even to terms of penal labour. Acts of defiance by administrative exiles were met with still harsher sentences, setting a pattern of mounting resistance and intensifying punishment.[55]

Within this cycle of escalating confrontation, 1889 would prove a decisive year. Two violent showdowns between the exiles and their captors were to have far-reaching consequences in the struggle for political power in Russia. Each would severely damage the moral and political authority of the tsarist regime and feed the outrage and hatred that were fast becoming the psychological animus of the revolutionary movement.

In the 1880s and 90s, in addition to being a destination for political exiles, the town of Yakutsk became a staging post for the exiles' deportation to the desolate snowbound settlements of Vilyusk, Verkhoyansk and Kolyma, in the frozen wilderness of the Arctic Circle.[56] Eager to clear a backlog of exiles that had accumulated in Yakutsk over the winter of 1888–9, the acting provincial governor, Pavel Ostashkin, ordered the local authorities to press ahead with the deportation of the exiles in temperatures below −20°C. Ostashkin further imposed restrictions on the size of the parties allowed to travel together under armed guard. No more than four exiles were permitted in a single group. He also drastically cut the weight of luggage and provisions that the exiles were allowed to take with them further north.[57]

This new deportation regime was scarcely intended to find favour with the exiles. The first to face an onward journey under these conditions was a group of some thirty administrative exiles, including almost a dozen women and children. On 22 March 1889, the exiles refused point blank to proceed and delivered a petition insisting that the governor rescind the order to force them to continue their journey in such lethal temperatures. They then barricaded themselves in a large wooden house, in the apartment of one of Yakutsk's resident exiles, and awaited the governor's response. Their protests fell on deaf ears, for the Yakutsk authorities were suspicious that the exiles wished to remain in Yakutsk until the spring, simply in order to escape.[58]

When Ostashkin's instructions to surrender were ignored, the gov-

ernor ordered a unit of Cossacks to surround the building and to drag
the exiles into the yard by force. In the ensuing struggle, the exiles
attempted to defend themselves with sticks and knives, and one of them
produced a revolver and opened fire on the soldiers, who fled. When
the governor arrived to take charge of the situation, there was a further
exchange of fire that culminated in the assembled troops shooting at
the building for several minutes until the revolutionaries surrendered.
According to some estimates, as many as several hundred rounds were
fired. By the time the exiles capitulated and the acrid smoke cleared
from the apartment, six exiles, a police officer and a soldier lay dead;
several more, including Ostashkin himself, were wounded.[59]

In the aftermath, the exiles insisted that they had fired only in an
effort to defend themselves from violent assault by the soldiers; the
state meanwhile claimed that what had taken place was a premeditated rebellion against the lawful authority of the governor of Yakutsk.
The state turned over the surviving exiles to a military tribunal, which
determined that all those who had signed the petition were guilty of
"armed insurgency." In June, it sentenced the three alleged ringleaders to death, a further fourteen to lifelong penal labour and the rest
to fifteen-year terms of the same. On 7 August 1889, Lev Kogan-
Bernshtein, Albert Gausman and Nikolai Zotov were hanged in the
courtyard of the Yakutsk prison.[60] Each penned valedictory letters to
his family and comrades in the long night before the execution. Zotov
wrote to his parents:

> I am in good spirits, even elated, but I feel a terrible physical
> and nervous fatigue. The strain upon my nerves over the last
> two days has been unbearable. So many strong emotions! Well,
> my dearest ones, my family, my loved ones, I embrace you all
> for the very, very last time. I die very easily, conscious of the
> justice of my cause, with a feeling of strength in my breast. I
> fear only for those dear to me whom I will leave behind. What
> are my sufferings—they last but a few hours? What strength
> will they need to endure! . . . The guards have just entered.
> They have brought the convict's clothes and I have already
> changed into them. I am sitting here in a canvas shirt and I am
> frightfully cold. Do not think that my hands shake from fear.
> Farewell, farewell, my dear ones![61]

Desperate and surrounded, without the weapons necessary for defending themselves, the exiles had been no match for the armed force of the Russian state. The battle fought in Yakutsk on 22 March 1889 was, however, part of the wider war for public sympathy being waged in the pages of both the Russian and the international press. The "Yakutsk Tragedy" caused a scandal that reverberated around Russia and beyond. The revolutionaries understood the nature of this wider war for public opinion, and they pursued it skilfully. Even as he faced the gallows, Zotov grasped the power that the story of events in Yakutsk could wield. "Here is my testament," he declared in his final letter to his comrades back in Russia:

> Steel yourselves, and under the impression of the finale of these horrors, this slaughter, this butchery, make use of this drama, this colossal example of the cruelty, arbitrariness and inhumanity of Russian despotism with all the means at your disposal . . . Write to every corner of our motherland and abroad to all the [George] Kennans . . . This is the only way we can recoup our losses in this terrible act of state vengeance.[62]

By the autumn of 1889, revolutionary pamphlets detailing the "despotic cruelty" of the Yakutsk authorities were, indeed, circulating throughout Siberia and European Russia. Political exiles in Irkutsk province dispatched a letter to Alexander III himself denouncing Ostashkin's "outrageous and bloody punishment" of the political exiles.[63]

In Europe and the United States, the press was no more sympathetic to the authorities. The reactionary regime of Alexander III was widely reviled; Kennan's journalistic crusade against the exile system and the steady flow of memoir literature by political exiles in London, Paris and Geneva fanned the flames of anti-tsarist sentiment. The Russian-language émigré journal *Social Democrat,* published in London, declared that "the exploits of the tsarist cannibals are so eloquent that they require no commentary." *The Times* of London reported the incident on 26 December 1889, calling it a "slaughter of political prisoners in Siberia" and declaring that "this tale of blood and horrors is a story which the Russian government cannot afford to pass over. Superior to public opinion as it professes to be, there is a point beyond which it can not go in disregarding the verdict of mankind." *The New*

York Times followed in February with a lengthy article entitled "Men Shot Down Like Dogs: The True Story of the Yakutsk Massacre."[64] The tsarist state was creating a legion of Siberian martyrs, but seemed blind to this danger. A month after its bloody settling of scores with the survivors of the Yakutsk tragedy, the Siberian authorities were to be provoked into another blunder just as damaging for the government's credibility and legitimacy. The instigator was Yelizaveta Kovalskaya.

Adjutant General Baron Andrei Korf was governor-general of Priamursk, an office with direct responsibility for the political prisoners in Kara. Korf was a man of robustly conservative views and a critic of what he held to be St. Petersburg's excessive leniency in its dealings with "state criminals." On 5 August 1888, he made an official visit to the Ust-Kara prison and, coming across Kovalskaya sitting in the courtyard, ordered her to stand in his presence. She refused. "As a prisoner," she recalled, "I absolutely *could not* stand up before the enemy against whom I had not ceased to struggle, even in prison." Korf was outraged by this demonstration of defiance from a notorious political exile with a track record of having a "harmful influence" on other prisoners. Two days later, he instructed that Kovalskaya be transferred to the Verkhneudinsk prison, near Chita, and placed "under the strictest conditions," in solitary confinement. He was explicit that the punishment should "set an example to others."[65]

On 11 August, Masyukov, the commandant of the women's prison in Kara, had Kovalskaya manhandled, half-naked, from her prison cell in the dead of night. She was made to dress in regular convict clothing in the presence of male criminal exiles, carried out of the prison and transferred by boat to Sretensk. Kovalskaya's fellow women prisoners reacted with outrage. Maria Kaluzhskaya, Maria Kovalevskaya and Nadezhda Smirnitskaya denounced this "base mockery of a state criminal." They wrote to the authorities in Irkutsk demanding a formal investigation of this "scandalous violation of the law," and also Masyukov's removal from office. Relations between politicals and the prison authorities deteriorated sharply over the following year as the prisoners engaged in three separate hunger strikes only to abandon them on each occasion as death drew near. This was dangerous brinksmanship. On 31 May 1889, Gurevich, one of the Kara doctors sent to examine the female prisoners, reported that they were indeed "manifesting the symptoms of starvation . . . all have an increased heart rate and a very unpleasant smell from their mouths, quickened pulse, sleeplessness and apathy." Within days, however, the prisoners' resolve began to weaken and they were unable to refuse the food that was brought daily to their cells.[66]

Then another of Kara's female prisoners, Natalya Sigida, initiated a dramatic escalation in the conflict. The twenty-eight-year-old daughter of a merchant from Taganrog (her family and Anton Chekhov's were neighbours) and a member of the People's Will, Sigida had been sentenced to eight years of penal labour for operating an underground printing press. Recognizing that the women would not succeed through their hunger strike in forcing concessions from the authorities, she requested a meeting with Masyukov at the end of August 1889. Admitted into his office, Sigida declared, "I had hoped that you would be removed from your post, but the authorities have paid no attention to our declaration and so I will insult you personally." Walking up to Masyukov, Sigida slapped him in the face. In what had become, for both the revolutionaries and the prison authorities, an attritional contest over moral authority and political legitimacy, striking a senior prison official was a symbolic assault on the imperial state.[67]

Determined once and for all to stamp his authority on the unruly political prisoners in his charge, on 26 October, Korf ordered a clampdown at the Kara prison. The warders were informed that the regime would henceforth

> be fundamentally changed so that no indulgence would be shown. In the case of any further disturbances . . . they are all, *en masse*, to be placed on normal convict rations and deprived of everything they have been allowed to acquire with their own money, not excepting writing materials and such like. If any of the prisoners show any kind of resistance . . . it is to be met with armed force, regardless of the consequences. Troublemakers are to be subjected to corporal punishment without the slightest concession.[68]

Most scandalous for the revolutionaries, Korf ordered that Sigida receive 100 strokes of the birch rod. The impression made by this

uncompromising disregard of the traditional exemption of both educated Russians and women from corporal punishment is difficult to
overstate. Amid widespread public opposition to the use of corporal
punishments even on common criminals, to flog political prisoners
drawn from the educated ranks of Russian society was to transgress
accepted moral standards; to subject a young woman to 100 strokes
of the birch rod was to perpetrate an atrocity. The Kara physician
Gurevich refused either to sanction or to attend the flogging in view
of Sigida's poor health. Undeterred, the authorities proceeded with the
punishment in the absence of a doctor on 7 November 1889. In the
moments before the flogging, Sigida "declared that the punishment was
the equivalent of death and lay down voluntarily beneath the birch."[69]

These were not empty words. After she was returned to her cell
later that day, Sigida and her three fellow prisoners, Kovalevskaya,
Kaluzhskaya and Smirnitskaya, poisoned themselves. Sigida died that
evening, the others over the course of the following two days. When
news of the flogging reached the political prisoners in Kara, the suicidal
protests spread. Naum Gekker, a political exile who had already been
released to settlement beyond the walls of the prison, shot himself but
survived. Within a week, seven prisoners in the men's prison had also
attempted to overdose with morphine. More followed their example.
In total, twenty prisoners took poison and six died.[70]

The fatal drama that played out in Kara was a public contest
between revolutionaries and the state over control of the prisoners'
bodies. The radicals denied the state the right to punish them physically, and in so doing denied the authorities the right to treat them as
common criminals. By taking their own lives, Sigida and her fellow
revolutionaries used corporal punishment as a spectacle to underline
the illegitimate violence of the authorities and, by extension, the tyranny of autocracy itself. The Decembrist Ivan Sukhinov had hanged
himself in his cell in Nerchinsk in 1828 because to submit to a flogging
was to submit to humiliation *as a nobleman;* for the revolutionaries
of the 1880s, the same punishment was an assault on their dignity *as
human beings.* "I was left with no choice but to die," Sergei Dikovsky
explained in the aftermath of the mass poisoning, "because neither
my education nor my strong sense of human dignity *permit me to live*
under the permanent threat of such terrible humiliation and shame."[71]

An unrepentant Korf was, meanwhile, no less concerned with

dignity, but in his case this was with the dignity of his office. On 14 November, he sent a telegram to the minister of the interior, Ivan Durnovo:

> You know that I am not a cruel man, but if there were such a case again, and even if I knew what the results of the punishment would be, I would nevertheless order that it be carried out, so convinced am I that we must put an end to the disorder in our political prisons. It is humiliating that we have reached the stage where criminals can strike our senior officials. I believe that to tolerate any further the licentiousness that these monsters and regicides have enjoyed as a result of the softheartedness of Petersburg would be against my [coronation] oath. I understand very well that many in Petersburg and elsewhere will censure me, but I must fulfil my sacred obligations.[72]

Censure him they did. Together with the "Yakutsk Tragedy," the "Kara Tragedy," as it was quickly dubbed, dealt a body blow to the moral authority and legitimacy of the tsarist regime in its struggle with the revolutionary movement. Kennan reported on the case to a horrified audience in Europe and the United States: "Madame Sigida and her . . . companions were just as truly put to death by the East-Siberian officials as if their throats had been cut in the prison courtyard by the prison executioner."[73] In February 1890, *The Times* of London reported the fate of the "refined and highly educated woman" Sigida as follows:

> Such infamies were not perpetrated on ladies of rank and position even in the time of the Emperor Nicholas. The humiliation of this barbarous form of punishment so affected Madame Sigida that, in her distress and her fear of other tortures the future might hold in store, she poisoned herself. What can have happened is as yet a mystery—but evidently the women political prisoners, particularly those who by their position and education are especially susceptible to anything that could compromise their honour and sense of self-respect, thought they were no longer safe from the insults of the authorities.[74]

The New York Times gave detailed accounts under the headlines "Exiles Driven to Suicide: The Horrors of Siberian Political Prisons" and "Russia's Brutal Cruelty" of what it termed Sigida's "shocking official murder" and "the outrage in the political prison at Kara."[75] On 9 March 1890, "a very large demonstration" gathered in London's Hyde Park in protest at the "inhuman conduct of the Russian government in its treatment of political prisoners, who, without trial, are exiled to Siberia, the living tomb of countless thousands of noble men and noble women, whose only offence is that they aspire to enjoy the political freedom which we in England have inherited from our forefathers." To rousing cheers, one of the speakers declared:

> It was the duty of Englishmen to protest against, and to draw public attention to, the horrible state of social and political enslavement in which the Russian nation found itself . . . Scores of brilliant men and noble women in Russia, for the crime of asking for political freedom, were rotting in underground dungeons and in cells which were too low for them to stand up in and too small for them to lie down in . . . After a travesty of a trial, young men and beautiful women were dragged off to work in the silver and lead and salt mines, to be worse than beasts of burden, and to undergo frightful privations and cruelties. These poor prisoners, marching for miles through the snow, laden with chains and handcuffed, dropped down on the roadside like rotten sheep, and those who lived, and particularly the women, were subjected to the foulest indignities. Could Englishmen look on these things with equanimity?[76]

Kennan's fierce criticisms of the exile system also fed into a rising tide of sympathy for the revolutionaries abroad. Upon his return to the United States from his travels in Siberia, Kennan lectured to audiences on the exile system, often appearing onstage with half his head shaved and clad in rags and chains, like a Siberian convict. His message was clear: "The Siberian exiles are not wild fanatics, they are men and women who have given up all that is dear to them and have laid down their lives on what we regard as the essential and fundamental rights of a human being." The Siberian Exile Petition Association had chapters in fifty American cities in the 1890s and gathered over 1 million signatures on petitions protesting against the tsarist treatment of political prisoners. At Kennan's lecture in Boston in 1890, Mark Twain rose from his seat and tearfully exclaimed: "If such a government cannot be overthrown otherwise than by the use of dynamite, then thank God for dynamite!"[77]

After his arrival in London in July 1884, the revolutionary Sergei Kravchinsky, the assassin in 1878 of the chief of Russia's political police, General Nikolai Mezentsev, began raising the profile of Russian radicals languishing in tsarist penal settlements and prisons. His publications, among them *The Russian Storm Cloud* (1886) and the largely autobiographical *The Career of a Nihilist* (1889), were warmly received by the English public. Together with the famous Russian anarchist Peter Kropotkin, himself a fugitive from Siberia, Kravchinsky helped to establish the Society of Friends of Russian Freedom in London on 31 March 1890. The stated goals of the society were to help the victims of tsarist abuses, to arrange financing for escapes of political prisoners and to call attention in the West to the need for reform in Russia. In August 1890, the society published its first English-language newspaper, which, by November, had over 100,000 subscribers. Such excoriating condemnation could not but damage the Russian autocracy, consolidating on the international stage the view of a brutal and tyrannical regime. So widespread and resonant was the image of the sympathetic Russian political dissident in Victorian Britain that it even found its way, in the character of Mr. Szczepansky, into Edith Nesbit's *The Railway Children* (1905).[78]

Responding to widespread international sympathy for the plight of political prisoners in Russia, the British, French and Swiss governments refused to extradite radicals to face a tsarist justice system that was widely believed to flout the most basic principles of legality and to subject its prisoners to inhumane treatment. As a consequence, Georgy Plekhanov (the father of Russian Marxism), Yury Martov, Lenin and Josef Stalin were all able to pursue their revolutionary activity abroad without fear of interference from European governments.[79]

At home, as soon as censorship preventing the open discussion of events in the domestic Russian press collapsed in the 1905 Revolution, news of the tragic events in Kara and Yakutsk filled the pages of both radical and liberal publications. At the very moment when the tsarist regime was fighting for its survival, tales of brutality and despotism in

Siberia only further damaged its credibility in the eyes of the Russian reading public.[80]

Perceptive members of the government were quite aware of what was happening. The governor-general of Western Siberia, Nikolai Kazna-kov, reported that the exile system was only incubating sedition in Siberia. It was quite impossible to keep the thousands of administrative exiles dispersed across the continent's towns and villages under effective surveillance, he argued, and banishing them to Siberia "hardly has the effect of convincing them of the error of their ways but rather only further embitters them." The administrative exile of subversives, Ministry of the Interior official De-Karrer observed, served to forge revolutionaries into cohesive groups, "feeding their conviction that they have suffered an injustice and bolstering their spirit of resistance."[81]

The revolutionaries themselves agreed. Gekker, whose own suicide attempt in the wake of Sigida's flogging had failed, looked back on his time in the Lower Kara prison with something approaching a sense of pride: "Entire generations of our revolutionary youth passed through Kara, and for many dozens . . . it was an alma mater, a higher school of development and education." Alarmingly for the authorities, Siberia's political exiles were keen to share this education with the towns-people and villagers among whom they lived, as Dmitry Anuchin, the governor-general of Eastern Siberia, observed in 1882: "It must be said that by means of exile, the government is itself and at its own expense spreading anarchist teachings in places like Eastern Siberia that had never heard of anything of the sort."[82]

Kennan was convinced that "it was not terrorism that necessitated administrative exile in Russia; it was merciless severity and banishment without due process of law that provoked terrorism."[83] Surveying the violence that engulfed the Russian Empire during the 1905 Revolution, the liberal legal theorist Vladimir Gessen—no fanatical revolutionary himself—was clear in his own mind that:

> The future historian . . . if he wishes to understand the impla-
> cable hatred and the insane brutalisation of the masses that
> have given rise to an anarchy of bloodshed and terror, will of
> course remember that the generation to which the difficult his-

torical task of renewing the state in Russia has been given is a sick, politically and morally corrupted generation. It is a generation that has never seen any state order other than one of emergency police measures, exceptional for their cruelty.[84]

In 1889, the writing was already on the wall. The revolutionary journal *Social Democrat* issued a warning in its commentary on the violent showdown in Yakutsk that year: " 'Woe to the vanquished!'— that is what the government wishes to say with its barbaric and cruel treatment of the revolutionaries who have fallen into its hands. So be it! There will come a time when it will feel all the merciless severity of that rule."[85] The government would have approximately a decade to wait. If guilt had been the inspiration of the revolution, vengeance would prove its lifeblood.

13

The Shrinking Continent

On the afternoon of 19 November 1877, an undistinguished-looking 17-metre schooner named *Dawn* dropped anchor alongside the Customs House on the bank of the Neva River in St. Petersburg. An excited crowd of onlookers had gathered to catch a glimpse of the ship. The *Dawn* had just completed the first successful maritime voyage from the Yenisei River in Eastern Siberia to St. Petersburg. It had crossed the Kara and Barents seas, before circumnavigating Scandinavia by way of Vardø, Christiania (Oslo), Stockholm and Helsingfors (Helsinki) to finally reach the Russian capital. By common consensus both in Russia and abroad, this was a prodigious feat of seamanship: a half-decked sailing boat without a keel and with a crew of only five had navigated the ice floes and storms of the barely charted, and notoriously dangerous, Arctic seas. The ship had already enjoyed a triumphal passage through the coastal towns and cities of Norway, Sweden and the Grand Duchy of Finland, where it had been enthusiastically received by crowds of well-wishers; its crew had been celebrated in the national press and treated to feasts in its honour.

By the time the *Dawn* reached the Customs House on Vasilevsky Island, however, it bore only four of the five crew members who had set out from the Yenisei on 9 August. Andrei Tsybulenko was absent, as the daily *St. Petersburg News* drily noted, "for reasons beyond his control."[1] Tsybulenko had been arrested that morning when the ship docked in the naval base of Kronstadt, following a tip-off from the Russian consul in Christiania. Tsybulenko was, it had emerged, an exile from Yenisei province who had illegally made the passage from Siberia back to European Russian and was, therefore, a fugitive from justice. On orders from the minister of the interior, Aleksandr Timashev, he had been taken into custody and detained in the Kronstadt fortress.

The authorities intended to deport Tsybulenko back to Yenisei province, where he would remain in exile for the rest of his life, but by January 1878, Tsybulenko had been released from custody and had received an official pardon from Alexander II and even awards and commendations from both the influential Imperial Society for the Advancement of Russian Merchant Shipping and the Ministry of Trade.

Tsybulenko's remarkable reversals in fortune—from exile in Eastern Siberia, to member of a celebrity crew of intrepid seamen, to prisoner of the state in Kronstadt, and finally to pardoned fugitive—reflect mounting public opposition to the use of Siberia as a penal colony. From the 1850s, leading figures in Russia's scientific, commercial and political elites began to challenge the established view of Siberia as a frozen, inhospitable wasteland, suitable only as a place of banishment for the empire's criminals. They argued for a re-imagining of Siberia as a rich economic colony, one which had been neglected by the state and crippled by the exile system but which harboured, in fact, a wealth of natural resources awaiting exploration and development. These strategic criticisms of the government's use of Siberia as a continental prison joined the rising tide of moral opposition to a system characterized by brutal floggings, by destitution and degradation of the blameless wives and children of convicts and by the martyrdom of revolutionaries.

Perceptions of Siberia in imperial Russia were unstable and constantly evolving. In the middle of the eighteenth century, most Russians had seen Siberia as a mercantile colony of the state, a view which chimed with Russia's new-found identity as a colonial empire.[2] Comparing Siberian rivers such as the Lena to the Nile, for example, the great polymath Mikhail Lomonosov had dedicated odes to the natural riches of the continent and declared in the early 1760s that "Siberia will foster the growth of Russian imperial grandeur." Catherine the Great herself had envisioned Siberia as a self-sufficient colonial realm.[3] By the end of Catherine's reign, though, much of Siberia's alluring lustre, and the colonial optimism it sustained, had begun to dim.

The fur trade, which had driven expansion eastwards in the sixteenth and seventeenth centuries, had declined precipitously in the eighteenth, while the metallurgical works that had been pioneered under Peter the Great could not match the economic importance of that "soft gold." As Siberia's economic significance diminished, its status as a penal colony increased. At the same time, for both the Russian government and much of the Russian educated public, the image of Siberia as a gold mine was gradually displaced by a menacing picture of an Asiatic wasteland of barren, frozen expanses.[4] In 1841, the journal *Notes of the Fatherland* aptly summarized the baleful and pessimistic image of the Siberian continent that had taken hold in the popular imagination. It dwelt on the inaccessibility of Siberia to trade routes: "As long as the current laws of nature obtain in our world, the mouths of the Ob and Lena will be blocked up with ice . . . Siberia will long be fated to remain a wasteland." Russia would be better off, the author averred, if the continent's "ocean of snow" were replaced with a real body of water, which would at the very least facilitate maritime trade with the Far East. These images of an ice-bound and impenetrable Siberia were subject to radical revision in the 1860s and 70s. The opening of a sea route to Eastern Siberia forged not only real but also imaginary links between Siberia and European Russia.[5]

The exile system occupied an ambiguous position within these shifting views of Siberia. On the one hand, punishment and colonization in Siberia were in theory compatible, and this presumption was embedded in the very nature of the exile system. Mikhail Speransky's reforms of 1822 had envisioned the exiles' and penal labourers' eventual conversion into disciplined and motivated settlers who would populate Siberia and bind it to Russia with their culture and their industry. On the other hand, it was only by virtue of its backwardness and the harshness of conditions for its exiles that Siberia retained its punitive qualities. This unresolved contradiction, already familiar from Britain's Australian penal colonies, remained at the heart of the exile system over the nineteenth century.

Whatever the wider vision of Siberia in the empire, the very idea of penal colonization was unravelling on the ground. Official disquiet was mounting about the costs, the inefficiency and the wholly disruptive effects of disgorging hundreds of thousands of exiles into Siberia. Report after report and commission after commission stressed the almost intolerable burden the exiles—deracinated, destitute, often sick or crippled and frequently hardened criminals—were imposing on the native population of Siberia and the voluntary migrants who had settled there.[6] Regional governors and government inspectors repeatedly lamented the ways in which the exile system was not merely failing to develop the untapped potential of Siberia but actively impeding the colonization of the continent by the genuine settlers, the local peasantry. These officials, often very clear-sighted about the contradictions inherent in the policy of penal colonization, argued for a range of reforms, from restricting the numbers being exiled, to a complete abolition of Siberian exile. In 1835, one major investigation concluded that the government's ambition to colonize Siberia with criminals was foundering:

> The best of intentions and the most noble of goals frequently prove unworkable because they are not matched by the resources necessary to implement them. It is enough to examine the physical and moral condition of the exile settlers in recent times to convince oneself of this truth. An exile settler is a man you will meet on the road, almost naked in spite of the ferocity of the Siberian winter, withered by hunger, filthy, downcast and with a clear expression of suffering in his eyes . . . The death penalty would be a blessing in comparison with the life of torture and exhaustion that destroys all the strength of his body and spirit.[7]

Beyond the failure of penal colonization, officials frequently argued that exiles were significantly impeding the economic development of Siberia and, by extension, of the empire as a whole. One notable commission, headed by Adjutant General Nikolai Annenkov, recommended in 1851 that exile to settlement be abolished in favour of penal labour in which the convicts would be held exclusively in prisons, forts and factories. In the latter stages of his reign, Nicholas I also ordered officials to investigate "whether or not it might be possible to end exile to Siberia and leave it only for penal labourers." The state, however, merely tinkered at the margins of the system over the course of the 1850s and 60s. It introduced piecemeal improvements to the physical infrastructure of waystations and penal forts and attempted to address the most egregious cases of malfeasance and incompetence within the exile administration. These minor improvements were swept aside by the sharp increases in the numbers of criminals being exiled to Siberia each year, beginning with the crushing of the January Uprising in Poland in 1863.[8]

Why did the tsarist regime persist with the use of a penal system that was so manifestly damaging to the economy and society of Siberia itself? Part of the answer lies in bureaucratic inertia and in the perceived increased costs that would be occasioned by the construction of an alternative: a prison system to house European Russia's malefactors in their native regions. Yet the answer also lies in the fact that, in both the official and the public imagination, Siberia remained for the first half of the nineteenth century an inhospitable wasteland essentially unsuited to economic development. Its role as a sprawling, backward and impenetrable penal territory overshadowed any alternative role as an economic colony that could be successfully integrated into European Russia. Impenetrability was not without its benefits, after all. Conservatives in government were apt to see the primeval backwardness of Siberia as the very guarantor of its success as a "vast prison without a roof."[9] Nicholas I's long-serving minister of foreign affairs and leading conservative statesman in the Holy Alliance, Karl Nesselrode, expressed scepticism about the merits of annexing the Amur, on the grounds that it would render the Pacific too accessible to the exile population:

> Up to that time, remote Siberia had been for us a deep sack into which we tossed our social sins in the form of exiles and penal labourers and so on. With the annexation of the Amur, the bottom of this net would be torn open and our convicts might be offered a broad field for escape along the Amur to the Pacific.[10]

Nesselrode and other opponents of development were, however, fighting a losing battle to keep Siberia isolated. A fundamental reorientation of public interest in Siberia began to occur in the mid-nineteenth century. Impelled by humiliating defeat in the Crimean War (1853–6), nationalist sentiment prompted the educated classes to turn away from Europe and to look to Siberia as a site for imperial exploration, expansion and influence.[11]

Public champions of ethnographic, geographical, geological and commercial exploration in the middle of the nineteenth century, the empire's flourishing voluntary associations promoted the "discovery" of Siberia as a bountiful Russian colony. Driven by a combination of patriotic, scientific and entrepreneurial interests, these societies came to play an increasingly prominent role in the shaping of public debate about Russia's colonial mission in the East. Organizations such as the Imperial Russian Geographical Society, founded in 1845, were animated by a patriotic desire to see Russia fulfil its imperial destiny in Siberia, tap the boundless natural resources of the continent and establish itself as a great imperial power to rival the British and the French.[12] The governor-general of Eastern Siberia, Nikolai Muravyov (later Muravyov-Amursky), vice-president of the Geographical Society, declared to its members in 1850: "Siberia conceals in its depths such productive forces that await only man's enterprising hand to transform them into a never-ending source of richness for the state and the Russian people."[13]

Determined to pursue his great colonial ambitions for Siberia, Muravyov pushed for further Russian expansion into the Amur River Basin, which lay between the lands of Transbaikal and the shores of the Pacific. The territory was still nominally under the control of a weak and vulnerable Chinese Empire, but by marshalling both military power and diplomatic acumen, in 1858 Muravyov succeeded in orchestrating its annexation. Siberia now had a major waterway that flowed into the Pacific. Within a decade, steamships were ploughing the route, boosting Siberia's trade with the Far East. Muravyov's second cousin, the exiled anarchist Mikhail Bakunin, was effusive in his praise of what the Amur annexation heralded: "Through Amur, [Siberia] was linked to the Pacific and is no longer a wilderness without an outlet," he wrote to fellow radical Alexander Herzen. In moving "closer to America and Europe than to Russia, it is being ennobled and humanised. Siberia—a blessed country of the future, a land of renewal!"[14]

This re-evaluation of Siberia became more influential in the second half of the nineteenth century and found favour with other senior figures in the government who shared Muravyov's energy and ambition. The minister of transport, Konstantin Poset, was one such proponent of the empire's colonial mission in Siberia. In the 1870s, he laid plans for the construction of the Trans-Siberian railway, a project which was delayed until the 1890s by the costs of the Russo-Turkish War of 1877–8. Following his return to the capital from his third tour of Siberia, in May 1874, Poset wrote a report entitled "Ending Exile to Siberia," which made the case that the exile system was frustrating Russia's imperial ambitions in the East: "A gigantic territory, two and a half times the size of European Russia, the riches of which have not been properly assessed and explored, has been condemned to serve as a place of residence for all the criminals from a population of 70 million people." Such a policy had made sense, Poset continued, "when Siberia, ending in Kamchatka and the Sea of Okhotsk with only the barren Pacific Ocean beyond it, was itself considered a deserted land settled only by wild and nomadic peoples." Now, though, the Pacific Ocean was becoming each day more like the Mediterranean Sea and, following the annexation of the Amur River Basin in 1858, Russia extended directly to that sea. The states that neighboured Siberia had opened up and were developing quickly: "Now it was essential to give Siberia the opportunity of developing, to remove from it the brand of 'land of criminals.'"[15] It was no coincidence that Poset hurried aboard the *Dawn* when it dropped anchor in St. Petersburg to congratulate the crew on their successful voyage.

The voyage of the *Dawn* was the brainchild of Mikhail Sidorov, a millionaire industrialist, explorer and ethnographer. A man of expansive interests and of means expansive enough to pursue them, Sidorov made a signal contribution to the development of Eastern Siberia in the 1860s and 70s. Having married into a wealthy Siberian merchant family in 1858, he came to develop extensive gold and graphite mining operations in Yenisei province. Beyond his obvious commercial interest in the development of Siberia, Sidorov was also committed to the well-being and development of the Russian North and was the author of several books and articles on the region, its native peoples, wildlife and mineral resources. Sidorov was convinced of the possibilities of using commerce to drive forward the colonization of Siberia and, by the mid-1860s, he was actively lobbying senior figures in the administration of Siberia to adopt trade-friendly policies. He published a pamphlet in 1864 entitled "The Possibility of Settling Northern Siberia by Means of Industry and Trade and on the Development of Siberia's External Trade," which he presented to the governor of Tobolsk, the governor-general of Western Siberia and the minister of finance. Sidorov argued for the necessity of constructing a merchant fleet, for the introduction of a favourable tax regime for enterprises in Siberia and for the transformation of existing factories and mining industries.[16]

In the late 1860s and the 1870s, Sidorov sponsored a number of attempts by Norwegian and English explorers to navigate the waters of the Barents and Kara seas and, in 1869, he offered the princely sum of 14,000 roubles to the captain of the first vessel that transported some of his graphite down the Yenisei and into the Kara Sea, through the Kara Strait and the Barents Sea, around the northern coast of Scandinavia, and back to the capital. Then, in 1875–6, Sidorov himself organized an expedition to navigate a route from the Yenisei River to St. Petersburg. The successful opening of commercial navigation would enable him to export his graphite to Europe more easily (the Trans-Siberian railway was a still distant prospect and Siberia's roads, as ever, notoriously poor), but he had a wider ambition to promote the economic activity of Eastern Siberia by opening up new trade routes. This was not the first attempt at the perilous voyage. Ships had successfully reached the Yenisei and Ob rivers from the Kara Sea, but as yet no vessel had managed to complete the journey from Eastern Siberia to European Russia.[17] The difference was significant. Penetration into Siberia from European Russia was a matter of exploration; the movement of shipping *from* Eastern Siberia back *to* the capital implied boundless commercial opportunities. And in Siberia, enterprise was a patriotic endeavour.

In 1876, Sidorov ordered the construction in the town of Yeniseisk of a 25-metre ocean-going clipper, *Northern Lights,* from the only shipbuilder capable of constructing such a vessel on the Yenisei. Sidorov charged the Baltic German David Shvanenberg with captaining the ship, loaded with Sidorov's graphite, out of the mouth of the Yenisei and back to St. Petersburg. On his arrival overland in Yeniseisk in June of that year with Finnish first mate Gustav Numelin, Shvanenberg found that no sailors were available and so was obliged to put together a crew from local workmen with no experience of sailing. The ship finally set sail out of the Yenisei and into the Kara Sea on 6 September, but rapidly encountered ice and storms that tore the sail and forced the vessel back into the river. Shvanenberg took the decision to leave the ship anchored for the winter in the mouth of the Yenisei and, having failed to find the materials locally to repair the sail and re-equip the *Northern Lights,* to return to St. Petersburg. He left Numelin and the other three members of the crew—Chesnokov, Taburin and Korotkov—to maintain the ship through the winter months

in preparation for another attempt at the voyage the following summer. Shvanenberg had arranged for them to receive provisions from the
nearest settlement, 150 kilometres away, but the provisions were never
delivered and, for more than six months, Numelin and his companions
were left to fend for themselves.

Shvanenberg was able to dispatch a rescue party the following
spring, but when they finally reached the vessel on 29 April 1877, the
rescuers came across a pitiful scene. Korotkov and Taburin had died
of scurvy; wolves had eaten Chesnokov; and Numelin, who had succeeded in fending off the predators with the assistance of the ship's four
Siberian dogs while caring for his sick companions, was in a state of
delirium. The rescue party comprised another ship's mate, an Estonian
named Eduard Meivaldt, and one Andrei Tsybulenko, in addition to
two local hunters who had agreed to help locate the *Northern Lights*
from the town of Dudinka, some 360 kilometres away. Able to save
Numelin, the rescuers were unable to do the same for the ship. Confronted with temperatures that had dropped on 12 November 1876
to −46°C and that were still registering at −14°C on 5 May 1877, the
stricken crew had not managed to keep the ship free of snow and ice.
When the ice finally began to break up on 6 June, it gradually crushed
the trapped vessel as the Yenisei flooded. Numelin and his four companions were forced to take shelter at the riverbank on the roof of
the hut in which the Finn had spent the winter. There they remained
trapped for eight days on a surface measuring 4 square metres, working in shifts to fend off the ice floes (the waters rose to within 30 centimetres of the roof), while the river flooded for 30 kilometres in every
direction.[18]

Happily for Shvanenberg, the captain had meanwhile gained from
Sidorov the equivalent of a blank cheque to commission the construction of as many replacement vessels as were necessary "as long as I did
not return to Petersburg overland." Having completed his own perilous voyage through the Siberian forests, Shvanenberg himself finally
reached the *Northern Lights* on 16 July and supervised the evacuation
of the ship.[19] The ship proved damaged beyond repair, but Shvanenberg
succeeded in purchasing a new vessel, a river barge used for transporting goods up and down the Yenisei. Having unloaded what remained
of the cargo of the *Northern Lights,* the crew then spent two weeks
with the help of Siberian natives converting this barge into a primitive

schooner capable of sailing on the open seas. The alterations complete, Shvanenberg, showing no little optimism, renamed the ship *Dawn*.

Essentially unsuited to the open seas, the *Dawn* was only 17 metres long and 4 metres wide; it had no keel, only a half-deck that was badly equipped with navigational instruments and almost incapable of sailing against the wind. It was, however, a product of Siberia itself, built with local expertise. Able to find only one replacement sailor, a Finn named Kuzik, Shvanenberg turned to Tsybulenko, who also had never sailed before, as the fifth member of the crew.

A former army scribe in the 72nd Tula Infantry Regiment, Andrei Tsybulenko was an exile to Siberia. A military tribunal in Ryazan had convicted him in 1873 of "drunkenness, offending his sergeant major with foul language and manifesting disobedience and a lack of respect to his infantry commander." He had been stripped of all rights and properties and sentenced to four years in the Smolensk military-correctional battalion followed by exile to settlement in Siberia. Banished to a village in Yenisei province, in 1875 Tsybulenko received a permit to seek work more widely in the province and thereafter disappeared from official view, only to reappear a year later in the rescue party that saved Numelin. As an exile, Tsybulenko was forbidden from ever returning to European Russia, and this was a fact of which Shvanenberg was aware. Assisting an escapee would have made the captain an accessory, so Shvanenberg came up with the following solution: "I convinced Tsybulenko to sail with us only as far as the Baideratskaya Bay [on the shores of Tobolsk province in Western Siberia], from whence he could easily reach Obdorsk, and then travel up the Ob River back to Yenisei province."[20]

Having made final preparations and taken on board, in addition to graphite, a number of artefacts of ethnographic interest and examples of local wildlife, the *Dawn* set sail up the Yenisei from the settlement of Gochikha on 9 August 1877. Navigation in the poorly charted waters of the mouth of the Yenisei proved very difficult. On a number of occasions, the ship almost ran aground. As it approached Baideratskaya Bay on 13 August, storms and heavy ice floes prevented the ship from reaching the shore and thus made it impossible for Tsybulenko to disembark as planned.

The *Dawn* ploughed on through gales and rough seas teeming with ice that threatened to puncture its hull. The crew members were forced at all times to stand guard on deck in order to fend off the ice floes with their oars. Deprived of sleep, frozen stiff and utterly exhausted, the sailors almost perished in a storm that struck their vessel in the treacherous Kara Strait. Their determination, skill and endurance paid off, however, and they survived this brush with disaster before navigating the Barents Sea and finally reaching the Norwegian port of Vardø on 31 August.

The telegraph station in Vardø immediately began to broadcast news of the *Dawn*'s intrepid voyage, and the crew members were hailed as heroes in every Scandinavian town in which they docked. As news of the voyage spread, the tsar himself sent a message of congratulation to the Society for Merchant Shipping, and the Scandinavian and British press began to run with the story. In Christiania, Gothenburg and Stockholm, police were needed to control the crowds of well-wishers who gathered on the quayside, the crew were fêted by local dignitaries, and celebratory dinners were held in their honour. On their arrival in the Norwegian capital on 17 October, the crew was greeted by the Russian consul, who invited all the Norwegian ministers to attend a dinner in honour of the ship and her captain. The consuls of England, Germany and France also held separate dinners to celebrate the crew's achievement. The Russian consul's response to the arrival of the ship was not, however, confined to the raising of champagne flutes and the proposing of toasts. On 28 October, he wrote to the Ministry of Finance: "I consider it my duty to report . . . in advance the presence of an exile, Tsybulenko, on-board the schooner *Dawn*." This troubling news was passed on to the Ministry of the Interior, which, clearly embarrassed and irritated by the presence of an exile on board a ship that was garnering such attention at home and abroad, responded with an instruction on 11 November to arrest Tsybulenko and arrange "his overland deportation back to Siberia" as soon as the *Dawn* arrived in the capital.[21]

The *Dawn* finally sailed down the Neva and into St. Petersburg against the international backdrop of the Russo-Turkish War and while Russian society was rejoicing in a patriotic mood. In November 1877, Russian forces in the Balkans were laying siege to Pleven and had successfully captured the fortress of Kars on the Turkish-Armenian border in one of the decisive battles of the conflict.[22] The pages of the Russian press were full of jubilant reports from the theatre of war, and a mood of optimism gripped the empire. This new-found imperial self-confidence, coming as it did a mere twenty years after Russia's crushing humiliation in Crimea, bolstered the claims of those who argued that Russia had a great destiny to pursue in Siberia. For the development of "Our East" was an important geopolitical goal in the reign of Alexander II, and the assimilation of Siberia was central to the prosecution of the empire's commercial and strategic interests in the Far East.[23] The need to explore a sea passage between St. Petersburg and Siberia was further heightened when Alexander II's government took the decision in 1867 to sell Alaska to the United States, a move so unpopular that it created a public backlash. Ministers were accordingly eager to draw attention to the state's sponsorship of Siberian exploration and to foster entrepreneurship as a way of putting the controversy behind them. An unforeseen consequence of the sale of Russia's North American colonies was the rapid decline of the road network in north-eastern Siberia (these highways had previously been maintained by the Russian-American Company as a transport route for both goods and people to and from Alaska). Against this background, the opening of maritime routes in and out of Eastern Siberia acquired great practical as well as symbolic significance.[24]

More broadly, the European powers' incipient "Scramble for Africa" was also offering an object lesson in the relationship between exploration, colonization, economic power and imperial prestige (the Russian press even carried stories of Henry Morton Stanley's encounter with David Livingstone in the autumn of 1877). The voyage of the *Dawn* was evidence to the Russian public that the Russian Empire, like its British and French rivals, was no slouch when it came to the exploration and economic development of its own annexed territories. The broader imaginative canvas of Siberia as a colony that harboured a wealth of untapped resources infused the achievement of the *Dawn* with a significance beyond the undoubted heroism of the voyage itself.[25]

While Siberia's role in Russia's imperial destiny was being championed, the continent's role as a place of exile was being roundly criticized. The growth of abolitionist sentiment rehearsed arguments that had arisen in Britain's American colonies in the 1770s and, subsequently, in Australia in the 1830s. On both continents, the economic development of the colonies undermined the deterrent effect of penal deportations. What had previously appeared as harsh wildernesses over time transformed into what appeared to many to be desirable destinations, from which return was no longer so difficult if things did not work out. Rising prosperity in the colonies also generated a backlash among the colonists themselves, who protested against their land being used as a dumping ground for the mother country's criminals.[26]

The tsarist state's use of Siberia as a place of exile was first criticized by those best placed to judge its deficiencies: its administrators. By the 1870s, almost every senior official in Siberia was pleading with St. Petersburg to reduce the number of exiles being deported annually to the regions and towns in their charge. In 1871, the governor-general of Western Siberia, Aleksandr Khrushchev, requested that no more exiles be sent to the towns of Tobolsk province and that deportations to Tomsk province be halted for a period of ten years.[27] In 1875, the governor of Tobolsk, Yury Pelino, turned to the forthcoming construction of the Trans-Siberian railway to underline a central paradox at the heart of the state's attempts to both develop Siberia and use it as a place of exile: "Preparing to move closer to European Russia by means of a new railway, Western Siberia is about to enter a new phase of intellectual life and economic activity. It can, therefore, scarcely preserve the conditions suited to exile that it had when it was an almost uninhabited country." Pelino pointed out that, while the northern reaches of Western Siberia did remain only very sparsely populated, exiles flocked to the urban centres. Listing the familiar litany of complaints about feckless and criminal exiles parasitizing the hard-working Siberian peasants and merchants, Pelino appealed to St. Petersburg to end exile to Western Siberia and to settle its criminals in "another, more distant territory." The more distant territories (of Eastern Siberia) were, however, struggling to cope with their own quota of penal labourers and exiles without assuming additional responsibility for the thousands of administrative exiles entering Western Siberia every year.[28]

The contradiction was increasingly stark. Exiles were being concentrated in the more densely populated regions of Siberia that no longer required an influx of penal colonists. At the same time, due to lack of facilities and resources, the state was not sending significant numbers to less densely populated areas that were in greater need of colonization. Between 1887 and 1896, an annual average of some 5,600 people were being exiled to the more developed Western Siberian province of Tobolsk; an average of just 160 were being sent each year to Yakutsk province in Eastern Siberia. Ethnographer and journalist Nikolai Yadrintsev observed in 1889 that such a distribution "completely defies the colonial goals of exile."[29]

Various government commissions were established in the 1870s and 80s and charged with devising solutions to the state's reliance on Siberia as a dumping ground for criminals. Their findings were unanimous in their condemnation of a system that was no longer fulfilling its three punitive roles: "security, deterrence and correction." Each one proposed a series of reforms in legislation to reduce the numbers being exiled each year and to promote the construction of prisons. One influential commission, established in 1877 and drawing on senior officials from all the key ministries and legal experts, found after two years of regular sittings that "it is perfectly obvious that the reason for the disarray in the exile system lies in the very legislation governing it; in the unfeasibility of the very goals it has pursued up until now; in the shortage of funds, the shortage of experienced administrators; in the shortcomings of Siberia's location for penal colonization; and in the vast scale on which exile was used."[30] The commission further acknowledged that, if exile was an obstacle to the development of Siberia, the reverse was also true:

> There can be little doubt that exile has, to a large extent, expended its former punitive power. It used to be a terrible punishment when it was preceded by torturous corporal punishments, an exhausting journey via the waystations in fetters, which lasted between one and a half and two years . . . at a time when the exile used to have to search for a means of sustenance in almost deserted territories. Yet . . . with the introduction of improved means of transporting convicts by rail, by ship and by carriage, with the increasing population of Siberia, exile has simply become a form of population resettlement.[31]

The commission's proposals to abolish exile to settlement were rejected by the government "in view of the financial difficulties that would be associated with its abolition" (a reference to the costs of constructing the large-scale penitentiaries in European Russia). But the price of maintaining the exile system was also spiralling. By 1869, the deportation convoys operating between Nizhny Novgorod and

Achinsk, on the border between Western and Eastern Siberia, involved a total of 56 officers, 96 senior non-commissioned officers, 470 junior non-commissioned officers, 1,900 privates and 56 scribes. One government audit in 1876 estimated that the government spent 660,000 roubles on the transfer of exiles to Siberia: 94,500 roubles on feeding them and 46,500 on clothing them; 429,000 on transportation costs; 69,500 on treating the sick and so on. By this time, critics of the exile system were challenging the argument that it was a relatively cheap form of punishment. The government was spending, Yadrintsev claimed, no fewer than 800 roubles per exile per year.[32]

Government officials and, increasingly, the wider public were well aware that the right of peasant and merchant communities to administratively exile their own members deemed guilty of "immoral behaviour" was open to all manner of abuses. Between 1882 and 1898, more than half of the 148,000 men and women exiled to settlement in Siberia were administrative exiles, and the overwhelming majority (94 per cent) had been banished by their own communities. In Siberia itself, a chorus of senior officials was pleading with St. Petersburg to restrict the numbers of administrative exiles. The governors of Tomsk and Tobolsk provinces reported that, "given the flood of voluntary settlers, there were almost no more available areas suitable for the settlement of exiles" and that it was extremely difficult to assign any more exiles to existing peasant communities, which were already "absolutely inundated with criminals." Exiles already accounted for 25 per cent of the population of some of the districts of Irkutsk province, and officials there pronounced the addition of any more "extremely undesirable."[33]

In the era of the Great Reforms, these arguments were beginning to seep out to the public sphere, taken up in a range of publications denouncing the dysfunctions of the exile system. Public opposition grew ever louder. Yadrintsev's devastating critique, developed over the 1870s and 80s, exploded the official myths about the colonial and rehabilitative benefits of exile. Yadrintsev argued that the exile system effectively disgorged into Siberia hundreds of thousands of unproductive, violent criminals, who then proceeded to parasitize the local population before "dying out without a trace." Siberia's riches were ignored by Russia and the region had been left "as if forgotten, and with each passing day it falls further behind the neighbouring countries of the East."[34]

By the mid-1870s, Siberian towns were themselves loudly protesting the debilitating effects of the exile population thrust upon them by the state. The Tara town duma in Western Siberia complained in 1874 that the exiles from European Russia "had brought with them idleness, drunkenness, fraud, corruption, unruly conduct and even robbery and murder." The Chita town duma in Eastern Siberia lamented in 1881 that "the most unsuitable element is dispatched to us, the most hardened criminals, who . . . bring to the society and to the region as whole . . . debauchery, drunkenness and the science of crime."[35]

A now flourishing Siberian press carried a flood of denunciations of the exile system and calls for its abolition. The local population was begging the state, the Irkutsk weekly *Siberia* reported, to liberate it from the burden of having to deal with Russia's exiles:

> The territory is burdened with taxes to support the thousands of deportation convoys; its villages are swamped with exiles whom the peasants have to feed and support . . . thousands of exiles and penal labourers swarm down the roads and before them lie defenceless Siberian villages. There are up to 30,000 vagabonds scattered across Siberia whom the peasantry has to feed under the daily threat of armed robbery, murder and arson. Towns are awash with crime.[36]

The magazine *Eastern Review,* published in Irkutsk, insisted in 1891 that the government should strive for "the replacement of exile as a system of penal colonisation with a new system [of building prisons]—so common in Western Europe." Opposition to the exile system was one of the rallying cries of the Siberian regionalist movement, led by Yadrintsev and Grigory Potanin. The regionalists strove for greater autonomy from St. Petersburg and for an end to Siberia's second-class status as a colony of Russia.[37]

Nationally, the tide was also turning against exile. The influential "thick journals"—*Notes of the Fatherland, Herald of Europe, Russian Thought, Northern Herald, Russian Wealth*—which were the very imprint of civil society, produced a barrage of articles denouncing the failings of the exile system and its role as an obstacle to the colonization of Siberia. *Russian Thought* argued that "exile has not only failed to strengthen the colonial wave but it has rather impeded it, discrediting Siberia in the eyes of the Russian people as a land of criminals and renegades." Whereas Great Britain's penal colonization of Australia had established a prospering population of almost 3 million, Siberia's towns and cities had barely grown over the preceding decades: Yeniseisk still only numbered 12,000 residents, Tobolsk 20,000. The state's attempt to colonize Siberia with criminals had been a "complete fiasco."[38] *Russian Wealth,* meanwhile, claimed that the history of penal colonization across the globe had shown that, as soon as the colonies achieved a certain level of economic and civic development, "the new criminal element becomes an onerous burden for the colony and creates significant obstacles to its further development, and the colony tries with all its might to rid itself of these dangerous guests." Such had been the history of North America, Tasmania, Western Australia and New South Wales. The same process was now occurring in Siberia: "For several decades both Siberian society and expert studies have been demonstrating all the damage exile has caused to the civic development of Siberia, its pointlessness as a form of punishment and the necessity of abolishing it. Russia has, nevertheless, persisted with this system of reform and colonization, which has never yielded any of its intended benefits."[39]

When the *Dawn* docked at the Russian naval base of Kronstadt on the morning of 19 November 1877, Tsybulenko was arrested and taken down to the cells of the fortress. With the rest of his crew, Shvanenberg sailed on to St. Petersburg, "anxious that perhaps a similar fate awaited me if the *Dawn* were suspected of the deliberate transfer of exiles." Shvanenberg's doubts were quickly dispelled by the warm welcome he received from the director of the Customs House, Nikolai Kachalov, and by an inspection of his boat by Konstantin Poset, the minister of transport, who had long called for the abolition of Siberian exile. There then followed a dinner at Kachalov's residence that was attended by many dignitaries. As Shvanenberg later recalled, "No Russian skipper had seen the likes of such a reception in Russia since, of course, the glory days of Peter I and Catherine II."[40]

It was into this perverse set of contradictions—the ship's crew celebrated by senior figures within the imperial government and navy, while one of its members languished in a prison cell—that the expedition's financier Sidorov stepped, marshalling his forces for what would prove to be a sustained campaign not only for Tsybulenko's release from custody, but also for his eventual pardon by the emperor. In making their arguments, Sidorov and his allies emphasized the reinvigorated image of Siberia as a wealthy colonial territory whose riches could be unlocked by the daring and endeavour of patriotic men such as Shvanenberg and Tsybulenko. The image of Siberia as Russia's imperial destiny was thus pitched against the established, but eroding, image of the continent as a giant prison from which escape was an act of social and political defiance.

On the very day the *Dawn* finally dropped anchor at Vasilevsky Island in St. Petersburg, Sidorov learned from Shvanenberg of Tsybulenko's detention and wrote a letter to Timashev, the minister of the interior, appealing to him to revoke the arrest warrant. The petition was an artful example of political manipulation, and it spoke to a newly reinvigorated spirit of colonial enterprise in Siberia: "Andrei Tsybulenko . . . was one of the causes of Russia's current glory in merchant shipping, and with yet another important feat has adorned the history of the reign of Our Tsar-Liberator." The Society for Merchant Shipping would be especially delighted, Sidorov declared, if the minister agreed to intercede with the emperor to secure a pardon for Tsybulenko.[41]

Events were already unfolding very rapidly beyond the direct control of ministers. Even before the *Dawn* reached the Russian capital, the Russian press had picked up news of its voyage from the Scandinavian papers. On 18, 19 and 21 November, the daily *Voice* and *Stock Market News* both gave detailed accounts of the ship's exploits drawn from reports in the Swedish and Finnish press. The newspapers dwelt on the extraordinary bravery of the crew, the tragic fate of the *Northern Lights,* the triumph of the *Dawn* and the enthusiasm and admiration with which the ship was greeted on its passage through Scandinavia. *St. Petersburg News,* meanwhile, shifted attention to the crowds that had gathered around the ship on the quayside to see "the brave sailors and their fragile little boat."[42] The newspaper emphasized both the commercial and the patriotic significance of the voyage: "The passage, navigated from the Yenisei to the shores of Europe by a little sailing boat, shows the full possibility of establishing steamship navigation that connects the Yenisei, and thereby virtually the whole of Siberia, with Europe by a cheap trade route."[43]

It was against this background of mounting public interest in the voyage of the *Dawn* that the members of the empire's voluntary associations, including the most prestigious of them all, the Imperial Russian Geographical Society, gathered to celebrate the opening of a sea route between Siberia and the capital. The achievement was widely reported in the press, and the eulogies flowed thick and fast. At a crowded sitting of the Society for Merchant Shipping, the geographer Fyodor Studitsky declared: "Yes you, the *Dawn,* will be a dawn for all Siberia and for our merchant fleet! We can boldly declare that navigating out of the Siberian rivers is a new dawn for Siberia!" The society elected Shvanenberg and the two shipmates lifetime members and presented Kuzik and Tsybulenko with watches bearing a portrait of the tsar, the same tsar who had yet to pardon Tsybulenko.[44]

Two discordant narratives about Tsybulenko thus collided. The first was of a fugitive convict who had defied the will of the tsar and had fled his place of exile; the second and much more powerful narrative was of an intrepid seaman who had executed a daring voyage from the heart of Siberia to European Russia, a feat with important implications for Russia's ability to develop and exploit the continent to its east.

In a reflection of both Sidorov's personal influence and the mounting public attention drawn to Tsybulenko's case, senior figures within the government moved swiftly to secure a pardon. On 15 December, with the support of other senior ministers, Timashev took the case to Alexander II. On 13 January 1878, the tsar granted the exile a full pardon, and even had him presented with a silver medal bearing the inscription "for diligence." On 1 February, Tsybulenko signed his release papers as "Former Exile, Andrei Ivanovich Tsybulenko."[45]

It was against the background of changing public perceptions of Siberia that the state stepped up its colonial policies in the late 1880s and the 1890s. Laws were passed in 1889 encouraging the movement of settlers to state lands, and the construction of the Trans-Siberian railway in the 1890s projected the industry and culture of the "Russian nation" into Siberia.[46] The railway was intended, in the words of Nicholas II, "to connect the natural abundance of Siberian lands with Russia's network of rail communications," but it served no less to connect Siberia's exiles with the lands from which they had been expelled. As the iron road stretched out through the taiga, it linked towns and cities across Siberia, each with large numbers of settled exiles. By 1900, the locomotives of the Trans-Siberian were steaming through Tyumen, Omsk, Krasnoyarsk and Irkutsk. The numbers of voluntary migrants heading to Siberia to take advantage of the free land soared as trains began to run on its western sections. Each spring, when the government reduced the fare for a family of four to below a month's wages in a St. Petersburg or Moscow factory, special trains carried Russia's land-hungry peasant and working-class settlers eastwards in the tens of thousands. Contemporaries used the term "resettlement" rather than "colonization" to refer to what had indeed become a mass migration of Russian peasants within the existing borders of the empire.[47]

The Russian press hailed the construction of the railway as an "iron bridge" between Europe and Asia. If Peter the Great had "opened a window" onto Europe, the *St. Petersburg News* gushed, then Nicholas II had "opened the gates of the great ocean for us," leading Russia to a "new threshold of international life." After 1894, the annual influx of new migrants to Siberia fell below 100,000 only during the conflict with Japan in 1904–5. Siberia was booming, and as it boomed, the exile system appeared more and more starkly a relic from another era.[48]

By the 1890s, only Sakhalin and some of the more remote settlements in the far north of Siberia remained remote and inaccessible. For the rest of the continent, the Main Prison Administration acknowledged in 1899 that "the arduous nature of the journey and the impossibility of returning to European Russia" were no longer credible circumstances: "With the construction of the Siberian railway, exile has, it should be acknowledged, outlived its time."[49] In 1900, a wide-ranging government report likened the exile system to serfdom. A historical anachronism, it had long outlived its original purpose and was now hampering the modernization of the state:

> If exile is understood as a form of penal colonisation, then it harbours within itself basic obstacles to its own success . . . The continued transfer of exiles there is burdensome and harmful for a country which already has an independent life and can no longer be considered "a vast prison without a roof."[50]

By the end of the nineteenth century, the emerging consensus was that, if the empire were to unleash its slumbering colonial energies beyond the Urals, Siberia had to be liberated from the burden of supporting Russia's criminals. The government needed to abolish the exile system.

A growing chorus of moral outrage at conditions for Siberia's exiles bolstered these strategic considerations. The serious literary journals were awash with short stories by Chekhov, Vladimir Korolenko and a host of lesser-known writers that chronicled the brutalizing conditions in Siberia.[51] The publication of Chekhov's *Sakhalin Island* in 1893 delivered a devastating blow to the image of the exile system and to the legitimacy of the state that administered it. A series of autobiographical, ethnographic and journalistic works in the decade that followed, among them Pyotr Yakubovich's *In the World of the Outcasts* (1896) and Vlas Doroshevich's *Sakhalin* (1903), lined up to denounce the exile system for its inhumanity. George Kennan had, meanwhile, made a name for himself even in Russia as a ferocious critic of the exile system. Although the tsarist censor prevented the publication of Kennan's articles and books in Russia, they were still picked up, summarized and discussed in the pages of the Russian press.[52] The fate of women, children, administrative exiles, political prisoners and the hapless Siberians themselves commanded page after page of reportage clamouring for reform. Most educated Russians by now considered Siberian exile to be the embarrassing vestige of a barbaric past and evidence of Russia's backwardness among its European neighbours.

Perhaps the most influential condemnation of Siberian exile came in 1899 from the pen of Leo Tolstoy. His last great novel, *Resurrection,* offered an unflinching portrait of the degrading conditions in which men, women and children made the gruelling journey into exile and the destitution, depravity and violence they endured when they arrived. After three months in Siberia, the hero of the novel, Nekhlyudov, observes that the exile system:

> had been specially invented to create the highest degree of corruption and evil, unattainable by any other means, with the specific aim of disseminating the corruption and evil over the whole of society on as wide a front as possible. "It's as if they had run a competition for corrupting the greatest number of people in the most effective and infallible way," thought Nekhlyudov, contemplating all that was being done in the prisons and at the waystations. Every year hundreds of thousands of people were reduced to the lowest level of depravity, and when they had been thoroughly corrupted they were set free in order to communicate the corruption acquired in prison to the rest of the population.[53]

By the turn of the twentieth century, such views had become the common consensus in educated circles. Liberals condemned the abuse of individual rights; conservatives the moral and sexual corruption of exile families. Siberian exile was, perhaps, the only social issue of the day that had managed to unite in condemnation an otherwise polarized public sphere.

Faced with mounting pressure from within the state administration, from the population of Siberia and from Russian public opinion at large, the government finally grasped the necessity of reform. On 6 May 1899, Nicholas II ordered the establishment of a commission, chaired by the minister of justice, Nikolai Muravyov, "to address the urgent question of abolishing or limiting exile whether by the courts or administratively by rulings of merchant guilds and village assemblies." Across the political spectrum, the Russian and international press hailed Nicholas's edict as long overdue and as an important step in the right direction. The liberal daily *St. Petersburg News* reported that "all of Russia has learned with a sense of moral relief of the forthcoming abolition of exile, the ending of a centuries-old injustice." The conservative *New Times* was no less effusive: the imperial edict "will remove from Siberia the shameful brand of a land of exiles and penal labourers and is a sacred moment not only for Siberia but for all of Russia. It establishes the foundations of humaneness and justice in those spheres of Russian life that had hitherto lagged behind progressive trends and behind the humanitarian ideas of our times."[54]

The findings that the commission submitted to the State Council a year later scarcely lived up to this soaring rhetoric, however. The resulting legislation on 10 and 12 June 1900 retained "penal labour" but no longer stipulated that it had to be accompanied by exile to Siberia. The new laws also reduced exile to settlement. Half of the some 300,000 exiles in 1900 had been sent there by their own communities' administrative verdicts, bypassing the courts. The new legislation removed these powers from merchant guilds while retaining them for village assemblies. It did, though, remove the right of peasant communities to refuse to accept the return of an exile once an initial judicial sentence had been served, a provision that had accounted for over 43,000 administrative exiles between 1882 and 1898. Village assemblies continued, nevertheless, to wield the power to exile their own members for "immoral behaviour," a flexible category that covered everything from drunkenness to violent crime and accounted for nearly 27,000 administrative exiles passing through the Exile Office between 1882 and 1898. The legislation did reduce the scope for exile to settlement for common criminals and, following a programme of prison building in European Russia in the 1880s and 90s, ordered that greater numbers of them should be incarcerated in their native regions rather than exiled.[55]

Muravyov's commission was quite frank about the reasons for these half-measures. The state could not strip peasants of their extra-judicial powers of banishment because it was simply unable to offer any viable substitute in their place: the inadequacy of police protection in the gigantic territories of the empire, the dispersal of the population, the vast areas covered by law enforcement and the poor state of the roads meant that "many distant areas are for long periods of time quite inaccessible, and many criminals thus escape the retribution they deserve." The state's fundamental inability to govern its own rural population adequately thus obliged it to persist with a system of punishment that it had already acknowledged in 1879 to be "harmful and lacking any juridical foundation."[56]

The reforms of 1900 might have sought to reduce exile to settlement for common criminals, but they retained the use of exile to Siberia for both political and religious crimes. If the state no longer viewed Siberia as a kind of quarantine for criminality *tout court,* it continued to consider it as such for sedition: "The criminals cannot be tolerated in the areas where their agitation developed and spread. In order to root it out, the agitator himself must be removed to a different region where his propaganda cannot be disseminated." The emergency legislation enacted in the wake of Alexander II's assassination, the "Statute on Measures for the Preservation of Political Order and Social Tranquillity," which had given the authorities wide-ranging powers to exile subversives administratively, likewise remained in force.[57]

Patriotic enthusiasts had in 1877 hailed the voyage of the *Dawn* as the harbinger of a new age of Siberian exploration, transportation and economic development. Twenty years later, the construction of the Trans-Siberian railway appeared to fulfil that promise. The continent's future was not as a wasteland for criminal outcasts. Siberia was, in fact, an economically rich and strategically invaluable territory, which, if opened up with modern networks of communications and transport, would become a land of economic opportunity, destined to form an integral part of the Russian state. Migrant peasants now trundled across the Urals in cramped railway carriages in their tens of thousands. Each man, woman and child who made the journey was evidence that the forced migration of penal labourers had become a geopolitical absurdity. The railway also severely undermined the last-ditch defence of exile: containment. The distances separating Transbaikal from Moscow and St. Petersburg had suddenly shortened; a very simple escape route had opened up for any exile able to abscond and to secure forged papers.

Even as the gathering revolutionary storm was drastically raising the stakes in the conflict between the state and society, the government remained wedded to a system that was almost universally condemned as both morally odious and strategically blind. For the swelling ranks of tsarism's opponents at the turn of the twentieth century, the exile system had become a festering indictment of the inhumanity of the state. The government no longer touted colonialism as a rationale for the exile system. Exile to Siberia was henceforth redefined unambiguously as a matter of punishment and containment. The numbers exiled administratively for political crimes in the 1880s and 90s numbered only several hundred; they would surge into the tens of thousands in the wake of the 1905 Revolution.

14

The Crucible

When the future Bolshevik journalist and historian Yury Steklov was administratively exiled to Yakutsk province in July 1895, he felt he would be following in the footsteps of "unconquerable giants." He looked forward with keen anticipation to meeting "the old men," those representatives of the former revolutionary movement from the 1860s, 70s and 80s. "They appeared to us," he remembered, "like heroic demi-gods." Steklov was not alone in drawing inspiration from the older generation of political exiles. For the latest revolutionary cohort—many of them arrested for involvement in a new wave of unrest in Russia's universities and factories in the 1890s—encounters in Siberia with the "martyrs" of Kara and Yakutsk imbued them with a deep conviction that they were protagonists in a grand crusade that stretched back across the nineteenth century. Of the 100 leading figures in the October Revolution, more than sixty had been exiled, some as many as four or five times. By the turn of the twentieth century, Siberian exile had become a revolutionary rite of passage.[1]

Alexander III's repressive rule succeeded for more than a decade in suppressing small and fragile revolutionary parties with only the shallowest of support among Russian workers and peasants. What set the new generation of radicals apart from their revolutionary forebears was the breadth of their movement. By Alexander's death in 1894, industrialization, urbanization and the spread of literacy in both town and country had forged a new, politically conscious class of opponents among a combustible mass of impoverished peasants, exploited urban workers and disaffected ethnic and national minorities. Peasants suffering from rural overpopulation, poverty and repeated famines—most notably in 1892 and 1900—became receptive to the revolutionary theories of the revitalized Populist movement led by the Socialist Revolutionary Party. Established ideologies of agrarian socialism, anarchism and nationalism found a new challenge in Marxism, which came to exert a powerful appeal in the expanding industrial districts of Russian towns and cities. Across the empire, universities became engine rooms of radicalization. Protests over freedom of speech in 1899 were met with a government crackdown: baton-wielding detachments of mounted Cossacks were sent to break up student demonstrations, and the sweeping arrests that followed ensured that many educated middle- and upper-class Russian families were confronted for the first time with the arbitrary, coercive power of the state. When hundreds of students were detained in the prison cells of the Peter and Paul Fortress in 1901 for nothing more than a peaceful demonstration in the centre of St. Petersburg, many of them, and thousands of their supporters, came to the conclusion that gradual reform of the state was impossible. Fire had to be fought with fire.[2]

As the nineteenth century drew to a close, the imperial borderlands once again became restive. Alexander III's clumsily oppressive policies of Russification in schools and universities in Poland and the Western Borderlands radicalized a new generation of Poles who had already imbibed their parents' deep hostility towards the autocracy. Victims of repeated pogroms in the final decades of the nineteenth century, and now facing harsh restrictions on their residency rights, education and professions, many of the empire's Jews concluded that their future lay in revolution rather than in an accommodation with the tsarist state. Founded in 1897, the Bundist movement combined socialism with demands for Jewish cultural autonomy and drew tens of thousands of new recruits. Whether they pinned their hopes on the peasantry, the proletariat or the nation as an agent of historical change, all of Russia's radical parties were united in their determination to achieve revolution.[3]

In the reign of Nicholas II, the Russian government pressed on with the use of exile as a weapon in the struggle with sedition. Initially, the authorities showed that they had, at least in part, learned the lessons from the public relations disasters of the 1889 suicides and executions of political prisioners in Kara and Yakutsk. In the decade before the 1905 Revolution, officials sought to deny revolutionaries a platform on which to stage their protests and fashion narratives of martyrdom. They banished them not simply beyond the Urals but also beyond the public's gaze to remote settlements in the far north-east of Siberia. As the leadership of the empire's various revolutionary movements passed through the exile system, some suffered in obscurity while others struggled to re-create the acts of heroic defiance that their predecessors had staged in the 1880s. In other ways, administrative exile empowered political radicals. It forged among their ranks a sectarian sense of solidarity that built upon collective experiences of suffering and privation and that would galvanize their authority in the years of revolutionary struggle ahead. Exile colonies became academies of sedition in which new recruits could study doctrine and established figures could churn out a stream of revolutionary theory and journalism.

The 1905 Revolution cleaved Nicholas II's reign in two. From its secret printing presses, safe houses and congresses abroad, the revolutionary movement erupted across the empire. Faced with a campaign of terrorism, an insurgent peasantry and wide-scale urban unrest, the state once again began to exile its enemies to Siberia. But the authorities could not contain the tens of thousands of new battle-hardened revolutionaries, terrorists and often violent criminals in the obscurity of remote settlements over which they had little oversight and control. So they turned to Siberia's closed prisons and penal forts in order to house them. The exile system might have helped to quell Russia's first revolution, but it would foster the implacable hatred of the government that fuelled its second. If, at the outset of Nicholas II's reign, Siberia had served as a realm of political quarantine, by the eve of the First World War it had come to resemble a giant laboratory of revolution.

In 1889, the young revolutionary Mikhail Polyakov was banished to the far-eastern Siberian district of Kolyma (which would become notorious under Stalin as the site of a major network of Gulag camps), some 12,800 kilometres from St. Petersburg: "In this vast territory that is larger than France, there are only . . . 6,500 inhabitants," Polyakov observed. Fewer than 1,000 of them were Russians. Polyakov had been sent "to a living death in a land cut off from all the world by 2,000 kilometres of swamps and mountainous desert."[4] Sredne-Kolymsk itself was a settlement with eighteen political exiles, most of whom had been sent there in 1888. Foodstuffs and clothing were scarce and, if available at all, then only at extortionate prices that put them beyond the reach of most. By early September each year, the ground was already blanketed in snow and the temperatures were dropping to −30°C. The inhabitants of the region would spray their "lairs" with water to form an icy shell that protected them from the ferocity of the descending winter; the fish bladders that served as window-panes in the summer were replaced with chunks of translucent ice to admit light. But by the middle of November, these had lost any practical function, as the darkness never lifted: "The last brief hours of daylight vanish and you are condemned to live by the light of the fireplace . . . or the pitiful flickering of a tallow candle." Polyakov remembered "the absolute silence of a night" punctuated only by the howling of dogs:

> At these times, you feel like a pathetic, insignificant worm. You enter your uncomfortable abode and feel such a deathly despondency that even memories of prison appear like a sweet dream. It is like that for a whole one and a half months: you go to bed at night and you get up at night. At the beginning of January, the *sun is reborn*: initially in the form of a small crescent, which grows with each passing day. You look at it and feel such a deep sense of joy, understandable probably only to someone who has been locked up in dark cells when he finally leaves the walls of the jail.[5]

This was not the fate of all administrative exiles. The very arbitrariness of the exile system still offered those with connections the possibility of serving out their sentences in rather more congenial surroundings. The future architect of the October Revolution, Vladimir Ulyanov (Lenin), was one such radical who found himself banished in 1897 to a remote Siberian village, Shushenskoye, on the upper Yenisei River, in the foothills of the Sian Mountains that divided southern Siberia from Mongolia. Lenin spent three years in exile under conditions that would have astonished revolutionaries just a decade earlier. A hereditary nobleman and the son of a well-connected and assertive mother, Lenin was able to travel as far as Krasnoyarsk by rail. There, he rented a comfortable room in the home of a woman known to be sympathetic to the "politicals" and gathered material in the library of the celebrated bibliophile Gennady Yudin while he waited for his final destination to be decided. When he did finally arrive at his place of exile, Lenin was pleasantly surprised. Shushenskoye was, he wrote to his sister, "not a bad village. It is true that it is in a rather bare locality, but not far away . . . there is a forest, although much of it has been felled. There is no road to the Yenisei, but the River Shush flows right past the village, and there is a fairly large tributary of the Yenisei nearby . . . where you can bathe. The Sian Mountains, or their ridges, are visible on the horizon . . ."⁶

Shushenskoye consisted of 287 homes and a population of 1,400 residents. From here, Lenin marshalled a voluminous correspondence with activists in St. Petersburg, Moscow and various underground cells across Russia. He also received a steady stream of books on extended loan from libraries in St. Petersburg and Moscow, via the good offices of his sisters, to supply his voracious appetite for reading. Despite his frustrations with the speed of the postal system (it took about thirty-five days to send a letter to the capital and receive a reply), Lenin devoured texts on politics, economics, industrial history, agriculture and statistics, and, when he finally left Siberia at the beginning of 1900, he took with him 225 kilogrammes of books. It was from exile that Lenin wrote and, in 1899, published his influential *The Development of Capitalism in Russia,* which established him as a major Marxist thinker.⁷

In a manner that recalled both the Decembrists' resources and their appetites for consumer goods unavailable in Siberia's remoter regions, Lenin bombarded his mother and sisters with requests for creature comforts: warm socks, a mackintosh cape for when he went hunting. He needed a straw hat and kid gloves (essential protection from the dreaded Siberian mosquitoes, which made a brief but ferocious appearance each summer in this boggy region). When not immersed in study, Lenin took to bucolic pursuits, hunting and skating with the dozen or so fellow exiles in the vicinity of Shushenskoye. By the end of 1897 his companions were commenting on how he had put on weight, and that his healthy suntan made him look "just like a Siberian."⁸

The young Lev Bronshtein (Trotsky) was exiled in 1904 to the god-forsaken village of Ust-Kut, on the upper reaches of the River Lena, where he studied Marx's *Das Kapital* "while brushing the cockroaches off the pages." And yet here, too, conditions were a world away from those faced by radicals further north. Trotsky had the opportunity to father two children with his bride, Aleksandra, hone his formidable skills as a journalist through a steady stream of publications in the pro-gressive newspaper *Eastern Review*, and play croquet with a ferocious competitiveness.[9]

The relative leniency of the state's treatment of Lenin and Trotsky revealed not only the persistent power of social hierarchy and wealth to mitigate the worst features of Siberian exile, but also the state's igno-rance of the embryonic power of their bookish radicalism. Lenin might have complained impatiently about the delays in the delivery of books and letters, but he was connected to a web of conspiracy and subver-sion that stretched from Irkutsk and Krasnoyarsk to Moscow, Kiev, Geneva and London.[10]

Conditions for Kolyma's administrative exiles in the far north-east were a world apart. They endured an isolation that was punctured only three times a year, when the post arrived, Polyakov remembered, "like a jolt of electricity . . . transporting many into a state of delirious ecstasy." As the weeks passed, however, and the exiles had read and re-read the bales of newspapers, journals, books and letters from their loved ones, the euphoria subsided:

> All the news and events that had taken place six, nine, 12 months earlier are pored over and examined with anguished eagerness and partly talked through; the ecstasy abates and you once again fall into a state of hopeless despondency. You sit there with a book, concentrating on writing a letter, immersed in your work. And suddenly, you are struck by the thought: What is the point? What is it all for? The languages, and the lectures of brilliant scholars, and the wisdom of centu-ries and everything you have read and pondered? Because you still have another six, seven, eight years of languishing here! And what will remain of you by the end of your exile inside those lonely, damp walls, in the nightmarishly long, never-ending nights: nights that are like years . . . Is it worth it? Such gloomy thoughts can be overpowering and so you run to see your comrades.[11]

In such claustrophobic and static conditions, even comradeship could rapidly grow stale. Another of Kolyma's exiles, Social Demo-crat Grigory Tsyperovich, confided in a letter that everyone "knows

what the others will say on this or that topic; I don't feel like arguing, discussing anything, because it all boils down to the repetition of
well-known and well-rehearsed arguments. Oh, I'm so sick of all this
pointless vegetating, of this constant prancing around a dusty fireplace
with teapots!"[12]

Cut off from the world and from the revolutionary struggle that
had given meaning to their lives, the administrative exiles of the far
north quarrelled and feuded. Political disputes over revolutionary doctrine and tactics became animated by personal animosities, rivalries
and jealousies. Tsyperovich observed petty bickering that so infected
relationships that exiles had to move out of their shared cabins and live
separately. Such infighting could also have tragic consequences. One of
Lenin's comrades, Nikolai Fedoseyev, who had been sent to Verkholensk in north-eastern Siberia in 1897, was unable to endure, as Lenin
angrily wrote, "the calumnies of some monster or other" among his
fellow exiles. He shot himself in June 1898. Much of the Bolsheviks'
sectarianism was fostered in the claustrophobic confines of these exile
colonies. Distrust, resentments and personal rivalries, all magnified by
the shared isolation of exile, left an imprint on the psychology of the
men and women who would one day rule Russia. By the 1930s, personal slights and enmities would become a matter of life and death in
the Bolsheviks' fratricidal bloodletting.[13]

Monotony and claustrophobia ate away at the mental health of
some. Tsyperovich noted how his comrades appeared to be "covered
in a kind of dark mould. Their movements were lifeless; their extreme
nervous exhaustion was evident in their looks and words; and when
one of them did become excited, the signs of nervous suffering revealed
themselves in his every gesture and every word." Many fell into
despair; some took their own lives. Ludwig Janowicz had been exiled
to Sredne-Kolymsk in 1897 and endured five years of exile before being
summoned by the authorities to Yakutsk to testify in a trial. In a tragic
union with an earlier revolutionary martyr in Eastern Siberia, Janowicz
shot himself on the grave of Pappy Podbelsky, a member of the People's
Will who had been killed in the "Yakutsk Tragedy" of March 1889.
Janowicz left a note for his comrades: "My nerves are completely shot;
I become hysterical at the slightest trifle. I have become completely
spineless. So what's the point of exposing myself to ridicule?" His
exhaustion and despair were, he wrote, "the result of many years of

imprisonment and exile (altogether eighteen years) in extremely difficult conditions. In essence, it is the Russian government that has killed me. May the responsibility for my death and the death of countless legions of my comrades be laid at its door."[14]

In the decade following Nicholas II's accession to the throne, no fewer than 2,700 people were administratively exiled for political crimes. The incidence of sedition was rising exponentially: in 1894, fifty-six political cases were dealt with by imperial decree; by 1903 the number had risen to 1,500. By 1 January 1901, there was a total of 1,800 political exiles in Siberia. The newly appointed governor-general of Irkutsk, Pavel Kutaisov, complained that the influx of political prisoners to Eastern Siberia made adequate supervision of them virtually impossible. The current system, he argued, "only serves to spread revolutionary ideas all over Russia so that, in effect, the government itself is taking radical steps to ensure the dissemination of the very theories with which it is locked in struggle." Siberia's rapid development and the growth of its cities at the turn of the century meant that the arguments in favour of cleansing St. Petersburg and Moscow of subversives were now extended by Siberia's administrators to Krasnoyarsk and Irkutsk. Active revolutionaries were no more tolerable in what were fast becoming populous urban centres, occupying strategically vital positions in Russia's imperial expansion eastwards, than they had been in the capitals.[15]

Doubtful of the authorities' ability to cope with the influx of committed, well-organized and in many cases violent revolutionaries, Kutaisov wagered on repression. His solution was to cleanse Eastern Siberian cities of troublemakers by banishing them still further, beyond the Arctic Circle, to the snowbound Devil's Islands of Verkhoyansk and Kolyma. In August 1903, he issued an edict that amounted to a sudden repudiation of the state's relative leniency in its recent treatment of political exiles. He ordered that, henceforth, violations of official instructions were all to be punished with administrative exile to the interminably frozen wastelands of the far north. Prior to the crackdown, the authorities had turned a blind eye to minor infringements of the regulations; an exile who temporarily absconded from his registered place of banishment to seek provisions in Yakutsk might spend a symbolic day under arrest. Now, he or she would find themselves deported to Kolyma.[16]

Situated on the banks of the Lena, about 3,200 kilometres north-east of Irkutsk, Yakutsk remained the gateway to the Arctic Circle. This small town thus offered political exiles destined for oblivion in remote exile colonies a last chance to put on a show of strength and collective resolve. Intensified repression produced concentrations of highly motivated young men and women with little to lose. Pinkhus Rozental, a doctor from Wilno (Vilnius), had already spent fifteen months in a tsarist prison before receiving his six-year sentence of exile to Yakutsk for revolutionary agitation among the working classes and for the spread of subversive literature. He described the effects of Kutaisov's crackdown:

> As soon as the winter route to Yakutsk was established along the frozen Lena, the transportation of new groups of convicts resumed. Party after party arrived. It seemed like a great migration of peoples. Time and again, the new arrivals struggled for the right to meet with the local exiles . . . In each group there were several involuntary migrants from Irkutsk province, some exiled for resisting the police, some for assisting in escapes, some for failing to follow official instructions. All of them had been secretly denounced by officials and were on their way to the region of Yakutia, to Verkhoyansk and to Kolyma.[17]

In this already tense situation, Kutaisov's decision to withdraw state funds for the return journey of exiles who had already completed their sentences caused an uproar. It was impossible, the exiles protested, to save up the 300 roubles needed for the journey from a monthly subsistence of only twelve. The new instruction effectively meant that exiles would be forced to remain in Siberia for several years more in order to save up the money to go home.[18]

Their protest would be no mere reprise of the "Yakutsk Tragedy." The differences in 1904 were striking. As in the 1880s, these exiles had an eye on the wider public gallery, but their resistance to the state was better organized and better equipped. At the same time, the officials in Yakutsk displayed a tactical nous and a surer grasp of the political implications of a bloody showdown with the exiles.

The centre of exile life in Yakutsk was a large two-storey wooden house belonging to one of the local Yakuts, a man named Romanov.

The building accommodated several exiles on its upper floor, and those living in the wider district used the building as a meeting place and poste restante. There were only 150 soldiers in the Yakutsk garrison, half of whom were tasked with guarding various sites. On 17 February 1904, fifty-four political exiles—Bundists, Bolsheviks and Socialist Revolutionaries—barricaded themselves inside Romanov's house, provisioned with supplies and weapons. They sent a list of demands to the governor:

1. The return, at the state's expense, of exiles who have finished their sentences.
2. The abolition of administrative punishments for absences without leave.
3. The revocation of the instruction forbidding us from meeting our comrades-in-exile.
4. A guarantee of the personal inviolability of the signatories to this protest.[19]

Anxious to avoid a repeat of the international outrage caused by the bloody denouement of the exiles' protest in 1889, Nikolai Chaplin, the deputy governor who was temporarily in charge of the province, sought to avoid armed conflict. Having surrounded the house with troops, he entered the courtyard unarmed to negotiate with the exiles. He explained that he had no power to rescind Kutaisov's orders and that the exiles should appeal to St. Petersburg for legal redress. He insisted, however, that he had no intention of ordering his troops to open fire: "If you wish to sit in a locked apartment, do so! It makes no difference to me!" He even omitted to inform St. Petersburg of the standoff, in order to avoid an instruction to storm the building. When the exiles provocatively raised a red flag above the house, the governor stuck to his policy of "paying them no attention." The siege continued, and the revolutionaries, aware that theirs was a struggle for popular sympathy, began to issue proclamations to the inhabitants of Yakutsk, outlining the reasons for their resistance. The first, on 21 February, declared: "We cannot stand idle as the government turns the exile system into a system of drawn-out murder."[20]

Frustrated by Chaplin's apparent indifference to their protest, within a week the exiles were accusing him of an insidious attempt to break their will, as they explained to the residents of the town in another proclamation:

> We have now for a week been barricaded in this house and so far we have only been surrounded. The authorities wish to drive us out with hunger. Why has "order" not been restored by force? . . . The government fears that, by shooting us, it would provoke fury and indignation in all those in whom it has still to exterminate the ability to feel indignation.[21]

Running short of food and water, and repeatedly goaded by the soldiers laying siege to the house, the revolutionaries convened a meeting to discuss their options and decided to go on the offensive. And at three o'clock on 4 March, they opened fire, prompting a fierce reply from the soldiers surrounding the building; two soldiers and one revolutionary were killed. Sporadic shooting continued, but at no time did Chaplin give the order to storm the building. Cornered and faced with the choice between a slow death and surrender, the exiles voted for the latter and laid down their weapons on the morning of 7 March. The *Romanovtsy*, as they became known, had held out for eighteen days and had succeeded in eliciting a wave of protests among sympathetic fellow exiles in Eastern Siberia. Ultimately, however, the wily Chaplin's tactics had paid off. There was no massacre to fuel the exiles' claims of martyrdom at the hands of a barbaric state.[22]

In July 1904, the case was brought to trial. Amid the mounting anti-government mood in the empire that summer, while the imperial navy was suffering defeat after defeat at the hands of the Japanese, the government was eager to avoid a repetition of the public outcry that had accompanied the death sentences handed down to the "Yakutsk martyrs" in 1889. Kutaisov decided that this time the exiles would be tried by a civilian rather than a military court, a move which effectively precluded the possibility of death sentences. A spate of suicides among political exiles in the years leading up to 1905 had once again pushed the authorities onto the back foot and threatened to discredit their attempts to win public support for their struggle with subversion. The celebrated lawyer Aleksandr Zarudny represented the *Romanovtsy*, highlighting the desperation of those who sought merely to turn "the slow death of exile" into the "quick death of execution." After ten days of trial, the court handed down relatively lenient sentences. The mutinous exiles were condemned to various terms of penal labour in Siberia's central prisons.[23]

In the three or four decades before 1905, Siberia's political exiles had remained a small, if influential, minority. Many of these bookish radicals had been dedicated opponents of the tsarist regime, yet their exile in Siberia had revealed their isolation and, ultimately, their impotence. These generals of the revolution would have been nothing without their foot soldiers, and these were supplied in their tens of thousands by the crucible of the first Russian Revolution. The storm, which finally broke in 1905, had been gathering since the turn of the century. Radicalized by low-level government repression, the Socialist Revolutionaries set up a Combat Organization dedicated to waging a campaign of assassinations that claimed the lives of two ministers of the interior, Dmitry Sipyagin in 1902 and Vyacheslav von Plehve in 1904.[24] But the tipping point came on 9 January 1905, when soldiers guarding the Winter Palace in St. Petersburg opened fire on demonstrators, massacring hundreds of unarmed workers and their families.

Protests spread across the country and, by September 1905, the government was facing a general strike and a violent rural insurgency. Russian towns and cities echoed to the sounds of gunfire and explosions as revolutionaries waged an often indiscriminate war against representatives of the state. The Socialist Revolutionary Party had claimed responsibility for only six attacks between 1902 and 1904. The following year, its terrorist operations expanded to include fifty-one attacks, followed by seventy-eight in 1906 and sixty-two in 1907. Targets included state officials, gendarmes, governors and even the tsar's uncle and governor of Moscow, Grand Duke Sergei Aleksandrovich, on 4 February 1905. Beyond the direct control of the Combat Organization, terrorist violence, perpetrated by a host of other parties, splinter groups and lone assassins, was also spreading. Between 1 January and 20 August 1906, there were almost 1,800 terrorist acts, including numerous bombings, which killed and wounded almost 1,500 people, a third of them private citizens. One of the most notorious was the attempted assassination of Prime Minister Pyotr Stolypin at his dacha in St. Petersburg on 12 August 1906. Three members of the Maximalists, an offshoot of the Socialist Revolutionaries, entered the dacha, two dressed as officers and one as a civilian, carrying suitcases packed with explosives. When challenged by Stolypin's suspicious guards, they shouted "Long live freedom!" and "Long live anarchy!" and detonated their bombs. The result was carnage: twenty-seven people died instantly and another seventy, including two of Stolypin's own children, were badly wounded. Miraculously, Stolypin himself survived.[25]

Politically motivated violence often shaded into unvarnished criminality and senseless savagery. What one commentator referred to as "an epidemic of trauma"—violent assaults, acts of arson, rapes, pogroms and murders—tore through the empire. The "expropriations" conducted by revolutionary parties to replenish their coffers were often indistinguishable from the bank jobs carried out by criminals with pretentions to nothing more than personal gain. The "fury of the masses," as one horrified observer termed it, was directed at landed gentry, impoverished Jewish communities, village policemen, factory foremen and also countless ordinary citizens.[26]

St. Petersburg's imperial misadventures in the Russo-Japanese War only fanned the flames of the revolutionary unrest. Over eighteen months in 1904 and 1905, Russian forces were comprehensively beaten by an enemy whom they regarded as racially inferior, in the full glare of the world's press. The debacle exposed the incompetence of the government and fuelled the growing revolutionary discontent at home.[27]

Riven by the same social and political tensions as the rest of the empire, Siberia's cities were also the first to experience the revolutionary fallout of Russia's short, calamitous war. Following St. Petersburg's conclusion of a humiliating peace treaty with Japan in September 1905, Russian soldiers began to return home and passed through Siberian cities already in the grip of revolutionary unrest. Some joined exiles and workers from Siberian factories and railways in revolt. On 16 November 1905, some 4,000 people attended a meeting in Chita in Transbaikal and passed a resolution declaring a republic. In Irkutsk, revolutionaries endeavoured to win over the support of the city garrison and succeeded in electing a military strike committee; the committee demanded a constituent assembly, universal suffrage and an amnesty for political prisoners. In early November, revolutionary protests similarly gripped Krasnoyarsk, and workers and soldiers established their own revolutionary council, or soviet, declared a "Republic of Krasnoyarsk" beneath the red flag, and called for "liberty, equality and fraternity." On 8 December, the soviet took control of the provincial publishing house and began to publish the *Krasnoyarsk Worker*.[28]

Faced with widespread opposition from almost all sections of society, the autocracy offered concessions in October 1905 designed to split the moderate from the radical elements within the anti-government forces. Freedom of the press, freedom of assembly, an end to religious discrimination, the convocation of a consultative chamber, named the Duma, to debate new laws, and the legalization of political parties were all set out in the October Manifesto. Reform was coupled with repression. Bolstered by the gradual return of loyal troops, the government responded to the revolutionary violence with a savage crackdown across the empire. A decree issued the following month gave all governors-general, provincial governors and city governors the power to declare a state of emergency and even martial law within their jurisdictions.

By January 1907, martial law was in effect in twenty-three provinces, twenty-five districts, nine cities and along two railway lines. In February 1906, the Ministry of the Interior authorized governors to exile peasants who were merely suspected of involvement in the rural unrest. Military tribunals sentenced some 3,000 sailors and soldiers between 1905 and 1912 to lengthy, often lifelong, terms of penal labour for their part in the revolution. A mere forty-three civilians were tried in district military courts in 1903; by 1908, the number was around 7,000, of whom over 1,000 were sentenced to death. It was, as professor of law Mikhail Chubinsky observed, "the era of military tribunals and executions." Sealed convict trains began to disgorge thousands of new political prisoners into Siberia's jails.[29]

Between 1906 and 1912, some 60,000 individuals were tried for political crimes by both regular and military courts. The great majority were found guilty not just of rebellion and agitation but also of merely belonging to illegal organizations or spreading seditious literature. The number of penal labourers in the empire leapt from 6,100 in 1905 to 28,500 in 1910; the total of those sentenced to terms of exile in the same period surged from 6,500 to 30,000. Yakov Sverdlov, the future general secretary of the Bolshevik Party, remarked that, while before 1905 the state was exiling only "individual representatives of the masses, now the masses themselves were being exiled."[30]

The result of the government's counter-insurgency campaigns was an explosion in the Siberian prison population and a catastrophic decline in conditions for prisoners (the collapse of the penal labour colony on Sakhalin in 1905 had already left the administrators of the exile system struggling to rehouse convicts). In 1912, the prisons in Nerchinsk, which had space for 1,570 convicts, were in fact holding 3,560. Inspections described prisoners crammed into badly ventilated cells filled with an overpowering stench from the tubs of human waste. Mortality within the penal labour system soared as typhus and tuberculosis stalked overcrowded closed prisons, which became, in the words of one journalist, "reservoirs of infection." In the Aleksandrovsk Central Penal Labour Prison, rates of tuberculosis had more than doubled by 1914 and the prison hospital was now admitting only patients "with no hope of recovery." In 1911 in the various prisons of Tobolsk province, 5,200 or 38 per cent of the total of 13,500 inmates were recorded as being sick; 147 died in custody.[31]

Effectively 1905 sealed the fate of the autocracy. The government clawed back its power, but the brutality of the repression ensured that its victory was short-lived. The state's violent counter-insurgency fuelled a growing polarization between the Russian masses and their rulers that the concessions enshrined in the October Manifesto were unable to bridge. The government's subsequent attempts to refurbish its own legitimacy never escaped the very dark shadows cast by its use of bayonets and prisons.

Initially, the 1905 Revolution boded well for Siberia's prisoners. The promulgation of the October Manifesto was accompanied in Siberia on 21 October by a partial amnesty for exiled revolutionaries convicted of "state crimes" and a significant softening of the prison regime. On that day, prisoners in the Tobolsk Central Penal Labour Prison marched around the courtyard carrying red flags and singing revolutionary songs while a crowd of their supporters gathered in front of the prison gates to clamour for the immediate release of all political prisoners. The government stood firm, but its prisons became, for a time, in the words of one political convict, like "republics."[32]

As government repression gained momentum, however, this brief moment of liberalization proved short-lived. The government succeeded in re-imposing its authority in Siberia's mutinous cities in late December. In Krasnoyarsk, the governor had to wait for reinforcements to arrive from Omsk. They besieged the revolutionaries and eventually, on 2 January, deployed artillery to force their surrender. Around 400 were arrested for participation in the "armed uprising" and locked up in the city's prison.[33]

The re-imposition of discipline in Siberia's prisons was swift and brutal. On 18 January 1906, loyal troops arrived at the Tobolsk Central Penal Labour Prison, searched the cells, seized weapons, books, letters and personal belongings, clapped the convicts in irons and flogged many of them.[34] Over the course of 1906 and 1907, a succession of new officials was appointed to run many of Siberia's jails. This new breed tended to be far harsher in its treatment of the inmates than its predecessor had been. Prison warders found guilty of laxness in their treatment of prisoners were dismissed from their posts.[35]

In January 1907, the military governor of Transbaikal, Mikhail Yebelov, wrote to the head of the Nerchinsk Mining Region, Yuly Metus, that only the "most energetic" individuals should be recruited as prison warders and guards. Henceforth, "all measures should be taken to re-establish the proper regime in the prisons." These included keeping cell doors locked, following the letter of the law when punishing those guilty of violating prison discipline, prohibiting prisoners from keeping any funds of their own or any other possessions to which they were not legally entitled, and closing the prisoners' own store (the *maidan*). Metus hurried to pass on the additional instructions to the wardens in charge of the eight prisons in the Nerchinsk region: henceforth, prisoners were to be shackled and prison guards were to react to resistance with their firearms. Criticizing the lax regime in the Akatui prison, Metus declared that the "time for tenderness, for the illegal state of affairs permitted by a weak prison administration, has passed. If the warders do not have the stomach for imposing order, they had better quit!" Many, it seemed, found the stomach. Warders removed the political prisoners' personal linen, pillows and blankets, confiscated their writing materials, dismantled their libraries, banned tobacco and permitted correspondence only with close family members and sometimes not at all.[36]

But if the warders were a new breed in Siberia's jails after 1905, so too were the prisoners. Many had been bloodied in the strikes, mutinies, terrorist campaigns and rural unrest of the revolution. By 1908, 249 of Tobolsk's penal labourers had been sentenced for murder or attempted murder; a quarter were recidivists. Indeed, as Siberia's prisons filled to overflowing with insurgent peasants, striking workers, mutinous soldiers and sailors, bank robbers, pogromists, thieves and committed revolutionaries, the boundaries between the political and the criminal became blurred as never before. Many of the new political prisoners were radicalized not just by the revolutionary violence but also by the fire of revolutionary discourse. This new cohort of penal labourers in Siberia's jails was increasingly aware of its own rights. An official report into the state of the Nerchinsk prisons in the summer of 1906 observed that "today's penal labourer is more self-regarding and more attached to his own freedoms; he is more conscious in the defence of his dignity." No longer only the preserve of educated Russians, ideas of natural rights and inalienable human dignity were now shaping the mentality and conduct of the lower orders exiled for their part in the revolutionary unrest. What united most, if not all, prisoners was a visceral hatred of authority. Many, too, had little to lose. Of the 610 men and women serving terms of penal labour in Tobolsk in 1909, only 16 per cent had been sentenced to fewer than eight years; 62 per cent were serving between eight and twenty years and 12 per cent had been condemned to lifelong penal labour.[37]

By 1907, two hostile camps were facing off in Siberia's overcrowded prisons. On one side were the new prison warders who were determined to stamp the authority of the state on their unruly prison population; on the other were revolutionaries and criminals who were ready to use violence inside the prisons and who were now supported and abetted by networks of exiled revolutionaries outside.[38] In the decade between 1905 and the outbreak of the First World War, Siberia's prisons became the epicentres of a violent confrontation.

Nowhere was the confrontation starker and more violent than in Tobolsk. The authorities in the town were struggling to cope with the influx of political prisoners; in 1905, there were only twenty-one penal labourers sentenced for political crimes; by 1907, there were 250. Concerned with the mounting influence of political prisoners on ordinary criminals, Tobolsk's prison officials had most of them transferred, fol-

lowing a fire, from the central prison on the main square to the smaller
and older jail, known as Prison No. 2, on the edge of the town. The
regime in the old prison was, at first, relatively liberal. Attempts by the
warden, Bogoyavlensky, to reassert his authority in the wake of 1905
by insisting that prisoners leap to their feet in his presence and shout out
"We wish you health!" in the Russian military tradition were met with
a mocking refusal. The prisoners were housed in large cells in groups of
three; they enjoyed subscriptions to newspapers, were allowed books,
pens and paper; they were granted regular exercise and could wear
their own clothing; their loose fetters were removed at night; the food
was acceptable and the men were even permitted sometimes to enter
the kitchens to prepare their own meals. But relations between the prisoners and their guards began to deteriorate when, in January 1907, a
search of one of the cells revealed part of a beam that had been torn
from the wall in order to make way for a tunnel. Shortly afterwards, a
false passport was discovered in the seam of one of the exiles' books.
Bogoyavlensky responded by denying the exiles the right to correspond
with their relatives in any language other than Russian—a decision that
effectively denied several Poles, Jews and a Finn the chance to communicate with their families. This move provoked a spiral of escala-
tory measures by both the prisoners and the prison officials—a hunger
strike, the removal of mattresses, pens and paper, a "boycott" of all
instructions from the guards—that culminated with the ringleader of
the political prisoners, Dmitry Takhchoglo, being placed for two weeks
in solitary confinement.[39]

Born in 1877, Takhchoglo was a nobleman from Kherson province in south-west Russia. He had studied at the Faculty of Physics
and Mathematics at the St. Petersburg Imperial University, where he
became involved in the student movement and, from there, entered the
ranks of the Russian Social Democratic Workers' Party. In the midst of
the 1905 Revolution, Takhchoglo had been found guilty of attempting to kill a policeman in Yekaterinoslav and had been sentenced to
death. In the wake of the October Manifesto, however, his sentence
had been commuted to fifteen years of penal labour. As soon as Takhchoglo arrived in Tobolsk, the authorities found him "to be a stubborn
enemy of the prison regime who refused to follow the orders of the
warders and enjoyed huge authority among his fellow prisoners as a
great revolutionary figure with a university education."[40]

Fuelled by wider government repression across the empire, tensions in the prison erupted into open conflict on 16 July 1907. Once again, the detonator was the flogging of political prisoners. The revolutionaries in Prison No. 2 learned of the birching of three of their comrades on the other side of town in the Tobolsk Central Penal Labour Prison.[41] Outraged, a group of sixteen convicts resolved to mutiny and handed a declaration to Bogoyavlensky:

> Having learned of the punishment of three of our comrades . . . we declare that, with this act, the Tobolsk administration has thrown down the gauntlet to all political prisoners. We, the political prisoners in Prison No. 2, take up this gauntlet and declare that we prefer a bloody death at the hands of unbridled tyrants to the disgrace of the mockery and of the insult to those sacred rights of every man and citizen.[42]

That evening, the prisoners wrote letters to their friends and family. Takhchoglo wrote: "Alea jacta est! The Rubicon has been crossed!" One of his companions was Ivan Semyonov, a peasant from Tver province who had migrated to St. Petersburg and found both work and revolution in the city's vast Putilov works. For his part in a violent bank robbery on behalf of the Bolshevik Party, Semyonov had been sentenced to twenty years of penal labour. He wrote to his mother:

> Dear Mother,
>
> . . . By the time you receive this letter, it is possible that I will no longer be alive. I won't describe to you in detail what has happened. I will be brief. They took the birch rods to three of our comrades. We cannot stand for this disgrace and so we have decided to wash it away with our blood. Tomorrow we will stage a mutiny and they will probably run us through with their bayonets. We have no choice but to die. My dearest mother, I beg you, do not cry for me and do not reproach me that I am causing you a mountain of grief. I couldn't act differently. I won't explain why I couldn't because you anyway wouldn't understand. So then, forgive me, and farewell! I kiss you without end.
>
> Your loving son.[43]

As Semyonov had predicted, it was the last letter he ever wrote. The following day, having armed themselves with bed planks and furniture legs, the sixteen political prisoners refused to allow warders into their cells to search them, declaring: "You can carry out your search but you'll have to kill all of us first!" The guards summoned Bogoyavlensky, who appeared together with a further twenty soldiers and guards to cries of "Hangman! Bloodsucker!" The prison warden ordered his men to stand guard at the door of each cell and to show "the bastards" if they offered any resistance. Bogoyavlensky ordered the plank-wielding Takhchoglo and two of his comrades to be thrown into a punishment cell. In protest, the revolutionaries began to smash the windows of their cells and to break down their doors with planks, whereupon nervous soldiers opened fire on the rioting prisoners. By the time the frantic orders to cease fire were obeyed, Semyonov lay dead from a gunshot wound to the head and seven other prisoners had been injured.[44]

When brought before a military tribunal in November 1907, the mutinous exiles nevertheless received a sympathetic hearing. Sergei Anisimov, the celebrated lawyer and veteran of political trials, travelled from St. Petersburg to Tobolsk to mount their defence and gave an eloquent closing speech to the tribunal:

> In Russia, given the tragic peculiarities of our political life, the very character traits that confer on people a leading position in the social life of civilised countries turn them into political criminals. Life in Russia makes so-called "politicals" of everyone blessed with a particular sensitivity for the downtrodden and insulted, of everyone possessed of a certain moral independence and the ability to live without making huge compromises with their conscience. In the absence of the possibility of an open political struggle, sooner or later prison, exile, penal labour and fetters await each and every one of these politicals.

Appealing to the officers sitting in judgement of the politicals, Anisimov explained that the revolutionaries' sense of human dignity was no less important to them than a sense of military honour was to the officers. To submit to a flogging was to submit to their "destruction as human beings." Anisimov linked the revolutionaries' protest with the mass poisoning of the "Kara Tragedy" in 1889 and emphasized that revolutionaries like Ivan Semyonov were prepared to die in protest at the flogging of a comrade. Even the prosecuting counsel asked for leniency from the tribunal, and the men were duly sentenced to a token ten days in solitary confinement and to the extension of their sentences by six months. Such sentences were akin to an acquittal, and indicated a desire on the part of some in the administration to defuse rather than escalate confrontations with revolutionaries.[45] But this policy of restraint proved difficult, if not impossible, to maintain.

The story of a mass escape from the Aleksandrovsk Central Penal Labour Prison captures the increasingly brutal confrontation between the prisoners and their guards. Opened in 1873, Aleksandrovsk was until the twentieth century one of the most progressive penal institutions in Siberia. It boasted spacious, well-ventilated cells and workshops, a library and a school. Its liberal warden, Faddei Savitsky, even permitted the prisoners to assemble an orchestra and to stage performances in an improvised theatre.[46] This liberal regime was designed to accommodate prisoners who were already nearing the end of their sentences and so had little incentive to challenge the authority of their guards or to attempt an escape. But as a direct result of the government's suppression of the 1905 Revolution, the number of political prisoners entering its walls had swollen: by the end of 1907, the Aleksandrovsk Central Prison housed some 400 political prisoners sentenced to penal labour and, of them, a quarter had received life terms.[47]

Violence erupted on 10 April 1908. At a prearranged signal, a group of twenty prisoners in one of the blocks fell on their guards. They bludgeoned one to death with a blunt instrument smuggled out of the workshops and, having seized his revolver, shot dead two more. They then fought their way through the guardhouse, killing another warder and badly wounding two others; one of their own number was killed by a warder. The convicts eventually managed to flee the prison and head into the surrounding woodland. Their timing proved unfortunate, though: heavy snowfall that night slowed their progress and plummeting temperatures made survival in the forests difficult. Troops summoned to the prison managed to track down and capture several of them in short order.[48]

In September, a military tribunal in Irkutsk sentenced fifteen of the fugitives to death, and this time the authorities showed no inclination to accede to the families' pleas for clemency. On 9 February 1909, the prisoners themselves pre-empted their death sentences in the Irkutsk prison by taking poison (although only one of them died). The following month, Nicholas II commuted the survivors' sentences to lifelong penal labour.[49]

The tsar's occasional exercise of clemency did nothing to break the escalating cycle of brutality within Siberia's prisons. Buoyed by popular support and by networks of sympathizers, radicalized and embittered political prisoners showed themselves capable of staging armed jail-breaks and violent robberies when on the run. On the night of 10 October 1906, twenty-seven political prisoners launched a desperate attempt to escape from the Irkutsk prison. They overpowered their guards and disarmed, bound and gagged them before proceeding to throw open the doors of the common criminals' cells to release the inmates. When the prison warden arrived to investigate the commotion, he was attacked and beaten so badly that he died of his injuries five days later. His deputy also came down to the cells only to be fatally shot by one of the weapons that the prisoners had seized. Another injured guard was beaten to death in the corridor. The prisoners made their way into the courtyard and, finding the gates of the prison locked, clambered onto the roof of one of the workshops and leapt from there over the wall as the guards opened fire. Seventeen prisoners succeeded in fleeing, ten were killed and five were injured.[50]

Such escapes could lead to bloody, if brief, insurgencies. Between August 1908 and January 1909, exiled revolutionaries in Turukhansk district in Yenisei province waged a campaign of jail-breaks, robberies and murders. After two anarchist exiles were arrested on suspicion of the violent robbery of a shop and the theft of weapons and money, they were transported under guard to Yeniseisk. En route, a group of around twenty anarchists, Social Democrats and exiled Polish soldiers attacked the convoy with firearms, killed two guards and liberated the prisoners. The revolutionaries then embarked on a spree of armed robberies and murders in the district, "expropriating" tens of thousands of roubles from post offices, merchants and wealthy peasants. They left two police officials, two Cossacks and three merchants dead. On 20 December, they attacked the town of Turukhansk itself and liberated the political prisoners in the local jail before breaking into a police station and stealing stamps, uniforms and passports. It was only in February 1909 that reinforcements—a mounted regiment of Cossacks and riflemen—arrived and began to hunt down the insurgents. A few days later, the revolutionaries were cornered and several were shot dead before the rest surrendered. A wave of repression swept through the district as some 150 political exiles were arrested on suspicion of aiding and abetting the fugitives.[51] The violence and desperation of these bids for freedom and the casual brutality the political exiles inflicted on the local population would have been unthinkable a decade earlier.

Terrorism likewise flourished in Siberia's towns and cities as networks of revolutionaries took their revenge on those they held responsible for the prison regime. Wardens and guards might have had the upper hand inside the jails and penal forts, but beyond their walls they were extremely vulnerable to determined, well-organized and ruthless assassins.

In the summer of 1907, the military tribunal was not the only court sitting in judgement in the town of Tobolsk. On 14 July, the very day of the flogging of the three political prisoners, a note had been posted to Bogoyavlensky: "We have learned . . . that you have cruelly treated our comrades among the political and criminal exiles, and for that we are serving you with a death sentence that we shall carry out without delay." The note was signed "Incognito." Two weeks later, an unknown assassin shot Bogoyavlensky dead with a Browning pistol as he sat in his carriage in the Yermak Park. In the ensuing confusion, the gunman fled.[52]

The manner of Bogoyavlensky's assassination was remarkable for its demonstration of the reach, organization and power of the revolutionary movement in Siberia after 1905. The shooting was a premeditated execution carried out by radicals beyond the walls of the prison. In the 1880s and 90s, revolutionaries had appealed to the court of public opinion in their struggles with their jailers; now they claimed to act as agents of that court's judgement.[53]

Promoted from head of the Nerchinsk Mining Region to inspector of prisons throughout Transbaikal, Yuly Metus was in Chita on official business and, on 27 May 1907, had checked in to the New Central Hotel. A young woman arrived on the same train as Metus and also checked in to the same hotel, using a passport in the name of Lidia Yushkova, the twenty-one-year-old daughter of a parish priest.

The following morning, she called the concierge and informed him that she wished to visit Metus. The prison official agreed to meet her in the dining room, where the young woman handed Metus a petition that contained a request to visit a political prisoner confined in the Maltsev prison under Metus's command. Metus took the petition, stepped over to the window, and began to read it. At that moment, Yushkova pulled out a revolver and fired a single shot that struck him at the base of his skull. Metus fell lifeless to the floor.

Yushkova fled the building but was pursued by the hotel porter, Vasily Yefremenkov, who managed to catch up with and seize her near the market. Yefremenkov called on the crowd that gathered to help him but was met with the profound ambivalence of the Russian public to the forces of law and order. As the official investigation recorded, the porter "not only found no sympathy and no assistance in the crowd but, on the contrary, voices were heard saying that it was none of his business and that, if he persisted, he would be killed." Intimidated and outnumbered, Yefremenkov released Yushkova. With the parting cry of "Leave me! I did as my comrades instructed!," she leapt into a waiting carriage and vanished.[54]

A few days later, 1,500 copies of a proclamation by the Socialist Revolutionaries began to circulate throughout Eastern Siberia:

Citizens! What was fated to happen has now happened! On 28 May, by order of the Socialist Revolutionary Party, a member of its Flying Combat Organisation executed Metus, Inspector of Prisons in Transbaikal and former Head of the Nerchinsk Penal Region. The shot fired by our comrade was the final word of outrage of the people's court. Metus was the agent of, and even inspiration for, the government's murder and torture of our imprisoned comrades in Akatui and Algachi [in Nerchinsk], among whom there were women and the sick.

The representatives of the autocracy have claimed before the entire nation that turning their prisons into a bloodbath of violence and torture is nothing more than zealous tsarist executioners "faithfully carrying out the duties of their office" ... With its response, the government itself signed Metus' death sentence, which the Socialist Revolutionaries then considered themselves obliged to carry out.[55]

More such assassinations followed. A month later, four assailants fired on the warden of the Krasnoyarsk prison, Smirnov, as he was being driven through the city in his carriage. Smirnov survived the initial shots and fled on foot, but the terrorists pursued him through the streets and, catching up with him, shot him fifteen times. The authorities were quick to detain one suspect, Pyotr Rosyalkov, who had already been convicted of participating in the armed uprising in the city in December 1905 and had been imprisoned in Tomsk only to escape thereafter. Rosyalkov was arrested in a nearby tavern in possession of a Nagant revolver with three spent rounds still in the chamber and, pronounced by the governor of Yenisei province to be "a dangerous anarchist terrorist, capable of any crime," was turned over to a military tribunal. Rosyalkov was found guilty of the assassination and sentenced to hang. Despite the appeals of his mother, he was executed on 25 October 1908.[56]

In Tobolsk, meanwhile, Takhchoglo and his comrades might have found a sympathetic hearing before the military tribunal, but local officials held what they saw as a lack of discipline in the prisons responsible for their revolt. The murdered Bogoyavlensky's replacement, Ivan Mogilyev, was determined to bring the town's unruly prisoners to heel. This time, the confrontation would play out in the Tobolsk Central Penal Labour Prison, to which most politicals had been returned. Disputes over access to the kitchens and the wearing of fetters provoked the familiar cycle of protest and crackdown. These confrontations spilled over into the town square; Mogilyev went so far as to leave examples of the convicts' food in front of the gates of the prison in order to demonstrate to the residents of Tobolsk that the prisoners were not being mistreated. Such theatrical gestures could not, however, turn the tide of popular opinion. Reports of abuses in the jail were still circulating in the local press: Mogilyev was locking up prisoners in a "hot" punishment cell in which "they suffocated from the heat" and "died like flies."[57]

In the autumn of 1907, Mogilyev ordered that all the prisoners be fettered and their heads shaved, and he had three, who had defiantly removed their fetters, flogged. The brutality provoked a wave of protest in the prison. The inmates began banging on their windows, clattering their pots and tins against the bars of their cell windows and shouting at the top of their voices. The din could be heard across the town. Mogilyev had been upstaged.

Undeterred, the warden pressed on with his crackdown. The use of corporal punishment became widespread, inflicted for minor infractions such as a prisoner's refusal to remove his cap in the presence of a warder as well as for more serious offences such as attempted escapes. Tobolsk became known as the "realm of the birch." Mogilyev denied the prison doctor the right to have prisoners sent to the infirmary, insisted that even the sick wear their fetters at all times, began to set the rations for the sick himself and had some prisoners removed from the hospital and thrown into solitary confinement. He singled out Takhchoglo for particularly vindictive treatment, ordering the removal of the strips of leather that prevented the prisoner's iron fetters from rubbing against his ankles and wrists. Takhchoglo was denied books and writing materials for months, and he was deliberately placed in cells confining the most dangerous of the common criminals.[58]

The jail was, like many across Siberia, becoming what one contemporary journalist termed an "open area of political struggle." On 7 January 1908, an attempt by the warders to move an insubordinate prisoner to the punishment cells elicited a storm of protest among more than a dozen of his cellmates. "Arrest us all," they shouted. Mogilyev ordered the ringleaders arrested, a move that only fanned the flames of the riot throughout the prison. Having assembled reinforcements, Mogilyev demanded that the men be dragged from their cells but, this time, the guards suffered losses of their own. Seven prisoners were injured, but one managed to seize a revolver and, firing on the guards, killed one and wounded another.[59]

In March 1908, the thirteen prisoners in the mutinous cell were tried for murder by a military tribunal in the grounds of the prison. Invoking the state's law, the prosecutors portrayed the defendants as violent fanatics. By contrast, invoking natural law, the accused sought to draw a picture of the despotic and cruel regime that had driven them to revolt. Appealing to the court of public opinion, the men in the dock asked permission to lower their trousers to show the court their wounds from Mogilyev's repeated beatings, but the judge denied the request.

This time, the authorities would show no restraint and no leniency.

The prisoners were convicted of conspiring to murder their guards and of premeditated murder and were sentenced to hang. General Ivan Nadarov, the military governor of the Omsk region, withheld clemency, and the thirteen were hanged in the courtyard of the Tobolsk Central Penal Labour Prison. Conditions there had now become so dreadful that, when he finally saw the scaffold, one of the condemned men was heard to exclaim, "Ah, there you are, my sweet gallows, my beautiful sunshine, there you are at last!" The prison doctor attending the execution had a nervous breakdown and left his post.[60]

Even after the execution, the repression in the prison continued. In July, Takhchoglo attempted to kill himself by slashing his wrists with a sharpened pen; four others followed his example. The horrors of the execution and the suicides rippled beyond the prison and across the town. One of Tobolsk's Duma deputies, Nikolai Skalozubov, protested to Prime Minister Pyotr Stolypin about "the terrible nightmare that the Tobolsk prison, which stands in the centre of the town, has inflicted on its residents." In Passion Week, he wrote, "people have lost sleep, sobbing from nervous excitement. Services take place in the town's churches and in the [Sofia] cathedral, while next door, beyond the walls of the prison, there are thirteen gibbets." How could the residents of Tobolsk "live calmly around walls behind which men are mercilessly flogged, beaten, tortured in hot punishment cells and hanged?" The Socialist Revolutionaries in Tobolsk published proclamations to the residents and the soldiers of the local garrison denouncing the "bestialities" perpetrated inside the prison.[61]

Vengeance for the hangings was slow in coming, but come it surely did. Mogilyev survived for a full year and a half as the master of the Tobolsk Central Penal Labour Prison, but he was now a marked man. Despite reservations among some in the local party leadership that an assassination would only intensify repression of their comrades behind bars, a Socialist Revolutionary named Nikolai Shishmaryov travelled to Tobolsk in April 1909. He loitered outside the prison on the bustling square and, when Mogilyev arrived, stepped forward and shot him dead. Unlike his comrade in Chita, Shishmaryov did not benefit from the passivity of sympathetic onlookers and was seized by a crowd of residents.

The local committee of the Socialist Revolutionaries swiftly printed another proclamation under the epigraph, "Rights must be won through struggle!," and distributed it throughout Tobolsk:

On 20 April 1909, a member of the Urals Regional Combat Organisation of the Socialist Revolutionary Party killed the warden of the Tobolsk Penal Labour Prison, Mogilyev. The warden was sentenced to death by the SR Party for his outrageous tormenting and mockery of our brothers and comrades who are languishing in the prison.[62]

Sentenced to death by hanging, Shishmaryov succeeded in taking poison and died on the eve of his execution. Mogilyev was meanwhile buried next to the grave of his predecessor, Bogoyavlensky, in the town cemetery; his obituary was published in the official journal *Prison Herald*. The prison warders were now, like the revolutionaries arrayed against them, forging their own genealogy of martyrdom.[63]

Some three centuries after Boris Godunov had exiled the insurgent Uglichans and their silenced bell to political oblivion in Tobolsk, the town had itself become a stage in the very public struggle between the state and its internal enemies. The bloody drama that played itself out in Tobolsk between 1907 and 1909 was a microcosm of the 1905 Revolution. Militants provoked the regime into a brutal crackdown that served only to alienate further the tens of thousands of prisoners in custody and the hundreds of thousands of exiles and their families beyond the prisons. At his trial in 1907, Takhchoglo astutely observed that the government's crackdown in its prisons "only widened the gap between the authorities and the people."[64]

In the years leading up to the First World War, the government's repression showed no signs of abating. Siberia's prison regime was now, the radical journalist Venedikt Myakotin protested, "deliberately designed . . . to create as many privations, large and small, for the convicts as possible." In the Algachi jail in 1913, prisoners were thrown into punishment cells for refusing to respond to the warders' insulting use of the informal Russian "you." Refusals to stand to attention in the presence of warders were met with fetters, stints in dark, cramped punishment cells and the removal of writing materials, linen, books and so forth. Prisoners protested against these punishments through hunger strikes and suicides. In 1909, a penal labourer serving a life sentence in the Tobolsk Central Penal Labour Prison refused to allow his head to be shaved, as it was "humiliating." Locked in solitary confinement, he attempted to slit his wrists with a shard of glass; the following day, another prisoner tried to do the same. In Algachi, seven political prisoners attempted to kill themselves in protest at the flogging of one of their comrades.[65] In Nerchinsk's Kumatorsk prison in 1912, the flogging of a young Socialist Revolutionary terrorist, Izrael Brilon, for insubordination and for violently resisting his guards, sparked a string of protests among his comrades. A hunger strike was called, and when the warder refused to make any concessions, four of the men killed themselves, some using poison, others using knives. Ten convicts had committed suicide in prisons throughout Tobolsk province in 1900; in 1909, no fewer than 145 took their lives.[66] Prison suicides became a barometer of both the revolutionaries' pitiless struggle against the state and their furious impotence. The state had won the extended test of strength in the years between 1900 and 1914, but at a cost.

In the decade before 1905, arrest, exile and imprisonment succeeded in disrupting the activities of revolutionaries and in crushing many in health and spirit. But they also served to radicalize others by confirming their caste-like status as revolutionaries in the eyes of contemporaries. Martyrdom and suffering were to prove a source of moral authority in 1917 as Siberia's former exiles staked their claims to lead the revolution. The 1905 Revolution transformed Siberia's prisons from a mark of distinction for a sectarian elite of radicals into a fate shared by tens of thousands of politicized tsarist subjects drawn from every corner of the empire and from every social class and ethnic group.

Siberia's prisons also proved indispensable weapons in the government's campaign to crush the 1905 Revolution, but they were a double-edged sword. Crammed with embittered and hostile revolutionaries, they became not simply places of containment and punishment but also incubators of the vengeful, implacable hatred that would erupt across the empire in 1917.

On 1 July 1910, the Omsk Military Tribunal, sitting in Tobolsk, sentenced to death an obscure political prisoner named Sergei Vilkov for his alleged part in the murder of a prison guard. Vilkov returned to his punishment cell at four o'clock in the afternoon and sat down to write a final note to the prison authorities. There were echoes of the heroic suicide of Cato the Younger in the lines that Vilkov scrawled. In 46 BC, Cato had disembowelled himself rather than submit to Caesar's tyranny, even if that tyranny was expressed in "Caesar's favour."* Vilkov likewise refused both the state's justice and the tsar's clemency:

> You are the brigands and the murderers, not those on whom you sit in judgement! And so you have sentenced me to death for nothing, but I am finished with you! I know how to hang myself. I know how to hang myself and I can manage without your hangmen. I no longer wish to live even if my death sentence is replaced by penal labour. At least I will no longer see tyranny![67]

Vilkov killed himself not simply to defend his human dignity; with his suicide, he denied the state not only the power to kill him but also, in an even more radical challenge to the patriarchal authority of the crown, its power to grant him life through an act of clemency. In 1826, one of the Decembrists had written to Nicholas I to express his gratitude for "granting me life" by commuting his death sentence to penal labour. Almost a century later, the new cohort of revolutionaries would brook no such magnanimity. Vilkov's suicide note was a tormented, screaming refusal of mercy. The young prisoner took his own life not in order to cheat the gallows but rather to pre-empt the possibility of a reprieve. In so doing, he subverted perhaps the ultimate demonstration of sovereign power: the power not to take life, but to grant it.[68]

Vilkov's suicide note was also a death sentence on the state that had condemned him to die. The revolutionary killed himself in the fervent belief that the authority of the autocracy would eventually be stripped away, laying bare the state's corrupt core. At that moment, the power of the tsar would be exposed for the conjuring trick it really was and the deluded supporters of the regime would turn on their rulers:

> You thieves and murderers rejoice that you have seized so much power! . . . You hangmen have killed thousands upon

---

* " 'For as to myself,' said he, 'if I would be preserved by Caesar's favour, I should myself go to him; but I would not be beholden to a tyrant, for his acts of tyranny. For it is but usurpation in him to save, as their rightful lord, the lives of men over whom he has no title to reign.' " *Plutarch's Lives,* trans. John Dryden, vol. 2 (New York, 2001), p. 313.

thousands and continue to kill! You parasites feed off honest, hard-working people, and take away life just so that you can drink even more blood! The peasants feed you, and you rule over them by means of dark masses of soldiers. But there will come a time when they will see you for the swindlers, thieves, murderers and debauchees you are! And then you will be shown no mercy!

Vilkov's body was discovered at nine o'clock on the evening of 1 July 1910. He had tied a length of rope to a ring in the wall that supported his bed and, while lying on the floor, had slowly strangled himself to death.[69] The young revolutionary had not only refused clemency; he had also vowed never to grant it. And indeed, after 1917, the Bolsheviks would show their own enemies no mercy, only vengeance. The autocrat, whose sovereign gift of life Vilkov had spurned, would himself die in a Siberian cellar in a hail of revolutionary bullets.[70]

Red Siberia

On 2 March 1917, Nicholas II abdicated the throne, and power was transferred to the Provisional Government. Russia was declared "the freest country in the world." The exile system, widely reviled as a symbol of despotism, imploded. The new government declared an amnesty resulting in the release of 88,000 prisoners, including nearly 5,700 political prisoners and some 68,000 criminals. An additional 14,500 prisoners were released by revolutionary mobs. Mass escapes also became an everyday occurrence in the ensuing months. On 25 April, the Provisional Government formally abolished exile as a punishment.[1]

As Siberia's jails opened their doors, the political prisoners who emerged from them often harboured a ruthless determination to destroy the remnants of the old regime. Revolutionary crowds in Irkutsk gave a heroes' welcome to political prisoners released from the Aleksandrovsk Central Penal Labour Prison, who took to a tribune to make speeches. "Their eyes blazed feverishly, the emaciated faces of many spoke of the sufferings they had endured," the ethnographer Ivan Serebrennikov observed. "Their speeches were those of fanatics, full of unshakeable conviction . . . Slaves to their ideas, they were the modern archpriests . . . of socialism, born of the [revolutionary] underground and of the tsar's prisons."[2]

It is one of the ironies of 1917 that the revolution should have overwhelmed the exile system that the autocracy had for so long wielded as a weapon against subversion. Warders, exile officials and guards suddenly found themselves stripped of their authority and vulnerable to the vengeful retribution of their former captives. What little semblance of order remained in Siberia's exile and prison system by the end of 1917 was torn up by the civil war that engulfed the continent between 1918 and 1920. Exiles, prisoners, their families and officials were sucked into a maelstrom of battles, refugee columns, famine and epidemics. It was a fittingly ignominious end to a system that had achieved so little at such a colossal expense.[3]

Yet Siberia surrendered its prisoners only temporarily. After 1917, exile and penal labour would be reinvented and punishments would be revamped for an age of science, rationality and industrialization. The Bolsheviks did not inherit a functioning penal system from their tsarist predecessors, but they did inherit a very similar set of practical dilemmas: how to extract the vast and valuable mineral resources from the far-flung frozen expanses of the taiga and tundra and, also, how to contain crime and subversion within the Soviet state. After 1917, the Bolsheviks rose to meet these challenges with a zeal and a brutality all their own.

No longer would deportation to Siberia be primarily about the enforced isolation and penal settlement of criminals and dissenters, with forced labour reserved for a particularly dangerous minority. It would now involve the ruthless exploitation of convict labour on an industrial scale justified by the need for a "purification of society" and by the prospect of "individual rehabilitation." Far-flung tsarist-era exile settlements such as Sredne-Kolymsk and prisons like Omsk were expanded into major centres of forced labour. The Gulag was celebrated in the press as a workshop of the new citizenry, and its camps were hailed as "curative labour camps."[4]

As part of the Bolshevik Party's cultural campaigns to consolidate its own legitimacy and to sanctify the October Revolution, state publishing houses in the 1920s and 1930s produced a stream of hagiographical texts commemorating the martyrdom of pre-revolutionary political prisoners. Memoirs, historical studies and archival documents established an inspiring genealogy of tsarist oppression and revolutionary heroism—a genealogy that stretched back in time, linking the Bolsheviks with their revolutionary forebears and representing the victory of Soviet power as the culmination of a century-old struggle with tyranny. The experience of Siberian exile formed an important thread of continuity linking the new rulers of the lands of the Russian Empire with cohorts of illustrious radicals from the 1860s like Nikolai Chernyshevsky, and, ultimately, with the Decembrists of the 1820s. The Society of Former Political Penal Labourers was established in 1921 and began to publish a journal, *Penal Labour and Exile*, devoted to recording the experiences of political exiles and penal labourers. Yet ironically, at the very moment when the Bolsheviks were emphasizing the martyrdom of Siberian exiles and the cruel tyranny of the tsarist state, they were casting their own rivals, dissenters, and the human detritus of the *ancien régime* into forced labour camps on a scale that would have defied the imagination of tsarist penal administrators.[5]

Many radicals from the pre-revolutionary underground—especially Socialist Revolutionaries and Mensheviks, but increasingly Bolshevik oppositionists as well—were thus offered a vantage point from which to compare both tsarist and Soviet prisons in Siberia. The majority would look back wistfully on the conditions of their incarceration before the revolution. One such "Old Bolshevik" was Iwan Teodorowicz.[6]

Teodorowicz had been born in 1875 into a family of Polish aristocrats with a proud history of revolutionary struggle against the autocracy. His great-grandfather had played an active part in the November Insurrection of 1830 in Warsaw; his father and two older brothers had fought in the January Uprising of 1863. Captured by tsarist forces, one brother had been exiled to the Caucasus and the other to Siberia. Teodorowicz had been raised "to hate Russian tsarism." By the time he finished high school, this scion of a long line of rebels was convinced that he would live his life as a "professional revolutionary." Studying in Moscow in the 1890s, he became a Marxist and joined the Russian Social Democratic Workers' Party, which would, in 1903, split into the Bolsheviks and the Mensheviks.

Active in the revolutionary underground in Moscow at the turn of the twentieth century, Teodorowicz was denounced by an informer, arrested in 1902 and exiled to Yakutsk. He escaped from exile three years later and made his way to Geneva, before returning to St. Petersburg in October 1905, where he went on to play a leading role in the revolutionary underground. He was again arrested in 1908 and sentenced to five years of penal labour followed by exile in Irkutsk province. Nine years later, he returned to Petrograd in the midst of the February Revolution, now as a leading Bolshevik. Teodorowicz was a member of the party's Central Executive Committee, which issued a proclamation on 19 July 1918 reporting and approving the murder of Nicholas II. He became deputy commissar of agriculture in 1922, played a leading role in setting up the Society of Former Political Penal Labourers and, from 1929, was the editor of *Penal Labour and Exile*.

In 1929, the Soviet regime ordered the construction of a large modernist apartment building on the edge of Leningrad's Revolution Square (today's Trinity Square) for the members of the Society of Former Political Penal Labourers. At last, these ageing revolutionaries found affirmation of their struggle in this impressive edifice on the banks of the Neva, dubbed the "House of the Political Penal Labourers." From their well-appointed balconies they could look across the square on to the Peter and Paul Fortress, from whose casements, more than 100 years earlier, the Decembrists had been led out in chains to begin their journey to Siberia.

Today, a diminutive stone memorial stands beneath the House of the Political Penal Labourers in the centre of Trinity Square. Erected in 2002, it bears the inscription "To the Prisoners of the Gulag." The location is significant. Within a few years of taking up residence in their new apartment building, the former political prisoners had every reason to envy the Decembrists their years of Siberian exile.

As state repression intensified in the 1930s, the Society of Former Political Penal Labourers, which represented a more inclusive and pluralist vision of the revolutionary past, fell foul of the increasingly shrill intolerance of ideological difference. In 1935, it was disbanded and its journal was shut down. Finally, on 11 June 1937, Teodorowicz was, like many of his colleagues, arrested. The careworn veteran of Siberia's penal settlements once again found himself locked in a prison cell, charged with plotting to overthrow the state. But this time, there would be no escape and no release. One hundred and thirty members of the society were executed during the Great Terror, and a further ninety were sent to the forced labour camps of a revolutionary regime many had struggled to bring to power. Teodorowicz, however, never reached the camps. On 20 September 1937, he was executed by firing squad.[7]

Notes

ARCHIVAL ABBREVIATIONS

St. Petersburg

RGIA (*Rossiiskii gosudarstvennyi istoricheskii arkhiv*)—Russian State Historical Archive

IRLI RAN (*Institut russkoi literatury Rossiiskoi Akademii Nauk*)—Institute of Russian Literature, Russian Academy of Sciences

AAN SPb (*Sankt Peterburgskii filial arkhiva Akademii Nauk*)—St. Petersburg Branch of the Archive of the Academy of Sciences

TsGIA SPb (*Tsentral'nyi gosudarstvennyi istoricheskii arkhiv Sankt Peterburga*)— Central State Historical Archive of St. Petersburg

Moscow

GARF (*Gosudarstvennyi arkhiv Rossiiskoi Federatsii*)—State Archive of the Russian Federation

RGVIA (*Rossiiskii gosudarstvennyi voenno-istoricheskii arkhiv*)—Russian State Military–Historical Archive

Tobolsk

GATOvgT (*Gosudarstvennyi arkhiv Tiumen'skoi oblasti v gorode Tobol'sk*)— State Archive of Tyumen province in the town of Tobolsk

Irkutsk

GAIO (*Gosudarstvennyi arkhiv Irkutskoi oblasti*)—State Archive of Irkutsk province

Archival references use the following abbreviations:

f. (*fond*)

op. (*opis'*)

d. (*delo*)
k. (*karton*)
n. (*nomer*)
ch. (*chast'*)
dp. (*deloproizvodstvo*)
eksp. (*ekspeditsiia*)
t. (*tom*)
sv. (*svodka*)
o. o. (*osoboe otdelenie*)
l. or ll. (*list* or *listy*)

EPIGRAPH

1. F. M. Dostoevskii, "Zapiski iz Mertvogo doma," in idem, *Polnoe sobranie sochinenii*, 30 vols. (Leningrad, 1972–90), vol. 4, p. 9.

PROLOGUE: THE BELL OF UGLICH

1. K. Iaroslavskii, *Vozvrashchennyi iz Sibiri uglichskii kolokol* (Uglich, 1892); D. V. Lavrov, *Uglichskii ssyl'nyi kolokol* (Uglich, 1913); A. M. Lobashkov, *Istoriia ssyl'nogo kolokola* (Yaroslavl, 1988), pp. 32–45.
2. Lobashkov, *Istoriia ssyl'nogo kolokola*, pp. 9–27; Andrew A. Gentes, *Exile to Siberia, 1590–1822* (Basingstoke, 2008), pp. 36–7.
3. Ippolit Zavalishin, *Opisanie Zapadnoi Sibiri*, 2 vols. (Moscow, 1862), vol. 1, pp. 317–18.
4. Galina Shebaldina, *Shvedskie voennoplennye v Sibiri (Pervaia chetvert' XVIII veka)* (Moscow, 2005), ch. 1; A. P. Mikheev, *Tobol'skaia katorga* (Omsk, 2007), pp. 24–5.
5. F. Kudriavtsev and G. Vendrikh, *Irkutsk: ocherki po istorii goroda* (Irkutsk, 1971), pp. 105–6; L. M. Dameshek (ed.), *Irkutsk v panorame vekov* (Irkutsk, 2002), pp. 139, 146; N. V. Kulikauskene (ed.), *Letopis' goroda Irkutska XVII—XIX vv.* (Irkutsk, 1996), pp. 233–6.
6. Alexander Solzhenitsyn, *The Gulag Archipelago: 1918–1956*, trans. Thomas P. Whitney and Harry Willetts (London, 1995); Anne Applebaum, *Gulag: A History* (London, 2004); Steven A. Barnes, *Death and Redemption: The Gulag and the Shaping of Soviet Society* (Princeton, 2011).
7. Yuri Slezkine and Galya Diment, "Introduction," in idem (eds.), *Between Heaven and Hell: The Myth of Siberia in Russian Culture* (New York, 1993), p. 2; Valerie Kivelson, *Cartographies of Tsardom: The Land and Its Meanings in Seventeenth-Century Russia* (Ithaca, 2006), ch. 4.
8. Robert Hughes, *The Fatal Shore: A History of the Transportation of Convicts to Australia, 1787–1868* (London, 1986), p. xi; Stephen A. Toth, *Beyond Papillon: The French Overseas Penal Colonies, 1854–1952* (Lincoln, NE, 2006), p. 12.

9. A. P. Chekhov, "V ssylke," *Polnoe sobranie sochinenii i pisem*, 20 vols. (Moscow, 1944–51), vol. 8, p. 87.

10. *Iaroslavskie eparkhial'nye vedomosti*, 1892, no. 24, pp. 373–5; Lobashkov, *Istoriia ssyl'nogo kolokola*, pp. 39–41.

11. Frith Maier, "The Forgotten George Kennan: From Cheerleader to Critic of Tsarist Russia," *World Policy Journal*, vol. 19, no. 4 (Winter 2002–3), pp. 79–84; Jane E. Good, "America and the Russian Revolutionary Movement, 1888–1905," *The Russian Review*, vol. 41, no. 3 (July 1982), p. 274.

12. George L. Yaney, *The Systematization of Russian Government: Social Evolution in the Domestic Administration of Imperial Russia, 1711–1905* (Urbana, IL, 1973); Richard Pipes, *Russia Under the Old Regime*, 2nd edn (London, 1995), ch. 11.

I   ORIGINS OF EXILE

1. George V. Lantzeff and Richard A. Pierce, *Eastward to Empire: Exploration and Conquest on the Russian Open Frontier, to 1750* (Montreal, 1973).

2. Michael Khodarkovsky, *Russia's Steppe Frontier: The Making of a Colonial Empire, 1500–1800* (Bloomington, IN, 2002), ch. 3; George V. Lantzeff, *Siberia in the Seventeenth Century* (New York, 1972), pp. 87–8; Andrew A. Gentes, *Exile to Siberia, 1590–1822* (Basingstoke, 2008), pp. 22–5; Janet M. Hartley, *Siberia: A History of the People* (New Haven, 2014), pp. 5–11.

3. James Forsyth, *A History of the Peoples of Siberia: Russia's North Asian Colony, 1581–1990* (Cambridge, 1992), pp. 6–10; Andrew A. Gentes, *Exile, Murder and Madness in Siberia, 1823–61* (Basingstoke, 2010), pp. 1–4.

4. W. Bruce Lincoln, *The Conquest of a Continent: Siberia and the Russians* (Ithaca, 1994), pp. 48–56; Forsyth, *A History of the Peoples of Siberia*, pp. 10–28; Piers Vitebsky, *Reindeer People: Living with Animals and Spirits in Siberia* (London, 2011), chs. 1–2.

5. Robert J. Kerner, *The Urge to the Sea; the Course of Russian History. The Role of Rivers, Portages, Ostrogs, Monasteries, and Furs* (New York, 1970), p. 86; Raymond H. Fisher, *The Russian Fur Trade, 1550–1700* (Berkeley, 1943), chs. 1–3; Mark Bassin, "Expansionism and Colonialism on the Eastern Frontier: Views of Siberia and the Far East in Pre-Petrine Russia," *Journal of Historical Geography*, vol. 14, no. 1 (1988), pp. 3–21.

6. Lantzeff, *Siberia in the Seventeenth Century*, pp. 87–91; Hartley, *Siberia*, pp. 38–41; Lincoln, *The Conquest of a Continent*, pp. 45–6, 61; Forsyth, *A History of the Peoples of Siberia*, pp. 33–5, 61–6; Valerie Kivelson, "Claiming Siberia: Colonial Possession and Property Holding in the Seventeenth and Early Eighteenth Centuries," in Nicholas B. Breyfogle et al. (eds.), *Peopling the Russian Periphery: Borderland Colonization in Eurasian History* (London, 2007), pp. 27–32.

7. Lincoln, *The Conquest of a Continent*, pp. 81–2; Fisher, *The Russian Fur Trade*, ch. 6; Janet Martin, *Treasure from the Land of Darkness: The Fur Trade and Its Significance for Medieval Russia* (Cambridge, 1986); Christoph

Witzenrath, *Cossacks and the Russian Empire, 1598–1725: Manipulation, Rebellion and Expansion into Siberia* (London, 2007), pp. 62–70; ch. 4.

8. A. P. Shchapov, "Sibirskoe obshchestvo do Speranskogo," *Sochineniia*, 4 vols. (St. Petersburg, 1906–8), vol. 3, p. 673; Lantzeff, *Siberia in the Seventeenth Century*, ch. 5; Lincoln, *The Conquest of a Continent*, pp. 83–4; Gentes, *Exile to Siberia*, pp. 29–31, 82–4, 135, 142–5; Richard Pipes, *Russia Under the Old Regime*, 2nd edn (London, 1995), p. 282; Witzenrath, *Cossacks and the Russian Empire*, chs. 1, 4.

9. I. V. Shcheglov, *Khronologicheskii perechen' vazhneishikh dannykh iz istorii Sibiri: 1032–1882 gg.* (Irkutsk, 1883), pp. 44–5; Lincoln, *The Conquest of a Continent*, pp. 59–63; Witzenrath, *Cossacks and the Russian Empire*, p. 18.

10. V. A. Aleksandrov, *Rossiia na dal'nevostochnykh rubezhakh (vtoraia polovina XVII v.)* (Khabarovsk, 1984), pp. 37–8; Forsyth, *A History of the Peoples of Siberia*, p. 45; Gentes, *Exile to Siberia*, p. 17.

11. Forsyth, *A History of the Peoples of Siberia*, pp. 67–9; Lincoln, *The Conquest of a Continent*, p. 88; Witzenrath, *Cossacks and the Russian Empire*, p. 69.

12. N. M. Iadrintsev, *Sibir' kak koloniia v geograficheskom, etnograficheskom i istoricheskom otnoshenii* (St. Petersburg, 1882), p. 165.

13. Cited in A. A. Alekseev, "Istoriia slova grazhdanin v XVIII v.," *Izvestiia Akademii Nauk SSSR*, vol. 31, no. 1 (1972), p. 68; Bassin, "Expansion and Colonialism," pp. 3–21.

14. William Coxe, *Travels into Poland, Russia, Sweden and Denmark*, 4th edn, 5 vols. (London, 1792), vol. 3, pp. 120–22. Coxe was not the only foreigner at the end of the eighteenth century to witness knoutings, mutilations and brandings with a mixture of fascination and horror. See the memoirs of the Japanese captain Katsuragav Khosiu, *Kratkie vesti o skitaniiakh v severnykh vodakh*, trans. V. M. Konstantinov (Moscow, 1978), pp. 187–8.

15. E. Anisimov, *Dyba i knut: politicheskii sysk i russkoe obshchestvo v XVIII veke* (Moscow, 1999), pp. 498–500; Cyril Bryner, "The Issue of Capital Punishment in the Reign of Elizabeth Petrovna," *The Russian Review*, vol. 49, no. 4 (October 1990), pp. 389–416; John P. LeDonne, *Absolutism and Ruling Class: The Formation of the Russian Political Order, 1700–1825* (Oxford, 1991), pp. 216–17; Alan Wood, "Siberian Exile in the Eighteenth Century," *Sibirica*, vol. 1, no. 1 (Summer 1990), pp. 45–6.

16. Abby Schrader, *Languages of the Lash: Corporal Punishment and Identity in Imperial Russia* (DeKalb, IL, 2002), ch. 1.

17. Coxe, *Travels into Poland*, pp. 129–30.

18. P. A. Slovtsov, *Istoricheskoe obozrenie Sibiri. Stikhotvoreniia. Propovedi*, ed. V. A. Kreshchik (Novosibirsk, 1995), p. 149.

19. N. D. Sergeevskii, *O ssylke v drevnei Rossii* (St. Petersburg, 1887), p. 15; Gentes, *Exile to Siberia*, ch. 3; Anisimov, *Dyba i knut*, pp. 503–10; idem, *The Reforms of Peter the Great: Progress Through Coercion in Russia*, trans. John T. Alexander (Armonk, NY, 1993), p. 229.

20. M. G. Levin and L. P. Potapov (eds.), *Narody Sibiri* (Moscow, 1956), p. 140; Lincoln, *The Conquest of a Continent*, p. 149; Hartley, *Siberia*, pp. 24–5.

21. Stephen D. Watrous (ed.), *John Ledyard's Journey through Russia and Siberia, 1787–1788* (Madison, WI, 1966), pp. 77–8, 152; Edward G. Gray, *The Making of John Ledyard: Empire and Ambition in the Life of an Early American Traveler* (New Haven, 2007), chs. 8–9.

22. V. K. Andreevich, *Istoricheskii ocherk Sibiri*, 6 vols. (St. Petersburg, 1889), vol. 5, pp. 159–69; Lincoln, *The Conquest of a Continent*, p. 142.

23. Robert Hughes, *The Fatal Shore: A History of the Transportation of Convicts to Australia, 1787–1868* (London, 1986), p. xi.

24. David Moon, "Peasant Migration and the Settlement of Russia's Frontiers, 1550–1897," *The Historical Journal*, vol. 40, no. 4 (1997), p. 863; L. G. Beskrovnyi (ed.), *Opisanie Tobol'skogo namestichestva, sostavlennoe v 1789–1790 gg.* (Novosibirsk, 1982), pp. 246–51.

25. John Dundas Cochrane, *Narrative of a Pedestrian Journey Through Russia and Siberian Tartary, from the Frontiers of China to the Frozen Sea of Kamchatka; Performed During the Years 1820, 1821, 1822 and 1823* (Philadelphia, 1824), p. 86.

26. Hartley, *Siberia*, pp. 24–5; *Aziatskaia Rossiia*, vol. 2, pp. 501–3; Lincoln, *The Conquest of a Continent*, pp. 147–9; Cochrane, *Narrative of a Pedestrian Journey*, pp. 133–4.

27. L. M. Dameshek and A. V. Remnev (eds.), *Sibir' v sostave Rossiiskoi Imperii* (Moscow, 2007), appendix 2; Hartley, *Siberia*, pp. 55–69.

28. N. M. Iadrintsev, *Russkaia obshchina v tiur'me i ssylke* (St. Petersburg, 1872), pp. 508–9; Adele Lindenmeyr, *Poverty Is Not a Vice: Charity, Society, and the State in Imperial Russia* (Princeton, 1996), ch. 2; Wood, "Siberian Exile in the Eighteenth Century," p. 54; Alison K. Smith, "'The Freedom to Choose a Way of Life': Fugitives, Borders, and Imperial Amnesties in Russia," *The Journal of Modern History*, vol. 83 (June 2011), pp. 243–71; RGIA, f. 1374, op. 6, d. 1366 (1800), ll. 1–19.

29. Paul Avrich, *Russian Rebels, 1600–1800* (New York, 1972), parts 3–4; Isabel de Madariaga, *Russia in the Age of Catherine the Great* (New Haven, 1981), ch. 16; Gentes, *Exile to Siberia*, pp. 111–14.

30. E. N. Anuchin, *Issledovaniia o protsente soslannykh v Sibir' v period 1827–1846 godov. Materialy dlia ugolovnoi statistiki Rossii* (St. Petersburg, 1873), pp. 309–10; Gentes, *Exile, Murder and Madness*, pp. 22, 26–34; idem, "Vagabondage and the Tsarist Siberian Exile System: Power and Resistance in the Penal Landscape," *Central Asian Survey*, vol. 30, nos. 3–4 (2011), pp. 407–21.

31. Gentes, *Exile to Siberia*, pp. 115–16; Laura Engelstein, *Castration and the Heavenly Kingdom: A Russian Folktale* (Ithaca, 1999).

32. Madariaga, *Russia in the Age of Catherine the Great*, pp. 542–5; Wood, "Siberian Exile in the Eighteenth Century," pp. 52–3.

33. Iadrintsev, *Russkaia obshchina*, p. 523; Gentes, *Exile to Siberia*, pp. 117–18; RGIA, f. 1264, op. 1, d. 400 (1824), ll. 1–4; RGIA, f. 1281, op. 6, d. 27 (1856), 14 ob–15.

34. *Ssylka v Sibir'. Ocherk ee istorii i sovremennogo polozheniia* (St. Petersburg, 1900), pp. 46–7; Alan Wood, "The Use and Abuse of Administrative Exile

to Siberia," *Irish Slavonic Studies* (1985), no. 6, p. 69; V. N. Dvorianov, *V sibirskoi dal'nei storone . . . (Ocherki istorii politicheskoi katorgi i ssylki. 60-e gody XVIII v.—1917 g.)* (Minsk, 1985), p. 27; Ivan Turgenev, "Punin and Baburin" in *Youth and Age: Three Short Novels by Ivan Turgenev,* trans. Marion Mainwaring (London, 1968), pp. 31–4.

35. Jerome Blum, *Lord and Peasant in Russia: From the Ninth to the Nineteenth Century* (Princeton, 1961), p. 430.

36. Andrew A. Gentes, "'Completely Useless': Exiling the Disabled to Tsarist Siberia," *Sibirica,* vol. 10, no. 2 (Summer 2011), p. 33; *Ssylka v Sibir',* pp. 54–6; RGIA, f. 1286, op. 10, d. 1090 (1846), ll. 7–8; RGIA, f. 1286, op. 16, d. 671 (1855), ll. 4–7.

37. Robert J. Abbott, "Police Reform in the Russian Province of Iaroslavl, 1856–1876," *Slavic Review,* vol. 32, no. 2 (1973), p. 293; Neil Weissman, "Regular Police in Tsarist Russia, 1900–1914," *The Russian Review,* vol. 44, no. 1 (January 1985), p. 49; Stephen P. Frank, *Crime, Cultural Conflict and Justice in Rural Russia, 1856–1914* (Berkeley, 1999), pp. 30–36, 236–41.

38. Wood, "The Use and Abuse," pp. 69–70; Anuchin, *O protsente soslannykh,* pp. 310–12; *Ssylka v Sibir',* ch. 2; Hughes, *The Fatal Shore,* pp. 72–3, 163.

39. David F. Lindenfeld, *The Practical Imagination: The German Sciences of the State in the Nineteenth Century* (Chicago, 1997), ch. 1; Marc Raeff, *The Well-Ordered Police State: Social and Institutional Change through Law in the Germanies and Russia, 1600–1800* (New Haven, 1983), pp. 204–50; Pipes, *Russia Under the Old Regime,* p. 128.

40. RGIA, f. 1374, op. 6, d. 1366 (1800), ll. 1–19; *Ssylka v Sibir',* pp. 47–8; A. D. Kolesnikov, "Ssylka i zaselenie Sibiri," in L. M. Goriushkin (ed.), *Ssylka i katorga v Sibiri (XVIII—nachalo XX v.)* (Novosibirsk, 1975), p. 42; Gentes, "'Completely Useless,'" p. 31; Daniel Beer, "Penal Deportation to Siberia and the Limits of State Power, 1801–1881," *Kritika: Explorations in Russian and Eurasian History,* vol. 16, no. 3 (2015), pp. 621–50.

41. Marc Raeff, *Siberia and the Reforms of 1822* (Seattle, 1956), pp. 59–62; Marc Raeff, *Michael Speransky: Statesman of Imperial Russia, 1772–1839* (The Hague, 1957); Gentes, *Exile to Siberia,* pp. 156–201.

42. Andrew Gentes, "'Licentious Girls' and Frontier Domesticators: Women and Siberian Exile from the Late Sixteenth to the Early Nineteenth Centuries," *Sibirica,* vol. 3, no. 1 (2003), pp. 3–20; Abby M. Schrader, "Unruly Felons and Civilizing Wives: Cultivating Marriage in the Siberian Exile System, 1822–1860," *Slavic Review,* vol. 66, no. 2 (Summer 2007), pp. 230–56.

43. Wood, "Siberian Exile in the Eighteenth Century," p. 59; *Aziatskaia Rossiia,* vol. 1, p. 81; *Ssylka v Sibir',* appendix 4; Dameshek and Remnev (eds.), *Sibir',* p. 279.

44. *Ssylka v Sibir',* appendix 1; A. D. Margolis, 'Chislennost' i razmeshchenie ssyl'nykh v Sibiri v kontse XIX veka," in idem, *Tiur'ma i ssylka v impera-torskoi Rossii. Issledovaniia i arkhivnye nakhodki* (Moscow, 1995), p. 41; Andrew A. Gentes, "Towards a Demography of Children in the Tsarist Siberian Exile System," *Sibirica,* vol. 5, no. 1 (Spring 2006), p. 1; Frank, *Crime, Cultural Conflict, and Justice,* ch. 2.

2 THE BOUNDARY POST

1. Petr Kropotkin, *In Russian and French Prisons* (London, 1887), pp. 124–5.
2. George Kennan, *Siberia and the Exile System*, 2 vols. (New York, 1891), vol. 1, pp. 52–4.
3. I. P. Belokonskii [Petrovich], *Po tiur'mam i etapam. Ocherki tiuremnoi zhizni i putevye zametki ot Moskvy do Krasnoiarska* (Oryol, 1887), pp. 107–8.
4. Cited in Andrew A. Gentes, *Exile to Siberia, 1590–1822* (Basingstoke, 2008), p. 48.
5. Robert Hughes, *The Fatal Shore: A History of the Transportation of Convicts to Australia, 1787–1868* (London, 1986), p. 145; Gwenda Morgan and Peter Rushton, *Banishment in the Early Atlantic World: Convicts, Rebels and Slaves* (London, 2013), ch. 6. On the deportations of penal colonists to French Guiana, see Stephen A. Toth, *Beyond Papillon: The French Overseas Penal Colonies, 1854–1952* (Lincoln, NE, 2006); Michel Pierre, *La terre de la grande punition* (Paris, 1982).
6. Hughes, *The Fatal Shore*, pp. 129–57; J. McDonald and R. Shlomowitz, "Mortality on Convict Voyages to Australia, 1788–1868," *Social Science History*, vol. 13, no. 3 (1989), pp. 285–313; James J. Willis, "Transportation versus Imprisonment in Eighteenth- and Nineteenth-Century Britain: Penal Power, Liberty, and the State," *Law and Society Review*, vol. 39, no. 1 (2005), pp. 171–210; Hamish Maxwell-Stewart, "Convict Transportation from Britain and Ireland, 1615–1870," *History Compass*, vol. 8, no. 11 (2010), pp. 1221–42.
7. Anton Chekhov, *Sakhalin Island*, trans. Brian Reeve (Richmond, 2007), p. 26; N. Rumiantsev, *Istoricheskii ocherk peresylki arestantov v Rossii* (St. Petersburg, 1876), p. 10; William L. L. D. Spottiswoode, *A Tarantasse Journey through Eastern Russia in the Autumn of 1856* (London, 1857), p. 37.
8. Gryts'ko [G. Z. Eliseev], "Ugolovnye prestupniki," *Sovremennik*, 1860, vol. 74, p. 286; A. A. Vlasenko, "Ugolovnaia ssylka v Zapadnuiu Sibir' v politike samoderzhaviia XIX veka," Kandidatskaia diss. (Omsk State University, 2008), pp. 63, 69.
9. "Rasskazy Praskov'i Egorovny Annenkovoi," *Russkaia starina*, 1888, no. 4, p. 3.
10. RGIA, f. 383, op. 29, d. 924 (1806), ll. 27, 29; G. Peizen, "Istoricheskii ocherk kolonizatsii Sibiri," *Sovremennik*, 1859, no. 9, pp. 29–30; RGIA, f. 383, op. 29, d. 953 (1818), ll. 2, 24.
11. RGIA, f. 468, op. 20, d. 273 (1787), ll. 2, 8, 22; RGIA, f. 383, op. 29, d. 924 (1806), l. 29.
12. RGIA, f. 383, op. 29, d. 938 (1811), ll. 88–9; RGIA, f. 383, op. 29, d. 953 (1818), ll. 1, 12–14. On the wider problem of the incapacitated exiles reaching Siberia, see Andrew A. Gentes, " 'Completely Useless': Exiling the Disabled to Tsarist Siberia," *Sibirica*, vol. 10, no. 2 (Summer 2011), pp. 26–49.
13. RGIA, f. 1149, op. 1, d. 10 (1828), ll. 2–6; "Arestanty v Sibiri," *Sovremennik*, 1863, no. 11, p. 146.

14. RGIA, f. 383, op. 29, d. 924 (1806), l. 29; Rumiantsev, *Istoricheskii ocherk peresylki*, pp. 12–13.

15. O. N. Bortnikova, *Sibir' tiuremnaia: penitentsiarnaia sistema Zapadnoi Sibiri v 1801–1917 gg.* (Tyumen, 1999), p. 45; RGIA, f. 1286, op. 1, d. 195 (1804), l. 1.

16. S. M. Shtutman, *Na strazhe tishiny i spokoistviia: iz istorii vnutrennykh voisk Rossii (1811–1917 gg.)* (Moscow, 2000), pp. 107–9; RGIA, f. 1286, op. 1, d. 195 (1804), ll. 51, 53, 64; RGIA, f. 1286, op. 2, d. 245 (1817), l. 1; "O prestupleniiakh po vsei Sibiri, v koikh uchastvovali ssyl'nye s 1823 po 1831 god," *Zhurnal Ministerstva Vnutrennykh Del*, 1833, no. 8, pp. 224–33.

17. *Ssylka v Sibir'. Ocherk ee istorii i sovremennogo polozheniia* (St. Petersburg, 1900), appendix no. 1; Gentes, *Exile to Siberia*, p. 137.

18. Bortnikova, *Sibir' tiuremnaia*, p. 47; H. G. Stepanov (Shenmaier), "Upravlenie katorgoi v Sibiri v nachale XIX veka (pravovoi aspekt)," *Sibirskaia ssylka* (Irkutsk, 2011), no. 6 (18), pp. 92–107; "Ustav ob etapakh v sibirskikh guberniiakh," *Uchrezhdenie dlia upravleniia sibirskikh gubernii* (St. Petersburg, 1822), pp. 4–5; Ippolit Zavalishin, *Opisanie Zapadnoi Sibiri*, 2 vols. (Moscow, 1862), vol. 1, pp. 355–6.

19. S. V. Maksimov, *Sibir' i katorga*, 3rd edn (St. Petersburg, 1900), p. 14; Rumiantsev, *Istoricheskii ocherk peresylki*, p. 12; N. M. Iadrintsev, *Russkaia obshchina v tiur'me i ssylke* (St. Petersburg, 1872), p. 320; Vlasenko, "Ugolovnaia ssylka," p. 63.

20. "Ustav ob etapakh v sibirskikh guberniiakh," p. 26; L. M. Dameshek and A. V. Remnev (eds.), *Sibir' v sostave Rossiiskoi Imperii* (Moscow, 2007), pp. 277–8.

21. "Ustav o ssyl'nykh," articles 210–13; Marc Raeff, *Siberia and the Reforms of 1822* (Seattle, 1956), p. 60; RGIA, f. 1286, op. 21, d. 1118 (1860), l. 1; Gentes, *Exile to Siberia*, pp. 198–9. In 1870, the Exile Office was transferred from Tobolsk to Tyumen. See Vlasenko, "Ugolovnaia ssylka," pp. 81–2.

22. RGIA, f. 1264, op. 1, d. 414 (1825), l. 6; RGIA, f. 1264, op. 1, d. 71 (1835), l. 138.

23. "Ustav ob etapakh v sibirskikh guberniiakh," no. 22; RGIA, f. 1264, op. 1, d. 71 (1835), ll. 136 ob–137; Gentes, *Exile to Siberia*, pp. 195–6.

24. Rumiantsev, *Istoricheskii ocherk peresylki*, pp. 10–11; GARF, f. 109, op. 8, 1 eksp., d. 357 (1833), l. 10; GATOvgT, f. 152, op. 31, d. 127 (1849), l. 18; RGIA, f. 1286, op. 29, d. 836 (1868), l. 8.

25. "Arestanty v Sibiri," pp. 153–4; Iadrintsev, *Russkaia obshchina*, pp. 2–5, 304. Kennan reported a similar improvised decoration in the prison in Algachi in the 1880s. Kennan, *Siberia and the Exile System*, vol. 2, pp. 292–3.

26. V. P. Kolesnikov, "Zapiski neschastnogo, soderzhashchie puteshestvie v Sibir' po kanatu," *Zaria*, 1869, no. 5, pp. 25–6.

27. Vlasenko, "Ugolovnaia ssylka," pp. 66–7; Gentes, *Exile to Siberia*, p. 198; Kennan, *Siberia and the Exile System*, vol. 1, p. 378; RGIA, f. 1286, op. 22, d. 925 (1857), l. 8 ob; Gryts'ko [Eliseev], "Ugolovnye prestupniki," p. 286; RGIA, f. 1286, op. 29, d. 771 (1868), l. 2.

28. Iu. Ruchin'skii, "Konarshchik, 1838–1878: vospominaniia o sibirskoi

ssylke," in B. S. Shostakovich (ed.), *Vospominaniia iz Sibiri: memuary, ocherki, dnevnikovye zapiski pol'skikh politicheskikh ssyl'nykh v vostochnuiu Sibir' pervoi poloviny XIX stoletiia* (Irkutsk, 2009), p. 374; V. L. Seroshevskii, "Ssylka i katorga v Sibiri," in I. S. Mel'nik (ed.), *Sibir': ee sovremennoe sostoianie i ee nuzhdy. Sbornik statei* (St. Petersburg, 1908), p. 209; Nikolai Leskov, *Lady Macbeth of Mtsensk and Other Stories*, trans. David McDuff (London, 1987), pp. 158–71.

29. RGIA, f. 1263, op. 1, d. 415 (1825), ll. 296, 298; RGIA, f. 1264, op. 1, d. 414 (1825), l. 1; RGIA, f. 1286, op. 7, d. 341 (1840), l. 30; GAIO, f. 32, op. 1, d. 199 (1877), l. 2; Vlasenko, "Ugolovnaia ssylka," p. 66; L. Mel'shin [P. F. Iakubovich], *V mire otverzhennykh: zapiski byvshego katorzhnika* (St. Petersburg, 1896), p. 14.

30. RGIA, f. 1286, op. 7, d. 377 (1840), l. 71; Vlasenko, "Ugolovnaia ssylka," p. 299.

31. GARF, f. 109, 1 eksp., op. 8, d. 357 (1833), l. 15; RGIA, f. 1286, op. 7, d. 377 (1840), l. 38.

32. Andrew A. Gentes, *Exile, Murder and Madness in Siberia, 1823–61* (Basingstoke, 2010), p. 52; RGIA, f. 1286, op. 10, d. 1428 (1846), ll. 15–22.

33. GATOvgT, f. 152, op. 39, d. 114 (1864), l. 4.

34. "Arestanty v Sibiri," pp. 139–40, 149.

35. RGIA, f. 1286, op. 22, d. 925 (1861), ll. 10–12.

36. RGIA, f. 1286, op. 22, d. 925 (1861), ll. 13–13 ob; RGIA, f. 468, op. 20, d. 1198 (1855), ll. 1–6; RGIA, f. 1286, op. 24, d. 941 (1863), ll. 1–2; RGIA, f. 1286, op. 29, d. 771 (1868), l. 10.

37. RGIA, f. 1286, op. 29, d. 771 (1868), ll. 19–20; RGIA, f. 1286, op. 9, d. 719 (1844), ll. 1–2, 17–18. In 1875, the inspector of the Nizhegorodsk–Tyumen highway reported on the rotten fish distributed to prisoners in marching convoys. See RGIA, f. 1286, op. 36, d. 686 (1875), l. 14.

38. Maksimov, *Sibir' i katorga*, p. 14; Iadrintsev, *Russkaia obshchina*, pp. 151–2.

39. Andrew A. Gentes, "Vagabondage and the Tsarist Siberian Exile System: Power and Resistance in the Penal Landscape," *Central Asian Survey*, vol. 30, nos. 3–4 (2011), p. 410.

40. Iadrintsev, *Russkaia obshchina*, p. 179.

41. Maksimov, *Sibir' i katorga*, p. 3.

42. "Ustav ob etapakh v sibirskikh guberniiakh," no. 61; Iadrintsev, *Russkaia obshchina*, p. 176; Maksimov, *Sibir' i katorga*, pp. 17–18.

43. Iadrintsev, *Russkaia obshchina*, p. 276; GATOvgT, f. i376, op. 1, d. 56 (1848), ll. 38–40.

44. Fyodor Dostoevsky, *The House of the Dead*, trans. David McDuff (London, 2003), pp. 99–102 [translation modified].

45. Kennan, *Siberia and the Exile System*, vol. 1, pp. 391–2.

46. GAIO, f. 24, op. 3, k. 2, d. 23 (1827), l. 9; RGIA, f. 1149, op. 2, d. 99 (1838), l. 6; RGIA, f. 1286, op. 8, d. 1086 (1843), l. 6; RGIA, f. 1286, op. 7, d. 341 (1840), l. 112 ob; RGIA, f. 383, op. 29, d. 924 (1806), l. 28; RGIA, f. 1264, op. 1, d. 51 (1828), ll. 187–8 ob; *Polnoe sobranie zakonov Rossiiskoi Imperii* II (55 vols.), vol. 3, no. 2286; vol. 4, no. 3377; vol. 28, section 1, no. 27736;

A. D. Margolis, "Soldaty-dekabristy v Petropavlovskoi kreposti i sibirskoi ssylke," in idem, *Tiur'ma i ssylka v imperatorskoi Rossii: Issledovaniia i arkhivnye nakhodki* (Moscow, 1995), p. 73.

47. RGIA, f. 1264, op. 1, d. 71 (1835), l. 150.

3   BROKEN SWORDS

1. I. D. Iakushkin, *Memuary, stat'i, dokumenty* (Irkutsk, 1993), p. 151; S. P. Trubetskoi, *Materialy o zhizni i revoliutsionnoi deiatel'nosti*, 2 vols. (Irkutsk, 1983–7), vol. 1, pp. 281–2; Mariia Volkonskaia, *Zapiski Marii Volkonskoi* (St. Petersburg, 1904), p. 14; N. M. Iadrintsev, *Russkaia obshchina v tiur'me i ssylke* (St. Petersburg, 1872), p. 537; A. N. Murav'ev, *Sochineniia i pis'ma* (Irkutsk, 1986), p. 263.

2. N. V. Basargin, *Zapiski* (Krasnoyarsk, 1985), p. 79.

3. Allison Blakely, "American Influences on Russian Reformist Thought in the Era of the French Revolution," *The Russian Review*, vol. 52, no. 4 (October 1993), pp. 451–71; Orlando Figes, *Natasha's Dance: A Cultural History of Russia* (London, 2002), pp. 74–5; Krista Agnew, "The French Revolutionary Influence on the Russian Decembrists," *Consortium on Revolutionary Europe*, vol. 22 (1993), pp. 333–9; Julie Grandhaye, *Les décembristes: une génération républicaine en Russie autocratique* (Paris, 2011), pp. 74–8.

4. G. A. Rimskii-Korsakov, "Extrait de la lettre d'un russe refugié en Allemagne," in Gennadii Nevelev (ed.), *Dekabristskii kontekst* (St. Petersburg, 2012), p. 33; Richard Stites, *The Four Horsemen: Riding to Liberty in Post-Napoleonic Europe* (Oxford, 2014), pp. 256–7; Figes, *Natasha's Dance*, pp. 84–5; Marc Raeff, *The Decembrist Movement* (Englewood Cliffs, NJ, 1966), ch. 2.

5. M. V. Dovnar-Zapol'skii, *Idealy dekabristov* (Moscow, 1907), p. 94.

6. Cited in Theophilus Prousis, *Russian Society and the Greek Revolution* (DeKalb, IL, 1994), p. 47; Stites, *The Four Horsemen*, pp. 272–89; Isabel de Madariaga, "Spain and the Decembrists," *European Studies Review*, vol. 3, no. 2 (1973), pp. 141–56.

7. Andrzej Walicki, *Philosophy and Romantic Nationalism: The Case of Poland* (Oxford, 1982), pp. 33, 81; Franklin Walker, "Poland in the Decembrists' Strategy of Revolution," *Polish Review*, vol. 15, no. 2 (Spring 1970), pp. 43–54.

8. S. G. Volkonskii, *Zapiski* (Irkutsk, 1991), p. 383.

9. V. A. Fedorov (ed.), "Arest dekabristov," *Vestnik Moskovskogo Universiteta. Seriia VIII: Istoriia*, vol. 5 (1985), pp. 59–71.

10. Stites, *The Four Horsemen*, pp. 293–314.

11. Anatole Mazour, *The First Russian Revolution, 1825: The Decembrist Movement, Its Origins, Development, and Significance* (Stanford, 1937), ch. 8; Grandhaye, *Les décembristes*, ch. 7.

12. Aleksander Pushkin, *Eugene Onegin* (1833), trans. Stanley Mitchell (London, 2008), p. 213.

13. Mazour, *The First Russian Revolution*, ch. 4; Patrick O'Meara, *The Decembrist Pavel Pestel: Russia's First Republican* (Basingstoke, 2003), ch. 6; Glynn R. V. Barratt (ed.), *Voices in Exile: The Decembrist Memoirs* (Montreal, 1974), pp. 1–10; Susanna Rabow-Edling, "The Decembrists and the Concept of a Civic Nation," *Nationalities Papers*, vol. 35, no. 2 (May 2007), pp. 369–91; Grandhaye, *Les décembristes*, ch. 6; Raeff, *The Decembrist Movement*, chs. 4–6. For a general discussion of patriotism at the beginning of the nineteenth century see Maurizio Viroli, *For Love of Country: An Essay on Patriotism and Nationalism* (Oxford, 1995).

14. W. Bruce Lincoln, *Nicholas I: Emperor and Autocrat of All the Russias* (Bloomington, IN, 1978), p. 79; Figes, *Natasha's Dance*, pp. 72–3; Stites, *The Four Horsemen*, p. 256.

15. N. M. Karamzin, *Zapiski o drevnei i novoi Rossii* (St. Petersburg, 1914), p. 122.

16. Pavla Miller, *The Transformations of Patriarchy in the West, 1500–1900* (Bloomington, IN, 1998); Susan K. Morrissey, *Suicide and the Body Politic in Imperial Russia* (Cambridge, 2006), pp. 11–12; Richard S. Wortman, *Scenarios of Power: Myth and Ceremony in Russian Monarchy*, 2 vols. (Princeton, 1995), vol. 1, ch. 9.

17. " 'Gosudar'! Ispoveduiu tebe iako boiashchiisia boga," *Istoricheskii arkhiv*, 2006, no. 1, pp. 166–7, 174.

18. IRLI RAN, f. 57, op. 5, n. 2, ll. 27, 273; B. Syroechkovskii, "Iz zapisok Nikolaia I o 14 dekabria 1825 g.," *Krasnyi arkhiv*, 1924, no. 4, pp. 230–31; N. F. Karash, *Kniaz' Sergei Volkonskii: istoriia zhizni dekabrista* (Irkutsk, 2006), pp. 161–2.

19. Roman Koropeckyj, *Adam Mickiewicz: The Life of a Romantic* (Ithaca, 2008), p. 72.

20. N. K. Shil'der, *Imperator Nikolai Pervyi: ego zhizn' i tsarstvovanie*, 2 vols. (St. Petersburg, 1897), vol. 1, pp. 453–4.

21. A. I. Gertsen, "Byloe i dumy," *Sobranie sochinenii*, 30 vols. (Moscow, 1954–65), vol. 8, p. 61; "Manifest 13 iulia 1826," in Nevelev (ed.), *Dekabristskii kontekst*, p. 25.

22. "Kazn' 14 iiulia 1825 goda," *Poliarnaia zvezda*, 1861, no. 6, pp. 72–5; Mazour, *The First Russian Revolution*, p. 213.

23. N. Ramazanov, "Kazn' dekabristov. Rasskazy sovremennikov," *Russkii arkhiv*, 1881, no. 2, pp. 341–6; Ludmilla A. Trigos, "The Spectacle of the Scaffold: Performance and Subversion in the Execution of the Decembrists," in Marcus Levitt and Tatyana Novikov (eds.), *Times of Trouble: Violence in Russian Literature and Culture* (Madison, WI, 2007), pp. 42–56. In fact, it was precisely because the death penalty had barely been used for some seventy years that Russia had needed to summon specialist hangmen from Sweden; it had none of its own. Mikhail Zetlin, *The Decembrists* (New York, 1958), p. 277.

24. "Manifest 13 iulia 1826," in Nevelev (ed.), *Dekabristskii kontekst*, p. 25.

25. V. M. Bokov (ed.), *Dekabristy i ikh vremia. Trudy moskovskoi i leningradskoi sektsii po izucheniiu dekabristov i ikh vremia*, 2 vols. (Moscow, 1929–

32), vol. 1, p. 209; Gertsen, "Byloe i dumy," p. 59; *Arkhiv dekabrista S. G. Volkonskogo*, vol. 1: *Do Sibiri* (Petrograd, 1918), p. xix; Raeff, *The Decembrist Movement*, p. 163.

26. Jacques-François Ancelot, *Six mois en Russie: Lettres écrites à M. X.-B. Saintines en 1826* (Paris, 1827), pp. 411–12.

27. IRLI RAN, f. 57, op. 1, n. 61, ll. 27, 42.

28. Nikita Murav'ev, *Pis'ma dekabrista 1813–1826 gg.* (Moscow, 2001), pp. 212–13; GARF, f. 1153, op. 1, d. 135 (1825), l. 1. Volkonsky expressed similar feelings of remorse. See O. Popova, "Istoriia zhizni M. N. Volkonskoi," *Zven'ia*, nos. 3–4 (Moscow, 1934), p. 54.

29. Nikolai Nekrasov, "Russkie zhenshchiny," *Sobranie sochinenii v vos'mi tomakh*, 8 vols. (Moscow, 1965–7), vol. 3, pp. 21–87; Christine Sutherland, *The Princess of Siberia: The Story of Maria Volkonsky and the Decembrist Exiles* (London, 1984); Anatole Mazour, *Women in Exile: Wives of the Decembrists* (Tallahassee, FL, 1975); Mikhail Filin, *Mariia Volkonskaia: "utaennaia liubov'" Pushkina* (Moscow, 2006).

30. Trubetskoi, *Materialy*, vol. 1, pp. 110, 112, 166, 177, 204–5.

31. Filin, *Mariia Volkonskaia*, pp. 143–53.

32. Popova, "Istoriia zhizni M. N. Volkonskoi," pp. 28–60; Sutherland, *The Princess of Siberia*, p. 108.

33. E. Anisimov, *Dyba i knut: politicheskii sysk i russkoe obshchestvo v XVIII veke* (Moscow, 1999), pp. 621–30.

34. Iu. M. Lotman, "Dekabrist v povsednevnoi zhizni," in idem, *Besedy o russkoi kul'ture: byt i traditsii russkogo dvorianstva (XVIII–nachalo XIX veka)* (St. Petersburg, 2011), pp. 353–4.

35. Basargin, *Zapiski*, p. 39; Volkonskaia, *Zapiski*, p. 10.

36. Popova, "Istoriia zhizni M. N. Volkonskoi," p. 36; IRLI RAN, f. 57, op. 5, n. 2, l. 203.

37. Popova, "Istoriia zhizni M. N. Volkonskoi," pp. 42–3.

38. Volkonskaia, *Zapiski*, p. 20.

39. V. A. Fedotov (ed.), "Krestnyi put' dekabristov v Sibir': Dokumenty ob otpravke osuzhdennykh na katorgu i v ssylku i ob usloviiakh ikh soderzhaniia 1826–1837 gg.," *Istoricheskii arkhiv*, 2006, no. 6, p. 48; D. I. Zavalishin, *Zapiski dekabrista*, 2nd edn (St. Petersburg, 1906), p. 249.

40. "Vospominaniia o 1826-m i 1827-m godakh Kniazia Evgeniia Petrovicha Obolenskogo," in V. A. Fedotov (ed.), *Memuary dekabristov* (Moscow, 1981), p. 97; I. I. Gorbachevskii, "Zapiski," in A. S. Nemzer (ed.), *Memuary dekabristov* (Moscow, 1988), p. 395; A. E. Rozen, *Zapiski dekabrista* (Leipzig, 1870), p. 197.

41. Zavalishin, *Zapiski*, p. 255.

42. Basargin, *Zapiski*, p. 52; Murav'ev, *Pis'ma dekabrista 1813–1826 gg.*, p. 215; B. E. Syroechkovskii, *Mezhdutsarstvie 1825 goda i vosstanie dekabristov v memuarakh i perepiske chlenov tsarskoi sem'i* (Moscow, 1926), p. 62; Trubetskoi, *Materialy*, vol. 1, pp. 113–14; Iakushkin, *Memuary*, p. 177; Barratt (ed.), *Voices in Exile*, p. 19; Karash, *Kniaz' Sergei Volkonskii*, p. 170.

43. A. D. Margolis, "Etapirovanie dekabristov v Sibir'," in idem, *Tiur'ma i ssylka*

v imperatorskoi Rossii. Issledovaniia i arkhivnye nakhodki (Moscow, 1995), p. 60; Fedotov (ed.), "Krestnyi put' dekabristov," p. 49.

44. M. K. Azadovskii (ed.), *Vospominaniia Bestuzhevykh* (Moscow, 1951), pp. 139, 140, 142; Fedotov (ed.), "Krestnyi put' dekabristov," p. 52; P. E. Shchegolev, "Dekabristy na puti v Sibir': Po neizdannym materialam. Otkliki," no. 22 Prilozhenie k no. 150 gazety *Den'*, 1914, pp. 4–5.

45. M. M. Gedenshtrom, *Otryvki o Sibiri* (St. Petersburg, 1830), p. 4; Barratt (ed.), *Voices in Exile*, p. 209; Fedotov (ed.), "Krestnyi put' dekabristov," p. 52.

46. N. I. Lorer, "Zapiski moego vremeni: vospominanie o proshlom," in Nemzer (ed.), *Memurary dekabristov*, p. 397.

47. Fedotov (ed.), "Krestnyi put' dekabristov," p. 52; Basargin, *Zapiski*, p. 99.

48. Zavalishin, *Zapiski*, p. 256; S. V. Kodan, *Sibirskaia ssylka dekabristov* (Irkutsk, 1983), p. 100; Fedotov (ed.), "Krestnyi put' dekabristov," p. 49; T. A. Pertseva, "Nakazanie dekabristov: dolzhenstvuiushchee i real'noe," in *Sibirskaia ssylka* (Irkutsk, 2011), no. 6 (18), p. 117.

49. M. A. Fonvizin, *Sochineniia i pis'ma*, 2 vols. (Irkutsk, 1979), vol. 1, p. 134; Basargin, *Zapiski*, p. 98; S. V. Maksimov, *Sibir' i katorga*, 3rd edn (St. Petersburg, 1900), p. 392.

50. Basargin, *Zapiski*, p. 99.

51. Margolis, "Etapirovanie dekabristov," p. 57; Andrew A. Gentes, *Exile, Murder and Madness in Siberia, 1823–61* (Basingstoke, 2010), pp. 86–7.

52. Iadrintsev, *Russkaia obshchina*, p. 189; Fyodor Dostoevsky, *The House of the Dead*, trans. David McDuff (London, 2003), pp. 95–6; L. Mel'shin [P. F. Iakubovich], *V mire otverzhennykh: zapiski byvshego katorzhnika* (St. Petersburg, 1896), p. 16.

53. V. P. Kolesnikov, "Zapiski neschastnogo, soderzhashchie puteshestvie v Sibir' po kanatu," *Zaria*, 1869, no. 4, pp. 57–8, 60–63; RGIA, f. 468, op. 25, d. 244 (1828), l. 124 ob.

54. Kolesnikov, "Zapiski neschastnogo," no. 5, pp. 22, 25–6, 30.

55. Wortman, *Scenarios of Power*, vol. 1, ch. 9.

56. "Ustav o ssyl'nykh," nos. 758–9, in *Uchrezhdenie dlia upravleniia sibirskikh gubernii* (St. Petersburg, 1822); GARF, f. 109, 1 eksp., op. 1, d. 61, ch. 3 (1826), ll. 6–7. The statutes were still barring women who had followed their husbands to Nerchinsk from returning to Russia in the 1870s. See RGIA, f. 1286, op. 38, d. 334 (1877), l. 1.

57. "Dnevnik Anastasii Vasil'evny Iakushkinoi," *Novyi mir*, 1964, no. 12, pp. 138–59; Iakushkin, *Memuary*, pp. 51, 54, 165; GARF, f. 109, 1 eksp., op. 1, d. 61, ch. 56 (1826), ll. 6–7, 11, 18.

58. B. L. Mozdalevskii, "Dekabrist S. G. Volkonskii v katorzhnoi rabote v Blagodatskom rudnike," in Iu. G. Oskman (ed.), *Bunt Dekabristov* (Leningrad, 1926), pp. 340, 346.

59. Mozdalevskii, "Dekabrist S. G. Volkonskii," p. 351; Volkonskaia, *Zapiski*, p. 15; Filin, *Mariia Volkonskaia*, p. 172.

60. Sutherland, *The Princess of Siberia*, p. 124; W. Bruce Lincoln, *The Conquest of a Continent: Siberia and the Russians* (Ithaca, 1994), pp. 174–5; Figes,

Natasha's Dance, p. 92; Volkonskaia, *Zapiski*, p. 15. On Nicholas's orders, see GARF, f. 109, 1 eksp., op. 1, d. 61, ch. 3 (1826), ll. 6–7; M. O. Gershenzon (ed.), "Pis'ma kn. M. N. Volkonskoi iz Sibiri, 1827–1831," *Russkie propilei* (Moscow, 1915), p. 18; GARF, f. 1146, op. 1, d. 2028 (1826), l. 7; Popova, "Istoriia zhizni M. N. Volkonskoi," p. 58.

61. S. Wilson, "The Myth of Motherhood a Myth: The Historical View of European Child-Rearing," *Social History*, vol. 9, no. 2 (1984), pp. 81–98; P. D. Jimack, "The Paradox of Sophie and Julie: Contemporary Responses to Rousseau's Ideal Wife and Ideal Mother," in E. Jacobs et al (eds.), *Woman and Society in Eighteenth-Century France* (London, 1979), pp. 152–65; Carol Duncan, "Happy Mothers and Other New Ideas in French Art," *Art Bulletin*, vol. 55, no. 4 (1973), pp. 570–83; Michelle Lamarche Marrese, *A Woman's Kingdom: Noblewomen and the Control of Property in Russia, 1700–1861* (Ithaca, 2002), pp. 197–204; idem, "'The Poetics of Everyday Behavior' Revisited," *Kritika: Explorations in Russian and Eurasian History*, vol. 11, no. 4 (Fall 2010), p. 715; Figes, *Natasha's Dance*, pp. 120–21.

62. Mozdalevskii, "Dekabrist S. G. Volkonskii," p. 358.

63. Popova, "Istoriia zhizni M. N. Volkonskoi," p. 43; P. E. Shchegolev, "Iz razyskanii v oblasti biografii i teksta Pushkina," *Pushkin i ego sovremenniki*, vol. 14 (1911), p. 180; L. G. Frizman, *Dekabristy i russkaia literatura* (Moscow, 1988); Harriet Murav, "'Vo Glubine Sibirskikh Rud': Siberia and the Myth of Exile," in Galya Diment and Yuri Slezkine (eds.), *Between Heaven and Hell: The Myth of Siberia in Russian Culture* (New York, 1993), pp. 95–100.

64. Alexander S. Pushkin, "Message to Siberia," trans. Alan Myers, in idem, *The Complete Works of Alexander Pushkin*, 15 vols. (ed. I. Sproat et al) (Downham Market, 1999), vol. 3, p. 42.

65. M. V. Nechkina, *14oe dekabria 1825-ogo goda i ego tolkovateli: Gertsen i Ogarev protiv Barona Korfa* (Moscow, 1994); S. E. Erlikh, *Istoriia mifa: "Dekabristskaia legenda" Gertsena* (St. Petersburg, 2006); Stites, *The Four Horsemen*, pp. 328–9.

66. O'Meara, *The Decembrist Pavel Pestel*, pp. 124–38; K. F. Miziano, "Ital'ianskoe Risordzhimento i peredovoe obshchestvennoe dvizhenie v Rossii XIX veka," in *Rossiia i Italiia: iz istorii russko-ital'ianskikh kul'turnykh i obshchestvennykh otnoshenii* (Moscow, 1986), p. 97; B. S. Shostakovich, "Politicheskie ssyl'nye poliaki i dekabristy v Sibiri," *Ssyl'nye revoliutsionery v Sibiri (XIX v.–fevral' 1917)*, no. 1 (Irkutsk, 1973), pp. 245–53.

67. Basargin, *Zapiski*, pp. 77–8; Ludmilla A. Trigos, *The Decembrist Myth in Russian Culture* (Basingstoke, 2009), pp. 15–23, 31.

4   THE MINES OF NERCHINSK

1. William Coxe, *Travels into Poland, Russia, Sweden and Denmark*, 4th edn, 5 vols. (London, 1792), vol. 3, pp. 436–7; I. V. Shcheglov, *Khronologicheskii perechen' vazhneishikh dannykh iz istorii Sibiri: 1032–1882 gg.*

(Irkutsk, 1883), pp. 67–8; L. A. Puliaevskii, *Ocherk po istorii g. Nerchinska* (Nerchinsk, 1929), pp. 6–7; E. Anisimov, *Dyba i knut: politicheskii sysk i russkoe obshchestvo v XVIII veke* (Moscow, 1999), pp. 654–5; Andrew A. Gentes, *Exile to Siberia, 1590–1822* (Basingstoke, 2008), pp. 101, 108, 125.

2. RGIA, f. 1264, op. 1, d. 53 (1829), ll. 161 ob–4; RGIA, f. 468, op. 20, d. 668 (1829), ll. 36, 70; S. V. Maksimov, *Sibir' i katorga*, 3rd edn (St. Petersburg, 1900), pp. 52–3; Grigorii Spasskii, "Vzgliad na Dauriiu i v osobennosti na Nerchinskie gornye zavody v 1820," *Sibirskii vestnik*, vol. 9 (1823), p. 107.

3. Mariia Volkonskaia, *Zapiski Marii Volkonskoi* (St. Petersburg, 1904), p. 44.

4. "Novye svedeniia o prebyvanii vos'mi dekabristov v Nerchinskikh zavodakh v 1826–1827 godakh," *Istoricheskii vestnik*, vol. 45, no. 7 (1891), p. 223; Glynn R. V. Barratt (ed.), *Voices in Exile: The Decembrist Memoirs* (Montreal, 1974), p. 229; P. Trunev, "Dekabristy v nerchinskikh rudnikakh," *Istoricheskii vestnik*, vol. 97, no. 8 (1897), pp. 492–4; Volkonskaia, *Zapiski*, p. 144.

5. B. L. Mozdalevskii, "Dekabrist S. G. Volkonskii v katorzhnoi rabote v Blagodatskom rudnike," in Iu. G. Oskman (ed.), *Bunt Dekabristov* (Leningrad, 1926), p. 346.

6. M. V. Golovinskii, "Dekabrist kniaz' E. P. Obolenskii," *Istoricheskii vestnik*, 1890, no. 8, pp. 120–21; Barratt (ed.), *Voices in Exile*, p. 232.

7. GAIO, f. 24, op. 3, k. 49, d. 297 (1826), l. 33; GARF, f. 109, op. 1, 1 eksp., d. 61, ch. 1 (1826), l. 36.

8. Barratt (ed.), *Voices in Exile*, pp. 230–31; "Novye svedeniia o prebyvanii vos'mi dekabristov," p. 227.

9. F. G. Safronov, "Ssylka v Vostochnuiu Sibir' v pervoi polovine XVIII v.," in L. M. Goriushkin (ed.), *Ssylka i katorga v Sibiri (XVIII—nachalo XX v.)* (Novosibirsk, 1975), pp. 30–32.

10. Volkonskaia, *Zapiski*, p. 46.

11. Ibid., pp. 48, 72.

12. M. O. Gershenzon (ed.), "Pis'ma in M. N. Volkonskoi iz Sibiri 1827–1831," *Russkie propilei* (Moscow, 1915), p. 42.

13. Volkonskaia, *Zapiski*, p. 144.

14. Trunev, "Dekabristy v Nerchinskikh rudnikakh," pp. 492–4.

15. Volkonskaia, *Zapiski*, pp. 50–52, 144; "Novye svedeniia o prebyvanii," p. 223; Barratt (ed.), *Voices in Exile*, p. 231; Golovinskii, "Dekabrist kniaz' E. P. Obolenskii," p. 121; S. F. Koval' (ed.), *K Rossii liubov'iu goria: Dekabristy v Vostochnom Zabaikal'e* (Irkutsk, 1976), p. 17.

16. RGIA, f. 468, op. 20, d. 668 (1829), l. 27; John Dundas Cochrane, *Narrative of a Pedestrian Journey through Russia and Siberian Tartary from the Frontiers of China to the Frozen Sea and Kamchatka; Performed during the Years 1820, 1821, 1822, and 1823*, 2 vols. (Edinburgh, 1829), vol. 2, p. 111.

17. Spasskii, "Vzgliad na Dauriiu," pp. 81–2; Maksimov, *Sibir' i katorga*, p. 54.

18. RGIA, f. 468, op. 20, d. 669 (1829), ll. 40–43; Maksimov, *Sibir' i katorga*, pp. 56–7.

19. RGIA, f. 1149, op. 2, d. 99 (1838), ll. 3–6.

20. Maksimov, *Sibir' i katorga*, p. 49; L. Mel'shin [P. F. Iakubovich], *V mire*

otverzhennykh: zapiski byvshego katorzhnika (St. Petersburg, 1896), pp. 79–80.

21. Mel'shin [Iakubovich], *V mire otverzhennykh*, p. 57; "Arestanty v Sibiri," *Sovremennik*, 1863, no. 11, p. 159.

22. RGIA, f. 1286, op. 10, d. 1353 (1847), l. 59; Mel'shin [Iakubovich], *V mire otverzhennykh*, p. 57; A. A. Vlasenko, "Ugolovnaia ssylka v Zapadnuiu Sibir' v politike samoderzhaviia XIX veka," Kandidatskaia diss. (Omsk State University, 2008), p. 157; V. I. Semevskii, *Rabochie na sibirskikh zolotykh promyslakh: istoricheskoe issledovanie*, 2 vols. (St. Petersburg, 1898), vol. 1, p. 305.

23. RGIA, f. 468, op. 20, d. 667 (1827), l. 272.

24. GAIO, f. 24, op. 3, k. 5, d. 82 (1831), ll. 28–28 ob.

25. RGIA, f. 1264, op. 1, d. 609 (1833), ll. 2, 9; RGIA, f. 468, op. 25, d. 244 (1828), l. 18; RGIA, f. 468, op. 19, d. 291 (1847), ll. 5–7; RGIA, f. 468, op. 21, d. 16 (1857), l. 22; RGIA, f. 1149, op. 9, d. 3 (1877), l. 336 ob.

26. RGIA, f. 1264, op. 1, d. 382 (1808), l. 1; RGIA, f. 1263, op. 1, d. 52 (1813), ll. 416–17; RGIA, f. 468, op. 20, d. 543 (1818), ll. 1–2; RGIA, f. 468, op. 19, d. 547 (1828), ll. 4, 14, 22–3.

27. Semevskii, *Rabochie na sibirskikh zolotykh promyslakh*, vol. 1, p. 322.

28. RGIA, f. 468, op. 25, d. 244 (1828), l. 45 ob; RGIA, f. 468, op. 20 (326/487), d. 625 (1828), ll. 1–3.

29. RGIA, f. 1264, op. 1, d. 51 (1828), ll. 11–12 ob; RGVIA, f. 410, op. 1, d. 71 (1827), l. 2; RGIA, f. 468, op. 25, d. 244 (1828), ll. 10 ob–11. Proximity to the Chinese border proved an ongoing headache for administrators of Eastern Siberia as convicts repeatedly seeking to escape the clutches of the Russian state fled across the frontier. See RGIA, f. 1264, op. 1, d. 53 (1829), ll. 134–6; RGIA, f. 1286, op. 7, d. 334 (1840), ll. 1–11.

30. GAIO, f. 24, op. 3, k. 2, d. 23 (1827), ll. 2, 9, 26–7, 31, 111, 116–17 ob. See a similar denunciation from 1835: GAIO, f. 24, op. 3, d. 268 (1835), ll. 22–3, 48.

31. A. E. Rozen, *Zapiski dekabrista* (Leipzig, 1870), p. 197; D. I. Zavalishin, *Zapiski dekabrista*, 2nd edn (St. Petersburg, 1906), p. 250.

32. Olga Chayanova, *Teatr Maddoksa v Moskve 1776–1805* (Moscow, 1927).

33. Solomon Shtraikh, *Roman Medoks. Pokhozhdeniia russkogo avantiurista XIX veka* [1930] (Moscow, 2000), pp. 58, 71.

34. A. A. Orlov, "'Spasitel' otechestva' Roman Medoks—uznik dvukh imperatorov," *Voprosy istorii*, 2002, no. 12, p. 147; Iu. M. Lotman, *V shkole poeticheskogo slova: Pushkin, Lermontov, Gogol'* (Moscow, 1988), pp. 315–16.

35. M. K. Azadovskii (ed.), *Vospominaniia Bestuzhevykh* (Moscow, 1951), p. 145.

36. GARF, f. 109, 1 eksp., d. 61, ch. 1 (1826), ll. 136–9.

37. RGIA, f. 468, op. 25, d. 244 (1828), ll. 1 ob–2, 48 ob.

38. Daniel Beer, "Decembrists, Rebels and Martyrs in Siberian Exile: The 'Zerentui Conspiracy' of 1828 and the Fashioning of a Revolutionary Genealogy," *Slavic Review*, vol. 72, no. 3 (Autumn 2013), pp. 528–51.

39. RGIA, f. 468, op. 25, d. 244 (1828), l. 159.

40. RGIA, f. 468, op. 25, d. 244 (1828), ll. 52 ob, 55–7 ob.
41. RGIA, f. 468, op. 25, d. 244 (1828), ll. 158 ob, 70 ob, 68.
42. GARF, f. 109, 1 eksp., d. 61, ch. 154 (1826), ll. 1–8.
43. [V. N. Solov'ev], "I. I. Sukhinov. Odin iz dekabristov," *Russkii arkhiv*, 1870, nos. 4–5, pp. 918–19; Iu. G. Oksman, "V. N. Solov'ev, Zapiska o I. I. Sukhinove," in idem (ed.), *Vospominaniia i rasskazy deiatelei tainykh obshchestv 1820-kh gg.*, 2 vols. (Moscow, 1933), vol. 2, p. 46; RGVIA, f. 36, op. 4, sv. 17, d. 132 (1826), ll. 4–5 ob; Iu. G. Oksman, "Poimka poruchika I. I. Sukhinova," in B. L. Mozdalevskii and Iu. G. Oksman (eds.), *Dekabristy: neizdannye materialy i stat'i* (Moscow, 1925), pp. 64–70; "Otnoshenie upravliaiushchego ministerstvom vnutrennykh del arkhangel'skomu grazhdanskomu gubernatoru," *Russkaia starina*, 1899, no. 6, p. 586; B. Brazilevskii (ed.), *Gosudarstvennye prestupleniia v Rossii v XIX veke. Sbornik izvlechennykh iz ofitsial'nykh izdanii pravitel'stvennykh soobshchenii*, 3 vols. (St. Petersburg, 1906), vol. 1, p. 65; M. F. Shugurov, "O bunte Chernigovskogo polka," *Russkii arkhiv*, 1902, no. 2, pp. 298–301; "Vosstanie Chernigovskogo polka v pokazaniiakh uchastnikov," *Krasnyi arkhiv*, vol. 13 (1925), pp. 1–67.
44. Iu. G. Oksman, "Dekabrist V. N. Solov'ev i ego vospominaniia," in Mozdalevskii and Oksman (eds.), *Dekabristy*, pp. 16–17; B. A. Kurakin, "Dekabristy na puti v Sibir'," in Mozdalevskii and Oksman (eds.), *Dekabristy*, p. 114; GAIO, f. 24, op. 3, k. 49, d. 282 (1829), ll. 5–6; T. A. Pertseva, "Nakazanie dekabristov: dolzhenstvuiushchee i real'noe," in *Sibirskaia ssylka* (Irkutsk, 2011), no. 6 (18), pp. 119–22.
45. RGIA, f. 468, op. 25, d. 244 (1828), ll. 76, 80–81 ob; 161–2.
46. RGIA, f. 468, op. 25, d. 244 (1828), ll. 61 ob–63 ob; 69 ob.
47. RGVIA, f. 410, op. 1, d. 71 (1827), ll. 4–4 ob; RGIA, f. 468, op. 25, d. 244 (1828), ll. 45 ob, 148 ob; M. V. Nechkina, "Zagovor v zerentuiskom rudnike," *Krasnyi arkhiv*, vol. 13 (1925), p. 260.
48. RGIA, f. 468, op. 25, d. 244 (1828), ll. 48, 150; RGIA, f. 468, op. 20, d. 670 (1829), ll. 60 ob–61.
49. RGIA, f. 468, op. 25, d. 244 (1828), ll. 48 ob, 49 ob; John P. LeDonne, "Criminal Investigations Before the Great Reforms," *Russian History*, vol. 1, no. 2 (1974), p. 111. See, for example, Mel'shin [Iakubovich], *V mire otverzhennykh*, pp. 334–5.
50. RGIA, f. 468, op. 25, d. 244 (1828), ll. 55–7, 64, 66–7, 150–150 ob.
51. Nechkina, "Zagovor v Zerentuiskom rudnike," pp. 263, 269; RGIA, f. 468, op. 25, d. 244 (1828), ll. 27, 43 ob, 114–15 ob; M. Sokolovskii, "Imperator Nikolai I v voenno-sudnykh konfirmatsiiakh," *Russkaia starina*, Oct.–Dec. 1905, pp. 397–420.
52. John P. LeDonne, "The Administration of Military Justice Under Nicholas I," *Cahiers du monde russe et soviétique*, vol. 13, no. 2 (1972), p. 183. Such practices continued throughout the nineteenth century. See Samuel Kucherov, *Courts, Lawyers, and Trials under the Last Three Tsars* (New York, 1953); Samuel Kutscheroff, "Administration of Justice under Nicholas I of Russia," *American Slavic and East European Review*, vol. 7, no. 2 (April 1948),

p. 128; *Polnoe sobranie zakonov Rossiiskoi Imperii* (1830), vol. 20, art. 14309; "K istorii zagovora Sukhinova," *Byloe*, 1906, no. 8, p. 131.

53.   "K istorii zagovora Sukhinova," pp. 130–35.

54.   *Uchrezhdenie dlia upravleniia bol'shoi deistvuiushchei armii. Chast' pervaia* (St. Petersburg, 1812), p. 4; "K epilogu zagovora I. I. Sukhinova," *Byloe*, 1906, no. 5, pp. 37–8.

55.   RGIA, f. 468, op. 19, d. 547 (1828), l. 30.

56.   RGIA, f. 468, op. 25, d. 244 (1828), l. 132.

57.   [Solov'ev], "I. I. Sukhinov," pp. 920, 926.

58.   [I. I. Gorbachevskii], "Zapiski neizvestnogo iz Obshchestva Soedinennykh Slavian," *Russkii arkhiv*, 1882, no. 1, pp. 435–554; "Zapiski Barona Andreia Evgenievicha Rozena," *Otechestvennye zapiski*, 1876, no. 3, p. 48; "Vospominaniia Matveia Ivanovicha Murav'eva-Apostola," *Russkaia starina*, 1886, no. 5, p. 535; Volkonskaia, *Zapiski*, p. 86; "Rasskazy Praskov'i Egorovny Annenkovoi," *Russkaia starina*, 1888, no. 4, p. 374. Only Zavalishin expressed scepticism that a conspiracy had ever existed: Dmitrii Zavalishin, *Zapiski dekabrista*, 2nd edn (St. Petersburg, 1906), p. 287.

5   THE DECEMBRIST REPUBLIC

1.   "Neizdannaia rukopis' dekabrista N. V. Basargina," *Katorga i ssylka*, 1925, no. 5, p. 164; M. K. Azadovskii (ed.), *Vospominaniia Bestuzhevykh* (Moscow, 1951), pp. 248, 313–14.

2.   Geoffrey Hosking, *Russia: People and Empire, 1552–1917* (Cambridge, MA, 1998), p. 144; W. Bruce Lincoln, *Nicholas I: Emperor and Autocrat of All the Russias* (Bloomington, IN, 1978), ch. 4; Nicholas V. Riasanovsky, *Nicholas I and Official Nationality in Russia, 1825–1855* (Berkeley, 1959).

3.   Nicholas V. Riasanovsky, *A Parting of the Ways: Government and the Educated Public in Russia, 1801–1855* (Oxford, 1976).

4.   Mariia Volkonskaia, *Zapiski Marii Volkonskoi* (St. Petersburg, 1904), p. 70; Andrei Rozen, *Zapiski dekabrista* (Leipzig, 1870), pp. 218–19; GARF, f. 109, 1 eksp., d. 61, ch. 1 (1826), l. 140; Mikhail O. Gershenzon (ed.), "Pis'ma M. N. Volkonskoi iz Sibiri," *Russkie propilei* (Moscow, 1915), p. 44.

5.   Azadovskii (ed.), *Vospominaniia Bestuzhevykh*, p. 248; Rozen, *Zapiski*, p. 221; N. V. Basargin, *Zapiski* (Krasnoyarsk, 1985), p. 111.

6.   Volkonskaia, *Zapiski*, pp. 42–4.

7.   Gershenzon (ed.), "Pis'ma M. N. Volkonskoi," p. 55.

8.   Volkonskaia, *Zapiski*, pp. 76–8.

9.   V. A. Fedotov (ed.), "Krestnyi put' dekabristov v Sibir': Dokumenty ob otpravke osuzhdennykh na katorgu i v ssylku i ob usloviiakh ikh soderzhaniia 1826–1837 gg.," *Istoricheskii arkhiv*, 2006, no. 6, pp. 52–3; A. D. Kolesnikov, "Ssylka i zaselenie Sibiri," in L. M. Goriushkin (ed.), *Ssylka i katorga v Sibiri XVIII-nachalo XX v.* (Novosibirsk, 1975), p. 52.

10.   D. I. Zavalishin, *Zapiski dekabrista*, 2nd edn (St. Petersburg, 1906), pp. 264–5. See also Basargin, *Zapiski*, p. 113.

11. I. D. Iakushkin, *Memuary, stat'i, dokumenty* (Irkutsk, 1993), p. 176; M. V. Golovinskii, "Dekabrist kniaz' E. P. Obolenskii," *Istoricheskii vestnik*, 1890, no. 8, p. 126.

12. V. A. Fedotov (ed.), " 'U nas net nikakikh sviazei s vneshnim mirom': Pis'ma dekabrista P. N. Svistunova k bratu Alekseiu. 1831–1832 gg.," *Istoricheskii arkhiv*, 1993, no. 1, pp. 188–9.

13. Fedotov (ed.), "Krestnyi put' dekabristov," pp. 52–3; F. G. Safronov, "Ssylka v Vostochuiu Sibir' v pervoi polovine XVIII v.," in Goriushkin (ed.), *Ssylka i katorga*, pp. 31–2; Andrew A. Gentes, *Exile, Murder and Madness in Siberia, 1823–61* (Basingstoke, 2010), p. 93.

14. Iakushkin, *Memuary*, pp. 187–8; Rozen, *Zapiski*, pp. 215, 221, 235.

15. Azadovskii (ed.), *Vospominaniia Bestuzhevykh*, p. 198.

16. Rozen, *Zapiski*, p. 223.

17. Basargin, *Zapiski*, pp. 115–16.

18. Jeanne Haskett, "Decembrist N. A. Bestuzhev in Siberian Exile, 1826–55," *Studies in Romanticism*, vol. 4, no. 4 (Summer 1965), p. 190.

19. N. Kuchaev, "Stanislav Romanovich Leparsky, komendant Nerchinskikh rudnikov s 1826 po 1837 god," *Russkaia starina*, vol. 28 (August 1880), p. 717; Glynn R. V. Barratt (ed.), *Voices in Exile: The Decembrist Memoirs* (Montreal, 1974), p. 242.

20. "Pis'ma M. N. Volkonskoi," pp. 28, 37, 40, 75–6.

21. S. Gessen and A. Predtechenskii (eds.), *Vospominaniia Poliny Annenkovoi* (Moscow, 1929), chs. 4–10.

22. Volkonskaia, *Zapiski*, p. 74; Basargin, *Zapiski*, p. 128.

23. Volkonskaia, *Zapiski*, p. 78.

24. O. Popova, "Istoriia zhizni M. N. Volkonskoi," *Zven'ia*, vol. 3–4 (Moscow, 1934), pp. 66–7; S. Volkonskii, *O dekabristakh: po semeinym vospominaniiam* (Paris, 1921), p. 84.

25. A. D. Margolis, "Pis'ma zhen dekabristov A. Kh. Benkendorfu," in idem, *Tiur'ma i ssylka v imperatorskoi Rossii. Issledovaniia i arkhivnye nakhodki* (Moscow, 1995), p. 80. Iakushkin, *Memuary*, pp. 178, 188; Popova, "Istoriia zhizni M. N. Volkonskoi," p. 71.

26. Gessen and Predtechenskii (eds.), *Vospominaniia Poliny Annenkovoi*, pp. 161–3.

27. "Perekhod dekabristov iz Chity v Petrovskii Zavod," in B. L. Mozdalevskii and Iu. G. Oksman (eds.), *Dekabristy: Neizdannye materialy i stat'i* (Moscow, 1925), pp. 128–48; Basargin, *Zapiski*, p. 137.

28. Basargin, *Zapiski*, p. 141; Azadovskii (ed.), *Vospominaniia Bestuzhevykh*, pp. 166, 335; Barratt (ed.), *Voices in Exile*, p. 274.

29. Margolis, "Pis'ma zhen dekabristov," pp. 82, 86–7.

30. Ibid., p. 84.

31. Iakushkin, *Memuary*, pp. 203, 213–14.

32. M. A. Rakhmatullin, "Imperator Nikolai I i sem'i dekabristov," *Otechestvennye zapiski*, 1995, no. 6, pp. 3–20.

33. A. I. Gertsen, "Byloe i dumy," *Sobranie sochinenii*, 30 vols. (Moscow, 1954–65), vol. 8, p. 59.

34. *Poems by Nikolai Nekrasov*, trans. Juliet M. Soskice (Oxford, 1938), p. 82; Anna Biel, "Nikolai Nekrasov's Representation of the Decembrist Wives," *Australian Slavonic and East European Studies*, vol. 25, nos. 1–2 (2011), pp. 39–59.

35. M. M. Khin, "Zheny dekabristov," *Istoricheskii vestnik*, vol. 18 (1884), pp. 650–83; P. E. Shchegolev, "Zheny dekabristov," in idem, *Istoricheskie etiudy* (St. Petersburg, 1913); Nikolai Nekrasov, "Russkie zhenshchiny," *Sobranie sochinenii*, 8 vols. (Moscow, 1965–7), vol. 3, pp. 27, 40; Iu. M. Lotman, "Dekabrist v povsednevnoi zhizni" in idem, *Besedy o russkoi kul'ture: byt i traditsii russkogo dvorianstva (XVIII–nachalo XIX veka)* (St. Petersburg, 2011), pp. 353–4.

36. Vera Figner, "Zheny dekabristov," *Katorga i ssylka*, vol. 21 (1925), p. 18.

37. Golovinskii, "Dekabrist kniaz' E. P. Obolenskii," pp. 124–5.

38. Popova, "Istoriia zhizni M. N. Volkonskoi," pp. 65–6, 72; RGIA, f. 914, op. 1, d. 38 (1848), l. 1; N. F. Karash, *Kniaz' Sergei Volkonskii: istoriia zhizni dekabrista* (Irkutsk, 2006), pp. 244–5; IRLI RAN, f. 57, op. 1, n. 61, l. 42; M. P. Volkonskii, "Pis'ma S. G. Volkonskogo," *Zapiski otdela rukopisei gosudarstvennoi biblioteki SSSR*, 1961, no. 24, p. 371; Basargin, *Zapiski*, p. 233.

39. Azadovskii (ed.), *Vospominaniia Bestuzhevykh*, p. 146.

40. Basargin, *Zapiski*, pp. 211–12.

41. Karash, *Kniaz' Sergei Volkonskii*, p. 215; Basargin, *Zapiski*, pp. 144–5; Julie Grandhaye, *Les décembristes: une génération républicaine en Russie autocratique* (Paris, 2011), pp. 277–8.

42. Fedotov (ed.), " 'U nas net nikakikh sviazei,' " p. 186.

43. Rozen, *Zapiski*, p. 230; Basargin, *Zapiski*, p. 165; O. S. Tal'skaia, "Ssyl'nye dekabristy o vneshnei politike Rossii vtoroi chetverti XIX v.," *Sibir' i dekabristy*, no. 2 (1981), pp. 28–9; T. A. Pertseva, "Pol'skii vopros v publitsistike M. S. Lunina," *Sibir' i dekabristy*, no. 2 (1981), pp. 46–53; Zavalishin, *Zapiski*, p. 268.

44. Haskett, "Decembrist N. A. Bestuzhev," p. 189; Zavalishin, *Zapiski*, pp. 268–9. Ironically, Rousseau wrote voluminously on botany. See J.-J. Rousseau, *Letters on the Elements of Botany* (1787).

45. Glynn R. Barratt, "A Note on N. A. Bestuzhev and the Academy of Chita," *Canadian Slavonic Papers*, vol. 12, no. 1 (1970), p. 56; Zavalishin, *Zapiski*, p. 269; Rozen, *Zapiski*, p. 231; A. P. Beliaev, *Vospominaniia dekabrista o perezhitom i perechuvstvovannom* (Krasnoyarsk, 1990), p. 170.

46. S. I. Cherepanov, "Otryvki iz vospominanii sibirskogo kazaka," *Drevniaia i novaia Rossiia* (1876), vol. 2, p. 267 (cited in Barratt, "A Note on N. A. Bestuzhev," p. 59); Grandhaye, *Les décembristes*, pp. 275–6.

47. M. V. Nechkina (ed.), *Zapiski dekabrista N. I. Lorera* (Moscow, 1931), p. 148; Haskett, "N. A. Bestuzhev," pp. 191–2; Golovinskii, "Dekabrist kniaz' E. P. Obolenskii," p. 126; Gershenzon (ed.), "Pis'ma M. N. Volkonskoi," p. 68.

48. N. A. Bestuzhev, *Sochineniia i pis'ma* (Irkutsk, 2003), pp. 245–6.

49. V. N. Dvorianov, *V sibirskoi dal'nei storone . . . (Ocherki istorii politicheskoi katorgi i ssylki. 60-e gody XVIII v.—1917 g.)* (Minsk, 1985), p. 56.

50. Zavalishin, *Zapiski*, pp. 272, 333, 314, 347.

51. Barratt, "A Note on N. A. Bestuzhev," p. 57; Anatole Mazour, *The First Russian Revolution 1825: The Decembrist Movement, Its Origins, Development and Significance* (Stanford, 1937), p. 246.

52. Azadovskii (ed.), *Vospominaniia Bestuzhevykh*, pp. 220, 232; Zavalishin, *Zapiski*, pp. 362–5; N. M. Druzhinin, "Dekabrist I. D. Iakushkin i ego lankasterskaia shkola," *Uchenye zapiski Moskovskogo gorodskogo pedagogicheskogo instituta*, 1941, vol. 2, no. 1, pp. 33–96; Mazour, *The First Russian Revolution*, pp. 244–6.

53. Karash, *Kniaz' Sergei Volkonskii*, pp. 233–90; Mazour, *The First Russian Revolution*, p. 247.

54. Barratt, "A Note on N. A. Bestuzhev," p. 58; O. S. Tal'skaia, "Bor'ba administratsii s vliianiem dekabristov v Zapadnoi Sibiri," in Goriushkin (ed.), *Ssylka i katorga*, p. 90; D. I. Zavalishin, "Amurskoe delo i vliianie ego na vostochnuiu Sibir' i gosudarstvo," *Russkaia starina*, 1881, no. 9, pp. 75–100; Zavalishin, *Zapiski*, pp. 389–424; Mazour, *The First Russian Revolution*, pp. 249–52; O. S. Tal'skaia, "Ssyl'nye dekabristy," in L. M. Goriushkin (ed.), *Ssylka i obshchestvenno-politicheskaia zhizn' v Sibiri* (Novosibirsk, 1978), pp. 231–51.

55. Basargin, *Zapiski*, p. 217.

56. Tal'skaia, "Bor'ba administratsii," pp. 75, 85; Bestuzhev, *Sochineniia*, pp. 422, 432.

57. GARF, f. 109, eksp., 1, d. 61, ch. 43 (1826), ll. 1–5; Glynn R. V. Barratt, *The Rebel on the Bridge: A Life of the Decembrist Baron Andrey Rozen, 1800–1884* (London, 1975), pp. 160–63; Volkonskii, "Pis'ma S. G. Volkonskogo," p. 365.

58. Azadovskii (ed.), *Vospominaniia Bestuzhevykh*, p. 145; M. K. Azadovskii (ed.), *Sibir' i dekabristy* (Irkutsk, 1925), p. 142; Barratt (ed.), *Voices in Exile*, p. 304; Dvorianov, *V sibirskoi dal'nei storone*, p. 58.

59. Rozen, *Zapiski*, p. 262; Fedotov (ed.), "Krestnyi put' dekabristov," p. 55.

60. M. S. Lunin, *Sochineniia, pis'ma, dokumenty* (Irkutsk, 1988), pp. 81–116, 285–8.

61. Ibid., pp. 246, 82, 285.

62. Ibid., pp. 101, 103, 112, 84, 251.

63. Glynn V. R. Barratt, *M. S. Lunin: Catholic Decembrist* (The Hague, 1976), pp. 112–18; Lunin, *Sochineniia*, p. 181.

64. Lunin, *Sochineniia*, pp. 293, 372; T. A. Pertseva, "Dekabrist M. S. Lunin v Akatue," in L. M. Goriushkin (ed.), *Ssyl'nye dekabristy v Sibiri* (Novosibirsk, 1985), pp. 148–9.

65. S. V. Maksimov, *Sibir' i katorga*, 3rd edn (St. Petersburg, 1900), p. 398; Gessen and Predtechenskii (eds.), *Vospominaniia Poliny Annenkovoi*, p. 166; Pertseva, "Dekabrist M. S. Lunin," p. 150.

66. GAIO, f. 24, op. 3, k. 32, d. 67 (1844), l. 2; Lunin, *Sochineniia*, pp. 262–3.

67. Lunin, *Sochineniia*, pp. 262–3, 265, 268, 272, 350, 362; V. A. D'iakov, "Smert' dekabrista Lunina," *Voprosy istorii*, 1988, no. 2, pp. 99–106.

68. E. A. Iakushkin (ed.), *Dekabristy na poselenii (v 1839–1855)* (Moscow, 1926), p. 67; Dvorianov, *V sibirskoi dal'nei storone*, p. 48.

69. Trans. Valentine Snow in John Simpson (ed.), *The Oxford Book of Exile* (Oxford, 1995), p. 80.

70. S. V. Kodan, "Amnistiia Dekabristam (1856 g.)," *Voprosy istorii*, 1982, no. 4, pp. 178–82; B. G. Kubalov, *Dekabristy i amnistiia* (Novonikolaevsk, 1925); L. A. Sokol'skii, "Vozvrashchenie dekabristov iz sibirskoi ssylki," in Iu. G. Oksman (ed.), *Dekabristy v Moskve* (Moscow, 1963), pp. 220–40; Orlando Figes, *Natasha's Dance: A Cultural History of Russia* (London, 2002), p. 141; Rosamund Bartlett, *Tolstoy: A Russian Life* (London, 2010), pp. 141–8, 165.

71. A. I. Gertsen, "Kniaz' Sergei Grigor'evich Volkonskii," *Sobranie sochinenii*, 30 vols. (Moscow, 1954–65), vol. 19, p. 16.

72. S. G. Volkonskii, "Iz vospominanii," in I. Ia. Shchipanov (ed.), *Izbrannye sotsial'no-politicheskie i filosofskie proizvedeniia dekabristov*, 3 vols. (Moscow, 1951), vol. 2, p. 265.

6 SYBIRACY

1. Vintsenty Migurskii, "Zapiski iz Sibiri," in B. S. Shostakovich (ed.), *Vospominaniia iz Sibiri: memuary, ocherki, dnevnikovye zapiski pol'skikh politicheskikh ssyl'nykh v vostochnuiu Sibir' pervoi poloviny XIX stoletiia* (Irkutsk, 2009), pp. 175–83.

2. L. Bol'shakov and V. A. D'iakov, "I eto byla pravda. Strogo dokumental'naia povest' o shiroko izvestnom rasskaze L. N. Tolstogo 'Za chto?' i podlinnykh sud'bakh ego nepridumannykh personazhei," *Prostor*, 1979, no. 7, p. 99; Andrzej Walicki, *The Enlightenment and the Birth of Modern Nationhood: Polish Political Thought from Noble Republicanism to Tadeusz Kościuszko*, trans. Emma Harris (Notre Dame, IN, 1989), ch. 1; Andrzej Walicki, *Philosophy and Romantic Nationalism: The Case of Poland* (Oxford, 1982), pp. 11–30; Dominic Lieven, *Russia Against Napoleon: The True Story of the Campaigns of* War and Peace (London, 2009), pp. 242–328; B. P. Milovidov, "Voennoplennye poliaki v Sibiri v 1813–1814 gg.," *Otechestvennaia voina 1812 goda. Istochniki, pamiatniki, problemy* (Mozhaisk, 2009), pp. 325–59; S. V. Shvedov, "Plennye Velikoi armii v Rossii," *Otstuplenie Velikoi Armii Napoleona iz Rossii* (Maloyaroslavets, 2000), pp. 69–70.

3. Walicki, *Philosophy and Romantic Nationalism*, pp. 64–85; RGIA, f. 733, op. 62, d. 644 (1823), ll. 1–2, 8–9, 12, 30, 38, 57, 138, 155.

4. W. Bruce Lincoln, *Nicholas I: Emperor and Autocrat of All the Russias* (Bloomington, IN, 1978), pp. 135–43.

5. R. F. Leslie, *Polish Politics and the Revolution of November 1830* (Westport, CT, 1969), p. 155; Adam Zamoyski, *Holy Madness: Romantics, Patriots and Revolutionaries, 1776–1871* (London, 1999), p. 276.

6. Leslie, *Polish Politics*, p. 155; Philippe Darriulat, *Les Patriotes: La gauche républicaine et la nation 1830–1870* (Paris, 2001), ch. 3; Walicki, *Philosophy and Romantic Nationalism*, pp. 78–80; Robert E. Spiller, "Fennimore Cooper and Lafayette: Friends of Polish Freedom, 1830–1832," *American*

Literature, vol. 7, no. 1 (1935), pp. 58–9; *The Times* cited in Orlando Figes, *Crimea* (London, 2010), p. 80; Joseph W. Wieczerzak, "The Polish Insurrection of 1830–1831 in the American Press," *The Polish Review*, vol. 6, nos. 1–2 (1961), pp. 53–72; Jill Harsin, *Barricades: The War of the Streets in Revolutionary Paris* (New York, 2002).

7. R. F. Leslie, "Polish Political Divisions and the Struggle for Power at the Beginning of the Insurrection of November 1830," *Slavonic and East European Review*, vol. 31, no. 76 (Dec. 1952), pp. 113–32; Norman Davies, *God's Playground: A History of Poland*, 2 vols. (Oxford, 1981), vol. 2, pp. 315–33.

8. A. S. Nagaev, *Omskoe delo, 1832–1833* (Krasnoyarsk, 1991), p. 4; RGIA, f. 1286, op. 5, d. 483 (1833), l. 93; F. F. Bolonev, A. A. Liutsidarskaia and A. I. Shinkovoi, *Ssyl'nye poliaki v Sibiri: XVII, XIX vv.* (Novosibirsk, 2007), p. 61; S. V. Kodan, "Sibirskaia ssylka uchastnikov oppozitsionnykh vystuplenii i dvizhenii v tsarstve pol'skom 1830–1840-kh gg. (Politiko-iuridicheskii srez)," p. [3] (http://textarchive.ru/c-1413151.html, accessed 15 February 2014).

9. V. A. D'iakov, "Petr Vysotskii na sibirskoi katorge (1835–1856), in idem and V. S. Bol'shakov (eds.), *Ssyl'nye revolutsionery v Sibiri (XIX v.–fevral' 1917 g.)* (Irkutsk, 1979), p. 4.

10. S. V. Kodan and B. S. Shostakovich, "Pol'skaia ssylka v Sibir' vo vnutrennei politike samoderzhaviia (1830–1850-e gody), *Slavianovedenie*, 1992, no. 6, p. 4; RGIA, f. 1286, op. 5, d. 483 (1833).

11. R. F. Leslie, "Left-Wing Political Tactics in Poland, 1831–1846," *Slavonic and East European Review*, vol. 33, no. 80 (December 1954), pp. 120–39; Idesbald Goddeeris, *La grande émigration polonaise en belgique (1831–1870): Élites et masses en exil à l'époque romantique* (Frankfurt, 2013); Roman Koropeckyj, *Adam Mickiewicz: The Life of a Romantic* (Ithaca, 2008), pp. 190–91.

12. Karma Nabulsi, "Patriotism and Internationalism in the 'Oath of Allegiance' to Young Europe," *European Journal of Political Theory*, vol. 5, no. 1 (2006), pp. 61–70; Roland Sarti, "Giuseppe Mazzini and Young Europe," in C. A. Bayly and E. F. Biagini (eds.), *Giuseppe Mazzini and the Globalisation of Democratic Nationalism, 1830–1920* (Oxford, 2008), pp. 275–98; Walicki, *Philosophy and Romantic Nationalism*, p. 81.

13. Leslie, "Left-Wing Political Tactics in Poland," pp. 120–39; Anna Procyk, "Polish Émigrés as Emissaries of the *Risorgimento* in Eastern Europe," *Harvard Ukrainian Studies*, vol. 25, no. 1/2 (Spring 2001), pp. 7–29; Migurskii, "Zapiski iz Sibiri," pp. 71–81.

14. Migurskii, "Zapiski iz Sibiri," pp. 98–9, 107–8, 111; Bol'shakov and D'iakov, "I eto byla pravda," p. 105.

15. B. S. Shostakovich, "Konarshchik Iustyn'ian Ruchin'skii," in idem (ed.), *Vospominaniia iz Sibiri*, pp. 302–4; Thomas Frost, *The Secret Societies of the European Revolution, 1776–1876*, 2 vols. (London, 1876), vol. 2, pp. 255–61; G. N. Marakhov, "Deiatel'nost' Sodruzhestva pol'skogo naroda na Pravoberezhnoi Ukraine v 1835–1839 gg. (po materialam kievskogo arkh-

iva)," in *Sviazi revoliutsionerov Rossii i Pol'shi XIX–nachala XX v.* (Moscow, 1968), pp. 166–93.

16. RGIA, f. 1286, op. 5, d. 483 (1833), ll. 81–2; Bolonev et al, *Ssyl'nye poliaki v Sibiri*, p. 86; B. S. Shostakovich, *Istoriia poliakov v Sibiri (XVII–XIX vv.)* (Irkutsk, 1995), pp. 60–62; Andrew A. Gentes, *Exile, Murder and Madness in Siberia, 1823–61* (Basingstoke, 2010), p. 136.

17. B. S. Shostakovich, "Eva Felin'skaia—vidnaia predstavitel'nitsa politssylki poliakov v Sibir' pervoi poloviny XIX v., obshchestvennyi deiatel', memuarist," in V. G. Datsyshen (ed.), *Zhenshchina v istorii Rossii XVIII–XXI vekov* (Irkutsk, 2010), p. 31; Viktoria Slivovskaia, "Sibirskie teni: o pol'skikh zhenshchinakh v mezhpovstancheskii period ssylki," *Sibirskaia ssylka* (Irkutsk, 2000), no. 1 (13), pp. 99–102; Eva Felinska, *Revelations of Siberia. By a Banished Lady*, trans. Colonel Lach Szyrma, 2 vols. (London, 1852).

18. Gentes, *Exile, Murder and Madness*, pp. 133–5; Piotr Wandycz, *The Lands of Partitioned Poland, 1795–1918* (Seattle, 1974), pp. 125–6; RGIA, f. 1286, op. 5, d. 483 (1833), l. 1.

19. Kodan and Shostakovich, "Pol'skaia ssylka v Sibir'," p. 4; Iu. Ruchin'skii, "Konarshchik, 1838–1878: vospominaniia o sibirskoi ssylke," in Shostakovich (ed.), *Vospominaniia iz Sibiri*, pp. 328, 331.

20. Shostakovich, *Istoriia poliakov v Sibiri*, pp. 58–63.

21. Migurskii, "Zapiski iz Sibiri," pp. 119–27, 141.

22. Anton Chekhov, *The Steppe and Other Stories, 1887–1891*, trans. Ronald Wilks (London, 2001); idem, *Ward No. 6 and Other Stories, 1892–1895*, trans. Ronald Wilks (London, 2002); idem, *The Lady with the Little Dog and Other Stories, 1896–1904*, trans. Ronald Wilks (London, 2002); Migurskii, "Zapiski iz Sibiri," p. 142.

23. Migurskii, "Zapiski iz Sibiri," pp. 147–8.

24. Ibid., p. 149.

25. Kodan and Shostakovich, "Pol'skaia ssylka v Sibir'," p. 7; M. D. Filin, "Pol'skie revoliutsionery v Zabaikal'skoi politicheskoi ssylke v 30–40 gg. XIX v.," in L. M. Goriushkin (ed.), *Politicheskie ssyl'nye v Sibiri (XVIII—nachalo XX v.)* (Novosibirsk, 1983), p. 173.

26. D'iakov, "Petr Vysotskii," pp. 3–30.

27. RGIA, f. 468, op. 18, d. 489 (1803), ll. 1–12; Leo Tolstoy, *The Death of Ivan Ilyich and Other Stories*, trans. David McDuff (London, 2008), pp. 221–32; John P. LeDonne, "The Administration of Military Justice under Nicholas I," *Cahiers du monde russe et soviétique*, vol. 13, no. 2 (1972), pp. 180–91; John Keep, "No Gauntlet for Gentlemen: Officers' Privileges in Russian Military Law, 1716–1855," *Cahiers du monde russe et soviétique*, vol. 34, nos. 1–2 (1993), pp. 171–92; Abby Schrader, *Languages of the Lash: Corporal Punishment and Identity in Imperial Russia* (DeKalb, IL, 2002), pp. 105–6; RGIA, f. 1286, op. 9, d. 493 (1845), l. 29; Nagaev, *Omskoe delo*, p. 34.

28. L. M. Goriushkin (ed.), *Politicheskaia ssylka v Sibiri. Nerchinskaia katorga*, vol. 1, no. 2 (Novosibirsk, 1993), pp. 48–9, 100–101; Kodan and Shostakovich, "Pol'skaia ssylka v Sibir'," p. 8; B. S. Shostakovich, "Politicheskie

ssyl'nye poliaki i dekabristy v Sibiri," *Ssyl'nye revoliutsionery v Sibiri (XIX v.–fevral'' 1917)*, no. 1 (Irkutsk, 1973), pp. 279–80.

29. A. A. Ivanov, "Politicheskie ssyl'nye v Vostochnoi Sibiri v XIX v.," in L. M. Korytnyi (ed.), *Vklad pol'skikh uchenykh v izuchenie Vostochnoi Sibiri i ozera Baikal* (Irkutsk, 2011), pp. 108–9.

30. S. V. Kodan, *Politicheskaia ssylka v sisteme karatel'nykh mer samoderzhaviia pervoi poloviny XIX v.* (Irkutsk, 1980), p. 71; Kodan and Shostakovich, "Pol'skaia ssylka v Sibir'," pp. 8–9.

31. Migurskii, "Zapiski iz Sibiri," pp. 160, 177.

32. L. Bol'shakov, "Delo Migurskikh: povest' v dokumentakh," *Prometei*, 1971, vol. 8, pp. 135–6.

33. Ibid., pp. 139–140.

34. Migurskii, "Zapiski iz Sibiri," pp. 206–11; Bol'shakov, "Delo Migurskikh," p. 141.

35. Bol'shakov and D'iakov, "I eto byla pravda," pp. 112–13.

36. Ibid., p. 117.

37. Ibid., p. 118.

38. Migurskii, "Zapiski iz Sibiri," pp. 262–3.

39. Ibid., pp. 264–9; Goriushkin (ed.), *Politicheskaia ssylka*, p. 94.

40. V. I. Dal', "Ssyl'nyi," *Otechestvennye zapiski*, 1846, vol. 46, no. 5, pp. 153–6; Migurskii, "Zapiski iz Sibiri," p. 59; Wincenty Migurski, *Pamiętniki z Sybiru spisane przez Wincentego Migurskiego* (Lviv, 1863); S. V. Maksimov, *Sibir' i katorga*, 3rd edn (St. Petersburg, 1900), p. 346.

41. Maksimov, *Sibir' i katorga*, p. 356; L. N. Tolstoi, "Za chto," in idem, *Polnoe sobranie sochinenii*, 91 vols. (Moscow, 1928–64), vol. 42, pp. 84–106.

42. B. S. Shostakovich, "Eti neizvestnye izvestnye Migurskie," in idem (ed.), *Vospominaniia iz Sibiri*, p. 41.

43. Goriushkin (ed.), *Politicheskaia ssylka*, pp. 92, 113–17; Maksimov, *Sibir' i katorga*, pp. 344, 346.

44. Maksimov, *Sibir' i katorga*, p. 346. Such debates continued in the 1860s and 70s. See Shostakovich, *Istoriia poliakov v Sibiri*, pp. 93–4.

45. Ruchin'skii, "Konarshchik," p. 384.

46. M. S. Lunin, *Sochineniia, pis'ma, dokumenty* (Irkutsk, 1988), p. 105; Gentes, *Exile, Murder and Madness*, p. 139; F. F. Bolonev (ed.), *Ssyl'nye poliaki v Sibiri: XVII, XIX vv.* (Novosibirsk, 2007), pp. 149–52; Kodan and Shostakovich, "Pol'skaia ssylka v Sibir'," p. 13.

47. Richard S. Wortman, *Scenarios of Power: Myth and Ceremony in the Russian Monarchy*, 2 vols. (Princeton, 1995), vol. 1; Andrew A. Gentes, "Siberian Exile and the 1863 Polish Insurrectionists According to Russian Sources," *Jahrbücher für Geschichte Osteuropas*, vol. 51, no. 2 (2003), pp. 200, 216; RGIA, f. 1341, op. 51, d. 449 (1843), ll. 1–3, 10–10 ob.

48. Goriushkin (ed.), *Politicheskaia ssylka*, pp. 104–5, 108.

49. RGIA, f. 1286, op. 10, d. 1089 (1846), ll. 2–3, 14, 20; S. V. Kodan, "Amnistiia Dekabristam (1856)," *Voprosy istorii*, 1982, no. 4, pp. 178–82; Maksimov, *Sibir' i katorga*, p. 346.

50. RGIA, f. 1265, op. 9, d. 229 (1860), l. 2.

51. RGIA, f. 1265, op. 9, d. 229 (1860), ll. 3–3 ob.

52. Muravyov was granted the title "Amursky" (of the Amur), in honour of his successful 1858 negotiation of the Aigun Treaty, in which China ceded control of the Amur Basin to Russia. See W. Bruce Lincoln, *The Conquest of a Continent: Siberia and the Russians* (Ithaca, 1994), pp. 190–96.

53. RGIA, f. 1265, op. 9, d. 229 (1860), ll. 3 ob–8.

54. D'iakov, "Petr Vysotskii," p. 29.

55. Ruchin'skii, "Konarshchik," pp. 475–6.

56. Adam Mickiewicz, "The Books of the Polish Nation and of the Polish Pilgrimage," in idem, *Konrad Wallenrod and Other Writings of Adam Mickiewicz*, trans. Jewell Parish et al (Berkeley, 1925), pp. 142–3; Zofia Stefanowska, "Romantic Messianism," *Dialogue and Universalism*, nos. 5–6 (2000), pp. 31–8; Walicki, *Philosophy and Romantic Nationalism*, pp. 247–76; Serhiy Bilenky, *Romantic Nationalism in Eastern Europe: Russian, Polish, and Ukrainian Political Imaginations* (Stanford, 2012), ch. 4.

57. Lubov Keefer, "The Influence of Adam Mickiewicz on the Ballades of Chopin," *American Slavic and East European Review*, vol. 5, nos. 1–2 (1946), pp. 38–50.

58. Zamoyski, *Holy Madness*, pp. 291–2.

59. Martin Malia, *Russia Under Western Eyes: From the Bronze Horseman to the Lenin Mausoleum* (Cambridge, MA, 1999), pp. 93–4.

60. Michel Cadot (ed.), *Publications de Jules Michelet: légendes démocratiques du Nord* (Paris, 1968); Walicki, *Philosophy and Romantic Nationalism*, pp. 80–81; Darriulat, *Les Patriotes*, ch. 3; Ervin C. Brody, "The 1830 Polish Uprising in the Mirror of Hungarian Literature," *The Polish Review*, vol. 17, no. 2 (1972), pp. 56–8; Zamoyski, *Holy Madness*, p. 277.

61. Malia, *Russia Under Western Eyes*, chs. 1–2.

62. George F. Kennan, *The Marquis de Custine and His Russia in 1839* (London, 1972), pp. 19–29.

63. Astolphe de Custine, *Letters from Russia*, anonymous trans., ed. Anka Muhlstein (New York, 2002), p. 377.

64. Kennan, *The Marquis de Custine*, pp. 95–8; Figes, *Crimea*, pp. 86–99.

65. Custine, *Letters from Russia*, p. 376.

7   THE PENAL FORT

1. W. Bruce Lincoln, *Nicholas I: Emperor and Autocrat of All the Russias* (Bloomington, IN, 1978), p. 290.

2. "Pokazaniia F. M. Dostoevskogo po delu petrashevtsev," *Krasnyi arkhiv*, 1931, no. 2, pp. 130–46; no. 3, pp. 160–78; J. H. Seddon, *The Petrashevtsy: A Study of the Russian Revolutionaries of 1848* (Manchester, 1985).

3. Joseph Frank, *Dostoevsky: The Years of Ordeal, 1850–1859* (Princeton, 1983), pp. 51–2.

4. Ibid., p. 55.

5. Fyodor Dostoevsky, *The Idiot*, trans. David McDuff (London, 2004), pp. 71–2.

6. L. Grossman, "Grazhdanskaia smert' F. M. Dostoevskogo," *Literaturnoe nasledstvo*, vols. 22-4 (Moscow, 1935), pp. 683-92.

7. "M. V. Butashevich-Petrashevskii v Sibiri," *Krasnyi arkhiv*, vol. 10, 1925, p. 188; Frank, *Dostoevsky*, pp. 51-9; Grossman, "Grazhdanskaia smert'," p. 683.

8. N. Bel'chikov, "Pis'mo F. M. Dostoevskogo iz kreposti," *Krasnyi arkhiv*, vol. 2, 1922, pp. 237-8.

9. F. M. Dostoevskii, "Pis'ma," in idem, *Polnoe sobranie sochinenii*, 30 vols. (Leningrad, 1972-90), vol. 28, pp. 163-4.

10. Fyodor Dostoevsky, *A Writer's Diary. Volume 1, 1873-1876*, trans. Kenneth Lantz (Evanston, IL, 1994), p. 130.

11. Frank, *Dostoevsky: The Years of Ordeal*, p. 73.

12. Joseph Frank, *Dostoevsky: The Stir of Liberation, 1860-1865* (Princeton, 1986), p. 215; L Tolstoi, "Pis'ma," in *Polnoe sobranie sochinenii*, 91 vols. (Moscow, 1928-64), vol. 63, p. 24; Nancy Ruttenburg, *Dostoevsky's Democracy* (Princeton, 2008), pp. 72-81.

13. Gryts'ko [G. Z. Eliseev], "Ugolovnye prestupniki," *Sovremennik*, 1860, vol. 74, pp. 283-4; V. L. Seroshevskii, "Ssylka i katorga v Sibiri," in I. S. Mel'nik (ed.), *Sibir': ee sovremennoe sostoianie i ee nuzhdy. Sbornik statei* (St. Petersburg, 1908), pp. 220-21; Frank, *Dostoevsky: The Stir of Liberation*, pp. 214-20; V. A. Zelenskii (ed.), *Kriticheskii kommentarii k sochineniiam F. M. Dostoevskogo. Sbornik kriticheskikh statei*, vol. 2 (Moscow, 1901), p. 38.

14. Fyodor Dostoevsky, *The House of the Dead*, trans. David McDuff (London, 2003), p. 27.

15. Dostoevskii, "Pis'ma," p. 170.

16. L. Mel'shin [P. F. Iakubovich], *V mire otverzhennykh: zapiski byvshego katorzhnika* (St. Petersburg, 1896), p. 122; S. V. Maksimov, *Sibir' i katorga*, 3rd edn (St. Petersburg, 1900), pp. 32, 34; George Kennan, *Siberia and the Exile System*, 2 vols. (New York, 1891), vol. 2, pp. 145-6.

17. Dostoevsky, *The House of the Dead*, pp. 29-31; Mel'shin [Iakubovich], *V mire otverzhennykh*, p. 29.

18. N. M. Iadrintsev, *Russkaia obshchina v tiur'me i ssylke* (St. Petersburg, 1872), p. 57.

19. Mel'shin [Iakubovich], *V mire otverzhennykh*, p. 112; Dostoevsky, *The House of the Dead*, p. 30; Dostoevskii, "Pis'ma," p. 171.

20. Shimon Tokarzhevskii, "Sem' let katorgi" (1907), in idem, *Sibirskoe likholeti'e* (Kemerovo, 2007), p. 190; Nina Perlina, "Dostoevsky and his Polish Fellow Prisoners from the House of the Dead," in David L. Ransel and Bożena Shallcross (eds.), *Polish Encounters, Russian Identity* (Bloomington, IN, 2005), pp. 100-109; Abby Schrader, *Languages of the Lash: Corporal Punishment and Identity in Imperial Russia* (DeKalb, IL, 2002), p. 109; Dostoevsky, *The House of the Dead*, p. 50.

21. Dostoevsky, *The House of the Dead*, p. 93.

22. Dostoevskii, "Pis'ma," p. 170; "Ocherki nevol'nogo turista," *Knizhki nedeli*, 1895, no. 1, pp. 126-7; Mel'shin [Iakubovich], *V mire otverzhennykh*, p. 50.

23. Dostoevsky, *The House of the Dead*, p. 33; Mel'shin [Iakubovich], *V mire otverzhennykh*, pp. 60-61.

24. Mel'shin [Iakubovich], *V mire otverzhennykh*, p. 29; "Ocherki nevol'nogo turista," 1895, no. 3, p. 57.

25. Stephen P. Frank, *Crime, Cultural Conflict and Justice in Rural Russia, 1856–1917* (Berkeley, 1999); Christine Worobec, *Possessed: Women, Witches, and Demons in Imperial Russia* (DeKalb, IL, 2001); Christine Worobec, "Horse Thieves and Peasant Justice in Post-Emancipation Imperial Russia," *Journal of Social History*, vol. 21, no. 2 (Winter 1987), pp. 281–93; Orlando Figes, *A People's Tragedy: The Russian Revolution, 1891–1924* (London, 1996), pp. 87–9; Richard S. Wortman, *The Development of a Russian Legal Consciousness* (Chicago, 1976); Daniel Beer, *Renovating Russia: The Human Sciences and the Fate of Liberal Modernity, 1880–1930* (Ithaca, 2008), pp. 19–21.

26. I. V. Efimov, *Iz zhizni katorzhnykh Ilginskogo i Aleksandrovskogo togda kazennykh, vinokurennykh zavodov, 1848–1853 gg.* (St. Petersburg, 1899), p. 17; Dostoevsky, *The House of the Dead*, p. 231; Mel'shin [Iakubovich], *V mire otverzhennykh*, p. 161.

27. Mel'shin [Iakubovich], *V mire otverzhennykh*, p. 60.

28. Dostoevsky, *The House of the Dead*, pp. 72–3.

29. "Arestanty v Sibiri," *Sovremennik*, 1863, no. 11, p. 162.

30. E . . . . . . v, "Ocherki, rasskazy i vospominaniia: ssyl'no-katorzhnye v Okhotskom solevarennom zavode," *Russkaia starina*, vol. 22, 1878, pp. 306–7.

31. Efimov, *Iz zhizni katorzhnykh*, pp. 31–2; GAIO, f. 24, op. 2, k. 2619, d. 233 (1884), ll. 62–3.

32. Maksimov, *Sibir' i katorga*, pp. 44–5; Dostoevsky, *The House of the Dead*, pp. 86, 94.

33. Iadrintsev, *Russkaia obshchina*, pp. 64–5, 472–5; V. Moskvich, "Pogibshie i pogibaiushchie. Otbrosy Rossii na sibirskoi pochve," *Russkoe bogatstvo*, 1895, no. 7, pp. 65–6.

34. Dostoevsky, *The House of the Dead*, pp. 108–9.

35. Andrew A. Gentes, " 'Beat the Devil!': Prison Society and Anarchy in Tsarist Siberia," *Ab Imperio*, 2009, no. 2, p. 209; Tokarzhevskii, "Sem' let katorgi," p. 180.

36. Dostoevsky, *The House of the Dead*, p. 66; Maksimov, *Sibir' i katorga*, pp. 12, 43; Iadrintsev, *Russkaia obshchina*, pp. 59–61, 92; Moskvich, "Pogibshie i pogibaiushchie," pp. 69–71.

37. Tokarzhevskii, "Sem' let katorgi," p. 179; "Arestanty," pp. 136–7; Iadrintsev, *Russkaia obshchina*, pp. 60–61.

38. Kennan, *Siberia and the Exile System*, vol. 1, p. 364; Maksimov, *Sibir' i katorga*, pp. 40–41; Gentes, " 'Beat the Devil!,' " p. 214.

39. Dostoevsky, *The House of the Dead*, p. 84; Maksimov, *Sibir' i katorga*, p. 41.

40. Vasilii Vlasov, *Kratkii ocherk neustroistv sushchestvuiushchikh na katorge* (St. Petersburg, 1873), p. 4.

41. Charles Henry Hawes, *The Uttermost East; Being an Account of Investigations Among the Natives and Russian Convicts of the Island of Sakhalin, with Notes of Travel in Korea, Siberia, and Manchuria* (London, 1904), p. 150.

42. I. P. Belokonskii, *Po tiur'mam i etapam: Ocherki tiuremnoi zhizni i putevye*

zametki ot Moskvy do Krasnoiarska (Oryol, 1887), p. 157; Dostoevsky, *The House of the Dead*, pp. 84–5; Vlas M. Doroshevich, *Sakhalin*, 2 parts (Moscow, 1903), part 1, p. 340; Gentes, " 'Beat the Devil!,' " pp. 213–14.

43. Maksimov, *Sibir' i katorga*, p. 39; Mel'shin [Iakubovich], *V mire otverzhennykh*, p. 34.
44. Dostoevsky, *The House of the Dead*, p. 110.
45. Kennan, *Siberia and the Exile System*, vol. 1, p. 391.
46. Seroshevskii, "Ssylka i katorga v Sibiri," in Mel'nik (ed.), *Sibir'*, p. 219; Iadrintsev, *Russkaia obshchina*, pp. 152–3; Maksimov, *Sibir' i katorga*, p. 36.
47. Maksimov, *Sibir' i katorga*, p. 38.
48. Kennan, *Siberia and the Exile System*, vol. 1, p. 391; Belokonskii, *Po tiur'mam i etapam*, p. 155; Doroshevich, *Sakhalin*, part 1, pp. 271–2.
49. Frank, *Crime, Cultural Conflict*; Figes, *A People's Tragedy*, pp. 95–8.
50. Iadrintsev, *Russkaia obshchina*, pp. 93–4.
51. Ibid., p. 149.
52. Maksimov, *Sibir' i katorga*, p. 36.
53. "Ocherki nevol'nogo turista," 1895, no. 1, p. 131; Maksimov, *Sibir' i katorga*, p. 43.
54. Belokonskii, *Po tiur'mam i etapam*, p. 35.
55. "Arestanty," p. 138.
56. Dostoevsky, *The House of the Dead*, p. 354.
57. Ruttenburg, *Dostoevsky's Democracy*, pp. 185–95; Joseph Frank, *Dostoevsky: The Miraculous Years, 1865–1871* (Princeton, 1995); idem, *Dostoevsky: The Mantle of the Prophet, 1871–1881* (Princeton, 2002); Anna Schur, *Wages of Evil: Dostoevsky and Punishment* (Evanston, IL, 2012).
58. Orlando Figes, *Natasha's Dance: A Cultural History of Russia* (London, 2002), chs. 4, 6; Andrzej Walicki, *A History of Russian Thought: From the Enlightenment to Marxism*, trans. Hilda Andrews-Rusiecka (Stanford, 1979), chs. 6–12; Martin Malia, *Alexander Herzen and the Birth of Russian Socialism, 1812–1855* (London, 1961); Franco Venturi, *Roots of Revolution: A History of the Populist and Socialist Movements in Nineteenth-Century Russia*, trans. Francis Haskell (London, 1972); Tibor Szamuely, *The Russian Tradition* (New York, 1974); Isaiah Berlin, *Russian Thinkers* (London, 2008); Laura Engelstein, *Slavophile Empire: Imperial Russia's Illiberal Path* (Ithaca, 2009), ch. 4.
59. Dostoevsky, *A Writer's Diary*, p. 349 [translation modified].
60. Dostoevskii, "Pis'ma," pp. 172–3.
61. Ibid., p. 169; Dostoevsky, *The House of the Dead*, pp. 35–6.
62. A. I. Gertsen, "Le peuple et le socialisme," in idem, *Sobranie sochinenii*, 30 vols. (Moscow, 1954–65), vol. 7, pp. 271–306.
63. Dostoevskii, "Pis'ma," pp. 169–70.
64. Ibid., p. 172.
65. Fyodor Dostoevsky, *Crime and Punishment*, trans. David McDuff (London, 2003), pp. 647–56.
66. Fyodor Dostoevsky, *The Brothers Karamazov*, trans. David McDuff (London, 2003), p. 756.
67. Aileen Kelly, "Dostoevsky and the Divided Conscience," in idem, *Toward*

Another Shore: Russian Thinkers Between Necessity and Chance (New Haven, 1998), pp. 55–79.

68. Dostoevsky, *A Writer's Diary*, p. 354; Frank, *Dostoevsky: The Years of Ordeal*, chs. 9–10; Schur, *Wages of Evil*, pp. 137–44.

69. Dostoevsky, *A Writer's Diary*, p. 139.

70. Ibid., p. 289 [translation modified].

71. Harriet Murav, "Dostoevskii in Siberia: Remembering the Past," *Slavic Review*, vol. 50, no. 4 (Winter 1991), pp. 858–66; Figes, *Natasha's Dance*, pp. 329–31; Wayne Dowler, *Dostoevsky, Grigor'ev and Native Soil Conservatism* (Toronto, 1982); Gary Morson, *The Boundaries of Genre: Dostoevsky's Diary of a Writer and the Traditions of Literary Utopia* (Austin, 1981); Hans Kohn, "Dostoyevsky and Danilevsky: Nationalist Messianism," in E. J. Simmons (ed.), *Continuity and Change in Russian and Soviet Thought* (Cambridge, MA, 1955), pp. 500–515.

8   "IN THE NAME OF FREEDOM!"

1. Adam Zamoyski, *Holy Madness: Romantics, Patriots and Revolutionaries, 1776–1871* (London, 1999), pp. 413–17.

2. Stefan Kieniewicz, "Polish Society and the Insurrection of 1863," *Past and Present*, no. 37 (July 1967), pp. 130–48.

3. RGIA, f. 1286, op. 25, d. 1182 (1864), l. 32; Norman Davies, *God's Playground: A History of Poland*, 2 vols. (Oxford, 1981), vol. 2, pp. 347–68.

4. P. L. Kazarian, *Chislennost' i sostav uchastnikov pol'skogo vosstaniia 1863–1864 gg. v iakutskoi ssylke* (Yakutsk, 1999), pp. 12–13; N. P. Mitina, *Vo glubine sibirskikh rud. K stoletiiu vosstaniia pol'skikh ssyl'nykh na Krugobaikail'skom trakte* (Moscow, 1966), p. 10; L. P. Rochevskaia, *Istoriia politicheskoi ssylki v Zapadnoi Sibiri vo vtoroi polovine XIX v. (60-kh–80-kh godov)* (Tyumen, 1976), p. 43; Davies, *God's Playground*, p. 368.

5. Helena Boczek, *Aleksander Sochaczewski, 1843–1923, malarz syberyjskiej katorgi: Życie, twórczość i dzieje kolekcji* (Warsaw, 1993).

6. I. P. Belokonskii (Petrovich), *Po tiur'mam i etapam: Ocherki tiuremnoi zhizni i putevye zametki ot Moskvy do Krasnoiarska* (Oryol, 1887), p. 80; RGIA, f. 1286, op. 38, d. 467 (1877), l. 34; RGIA, f. 1286, op. 28, d. 917 (1867), l. 2; RGIA, f. 1286, op. 25, d. 229 (1864), ll. 1–68; RGIA, f. 1286, op. 25, d. 99 (1864), l. 18.

7. RGIA, f. 1286, op. 25, d. 862 (1865), l. 1.

8. GARF, f. 122, 3 dp., op. 5, d. 1 (1864), ll. 17–18; L. M. Goriushkin (ed.), *Politicheskaia ssylka v Sibiri. Nerchinskaia katorga*, vol. 1, no. 2 (Novosibirsk, 1993), pp. 156, 160–61, 167–9.

9. Mitina, *Vo glubine sibirskikh rud*, pp. 13, 30; Andrew A. Gentes, "Siberian Exile and the 1863 Polish Insurrectionists According to Russian Sources," *Jahrbücher für Geschichte Osteuropas*, vol. 51, no. 2 (2003), pp. 203–4, 209; Goriushkin (ed.), *Politicheskaia ssylka*, pp. 177–8, 208–9; B. S. Shostakovich, *Istoriia poliakov v Sibiri (XVII–XIX vv.)* (Irkutsk, 1995), p. 88.

10. Gentes, "Siberian Exile and the 1863 Polish Insurrectionists," p. 205.

11. Mitina, *Vo glubine sibirskikh rud*, pp. 16–17; I. N. Nikulina, "Pol'skaia politicheskaia ssylka na Altai v XIX v.," in *Sibirskaia ssylka* (Irkutsk, 2011), no. 6 (18), pp. 415–16; E. Semenov, "Khoziaistvennaia deiatel'nost' pol'skikh politicheskikh ssyl'nykh v Zabaikal'e v 1860-kh–1880-kh gg.," *Vlast'*, 2010, no. 11, pp. 131–3; Gentes, "Siberian Exile and the 1863 Polish Insurrectionists," p. 208.

12. S. V. Maksimov, *Sibir' i katorga*, 3rd edn (St. Petersburg, 1900), p. 361.

13. Mitina, *Vo glubine sibirskikh rud*, p. 15.

14. RGIA, f. 1286, op. 25, d. 1182 (1864), ll. 1–5, 14.

15. GAIO, f. 24, op. 3, k. 1760, d. 23 (1864), ll. 7–8; GAIO, f. 24, op. 3, k. 1764, d. 57 (1866), ll. 18–19, 25–6.

16. GAIO, f. 24, op. 3, k. 1764, d. 57 (1866), ll. 35, 41–2.

17. GAIO, f. 24, op. 3, k. 1764, d. 57 (1866), l. 76.

18. RGIA, f. 1286, op. 25, d. 1296 (1864), ll. 21, 114–16, 127; RGIA, f. 1286, op. 25, d. 1189 (1864), ll. 1–2.

19. V. A. D'iakov, "Peterburgskaia ofitserskaia organizatsiia," in *Russko-pol'skie revoliutsionnye sviazi*, 3 vols. (Moscow, 1961–3), vol. 1, pp. 197–351; V. A. D'iakov, *Iaroslav Dombrovskii* (Moscow, 1969), pp. 46–7, 134; Jerzy Zdrada, *Jarosław Dombrowski, 1836–1871* (Krakow, 1973); RGIA, f. 1282, op. 1, d. 140 (1863), ll. 126–7 ob.

20. D'iakov, *Iaroslav Dombrovskii*, pp. 139–40.

21. RGIA, f. 1286, op. 25, d. 1481 (1864), ll. 10–13.

22. RGIA, f. 1286, op. 25, d. 1481 (1864), ll. 15–15 ob; 29–29 ob.

23. RGIA, f. 1286, op. 25, d. 1481 (1864), ll. 34–41.

24. Andrzej Walicki, "The Slavophile Thinkers and the Polish Question in 1863," in David L. Ransel and Bożena Shallcross (eds.), *Polish Encounters, Russian Identity* (Bloomington, IN, 2005), pp. 90–91; Edyta M. Bojanowska, "Empire by Consent: Strakhov, Dostoevskii and the Polish Uprising of 1863," *Slavic Review*, vol. 71, no. 1 (Spring 2012), pp. 1–24; Alexis E. Pogorelskin, "*Vestnik Evropy* and the Polish Question in the Reign of Alexander II," *Slavic Review*, vol. 46, no. 1 (Spring 1987), pp. 87–105; Svetlana Ivanova, "Obsuzhdenie 'pol'skogo voprosa' na stranitsakh periodicheskikh izdanii 60-kh godov XIX veka," *Rocznik Instytutu Polsko-Rosyjskiego*, 2012, no. 1, pp. 13–14; Andreas Renner, "Defining a Russian Nation: Mikhail Katkov and the 'Invention' of National Politics," *Slavonic and East European Review*, vol. 81, no. 4 (2003), pp. 674–5; Olga Maiorova, *From the Shadow of Empire: Defining the Russian Nation through Cultural Mythology* (Madison, WI, 2010), pp. 94–127.

25. D'iakov, *Iaroslav Dombrovskii*, pp. 150–51; A. A. Kornilov, *Obshchestvennoe dvizhenie pri Aleksandre II (1855–1881)* (Paris, 1905), p. 128.

26. *The Times*, 22 September 1863, p. 6; Mieczyslaw Giergielewicz, "Echoes of the Polish January Rising in 'Punch,'" *The Polish Review*, vol. 8, no. 2 (Spring 1963), pp. 3–27; J. H. Harley, "Great Britain and the Polish Insurrection of 1863," *Slavonic and East European Review*, vol. 16, no. 46 (July 1937), pp. 155–67; vol. 16, no. 47 (January 1938), pp. 425–38; K. S. Pasieka, "The

British Press and the Polish Insurrection of 1863," *Slavonic and East European Review*, vol. 42, no. 98 (December 1963), pp. 15–37.

27. Andrzej Walicki, *Philosophy and Romantic Nationalism: The Case of Poland* (Oxford, 1982), p. 371; Zamoyski, *Holy Madness*, pp. 438–9.

28. Alice Bullard, *Exile to Paradise: Savagery and Civilization in Paris and the South Pacific, 1790–1900* (Stanford, 2001), p. 186; D'iakov, *Iaroslav Dombrovskii*, chs. 7–8; Robert Tombs, *The Paris Commune 1871* (London, 1999); Alistair Horne, *The Fall of Paris: The Siege and the Commune 1870–71* (London, 2007), pp. 318–19; Hugh Thomas, *The Spanish Civil War* (London, 1961), p. 324.

29. Orlando Figes, *Crimea* (London, 2011), pp. 177–9; A. S. Gulin, "Garibal'diitsy na Nerchinskoi katorge 1863–1867 gg.," in *Sibirskaia ssylka* (Irkutsk, 2011), no. 6 (18), p. 262.

30. Gulin, "Garibal'diitsy," pp. 262–3.

31. K. Ferlej-Bielańska, *Nullo i jego towarzysze* (Warsaw, 1923), p. 186; B. G. Kubalov, "Stranitsy iz zhizni garibal'diitsev v Petrovskom zavode," *Svet nad Baikalom* (Ulan Ude, 1960), no. 4, pp. 139–41.

32. Ferlej-Bielańska, *Nullo*, p. 137; B. G. Kubalov, "N. G. Chernyshevskii, M. L. Mikhailov i garibal'diitsy na Kadainskoi katorge," *Sibirskie ogni*, 1959, no. 6, pp. 139–44.

33. Rozanna Kazari, "N. G. Chernyshevskii i garibal'diitsy iz Bergamo," in O. B. Lebedeva (ed.), *Obrazy Italii v russkoi slovesnosti* (Tomsk, 2009), p. 156; Goriushkin (ed.), *Politicheskaia ssylka*, pp. 146–7; Monica Gardner, "An Italian Tragedy in Siberia," *Sewanee Review*, vol. 34, no. 3 (July–Sept. 1926), pp. 329–38; Gulin, "Garibal'diitsy," p. 271; Gavin Jacobson, "Fraternity in Combat: An Intellectual History of the Republican Tradition from the Republic of Virtue to the Republic of Silence," DPhil dissertation, University of Oxford (2015), pp. 212–13.

34. A. S. Gulin, "Novye fakty k biografii A. A. Krasovskogo po arkhivnym i memuarnym istochnikam. Versiia pobega i gibeli," http://sibir-ssylka.ucoz .com (accessed 3 March 2014).

35. N. Bykhovskii, "'Son katorzhnika' i ego avtor," *Literaturnoe nasledstvo*, vols. 25–6 (Moscow, 1936), p. 459; Goriushkin (ed.), *Politicheskaia ssylka*, p. 150.

36. GAIO, f. 24, op. 3, k. 1760, d. 23 (1864), ll. 67–8; Bykhovskii, "'Son katorzhnika,'" p. 459.

37. Bykhovskii, "'Son katorzhnika,'" p. 459; GAIO, f. 24, op. 3, k. 1760, d. 23 (1864), l. 67; V. A. D'iakov, "Zapisnye knizhki A. A. Krasovskogo i V. V. Khreshchetskogo," in *Revoliutsionnaia situatsiia v Rossii 1859–1861 gg.* (Moscow, 1962), pp. 418–22.

38. Goriushkin (ed.), *Politicheskaia ssylka*, pp. 149–50 [emphasis in original].

39. Ibid., p. 150.

40. GAIO, f. 24, op. 3, k. 1760, d. 23 (1864), ll. 67–8; "Dukhovnoe zaveshchanie Krasovskogo," *Krasnyi arkhiv*, 1929, no. 6, p. 233.

41. "Dukhovnoe zaveshchanie Krasovskogo," p. 232; GAIO, f. 24, op. 3, k. 1760, d. 23 (1864), ll. 67–8; Goriushkin (ed.), *Politicheskaia ssylka*, pp. 204–6.

42. Goriushkin (ed.), *Politicheskaia ssylka*, pp. 167–9.
43. Mitina, *Vo glubine sibirskikh rud*, p. 105.
44. Goriushkin (ed.), *Politicheskaia ssylka*, pp. 173–4; GAIO, f. 24, op. 3, k. 1766, d. 65 (1866), ll. 6–8, 42, 61–4.
45. GAIO, f. 24, op. 3, k. 1766, d. 65 (1866), ll. 95–7.
46. Goriushkin (ed.), *Politicheskaia ssylka*, p. 175.
47. A. V. Volochaeva, "Vidy truda na Nerchinskoi katorge vo vtoroi polovine XIX v.," in *Sibirskaia ssylka* (Irkutsk, 2011), no. 6 (18), pp. 237–40; Gentes, "Siberian Exile and the 1863 Polish Insurrectionists," p. 212.
48. GAIO, f. 24, op. 3, d. 501 (1866), ll. 60–120; "Vosstanie poliakov v Sibiri 1866 goda," *Sibirskii arkhiv*, 1912, no. 3, pp. 176–84; Mitina, *Vo glubine sibirskikh rud*, pp. 121–31.
49. "Vosstanie na Krugobaikal'skoi doroge 1866 goda," *Byloe*, 1921, no. 17, pp. 134–5.
50. Mitina, *Vo glubine sibirskikh rud*; Gentes, "Siberian Exile and the 1863 Polish Insurrectionists," p. 213; A. I. Gertsen, "Pol'sha v Sibiri i Karakozovskoe delo," in idem, *Sobranie sochinenii*, 30 vols. (Moscow, 1954–65), vol. 19, p. 127.
51. Boczek, *Aleksander Sochaczewski*.
52. Émile Andreoli, "La clémence du tsar," *Le temps*, 23 September 1868, p. 5; idem, "De Pologne en Sibérie," *Revue moderne*, 1868, vol. 48, p. 163.
53. Andreoli, "De Pologne en Sibérie," pp. 124, 529, 748.
54. Ibid., p. 748.

9   GENERAL CUCKOO'S ARMY

1. V. Moskvich, "Pogibshie i pogibaiushchie. Otbrosy Rossii na sibirskoi pochve," *Russkoe bogatstvo*, 1895, no. 7, p. 49.
2. A. A. Vlasenko, "Ugolovnaia ssylka v Zapadnuiu Sibir' v politike samoderzhaviia XIX veka," Kandidatskaia diss. (Omsk State University, 2008), p. 204; N. M. Iadrintsev, *Sibir' kak koloniia v geograficheskom, etnograficheskom i istoricheskom otnoshenii* (St. Petersburg, 1882), p. 190.
3. L. M. Goriushkin (ed.), *Politicheskaia ssylka v Sibiri. Nerchinskaia katorga*, vol. 1, no. 2 (Novosibirsk, 1993), p. 139; RGIA, f. 1149, op. 9, d. 3 (1877), l. 773 ob.
4. "Ob izmeneniiakh poriadka raspredeleniia ssylaemykh v Sibir' iz Evropeiskoi Rossii," *Tiuremnyi vestnik*, 1898, no. 9, p. 447; A. D. Margolis, "Chislennost' i razmeshchenie ssyl'nykh v Sibiri v kontse XIX veka," in idem, *Tiur'ma i ssylka v imperatorskoi Rossii. Issledovaniia i arkhivnye nakhodki* (Moscow, 1995), p. 37; N. M. Iadrintsev, *Russkaia obshchina v tiur'me i ssylke* (St. Petersburg, 1872), p. 363; Alan Wood, "Russia's 'Wild East': Exile, Vagrancy and Crime in Nineteenth-Century Siberia," in idem (ed.), *The History of Siberia from Russian Conquest to Revolution* (London, 1991), p. 124.
5. Iadrintsev, *Russkaia obshchina*, pp. 351–5; Wood, "Russia's 'Wild East,'" p. 120; Andrew A. Gentes, *Exile, Murder and Madness in Siberia, 1823–61*

(Basingstoke, 2010), p. 34; idem, "Vagabondage and the Tsarist Siberian Exile System: Power and Resistance in the Penal Landscape," *Central Asian Survey*, vol. 30, nos. 3–4 (2011), p. 408; RGIA, f. 468, op. 18, d. 489 (1803), ll. 1–12.

6.   George Kennan, *Siberia and the Exile System*, 2 vols. (New York, 1891), vol. 1, p. 382; Iadrintsev, *Russkaia obshchina*, pp. 364, 415–17.

7.   "Arestanty v Sibiri," *Sovremennik*, 1863, no. 11, pp. 169–74; Iadrintsev, *Russkaia obshchina*, pp. 385–95.

8.   RGIA, f. 1264, op. 1, d. 438 (1831), l. 1 ob; RGIA, f. 1149, op. 3, d. 114 (1842), l. 5 ob; RGIA, f. 1405, op. 83, d. 2697 (1883), l. 3; RGIA, f. 1149, op. 3, d. 74 (1848), l. 2; Iadrintsev, *Russkaia obshchina*, pp. 363–4, 567.

9.   Iadrintsev, *Russkaia obshchina*, pp. 366, 371.

10.   RGIA, f. 1286, op. 33, d. 633 (1872), ll. 1–18, 27–34, 39–43, 52–68.

11.   Anton Chekhov, *Sakhalin Island*, trans. Brian Reeve (London, 2007), p. 306; RGIA, f. 1409, op. 2, d. 5247 (1828), ll. 1–7.

12.   RGIA, f. 1286, op. 5, d. 650 (1830), ll. 18–19; GAIO, f. 24, op. 3, k. 5, d. 96 (1831), l. 3.

13.   GAIO, f. 24, op. 2, k. 2619, d. 233 (1884), l. 50; Iadrintsev, *Sibir' kak koloniia*, p. 192; Kennan, *Siberia and the Exile System*, vol. 2, p. 156.

14.   RGIA, f. 1286, op. 38, d. 405 (1877), ll. 1, 5, 10, 19, 22, 42; RGIA, f. 1286, op. 38, d. 348 (1877), ll. 27, 31; RGIA, f. 1286, op. 38, d. 326 (1877), ll. 3, 9, 10, 12, 16–17; GARF, f. 122, 3 dp., op. 5, d. 1455 (1890), l. 8; GARF, f. 122, 3 dp., op. 5, d. 1000 (1883), ll. 1–4.

15.   RGIA, f. 1286, op. 33, d. 529 (1872), ll. 1, 6 ob–7 ob, 9, 58; Iadrintsev, *Russkaia obshchina*, p. 374; RGIA, f. 1286, op. 2, d. 245 (1817), ll. 1–2; RGIA, f. 1149, op. 9, d. 3 (1877), l. 70; Chekhov, *Sakhalin Island*, p. 302; S. V. Maksimov, *Sibir' i katorga*, 3rd edn (St. Petersburg, 1870), p. 65.

16.   Maksimov, *Sibir' i katorga*, pp. 47–8.

17.   RGIA, f. 1286, op. 38, d. 326 (1877), l. 12; Iadrintsev, *Russkaia obshchina*, pp. 373–4.

18.   Maksimov, *Sibir' i katorga*, p. 51; Chekhov, *Sakhalin Island*, p. 300 [translation modified].

19.   Kennan, *Siberia and the Exile System*, vol. 2, pp. 154–5.

20.   "Arestanty," p. 165; GARF, f. 122, op. 5, d. 64 (1879), ll. 15–16. For similar cases, see GARF, f. 102, 3 dp., op. 77, d. 1210 (1881), ll. 1–6.

21.   Maksimov, *Sibir' i katorga*, p. 86; Iadrintsev, *Russkaia obshchina*, p. 593.

22.   Iadrintsev, *Russkaia obshchina*, p. 594.

23.   Ibid., pp. 364–5, 463–4; GATOvgT, f. i378, op. 1, d. 59 (1829), ll. 10–12; GAIO, f. 32, op. 1, d. 1020 (1881), ll. 1, 11, 17, 42–42 ob.

24.   Maksimov, *Sibir' i katorga*, p. 86; Iadrintsev, *Russkaia obshchina*, pp. 450–72.

25.   RGIA, f. 1149, op. 2, d. 99 (1838), ll. 4–6.

26.   Fyodor Dostoevsky, *The House of the Dead*, trans. David McDuff (London, 2003), p. 255.

27.   V. Ia. Kokosov, *Rasskazy o kariiskoi katorge (iz vospominanii vracha)* (St. Petersburg, 1907), p. 120.

28. RGIA, f. 1149, op. 3, d. 74 (1848), ll. 2–3.

29. RGIA, f. 1405, op. 83, d. 2697 (1883), l. 39; *Ssylka v Sibir.'" Ocherk ee istorii i sovremennogo polozheniia* (St. Petersburg, 1900), p. 277.

30. RGIA, f. 1286, op. 3, d. 323 (1824), ll. 43–43 ob; RGIA, f. 1286, op. 30, d. 1000 (1869), ll. 2–11; RGIA, f. 1405, op. 535, d. 135 (1883), ll. 1–12; Iadrintsev, *Russkaia obshchina*, pp. 609–10.

31. RGIA, f. 1286, op. 7, d. 438 (1840), l. 56; RGIA, f. 1286, op. 7, d. 341 (1840), l. 5; Abby M. Schrader, *Languages of the Lash: Corporal Punishment and Identity in Imperial Russia* (DeKalb, IL, 2002), pp. 92–5.

32. RGIA, f. 1286, op. 7, d. 438 (1840), ll. 56, 60; RGIA, f. 1286, op. 15, d. 1293 (1855), ll. 1–2.

33. Iadrintsev, *Russkaia obshchina*, pp. 372, 438; Maksimov, *Sibir' i katorga*, p. 49.

34. RGIA, f. 1264, op. 1, d. 71 (1835), ll. 143–4; RGIA, f. 1286, op. 33, d. 369 (1872), ll. 37–41; GARF, f. 102, o. o., d. 910 (1901), ll. 9–10.

35. GATOvgT, f. 378, op. 1, d. 62 (1829), ll. 1–8; Maksimov, *Sibir' i katorga*, p. 84; RGIA, f. 1149, op. 9, d. 3 (1877), l. 775; Iadrintsev, *Sibir' kak koloniia*, p. 193; S. Chudnovskii, "Kolonizatsionnoe znachenie sibirskoi ssylki," *Russkaia mysl'*, 1886, no. 10, p. 48; Vlasenko, "Ugolovnaia ssylka," p. 197.

36. Iadrintsev, *Russkaia obshchina*, p. 194; Maksimov, *Sibir' i katorga*, p. 83; I. Ia. Foinitskii, *Na dosuge. Sbornik statei*, 2 vols. (St. Petersburg, 1900), vol. 2, p. 430.

37. *Ssylka v Sibir'*, pp. 265–6.

38. Vlasenko, "Ugolovnaia ssylka," p. 197; *Sibir'*, 17 August 1875, no. 8, p. 6; RGIA, f. 1149, op. 9, d. 3 (1877), l. 775; Maksimov, *Sibir' i katorga*, p. 82; GARF, f. 122, 3 dp., op. 5, d. 1059 (1884), ll. 1–29; GARF, f. 122, 3 dp., op. 5, d. 1255 (1887), ll. 1–10.

39. Iadrintsev, *Russkaia obshchina*, pp. 387–8, 453.

40. Edmund Noble, "No American Siberia," *North American Review*, vol. 145, no. 370 (Sept. 1887), p. 327; Iadrintsev, *Russkaia obshchina*, p. 618.

41. Iadrintsev, *Russkaia obshchina*, pp. 566, 618; RGIA, f. 1286, op. 22, d. 1000 (1861), ll. 1–3, 7–8; GARF, f. 122, 3 dp., op. 5, d. 2601 (1893), l. 1.

42. RGIA, f. 1149, op. 9, d. 3 (1877), l. 337; GATOvgT, f. 378, op. 1, d. 38 (1827), ll. 18–21; Foinitskii, *Na dosuge*, p. 409.

43. Moskvich, "Pogibshie i pogibaiushchie," p. 48; Maksimov, *Sibir' i katorga*, p. 69; Iadrintsev, *Russkaia obshchina*, pp. 447–8.

44. RGIA, f. 1286, op. 1, d. 195 (1804), l. 24; RGIA, f. 1286, op. 1, d. 120 (1805), l. 3; RGIA, f. 1264, op. 1, d. 71 (1835), ll. 149 ob, 152; *Statisticheskie svedeniia o ssyl'nykh v Sibiri za 1833 i 1834 gody* (St. Petersburg, 1837), p. 22.

45. RGIA, f. 1652, op. 1, d. 197 (1877), l. 10 ob; RGIA, f. 1149, op. 9, d. 3 (1877), l. 773; GAIO, f. 25, op. 6, k. 450, d. 228 (1899), ll. 5–7; GAIO, f. 25, op. 6, k. 452, d. 335 (1899), ll. 6–6 ob; RGIA, f. 1286, op. 33, d. 369 (1872), ll. 5–6.

46. GAIO, f. 25, op. 6, k. 449, d. 185 (1898), ll. 7–7 ob.

47. *Sibir'*, 3 August 1875, p. 4; 31 August 1875, p. 1; 19 October 1875, pp. 3–4;

9 January 1877, p. 3; *Sibirskaia gazeta*, 20 March 1888, p. 10; 26 May 1888, p. 11; *Vostochnoe obozrenie*, 1889, no. 47, p. 7.

48. RGIA, f. 1286, op. 9, d. 493 (1845), ll. 1–38.

49. *Sibir'*, 19 October 1875, pp. 3–4; Iadrintsev, *Russkaia obshchina*, p. 626; "Sibirskaia bezopasnost' v gorodakh i na dorogakh," *Vostochnoe obozrenie*, 1886, no. 40, pp. 1–23; *Zabaikal'skaia nov'*, 8 June 1907, p. 4.

50. Maksimov, *Sibir' i katorga*, p. 46; Iadrintsev, *Russkaia obshchina*, pp. 485–7, 615–16; V. Ptitsyn, "Zabaikal'skie razboiniki," *Istoricheskii vestnik*, 1890, vol. 40, pp. 237–9.

51. Iadrintsev, *Russkaia obshchina*, pp. 621–2; Iadrintsev, *Sibir' kak koloniia*, pp. 202–3; Stephen P. Frank, *Crime, Cultural Conflict and Justice in Rural Russia, 1856–1914* (Berkeley, 1999).

52. Iadrintsev, *Russkaia obshchina*, pp. 410–11; idem, *Sibir' kak koloniia*, p. 202; *Sibirskaia gazeta*, 20 March 1888, p. 10; V. L. Seroshevskii, "Ssylka i katorga v Sibiri," in I. S. Mel'nik (ed.), *Sibir': ee sovremennoe sostoianie i ee nuzhdy. Sbornik statei* (St. Petersburg, 1908), p. 224.

53. *Sankt-Peterburgskie Vedomosti*, 26 November 1871, no. 326, vtoroi list, p. 1.

54. *Ssylka v Sibir'*, pp. 304–5.

55. Maksimov, *Sibir' i katorga*, p. 69; Iadrintsev, *Russkaia obshchina*, pp. 450–55; Moskvich, "Pogibshie i pogibaiushchie," p. 60; RGIA, f. 1149, op. 9, d. 3 (1877), l. 773.

56. RGIA, f. 1263, op. 1, d. 52 (1813), ll. 416–17.

57. Moskvich, "Pogibshie i pogibaiushchie," p. 61; L. Mel'shin [P. F. Iakubovich], *V mire otverzhennykh: zapiski byvshego katorzhnika* (St. Petersburg, 1896), p. 168; Iadrintsev, *Russkaia obshchina*, p. 499.

58. *Sibirskaia gazeta*, 29 April 1879, p. 3; 16 January 1883, p. 70; 31 March 1885, p. 325; Kennan, *Siberia and the Exile System*, vol. 2, p. 464; Seroshevskii, "Ssylka i katorga v Sibiri," p. 222; Iadrintsev, *Russkaia obshchina*, p. 492.

59. RGIA, f. 1284, op. 241, d. 42 (1879), ll. 154–6; *Ssylka v Sibir'*, p. 264.

60. RGIA, f. 468, op. 19, d. 291 (1847), ll. 5–7; GARF, f. 122, 3 dp., op. 5, d. 1455 (1890), l. 14; Chekhov, *Sakhalin Island*, p. 310; Maksimov, *Sibir' i katorga*, pp. 74–5; Iadrintsev, *Russkaia obshchina*, p. 497; Moskvich, "Pogibshie i pogibaiushchie," pp. 47–8; A. N. Krasnov, "Na ostrove izgnaniia," *Knizhka nedeli*, 1893, no. 8, p. 166; Kennan, *Siberia and the Exile System*, vol. 2, p. 464; *Ssylka v Sibir'*, p. 263.

61. RGIA, f. 1652, op. 1, d. 197 (1877), l. 6 ob.

62. *Sibirskaia gazeta*, 12 October 1875, p. 5.

63. Iadrintsev, *Sibir' kak koloniia*, p. 205; idem, *Russkaia obshchina*, p. 500.

10 SAKHALIN ISLAND

1. Vlas M. Doroshevich, *Kak ia popal na Sakhalin* (Moscow, 1903), p. 20.

2. Anton Chekhov, *Sakhalin Island*, trans. Brian Reeve (London, 2007), p. 234; N. Ia. Novombergskii, *Ostrov Sakhalin* (St. Petersburg, 1903), p. 94.

3. Richard Wortman, "The Russian Imperial Family as Symbol," in Jane Burbank and David L. Ransel (eds.), *Imperial Russia: New Histories for the Empire* (Bloomington, IN, 1998), pp. 60–86; William G. Wagner, *Marriage, Property and Law in Late Imperial Russia* (Oxford, 1994); Pavla Miller, *Transformations of Patriarchy in the West, 1500–1900* (Bloomington, IN, 1998); Susan K. Morrissey, *Suicide and the Body Politic in Imperial Russia* (Cambridge, 2006), ch. 5.

4. Andrew A. Gentes, "'Licentious Girls' and Frontier Domesticators: Women and Siberian Exile from the Late Sixteenth to the Early Nineteenth Centuries," *Sibirica*, vol. 3, no. 1 (2003), pp. 3–20.

5. Michel Foucault, *Discipline and Punish: The Birth of the Prison*, trans. Alan Sheridan (New York, 1995); RGIA, f. 1149, t. 5, d. 68 (1860), ll. 16–17; RGIA, f. 1149, op. 9, d. 3 (1877), l. 758.

6. Abby M. Schrader, "Unruly Felons and Civilizing Wives: Cultivating Marriage in the Siberian Exile System, 1822–1860," *Slavic Review*, vol. 66, no. 2 (Summer 2007), pp. 230–56; Andrew A. Gentes, "Sakhalin's Women: The Convergence of Sexuality and Penology in Late Imperial Russia," *Ab Imperio*, 2003, no. 2, pp. 115–37.

7. RGIA, f. 1149, t. 5, d. 68 (1860), ll. 17 ob–18 ob.

8. E. N. Anuchin, *Issledovaniia o protsente soslannykh v Sibiri' v period 1827–1846 godov. Materialy dlia ugolovnoi statistiki Rossii* (St. Petersburg, 1873), p. 310; RGIA, f. 1264, op. 1, d. 427 (1828), l. 14 ob; RGIA, f. 1264, op. 1, d. 53 (1829), ll. 161–2; *Statisticheskie svedeniia o ssyl'nykh v Sibiri za 1833 i 1834 gody* (St. Petersburg, 1837), pp. 57, 64, 66–7.

9. Chekhov, *Sakhalin Island*, p. 226; RGIA, f. 1652, op. 1, d. 197 (1877), l. 2 ob; *Ssylka v Sibir'. Ocherk ee istorii i sovremennogo polozheniia* (St. Petersburg, 1900), appendices 2–3; A. D. Margolis, "Chislennost' i razmeshchenie ssyl'nykh v Sibiri v kontse XIX veka," in idem, *Tiur'ma i ssylka v imperatorskoi Rossii. Issledovaniia i arkhivnye nakhodki* (Moscow, 1995), p. 32.

10. RGIA, f. 1264, op. 1, d. 51 (1828), l. 186; "Smes'," *Zhurnal Ministerstva Vnutrennykh Del*, 1833, part 5, no. 8, pp. 226–7.

11. RGIA, f. 1264, op. 1, d. 427 (1828), l. 101; RGIA, f. 1264, op. 1, d. 427 (1828), ll. 116–18, 125 ob–128, 182; Schrader, "Unruly Felons and Civilizing Wives," pp. 249–50; RGIA, f. 1286, op. 7, d. 341 (1840), l. 36 ob.

12. *Statisticheskie svedeniia o ssyl'nykh*, p. 67.

13. Margolis, "Chislennost' i razmeshchenie ssyl'nykh," p. 31; Schrader, "Unruly Felons and Civilizing Wives," p. 247.

14. GARF, f. 122, 3 dp., op. 5, d. 1534 (1891), ll. 1, 7; GATOvgT, f. 330, op. 2, d. 157 (1890), ll. 894, 1394–5.

15. "Ustav o ssyl'nykh," no. 759, in *Uchrezhdenie dlia upravleniia sibirskikh gubernii* (St. Petersburg, 1822).

16. RGIA, f. 1286, op. 8, d. 426 (1841), ll. 6–7, 16–17.

17. RGIA, f. 1286, op. 38, d. 334 (1877), ll. 1–7.

18. Chekhov, *Sakhalin Island*, p. 234; GARF, f. 122, 3 dp., op. 5, d. 1154 (1885), ll. 293–4.

19. RGIA, f. 1405, op. 90, d. 7654 (1889), ll. 2–4.

20. RGIA, f. 1652, op. 1, d. 197 (1877), l. 2.

21. RGIA, f. 1149, op. 9, d. 3 (1877), ll. 752–752 ob.

22. RGIA, f. 468, op. 39, d. 105 (1857), ll. 25–6 ob; RGIA, f. 1149, op. 9, d. 3 (1877), ll. 749–51; Stephen G. Marks, "Conquering the Great East: Kulomzin, Peasant Resettlement, and the Creation of Modern Siberia," in Stephen Kotkin and David Wolff (eds.), *Rediscovering Russia in Asia: Siberia and the Russian Far East* (New York, 1995), pp. 23–39; Donald W. Treadgold, *The Great Siberian Migration: Government and Peasant in Resettlement from Emancipation to the First World War* (Princeton, 1957), pp. 67–106.

23. RGIA, f. 1263, op. 1, d. 4236 (1882), ll. 462–4; RGIA, f. 1149, op. 9, d. 3 (1877), ll. 337–8, 753–4; RGIA, f. 560, op. 22, d. 121 (1882), l. 175.

24. A. P. Gorkin, *Geografiia Rossii* (Moscow, 1998), pp. 515–16.

25. Andrew A. Gentes, "The Institution of Russia's Sakhalin Policy, from 1868 to 1875," *Journal of Asian History*, vol. 36, no. 2 (2002), p. 1; idem, "No Kind of Liberal: Alexander II and the Sakhalin Penal Colony," *Jahrbücher für Geschichte Osteuropas*, vol. 54, no. 3 (2006), pp. 328–43.

26. Bruce F. Adams, *The Politics of Punishment: Prison Reform in Russia, 1863–1917* (DeKalb, IL, 1996), ch. 4; RGIA, f. 1149, op. 9, d. 3 (1877), ll. 751–7; Gentes, "No Kind of Liberal," p. 340; Gentes, "The Institution of Russia's Sakhalin Policy," pp. 5–6.

27. RGIA, f. 560, op. 22, d. 121 (1881), l. 176; Gentes, "The Institution of Russia's Sakhalin Policy," pp. 4–6.

28. Konstantin Korablin, "Katorga na Sakhaline kak opyt prinuditel'noi kolonizatsii," *Vestnik DVO RAN*, 2005, no. 2, p. 75; GATOvgT, f. 152, op. 35, d. 362 (1885), ll. 1–1 ob; Vlas M. Doroshevich, *Sakhalin*, 2 parts (Moscow, 1903), part 1, p. 3; *Otchet po Glavnomu Tiuremnomu Upravleniiu za 1889* (St. Petersburg, 1891), p. 153; A. A. Plotnikov, "Etapirovanie ssylnokatorzhnykh na ostrov Sakhalin vo vtoroi polovine XIX v.," in *Sibirskaia ssylka* (Irkutsk, 2011), no. 6 (18), pp. 125–6.

29. F. Avgustinovich, *Zametki ob ostrove Sakhaline* (St. Petersburg, 1880); Gentes, "The Institution of Russia's Sakhalin Policy," pp. 26, 28; D. A. Dril', *Ssylka i katorga v Rossii (Iz lichnykh nabliudenii vo vremia poezdki v Priamurskii krai i Sibir')* (St. Petersburg, 1898), pp. 30–31; A. P. Salomon, "O Sakhaline," *Tiuremnyi vestnik*, 1901, no. 1, p. 21.

30. Anton Chekhov, *A Life in Letters*, trans. and ed. Rosamund Bartlett (London, 2004), p. 225.

31. Ibid., pp. 204–5.

32. Ibid., p. 248; A. P. Chekhov, "Ostrov Sakhalin," *Russkaia mysl'*, 1893, no. 10, pp. 1–33; no. 11, pp. 149–70; no. 12, pp. 77–114; 1894, no. 2, pp. 26–60; no. 3, pp. 1–28; no. 5, pp. 1–30; no. 6, pp. 1–27; no. 7, pp. 1–30.

33. Gentes, "Sakhalin's Women," p. 129; Doroshevich, *Kak ia popal na Sakhalin*, p. 5.

34. RGIA, f. 1374, op. 6, d. 1366 (1800), ll. 1–19; L. V. Poddubskii, "Sakhalinskie deti i ikh materi," *Pravo*, 1899, no. 50, p. 2354; N. S. Lobas, *Katorga i poselenie na o-ve Sakhaline. Neskol'ko shtrikhov iz zhizni russkoi shtrafnoi kolonii* (Pavlograd, 1903), p. 113; Cathy A. Frierson, *All Russia Is Burning!*

A Cultural History of Fire and Arson in Late Imperial Russia (Washington, 2002), ch. 5; Stephen P. Frank, "Narratives Within Numbers: Women, Crime and Judicial Statistics in Imperial Russia, 1834–1913," *The Russian Review*, vol. 55, no. 4 (October 1996), pp. 541–66; Laurie Bernstein, *Sonia's Daughters: Prostitutes and Their Regulation in Imperial Russia* (Berkeley, 1995).

35. Chekhov, *Sakhalin Island*, p. 230; RGIA, f. 1286, op. 4, d. 413 (1828), l. 12; RGIA, f. 1264, op. 1, d. 414 (1825), ll. 4–5; I. V. Efimov, *Iz zhizni katorzhnykh Ilginskogo i Aleksandrovskogo togda kazennykh, vinokurennykh zavodov, 1848–1853 gg.* (St. Petersburg, 1899), p. 51; L. Mel'shin [P. F. Iakubovich], *V mire otverzhennykh: zapiski byvshego katorzhnika* (St. Petersburg, 1896), p. 17; Dril', *Ssylka i katorga v Rossii*, pp. 32, 35.

36. RGIA, f. 1149, op. 2, d. 97 (1837), l. 14 ob; Vasilii Vlasov, *Kratkii ocherk neustroistv sushchestvuiushchikh na katorge* (St. Petersburg, 1873), p. 39.

37. RGIA, f. 1263, op. 1, d. 1067 (1836), ll. 134–5; GARF, f. 122, 3 dp., op. 5, d. 1154 (1885), l. 91.

38. I. P. Belokonskii (Petrovich), *Po tiur'mam i etapam: Ocherki tiuremnoi zhizni i putevye zametki ot Moskvy do Krasnoiarska* (Oryol, 1887), p. 57; George Kennan, *Siberia and the Exile System*, 2 vols. (New York, 1891), vol. 1, p. 108; RGIA, f. 1286, op. 36, d. 686 (1875), l. 20; RGIA, f. 1286, op. 38, d. 467 (1877), l. 41 ob; N. M. Iadrintsev, *Sibir' kak koloniia v geograficheskom, etnograficheskom i istoricheskom otnoshenii* (St. Petersburg, 1882), p. 175.

39. Chekhov, *A Life in Letters*, p. 261; Vlasov, *Kratkii ocherk neustroistv*, p. 38.

40. S. V. Maksimov, *Sibir' i katorga*, 3rd edn (St. Petersburg, 1900), p. 24; Alexandra Oberländer, *Unerhörte Subjekte: die Wahrnehmung sexueller Gewalt in Russland, 1880–1910* (Frankfurt, 2013), ch. 4.

41. V. I. Semevskii, *Rabochie na sibirskikh zolotykh promyslakh: istoricheskoe issledovanie*, 2 vols. (St. Petersburg, 1898), vol. 1, pp. xvii–xviii; Vlasov, *Kratkii ocherk neustroistv*, pp. 33, 36–8.

42. Vlasov, *Kratkii ocherk neustroistv*, pp. 33, 36.

43. GARF, f. 122, op. 5, d. 2807 (1899), ll. 5–6; Poddubskii, "Sakhalinskie deti," pp. 2351–3; IRLI RAN, f. 134, op. 4, d. 319, ll. 61–70.

44. Chekhov, *Sakhalin Island*, pp. 228–30; Lobas, *Katorga i poselenie*, pp. 105–10.

45. Chekhov, *Sakhalin Island*, p. 229.

46. Lobas, *Katorga i poselenie*, pp. 107–8.

47. Chekhov, *Sakhalin Island*, p. 232; Dril', *Ssylka i katorga v Rossii*, p. 32.

48. Poddubskii, "Sakhalinskie deti," pp. 2352–3.

49. A. P. Salomon, "O Sakhaline," *Tiuremnyi vestnik*, 1901, no. 2, pp. 75–7.

50. Ibid., p. 76; Krasnov, "Na ostrove izgnaniia," p. 168; Doroshevich, *Sakhalin*, part 1, p. 316; Dril', *Ssylka i katorga v Rossii*, p. 35.

51. N. M. Iadrintsev, *Russkaia obshchina v tiur'me i ssylke* (St. Petersburg, 1872), pp. 76–86; 424; Krasnov, "Na ostrove izgnaniia," p. 169.

52. Chekhov, *Sakhalin Island*, p. 235.

53. Salomon, "O Sakhaline," pp. 68–9.

54. Chekhov, *Sakhalin Island*, pp. 71, 126.

55. Ibid., p. 127.

56. Krasnov, "Na ostrove izgnaniia," p. 168; Salomon, "O Sakhaline," p. 77.

57. Vlasov, *Kratkii ocherk neustroistv*, pp. 29–30.

58. Ibid., p. 53; Doroshevich, *Sakhalin*, part 1, p. 98.

59. Chekhov, *Sakhalin Island*, p. 236; Poddubskii, "Sakhalinskie deti," p. 2357; Dril', *Ssylka i katorga v Rossii*, pp. 31–2.

60. GARF, f. 122, 3 dp., op. 5, d. 641 (1880), l. 2 ob.

61. Novombergskii, *Ostrov Sakhalin*, pp. 31–2; Poddubskii, "Sakhalinskie deti," p. 2350.

62. Vlasov, *Kratkii ocherk neustroistv*, pp. 33, 36; Charles Henry Hawes, *In the Uttermost East; Being an Account of Investigations Among the Natives and Russian Convicts of the Island of Sakhalin, with Notes on Travel in Korea, Siberia, and Manchuria* (London, 1904), p. 145; Novombergskii, *Ostrov Sakhalin*, p. 31; Dril', *Ssylka i katorga v Rossii*, p. 35.

63. Chekhov, *A Life in Letters*, p. 261 [translation modified].

64. Hawes, *In the Uttermost East*, p. 145; Novombergskii, *Ostrov Sakhalin*, p. 95; Dril', *Ssylka i katorga v Rossii*, pp. 34–5.

65. Dril', *Ssylka i katorga v Rossii*, p. 35; Lobas, *Katorga i poselenie*, pp. 150–51; A. A. Vlasenko, "Ugolovnaia ssylka v Zapadnuiu Sibir'," p. 174; V. G. Korolenko, "Fedor Bespriiutnyi," in idem, *Sobranie sochinenii v desiati tomakh*, 10 vols. (Moscow, 1953–6), vol. 1, pp. 176–220.

66. B. Savrimovich, *K voprosu po ustroistvu ssyl'nykh na o. Sakhalin* (1896), no. 4721, p. 9; RGIA, f. 892, op. 3, d. 54 (1915), l. 1.

67. M. N. Galkin-Vraskoi, "Poezdka v Sibir' i na ostrov Sakhalin," *Russkaia starina*, 1901, no. 1, pp. 163–4; Chekhov, *Sakhalin Island*, p. 63. The office of the governor-general of Priamursk, which covered the Amur Region, Transbaikal and Sakhalin, was established in 1884.

68. Poddubskii, "Sakhalinskie deti," p. 2353; Chekhov, *Sakhalin Island*, p. 245.

69. Salomon, "O Sakhaline," pp. 75–7; Dril', *Ssylka i katorga v Rossii*, pp. 16–19; Lobas, *Katorga i poselenie*, pp. 118–21; Chekhov, *Sakhalin Island*, p. 126; Doroshevich, *Sakhalin*, part 1, p. 91.

70. Dril', *Ssylka i katorga v Rossii*, p. 10; Korablin, "Katorga na Sakhaline," pp. 79–80; Lobas, *Ostrov Sakhalin*, pp. 42–3.

71. Chekhov, *A Life in Letters*, p. 252; V. M. Latyshev, "Sakhalin posle A. P. Chekhova (Reviziia Sakhalinskoi katorgi generalom N. I. Grodekovym v 1894)," *Vestnik Sakhalinskogo Muzeia*, 2000, no. 7, pp. 157–62; Andrew A. Gentes, "Sakhalin as *Cause Célèbre*: The Re-signification of Tsarist Russia's Penal Colony," *Acta Slavica Iaponica*, vol. 32, 2012, pp. 55–72; Sharyl M. Corrado, "The 'End of the Earth': Sakhalin Island in the Russian Imperial Imagination," Ph.D. dissertation, University of Illinois at Urbana-Champaign, 2010, ch. 4.

72. GARF, f. 122, op. 5, d. 2807 (1899), l. 1; V. M. Latyshev, "Vrach L. V. Poddubskii i ego zapiski o sakhalinskoi katorge," *Vestnik Sakhalinskogo Muzeia*, 2004, no. 11, pp. 141–8; Corrado, "The 'End of the Earth,'" p. 114; "K voprosu o budushchnosti i ustroistve o. Sakhalina," *Tiuremnyi vestnik*, 1901, no. 6, pp. 271–95.

73. "Rech' nachal'nika Glavnogo Tiuremnogo Upravleniia na o. Sakhaline," *Tiuremnyi vestnik*, 1899, no. 1, p. 10.

74. Salomon, "O Sakhaline," p. 69.

75. David Schimmelpenninck van der Oye, *Toward the Rising Sun: Russian Ideologies of Empire and the Path to War with Japan* (DeKalb, IL, 2001), chs. 11–12.

76. Iuliia Ul'iannikova, "Chuzhie sredi chuzhikh, chuzhie sredi svoikh: Russko-iaponskaia voina i evakuatsiia Sakhalinskoi katorgi v kontekste imperskoi politiki na Dal'nem Vostoke," *Ab Imperio*, 2010, no. 4, pp. 185–93; Corrado, "The 'End of the Earth,'" p. 164.

77. Doroshevich, *Sakhalin*, part 1, pp. 28, 30–31.

11   THE LASH

1. Anton Chekhov, *Sakhalin Island*, trans. Brian Reeve (London, 2007), p. 293.

2. On the moves to abolish corporal punishment, see Bruce F. Adams, *The Politics of Punishment: Prison Reform in Russia, 1863–1917* (DeKalb, IL, 1996), ch. 1; N. M. Iadrintsev, *Russkaia obshchina v tiur'me i ssylke* (St. Petersburg, 1872), p. 284; Richard S. Wortman, *The Development of a Russian Legal Consciousness* (Chicago, 1976), ch. 9; Abby M. Schrader, *Languages of the Lash: Corporal Punishment and Identity in Imperial Russia* (DeKalb, IL, 2002), ch. 6.

3. Iadrintsev, *Russkaia obshchina*, p. 438; Schrader, *Languages of the Lash*, pp. 3–4, 80–81.

4. N. N. Evreinov, *Istoriia telesnykh nakazanii v Rossii* (St. Petersburg, 1913), pp. 100–101.

5. Schrader, *Languages of the Lash*, pp. 105, 119–20; Evreinov, *Istoriia telesnykh nakazanii*, p. 98; Andrew A. Gentes, *Exile, Murder and Madness in Siberia, 1823–61* (Basingstoke, 2010), p. 50; Fyodor Dostoevsky, *The House of the Dead*, trans. David McDuff (London, 2003), pp. 229–30; V. M. Doroshevich, *Sakhalin*, 2 parts (Moscow, 1903), part 1, pp. 257–8.

6. Stephen P. Frank, *Crime, Cultural Conflict and Justice in Rural Russia, 1856–1914* (Berkeley, 1999), pp. 226–35; Orlando Figes, *A People's Tragedy: The Russian Revolution, 1891–1924* (London, 1996), p. 96; Schrader, *Languages of the Lash*, pp. 102, 105, 157; W. Bruce Lincoln, *Nicholas I: Emperor and Autocrat of All the Russias* (Bloomington, IN, 1978), pp. 103–4.

7. Schrader, *Languages of the Lash*, p. 216, n. 65.

8. RGIA, f. 1263, op. 1, d. 1067 (1836), ll. 268–9, 308 ob.

9. Chekhov, *Sakhalin Island*, p. 290.

10. N. S. Lobas, *Katorga i poselenie na o-ve Sakhaline. Neskol'ko shtrikhov iz zhizni russkoi shtrafnoi kolonii* (Pavlograd, 1903), p. 94.

11. Chekhov, *Sakhalin Island*, pp. 289–90.

12. Ibid., p. 287.

13. Joseph Frank, *Dostoevsky: The Years of Ordeal, 1850–1859* (Princeton, 1983), p. 78.

14. Shimon Tokarzhevskii, "Sem' let katorgi" (1907), in idem, *Sibirskoe likholeti'e* (Kemerovo, 2007), p. 173.

15. V. A. D'iakov, "Katorzhnye gody F. M. Dostoevskogo," in L. M. Goriushkin (ed.), *Politicheskaia ssylka v Sibiri XIX–nachalo XX v.* (Novosibirsk, 1987),

p. 201; K. Nikolaevskii, "Tovarishchi F. M. Dostoevskogo po katorge," *Istoricheskii vestnik*, January 1901, pp. 220–21; Tokarzhevskii, "Sem' let katorgi," pp. 177–8.

16. Tokarzhevskii, "Sem' let katorgi," pp. 173–4.

17. Chekhov, *Sakhalin Island*, p. 294.

18. N. M. Iadrintsev, *Sibir' kak koloniia v geograficheskom, etnograficheskom i istoricheskom otnoshenii* (St. Petersburg, 1882), p. 207; Vasilii Vlasov, *Kratkii ocherk neustroistv sushchestvuiushchikh na katorge* (St. Petersburg, 1873), p. 9.

19. Tokarzhevskii, "Sem' let katorgi," p. 172; Chekhov, *Sakhalin Island*, p. 278; Vlasov, *Kratkii ocherk neustroistv*, p. 23.

20. RGIA, f. 1286, op. 5, d. 508 (1832), ll. 1–2; GARF, f. 122, 3 dp., op. 5, d. 837 (1881), ll. 7–8.

21. Doroshevich, *Sakhalin*, part 1, p. 168; RGIA, f. 1341, op. 65, d. 565 (1847), ll. 13–14, 18.

22. Iadrintsev, *Russkaia obshchina*, pp. 101–102.

23. Doroshevich, *Sakhalin*, part 1, pp. 251–3.

24. V. Ia. Kokosov, *Rasskazy o kariiskoi katorge (iz vospominanii vracha)* (St. Petersburg, 1907), pp. 107–12.

25. Ibid., p. 193.

26. Dostoevsky, *The House of the Dead*, pp. 248, 250–51.

27. Ibid., pp. 81, 227.

28. I. V. Efimov, *Iz zhizni katorzhnykh Ilginskogo i Aleksandrovskogo togda kazennykh, vinokurennykh zavodov, 1848–1853 gg.* (St. Petersburg, 1899), pp. 35–7.

29. Doroshevich, *Sakhalin*, part 2, p. 57; part 1, p. 271

30. Iadrintsev, *Russkaia obshchina*, p. 371; Lev Deich, *Sixteen Years in Siberia*, trans. Helen Chisholm (London, 1903), pp. 177–8; Doroshevich, *Sakhalin*, part 1, p. 275.

31. V. Moskvich, "Pogibshie i pogibaiushchie. Otbrosy Rossii na sibirskoi pochve," *Russkoe bogatstvo*, 1895, no. 7, p. 53; Iadrintsev, *Russkaia obshchina*, p. 440; D. A. Dril', *Ssylka i katorga v Rossii (Iz lichnykh nabliudenii vo vremia poezdki v Priamurskii krai i Sibir')* (St. Petersburg, 1898), pp. 237–8; Chekhov, *Sakhalin Island*, p. 289.

32. *Ob otmene tiazhkikh telesnykh nakazanii za prestupleniia sovershaemye ssyl'nymi* (St. Petersburg, 1867), p. 8.

33. Schrader, *Languages of the Lash*, p. 156.

34. Tokarzhevskii, "Sem" let katorgi," p. 172; Schrader, *Languages of the Lash*, p. 157.

35. L. Mel'shin [P. F. Iakubovich], "Russkaia katorga pered sudom kafedral'noi nauki," *Russkoe bogatstvo*, 1900, no. 7, part 2, pp. 1–19; I. Ia. Foinitskii, "Ssylka ili tiur'ma?," *Iuridicheskii vestnik*, 1881, no. 4, pp. 386–98; I. Ia. Foinitskii, *Uchenie o nakazanii v sviazi s tiur'movedeniem* (St. Petersburg, 1889), pp. 155–62; Daniel Beer, *Renovating Russia: The Human Sciences and the Fate of Liberal Modernity, 1880–1930* (Ithaca, 2008), ch. 3; Adams, *The Politics of Punishment*.

36. N. Lobas, "K voprosu o telesnykh nakazaniiakh," *Vrach*, 27 June 1898, no. 26, pp. 760–63; Dr Lobas, "Flogging in Siberia," *Current Literature*, vol. 24, no. 6 (December 1898), pp. 553–4; "The Knout at Sakhalin," *The New York Times*, 29 May 1898, p. 23.

37. V. N. Gartevel'd, *Katorga i brodiagi Sibiri* (Moscow, 1912), p. 56.

38. Kokosov, *Rasskazy o kariiskoi katorge*, pp. 18–19.

39. Ibid., pp. 24–9.

40. RGIA, f. 1286, op. 8, d. 1086 (1843), l. 19 ob; RGIA, f. 1286, op. 10, d. 1154 (1847), ll. 3–3 ob, 6–6 ob.

41. S. V. Maksimov, *Sibir' i katorga*, 3rd edn (St. Petersburg, 1900), pp. 90–92; RGIA, f. 1265, op. 1, d. 206 (1852), l. 122 ob.

42. Efimov, *V zhizni katorzhnykh*, p. 29; Maksimov, *Sibir' i katorga*, p. 91; Iadrintsev, *Russkaia obshchina*, pp. 40–44.

43. Chekhov, *Sakhalin Island*, p. 124; George Kennan, *Siberia and the Exile System*, 2 vols. (New York, 1891), vol. 2, p. 207.

44. N. Ia. Novombergskii, *Ostrov Sakhalin* (St. Petersburg, 1903), p. 247.

45. Vlasov, *Kratkii ocherk neustroistv*, p. 54; I. P. Belokonskii [Petrovich], *Po tiur'mam i etapam: Ocherki tiuremnoi zhizni i putevye zametki ot Moskvy do Krasnoiarska* (Oryol, 1887), pp. 66–7; Iadrintsev, *Russkaia obshchina*, pp. 172–3; Dril', *Ssylka i katorga v Rossii*, p. 28; A. N. Krasnov, "Na ostrove izgnaniia," *Knizhka nedeli*, 1893, no. 8, p. 161.

46. Doroshevich, *Sakhalin*, part 2, p. 56; M. Finnov, "'Mrachnoe Onorskoe delo': Po stranitsam knigi A. P. Chekhova 'Ostrov Sakhalin,'" in *Ostrov Chekhova: Ot Melikhova do Sakhalina: liudi, sud'by, vstrechi* (Moscow, 1990), pp. 227–55.

47. N. S. Lobas, "K istorii russkoi shtrafnoi kolonii. 1. Sudebnaia ekspertiza na ostrove (Iz pamiatnoi knizhki byvshego sakhalinskogo vracha)," *Vrachebnaia gazeta*, 1904, no. 42, pp. 1199–202.

48. Lobas, "K istorii russkoi shtrafnoi kolonii," *Vrachebnaia gazeta*, 1904, no. 43, pp. 1238–42; Lobas, *Katorga i poselenie*, pp. 54–63.

49. Doroshevich, *Sakhalin*, part 2, pp. 54–67.

50. V. M. Latyshev, "Sakhalin posle A. P. Chekhova (Reviziia Sakhalinskoi katorgi generalom N. I. Grodekovym v 1894)," *Vestnik Sakhalinskogo Muzeia*, 2000, no. 7, pp. 157–62; Sharyl M. Corrado, "The 'End of the Earth': Sakhalin Island in the Russian Imperial Imagination," Ph.D. dissertation (University of Illinois at Urbana-Champaign, 2010), p. 116; Krasnov, "Na ostrove izgnaniia," p. 161; *Vladivostok*, 15 August 1893, p. 7; 21 November 1893, p. 10; Chekhov, *Sakhalin Island*, p. 281; *Evening Standard*, 10 February 1894.

51. *The New York Times*, 10 February 1894, p. 5 [spelling modified].

12 "WOE TO THE VANQUISHED!"

1. V. N. Shaganov, *Nikolai Chernyshevskii na katorge i v ssylke* (St. Petersburg, 1907), pp. 1–3; Mikhail Gernet, *Istoriia tsarskoi tiur'my*, 5 vols. (Moscow,

1951–6), vol. 2, pp. 277–81; A. D. Margolis, "N. G. Chernyshevskii v doroge na katorgu," in idem, *Tiur'ma i ssylka v Imperatorskoi Rossii. Issledovaniia i arkhivnye nakhodki* (Moscow, 1995), p. 95.

2.   Nikolai Chernyshevsky, *What Is to Be Done?*, trans. Michael R. Katz (Ithaca, 1989); Orlando Figes, *A People's Tragedy: The Russian Revolution, 1891–1924* (London, 1996), p. 127.

3.   GARF, f. 109, 3 eksp., op. 154, d. 115 (1869), ll. 21–3; RGIA, f. 1405, op. 521, d. 410 (1882), ll. 11–12, 22–32, 405–6; RGIA, f. 1405, op. 521, d. 430 (1888), ll. 1–8, 248–50.

4.   James Allen Rogers, "Darwinism, Scientism, and Nihilism," *The Russian Review*, vol. 19, no. 1 (1960), pp. 10–23; Philip Pomper, *The Russian Revolutionary Intelligentsia* (Arlington Heights, IL, 1970); James H. Billington, *Fire in the Minds of Men: Origins of the Revolutionary Faith* (New York, 1980), ch. 14.

5.   Franco Venturi, *Roots of Revolution: A History of the Populist and Socialist Movements in Nineteenth-Century Russia*, trans. Francis Haskell (London, 1972), ch. 18; Daniel Field, "Peasants and Propagandists in the Russian Movement to the People of 1874," *The Journal of Modern History*, vol. 59, no. 3 (1987), pp. 415–38.

6.   K. P. Pobedonostsev, "Bolezni nashego vremeni," in idem, *Moskovskii sbornik* (Moscow, 1896), p. 125; Daniel Beer, *Renovating Russia: The Human Sciences and the Fate of Liberal Modernity, 1880–1930* (Ithaca, 2008), pp. 12–13.

7.   Margolis, "N. G. Chernyshevskii," p. 98; GAIO, f. 24, op. 3, k. 45, d. 160 (1866), ll. 1–3; L. M. Goriushkin (ed.), *Politicheskaia ssylka v Sibiri. Nerchinskaia katorga*, vol. 1, no. 2 (Novosibirsk, 1993), p. 176; E. A. Skripilev, "N. G. Chernyshevskii na Nerchinskoi katorge," *Politicheskie ssyl'nye v Sibiri (XVIII–nachalo XX v.)* (Novosibirsk, 1983), pp. 80–82.

8.   GARF, f. 102, 3 dp., op. 77, d. 1143 (1881), l. 6.

9.   Jonathan W. Daly, *Autocracy Under Siege: Security Police and Opposition in Russia, 1866–1905* (DeKalb, IL, 1998), p. 23; Jay Bergman, *Vera Zasulich: A Biography* (Stanford, 1983); Jonathan W. Daly, "On the Significance of Emergency Legislation in Late Imperial Russia," *Slavic Review*, vol. 54, no. 3 (Autumn 1995), p. 608.

10. Daly, *Autocracy Under Siege*, ch. 3; John D. Klier, *Russians, Jews and the Pogroms of 1881–1882* (Cambridge, 2011).

11. V. I. Lenin, "Tri zaprosa" (December 1911), *Polnoe sobranie sochinenii*, 5th edn, 55 vols. (Moscow, 1958–65), vol. 21, p. 114.

12. George Kennan, *Siberia and the Exile System*, 2 vols. (New York, 1891), vol. 1, pp. 242–3.

13. Daly, *Autocracy Under Siege*, ch. 3.

14. Daly, "Emergency Legislation," p. 615; *Ssylka v Sibir'. Ocherk ee istorii i sovremennogo polozheniia* (St. Petersburg, 1900), appendix 4, p. 18; RGIA, f. 1405, op. 521, d. 410 (1882), ll. 11–12, 22–32, 405–6; M. Borodin, "Mertvaia petlia," *Otechestvennye zapiski*, 1880, no. 7, pt. 2, pp. 40–63; Kennan, *Siberia and the Exile System*, vol. 1, p. 246; Lev Deich, *Sixteen Years in Siberia*, trans. Helen Chisholm (London, 1903), p. 188.

15. N. Gekker, "Politicheskaia katorga na Kare," *Byloe*, 1906, no. 9, p. 72; D. M. Nechiporuk, "Zagranichnaia agitatsiia russkikh revoliutsionerov v organizatsii pobegov iz Sibiri v Ameriku v nachale 1890-kh godov," *Istoricheskii ezhegodnik*, 2009, pp. 57–72; GAIO, f. 24, op. 3, k. 2643, d. 82 (1881), ll. 21–21 ob.

16. RGIA, f. 1284, op. 241, d. 42 (1879), ll. 163–163 ob; GAIO, f. 24, op. 3, k. 2244, d. 810 (1880), ll. 36–7, 43; GARF, f. 102, 3 dp., op. 77, d. 1038 (1881), ll. 1–3, 11–17; GATOvgT, f. 152, op. 12, d. 95 (1888), ll. 3–9; GAIO, f. 32, op. 1, d. 417 (1887), ll. 1–1 ob.

17. A. Levandovskii, *Elizaveta Nikolaevna Koval'skaia* (Moscow, 1928).

18. GAIO, f. 32, op. 1, d. 753 (1879), ll. 7–7 ob; Elizaveta Koval'skaia, "Zhenskaia katorga," in *Kariiskaia tragediia (1889): Vospominaniia i materialy* (Petrograd, 1920), pp. 5–6; GAIO, f. 32, op. 1, d. 1394 (1882), ll. 25–8, 60–61; GAIO, f. 32, op. 2, d. 142 (1882), ll. 1–30; Elizaveta Koval'skaia, "Pobeg," *Katorga i ssylka*, 1929, no. 5, pp. 130–31.

19. RGIA, f. 1405, op. 535, d. 158 (1884), ll. 1–9; Koval'skaia, "Zhenskaia katorga," pp. 18–19; idem, "Pobeg," *Katorga i ssylka*, 1932, no. 10, pp. 110–28.

20. GARF, f. 102, 3 dp., d. 5, ch. 1 (1884), ll. 56–56 ob; GAIO, f. 32, op. 1, d. 171 (1884), ll. 89–90, 121.

21. V. G. Korolenko, "Istoriia moego sovremmenika," *Sobranie sochinenii*, 10 vols. (Moscow, 1953–6), vol. 7, pp. 197–205; RGIA, f. 1286, op. 40, d. 321 (1879), ll. 1–8; GAIO, f. 24, op. 3, k. 2643, d. 65 (1880), ll. 9–11, 30–33.

22. Kennan, *Siberia and the Exile System*, vol. 2, pp. 24–7.

23. GARF, f. 102, 5 dp., d. 7765 (1888), l. 257; Koval'skaia, "Zhenskaia katorga," pp. 15–16.

24. GARF, f. 102, 3 dp., d. 1012 (1892), ll. 37–41.

25. Anton Chekhov, *A Life in Letters*, trans. and ed. Rosamund Bartlett (London, 2004), p. 241.

26. Goriushkin (ed.), *Politicheskaia ssylka v Sibiri*, pp. 223–5; V. I. Zorkin, *Vklad politicheskikh ssyl'nykh v izuchenie fol'klora Sibiri (vtoraia polovina XIX— nachalo XX v.* (Novosibirsk, 1985); A. I. Arkhipov, "Uchastie politicheskikh ssyl'nykh v podgotovke proekta zemel'noi reformy gubernatora V. N. Skrypitsyna v Iakutskoi oblasti," in *Sibirskaia ssylka* (Irkutsk, 2011), no. 6 (18), pp. 307–12.

27. Bruce Grant, "Empire and Savagery: The Politics of Primitivism in Late Imperial Russia," in Daniel R. Brower and Edward J. Lazzerini (eds.), *Russia's Orient: Imperial Borderlands and Peoples, 1700–1917* (Bloomington, IN, 1997), pp. 292–310; V. M. Andreev, "O zhurnalistskoi deiatel'nosti predshestvennikov sotsial-demokratii (ssyl'nykh narodnikov) v Sibiri v 70–80-kh gg. XIX v.," in P. V. Zabelin (ed.), *Zhurnalistika v Sibiri* (Irkutsk, 1972), pp. 75–85.

28. L. S. Chudnovskii, "Shkoly v Sibiri," *Zhurnal Ministerstva narodnogo prosveshcheniia*, 1892, no. 1, pp. 1–45, 107–40; S. P. Shevtsov, "Kul'turnoe znachenie politicheskoi ssylki v Zapadnoi Sibiri," *Katorga i ssylka*, 1928, no. 3, pp. 57–87; A. I. Blek, "Biblioteka i muzei v Semipalatinske," *Sibirskaia gazeta*, 1884, no. 24, p. 1.

29. Kennan, *Siberia and the Exile System*, vol. 2, pp. 45–51; *The Times*, 11 January 1884.

30. GAIO, f. 32, op. 1, d. 1299 (1883), ll. 1–4; GAIO, f. 32, op. 1, d. 753 (1880), ll. 2–2 ob.

31. GARF, f. 102, 2 dp., d. 186 (1883), l. 7; GARF, f. 102, 5 dp., d. 7765 (1888), ll. 261–261 ob; RGIA, f. 1405, op. 86, d. 8716 (1885), ll. 1–14.

32. RGIA, f. 1405, op. 535, d. 235 (1888), l. 11.

33. RGIA, f. 1405, op. 535, d. 235 (1888), ll. 10–25.

34. GARF, f. 102, 5 dp., d. 7765 (1888), ll. 258–258 ob. For examples of the press coverage, see V. I. Fedorova, *Narodnicheskaia ssylka Sibiri v obshchestvenno-politicheskoi i ideinoi bor'be v Rossii v poslednei chetverti XIX veka* (Krasnoyarsk, 1996), ch. 1.

35. GARF, f. 102, 5 dp., d. 7765 (1888), l. 259 ob.

36. RGIA, f. 1263, op. 1, d. 4236 (1882), l. 466; GARF, f. 102, 2 dp., d. 186 (1883), l. 26.

37. Goriushkin (ed.), *Politicheskaia ssylka v Sibiri*, p. 266.

38. GARF, f. 102, 2 dp., d. 436 (1883), ll. 12–13; Goriushkin (ed.), *Politicheskaia ssylka v Sibiri*, pp. 256–61; Julia Mannherz, *Modern Occultism in Late Imperial Russia* (DeKalb, IL, 2013).

39. Goriushkin (ed.), *Politicheskaia ssylka v Sibiri*, pp. 239–40; GARF, f. 102, 5 dp., d. 2835 (1882), l. 25; M. R. Popov, "K biografii Ippolita Nikiticha Myshkina," *Byloe*, 1906, no. 2, pp. 252–71.

40. GARF, f. 102, 5 dp., d. 2835 (1882), l. 26; GARF, f. 102, 5 dp., d. 2378 (1881), ll. 29–30; GATOvgT, f. 1686, op. 1, d. 114 (1882), ll. 1–3; N. Levchenko, "Pobeg s Kary," in A. Dikovskaia-Iakimova et al (eds.), *Kara i drugie tiur'my Nerchinskoi katorgi* (Moscow, 1927), pp. 55–72.

41. Goriushkin (ed.), *Politicheskaia ssylka v Sibiri*, pp. 245–7, 253–64.

42. GARF, f. 102, 3 dp., op. 77, d. 1288 (1881), ll. 6–8; M. I. Drei, "Kariets I. N. Tsiplov," *Katorga i ssylka*, 1926, no. 1, pp. 218–26; Goriushkin (ed.), *Politicheskaia ssylka v Sibiri*, pp. 241–2.

43. Goriushkin (ed.), *Politicheskaia ssylka v Sibiri*, pp. 262–3.

44. Popov, "K biografii," pp. 270–71.

45. F. Bogdanovich, "Posle pobega," in Dikovskaia-Iakimova et al (eds.), *Kara i drugie tiur'my Nerchinskoi katorgi*, pp. 82–4; GARF, f. 102, 5 dp., d. 2835 (1882), ll. 46–7.

46. N. N. Evreinov, *Istoriia telesnykh nakazanii v Rossii* (St. Petersburg, 1913), pp. 133–55; Anton Chekhov, *Sakhalin Island*, trans. Brian Reeve (London, 2007), p. 293; V. Ia. Kokosov, *Rasskazy o kariiskoi katorge (iz vospominanii vracha)* (St. Petersburg, 1907), pp. 107–12; A. Fomin, "Kariiskaia tragediia," in Dikovskaia-Iakimovaia et al (eds.), *Kara i drugie tiur'my Nerchinskoi katorgi*, p. 134.

47. Belokonskii, *Po tiur'mam i etapam*, pp. 167–80.

48. RGIA, f. 1286, op. 28, d. 917 (1867), ll. 16–18; Belokonskii, *Po tiur'mam i etapam*, p. 86.

49. *Ssylka v Sibir'*, appendix 1; RGIA, f. 1286, op. 38, d. 380 (1877), ll. 3–4; RGIA, f. 1286, op. 28, d. 917 (1867), ll. 48–9; RGIA, f. 1286, op. 37, d. 609

(1876), ll. 41. For a description of the barges, see Kennan, *Siberia and the Exile System*, vol. 1, ch. 5.

50. RGIA, f. 1286, op. 36, d. 686 (1875), ll. 13–14, 45 ob; GAIO, f. 32, op. 1, d. 199 (1877), l. 1; RGIA, f. 1286, op. 38, d. 467 (1876), l. 49 ob.

51. RGIA, f. 1286, op. 29, d. 836 (1868), ll. 8–8 ob; V. L. Seroshevskii, "Ssylka i katorga v Sibiri," in I. S. Mel'nik (ed.), *Sibir': ee sovremennoe sostoianie i ee nuzhdy* (St. Petersburg, 1908), pp. 210–11.

52. RGIA, f. 1286, op. 36, d. 686 (1875), l. 20; GARF, f. 122, op. 5, d. 619 (1880), ll. 1–2; GATOvgT, f. 330, op. 2, d. 1 (1888); GATOvgT, f. 330, op. 2, d. 629 (1890); GATOvgT, f. 333, op. 3, d. 1110 (1894); GAIO, f. 32, op. 1, d. 199 (1877), l. 1; GARF, f. 122, 3 dp., op. 5, d. 1328 (1887), ll. 2–4; D. A. Dril', *Ssylka i katorga v Rossii (Iz lichnykh nabliudenii vo vremia poezdki v Priamurskii krai i Sibir')* (St. Petersburg, 1898), p. 24; RGIA, f. 1024, op. 1, d. 100 (1893), ll. 2–3.

53. Ia. Stefanovich, "Po etapam. Iz zapisok semidesiatnika (s Kary do Irkutska)," *Vestnik Evropy*, 1916, no. 7, pp. 79–131; A. V. Pribylev, *Ot Peterburga do Kary v 80-kh gg.* (Moscow, 1923); L. Mel'shin [P. F. Iakubovich], *V mire otverzhennykh: zapiski byvshego katorzhnika* (St. Petersburg, 1896), p. 10; RGIA, f. 1405, op. 535, d. 135 (1883), ll. 11–12.

54. RGIA, f. 1405, op. 535, d. 239 (1888), ll. 1–44.

55. RGIA, f. 1405, op. 535, d. 239 (1888), ll. 47, 55; GAIO, f. 32, op. 1, d. 2412 (1888), ll. 28–9.

56. P. L. Kazarian, *Iakutiia v sisteme politicheskoi ssylki Rossii, 1826–1917 gg.* (Yakutsk, 1998), pp. 252–4.

57. "Doklad Ostashkina Depart. Pol. o dele 22 marta 1889 g.," in M. A. Braginskii et al (eds.), *Iakutskaia tragediia 22 marta (3 aprelia) 1889 goda. Sbornik vospominanii i materialov* (Moscow, 1925), pp. 210–23.

58. GARF, f. 102, o. o. 5 dp., d. 7732 (1889), l. 13.

59. GARF, f. 102, o. o. 5 dp., d. 7732 (1889), ll. 13–15; "Dokumenty po iakutskomu delu 22 marta 1889 goda," in Braginskii et al (eds.), *Iakutskaia tragediia 22 marta*, pp. 188–203.

60. GARF, f. 102, o. o. 5 dp., d. 7732 (1889), l. 49; M. Bramson, "Iakutskaia tragediia," in Braginskii et al (eds.), *Iakutskaia tragediia 22 marta*, pp. 26–7.

61. "Pis'ma osuzhdennykh iakutian," in Braginskii et al (eds.), *Iakutskaia tragediia 22 marta*, pp. 78–9.

62. Ibid., p. 79.

63. GARF, f. 102, 3 dp., op. 87, d. 373 (1889), ll. 2–4, 11; Fedorova, *Narodnicheskaia ssylka Sibiri*, pp. 58–74.

64. "Izbienie politicheskikh ssyl'nykh v Iakutske," in Braginskii et al (eds.), *Iakutskaia tragediia 22 marta*, p. 34; *The Times*, 26 December 1889, p. 7; *The New York Times*, 8 February 1890; The Society of Friends of Russian Freedom, *The Slaughter of Political Prisoners in Siberia* (Gateshead, 1890), pp. 14–16.

65. Koval'skaia, "Zhenskaia katorga," p. 26 [emphasis in original]; V. Pleskov, "Iz nedra arkhiva," in Dikovskaia-Iakimova et al (eds.), *Kara i drugie tiur'my Nerchinskoi katorgi*, p. 192.

66. "Kariiskie sobytiia po ofitsial'nym dannym V. Petrovskogo," in *Kariiskaia tragediia (1889). Vospominaniia i materialy* (St. Petersburg, 1920), p. 73; Fomin, "Kariiskaia tragediia," pp. 122–7.

67. Kennan, *Siberia and the Exile System*, vol. 2, p. 269; Fomin, "Kariiskaia tragediia," p. 128.

68. Fomin, "Kariiskaia tragediia," p. 131.

69. Ibid., pp. 130–31; GARF, f. 102, 5 dp., op. 107, d. 7961 (1889), ll. 63–63 ob.

70. Fomin, "Kariiskaia tragediia," p. 132.

71. Ibid., pp. 134–7.

72. GARF, f. 102, 5 dp., op. 127, d. 7961 (1889), ll. 20–21.

73. Kennan, *Siberia and the Exile System*, vol. 2, p. 272.

74. *The Times*, 28 February 1890, p. 13 [spelling modified].

75. *The New York Times*, 16 February 1890; 23 February 1890.

76. *The Times*, 10 March 1890, p. 6.

77. Jane E. Good, "America and the Russian Revolutionary Movement, 1888–1905," *The Russian Review*, vol. 41, no. 3 (July 1982), p. 274.

78. Haia Shpayer-Makov, "The Reception of Peter Kropotkin in Britain, 1886–1917," *Albion*, vol. 19, no. 3 (Autumn 1987), pp. 373–90; Barry Hollingsworth, "The Society of Friends of Russian Freedom," *Oxford Slavonic Papers*, vol. 3 (1970), pp. 45–64; Good, "America and the Russian Revolutionary Movement," p. 276; John Slatter, "Bears in the Lion's Den: The Figure of the Russian Revolutionary Emigrant in English Fiction, 1880–1914," *Slavonic and East European Review*, vol. 77, no. 1 (January 1999), pp. 30–55.

79. Robert Service, *Lenin: A Biography* (London, 2000), chs. 8–10.

80. G. F. Oslomovskii, "Kariiskaia tragediia," *Byloe*, 1906, no. 6, pp. 59–80; Viliuts, "Iakutskaia tragediia 1889 g. (Po vospominaniiam ssyl'nogo)," *Russkaia mysl'*, 1906, no. 3, pp. 55–77; L. Mel'shin [P. F. Iakubovich], "Vae Victis! (Dve tragedii v Sibiri)," *Sovremennye zapiski*, 1906, no. 1, pp. 1–18; Minor, "Iakutskaia drama 22-ogo marta 1889 goda," *Byloe*, 1906, no. 9, pp. 129–57; Gekker, "Politicheskaia katorga na Kare."

81. GARF, f. 102, 5 dp., d. 7765 (1888), ll. 261–2.

82. Gekker, "Politicheskaia katorga na Kare," pp. 69–70; RGIA, f. 1263, op. 1, d. 4236 (1882), ll. 468 ob–469.

83. Kennan, *Siberia and the Exile System*, vol. 1, p. 258.

84. V. M. Gessen, *Iskliuchitel'noe polozhenie* (St. Petersburg, 1908), pp. 170–71; Eric Lohr, "The Ideal Citizen and Real Subject in Late Imperial Russia," *Kritika: Explorations in Russian and Eurasian History*, vol. 7, no. 2 (Spring 2006), pp. 173–94.

85. "Izbienie politicheskikh ssyl'nykh v Iakutske," in Braginskii et al (eds.), *Iakutskaia tragediia 22 marta*, p. 34.

13   THE SHRINKING CONTINENT

1. *Sankt-Peterburgskie Vedomosti*, 21 November 1877, no. 322, p. 2; 24 November 1877, no. 325, p. 3.

2. Mark Bassin, "Inventing Siberia: Visions of the Russian East in the Early Nineteenth Century," *American Historical Review*, vol. 96, no. 3 (June 1991), pp. 767, 770; Alexander Martin, *Enlightened Metropolis: Constructing Imperial Moscow, 1762–1855* (Oxford, 2013).

3. M. V. Lomonosov, "Kratkoe opisanie raznykh puteshestvii po severnym moriam i pokazanie vozmozhnogo prokhoda sibirskim okeanom v Vostochnuiu Indiiu" (1762–3), in idem, *Polnoe sobranie sochinenii*, 11 vols. (Moscow-Leningrad, 1950–83), vol. 6, p. 498 (cited in Bassin, "Inventing Siberia," p. 770).

4. Raymond H. Fisher, *The Russian Fur Trade, 1550–1700* (Berkeley, 1943); W. Bruce Lincoln, *The Conquest of a Continent: Siberia and the Russians* (Ithaca, 1994), pp. 54–6; Bassin, "Inventing Siberia," p. 771; M. M. Gedenshtrom, *Otryvki o Sibiri* (St. Petersburg, 1830), p. 4.

5. N. B. Gersevanov, "Zamechaniia o torgovykh otnosheniiakh Sibiri k Rossii," *Otechestvennye zapiski*, 1841, vol. 14, part 4, pp. 26, 33–34, 30; Mark Bassin, *Imperial Visions: Nationalist Imagination and Geographical Expansion in the Russian Far East, 1840–1865* (Cambridge, 1999), ch. 5.

6. A. V. Remnev, *Samoderzhavie i Sibir': Administrativnaia politika v pervoi polovine XIX v.* (Omsk, 1995), pp. 161–97.

7. RGIA, f. 1264, op. 1, d. 71 (1835), ll. 164 ob–165.

8. A. A. Vlasenko, "Ugolovnaia ssylka v Zapadnuiu Sibir' v politike Samoderzhaviia XIX veka," Kandidatskaia diss. (Omsk State University, 2008), pp. 163–210; Andrew A. Gentes, *Exile, Murder and Madness in Siberia, 1823–61* (Basingstoke, 2010), pp. 68–71; L. M. Dameshek and A. V. Remnev (eds.), *Sibir' v sostave Rossiiskoi Imperii* (Moscow, 2007), p. 286.

9. N. M. Iadrintsev, *Sibir' kak koloniia v geograficheskom, etnograficheskom i istoricheskom otnoshenii* (St. Petersburg, 1882), p. 165.

10. Ivan Barsukov, *Graf Nikolai Nikolaevich Murav'ev-Amurskii po ego pis'mam, ofitsial'nym dokumentam, rasskazam sovremennikov i pechatnym istochnikam*, 2 vols. (Moscow, 1891), vol. 1, p. 671.

11. Bassin, *Imperial Visions*.

12. Nathaniel Knight, "Science, Empire and Nationality: Ethnography in the Russian Geographical Society, 1845–1855," in Jane Burbank and David L. Ransel (eds.), *Imperial Russia: New Histories for the Empire* (Bloomington, IN, 1998), pp. 108–41; Claudia Weiss, *Wie Sibirien "unser" wurde: Die Russische Geographische Gesellschaft und ihr Einfluß auf die Bilder und Vorstellungen von Sibirien im 19. Jahrhundert* (Göttingen, 2007), chs. 1–2; Joseph Bradley, *Voluntary Associations in Tsarist Russia: Science, Patriotism and Civil Society* (Cambridge, MA, 2009), ch. 3; Mark Bassin, "The Russian Geographical Society, the 'Amur Epoch,' and the Great Siberian Expedition 1855–1863," *Annals of the Association of American Geographers*, vol. 73, no. 2 (1983), pp. 240–56.

13. *Otchet Imperatorskogo Russkogo Geograficheskogo Obshchestva za 1850 g.* (St. Petersburg, 1851), p. 43.

14. Cited in Yuri Semyonov, *The Conquest of Siberia: An Epic of Human Passions*, trans. E. W. Dickes (London, 1947), p. 303.

15. Steven G. Marks, *Road to Power: The Trans-Siberian Railroad and the Colonization of Asian Russia, 1850–1917* (London, 1991), pp. 13–57; David Schimmelpenninck van der Oye, *Russian Orientalism: Asia in the Russian Mind from Peter the Great to the Emigration* (New Haven, 2010), pp. 59, 69–70; K. N. Pos'et, "Prekrashchenie ssylki v Sibir'," *Russkaia starina*, 1899, no. 7, p. 54.

16. M. K. Sidorov, *Sever Rossii* (St. Petersburg, 1870); idem, *O bogatstvakh severnykh okrain Sibiri i narodov tam kochuiushchikh* (St. Petersburg, 1873); M. K. Sidorov, *Proekt o vozmozhnosti zaseleniia severa Sibiri putem promyshlennosti i torgovli i o razvitii vneshnei torgovli Sibiri* (Tobolsk, 1864). On Sidorov, see special issue devoted to his activities, *Izvestiia obshchestva dlia sodeistviia russkomu torgovomu morekhodstvu*, 1889, no. 21, pp. 1–95; V. Korolev, *Rossii bespokoinyi grazhdanin* (Moscow, 1987).

17. K. Staritskii, "Ocherk istorii plavaniia po Karskomu moriu i ust'iam Eniseiia i Obi," *Izvestiia Imperatorskogo Russkogo Geograficheskogo Obshchestva*, 1877, vol. 13, no. 6, p. 435. On the history of Arctic navigation, see Lincoln, *The Conquest of a Continent*, ch. 14.

18. AAN SPb, f. 270, op. 1, d. 421, 1877–8, ll. 9–26; AAN SPb, f. 270, op. 1, d. 409, ll. 1–4; D. I. Shvanenberg, "O plavanii iakhty 'Utrenniaia Zaria' iz Enisei cherez Karskoe more i Severnyi okean do Varde," in *Trudy S-Peterburgskogo otdeleniia Imperatorskogo obshchestva dlia sodeistviia russkomu torgovomu morekhodstvu za 1877 god* (St. Petersburg, 1877), p. 439; idem, "V poliarnykh l'dakh," *Sbornik morskikh statei i rasskazov. Ezhemesiachnoe pribavlenie morskoi gazety "Iakhta,"* December 1877, pp. 507–18; idem, "Rasskaz kapitana D. I. Shvanenberga o plavanii skhun 'Severnoe Siianie' i 'Utrenniaia Zaria' v nizov'iakh Eniseia, v Karskom more v Severnom Ledovitom Okeane," *Izvestiia Imperatorskogo Russkogo Geograficheskogo Obshchestva*, 1877, vol. 13, no. 6, pp. 439–48.

19. Shvanenberg, "O plavanii iakhty 'Utrenniaia Zaria,'" pp. 248–9.

20. RGIA, f. 1286, op. 38, d. 465 (1877), ll. 25, 35; Shvanenberg, "O plavanii iakhty 'Utrenniaia Zaria,'" p. 251.

21. M. K. Sidorov, "O plavanii russkikh moriakov na iakhte 'Utrenniaia Zaria' ot Varde do Peterburga," *Trudy S-Peterburgskogo otdeleniia*, pp. 229–33; *The Times*, 29 October 1877, p. 8; RGIA, f. 1286, op. 38, d. 465 (1877), ll. 2–4.

22. Hakan Yavuz and Peter Sluglett (eds.), *War and Diplomacy: The Russo-Turkish War of 1877–1878 and the Treaty of Berlin* (Salt Lake City, UT, 2012).

23. Orlando Figes, *Crimea* (London, 2011); Schimmelpenninck van der Oye, *Russian Orientalism*, pp. 229–40; Alberto Masoero, "Territorial Colonization in Late Imperial Russia: Stages in the Development of a Concept," *Kritika: Explorations in Russian and Eurasian History*, vol. 14, no. 1 (Winter 2013), pp. 64–5; David Schimmelpenninck van der Oye, *Toward the Rising Sun: Russian Ideologies of Empire and the Path to War with Japan* (DeKalb, IL, 2001), ch. 2.

24. A. V. Remnev, *Rossiia Dal'nego Vostoka: imperskaia geografiia vlasti XIX–*

nachala XX vekov (Omsk, 2004), pp. 399–410; Ilya Vinkovetsky, *Russian America: An Overseas Colony of a Continental Empire* (New York, 2011), pp. 65–6.

25. Willard Sunderland, "The 'Colonization Question': Visions of Colonization in Late Imperial Russia," *Jahrbücher für Geschichte Osteuropas*, vol. 48, no. 2 (2000), pp. 210–32; A. V. Remnev, "Colonization and 'Russification' in the Imperial Geography of Asiatic Russia: From the Nineteenth to the Early Twentieth Centuries," in Uyama Tomohiko (ed.), *Asiatic Russia: Imperial Power in Regional and International Contexts* (London, 2012), pp. 108–9.

26. A. Roger Ekirch, *Bound for America: The Transportation of British Convicts to the Colonies, 1718–1775* (Oxford, 1987), pp. 207–12; Robert Hughes, *The Fatal Shore: A History of the Transportation of Convicts to Australia, 1787–1868* (London, 1986), ch. 14: Kirsten McKenzie, *Scandal in the Colonies: Sydney and Cape Town, 1820–1850* (Carlton, 2004); Hamish Maxwell-Stewart, *Closing Hell's Gates: The Death of a Convict Station* (Sydney, 2008); D. Meredith and D. Oxley, "Condemned to the Colonies: Penal Transportation as the Solution to Britain's Law and Order Problem," *Leidschrift*, vol. 22, no. 1 (April 2007), pp. 36–9.

27. Vlasenko, "Ugolovnaia ssylka," p. 212.

28. RGIA, f. 1652, op. 1, d. 197 (1877), l. 10; RGIA, f. 1149, op. 9, d. 3 (1877), l. 775; RGIA, f. 1586, op. 1, d. 1 (1885), l. 62.

29. N. M. Iadrintsev, "Statisticheskie materialy k istorii ssylki v Sibiri," *Zapiski Irkutskogo otdela geograficheskogo obshchestva* (St. Petersburg, 1889), vol. 6, p. 330; A. D. Margolis, "Chislennost' i razmeshchenie ssyl'nykh v Sibiri v kontse XIX veka," in idem, *Tiur'ma i ssylka v imperatorskoi Rossii. Issledovaniia i arkhivnye nakhodki* (Moscow, 1995), pp. 33–4.

30. RGIA, f. 1149, op. 9, d. 3 (1877), ll. 337–777; *Ssylka v Sibir', Ocherk ee istorii i sovremennogo polozheniia* (St. Petersburg, 1900), pp. 78–80; Bruce F. Adams, *The Politics of Punishment: Prison Reform in Russia, 1863–1917* (DeKalb, IL, 1996), pp. 97–120.

31. E. Frish, *Prilozhenie k predstavleniiu v Gosurdarstvennyi sovet o sokrashchenii ssylki v Sibir'* (St. Petersburg, 1887), p. 4.

32. RGIA, f. 1286, op. 28, d. 920 (1869), l. 122; RGIA, f. 1286, op. 38, d. 380 (1877), l. 5; N. M. Iadrintsev, *Russkaia obshchina v tiur'me i ssylke* (St. Petersburg, 1872), pp. 541–2.

33. RGIA, f. 1405, op. 88, d. 10215 (1879), ll. 447–53; Margolis, "Chislennost' i razmeshchenie ssyl'nykh," p. 31; GARF, f. 122, 3 dp., op. 5, d. 2786a (1895), l. 15 ob.

34. "Arestanty v Sibiri," *Sovremennik*, 1863, no. 11, pp. 133–75; S. V. Maksimov, *Sibir' i katorga* (St. Petersburg, 1871); Grigorii Fel'dshtein, *Ssylka. Ocherki ee genezisa, znacheniia, istorii i sovremennogo sostoianiia* (Moscow, 1893), pp. 185–91; Iadrintsev, *Russkaia obshchina*, p. 582; N. M. Iadrintsev, "Polozhenie ssyl'nykh v Sibiri," *Vestnik Evropy*, November 1875, no. 10, pp. 283–312; no. 12, pp. 529–56; Iadrintsev, *Sibir' kak koloniia*, pp. 220–21.

35. RGIA, f. 1652, op. 1, d. 197 (1877), l. 7 ob; RGIA, f. 1287, op. 38, d. 2104 (1881), l. 6.

36. *Sibir'*, 5 October 1875, no. 15, p. 5; 2 October 1877, no. 40, p. 3; 11 September 1877, no. 37, p. 1.

37. *Vostochnoe obozrenie*, 15 September 1891, no. 38, p. 2; *Sibirskaia zhizn'*, 12 December 1897, no. 262, p. 2; Iadrintsev, *Sibir' kak koloniia*; G. N. Potanin, "Proekt otmeny ssylki v Sibiri," in idem, *Izbrannye sochineniia v trekh tomakh*, 3 vols. (Pavlodar, 2005), vol. 2, pp. 170–76; A. A. Ivanov, "Samyi nasushchnyi vopros Sibiri," www.penpolit.ru (accessed 19 July 2015); Alan Wood, "Chernyshevskii, Siberian Exile and *Oblastnichestvo*," in Roger Bartlett (ed.), *Russian Thought and Society, 1800–1917* (Keele, 1984), pp. 42–66; Stephen Watrous, "The Regionalist Conception of Siberia, 1860 to 1920," in Yuri Slezkine and Galya Diment (eds.), *Between Heaven and Hell: The Myth of Siberia in Russian Culture* (New York, 1993), pp. 113–32; Yuri Slezkine, *Arctic Mirrors: Russia and the Small Peoples of the North* (Ithaca, 1994), ch. 4.

38. S. Chudnovskii, "Kolonizatsionnoe znachenie sibirskoi ssylki," *Russkaia mysl'*, 1886, no. 10, pp. 51, 58; Iadrintsev, "Polozhenie ssyl'nykh v Sibiri"; V. Moskvich, "Pogibshie i pogibaiushchie: Otbrosy Rossii na sibirskoi pochve," *Russkoe bogatstvo*, 1895, no. 7, pp. 46–81; A. N. Rodigina, *"Drugaia Rossiia": Obraz Sibiri v russkoi zhurnal'noi presse vtoroi poloviny XIX–nachala XX v.* (Novosibirsk, 2006), p. 204.

39. S. Dizhur, "Russkaia ssylka. Ee istoriia i ozhidaemaia reforma," *Russkoe bogatstvo*, 1900, no. 4, pp. 45–6.

40. Shvanenberg, "V poliarnykh l'dakh," p. 517.

41. RGIA, f. 1286, op. 38, d. 465 (1877), ll. 6–8.

42. *Golos*, 18 November 1877, no. 280, p. 3; 19 November 1877, no. 281, p. 3; *Birzhevye Vedomosti*, 21 November 1877, no. 298, pp. 1–2; *Sankt-Peterburgskie Vedomosti*, 21 November 1877, no. 322, p. 2.

43. *Sankt-Peterburgskie Vedomosti*, 24 November 1877, no. 325, p. 3.

44. Ibid., 27 November 1877, no. 328, p. 3; *Severnyi Vestnik*, 27 November 1877, no. 210, p. 2; *Peterburgskaia Gazeta*, 25 November 1877, no. 216, p. 2; "Privetstvie F. D. Studitskogo moriakam, pribyvshim iz Eniseia na Nevu na iakhte 'Utrenniaia Zaria' v zasedanii 22 noiabria," *Trudy S-Peterburgskogo otdeleniia*, p. 222; "Zhurnal obshchego sobraniia Imperatorskogo Russkogo Geograficheskogo Obshchestva 7-ogo dekabria 1877 goda," *Izvestiia Imperatorskogo Russkogo Geograficheskogo Obshchestva*, 1878, no. 1, pp. 32–4; Staritskii, "Ocherk istorii plavaniia," p. 437; Glenn M. Stein and Lydia I. Iarukova, "Polar Honours of the Russian Geographical Society 1845–1995," *Journal of the Hakluyt Society* (December 2008), p. 34; F. D. Studitskii (ed.), *Istoriia otkrytiia morskogo puti iz Evropy v sibirskie reki i do Beringova proliva*, 2 vols. (St. Petersburg, 1883), vol. 1, pp. 198–9.

45. RGIA, f. 1286, op. 38, d. 465 (1877), l. 33; Studitskii (ed.), *Istoriia otkrytiia morskogo puti*, vol. 1, p. 200; TsGIA SPb, f. 254, op. 1, d. 10688 (1877–8), l. 1; AAN SPb, f. 270, op. 1, d. 417 (1878), l. 21; AAN SPb, f. 270, op. 1, d. 417 (1878), l. 9.

46. Dameshek and Remnev (eds.), *Sibir' v sostave Rossiiskoi Imperii*, pp. 40–72; Frithjof Benjamin Schenk, *Russlands Fahrt in die Moderne: Mobilität und*

sozialer Raum im Eisenbahnzeitalter (Stuttgart, 2014), pp. 92–6; Sunderland, "The 'Colonization Question,'" pp. 217–26; Remnev, "Colonization and 'Russification,'" pp. 102–8.

47. Lincoln, *The Conquest of a Continent*, p. 259; L. M. Goriushkin, "Migration, Settlement and the Rural Economy of Siberia, 1861–1914," in Alan Wood (ed.), *The History of Siberia from Russian Conquest to Revolution* (London, 1991), pp. 140–57; Donald W. Treadgold, *The Great Siberian Migration: Government and Peasant Resettlement from Emancipation to the First World War* (Princeton, 1957); Sunderland, "The 'Colonization Question,'" pp. 211–13.

48. Charles Steinwedel, "Resettling People, Unsettling the Empire: Migration and the Challenge of Governance, 1861–1917," in Nicholas B. Breyfogle, Abby Schrader and Willard Sunderland (eds.), *Peopling the Periphery: Borderland Colonization in Eurasian History* (London, 2007), pp. 129–31; *Sankt-Peterburgskie vedomosti*, 13 January 1904 (cited in Anatolyi Remnev, "Siberia and the Russian Far East in the Imperial Geography of Power," in Jane Burbank, Mark von Hagen and Anatolyi Remnev (eds.), *Russian Empire: Space, People, Power, 1700–1930* (Bloomington, 2007), p. 445.

49. "Po povodu predstoiashchego preobrazovaniia katorgi i ssylki," *Tiuremnyi vestnik*, 1899, no. 6, p. 249.

50. *Ssylka v Sibir'*, pp. 134–5, 333–4, 337.

51. A. P. Chekhov, "V ssylke," in idem, *Polnoe sobranie sochinenii i pisem*, 20 vols. (Moscow, 1944–51), vol. 8, pp. 79–87; F. Kriukov, "V rodnykh mestakh," *Russkoe bogatstvo*, 1903, no. 9, pp. 5–34; V. Krylov, "V glushi Sibiri," *Vestnik Evropy*, 1893, no. 5, pp. 65–95; L. Mel'shin [P. F. Iakubovich], "Kobylka v puti," *Russkoe bogatstvo*, 1896, no. 8, pp. 5–37; M. Paskevich, "Katorzhnaia," *Zhenskoe delo*, 1900, no. 2, pp. 46–63; P. Khotymskii, "Na novom meste," *Vestnik Evropy*, 1903, no. 5, pp. 156–80; no. 6, pp. 562–83; Lauren Leighton, "Korolenko's Stories of Siberia," *Slavonic and East European Review*, vol. 49, no. 115 (April 1971), pp. 200–213; Harriet Murav, "'Vo Glubine Sibirskikh Rud': Siberia and the Myth of Exile," in Diment and Slezkine (eds.), *Between Heaven and Hell*, pp. 95–111.

52. *Vostochnoe obozrenie*, 1 October 1889, no. 4, p. 9.

53. Leo Tolstoy, *Resurrection*, trans. Anthony Briggs (London, 2009), p. 472 [translation modified].

54. A. D. Margolis, "Sistema sibirskoi ssylki i zakon ot 12 iiunia 1900 goda," in idem (ed.), *Tiur'ma i ssylka v imperatorskoi Rossii*, p. 21; "Otzyvy pechati po voprosu ob otmene ssylki," *Tiuremnyi vestnik*, 1899, no. 8, p. 358.

55. Margolis, "Sistema sibirskoi ssylki," p. 23; GARF, f. 122, 3 dp., op. 5, d. 2786a (1895), l. 17; *Polnoe sobranie zakonov Rossiiskoi Imperii*, 3rd compendium (1881–1913), 10 June 1900, no. 18777, p. 633; 12 June, no. 18839, p. 757; Margolis, "Chislennost' i razmeshchenie ssyl'nykh," pp. 31–2.

56. Margolis, "Sistema sibirskoi ssylki," pp. 27, 19.

57. Adams, *The Politics of Punishment*, pp. 130–33; Stephen G. Wheatcroft, "The Crisis of the Late Tsarist Penal System," in idem (ed.), *Challenging Traditional Views of Russian History* (Basingstoke, 2002), pp. 33–9; Mar-

golis, "Sistema sibirskoi ssylki," p. 26; Vlasenko, "Ugolovnaia ssylka," pp. 178–210; B. Mironov, "Prestupnost' v Rossii v XIX–nachale XX veka," *Otechestvennaia istoriia*, 1998, no. 1, p. 35.

14   THE CRUCIBLE

1. Iu. Steklov, "Vospominaniia o iakutskoi ssylke," *Katorga i ssylka*, 1923, no. 6, p. 72; Volker Rabe, *Der Widerspruch von Rechtsstaatlichkeit und strafender Verwaltung in Russland, 1881–1917: Motive, Handhabung und Auswirkungen der administrativen Verbannung von Revolutionären* (Karlsruhe, 1985), pp. 342–3; Jonathan Daly, "Political Crime in Late Imperial Russia," *The Journal of Modern History*, vol. 74, no. 1 (March 2002), p. 93.

2. Susan K. Morrissey, *Heralds of Revolution: Russian Students and the Mythologies of Radicalism* (Oxford, 1998), ch. 2; Orlando Figes, *A People's Tragedy: The Russian Revolution, 1891–1924* (London, 1996), pp. 166–8.

3. Theodore R. Weeks, *Nation and State in Late Imperial Russia: Nationalism and Russification on the Western Frontier, 1863–1914* (DeKalb, IL, 1996), pp. 112–21; John D. Klier and Shlomo Lambroza (eds.), *Pogroms: Anti-Jewish Violence in Modern Russian History* (Cambridge, 1992); Figes, *A People's Tragedy*, pp. 79–83, 139–54.

4. RGIA, f. 1405, op. 535, d. 235 (1888), ll. 10–25; M. Poliakov, "Vospominaniia o kolymskoi ssylke," *Katorga i ssylka*, 1928, nos. 8–9, pp. 158, 160.

5. Poliakov, "Vospominaniia o kolymskoi ssylke," p. 169 [emphasis in original].

6. V. I. Lenin "Pis'ma," *Polnoe sobranie sochinenii*, 5th edn, 55 vols. (Moscow, 1958–65), vol. 55, p. 35.

7. Robert Service, *Lenin: A Biography* (London, 2000), ch. 7; W. Bruce Lincoln, *The Conquest of a Continent: Siberia and the Russians* (Ithaca, 1994), ch. 27; V. N. Dvorianov, *V sibirskoi dal'nei storone . . . (Ocherki istorii politicheskoi katorgi i ssylki. 60-e gody XVIII v.—1917 g.)* (Minsk, 1985), ch. 4.

8. Lincoln, *The Conquest of a Continent*, p. 219; Lenin, "Pis'ma," vol. 55, p. 55.

9. Lincoln, *The Conquest of a Continent*, p. 221; Robert Service, *Trotsky: A Biography* (London, 2009), ch. 6; Isaac Deutscher, *The Prophet Armed: Trotsky, 1879–1921* (Oxford, 1970), pp. 42–56.

10. Service, *Lenin*, ch. 7.

11. Poliakov, "Vospominaniia o kolymskoi ssylke," p. 171.

12. G. Tsyperovich, *Za poliarnym krugom. Desiat' let ssylki v Kolymske* (St. Petersburg, 1907), p. 110.

13. Ibid., p. 92; Lenin, "Pis'ma," vol. 55, p. 98; Dvorianov, *V sibirskoi dal'nei storone . . .*, pp. 127–32.

14. Tsyperovich, *Za poliarnym krugom*, pp. 50, 146; M. A. Braginskii et al (eds.), *Iakutskaia tragediia 22 marta (3 aprelia) 1889 goda. Sbornik vospominanii i materialov* (Moscow, 1925), pp. 108–16.

15. Daly, "Political Crime," p. 82; A. D. Margolis, "Chislennost' i razmeshchanie ssyl'nykh v Sibiri v kontse XIX veka," in idem, *Tiur'ma i ssylka v imperator-*

skoi Rossii. Issledovaniia i arkhivnye nakhodki (Moscow, 1995), pp. 38–40; Dvorianov, *V sibirskoi dal'nei storone* . . . , p. 155.

16. P. Teplov, *Istoriia iakutskogo protesta* (St. Petersburg, 1906), p. 453; GARF, f. 102, o. o., d. 9, ch. 8 (1904), ll. 14–14 ob.

17. P. I. Rozental', *"Romanovka" (Iakutskii protest 1904 goda. Iz vospominaniia uchastnika* (Moscow, 1924), pp. 14–15.

18. GARF, f. 102, o. o., d. 9, ch. 8 (1904), ll. 14–14 ob.

19. GARF, f. 124, op. 13, d. 1762 (1904), l. 3; Rozental', *"Romanovka,"* p. 23.

20. GARF, f. 102, op. o. o., d. 9, ch. 8 (1904), l. 12; GARF, f. 124, op. 13, d. 1762 (1904), l. 3.

21. "Romanovskii protest v proklamatsiiakh iakutskikh politicheskikh ssyl'nykh," *Katorga i ssylka*, 1924, no. 5, pp. 169–70.

22. Rozental', *"Romanovka,"* pp. 63–9.

23. Ibid., pp. 74–5, 78–9.

24. V. M. Chernov, "Terroristicheskii element v nashei programme," *Revoliutsionnaia Rossiia*, no. 7 (June 1902), pp. 3–4; R. A. Gorodnitskii, *Boevaia organizatsiia partii sotsialistov-revoliutsionerov v 1901–1911 gg.* (Moscow, 1998); Konstantin Morozov, *Partiia sotsialistov-revoliutsionerov v 1907–1911* (Moscow, 1998).

25. Susan K. Morrissey, "The 'Apparel of Innocence': Toward a Moral Economy of Terrorism in Late Imperial Russia," *The Journal of Modern History*, vol. 84 (September 2012), pp. 607, 613–14, 628–36; Anna Geifman, *Thou Shalt Kill: Revolutionary Terrorism in Russia, 1894–1917* (Princeton, 1993), p. 74; Abraham Ascher, *P. A. Stolypin: The Search for Stability in Late Imperial Russia* (Stanford, 2001), pp. 138–9.

26. D. N. Zhbankov, "Travmaticheskaia epidemiia v Rossii (aprel'-mai 1905 g.), *Prakticheskii vrach*, vol. 4, nos. 32–5 (1907), pp. 633–7; M. O. Gershenzon, "Tvorcheskoe samosoznanie," in *Vekhi. Intelligentsiia v Rossii: sbornik statei, 1909–1910*, 2nd edn (Moscow, 1909), p. 89; Charters Wynn, *Workers, Strikes, and Pogroms: The Donbass–Dnepr Bend in Late Imperial Russia* (Princeton, 1992); Joan Neuberger, *Hooliganism: Crime, Culture and Power in St. Petersburg, 1900–1914* (Berkeley, 1993).

27. Abraham Ascher, *The Revolution of 1905: Russia in Disarray* (Stanford, 1988), ch. 2.

28. L. Martov, L. Maslov and A. Potresov (eds.), *Obshchestvennoe dvizhenie v Rossii v nachale XX veka*, 4 vols. (St. Petersburg, 1909–14), vol. 2, part 1, pp. 166–74; Ascher, *The Revolution of 1905*, pp. 291–2.

29. Jonathan W. Daly, "On the Significance of Emergency Legislation in Late Imperial Russia," *Slavic Review*, vol. 54, no. 3 (Autumn 1995), pp. 622–5; E. Nikitina, "Matrosy-revoliutsionery na katorge," *Tsarskii flot pod krasnym flagom* (Moscow, 1931), p. 186; A. P. Mikheev, "Voennosluzhashchie v sostave uznikov tobol'skoi katorgi," *Vestnik Omskogo Gosurdarstvennogo Universiteta*, 2006, p. 1; William C. Fuller Jr, *Civil–Military Conflict in Imperial Russia, 1881–1914* (Princeton, 1985), p. 171; M. P. Chubinskii, "Smertnaia kazn' i voennye sudy," in M. N. Gernet, O. B. Gol'dovskii and I. N. Sakharov (eds.), *Protiv smertnoi kazni*, 2nd edn (Moscow, 1907), p. 112.

30. Stephen G. Wheatcroft, "The Crisis of the Late Tsarist Penal System," in idem (ed.), *Challenging Traditional Views of Russian History* (Basingstoke, 2002), pp. 46–8; Daly, "Political Crime," pp. 84–6; Ia. Sverdlov, "Massovaia ssylka" (1916), in idem, *Izbrannye proizvedeniia*, 3 vols. (Moscow, 1957–60), vol. 1, pp. 66–7.

31. E. Nikitina, "Tornaia doroga (tiur'ma i katorga 1905–1913 godov)," in V. Vilenskii (ed.), *Deviatyi val: k desiatiletiiu osvobozhdeniia iz tsarskoi katorgi i ssylki* (Moscow, 1927), p. 38; GAIO, f. 25, op. 6, k. 502, d. 2960 (1906), ll. 5 ob–6 ob; V. Miakotin, "O sovremennoi tiur'me i ssylke," *Russkoe bogatstvo*, 1910, no. 9, part 2, p. 129; GAIO, f. 226, op. 1, d. 279 (1915), ll. 5, 8, 39; A. P. Mikheev, *Tobol'skaia katorga* (Omsk, 2007), p. 80.

32. Ascher, *The Revolution of 1905*, pp. 247–8; S. Kallistov, "Iz zhizni tobol'skoi katorgi (Vospominaniia 1908–1910 gg.)," *Katorga i ssylka*, 1923, no. 6, p. 230; A. Fomin, "Nerchinskaia katorga poslednikh desiatiletii (1888–1917 gg.)," in A. Dikovskaia-Iakimova (ed.), *Kara i drugie tiur'my Nerchinskoi katorgi* (Moscow, 1927), p. 25; Mikheev, *Tobol'skaia katorga*, pp. 88, 92, 162.

33. GAIO, f. 25, op. 6, k. 502, d. 2962 (1906), ll. 1–2.

34. Mikheev, *Tobol'skaia katorga*, p. 163.

35. GAIO, f. 25, op. 6, k. 501, d. 2950 (1906), ll. 3–4.

36. Fomin, "Nerchinskaia katorga," pp. 25–6; Miakotin, "O sovremennoi tiur'me i ssylke," pp. 128–9; "Khronika," *Sibirskie voprosy*, 1909, no. 19, p. 33.

37. James H. Billington, *Fire in the Minds of Men: Origins of the Revolutionary Faith* (New York, 1980), ch. 14; GAIO, f. 25, op. 6, k. 502, d. 2960 (1906), l. 17; M. K., "Politicheskaia katorga," *Sibirskie voprosy*, 1912, no. 26, pp. 14–15; Mikheev, *Tobol'skaia katorga*, pp. 94, 96–7.

38. GARF, f. 100, o. o., d. 100, t. 3 (1907), ll. 301–301 ob.

39. Mikheev, *Tobol'skaia katorga*, p. 122; "Bunt v tobol'skoi katorzhnoi tiur'me," *Katorga i ssylka*, 1923, no. 6, pp. 199–203.

40. GAIO, f. 226, op. 2, d. 108 (1912), ll. 5, 11, 15–15 ob.

41. These instances of the flogging of political prisoners in Siberia contradict Daly's confident assertion that "corporal punishment was almost never used against political prisoners." Daly, "Political Crime," p. 91.

42. "Bunt v tobol'skoi katorzhnoi tiur'me," pp. 209–10.

43. Ibid., p. 209.

44. GATOvgT, f. 151, op. 1, d. 10 (1907), ll. 1–2; Mikheev, *Tobol'skaia katorga*, p. 165.

45. "Bunt v tobol'skoi katorzhnoi tiur'me," pp. 213–15.

46. F. Savitskii, "Aleksandrovskaia tsentral'naia katorzhnaia tiur'ma," *Tiuremnyi vestnik*, 1908, no. 1, p. 62; F. Kudriavtsev, *Aleksandrovskii tsentral (iz istorii sibirskoi katorgi)* (Irkutsk, 1936), pp. 19–33.

47. GAIO, f. 25, op. 6, k. 538, d. 3754 (1908), ll. 30–31.

48. GAIO, f. 25, op. 6, k. 538, d. 3754 (1908), ll. 4–6, 28–30; RGIA, f. 1405, op. 539, d. 499 (1908), ll. 1–1 ob; F. Savitskii, "Pobeg arestantov iz aleksandrovskoi katorzhnoi tiur'my," *Tiuremnyi vestnik*, 1909, no. 5, pp. 608–31; P.

Fabrichnyi, "Vooruzhennyi pobeg iz aleksandrovskogo tsentrala," *Katorga i ssylka*, 1922, no. 4, pp. 122–3.

49. GAIO, f. 25, op. 6, k. 538, d. 3754 (1908), ll. 82, 87, 103–9; Kudriavtsev, *Aleksandrovskii tsentral*, pp. 54–8.

50. GAIO, f. 25, op. 6, k. 488, d. 2665 (1906), ll. 32–32 ob, 46–8. For a similarly violent escape in Tobolsk province, see GATOvgT, f. i151, op. 1, d. 7 (1907), ll. 1–9.

51. GATOvgT, f. 171, op. 1, d. 137 (1909), ll. 5, 9–13, 18; I. P. Serebrennikov, "Terroristicheskaia deiatel'nost' ssyl'nykh revoliutsionerov v Vostochnoi Sibiri v mezhrevoliutsionnyi period (1907–1916 gg.)," in *Sibirskaia ssylka* (Irkutsk, 2011), no. 6 (18), pp. 340–41; D. I. Ermakovskii, *Turukhanskii bunt* (Moscow, 1930); D. A. Batsht, "Podavlenie 'Turukhanskogo bunta': karatel'nyi apparat tsarskoi Rossii za poliarnym krugom," in *Sibirskaia ssylka*, pp. 137–44.

52. "Bunt v tobol'skoi katorzhnoi tiur'me," p. 212; Sergei Anisimov, *Kak eto bylo. Zapiski politicheskogo zashchitnika o sudakh Stolypina* (Moscow, 1931), p. 73.

53. A. P. Tolochko, "O roli terrora v deiatel'nosti eserovskogo podpol'ia v Sibiri (1905-fevral' 1917 gg.)," *Istoricheskii ezhegodnik* (Omsk, 1997), pp. 14–24; A. A. Tsindik, "Zapadnosibirskie esery i anarkhisty v period reaktsii 1907–1910 gg. (voennaia rabota)," *Omskii nauchnyi vestnik*, 2009, no. 5, pp. 23–6; S. V. Desiatov, "Politicheskii ekstremizm v tobol'skoi gubernii na primere boevoi deiatel'nosti partii sotsialistov-revoliutsionerov (1906–1913 gg.)," *Omskii nauchnyi vestnik*, 2013, no. 3, pp. 33–5.

54. GAIO, f. 25, op. 6, k. 512, d. 3227 (1907), ll. 8–10.

55. GAIO, f. 25, op. 6, k. 512, d. 3227 (1907), l. 19.

56. GAIO, f. 25, op. 6, k. 507, d. 3115 (1907), ll. 18–21, 34–5, 52–4.

57. GATOvgT, f. 151, op. 1, d. 15 (1907), l. 2.

58. Mikheev, *Tobol'skaia katorga*, pp. 73–4; GATOvgT, f. 151, op. 1, d. 15 (1907), l. 4.

59. GATOvgT, f. 151, op. 1, d. 15 (1907), l. 3; I. Genkin, "Tobol'skii tsentral," *Katorga i ssylka*, 1924, no. 3, pp. 167–73; V. N. Gartevel'd, *Katorga i brodiagi Sibiri* (Moscow, 1912), p. 56; L. Kleinbort, "Ravenstvo v bezpravii," *Obrazovanie*, 1909, no. 3, p. 28; GATOvgT, f. 151, op. 1, d. 20 (1908), l. 1 ob; Mikheev, *Tobol'skaia katorga*, p. 167.

60. GATOvgT, f. 15, op. 1, d. 49 (1908), l. 2; Kallistov, "Iz zhizni tobol'skoi katorgi," p. 230; GATOvgT, f. 151, op. 1, d. 15 (1907), l. 4.

61. GATOvgT, f. 151, op. 1, d. 15 (1907), ll. 3 ob–5; GARF, f. 102, o. o., d. 9, ch. 64 (1908), ll. 11–11ob.

62. A. A. Tsindik, *Voennaia i boevaia rabota revoliutsionnogo podpol'ia v Zapadnoi Sibiri v 1907–1914 gg.*, Kandidatskaia diss. (Omsk University, 2002), pp. 77–8.

63. Genkin, "Tobol'skii tsentral," pp. 176–7; P. Vitiazev, "Pamiati N. D. Shishmareva. Iz vospominanii," *Katorga i ssylka*, 1923, no. 6, pp. 249–59; A. P. Mikheev, "Demony revoliutsii: iz istorii revoliutsionnogo ekstremizma v Zapadnoi Sibiri," *Izvestiia Omskogo Gosudarstvennogo Istoriko-*

kraevedicheskogo muzeia, 1997, no. 5, pp. 205–6; "Nekorolog. I. S. Mogiliev," *Tiuremnyi vestnik*, 1909, no. 5, pp. 576–7.

64. "Bunt v tobol'skoi katorzhnoi tiur'me," p. 218.

65. Miakotin, "O sovremennoi tiur'me i ssylke," p. 133; GARF, f. 102, op. 265, d. 881 (1913), ll. 150–52; GAIO, f. 226, op. 1, d. 86 (1911), ll. 3–5; GAIO, f. 266, op. 1, d. 33 (1909), ll. 146, 149; GATOvgT, f. 331, op. 16, d. 20 (1909), ll. 30–31.

66. GAIO, f. 25, op. 6, k. 584, d. 4678 (1912), ll. 12–13; I. Bril'on, *Na katorge. Vospominaniia revoliutsionera* (Petrograd, 1917), pp. 127–36; Mikheev, *Tobol'skaia katorga*, p. 81.

67. GATOvgT, f. 1, op. 1, d. 1074 (1910), ll. 1 ob–2. On the influence of Cato's suicide on Russia, see Susan K. Morrissey, *Suicide and the Body Politic in Imperial Russia* (Cambridge, 2006), pp. 53–60.

68. A. N. Murav'ev, *Sochineniia i pis'ma* (Irkutsk, 1986), p. 263; Vladimir Korolenko recorded other cases of revolutionaries killing themselves in order to spurn the mercy of the state: V. G. Korolenko, "Bytovoe iavlenie" (1910), in idem, *Sobranie sochinenii*, 10 vols. (Moscow, 1953), vol. 9, pp. 487–8; Morrissey, *Suicide and the Body Politic*, pp. 306–7; GATOvgT, f. 1, op. 1, d. 1074 (1910), l. 3.

69. See also Claudia Verhoeven, *The Odd Man Karakozov: Imperial Russia, Modernity, and the Birth of Terrorism* (Ithaca, 2009), p. 179; GATOvgT, f. 1, op. 1, d. 1074 (1910), l. 4 ob.

70. Richard Pipes, *The Russian Revolution, 1899–1919* (New York, 1990), ch. 17; Figes, *A People's Tragedy*, pp. 635–42; Helen Rappaport, *Ekaterinburg: The Last Days of the Romanovs* (London, 2009).

EPILOGUE: RED SIBERIA

1. GARF, f. 122, op. 5, d. 3307 (1917), ll. 38–40; M. G. Detkov, *Soderzhanie penitentsiarnoi politiki Rossiiskogo gosudarstva i ee realizatsiia v sisteme ispolneniia ugolovnogo nakazaniia v vide lisheniia svobody v period 1917–1930 godov* (Moscow, 1992), pp. 5–12; V. N. Dvorianov, *V sibirskoi dal'nei storone . . . (Ocherki istorii politicheskoi katorgi ssylki. 60-e gody XVIII v.–1917 g.)* (Minsk, 1985), pp. 243–4; Galina Ivanova, *Labour Camp Socialism: The Gulag in the Soviet Totalitarian System*, trans. Carol Faith (Armonk, NY, 2000), pp. 9–11; Orlando Figes, *A People's Tragedy: The Russian Revolution, 1891–1924* (London, 1996), ch. 9.

2. I. I. Serebrennikov, "Moi vospominaniia: 1917–1922," Hoover Institution Archives, Ivan I. Serebrennikov Papers, box 10, p. 8 [I am grateful to Prof. Robert Service for supplying me with this reference]; L. V. Shapova, "Amnistii i nachalo reorganizatsii penitentsiarnoi sistemy v Irkutskoi gubernii v 1917 g.," in *Sibirskaia ssylka* (Irkutsk, 2011), no. 6 (18), pp. 170–80.

3. P. Klimyshkin, "K amnistii," *Katorga i ssylka*, 1921, no. 1, pp. 8–20; G. Sandomirskii, "Na poslednei stupeni," *Katorga i ssylka*, 1921, no. 1, pp. 41–4; P. Fabrichnyi, "Tak bylo," *Katorga i ssylka*, 1921, no. 1, pp. 45–9; Jona-

than D. Smele, *Civil War in Siberia: The Anti-Bolshevik Government of Admiral Kolchak, 1918–1920* (Cambridge, 2006).

4. Anne Applebaum, *Gulag: A History* (London, 2004); Steven A. Barnes, *Death and Redemption: The Gulag and the Shaping of Soviet Society* (Princeton, 2011); M. Gor'kii, L. Averbakh and S. Firin (eds.), *Belomorsko-Baltiiskii Kanal imeni Stalina. Istoriia stroitel'stva 1931–1934 gg.* (Moscow, 1934; repr. 1998), pp. 593–5; Alexander Solzhenitsyn, *The Gulag Archipelago: 1918–1956*, trans. Thomas P. Whitney and Harry Willetts (London, 1995), p. 175; Golfo Alexopoulos, "Destructive-Labor Camps: Rethinking Solzhenitsyn's Play on Words," *Kritika: Explorations in Russian and Eurasian History*, vol. 16, no. 3 (2015), pp. 499–526.

5. Ludmilla A. Trigos, *The Decembrist Myth in Russian Culture* (Basingstoke, 2009), chs. 4–5. The journal *Katorga i ssylka* was published from 1921 to 1935.

6. Jonathan Daly, "Political Crime in Late Imperial Russia," *The Journal of Modern History*, vol. 74, no. 1 (March 2002), p. 93.

7. Ivan Teodorovich, "Avtobiografiia," *Entsiklopedicheskii slovar' Granat*, vol. 41, part 3, appendix, pp. 141–5; Marc Junge, *Die Gesellschaft ehemahliger politischer Zwangsarbeiter und Verbannter in der Sowjetunion: Gründung, Entwicklung und Liquidierung (1921–1935)* (Berlin, 2009), p. 442; L. Dolzhanskaia, "Repressii 1937–1938 gg. v moskovskikh artel'iakh OPK," in Ia. Leont'ev and Marc Iunge (eds.), *Vsesoiuznoe obshchestvo politkatorzhan i ssyl'noposelentsev. Obrazovanie, razvitie, likvidatsiia, 1921–1935* (Moscow, 2004), pp. 278–308.

Acknowledgements

This book has been a long time in the making, and along the way I have accumulated a great many debts that it gives me pleasure to acknowledge. Grants from Royal Holloway College, University of London and the Leverhulme Trust generously supported a year and a half of archival research in the Russian Federation. The pioneering work on Siberian exile by A. D. Margolis, Anatoly Remnev, Abby Schrader, Alan Wood and especially Andrew Gentes proved invaluable in framing my approach to the subject and in navigating the primary sources.

I am grateful to the staff of the archives I visited in St. Petersburg, Moscow, Tobolsk and Irkutsk and especially to Marina Pavlovna Podvigina and her colleagues at the Library of the Academy of Sciences in St. Petersburg. Ilya Magin offered invaluable assistance in both locating and deciphering archival materials in St. Petersburg, and he offered sound critical advice as my ideas took shape. He was also enormously helpful in identifying some of the more obscure individuals who appear in this book. Ivan Babitsky helped me gather information in the State Archive of the Russian Federation in Moscow. Over the summer of 2012, Yulia Popova assisted me in transcribing archival files in Tobolsk and Irkutsk. She also spent long hours patiently explaining colloquial or obsolete Russian expressions. Back in the United Kingdom, I benefited greatly from discussing revolutionary memoirs with Anatoly Mikhailovich Artamonov.

Some of the material and arguments of the book have been presented at seminars and conferences at the universities of London, Oxford, Leiden, Munich, Georgetown and Illinois at Urbana-Champaign, and at the European University at St. Petersburg, and in article form in *Slavic Review* and *Kritika: Explorations in Russian and Eurasian History*. I am very grateful to the participants in these colloquia and the editors and anonymous readers of these journals for their incisive questions and criticisms. Friends, family and colleagues read drafts of chapters and in some cases the entire manuscript. For their commentaries and suggestions, I thank Tobin Auber, Alex Barber, Richard Beer, Robert Beer, Alexandru Chirmiciu, Orlando Figes, James Grosvenor, Peter Kremmer, Gavin Jacobson, Stephen Lovell, Rudolf Muhs, Alexandra Oberländer, Amanda Vickery and Jonathan Waterlow. In addition to everything else she has given me, Rebecca Reich brought her own formidable critical skills to bear on the manuscript, saved me from numerous infelicities and much improved the clarity of my prose and of my arguments.

My agent Peter Robinson deftly steered this project from its inception over a cup of coffee in 2010 to its completion six years later. At Penguin, Simon Winder saw the potential in my book proposal and has, ever since, been a supportive and tolerant editor. George Andreou at Knopf offered excellent advice on redrafting parts of the manuscript. My wonderful copy-editor, Bela Cunha, endured my last-minute rewrites with equanimity.

Lastly, I thank my late friend and colleague David Cesarani for encouraging me to pursue this topic. I dedicate the book to my son, Gusztáv Milotay.

Cambridge, January 2016

PERMISSIONS

Some of the chapters expand upon material I have presented in the form of academic articles:

"The Exile, the Patron and the Pardon: The Voyage of the *Dawn* and the Politics of Punishment in an Age of Nationalism and Empire," *Kritika: Explorations in Russian and Eurasian History*, vol. 14, no. 1 (Winter 2013), pp. 5–30. "Decembrists, Rebels and Martyrs in Siberian Exile: The 'Zerentui Conspiracy' of 1828 and the Fashioning of a Revolutionary Genealogy," *Slavic Review*, vol. 72, no. 3 (Fall 2013), pp. 528–51. "Penal Deportation to Siberia and the Limits of State Power, 1801–1881," *Kritika: Explorations in Russian and Eurasian History*, vol. 16, no. 3 (Summer 2015), pp. 621–50.

Index

A NOTE ON THE TYPE

The text of this book was set in Sabon, a typeface designed by Jan Tschichold (1902–1974), the well-known German typographer. Based loosely on the original designs by Claude Garamond (ca. 1480–1561), Sabon is unique in that it was explicitly designed for hot-metal composition on both the Monotype and Linotype machines as well as for filmsetting. Designed in 1966 in Frankfurt, Sabon was named for the famous Lyons punch cutter Jacques Sabon, who is thought to have brought some of Garamond's matrices to Frankfurt.

Composed by North Market Street Graphics,
Lancaster, Pennsylvania

Printed and bound by Berryville Graphics,
Berryville, Virginia